THE
REVOLUTION
IN
AMERICAN
FOREIGN POLICY

―――――

Its Global Range

THE
REVOLUTION
IN
AMERICAN
FOREIGN POLICY

Its Global Range

WILLIAM G. CARLETON

RANDOM HOUSE · NEW YORK · 1964

For May and Will

THIRD PRINTING

© *Copyright, 1963, 1964, by Random House, Inc.*

All rights reserved under International and Pan-American Copyright Conventions. Published in New York by Random House, Inc., and simultaneously in Toronto, Canada, by Random House of Canada, Limited.

Library of Congress Catalog Card Number: 64-18312

Manufactured in the United States of America by
The Colonial Press Inc., Clinton, Mass.

Portions of this book are derived from the author's previous book of the same title, Copyright, 1954, © 1957, by Random House, inc.

Design by Jeanette Young

PREFACE

THIS IS the story of our turbulent crisis world since 1945 and how American foreign policy has attempted to deal with it. Foreign policy is thought of not merely as diplomacy, military strategy, and international organization but as functional in the widest sense, a subject as broad as history and life itself, including materials not only from political science and history as conventionally conceived but also from economics, sociology, anthropology, social psychology, practical and party politics, public opinion and propaganda, public relations, and so forth.

The range is truly global. An attempt has been made to avoid a too ethnocentric approach, and about as much attention is given to Asia or the Middle East or Africa or Latin America as is given to the United States or Europe. The political and social currents and cross-currents within and among all the continents, constantly and simultaneously reacting on one another, are, it is hoped, brought into balanced focus.

The positions on foreign affairs of the various countries and of the movements, groups, parties, and leaders within the countries are described, and the reasons for their positions are analyzed. This holds for the various Communist and neutral countries as well as for the countries in the Western bloc.

This book is a combination of narrative and interpretation, the specific and the abstract, the concrete and the conceptual. The aim is to put recent and contemporary events into historical perspective, to treat the present as history.

Moreover, I have attempted to accomplish all this in a readable and integrated way so that the busy student or the interested citizen might in relatively short space grasp the essential facts and forces of our amazingly complex and fast-moving world. I leave to the reader whether I have been measurably successful in this undertaking.

This volume is based on the indispensable yearbooks of the Council on Foreign Relations, of the United Nations, of the Royal Institute of International Affairs, of the Council of Europe; specialized works in specialized areas; many interpretive books and essays; the memoirs of politicians, diplomats, generals, and admirals; and a wide range of newspapers and periodicals both in the United States and abroad.

Many of the views reflected in this book have been expressed by me before in scores of essays and articles which have appeared in *The Yale Review, The American Scholar, The Virginia Quarterly Review, The Antioch Review, Harper's, Current History, World Politics, The Round Table* of London, and other periodicals.

WILLIAM G. CARLETON

CONTENTS

4. THE PERIOD OF ATTEMPTED COOPERATION (1945-1947)

5. CONTAINMENT AND COLD WAR

THE
REVOLUTION
IN
AMERICAN
FOREIGN POLICY

Its Global Range

INTRODUCTION

On the Nature of World Politics
A Brief Note

INTERNATIONAL RELATIONS are never simple. They are pluralistic, complex, and in constant flux.

American foreign policy today is a combination of various approaches and means: military strength; "power-politics" alliances; collective security in the United Nations; foreign economic aid; social politics (foreign technical assistance and economic aid directed to social and political ends); economic incentives and reprisals; trading policies designed to benefit some nations and injure others; ideological, cultural, and psychological appeals; and many more.

Foreign policy responds to many groups, interests, values, and pressures both at home and abroad. The pressures from abroad come from nations (some friendly, some unfriendly, some of varying shades of neutrality), from revolutionary and counter-revolutionary movements, from alliances, and from regional and international organizations, all of which in turn must respond to internal pressures.

The interests and values, groups and pressures, situations within situations, elements and factors, approaches and means operate simultaneously and continuously. However, the attention paid to a particular pressure, the emphasis given to this or that factor, the extent to which an approach or an instrument is used are constantly shifting as conditions change and influences rise and fall.

The territorial units which have been or are the players—city states, nation states, and empires—pursue a variety of goals: to survive, to extend the margin of survival, to defend or expand collective welfare and power, to further the interests of influential groups within, to advance basic institutional change or to prevent it.

Before institutional change can take place there must be first a proposal of change, an idea, and the conflict over the idea or over effectuating the idea is the ideological conflict, which often involves revolutions within states, and these not infrequently spill over into and complicate international relations. (A basic institutional change inside a country is not always the result of revolutionary upthrust or an idea; just as commonly it is the product of evolutionary growth. But by the time some groups in other countries want to adopt it in their own countries, it has been rationalized and become an idea, a doctrine, an ideology, which may spark revolutions and affect world politics.)

Most of the time international relations mainly entail adjusting the interests of established states and of the established groups, interests, and values within them (the ordinary process of accommodating vested power interests), but in a revolutionary age the ideological factor has a way of entwining with the power factor, indeed of representing new and upthrusting power elements challenging the older power elements, and then the power conflict among the nations and the ideological conflict are so interwoven as to become almost indistinguishable.

Nationalism itself is at first merely an idea, an ideology, which seeks, usually through revolution and the disruption of existing arrangements, to revive an old nation or give birth to a new one. Whether existing nations will favor or oppose the emergence of a new nation will depend upon their own group, national, and international interests. (In Western Europe nationalism was the result of slow domestic development later intensified by self-conscious rationalization; in most of the rest of the world, it was largely imported and became revolutionary ideology.)

Another form of ideological conflict takes place over change in basic religious, political, economic, and social institutions within nations. Agitation and action to make fundamental change in a given institution has a way of taking place at the same time in a number of nations, but the change will be far advanced in some, moderately advanced or just beginning in others, and completely without appeal in still others. States in which change has been accomplished may exploit this to extend the new ideology (and their own influence) among the states and groups where that ideology has an appeal. States in which change has little or no appeal may use resistance to change to extend their influence among the states and groups everywhere which are opposing change. Conflict over change may bring a new unity (for or against it) to some states and may disrupt other states. Within a country the groups favoring change have a way of sympathizing and cooperating with groups in other countries favoring change, while groups opposing change manifest a similar tendency. Thus proponents and opponents of change in states where the ideological conflict is unresolved may become or appear to become fifth columnists of states which are more unified in favor of change or in opposition to it. (During the French Revolution, Federalists in the United States thought Jeffersonians were fifth columnists of Jacobin France, and Jeffersonians thought Federalists were fifth columnists of Tory Britain.)

In the sixteenth and seventeenth centuries the ideological conflict which entwined with the ordinary conflict of the territorial entities was the religious one of Protestants against Catholics; in the eighteenth century it was that of constitutional government against absolute monarchy; in the nineteenth century it involved political democracy; and in the twentieth century it has been over economic collectivism, the degree to which government responsibility in economic and social matters should be carried and the methods used to achieve this degree.

Sometimes states make international alliances on the basis of a common ideology (Christian states versus Moslem, Catholic versus Protestant, legitimist versus revolutionary), but usually national power interests are of greater importance in determining such alliances, and not infrequently alliances are made in the national interest which defy sharp ideological differences. In the seventeenth century, Catholic France was in alliance with the Protestant states of Germany against the Catholic Hapsburgs and their Catholic allies, for France feared the power of the Hapsburg empire. At the same time Protestant Sweden, primarily on the basis of common ideology, was in alliance with the Protestant German states which were allies of France. In the eighteenth century, Britain, farthest advanced in constitutional government, was usually allied with the absolute monarchs of Central and Eastern Europe against the absolute monarchy of France, which both Britain and the Central European monarchs feared would upset the balance of power. By late nineteenth century, tsarist Russia and democratic France were in alliance against Germany, whose growing power both feared. It has often been said that in the face of the threat to the national security, states will make an alliance with the ideological devil.

There was a time when alliances which cut across drastically different cultures were thought by ordinary citizens to be infernal indeed, as when Catholic France in the seventeenth century made an alliance with the Islamic Sultan of Turkey against the Catholic Hapsburg empire; and even as late as 1902 there were misgivings when Britain made an "equal" alliance with Japan. Alliances which cut across all the continents and cultures are commonplace today.

(The Anglo-Japanese alliance came in for another sort of criticism, for in it Britain was backing Japan against Russia in the Far East, at the very time Britain was getting closer to France, Russia's ally, and even to Russia itself in opposition to Germany in Europe. But this sort of cross-play is not infrequent, for nations not only change allies—the ally of yesterday becomes the enemy of today, the enemy of yesterday the ally of today—but they also at times make one set of arrangements for one part of the world, a different set for another part of the world. In recent years the United States and Britain, the closest of allies, have had different policies with respect to Communist China. But all of this does not differ from domestic politics where groups, factions, and parties shift alliances and also cooperate in limited ways for specific objectives with groups they oppose in other ways.)

Alliances between states of common ideology are more comfortable and more easily made (as in the case of the United States and Britain in the twentieth century), and sometimes even in the face of an alarming threat to the balance of power and the national security, differences in ideology make the formation of countervailing protective alliances most difficult. The Grand Alliance against Hitler, like the Grand Alliance against Napoleon, was held together not by a common ideology of its own but by a common fear of the opposition's ideology and threat to the balance of power. In the war against Hitler, the Western democracies worked easily together, but ideological differences between the Western democracies and Communist Russia made the formation of a common alliance extremely difficult (so difficult that Hitler almost won his victory by default), and the maintenance of the alliance even during the heat of war was precarious.

During the late 1940's and the decade of the 1950's, the Western alliance of non-Communist states and the Eastern alliance of Communist states represented about as clear-cut a division on the basis of ideology as history affords. Some even conjectured that ideology had emerged as the most important single factor in international relations. But even during this period there was never absolute ideological purity. Tito, a confirmed Communist, took Yugoslavia out of the Soviet alliance for a number of reasons, and most of the new nations, while non-Communist, refused to join the Western alliance against the Communist states. In recent years the rift between the Soviet Union and Communist China, based in part on ideological differences within the Communist world itself and in part on non-ideological considerations, has further impaired the ideological solidarity of the rival alliances and demonstrated again the everlasting pluralism, flexibility, and complexity of international relations.

Collective security, too, is not a recent element in international relations; it did not begin with the League of Nations. Neither is it an independent element; along with its collective-security features may be mixed other elements. Some of the old Greek federations represented balance-of-power alliances; some, germinal Greek nationalism; some, embryonic collective security; and some were a combination of these elements. The Holy Roman Empire at times operated as a balance-of-power alignment for pope or emperor against other parts of Europe; at times as a battleground between pope and emperor or other warring contestants; at times as budding German nationalism; at times as a collective-security organization bound by laws of restraint above the states which composed it; and many times as a mixture of these elements. Following the Peace of Vienna in 1815, the Concert of Europe represented a significant interplay of power politics, legitimist (conservative) ideology, and an embryonic (and perverse) kind of collective security which sought to preserve peace by freezing the *status quo.* And the League of Nations and the United Nations, among other things, often afforded an additional arena for the conflict of the international power blocs.

The complicated and flexible nature of international relations can best be understood by examining concrete situations, by analyzing the operations of some of its most conspicuous practitioners who stood at the very vortex of international affairs in times of crisis. The following examples, drawn from hundreds of possible illustrations, are merely impressionistically suggestive.

There was Pericles, leader of the Athenian state during the trying days of the Peloponnesian War. At home, Pericles had to maneuver between the old aristocratic party of Cimon and the parvenu people's party of Cleon. Abroad, Athens was engaged in a life-and-death struggle with Sparta, Persia, and the aristocratic agrarian states in alliance with them. The enemies of Athens frequently made successful ideological appeals to the agrarian and aristocratic groups still surviving in commercial Athens and in the commercial, democratic states in alliance with her, thus producing fifth-column subversion. The war went badly for Athens. In his extremity, Pericles made an appeal to a pan-Hellenic patriotism in urging all Greece to unite in a common federation. Plutarch called this noble, and noble it may have been, but it appears a bold stroke of national ideological politics to extricate Athens from an increasingly difficult class ideological-power situation.

There was Marlborough, political as well as military leader of England in the War of the Spanish Succession waged to check Louis XIV and insure a workable balance of power. In addition to his superb military achievements, Marlborough was active on scores of political and diplomatic fronts: making and unmaking cabinet ministers; intriguing in the petticoat politics of Queen Anne's court; mediating between the petty German princes and balancing the interests of his other heterogeneous allies; over and again cajoling the Dutch deputies into allowing the Dutch armies to fight; reconciling the Emperor to his Protestant subjects in Hungary; stirring the Calvinists of the Cévennes and the Catalonians in Spain into fifth-column rebellions.

There was Frederick the Great, fighting all the continent in the Seven Years' War and engrossed not only in the military leadership of the war but in all phases of its political and diplomatic activity: winning the support of his new Silesian subjects by stopping religious persecutions; moving to separate the Protestant Saxons from their Catholic ruler; pursuing a sedulously "correct" policy in Hanover with an eye to reassuring Britain's Hanoverian kings; attempting to reach into French policy by bribing the Pompadour; sowing dissension between the Tsarina Elizabeth and her chief military commander; proclaiming himself the defender of Protestant Europe against "Jesuit Austria and France"; repeatedly appealing from the Diet of the Empire and over the heads of the German princes for the ideological national support of the German people.

There was Talleyrand, a true artist in international politics, accurately appraising the power balance as it shifted during the Revolutionary, Napoleonic, and Restoration eras, and adroitly using first the revolutionary ideology and then the legitimist one to the national interests of France.

There was the Younger Pitt, whose career from 1792 to 1806 is most instructive for mid-twentieth-century Americans. Pitt's task was analogous to our own at this time: how to check a great revolutionary power from upsetting the balance of power by direct military aggression, how to prevent the undermining of governments through ideological fifth-column subversion, how to avoid being tied too closely to moth-eaten and reactionary allies, and how to defeat a leftist movement abroad without at home bowing to reactionary hysteria and closing the door to domestic reform.

There was Bismarck, whose career yields rich insights: how in the interest of unifying Germany he adroitly created the War of 1866 with Austria and the War of 1870 with France and in each case isolated his victim diplomatically; and how, during the years of German unification, he kept the Tsar neutral, and during the years after 1871, kept Russia's friendship and even Russia's acquiescence in Germany's repeated mediation between Russian and Austrian interests. Equally instructive are the maladroit activities of that august dreamer, Napoleon III, for we can learn from the bunglers as well as from the artists. Bismarck used the ideology of nationalism to build Germany; but the third Napoleon misused it in Italy and in Poland to alienate the two powers, Austria and Russia, he needed most to help him check the rising Germany. Napoleon's record of disaster is unmistakable: it runs clear and unbroken from Solferino to Sadowa to Sedan.

These thumbnail sketches do not of course do justice to all the pressures, elements, and approaches involved in any of these crises; but they do suggest the complexity of international politics, a complexity emphatically not peculiar to our times, and the resiliency required to deal with them. They do not adequately suggest the continuing home pressures existing in the midst of international crisis, and it is significant that many of the most eminent of the practitioners of international relations lost control of domestic politics or fell from power because of a neglect of the home front at the very time of brilliant achievement abroad: Marlborough, Chatham, Talleyrand, Disraeli, Bismarck, Wilson, Clemenceau, Churchill.

The enormously complicated nature of international affairs did not become fully pertinent to American experience until first under Wilson and then under F.D.R. Americans themselves finally stood at the very center of world politics.

International relations, then, always involve many elements, and as foreign policy responds to changing conditions so do the relationships of the elements; they are combined in different ways and proportions, greater emphasis is given to this element rather than to that element. Since 1945 American foreign policy has made several significant shifts: from emphasis on the United Nations and diplomatic cooperation with Russia to large-scale economic aid to Europe, to rearmament and military alliances, to increasing use of economic aid and social politics in the underdeveloped countries while at the same time taking a "new look" at the military and relying less on conventional armaments and more on the nuclear deterrent. (However, through all these shifts many elements were being employed simultaneously.) Minor shifts take place from month to month, even from week to week, as between the various elements and within them.

When a nation makes a change in the direction of its foreign policy, all the elements of the combination undergo considerable shifts in their relationships to one another. Such changes of direction occurred, for example, when the Bourbons of France and the Hapsburgs of Austria buried their traditional enmity and became allies in 1756; when Britain moved from relative enmity with France and became an ally of France in the Crimean War of 1854; when Britain moved to relative isolation from the continent after the Crimean War; when Britain moved back from relative isolation and joined an entente with France and Russia in the first decade of this century; when the United States moved from isolation to virtual involvement and then to war in 1941; when the Allied cooperation of World War II was broken in 1947 and East and West moved into the Cold War.

This change of direction in 1947 required an entire reassessment of the existing elements—of the national power-politics element (an old and primary element in international relations), of group and class ideology (which had been raised to a place among the primary elements with the French Revolution and was intensified by the Russian Revolution), and of collective security (an element of some consequence with the League of Nations and more consequence with the United Nations, but which by and large still remained peripheral).

There are those who contend that while international relations are undeniably plural, no really new element ever enters the combination, that the more international relations seem to change the more they remain the same. This is egregiously mistaken. International relations, like everything else, are evolutionary. Sometimes world conditions change, converge, and climax in such a way that a new or revolutionary element emerges as a primary element in international relations, or an old element is so enormously increased in importance as in effect to become a new element, for the first time rising to a place among the primary elements.

It is the superlative realist who first perceives this new element and makes use of it. A great revolution in world politics took place in the seventeenth century when Cardinal Richelieu, France's great minister, used the new centralized monarchical nationalism to defeat France's enemies abroad who still were largely dependent on the old (and divisive) feudal and ecclesiastical elements. From that time on, as monarchical nationalism consolidated itself in country after country, national power politics increasingly became the central element in international relations.

Again, such a revolution occurred when the French Revolution raised group and class ideology (in this case middle-class democracy) and nationalism as ideology to primary places in international relations. Revolutionary France employed both these ideologies in its struggle with other states, and many other states used the counter-ideology of legitimacy to resist France. Thus there was an impressive extension of the ideological conflict which cuts across national boundaries, and ideology much more pervasively than before was used as a weapon of penetration and subversion, of counter-penetration and counter-subversion, and of repression and national solidification. The Russian Revolution in turn further intensified the use of class ideology in international relations. Thus the French Revolution and the Russian Revolution raised ideology to one of the indisputably primary elements in the world politics of modern times.

It is quite conceivable that the revolution in the technology of war will eventually raise collective security from one of the secondary elements in international relations to one of the primary elements, to even the central place.

Although an understanding of international relations depends on assimilating materials from many fields and intellectual disciplines, its essential ingredient is political. Effective foreign policy requires effective politics: the purposeful and skillful use of *all* the elements of power available in a given situation. Power inheres in many elements—technological, military, economic, social, cultural, psychological, ideological, legal, moral, and scores and scores of other things. The military is only one of these elements even in time of war. The art of politics consists in seeing the situation in its *totality*, in a way as inclusive and complex as history, as pluralistic and diverse as life, and in knowing what aspects and elements to emphasize and most exploit in any given moment in history. (The largely adventitious appearance of able political leadership, of political artistry, itself becomes an additional element of power, sometimes one of the most important.)

A doctrinaire approach to international affairs is fatal. There is no one correct approach. This is not to deny the continuing centrality of national "power politics," the importance of military strength and military alliances. But to over-emphasize

Realpolitik and to underestimate the other approaches is a distortion and is therefore unrealistic. There are those who maintain that the "Anglo-Saxon" powers are naive bunglers in international politics because they have never sufficiently absorbed *Realpolitik*. This is ironically gratuitous in the light of the past successes of the "Anglo-Saxon" powers and the failure of Germany, the country most addicted to *Realpolitik*. The Germans of the twentieth century failed because they were crippled by an approach to world politics that was monistic and doctrinaire, that through the decades had become more and more one-sided until at last it disguised its lack of realism by calling itself realistic.

What then *is* realism in international politics? It is the same as realism in any other kind of politics. It is the ability to use purposefully many factors, even seemingly contradictory ones, and to use them not singly and consecutively but interdependently and simultaneously, with timely shifting of the emphasis as conditions change.

There can never be a single approach to world politics, for the simple reason that the people themselves, the individual citizens, are not one-purpose, one-value units; they are motivated and moved by many purposes. The emphasis given to the various values differs from individual to individual, and it differs with individuals as conditions and circumstances change.

Even Germany, despite its stress on *Realpolitik*, could not in fact pursue an entirely single-track approach. Even those states today we denominate as "totalitarian" employ a more or less pluralistic approach to international relations. This must necessarily be the case because totalitarian states must deal with the peoples of non-totalitarian states, and besides even the most totalitarian of states has never succeeded in becoming monolithic, has never succeeded in suppressing the human imagination and reducing people to mere automatons and puppets. Since all states must of necessity pursue more or less flexible courses, those states not hobbled with doctrinaire views of foreign policy are the ones most likely, within the means and resources available to them, to attain a maximum effectiveness.

People, then, have many and mixed purposes, motives, interests, and values. Some purposes and values sustain power politics—patriotism, national interest, group and class interests that identify themselves with the national interest, and the fears and insecurities which are felt with respect to the external dangers from other nations. Some purposes and values sustain ideological politics—the desire for institutional change or the opposition to it, and the group and class interests which support change or reject it. Some purposes and values sustain a drive to more collective security (another form of ideology so long as collective security is not firmly established), others arouse resistance to it.

But people have moral values, too, human and humane values, and power politics and ideological politics cannot ignore popular moral evaluations. (Indeed, moral values may be said to represent a kind of over-all ideological concept which works to keep the other elements approximately within bounds.) Some of these moral values come from institutionalized religious experience, some from long historical humanistic experience, and some from both. Those derived from long historical humanistic experience are likely to be common to many societies of any given historical period. These values are broader and less orthodox than those derived from religious experience alone. Today most of our societies which have evolved out of long historical experience share an over-all general morality that expresses itself in a kind of pragmatic humanism: a respect for human life and a rejection of needless want, suffering, and cruelty.

These over-all cultural values about morality *do* constitute an element in international relations. They helped to defeat Germany in World War I. They helped mightily to mobilize nations and groups and ideologies against the monumental brutalities of Hitler. Even in the frenzy of wars and revolutions they can be ignored only to degrees. The Communists respect them more than we like to admit, and as Communist revolution moderates, the Communists pay more and more attention to them. Moreover, despite their practices, the Communists have a theoretical humanitarianism which must be matched in theory and practice by their opponents, but within a different system.

Obviously our "idealists," such as Gladstone and Wilson, are deeply motivated by the over-all cultural moralities of their time, and they exploit them, but even "sensible" politicians such as Walpole and Talleyrand and Bismarck do not ignore them. Sometimes quiet maneuver in the closet is more effective, sometimes crusading zeal. Talleyrand strove for peace no less than Wilson. Wilson was more practical and Talleyrand more moral than their stereotypes imply.

Sometimes there is a tortuous conflict in applying values. Were Truman and Stimson wise in ordering the dropping of the atom bomb on Hiroshima? Was the saving of the lives of Allied military personnel—on the assumption (at the time not verifiable either way) that the war would otherwise be a protracted one—a justification for the massive slaughtering of enemy civilians? Were long-time and basic interests sacrificed to the apparent advantage of the moment?

The statesman of a world power, at the very center of international affairs, who has the awful responsibility of making the big and ultimate decisions in foreign policy, must coordinate the world situation into an over-all pattern. Today, flanked by specialists, technicians, methodologists, and game theorists, "informed" by the opinion polls at home and abroad, the recipient of advice and reports from all over the world, he must make decisive moves on which there are time limits. He cannot wait until all the evidence is in, for all the evidence is never in. He must necessarily do some operating on "hunches," based on his political experience and his insights, on his "feel" for the total state of affairs, which is a composite of past, present, and future, of facts and values, of situations within situations.

The great decisions are not made with scientific precision, and they never will be. If made effectively, they are made with a kind of high artistry.

If this sounds like a species of mysticism, the reader can best disabuse himself of that notion by analyzing scores and scores of actual concrete situations, historical and contemporary.

[1]

THE EXTENT
OF THE REVOLUTION

IN THE 1940's the United States leaped into world leadership. No nation had ever quite done this before: not even Rome after the Second Punic War, not even France after Westphalia (1648), not even Britain after Waterloo (1815).

In the 1930's the United States had retreated into a pathological isolation: Americans had rejected even the non-compulsory jurisdiction of the World Court, made the decision to retire from the Philippines, refused to build up fortifications on Guam, and abandoned their neutral rights at sea, rights which were guaranteed by international law and for which in the past they had fought—all in the belief that this retreat would keep them out of "foreign wars." Yet during the following decade Americans fought a global war, led the mightiest coalition in history, became deeply involved politically in all parts of the earth, made the pivotal decisions that affected the future everywhere, and an American President bestrode the world like Caesar Augustus of old. In the light of its traditional foreign policy this sudden stupendous global influence of America constituted a veritable revolution, one of the most dramatic in history.

American Continentalism

America's traditional foreign policy was expressed in the Monroe Doctrine (1823). This policy was popularly called isolation, but Beard's term "American Continentalism" was more accurate. The Monroe Doctrine had been foreshadowed by Washington's Neutrality Proclamation (1793) and by his Farewell Address (1796). As colonial subjects of Britain, Americans had participated in the world balance of power and in the great world wars of the seventeenth and eighteenth centuries, but American leaders after the Revolution conceived American interests to be mainly confined to the North American continent, and only in small part global.

In essence, the Monroe Doctrine declared that the United States would keep out of the territories, wars, alliances, spheres of influence, and politics of the world outside the Western Hemisphere, but in return non-American powers would be expected to stay out of the political affairs of the Americas. Non-American countries with colonies in the Western Hemisphere could keep them, but they were to acquire no more colonies and to refrain from expanding those they had.

This brave, bold new doctrine addressed by a fledgling nation to the great powers of the world was undertaken on the fiat of the United States alone. No other nation joined in the declaration, not even any of the new Latin American republics. The Monroe Doctrine was the unilateral declaration of the United States and not the multilateral declaration of the Western Hemisphere republics.

How did it happen that this doctrine was never successfully challenged by Old World powers? Mainly because the Monroe Doctrine was proclaimed and "enforced" during the non-imperialist interlude between the old mercantilist imperialism of the seventeenth and eighteenth centuries and the new finance and industrial imperialism of the late nineteenth and early twentieth centuries. During this interlude the great European powers were mainly absorbed in developing their internal industrial revolutions. In addition, and connected with this non-imperialism, no power or combination of powers threatened the European or world balance of power from Waterloo (1815) to the German invasion of Belgium (1914). In short, the period of American continentalism was in general the period of world peace.

In the first decades following the enunciation of the Monroe Doctrine there was debate over just what it should effectively include. Was it actually to extend just to North America, or just to the bulge of Brazil, or clear to the tip of Cape Horn? As a matter of fact the United States never made a critical issue over any territory beyond the bulge.

It should be noted that the Monroe Doctrine made no promise of economic isolation. The United States wanted to trade in all parts of the world, and commercial treaties were eagerly negotiated. Indeed, even as early as 1844 the United States took advantage of the British opening up of China in the Opium War to acquire trading rights there, and in 1853 the Americans forcibly opened Japan to trade. Nevertheless, America's economic prosperity depended largely on exploiting and expanding a wealthy internal market, and America's high protective-tariff policies after the Civil War illustrated a general policy of economic nationalism.

It should also be noted that while the Monroe Doctrine warned non-American powers to refrain from expanding in the Western Hemisphere it did not require the United States or other American powers to refrain from such expansion. For the United States the Monroe Doctrine was no self-denying ordinance. In fact, the nation began expanding in 1803 with the Louisiana Purchase and continued to expand over the American continent at the expense of non-American powers and Mexico. Americans, in spite of their promise in the Monroe Doctrine that Europe could keep the American colonies it already had, actually liked to see the possessions of European powers in this hemisphere liquidated, for this meant the continued withdrawal of the European balance of power and greater security for the United States.

The Americans were not always able to liquidate European powers. In the War of 1812 an attempt was made to conquer Canada or a large part of it. (Incidentally, America's attack on Britain while the latter, back to the wall, was fighting to stop Napoleon from upsetting the world balance of power, illustrates the tendency of small powers to leave the maintaining of the balance of power to the big powers and to take advantage of the troubles of those big powers to gain advantages for themselves.) The attempt failed. But the idea that the American flag would some day wave from the Arctic to Panama grew in popular fancy and only died slowly with the decline of agrarian imperialism during the post-Civil War industrialization of the country.

In expanding over the continent, Americans displayed much realism. Their use of fifth-column American settlers in Florida, Texas, Oregon, and California to prepare the way for annexation was worthy of the most sagacious European *Realpolitik*. However, when Americans thought of international politics outside this hemisphere, they tended to moralize and to think in idealistic and ideological terms. Even President Monroe was tempted to apply his doctrine of non-intervention to the Greek Revolution and to warn the Metternich powers that America stood against re-establishment of the autocratic *status quo* in Greece, but his more realistic Secretary of State objected. Nevertheless, Americans welcomed the republican and liberal revolutions of the nineteenth century because these harmonized with their own traditions.

The Civil War was a deadly crisis for American continentalism. Up to that time it seemed clear that no North American balance of power, analogous to the European balance of power, would develop. The United States had emerged as by far the strongest power on the continent, and Canada and Mexico were in no way able to challenge American power. But what if the United States itself should split into two republics, and what if these, in turn, should split further? During the Civil War there was talk of a possible northwestern confederation separated from the North and of a possible southwestern confederation, with Texas as its center, separated from the South. A definite North American balance of power similar to that of Europe probably would have resulted from a Confederate victory; and had multiple powers emerged, the European balance of power, taking advantage of their rivalries, ultimately would have reinsinuated itself into the North American system. Indeed, the Southern Confederacy staked its success on the chance of English and French help, and during the war Napoleon III indulged his own quixotic imperialism and placed Maximilian on a Mexican throne. The French were expelled only after the danger of American fragmentation had passed. (The successful American Revolution, offspring of the European balance of power, had occurred during a period of intense British-French imperialist rivalry and because of that rivalry France had come to the aid of the American colonies, but the Confederate secession occurred during a period of relative non-imperialism, and hence European aid to the Confederacy was inadequate.)

A more unified and confident America emerged from the Civil War. As Americans more and more peopled the Pacific Coast and since no "protecting" British fleet policed the North Pacific as it did the North Atlantic, the Americans came more and more to take an interest in the defense of the Pacific. Besides, there was a school of American thought which held that China and the East would some day be a market for American goods in a way that the manufacturing countries of Europe would never be. In 1867 the United States purchased Alaska and the far-flung Aleutians, although the purchase was generally unpopular and was stigmatized as "Seward's folly." In 1889 the United States joined with Britain and Germany in a tripartite protectorate over the faraway Samoa Islands, a foreshadowing of the abandonment of continentalism. In 1893 an American fifth column spearheaded a revolution in Hawaii and raised the American flag. The new Hawaiian government asked for American annexation; but isolationist sentiment proved too strong and Cleveland hauled down the flag. In 1898, after Dewey had taken Manila, Hawaii was annexed by joint resolution of Congress.

The Departure from American Continentalism

It was the Spanish-American War of 1898, beginning as a crusade to liberate the Cubans and ending in military action to subjugate the Filipinos, which led to the general abandonment of American continentalism. As a result of that war America was left saddled with the Philippines, seven thousand miles away in the heart of the Far East. The arguments for retaining them were diverse: manifest destiny; the white man's burden; the opportunity to Christianize natives; the good fortune in having colonies near the mainland of Asia, where investments and markets beckoned; the fear that Germany would take the islands if the Americans surrendered them; the feeling that Americans were stuck with a responsibility they could not dodge. The argument that Americans could not scuttle and run probably had the greatest weight with ordinary Americans. It was the year of the grand partition of China, Kipling's poetry expressed the spirit of the times, and most of the arguments for retaining the Philippines were the familiar imperialist arguments then current in the Western world. Senator A. J. Beveridge was stumping the country telling Americans that Britain's greatest glory was not Magna Charta but her great civilizing work in India. American imperialism seemed most popular in the financial circles of the East and in the "isolationist" Middle West, which has always been strongly nationalist. Henry Cabot Lodge and Theodore Roosevelt were imperialist leaders in the East; but President McKinley, his successive Secretaries of State, the pro-imperialist Chairman of the Senate Foreign Relations Committee, and the ardent Senator Beveridge were all from the Middle West.

A galaxy of great names spoke out against the departure from continentalism: Grover Cleveland, Benjamin Harrison, Andrew Carnegie, William James, Mark Twain, Carl Schurz, William Jennings Bryan, Senators Hoar and Vest. Almost all the arguments in favor of American isolation were made then: the corrupting influence of ruling dependent peoples, the burden of maintaining large armies and navies, the danger of militarizing American politics and society, the certainty that America would become involved in foreign alliances and Asian and European wars. In the presidential election of 1900, with Bryan the Democratic nominee against McKinley, imperialism was the paramount issue, and the American electorate gave the decision to McKinley. Years later, writing of the emotional dilemma of the Americans of this time, George Santayana, himself the product of a riper civilization, observed that Americans seemed to be frightened of the uses of power and that William James was despairing of his country just when it was reaching puberty and beginning to play a part in world history.

But many of the old continentalist attitudes remained, and the non-militarism bred of America's relatively peaceful career and the pacifism inherent in many of America's pietistic sects persisted. For decades to come, isolationism would still be a force to be reckoned with in American affairs.

The decision of 1900, however, did mark a great departure in American foreign policy. In 1898 and 1899 the United States had gained control of Cuba (later converted into a legal protectorate over an "independent" nation), and sovereignty over Puerto

Rico, Guam, Hawaii, and the Philippines. Admiral Alfred T. Mahan succinctly described American foreign policy from the Spanish-American War to World War I as participation in Asia, a sphere of influence in the Caribbean, and continued non-participation in Europe.

In China the United States, having no sphere of influence of its own, took the lead in proclaiming the territorial integrity of China and the "open door," which was described cynically as "no special privileges for individual exploiting nations in China, equal opportunity for all exploiting nations." The United States was able to get formal recognition of these policies from the big powers, but their spheres of interest remained and in some cases were extended and the realities were little affected. At the same time, Japan was being supported by Britain and to a lesser extent by the United States in order to check Germany and Russia in the Far East. However, after Japan's victory over Russia in the war of 1904-1905, it was Japan that loomed as the chief challenger of the balance of power in China and Asia. American policy makers experienced great difficulties in the Far East, for they had to rely on diplomacy alone; Americans were still not willing to make binding alliances and commit themselves to the use of full-scale force in the interest of China policy, Asian trade, and the Philippines.

However, no uncertainty or ambivalence characterized American policy in the Caribbean Sea, which in the first decades of the twentieth century was reduced to "an American lake." The United States was steadily expanding its navy, which from 1880 to 1900 moved from twelfth to third place among the world's navies. To serve its expanding navy and growing world trade, the United States built the Panama Canal, and Americans came to think of the Virgin Islands, Puerto Rico, the Dominican Republic, Haiti, Cuba, Nicaragua, and the Republic of Panama, which was an American creation, as the outer defenses of the Canal route. Puerto Rico and the Virgin Islands became outright American possessions, Cuba and Panama legal protectorates, and the Dominican Republic, Haiti, and Nicaragua "veiled protectorates." An American naval base was built at Guantánamo and naval installations on the Corn Islands and on islands in the Gulf of Fonseca.

American economic penetration into the Caribbean area and the

Central American republics also increased enormously. New York banks became the chief creditors of these countries; the United Fruit Company came to be the most important single business enterprise in some of them; American corporations came to own extensive public utilities, plantations, ranches, sugar mills, oil refineries, and other large business enterprises. Wherever American influence penetrated on a large scale there was a perceptible advance in material conditions, but there were also further concentrations in land holdings and much wounding of national pride.

An instrument of American penetration was President Theodore Roosevelt's corollary to the Monroe Doctrine (1904) which in effect held that when governments in the Caribbean and Central America defaulted on their debts owed to European banks, the United States, rather than suffer European intervention, would itself intervene to collect them. And out of this emerged another "corollary," never officially expressed, which implied that since the United States would have to do the collecting in cases of default, the Caribbean and Central American countries should do their borrowing from New York banks rather than European banks. Sometimes American intervention took the form of merely appointing an American receiver of customs in a delinquent country to take over the customhouses, collect the duties, and divide a large percentage of the proceeds among the foreign creditors, but sometimes the intervention went beyond this. To protect foreign creditors and to maintain order, United States Marines occupied the Dominican Republic from 1916 to 1924, Haiti from 1915 to 1934, and Nicaragua from 1912 to 1925 and again from 1927 to 1933.

Even in Europe, despite Mahan's apt summary, the United States was taking a greater interest. The expanding American fleet gradually took over the policing of Western Hemisphere waters as more and more of the British fleet was assigned to the North Sea in response to the threat of the growing German navy. Theodore Roosevelt's administration, in both Asia and Europe, was drawing closer to Britain as Germany showed greater aggressiveness. In 1906, the United States was officially represented at the European "power-politics" conference at Algeciras, where the American delegation, behind the scenes, threw its weight in favor of France and Britain and against Germany in the dispute of France and Germany over Morocco.

As the armaments race intensified among the European powers and advances in technology made certain that war, if it came, would be the most disastrous in history, there was an enormous amount of discussion in Europe and the United States about international machinery to maintain peace. On the official level this evidenced itself in American participation in the Hague peace conferences of 1899 and 1907 and in Secretary of State Bryan's arbitration treaties of 1913. The pre-World War discussions were more honest and realistic than were the escapist and platonic "outlawry of war" gestures of the 1920's, but even so, the approach was almost exclusively legal rather than political.

When the World War broke in 1914, the first since 1815, thoughtful Americans saw that America's isolation had been made possible largely because for a century there had been no threat to the balance of power. Except for the German, Scandinavian, and Irish minorities, American opinion was overwhelmingly favorable to Britain and France, and American neutrality was predicated on the faith that if the Allies did not win they would certainly not lose.

President Wilson, in his famous "Peace without Victory" speech, articulated the belief that the future stability of the world would be best served if neither side pressed the war to victory and much of the old balance of power was preserved. But twentieth-century war, mobilizing all the resources and technology of the belligerent nations, had become total and it vengefully aroused the passions of mass populations to the point where moderation and compromise in war had become impossible.

The threat of German victory, of an upsetting of the balance of power in a way American leaders thought would be disadvantageous to the United States (a threat which became almost a certainty with the collapse of Russia and the Eastern front in the winter of 1916-1917 and the subsequent Russian Revolution), was the chief cause of America's entry into the war. However, the German submarine campaign got the most popular attention, and when President Wilson put American participation in the war on the grounds of violated neutral maritime rights and later converted the war into an ideological one to save and extend democracy, the dramatic opportunity to drive home to the American people the lesson that America's national security was fatefully involved in the menaced balance of power was not adequately exploited.

Woodrow Wilson was the first American statesman to stand at the very vortex of world politics. His influence at the time and for generations afterward was profound. The fact that the United States Senate refused to ratify his League of Nations obscured the tremendous impact of his leadership. Wilson aimed for a new world order, and he distilled his views in his famous Fourteen Points, which urged freedom of the seas, the reduction of trade barriers among the nations, self-determination of nations, preparation of the colonial areas for nationhood, disarmament, and an international collective-security system to keep peace and coordinate the increasing international activities of a shrinking world. Wilson believed that the revolution in the technology of weapons and warmaking had rendered war total and so disruptive and destructive that an international substitute for it would have to be found, and that the traditional balance of power was breaking down and could no longer serve the functions it had once served (however poorly) in preventing, limiting, and moderating wars. To Wilson, historical developments had by the twentieth century created a new set of realities which would have to be dealt with through international organization.

Wilson's Fourteen Points became the Allied war aims (even though they conflicted in many ways with the secret treaties of the European Allies distributing the spoils of war among themselves); they were a morale builder for Allied peoples and thrilled most of the world; in effect they were brilliant war propaganda, and directed over the heads of the enemy governments to the peoples of Germany, Austria-Hungary, Bulgaria, and Turkey, they undermined those governments, contributed to the popular revolutions which overthrew them, and therefore probably hastened the end of the war; and with the Russian Revolution and the challenge of Marxism they were an answer to Lenin and formed the basis of the ideology of the Western democracies in their long struggle with Communism, a struggle which would reverberate through the century. Even as late as the 1960's the ideology and the long-time program of the West continued to be largely Wilsonian.

At the Paris peace conference, Wilson fought valiantly for his aims. These aims came in conflict with the old imperialism, and he was forced at many points to compromise. Sometimes he was at odds with Lloyd George, Clemenceau, Orlando, and most of the other Allied delegations, but quite frequently the British delegations supported the Wilson position. Despite his defeats and compromises, as the Treaty of Versailles and the League of Nations finally emerged, they bore the imprint of Wilson's thinking.

Many of the subject nationalities of the old Russian, German, and Austro-Hungarian empires became independent states, and while this further weakened the old balance of power, Wilson regarded it as both inevitable and just, and he expected the League of Nations to be a stabilizing influence. Consistently with his belief in national self-determination and in order to salvage some of the old balance of power, Wilson fought successfully to save Germany as a power unit, to prevent her loss of the left bank of the Rhine. (To Wilson, a balance of power which did not violate national self-determination for the mere sake of larger power units was not incompatible with an international collective-security system but a supplement to it and helpful during the period of transition when the world organization was getting started and striving for greater effectiveness.) Wilson succeeded in limiting Germany's reparations payments to the civilian damage and the expenses of Allied war pensions. (The European Allies had first demanded that Germany be made to pay the whole cost of the war.) The colonies of Germany and the Arab territories of Turkey were not distributed outright to the victors but were made mandates of the League of Nations and were to be prepared for national statehood. The League of Nations, which became an integral part of the Treaty of Versailles, was largely the work of Wilson; and the League became the basis of the later United Nations. To protect France from any future German aggression until such time as the League of Nations would become effective, Wilson consented to a mutual assistance treaty of the United States, Britain, and France.

Wilson realized that the treaties which came out of the Paris conference contained some provisions of doubtful wisdom and left many problems unsolved, but the threat of Bolshevist revolution hung over Germany and Central Europe, there was need of haste and the stabilizing influence of immediate settlement, and

Wilson expected that the League of Nations and other international machinery set up by the treaties, in which the United States would participate, would later work out rectifications and solutions.

The United States Senate regarded the tripartite American-British-French treaty as an "entangling alliance" and it never had a chance of ratification. With respect to the Treaty of Versailles, including the League of Nations, the Senate was divided roughly into three groups. There were the Wilsonites, who wanted ratification without any changes. There were the isolationists, variously called the irreconcilables, the bitter-enders, the battalion of death, who were opposed to the treaty and the League in any form, with or without reservations. And there was the largest group of all, the Lodge reservationists, who favored ratification, provided certain conditions and clarifications, designed to safeguard American sovereignty from international encroachments, were written into the treaty. Had the Wilsonites and the reservationists succeeded in uniting, the treaty would have been ratified with reservations attached. But these two groups were never able to get together, and to this day a controversy has raged over whether Wilson should or should not have advised his followers to accept the reservations and unite with the reservationists to ratify the League. When the treaty came before the Senate without the reservations, the irreconcilables and the reservationists united to defeat it. When the treaty came before the Senate with the reservations, the irreconcilables and the Wilsonites united to prevent its getting a two-thirds majority.

The defeat of the League of Nations by the Senate probably represented popular sentiment, for there was a marked isolationist reaction after the end of the war. Many of those who saw clearly that America had entered the war to prevent the upsetting of the balance of power and to preserve its national security now felt, after the threat was over, that the danger had been exaggerated and probably would not arise again for another century. Others felt that the international bankers, big business, and the munitions makers had seduced the nation into war, that the best way to prevent involvement in European war in the future would be to shut off credit and munitions to both sides. It was this sort of thinking that produced the neutrality acts of the 1930's in which America surrendered its neutral commercial and maritime rights. Still others, who had believed literally in the Fourteen Points and a regenerated world, were disillusioned by the revival of "power politics"; by the territorial aggrandizement of the big powers and even the little ones, old and new, after the war; and by the Bolshevist Revolution in Russia. The truth was that America's plunge into full-scale international affairs took place at a time world politics had become extraordinarily complex, turbulent, and revolutionary; this leap was too abrupt (even the next one, with the experience of 1917-1920 behind it, would be difficult enough); American attitudes were not yet adjusted to so radical a departure from American practice and tradition.

Escapism: The Flight from the Twentieth Century (1920-1940)

For American foreign policy, the period between World War I and World War II represented one of the most curious situations in all history. The United States emerged from World War I the most powerful nation in the world—economically, financially, politically, militarily. Although its population represented only about 6 per cent of the world's peoples, it was producing close to one-third of the world's industrial products and about one-half of its steel. The United States was the world's foremost creditor nation. In the 1920's its private bankers loaned Western Europe the money for reconstruction, Germany the money with which to pay reparations, and Latin American and other underdeveloped countries the money to make beginnings in modernization and industrialization. Its giant corporations enormously extended their holdings in oil in the Middle East and in Latin America and their investments in Latin American public utilities, mines, banks, plantations, ranches, and refineries. Yet the United States government built higher and higher tariff walls, insisted that its wartime allies pay back their war debts, and made it almost a fetish to refrain from participation in international organizations (even the non-compulsory jurisdiction of the World Court was rejected) and international political commitments. So far as world politics were concerned, Americans attempted to turn the clock back not only beyond 1917 but even beyond 1898. Americans even gave up rights at international law for which officially they had fought in 1917 and in far-distant 1812.

Yet in no period of their history did Americans do so much verbalizing about world peace. A classic example of escapism was the Pact of Paris of 1928 (the Kellogg-Briand pact) which the United States government sponsored. In this treaty more than sixty signatory nations renounced war as an instrument of national policy and agreed to accept settlements or solutions of all disputes or conflicts, of whatever nature or origin, solely by peaceful means. The pact lacked any means of enforcement. This was precisely its appeal to the Americans of this period. The Americans had succeeded in making other nations cast off evil. Mystique was substituted for policy. Secretary of State Henry L. Stimson later proclaimed his own device for putting "teeth" in the pact. This came to be known as the Stimson Doctrine, which consisted in the refusal of the United States to recognize any situation, treaty, agreement, or change in territorial status which might be brought about by non-peaceful means. But mere non-recognition of the fact did not obliterate the fact.

Because of its deliberate policy of non-participation, the United States failed to make its weight felt in all of the situations and crises which led up to World War II. It was not present in 1923 to back Britain in her attempt to dissuade the French from their illegal invasion of the Ruhr to force Germany to pay reparations. This seizure of the Ruhr set up a chain of circumstances which led to Germany's disastrous inflation, the weakening of her middle classes, and the unleashing of the ugly forces of nihilism which contributed to the rise of Hitler to power. America's platonic doctrine of non-recognition did not stop Mussolini from seizing Ethiopia in 1935 or stop Hitler from sensationally upsetting the European balance of power in less than three years by militarizing the Rhineland in 1936, taking Austria in 1938 and later that year annexing the Sudetenland, and in 1939 dismembering the rest of Czechoslovakia, grabbing Danzig, the Corridor, and Memel, and making his extravagant demands on Poland which resulted in World War II. Moreover, by its neutrality legislation of 1935, 1936, and 1937, the United States had assured Mussolini and Hitler in advance that it would stay neutral in the event their actions led to war with Britain and France, that the United States would embargo arms to all belligerents and refuse them loans and credit, so that Britain and France would be deprived of the advantages they had enjoyed during America's neutrality in World War I.

America's non-participation in Asia was as disastrous as its non-participation in Europe. Since 1899 the Americans had espoused the open door in China and its territorial integrity, but in the 1930's they stood by while Japan absorbed China, upset the balance of power in Asia, and built one of the largest empires in history.

During World War I the prewar balance of power in Asia was seriously impaired. Japan now stood without real challenge, and it was soon clear that only a vigorous policy on the part of the United States could check her. Britain and France had been weakened by the war and were unable to exert their traditional influence. Japan had taken all of the German possessions in Asia and the Pacific, and German power had disappeared from the area. Russia was in the throes of revolution, furious civil wars, and then vast internal development, and the Western powers, including the United States, would not have welcomed Soviet power as a makeweight in the Far East even if such power were effectively available. Most important, China was in the midst of profound revolution and civil war and in no position to protect herself.

In 1912, the Nationalist party (Kuomintang) of Sun Yat-sen had led the revolution which had overthrown the Manchu dynasty and established a republic. Sun Yat-sen's movement, among the earliest of the anti-imperialist revolutions, sought to expel the foreign powers from their concessions and spheres of influence in China, unify the country, foster national consciousness, and develop the Chinese economy on a social-democratic basis with a mixture of state and private enterprise. But the new republic at Peking fell into the hands of the conservative Chinese, old government hands who had served the Manchus, and the feudal elements. In 1917 Sun Yat-sen set up a rival government at Canton, and from that time on civil war was waged between the Peking and the Canton governments. As strife spread, large parts of China fell into the hands of conservative Chinese local chieftains or warlords (tuchuns). Following the death of Sun in 1925 the confusion was worse compounded when his Kuomintang split between the majority wing led by Chiang Kai-shek and the minority wing of leftists and Communists. In the meantime the Japanese had profited by the troubles in China to increase their own concessions in that country. However, by 1930 Chiang Kai-shek seemed gradually to be extending Nationalist control over China, and the Japanese felt that they would have to strike while China was still weak and divided. And strike they did.

In 1931 and 1932 the Japanese took over political and military control of both north and south Manchuria, erected the puppet state of Manchukuo, and installed as their puppet ruler the heir of the Manchu dynasty. In 1933 they added the province of Jehol to Manchukuo. In 1935 Hopei (including the great cities of Peking and Tientsin) and Chahar provinces were virtually severed from China, and Japanese puppet governments were installed. In 1937 the Japanese struck farther south, and Shanghai and Nanking fell to them. In 1938 they captured Hankow and Canton. By 1939 all of China's great commercial cities were in Japanese hands. The war in Europe beginning in 1939 and the collapse of the Netherlands and France in 1940 beckoned the Japanese to even more empire in French Indochina, Thailand, the Dutch East Indies, and even the Philippines.

Meantime, what was the United States doing to check the growing might of Japan? Its one sagacious move took place back in 1922 when the treaties coming out of the Washington conference virtually froze the American, British, and Japanese navies to a 5:5:3 ratio. But this was the last of America's realistic measures with respect to Japan until the late 1930's. (In 1934 Japan renounced the Washington naval treaty and began a rapid expansion of her navy.) Stimson's non-recognition doctrine as applied to Manchukuo was futile. At the time of the Japanese takeover in Manchukuo there was talk in the League of Nations of putting an economic boycott on Japan, but the United States was not a member of the League, and several British statesmen announced that an economic boycott of Japan would be ineffective without American cooperation and that they would support no League boycott unless the United States consented to join in it. The United States gave no sign that it would take part in such a boycott. When the United States refused to build up its fortifications in Guam and Congress in 1934 passed an act granting independence to the Philippines, to take effect in 1946, the

Japanese were convinced that the Americans were losing interest in the Far East. (It was observed that the Americans were interested not so much in freedom *for* the Philippines as in freedom *from* them.) In fact, the United States contributed much to making Japan's conquest of China possible; American traders serviced the Japanese war machine with the necessary oil, scrap iron, steel, and other sinews of war which kept that machine going.

The Hitlerian expansion in Europe and the Japanese conquests in Asia seemed at first only to stiffen the American determination to remain aloof from world politics. Neutrality legislation was broadened and tightened, proposals for peacetime conscription were howled down, and all attempts to get an appreciable expansion in the navy were defeated until 1938. When in 1937 President Roosevelt suggested in a Chicago speech that the time had come for an international quarantine of aggressors, his proposal was met with a torrent of popular disapproval. The prevailing non-participationist sentiment was expressed in a proposed amendment to the United States Constitution (the so-called Ludlow Amendment), which provided that except in the case of foreign invasion or an attack on an American possession, a declaration of war by Congress would not become effective unless confirmed by a majority of voters in a national referendum. President Roosevelt declared that such an amendment would cripple any President in his conduct of foreign relations and encourage other nations to believe that they could violate American rights with impunity. Nevertheless, a reliable national poll revealed that 73 per cent of those polled favored a popular referendum of this type. The administration was forced to mobilize the last ounce of its political strength to defeat the Ludlow Amendment in the House of Representatives.

Sentiment for non-involvement in international affairs was not sectional; it was not confined to the Middle West; it was overwhelming and it represented opinion in all sections of the country. Some of the important votes in Congress on the neutrality acts were taken without prolonged debate, some even by voice vote. Americans were not going to be wheedled into pulling British chestnuts out of the fire this time; they were not going to be bamboozled twice in a generation!

And then through 1939, 1940, and 1941 occurred one of those

dramatic shifts in American public opinion, the kind of shift noted as an American characteristic by De Tocqueville over a century ago. As the Japanese built in Asia one of the great empires of history and the Germans steadily expanded in Europe, Americans became frightened, for this was an upsetting of the balance of power on the world's two most populous continents, swifter and more sensational then even Napoleon's. Nazi leadership was far more ruthless and contemptuous of American values than the Kaiser's Germany had ever been, and besides, the French and British defensive dikes were not as strong as they had been in 1914. Here was a lesson in the importance of the balance of power and its effect on American security and even survival that could not be misunderstood, and Roosevelt underscored it in a way that Wilson had never done. (The lesson of 1939-1941 made so vivid an impression on American opinion that after 1945 it kept insisting that Communist expansion, actually more ambiguous and amorphous, was the Hitlerian expansion all over again and should not be appeased as Hitler had been.)

After the fall of France and during the Battle of Britain, American opinion solidified behind Roosevelt's leadership, which was moving steadily toward intervention to save Britain and what was left of China. The Republican national convention of 1940 dramatically symbolized this shift in American opinion when it rejected Vandenberg, Dewey, and Taft because of their isolationism and made Wendell Willkie the Republican Presidential nominee. Willkie's nomination violated every rule of American politics: he was a big-business executive, he had had no political career, he had been a Democrat most of his life. Willkie, however, had one overriding virtue: he was the only interventionist before the convention.

After the shift in American opinion the United States moved rapidly from neutrality to virtual belligerency. The navy was expanded; conscription was voted; loans were extended to China; all scrap iron and steel except to the Western Hemisphere and Britain were embargoed; the neutrality legislation was modified in the interest of the Allies and then scuttled altogether; fifty "over-age" American destroyers were transferred to Britain by mere executive agreement; the Lend-Lease Act was passed and the United States henceforth virtually *gave* military equipment

to the countries fighting Hitler; and American naval units con-
voyed ships carrying Lend-Lease material and were ordered "to
shoot on sight" Italian and German vessels which entered the
American "defensive waters" from Greenland to Iceland. Thus
even before Pearl Harbor the United States had become an active
participant. After Pearl Harbor it became a fighting ally and the
leader of the grand coalition against Germany, Italy, and Japan.
For a second time in a generation, then, the United States became
the maintainer of the world balance of power, playing the role
Britain had played for centuries.

The Revolution in American Foreign Policy

From 1941 to 1945 the United States fought a global war, led
the mightiest alliance in history, became deeply and irrevocably
involved in all parts of the earth, and made the pivotal decisions
that affected the future everywhere. Americans engaged in operations on all continents and the seven seas; Americans built and
manned four hundred military, naval, and air bases in all parts
of the globe; American goods in American ships poured into strategic areas everywhere; and the United States gave to its allies
in Lend-Lease alone equipment and aid valued at over 50 billion
dollars. During World War I, the United States held aloof as an
"associated power," but in World War II the United States became a full-fledged ally, and Americans and Britons combined
their chiefs of staff and fought under single commanders in
Europe, Africa, and Asia.

President Roosevelt plunged into power politics to the hilt: he
defied the "Asia Firsters" and made Europe rather than Asia the
primary theater of war; he went contrary to Churchill in giving
a prominent place in the war to China and Chiang Kai-shek; he
played the Vichy side of the street (while Churchill more or less
played the Free French side) and thereby helped prevent North
Africa and the French fleet from falling into the hands of the Axis;
he vetoed Churchill's proposal to open another front in the
Balkans; and he treated Stalin's susceptibilities with the greatest
solicitude and sought above all to convince the Russian leader that
the Western Allies would make no separate peace, in order to
insure the fidelity of Russia to the grand alliance, ultimately bring

Russia into the war against Japan, and lay the basis for the cooperation of the Soviet Union and the West after the war.

The United States took the lead in the conferences which during the war shaped the power politics of the postwar era. At Casablanca (1943) Roosevelt and Churchill agreed that the immediate objective of the Allies was the "unconditional surrender" of the Axis powers. Undoubtedly this expressed the mood of the Allied peoples at the time; it was aimed at avoiding the "soft" German peace of 1919; and it was meant to persuade the Russians that the Western powers would not make a separate peace with Germany. However, even at that time it was asked anxiously if this would not create dangerous power vacuums, contrary to sound balance-of-power principles, destroy needed buffers, checkmates, and balancers among the nations. At Moscow (1943) decisions were taken to restore democratic government and civil liberties in Italy and insure a free and independent Austria. At Cairo (1943) it was decreed that Japan would be stripped of all islands in the Pacific taken from Germany during World War I, would be required to restore to China all territories she had taken from that country since 1895, including Formosa and the Pescadores Islands, and would be forced to surrender Korea, which was to become a free and an independent nation. At Teheran (1943) it was agreed that Poland would give up White Russian and Ukrainian areas to Russia and receive compensation in German territories to the Oder River.

At Yalta (1945) decisions were taken with respect to the prospective Allied zones of occupation in Germany and German reparations. Rumania, Bulgaria, and Hungary were to have governments "broadly representative of all democratic elements," and in Poland "free and unfettered elections would be held on the basis of universal suffrage and secret ballot." In the Far East, Stalin promised to bring Russia into the war against Japan and to conclude a treaty with Chiang Kai-shek, although the Chinese Communists were increasingly challenging Chiang's authority over large areas of China. In return, Russia was to receive from Japan southern Sakhalin and the Kurile Islands, a "pre-eminent" position at Dairen, the warm-water port in southern Manchuria, a lease for a naval base at Port Arthur, joint interest with China in the operation of the Chinese Eastern and the Southern Manchurian Railroads, and continued recognition of the Soviet-sponsored People's Republic in Outer Mongolia.

The Yalta agreements were later harshly criticized. It was charged that the United States paid too high a price in the Far East for Russian cooperation; but at the time the extent of Japan's weakness was not yet realized, the atom bomb was still to be born, and it was felt that Russian participation would shorten the war and reduce the cost of war, perhaps by as much as a million casualties. It was also charged that Yalta delivered Rumania, Bulgaria, Hungary, and Poland to the tender mercies of the Russians, but it was not realized that the Russians would interpret democratic government to be Communist government and that they would enforce this interpretation in whatever countries their armies occupied. The most serious charges against Yalta were that the agreements were too hard on Germany and made impossible a viable balance of power in Eastern Europe and in the Far East. However, this claim, if valid, was one that should have been charged to the whole conduct of the war and not just to Yalta. With the impending unconditional surrender of Germany and Japan, the countries which had been checkmates to Russia were going down. The old balance of power was collapsing. No new balance of power in this area was in sight, for Chiang's China was far from being an effective power. If Russia were to have been curbed, the victories over Germany and Japan would have had to have been limited victories, leaving those countries with sufficient power to check Russia. This, however, was not the mood in which the war had been waged and the postwar world envisaged. The Western democracies had banked heavily on Russian cooperation after the war. Besides, there was a feeling, explicitly expressed by Secretary Hull and President Roosevelt over and again, that in the future the United Nations would take the place of balance-of-power politics.

At the Potsdam conference (1945) the United States, the Soviet Union, and Britain drew up detailed plans for the military occupation of Germany, German reparations, and the denazification and demilitarization of the country. In the Potsdam Declaration, President Truman and Prime Minister Attlee demanded the unconditional surrender of the Japanese armed forces, the demilitarization of Japan, the punishment of war criminals, the removal of obstacles to democracy, and compliance with the Cairo Declaration. Japan was to be subjected to military occupation until these objectives were accomplished, but the Japanese were assured that they would not be destroyed as a nation and that the Emperor would not be required to abdicate. It was on the basis of the Potsdam Declaration—after the first atomic bombs in history had been dropped on Hiroshima and Nagasaki and Russia had declared war on Japan and her armies were deep in Manchuria and Korea—that Japan surrendered to American forces in September 1945 and World War II came to a close.

In addition to taking a leading role in the decisions which were inevitably shaping the power world of the years to follow the war, the United States initiated moves which it hoped would mold the ideological world of the future and effectively increase international cooperation and organization. Even before the United States became a formal belligerent, Roosevelt and Churchill had issued the Atlantic Charter (1941), which called for national self-determination, wider economic opportunities, freedom from fear and want, freedom of the seas, and disarmament. At the Moscow Conference (1943) the Soviet Union promised to cooperate with the Western powers in building a collective-security organization. At a conference held at Hot Springs, Virginia, in 1943, the decision was taken to establish the world Food and Agriculture Organization. At a conference held at Bretton Woods, New Hampshire, in 1944, the World Bank and the International Monetary Fund, two organizations which were to play an important part in the postwar world, were established. At the Conference of Dumbarton Oaks, Washington, D.C., in 1944, representatives of the United States, the Soviet Union, Britain, and China wrote the preliminary draft of the United Nations Charter, which in most respects became the basis for the official charter later adopted at San Francisco.

Even all these wartime conferences and measures gave no conception of the extent and depth of the commitments the United States was to carry after World War II. These would be truly staggering. In the decade after the war Americans took the lead in the United Nations and American soil became the site of the world's "capital." Americans ruled alien peoples in Germany, Austria, Italy, Trieste, Japan, and Korea. American generals, like

Roman generals of antiquity, became world famous as proconsuls. As late as 1939 President Roosevelt had been derided for saying at a private conference that America's frontier of security was at the Rhine, but after 1945 Americans came to take for granted that their security frontiers were at the Elbe, the Black Sea, the Himalayas, the Mekong, and the China Sea. American spheres of influence arose in Greece, Turkey, Jordan, Saudi Arabia, South Korea, South Vietnam, Thailand, and extended in circular moon fashion through the Japanese islands, the Ryukyus, Formosa, the Philippines, the Carolines, and the Marshalls. The United States had bases in the Arctic; in the New World from Newfoundland to Trinidad; in Greenland, in Iceland, in many countries of Western Europe including Spain, in the Azores, in Morocco, Libya, Greece, Turkey, and remote Dhahran in Saudi Arabia. American installations dotted the entire Pacific so as to make that ocean virtually an American lake. America had "entangling" military alliances, some bilateral and some multilateral, with over forty countries scattered throughout Europe, the Middle East, and the Far East, and as far away as Australia and New Zealand. By 1957, the American army had personnel stationed in over half a hundred countries overseas.

Americans shouldered the burdens of these vast commitments. During the first decade following World War II Americans spent more in military and economic aid to foreign countries than they had spent in their entire Lend-Lease program to win the war. Americans accepted as normal peacetime conscription, the mobilization of around 3 million personnel in the armed services, and annual defense budgets of from around 40 to 50 billion dollars. Even in 1953, when the numerical strength of their armed services stood at 3.5 million men and their budget reached the truly astronomical figure of nearly 85 billion dollars, with from 50 to 60 billion going to the armed services and their bases and equipment, Americans raised little complaint. In the early 1960's Americans would be spending billions on rockets, missiles, and earth satellites not only to keep abreast in the arms race but to conquer outer space and reach the other planets.

Such vast operations involved reorganization and expansion of the State Department; reorganization of the War and Navy departments into the combined Defense Department; new liaison arrangements between the State and Defense departments and other agencies; creation of the powerful decision-making National Security Council; wide extension of the ramifying, hidden bureaucracy which gathered undercover information; establishment of numerous new administrative agencies to deal with such matters as atomic energy, outer space, strategic materials, foreign economic aid and cooperation, and psychological and propaganda warfare. By 1960 the number of employees of the State Department had swollen from a prewar 5,000 to 23,000. By the same year there were 11,000 employees of the United States Information Agency, which dealt with the war of ideas, and 15,000 employees of the Agency for International Development.

Americans were painfully living in a world in which the election returns from Britain, France, Germany, Italy, and Japan or for that matter from Brazil, Greece, Turkey, Egypt, Iraq, India, and Indonesia had about as much effect on their lives as the election returns from New York and California. And since 1945 Europeans, according to the Ambassador in Theodore H. White's *Fire in the Ashes*, could not plan, think, or breathe without asking first, before anything else, what the Americans would do. The internal politics not only of European countries but also of Latin American, African, and Asian countries turned on American policies.

Here indeed was a revolution in American foreign policy difficult for most Americans to grasp. For American policy to be effective, Americans themselves would have to undergo a psychological revolution and learn to think in global terms, in terms of power politics, social politics, and propaganda politics.

It was well that most Americans as yet had no inkling of the immensity and complexity of the problems which would confront them in the postwar years. Americans were ready now to remain in world politics, but they were still thinking of foreign policy in simple, one-track terms. Some were inclined to choose the way of American imperialism, of the *pax americana*, and make the era that of "the American century" by using America's might and the persuasiveness of her atom bombs to impose an American settlement on the world. But the great majority believed that the postwar world would be one of peace and disarmament through collective security, an effective new League of Nations. The more discerning realized that much would depend on whether Russia and the Western democracies could work together after the war's end and that the degree of effectiveness of a world organization would be largely determined by this. Some others among the discerning, while ready to experiment with a new League of Nations, were already anticipating the Cold War and wanted to put first emphasis on a permanent alliance with Britain. As early as 1943, Governor Thomas E. Dewey of New York proposed such an alliance. Walter Lippmann saw clearly that the postwar world would have to be one of well-recognized spheres of influence. But most Americans, like Secretary of State Cordell Hull and President Roosevelt himself, believed that the long day of power-politics alliances and spheres of influence was at last drawing to its close and that a new era of peace, disarmament, world law, and international organization was at hand. In 1919 Americans had rejected the way of organized internationalism; in 1945 they overwhelmingly turned to it.

Americans were determined not to make the mistake of 1919. They felt that if the United States had been a member of the League of Nations, World War II would not have occurred. This, of course, was one of the great "ifs" of history, and there was no way of proving it. Some publicists believed that the Americans, even more fearful of Communism than the British and the French, would not have escaped the arguments for appeasing Fascism and Nazism as checks on Communism that had appealed so strongly to Chamberlain and the Cliveden set in Britain and to the "gravediggers" of France. But the majority of publicists believed that the Americans would have been saved by their very lack of sophistication in social politics, that with their moral and legal approach to international affairs and their country a signatory of the peace treaties and a member of the League of Nations, they would have been outraged by the flouting of treaties and League by the dictators. In any event, Americans in 1945 had a sense of guilt; they believed that their rejection of the League had caused the Hitlerian holocaust; and this belief was the most powerful drive in their determination to make a collective-security system work this time.

In the founding of the United Nations, the United States took the initiative. This lead came not only from the administration but also from the Senate and the House resolutions, from Republicans as well as Democrats. The American Dumbarton Oaks proposals largely became the basis of the United Nations Charter. The actual birth of the United Nations was on American soil at the San Francisco conference of the spring of 1945, and the American delegation contained leading Republicans as well as Democrats. Roosevelt had hoped to avoid two cardinal errors of 1919 when he worked for a non-partisan and even bipartisan approach to a collective-security organization and when he insisted that the world organization be divorced from the peace settlement and be established before a possible disintegration of the war alliance set in.

The United Nations Charter adopted at San Francisco set up an organization remarkably similar to the League of Nations. Its chief organs, like those of the League of Nations, were a council, a general assembly, a secretariat, and an international court of justice. The Council had the chief responsibility for enforcing peace. It consisted of five permanent members—the United States, the Soviet Union, Britain, France, and China—and six non-permanent members. The General Assembly had wide powers of discussion, and in it every member state was represented equally. The United Nations differed from the League of Nations in numerous details and in several significant ways. The United Nations' chief differences consisted in an Economic and Social Council to carry out and supervise the enlarged functions in economic and social matters, and in the complex voting arrangements in the Council. Great Britain was not enthusiastic about the big-power veto in the Council, which applied to matters of substance, even to enforcement measures against a big-five member itself, but both the United States and the Soviet Union regarded the veto as necessary to protect their interests.

When the United Nations Charter came before the United States Senate for ratification, only two senators were recorded in opposition. Nothing better illustrated the difference between 1919 and 1945. However, many Americans naively supposed that they were to be given another chance, that the world of 1945 was the world of 1919 all over again, whereas in fact the world of 1945 was incalculably more complex, revolutionary, and dangerous than even the world of 1919 had been.

[2]

THE CRISIS WORLD
OF MID-CENTURY
(1945-1955)

The Collapse of the German and Japanese Societies

The United States came to world leadership in the midst of a
most turbulent century. The vast Fascist imperialisms had just
been crushed, but the problem of what to do with the Japanese
and the Germans, dynamic peoples who had lost their way, remained. At the same time the Communist revolution was on the
march, and the Soviet Union, encouraging that revolution, was
expanding in the East and the West. Would the defeated peoples
turn to Communism? As Communism spread, would Communist
countries link themselves with expanding Russia and with one another and threaten the United States even before the world had
had a chance to recover from World War II?

What was to be done with Germany? How could Germany
be rendered a safe member of the international community? Was
it possible to shift the center of European industrial power from
Germany? If possible, what would be the time and cost required?
Could European recovery wait on such a drastic redistribution
of industry? If the industrial center of Europe remained in

Germany, the recovery of Europe would depend on the recovery of Germany; but how far could Germany be allowed to recover without endangering the peace of Europe and the world? Germany's future would determine the balance of power. Could Russia afford to see her oriented to the West? Could the West afford to see her oriented to the East? Would not a Germany independent of both East and West be in a position to play each against the other, regain her old power and initiative, and threaten both East and West again?

Japan posed much the same problem as Germany. If Japan were not allowed to recover industrially she would retard Asian and world recovery and be an economic drain on the occupying power. On the other hand, if Japan were allowed to recover, what would prevent her from again becoming a threat to peace? As Japan revived, would she incline to the East or to the West? If she inclined to one, would she not frighten the other? And if independent enough to incline to neither, would she not frighten both?

The Central Problem of the Soviet Union

However, what caused most anxiety to the United States was not the enemy countries but America's mighty war ally, Russia. The Russian government, product of the Bolshevik Revolution, had a different set of economic, social, and moral values; its regime was totalitarian; its intentions were enigmatic. Since the Revolution, Western governments had felt much uncertainty when dealing with Russia. The United States had not even recognized the Soviet government until 1933. So great was the suspicion of Russia and Communism that Britain and France in the 1930's had appeased the Axis dictators and gone to Munich in the hope that the Nazis would check the Communists. The Russians believed that the West had encouraged Hitler to attack Russia, and the West felt that the Hitler-Stalin pact had been an invitation to Hitler to attack the West. Mutual suspicions were not allayed even at the height of the war. Churchill had urged a British-American front in the Balkans so that Western troops would be there when peace came. Stalin had feared the West would conclude a separate peace with Germany, was suspicious when the invasion of France was delayed, and at times even accused the

West of secret overtures to the Germans. When the common enemy was defeated, mutual fears increased and came to the surface.

Americans felt baffled and frustrated when dealing with Russia, and while hoping for the best usually expected the worst. They oscillated between underestimating Russian strength and over-estimating it. When underestimating Soviet strength and ambitions they emphasized the frightful Russian war losses and the destruction of Russia's chief industrial cities (Russian losses in lives alone were estimated to be between 20 and 30 million); the relative inferiority of Russian science, industry, and technicians; the fact that Russia did not have the atomic bomb; the hope that Russia's continued industrialization and urbanization would develop articulate middle classes which would press for the liberalization of Soviet society; the belief that a totalitarian regime must eventually provoke mass discontent.

But mostly the Americans overemphasized Russian strength, and indeed the expansion of Russian power gave color to American fears. The U.S.S.R. covered one-sixth of the earth's surface; it bestrode the very center of the Eurasian land mass; it occupied the "Heartland" considered by geopoliticians to be so advantageous strategically for offense and defense, for expansion both East and West, and for an industrial revolution even more prodigious than the German or the American. It contained a rapidly growing population, and in fact it was experiencing the most rapid industrial revolution in history. Industrial centers were springing up not only in European Russia but beyond the Urals and even among the backward peoples of the Caspian. The power vacuums at the end of the war threatened to play into the hands of the Russians, indeed to invite Russian expansion.

Power politics in the postwar era became unprecedentedly difficult to engage in, for the old and more flexible multiple balance of power had been shattered by the two world wars. Important traditional balancers had disappeared, been seriously weakened, or themselves become power vacuums. Austria-Hungary had disintegrated in the first war. Germany, Italy, and Japan had been destroyed as great powers in the second. Britain and France, particularly France, though victors, had been seriously weakened. The two giants, the United States and the Soviet

Union, both comparative newcomers to world leadership and lacking experience and mellowness, faced each other in a perilous polarization of power. Britain, though regarded as the third power, was in no position really to mediate between the United States and Russia. Instead, in essentials Britain had no choice but to become a part of the American sphere. With time a powerful and independent China and a powerful and independent West European federal state might emerge to restore a multiple balance of power. However, such speculations on the possible future of the balance of power were of little value to American policy makers in 1945. They were confronted with active Russian expansion and the old barriers to Russian expansion no longer existed.

In the nineteenth century, Turkey and Austria-Hungary had provided such barriers. By 1945 Turkey was a third-class power and the Austro-Hungarian empire was gone. In the twentieth century Germany and Japan had provided such barriers. But in 1945 Germany and Japan were conquered provinces and themselves power vacuums. The Little Entente of the 1920's and 1930's was itself part of the Russian sphere. The Middle East, which touched Russian borders over a vast expanse of territory, was divided, troubled, unorganized, impotent. The United Nations was still too weak to function effectively in the balance of power.

By the end of the war massive Russian armies had penetrated deep into central Austria and Germany in the West and into Korea and Manchuria in the East. From East Germany, Austria, and Manchuria the Russians sent enormous amounts of industrial equipment back to Russia. As a victor in the war, Russia in the East had won recognition of her protectorate over Outer Mongolia, soon made some penetration of Sinkiang, and regained the Kuriles, southern Sakhalin, and a pre-eminent position in Manchuria; and Russia in the West had gained the Karelian Isthmus, Petsamo, Latvia, Estonia, Lithuania, the northern part of East Prussia, eastern Poland (western Byelorussia and western Ukraine), Bessarabia, northern Bukovina, and Carpathian Ruthenia. Even more important, Russian armies were in East Germany, Austria, Poland, Czechoslovakia, and the Balkan countries north of Greece; and Eastern Europe and the Balkans appeared to be in process of becoming a Russian sphere of influence integrated with the Russian economy.

While the West was impressed by Russia's enormous expansion, the Russians were impressed by their own restraint and pointed out that in their hour of triumph they had not even gained the Tsarist boundaries of 1914 (Finland and Poland were not territorially absorbed by Russia), that the Balkan countries were not pressed to become republics of the U.S.S.R. but still retained their national independence, and that Turkey was not forced to give Russia a share in the joint defense of the Straits, which the Russians claimed were as vital to their security as the Panama Canal to American security. By late 1946 the Russians also boasted that their troops had evacuated Danish Bornholm, Norway, Czechoslovakia, Yugoslavia, northern Iran, and Manchuria.

What particularly disturbed the West was the Russian position in Poland and the Balkan countries. In the past these countries had been oriented as much to the West as to the East. Some of them contained large Roman Catholic populations. Each had a highly developed sense of nationalism. The West claimed that national self-determination was being denied these countries, that the Yalta agreements guaranteeing broadly representative provisional governments and free elections were being flagrantly violated, that governments in these countries were moving toward one-party Communist monopolies, that their economies were being integrated into the Soviet economy. Russian ascendancy in Yugoslavia brought the Soviet threat to the Adriatic; in Bulgaria, to within striking distance of the Aegean and the Straits.

The Russians claimed that Poland and the Balkans were vital to their security. In the past, German invasions had been mounted in Poland, and in the 1930's Poland and the Balkans had rightist dictatorships hostile to neighboring Russia. There were common Slavic cultural ties between these countries and Russia; the "resurgent culturalism" noted by F. S. C. Northrop in all parts of the contemporary world was making itself felt there; the war had shown these peoples that their most effective defense from German aggression would come not from the West but from Russia. (Even the Czechs, the most Western-oriented of these peoples, seemed convinced of this.)

Communism, too, had more indigenous strength in the area than the West liked to admit. During the 1920's the middle way had been tried in most of these countries and measures of agrarian reform ("green socialism") had been enacted. Land had been taken from the big landowners and distributed to the peasants. But what usually happens in such movements had happened there: the land taken from the landlords was not sufficient, the patch of land provided the individual peasant was too small, and the vital credit required to buy equipment was not adequately provided. (In Radić's Yugoslavia, where land was already widely distributed, the difficulty had been largely that of inadequate credit facilities.) A counter movement had set in, land reverted to the landlords, and in the 1930's reactionary dictatorships rode to power on the fear of the propertied classes and the disillusionment of the peasants. (Czechoslovakia alone escaped such a dictatorship.) The oppression of rightist dictators had caused Communist and Socialist sentiment to grow, and Russia's decisive part in the wartime liberation movements produced greater mass sympathy for Communism. Nevertheless, it was highly doubtful whether at the end of the war Communists had a majority in any of these countries, even in Yugoslavia, and in the absence of free elections the doubt was not resolved. Moreover, even Polish, Czechoslovak, Rumanian, Hungarian, Bulgarian, and Yugoslav Communists had varying degrees of nationalism mixed with their Communism, and probably most of these aspired to adapt Communism to national conditions and cultures and not to slavishly follow the Soviet Union.

The Trend Toward Collectivism in Europe

The chief source of anxiety to Americans, however, was the apparent trend to collectivism in all Europe and Asia. Sometimes this trend manifested itself in totalitarian Communism, sometimes in milder socialism or social democracy. When countries went Communist would they link themselves to Russia and other Communist countries, present a unified international front, upset the bipolarized balance of power, and endanger American security and survival? To what extent was Communism an expression of Soviet imperialism? To what extent were Communist parties fifth columns for Russian aggression? To what extent were Socialists and Social Democrats sympathetic with Russia and Communism?

The trend which worried Americans represented a long-time historical movement. Marxist parties in Europe had been growing since the 1870's. By 1914 they represented strong mass movements in most European countries and cooperated across national boundaries in the Socialist International. The Russian Revolution of 1917 was a part of this general movement, and when the U.S.S.R. was formed it was expected that war suffering in Germany, Austria-Hungary, and Italy would soon produce revolutions which would cause these countries to become fellow members of a growing international proletarian state.

But Marxist revolutions outside Russia miscarried in 1918, 1919, and 1920, and the Socialist International split sharply between those who would bring the revolution the Russian way (these joined the Third or Communist International sponsored by Russia and claimed to be orthodox Marxists) and those who would carry it less far and bring it country by country in a peaceful, gradual, non-totalitarian way (these believed in the Second or Socialist International and were called revisionist Marxists or democratic Socialists).

The ruthlessness of the Russian Revolution helped prepare the way for Fascism in Italy and Nazism in Germany: it terrified the conservative and propertied classes, split the Marxists against themselves, in some countries paralyzed the movement toward democratic social reform, and provided the extreme right with the modern and streamlined techniques of revolution. The Fascists and Nazis promised to crush Marxist leaders, parties, and labor unions, but to win the masses by the dynamics of imperialist expansion and full employment.

During the war against Nazism (1939-1945) Communists, Socialists, liberals, democrats, and patriots generally fought together in the underground and liberation movements. The Communists, hating Nazism most bitterly and being highly organized and ruthless, often took leading parts in these movements. Conservatives frequently were identified in the public mind with Nazi appeasement and collaboration.

At the end of the war popular expectations ran high. *This* time there would be no miscarriage; basic social reforms would come no matter if bringing them meant socialism or even communism. There had been cooperation in time of war; then why not in peace to punish the gravediggers of reform and patriotism and to bring the good life long promised by science and the machine but impeded by the vested interests? Even parties of the center, like the Catholic Christian Democrats in Italy and the Catholic M.R.P. in France, were imbued with the urge to revolutionary change. Even De Gasperi, leader of Italy's Christian Democrats, was reported in 1945 as declaring dramatically: "Was not Christ the first communist?"

The more interdependent society produced by the machine had caused trends toward controlled economies and greater collectivism in all industrial countries. But why had such movements been much more marked and popular in Europe than in the United States? In Europe, capitalism had never been as free or as competitive as in America. Europe's population was large, economic opportunity restricted, capital harder to acquire. Fewer people could become capitalists and go into business for themselves. Europe's capitalism emerged out of guilds, trading associations, and mercantilistic monopolies. In the later industrial age, Europe had not escaped these earlier associative patterns and monopolistic practices. Big business in Europe had frequently been conducted by cartels, usually with government support. These cartels generally had preferred restricted output, low wages, and high prices to unlimited output, high wages, and low prices. They had resisted, too, high-pressure sales and distributive methods. Smaller businesses had often been family enterprises from generation to generation, preferring pinchpenny policies and old and easygoing productive and distributive methods to the more streamlined methods of American business. The gap between wages and prices had been wide in Europe and in the immediate postwar years it was so wide that wage and salary earners were hard put to sustain themselves and their families. American businessmen who swarmed over Europe during the Marshall Plan years to supervise American economic aid and to suggest new managerial techniques to European businessmen were struck by the feudal mentality of European businessmen and their frequent disregard of workers and consumers.

Since 1914 the European economy had been struck one hammer blow after another, causing distress and a decline in numbers and influence of the middle classes: the brunt of World War I, devastating inflation, well-nigh confiscatory taxation, world depression in the 1930's, the brunt of World War II,

again devastating inflation, the liquidating of European investments abroad, the disruption of world trading patterns. Most
discouraging, Europeans faced the loss of colonies, markets, and
investments as a result of the revolts against Western imperialism
of the underdeveloped peoples of Asia, Africa, and Latin America. (Since about 1500 the European economy had been an expanding one; it had been banker, investor, and manufacturer for
the rest of the world; it had lived in considerable part on the
markets of the world.) In addition, Europe faced the decline of
trade with countries beyond the Iron Curtain. In short, the European economy in relation to the world economy was now a
recoiling one. This recoil involved the prosperity of all Europeans
and a further decline of the middle classes.

Would socialism provide a more widespread distribution of
national income and make up in intensive markets at home what
was being lost in extensive markets abroad? Would not an economic federation of Western Europe provide more extensive
European markets? Would not both socialism and federation
provide both more intensive and extensive markets in Europe?
These questions were being earnestly debated by Europeans.

As conditions developed which made economic controls and
greater collectivism appealing to Europeans, as the middle classes
and middle-class attitudes declined, politicians, journalists, writers,
and artists mercilessly lampooned bourgeois society and bourgeois
values. Many of the post-1945 generation in Europe came to
know capitalist values only in caricature. While there were many
who defended a free economy, much of what was left of the old
system in Europe seemed to exist because of inertia and stalemate
and not because the people revered its values. The word *socialist*
had a magic in Europe that the word *democracy* had in America;
even the Nazis made use of it, and the French Radical Socialist
party was not France's socialist party although it gladly used the
socialist name. Many non-Marxists in Europe unwittingly came
to think in terms of Marxist vocabulary and Marxist values.

As soon as the war was over, Communist and Socialist parties
agitated for basic changes. The Socialists sympathized with many
of the Communist proposals and purposes but not with their
totalitarian methods. Even center and Catholic parties frequently
advocated economic controls and collectivist measures in a way

which puzzled free-enterprise Americans. Communism itself was viewed not as an aberration or a disease, as it was in the United States, but as a highly explicable movement which could better be combated by improved conditions than by incantations and inquisitions. There were even non-Communist Frenchmen and Italians who believed that France and Italy could absorb Communism into their national cultures just as the French Revolution had been absorbed.

In the immediate postwar years, a quasi-socialist revolution occurred in Western Europe. From 1945-1951 the Labour party was in power in Britain, and it nationalized the Bank of England, railroads, bus lines, air lines, internal water transport, coal mining, the gas industry, and the generation, transmission, and retail distribution of electricity. It also extended Keynesian controls, enormously widened the welfare state, and established the National Health Service (what Americans called "socialized medicine"). These great changes took place rather smoothly because the number of Communists was very small and British leftists were not split into two hostile camps of Communists and Socialists as they were in many continental countries. Britain thus became an extensive welfare state and a mixed economy, with some nationalization but with most enterprises still privately owned, an economy subject to government controls but much more of a market economy than an administered one.

In France, immediately after the Liberation, in 1944 and 1945, many industries were nationalized as punishment to Nazi collaborators. Among those which were confiscated were the Renault automobile works, the Berliet works, the leading companies manufacturing airplane engines, some of the chemical industries, and a large part of the motion picture producing industry. The railroads and a major part of the shipping and air lines had already been nationalized. In 1945 and 1946 the First Constituent Assembly passed acts nationalizing, with compensation to their private owners, the Bank of France and the four main commercial banks of the country and all their branches, the major insurance companies, the coal industry, gas, and electricity. Legislation was passed requiring that henceforth all changes in the prices of basic commodities, whether products of private or public enterprise, be approved by the government. Subsequently the French government built giant electric power stations along the Rhone, a kind of French TVA.

In Italy, the postwar government inherited the country's three leading banks (nationalized during an acute financial emergency by the Fascist government) together with all their assets and holding companies. It continued to hold these as government properties, although this constituted a curious situation in which some enterprises of a given industry were privately owned and operated and other enterprises of the same industry were government-owned and operated. The postwar government also nationalized some additional industries and began limited agrarian reforms which took land from big estates and distributed it in small plots to individual peasant proprietors. These agrarian measures were particularly important in southern Italy and Sicily, where virtually feudal conditions prevailed.

Both France and Italy thus became mixed economies, but they continued to operate much more as market economies than administered ones. However, government ownership in both countries was extensive enough and government controls were theoretically and legally so ramifying that both economies, without nationalizing a single additional industry or enacting any further legislation, could be shifted from market economies to administered ones should future developments and a swerve to the left in public opinion require it.

Communists and the more extreme Socialists were not satisfied with the reforms enacted. They maintained that these were inadequate, that more were necessary, that much of the reform legislation which had been enacted was not implemented, that even the nationalized industries were being run in a spirit of privatism rather than socialism, and that instead of the interests of the private sector being subordinated to the needs of the public sector the needs of the public sector were being subordinated to the interests of the private sector. They protested that the socialist revolution was being aborted, that what was emerging was at best a bastardized socialism, "a socialism without the Socialists."

By 1948 the urge to basic reform was slowing down. The revolutionary enthusiasm and national consensus born of the Liberation were oozing away. Conservatives began to find their voices again. Those in the liberal parties and in the Catholic and other center parties believed that reform had gone far enough. Marxists and leftists, who wanted more drastic changes, were not able to work together because of the rancorous division between Communists and Socialists. Large segments of opinion committed strongly to no party, but which had gone along with reform because of the ardor of the Liberation, began to feel that recovery was being impeded by reform, that Europe needed to revive economically before it could afford more social benefits. Moreover, these came increasingly to believe that to carry socialism further without really supplanting capitalism would destroy the incentives for capital accumulation of both systems and leave Europe without the urgent incentives of either system. It was more and more argued that Europeans, with their long tradition of private enterprise and their science, machine techniques, and skilled workers, would be able to recover their old momentum of production and saving through private enterprise and revive their entrepreneurial and middle classes if they could be given an immediate and large infusion of capital to get things going again. It was increasingly realized that European recovery needed American capital, machines, and goods, and that it was the part of wisdom to cooperate with American capitalism rather than antagonize it.

American business and political leaders, with the assent of conservative and other Europeans, were in effect saying this to Europe: "Three years after the end of the war you still have your ruined cities, your devastated areas, your personal hardships, your scarcities, your rationing, your inflation. Your reforms may have important bearings on your future economic well-being and they may eventually help you develop and maintain mass markets at home (although some of us with orthodox economic views doubt this), but at the moment recovery is more important than reform. Unless you make more rapid and decisive strides to recovery you will experience a new revolutionary wave, and next time it will probably carry you to Communism. What you need to do is to get rid of your obsolescent equipment and business methods, employ new managerial and sales techniques, dispense with your cartels and your cartel-managed prices, sell a greater volume of goods rather than depend on high profit per unit of goods on limited sales, develop a 'people's capitalism' like that in the United States, cut your tariffs and eliminate your quota systems and embargoes between European nations, facilitate the interconvertibility of European currencies, and develop as many synthetic raw materials as you can to prepare for the day when the underdeveloped nations industrialize and use more of their raw materials at home. Even so, you will always be a deficit area, you will always need to export or die (something you Europeans know full well), and the adoption of many of the foregoing measures will help you recover much of your former international trade and salvage your colonial trade even after the colonies have left you."

It was this kind of thinking which led the United States government, through its Marshall Plan during the years from 1948 to 1951, to pour into Western Europe large infusions of capital which greatly facilitated a remarkable European recovery under an economic system which, while mixed, was to be more of a market economy than an administered one, closer to traditional capitalism than to socialism. The Marshall Plan was the most important single measure of the postwar years; it contributed to the second miscarriage of Marxist revolution in Western Europe (the first one was following World War I); and in bringing America and Western Europe closer together, its impact on world politics was decisive. Many circumstances, then, slowed down the drive to collectivism in Western Europe, but the Marshall Plan was the most important of the specific measures which produced a more conservative opinion and trend.

It goes without saying that the Marshall Plan was not entirely altruistic on America's part. The American and the international economy could not be healthy as long as Europe's imports from America were so much larger than its exports, as long as the dollar gap was so wide that Europe had insuperable difficulties with its international balance of payments. Above all, Americans were vitally interested in alleviating the destitution in Europe in order to lessen the chances of Europe's going Communist. However, there was something of conscience in the Marshall Plan, something of propitiation. Informed Americans were aware that the United States had become producer of over 50 per cent of the world's steel, of over 30 per cent of its industrial products generally; that Americans had steadily encroached on Europe's old international markets; that during two world wars they had been the beneficiaries of Europe's woes to make further gains; and that United States tariff and other policies had not been adjusted to America's new position as chief creditor nation in the world.

However, even in the early 1950's the future of Western Europe was uncertain. There had not yet been complete recovery, inflation continued in some countries, and the premature lifting of price and rent controls caused suffering. There were complaints that the promises of the war years had not been fulfilled, that even some of the actual reforms of the immediate postwar years had not been implemented. The Communist party remained the largest single party in France, and in Italy the Communists and their Socialist allies controlled about one-third of the electorate. (Italy was the one country where Communists and majority Socialists cooperated.) The Italian election of 1953 resulted in such strength for the Communist coalition on the left and the neo-Fascists on the right that the democratic center found increasing difficulty governing, to say nothing of legislating and implementing agrarian and other basic reforms.

Americans were concerned about the over-all gains of collectivism in the world, even the mild collectivism of Western Europe; they were disturbed about the persistence of Communist strength in France and Italy; and they tended to exaggerate the part played by the Soviet Union. However, as European economies increasingly stabilized after 1948 the chances of immediate Communist revolution anywhere in Western Europe receded.

But in Asia Communism gained ground after 1945, the world's most populous nation was engulfed, and Americans saw in the spread of Communism a threat to the balance of power there. In Asia, as in other underdeveloped areas in the world, the anti-imperialist revolutions were in full swing, and the prospect loomed that in a number of countries anti-imperialist revolution and Communist revolution would merge.

The Anti-Imperialist Revolutions in Asia

By the end of the war the colonial peoples in Asia, the Middle East, Africa, and Latin America were stirring. Many were already in the midst of revolution. These revolutions usually expressed themselves in an extravagant nationalism. F. S. C. Northrop claimed that these revolutions represented a developing Buddhist, Brahmanist, Islamic, Slavic, Aztec, and Inca "resurgent culturalism." This was a questionable interpretation, but there could be no doubt that the anti-imperialist revolutions were immediate expressions of a vigorous national pluralism.

In Asia, the old British, French, and Dutch empires were breaking up. New nations were rapidly emerging among the underdeveloped colonial peoples. Most of these nations were internally unstable and beset with enormous difficulties. The Communists were confident that many of the new nations, out of their hatred of the old imperial powers and their need for rapid industrialization, would turn to Communism. The Soviet Union was an Asian as well as a European power; it was geographically close to many of the new nations; and in their propaganda the Russians made much of their own peasant origin, their anti-colonialism, and their lack of racism.

The empires now dissolving had ruled Asians for centuries. In the seventeenth and eighteenth centuries, during the early or mercantilist imperialism, Dutch, British, and French merchants had established trading posts in large parts of Asia from which had grown the Dutch empire in the East Indies and the British and French empires in India. Later the British expelled the French from India. In the late nineteenth century, during the second or finance-industrial imperialism, the British had extended their empire in Burma and Malaya, the French had established an empire in Indochina, and China had been carved up by the leading European powers into economic spheres of influence. The Europeans had left the Asian peoples producers and processors of foodstuffs and raw materials. Europeans had operated as exporters of these materials and as importers of Europe's manufactured goods. European traders, bankers, investors, and concessionaires had usually been in economic alliance with the native landlords and the numerically small native trading classes. Poverty, squalor, illiteracy, malnutrition, disease, and early death had been the common lot. What had been most galling to a native was his reduction to second-class citizenship, his status of inferiority in his own country. A color line had usually been drawn, and even educated and wealthy natives were made to feel it.

At the same time, European rule had gradually made an impact on the cultural lives of the people, felt even in the remote villages. The European had built some roads and railroads, introduced rudimentary sanitary and public health measures, and erected some schools. The European himself had planted the ideas and the methods with which the colonial peoples were later to oust him. Asians had come to imitate the nationalism of the Europeans, and the Europeans laid the basis of a native nationalism by suppressing internal disorder, opening up remote parts of the country, connecting many areas by communication and transportation systems, ruling the whole country through a centralized civil service, teaching people in schools to read and write their native tongue, and inducting men from all parts of the country into the imperial army. Although they had had little self-government in their homelands, the colonial peoples had learned about democracy, liberty, and civil rights from their rulers. Asians who could afford it had increasingly sent their sons to Britain or France to be educated. These had become familiar with Western thought and institutions and imbibed liberal and even socialist ideas. In addition to nationalism and democracy, the colonial peoples had learned from the West the vital importance of science and machine technology. They came to realize that the difference between a "backward" and an "advanced" people was not biologic or racial but the utilization by the "advanced" people of science and the machine. In short, the colonial peoples had learned rational, material, and industrial values from the West.

As far back as 1910, China's Sun Yat-sen had raised the banner of anti-imperialist revolution with his three principles of nationalism, democracy, and economic well-being. For over thirty years, Sun Yat-sen's Kuomintang had been fighting the Western imperialist powers and the reactionary traditional elements in China itself. As we have seen, the Kuomintang had become split by internal division, and the chaos in China had been worse compounded by the Japanese conquests. By the time of the Japanese collapse in 1945, the conflict in China had narrowed to an epic battle between the Communists and the majority wing of the Kuomintang, now grown conservative and led by Chiang Kai-shek.

During World War I the hold of the British and French on their Asian empires had been weakened, and both countries emerged from the war with decreased strength and influence. Nationalist independence movements had grown rapidly. The anti-imperialists had found an inspired leader in Mohandas K. Gandhi, whose philosophy bridged the gap between Asian traditionalism and Western modernity and whose techniques of revolution—passive resistance and non-violent non-cooperation— had proved marvelously effective in India and had spread to other revolutionary movements in Asia and Africa. During World War II the Japanese conquests of southeast Asia and the Dutch East Indies had shattered old imperial patterns, the hold of the European powers on their empires had been weakened still more, and nationalist movements had spread like wildfire. At the end of the war, it was clear that if the old imperial powers clung to their empires, there would be years of bloody struggle ahead.

While there was armed resistance on the part of the Dutch and the French to giving up their empires, actually Western rule in Asia was liquidated in the late 1940's and early 1950's with remarkable facility. The Westerners were war weary. Europeans were primarily interested in their own national reconstructions, and they were in no mood to carry on years of warfare with the nationalist movements, now grown to maturity. There was a general fear that protracted resistance would play into the hands of the Communists, allow them to capture the nationalist movements.

In 1946 the United States proclaimed the independence of the Philippines. In 1947 the British gracefully withdrew from the very heart of their empire, and that year both India and Pakistan were granted independence. The partition of old India into Moslem Pakistan and Hindu India was made necessary by fierce religious hostility, particularly on the part of the Moslems. The following year Burma and Ceylon became independent. The Labour party, committed to an anti-imperialist policy, was in power in Britain at the time. From 1945 to 1949 an intermittent war was waged between the Dutch and the Indonesian nationalists, but the Dutch yielded in 1949 and acknowledged the independence of Indonesia. The French hung on more tenaciously. Nevertheless, from 1949 to 1954, a series of agreements led finally to the independence of Laos and Cambodia. In 1954 the French finally gave way in Vietnam after military defeat and withdrew from both North and South Vietnam, although the prolonged resistance of France played into the hands of the Communists, allowed them to identify themselves with Vietnamese nationalism, and resulted in a Communist regime in North Vietnam. In 1957 the British acknowledged the independence of Malaya.

The problems faced by the newly independent countries were staggering. In most cases they were far from being "nations." Each usually contained a wide diversity of cultural, religious, ethnic, lingual, and communal groups; life and loyalty centered around the village and the cognate or collateral family. A strong administrative state would be necessary to wield these diversities into a modern nation, and the civil service and technical devices for doing this were scanty. Most of the new nations had popular suffrage and parliamentary machinery, but the substance of democracy was still lacking. There was pervasive poverty and illiteracy; a genuine middle class was small; and the landlords, the moneylenders, and even much of the old and small trading class accustomed to traditional ways were often opposed to the great economic and social changes promised by the nationalist leaders and were adept at manipulating the local electorate and creating other difficulties.

Sometimes the new nation was plagued with such a plethora of political parties as to make stable government impossible. Sometimes there was virtually only one party (the one that had led the revolution, with a mass composition that was largely peasant), and a contest was waged inside this party to determine how sweeping the changes were to be. Sometimes this same conflict took place inside the army. Sometimes the new nation seemed held together by the prestige of a single national leader, and there was a tendency to the cult of personality. Even in India, where democracy was better developed than in most of the new nations, Gandhi's Congress party had to operate in a paternal way. After Gandhi's assassination, Indian nationalism centered largely around the remarkable personality of Jawaharlal Nehru, an intellectual and idealist who had deeply imbibed Western liberalism and democratic socialism. Nehru was worshiped by the Indian masses.

The most important problem facing a new nation was how to break out of a poor and unbalanced economy based on archaic ways of producing and processing foodstuffs and raw materials and achieve a diversified, balanced, and up-to-date economy. This involved modernizing and mechanizing transportation, communications, and agriculture, building electric power plants, and making a beginning in industrialization. But the momentous take-off and breakthrough from a pre-industrial economy to an industrial economy required the rapid development of a whole complex of economic and social conditions and values operating through all of the community at the same time—an unprecedented amount of saving of investment capital from national income each year in a country already living on the margin of subsistence; the existence of a minimum of skilled labor; the disciplining of peasant labor to mechanical and industrial pursuits; a division of labor; popular education; specialization; the training of engineers, technicians, accountants, managers, and administrators; credit agencies; acceptance of rational and industrial attitudes. Were this complex once achieved a momentum would set in which would become cumulative in effect and carry the economy from poverty to economic well-being. But coordinate planning, heroic exertions, and outside help would be necessary to achieve such a complex.

The most important single factor was getting a supply of investment capital. These pre-industrial societies had a very small middle class, a very small capital-supplying class. There were not enough individuals with private savings to finance modern transportation, communication, agriculture, power plants, and the basic beginnings of industrialization. Foreign private capital was not available in sufficient amounts. Private capital was needed in the European countries for reconstruction, and the investment climate in the old nations was more favorable than in the new. Besides, the task of laying the groundwork for industrial societies in the new nations in a short span of time was beyond the scope and capacity of foreign private capital. Even when the imperial powers ruled the underdeveloped areas, the Western capitalists never attempted anything so ambitious. Foreign private capitalists were not interested in systematically transforming backward societies into advanced ones. This required an ordering of priorities on the basis of national need and development, making investments in projects in which there would be no profits, such as roads and schools, or in industries in which profits would be postponed to the long future, as in hydro-electric plants. Foreign private capitalists had an eye to more immediate profits and quick turnovers. Again, there was instability and revolutionary ferment in the new nations, and foreign entrepreneurs and bankers considered the investment climate there to be too risky. Finally, the leaders in the new nations were suspicious of foreign private capital in large amounts; they still had anti-imperialist mentalities and remembered only too well how in the past the penetration of foreign private capital had often been the forerunner of political pressures and even dictation; they recalled vividly how the foreign capitalists used their sweated labor and cheap raw materials to siphon off profits to the West.

The Russian Revolution exercised a powerful attraction for peoples in underdeveloped societies. As they saw it, the Russians only a generation ago suffered the same feudal conditions in which they found themselves. But the Russians within a single generation had pulled themselves up by their own bootstraps and deliberately planned and built an industrial society. Even in neighboring Siberia, even in Mongolia and the Caspian areas, Asians saw the rapid development of industry and modern cities. Before their very eyes they saw peoples in thirteenth-century conditions being catapulted into the twentieth century. Asians witnessed the phenomenally rapid rise of backward Russia to the second (some thought the first) industrial and political power in the world; they read that the Russian rate of economic growth had come to surpass that of the advanced capitalist countries, even the American; they heard predictions that by the late 1950's the average annual per capita income in Russia would be around $500, which would put Russia among the "rich" nations.

Some Asian leaders and intellectuals said in effect: "Here is something we can imitate. The American standard of living is wonderful, and of course we would like to have it; but the American system took centuries to build and its foundations were laid when capital equipment was relatively inexpensive. The American way is not within our reach, but the Russian way is; we can do what the Russians have done. We are told that bread without freedom is not worth the price, but our people have never had either bread or freedom. We will make bread first, the way we can make it, now, in this generation, and perhaps the freedoms will come later." Many in the new nations became Communists; Communist parties grew; and even non-Communists were impressed by the magnitude and the pertinence of the Russian achievement.

Throughout Asia, Russian Communists carried the message of the Russian Revolution. When talking to sophisticated leaders in the new nations they often dropped their Marxist jargon and in realistic and common-sense fashion said in effect this: "The surest and most self-reliant way to get an industrial revolution in a hurry is to adopt the planned (totalitarian) economics of Communism. That is what we did in the Soviet Union. We forced massive capital savings by collectivist methods, drastically curtailed consumption and the making of consumer goods, regimented capital and labor into the capital-goods making industries, and each year plowed back a large part of tax income and profits from state enterprises into capital investments for roads, railroads, trucks, power projects, tool and machine factories, steel mills, tractor plants, technical schools, and so forth. There were years when the Soviet Union devoted 30 per cent of national income to capital investment. Through the establishment of collective farms and the mechanization of agricultural equipment, we released peasants for work in the factories and through a planned (rigged) price system got food for the factory workers and raw materials for the factories cheaply and furnished finished goods to the agricultural collectives dearly. Yes, we squeezed capital savings out of agriculture, but how else does pre-industrial society industrialize except out of its agricultural surpluses? When the British were industrializing they released agricultural labor for the factories and increased agricultural production at the same time through the enclosure movements. And in the post-Civil War years in the United States (which we in Russia often call America's period of Stalinism), were not farm prices kept low at the very time agricultural exports were providing America's industrial revolution with the necessary foreign exchange? We broke peasants to factory discipline by all sorts of means—wholesale training on the job, overtime work, piecework, the stretch-out, the Stakhanov movement, the increasing rationalization of the labor process. We built hundreds of engineering and technical colleges, thousands of secondary technical schools. In the late 1920's and in the 1930's we experienced the most concentrated economic expansion in history. In scores of ways we used both the carrot and the stick as incentives to production; we drove ruthlessly and relentlessly; we evoked dedication, sacrifice, and superhuman efforts; we admittedly suffered much pain. But we made the historic breakthrough from pre-industrial primitivism to industrialism in a miraculously short time; and now the industries belong to us, the people, and our consumption has now gone up markedly and we can look forward in the future to an ever-rising standard of living. What we have done, you can do. Your salvation lies in adopting Communism."

Now, a follower of India's Nehru would probably make some such reply: "We do not minimize the magnitude of your achievements in the Soviet Union. But we think you went too far and too fast. Your ruthlessness required the savage dictatorship of Stalin. Even judged by your own purposes, you may have caused needless suffering. But humane considerations aside and from the strict economic point of view, we think you made some mistakes. You may have pressed your peasants so hard and so seriously under-allocated machinery to agriculture as to have produced a long-time agricultural imbalance. We prefer not to go so far and so fast. We do not want a police state and a dictatorship. Most of our people are peasants and we do not want to squeeze them to the extent you squeezed the Russian peasants. We believe we can make the breakthrough to industrialism by pursuing a middle way somewhere between American capitalism and Soviet Communism. Perhaps the best name for it—if it must have a name—is planned or social democracy. We know that the groundwork and the basic beginnings of industrialism must be done by government initiative and investment. But while the infrastructure and the key industries will be built by government, and credit and other controls will always be in the hands of government, we expect that a large amount of our economy— most small and medium-sized business concerns—will be carried on by private enterprise. We hope to build a mixed economy which will achieve both bread and freedom, both industrialism and a large measure of personal liberty. We hope to get grants and long-term loans from the governments of the advanced industrial countries to help our government make our initial investments. We hope to get aid from Britain's Colombo Plan and from the government of the United States, and since you say that the Soviet Union will soon be one of the 'rich' nations, perhaps we can eventually get help from the government of the Soviet Union too."

To this the Soviet exponent might rejoin: "You are seriously underestimating the difficulties in making the breakthrough to industrialism. That breakthrough has always been extremely painful. When commercial capitalism and then industrialism were coming to England, do you not recall the rack-renting and enclosures used to get the peasants off the land and then the dropping of the centuries-old dole to get them into the mines and factories? Surely you remember the hideous conditions in England's mines and factories in the early stages of industrialism, the long hours and low wages. England's rural folk were disciplined to industrialism by the most brutal methods. And remember, too, that the English had a relatively larger capital base from which to proceed than you have, they were the leading traders of the world, their population was small, they had in their homeland the kind of natural resources necessary to industrialism, and their transition to industrialism was spread over several generations. Even we in Russia were faced with fewer difficulties than you in India have. Our population was smaller. Our natural resources were greater. We had a wider industrial base from which to take off. We did not have to answer to a democratic electorate. Do you think that people will deliberately vote to continue to burden themselves with the enormous sacrifices entailed to achieve rapid industrialization when once the brunt of those burdens begins to be felt? People want the benefits of rapid industrialization without bearing the sacrifices to get them. We smashed the landlords and the other old feudal elements before we 'took off' and hence these reactionaries were powerless to stir up the people and throw obstacles in our way. We had already developed techniques for the rigid planning, coordinating, and rationalizing of the economy. We had drive, ruthlessness, yes even fanaticism, and you will need to apply these qualities even more intensively, for you are up against the massive inertia, the cultural debris, and the many thick layers of custom inherited from an ageless Oriental immobility.

"Tell me precisely how you are going to extract the necessary savings out of the Indian economy to make basic industrial beginnings. With your explosive rate of population increase you will have to invest around 9 per cent of your national income each year just to keep your standard of living where it is now. You are now not doing anywhere near that well, and if you are going to get ahead of your population increase, if you are going to accomplish a perceptible rise in your standard of living in spite of your population increase, you will have to invest at least 15 per cent of national income each year, and even then your progress will be slow and constantly menaced by population pressures. To really get over the hump to industrialism you ought to be investing each year during the next decade from around 20 to 30 per cent of your national income. How will you squeeze this out of your poor economy without adopting the discipline and forced savings of Communist economics? Do you think the advanced industrial countries will extend you economic aid sufficient to make up your own deficiencies in savings, even enough to boost your investments to 10 per cent of your national income? Again, how are you going to increase agricultural production to the extent you can release peasants for the factories and extract capital savings from the land? Whatever you do will meet the resistance of most of the landlords. If land is distributed to the peasants in individual plots, will each get enough land and have enough technical knowledge to become an efficient operator? Will the peasant get enough credit, tools, and machinery to produce economically? Can machinery be profitably used on small plots? And if you organize collectives, you will meet much peasant opposition, and under your so-called free and democratic society peasant opposition can wreck your plans.

"And what are you going to do when the inevitable reaction against the drive to industrialization sets in? Oh yes, it will set in even among many of those who now say they want rapid industrialization. When people are called on to make more and more sacrifices, when the old begins to slip away before the benefits of the new are visible, then people get a nostalgia for the old society of tradition, status, and 'security.' What propaganda machinery, what incentives, what coercive measures do you have to counteract this reaction and force a continuation of the drive to industrialism? And when the disillusioned make alliances with the old feudal elements, and perhaps the malcontents in the army, how are you going to maintain your so-called democratic regime in power?

"In short, I don't believe you can attain rapid industrialization by your easygoing and casual democratic methods. When you show signs of faltering, the reactionary right wing will take over. But a right-wing regime will eventually arouse more popular discontent than your so-called democratic one. Then your people, faced with a permanent miscarriage of their expectations of a better life, will turn to Communism to rid themselves of the reactionaries and adopt the realistic measures that will surely set them on the road to industrialism and rising living standards. Why not adopt Communism now rather than zig-zagging to industrialism through years of delay, confusion, waste, false expectations, and a probable interlude of right-wing reaction?"

Nehru's disciple would probably make a reply something like the following: "You see things in blacks and whites, in extremes; you are doctrinaire; the evolution you predict for us is too pat; you have little faith in people. The Soviet Union does not have the only road to industrialism or the only road to socialism. There are separate roads to industrialism, just as there are separate roads to socialism—something you will eventually have to acknowledge. Even your Communist way of industrializing is not a sure success; up to now the Soviet Union is the only example of its effectiveness; it may not be equally successful elsewhere; even the Stalin way nearly collapsed under the harsh impact of your first Five-Year Plan in the early 1930's. We know that any road to industrialism will entail sacrifices, and we are prepared to make them. Our methods are not as unsystematic as you think. We are at work on a coordinated Five-Year Plan, and the state will boldly take the lead in our economic development. Just what per cent of our national income we can each year set aside for investment capital we do not yet know. In part this will depend on the amount of economic aid our government gets from the governments of the advanced industrial nations. We will of course plow back some of the earnings of state enterprises into further investments. We are planning to distribute considerable land to the peasants, and we are at work on ways to provide the peasants with the credit, the techniques, and the tools for improved cultivation. We may have to undertake birth-control measures.

"What strikes me is that even before the war, before your present need to repair the ravages of war, so little of the Soviet Union's new wealth had gone into consumer goods and higher living standards. Your standards had gone up, yes, but not in proportion to what it seemed you could afford. Now that you have made the great breakthrough to industrialism, and after you recover from the war, what are you going to do with your high-geared totalitarian system? How will it continue to justify itself? Will your leaders claim you are still threatened by the capitalist powers? Will they use Soviet power to expand world Communism? Will they justify continuation of the totalitarian system by cultivating a sense of insecurity and insisting on a need for heavy armaments? Will they say the time has now come to move from socialism to a real communism and put Soviet citizens through another streamlined program designed to achieve a thoroughgoing communist system? And would such a program really have any genuine appeal to a people who have gotten a taste of modern industrial living and become accustomed to wide differences in income and to accumulating personal property and bank accounts? It will not be easy to dismantle your totalitarianism now that you have it, and your leaders may pursue programs which seek to justify its perpetuation.

"You delude yourself when you say that Russia is the only backward country which has achieved industrialism in a hurry. Japan, even before Russia, made the dramatic breakthrough to industrialism. From around 1870 to 1890 the Japanese ruling class, the old feudal elements, systematically and feverishly industrialized Japan. But Japanese industrial society bore the feudal and imperialistic stamp, just as your industrial society bears the totalitarian stamp. Means and ends cannot be separated. We in India believe that if we use democratic methods to achieve industrialism our future industrial society will be democratic."

The foregoing hypothetical discussion between an exponent of Soviet Communism and a follower of Nehru epitomizes the anxious questioning and probing taking place in the minds of Asian intellectuals and political leaders at the time of the anti-imperialist revolutions. Just how sweeping would be the economic and social changes of these revolutions? Would some of these revolutions go all the way to Communism? Would anti-imperialist revolutions and Communist revolutions merge? In the case of Asia's and the world's most populous nation, the answer came resoundingly in 1949 with the triumph of the Communists in China.

Sun Yat-sen's movement had early foreshadowed that combination of nationalism and social democracy (Sun's doctrine of livelihood or economic well-being) which by mid-century had captured the imagination of all the colonial and the under-developed peoples. In the 1920's Sun had moved more to the left and was on the friendliest terms with the Soviet Union. (His widow later took a leading part in China's Communist revolution.) But after Sun's death in 1925, the split in his revolutionary party, the Kuomintang, had become irreconcilable, and conservative and leftist wings engaged in civil war. Chiang Kai-shek's conservative faction controlled the Kuomintang, and Chiang more and more allied himself with China's small and wealthy bourgeois class in the coastal cities and with the landlords of the interior. The old left wing of the Kuomintang, now completely alienated, became more avowedly Marxist and Communist. After many vicissitudes and wanderings, the Communists, under the leadership of Mao Tse-tung, managed to set up a government, with its own army, in northwest China in the area around Yenan. This Yenan "government" maintained contacts with Communists in other parts of China. During the war with Japan, the Communists enlarged their territory, and by their bold guerrilla activities against the Japanese they appealed not only to those favoring social change but also to Chinese patriots. During that war, Chiang, to the annoyance of the Americans, who thought that an all-out effort should be made against the Japanese, concentrated some of his best troops along the borders of Communist-held territory in order to keep the Communists in check.

Unlike India, where the Congress party, analogous to the old Kuomintang under Sun Yat-sen, had managed to remain unified and had moved under Gandhi and Nehru in the direction of a moderate social-democratic position between extremes, China underwent a steady polarization to the extreme right and the extreme left. By 1945 the three best-known Chinese groups representing the liberal and the moderate leftist position were the Young China Party, the Social Democrats, and the Democratic League; but these commanded pitifully little popular support. The Democratic League moved in the direction of the Communists.

For two years following the collapse of Japan, both sides maneuvered for position, and from 1947 to 1949 a full-scale civil war raged between Chiang's Kuomintang and Mao's Communists. It seemed at first that Chiang held the advantage. The Communists, aside from their infiltrations into Manchuria, held only about 15 per cent of Chinese territory, regions in northwestern and central western China. Chiang's military forces numbered more than twice those of the Communists and their military equipment was three times as great. Chiang had American military advisers, military supplies, and financial assistance. Then why did Chiang fail?

Chiang failed because his leadership was inept and his policies alienated the great majority of the people. His loss of popular support was a slow and steady process. Back in the 1930's, after the Japanese had captured the coastal cities and cut him off from his bourgeois supporters, Chiang had become more and more dependent on the landlords and moneylenders of the interior, whose rapacious exploitation of the peasants increased with the spread of the war and the mounting inflation. By 1945 the landlords were taking as much as from 50 to 90 per cent of the peasant's crop for rent, and interest rates had risen to as high as 30 per cent. After the collapse of the Japanese and the reoccupation of the coastal cities by Chiang's forces, the Kuomintang government took over the Japanese-owned industries and ran them as government enterprises. Many of these properties had formerly belonged to Chinese, but Chiang's government failed to return them to the original owners. This outraged Chiang's former supporters among the commercial and industrial interests. American-aid funds were used to support some of the Kuomintang business enterprises, and Chiang's relatives and personal friends profited enormously. As the inflation became more devastating, more and more people suffered, and government officials, to make ends meet, became more flagrantly corrupt. As opposition mounted, Chiang's government became even more of a police state than it had been. Morale sagged; some defected to the Communists; but most Chinese withdrew into a passive and sullen indifference to the fate of the regime. Chiang's military leadership proved as disastrous as his political leadership, and he repeatedly went contrary to the advice of his American military advisers.

On the other hand, Mao proved to be a brilliant political and military leader. In the areas held by the Communists, agrarian reforms were instituted; rents and interest paid by peasants were drastically reduced; but the landlords and the moneylenders were not expropriated. The impression grew that the Communists were democratic social reformers, exponents of Sun Yat-sen's middle way. Although the Russians played a cagey game and outwardly carried out their Yalta agreements and their commitments to Chiang, when their armies swept over Manchuria in the closing days of the Japanese war they allowed the surrendered Japanese arms to fall into the hands of the Communists. As Chiang's unpopularity grew and the war turned against him, Chinese defecters to the Communists brought with them their American-supplied arms.

By early 1949 Chiang had definitely lost Manchuria. After his defeats in Manchuria, Chiang made no attempt to hold China proper or even south China. No defense at the Yangtze River was made. The collapse of morale and the will to fight was complete. Chiang simply forfeited the major part of China and withdrew to the island of Formosa. In the fall of 1949 Mao took over the mainland and proclaimed the People's Republic of China.

Like the Bolsheviks in Russia in 1917, the Chinese Communists, a distinct minority of their countrymen, had brilliantly taken advantage of virtual anarchy and a "revolutionary situation" to win control of their nation. The moderate middle approach of Sun Yat-sen had disappeared. In the eyes of most Chinese and most Asians, Chiang, who had inherited the mantle and party of Sun, had betrayed Sun's social-democratic revolutionary ideals and become the leader of the counter-revolutionary right. With no place to turn but to the discredited right or the still untried left, most Chinese, reeling from more than two decades of foreign and domestic wars, in dazed apathy were inclined to give the Communists the benefit of the doubt.

The impact on the rest of Asia of the Communist triumph in China was profound. Revolutionary movements in the other countries generally applauded the fall of Chiang, but they were still uncertain whether Mao's Communism would turn out to be the Soviet or a milder brand of Marxism. Most revolutionary leaders in Asia in the late 1940's and early 1950's were economic collectivists of one kind or another, but in their minds the differences between the various kinds of collectivism—Lenin's Communism, Stalin's Communism, Mao's Communism, national communism, socialism, and social democracy—were blurred. The following quotation from U Kyaw Nyein, a Burmese nationalist leader who for a time was Burma's minister of the interior, illustrates the vague but pragmatic Asian approach of this period: "Our immediate aim is a semi-socialist state, based first of all on radical agrarian reforms. In general our program is the same as Mao Tse-tung's program for the new democracy in China—adapted to Burmese conditions. We are Marxists but we are creative Marxists. We follow the line which is best for Burma, not what somebody who has never seen Burma decides is good for us."

In the years following World War II, then, Asia was in tempestuous revolutionary ferment. At one and the same time there were the anti-imperialist revolutions, new and unstable nations, untried democracies, dynamic drives for rapid industrialization and basic economic and social changes, the growth of nationalist and collectivist parties, and the triumph of Communism in China.

Would Communist Russia and Communist China operate as close partners in world affairs? Would there be other mergers of anti-imperialist revolution and Communist revolution? If so, would these join Russia and China in close cooperation in international politics? And how would all this affect the Asian and the world balance of power?

The Anti-Imperialist Revolutions in the Moslem World

At the end of World War II most of the vast territory in western Asia from Pakistan to Turkey, from the Arabian Sea to the

Aegean, and in North Africa from Egypt to Morocco was also in revolutionary ferment. This was the Moslem world, although there were millions of Moslems who lived outside it.

Of what did this Moslem world consist? There were the non-Arab lands of Afghanistan, Iran, and Turkey, which bordered directly on the Soviet Union. South of Iran and Turkey were the Arab lands of the Arabian peninsula and the Fertile Crescent.

Although Saudi Arabia occupied most of the Arabian peninsula, its eastern coast and the islands along the Persian Gulf were the sites of the oil-rich Sheikhdoms of Kuwait, Bahrain, and Qatar, its southern coast of the Sultanate of Muscat and Oman and of the British Crown Colony of Aden and the Aden Protectorate, and its southwest coast along the Red Sea of the independent state of Yemen. Except in Saudi Arabia and Yemen, British political and economic influence was dominant here.

The Arab lands of the Fertile Crescent, roughly the territories radiating from the Tigris-Euphrates area, were Lebanon, Syria, Iraq, Transjordan, and Palestine. Most of Palestine was to become the state of Israel.

In North Africa, along the southern coast of the Mediterranean, were the "less pure" Arab countries of Egypt, Libya, Tunisia, Algeria, and Morocco.

The vast area including Egypt and extending eastward to Pakistan was commonly known as the Middle East.

In many ways the Middle East was the most complicated area of the postwar's turbulent world. Here for centuries innumerable races, religions, and cultures had mingled and coexisted, for this area had been the crossroads of East and West since the dawn of history. Here there were imperialisms within imperialisms, the most tortuous of cross-currents, and dizzying inner conflicts. Here the withdrawal of Western imperialism was more protracted and grudging than elsewhere in the world. Moreover in the midst of the general retreat of Western imperialism there was actually a new Western penetration, for during and after World War I and World War II, Western oil companies had greatly extended their wells, refineries, and pipelines. The Arabs looked upon the large and continuing Jewish migration to Palestine as a new manifestation of Western imperialism.

The Soviet Union's long southern frontier bordered the northern part of the Middle East, and only little Turkey lay between Russia and the Turkish Straits, only weak and unstable Iran between Russia and the Persian Gulf, the gateway to Eastern seas whose coastlands contained the fabulously rich oil fields of Iran, Iraq, Kuwait, and Saudi Arabia.

In the decades before World War I most of the Moslem world had been subject to two layers of imperialism—Turkish and Western. The old Turkish empire had extended over the Arab lands of the Fertile Crescent, over Arabia, and over North Africa. But in North Africa, Turkish rule had either been supplanted or become nominal. However, in the Fertile Crescent, Turkish authority had been very real, and the Turks had ruled there in despotic, corrupt, and reactionary fashion. At the same time the British, French, Germans, Italians, and other Westerners had penetrated economically in all parts of the Turkish empire, including Turkey itself. Western countries had established extraterritoriality for their nationals (the capitulations), just as they had done in China, and in some countries the Western governments had controlled the customs revenues. Western bankers had owned the bonds and manipulated the credit of North African and Middle Eastern countries; Western capitalists and corporations had held railroad, oil, and other business concessions; and the Suez Canal was owned and operated by a private company whose shares were held by French and other European investors and by the British government. But in North Africa there had been Western political imperialism as well. The Europeans had pushed the Turks aside. Algeria had become a French colony, Egypt a British protectorate, Tunisia and Morocco French protectorates, and Libya an Italian colony. Persia and Afghanistan had not been parts of the Turkish empire, but both had been carved into Russian and British spheres of influence.

In the years before World War I Arab nationalism had had its beginnings among the intellectuals of Baghdad and Damascus who wanted to curb the tyranny of Turkish rule by the establishment of liberal institutions. During World War I the British, who wanted to undermine their Turkish enemy, encouraged the Arabs to revolt and organized an Arab legion to fight along with their armies. They induced Hussein, who was head of the Hashimite dynasty in the Hejaz, the Sharif of Mecca, and a direct descendant of the Prophet, to assume the Arab leadership. Hussein's son, Faisal, became the actual leader of the "revolt in the desert." Some of the earlier nationalists had misgivings about giving the movement an unmistakably Islamic character and handing over its leadership to a family from the more backward part of the Arab world. However, the British and Arab armies swept the Turks out of the Fertile Crescent and in 1918 Faisal proclaimed the Arab kingdom with its capital at Damascus. "Lawrence of Arabia" was the most colorful leader of this desert campaign.

But the Arab expectations were cruelly dashed. During the war the British and French had made a secret treaty dividing the Arab lands among themselves. The peace settlement substantially carried into effect this agreement, although both powers were compelled to take the territories as mandates of the League of Nations. France was assigned Lebanon and Syria, and Britain was assigned Iraq, Transjordan, and Palestine. The French expelled Faisal from Syria, and their mandates proved most unpopular. The Arabs charged that the French used their administration in the interest of France and its nationals and that they favored Christians (particularly the Maronites of Lebanon) over the Moslems. There were several armed rebellions in Syria.

The British made Faisal King of Iraq and his brother Abdullah ruler of Transjordan. The British acknowledged the "independence" of Transjordan in 1928 but retained control over finances, foreign affairs, and military matters. Something nearer "independence" was granted Iraq in 1932, but the British retained military bases and continued to train the Iraqi army and furnish it with military equipment. The pressures of international politics required the British to share Iraq's Mosul oil with other countries and the control of the Iraq Petroleum Company was divided four ways among British, Dutch, French, and American companies. Since Dutch Shell was mostly owned by British investors this gave the British virtually half of the Iraq Company. (It is also noteworthy that despite America's postwar isolationism, the American State Department did not hesitate to press the claims of the American companies; Standard Oil of New Jersey and Socony were the American companies "cut in" on the deal.) Arabs had mixed feelings about the two Hashimite states of Jordan and Iraq; some Arab nationalists felt that their rulers would little by little get full independence for their countries, but others regarded both Abdullah and Faisal as little better than British puppets.

The League of Nations mandate in Palestine enjoined the British to carry out the Balfour Declaration, which had promised to make that country a Jewish homeland. This proved a most difficult task, and the British were confronted with an increasingly tempestuous situation. The Arabs bitterly resented turning Palestine into a national home for the Jews, and they regarded Jewish immigration under the protection of Britain and the League of Nations as a new Western imperialism. In 1922 the Moslem Arabs constituted about 80 per cent of Palestine's population. In the following decade the Jewish population rose from around 80,000 to around 200,000. Continued immigration and the encroachments on scarce arable lands resulted in widespread strikes, civil disobedience, and even bloody clashes. Progress toward the establishment of self-governing institutions was blocked by this rancorous animosity.

The story in Egypt, the most populous and commercially advanced of the Arab states, was also a tortuous one. In 1919 and 1920 a great nationalist wave characterized by strikes, riots, and passive resistance swept over Egypt. The nationalist movement was led by the Wafd party, strong among Egypt's commercial and educated classes. This party wanted to make Egypt a fully independent nation with a constitutional monarchy and parliamentary government. In 1922 the British unilaterally proclaimed the termination of their protectorate and declared Egypt to be "an independent sovereign state." However, the realities of power were retained by the British. But by 1936 the Wafd was strong enough to induce Britain to make a treaty which removed most of the political controls over Egypt but which allowed Britain to maintain fortifications and troops in the Suez Canal Zone, to use Alexandria and Port Said as naval bases, to move British troops over Egyptian territory in time of war and threat of war, and to instruct the Egyptian army and equip it with arms. Thus Egypt was far from free.

During the period between the two world wars there were only five Middle Eastern countries free from Western *political* imperialism: Yemen, Saudi Arabia, Afghanistan, Iran, and Turkey. Yemen was isolated, medieval, Islamic, and absolutist with a population almost universally addicted to the narcotic habit of ghat-chewing. Saudi Arabia was almost entirely the product of one man, Ibn Saud of Nejd, who from 1913 to 1926 used the Arab tribes and the fanatical Wahhabi Moslems to conquer most of the Arab peninsula. His great triumph came in 1925 when he occupied the Hashimite realm of the Hejaz. Ibn Saud, who firmly believed Allah's word that the world is flat, was the last of the great patriarchs. He put together the largest state in Arabia since the days of Muhammad.

In Iran, a strong current of nationalism swept the country following World War I. The Bolshevist Revolution had brought the collapse of the Russian sphere in the north and now the Iranians turned their attention to undermining British influence in the south. The nationalist movement in 1921 brought to power Riza Khan, who overthrew the enfeebled Shah, proclaimed himself Shah, changed the name of his country from Persia to Iran, adopted Western administrative reforms, emphasized industrialization through state capitalism, built the Trans-Iranian Railway, and in 1933 reduced the concession area of the Anglo-Persian Oil Company (in which the British government had a controlling interest) and forced that company to pay higher royalties to the Iranian government. However, with all his feverish activities, Riza Shah was able to make scarcely a dent in the poverty, backwardness, and feudal nature of his country.

The most remarkable anti-imperialist revolution following World War I came in Turkey where the Nationalist movement under Mustafa Kemal (Atatürk) overthrew the Sultanate and the Caliphate and proclaimed a republic, separated mosque from government, abolished the wearing of the fez, encouraged Western dress and customs, emancipated women, abolished polygamy, substituted the Latin alphabet for the Arabic, made a massive drive on illiteracy, adopted Western legal codes, induced the Western powers to abolish the capitulations and other servitudes on Turkey, organized a strong central bank, erected a protective tariff, and sought rapid industrialization by establishing a number of state-owned enterprises and using state controls. Although Atatürk ruled as a dictator, he proclaimed popular suffrage and encouraged democratic practices. This thoroughly nationalist revolution adopted Western ways in order to deal effectively with the Westerners. It established a mixed economy, but one more capitalist than collectivist. Turkey, traditional national enemy of Russia, remained profoundly anti-Russian and became strongly anti-Communist. Despite the revolutionary changes of the 1920's, economic progress was slow, democracy had serious difficulties, Turkish society remained essentially conservative, and in fear of Russian Communism the Turks stood staunchly for the *status quo* in the Middle East and feared any kind of social revolution among their neighbors.

Following World War II Turkish resistance to a much more powerful Soviet Union stiffened and the Turkish government became even more conservative. On the other hand, in Iran the Tudeh party, the only genuine mass party to appear in that country and one of the few mass parties to emerge in the Middle East, gained rapidly. This party demanded basic economic and social reforms, and from 1944 to 1946 it looked as though this party would come to power and work a social revolution. But by 1946 the Communists had gained control of the Tudeh leadership, and when Russia for a time refused to get out of Iran's northern province of Azerbaijan, which she had occupied during the war, and the Tudeh supported the threatened Communist secession of that province from Iran, the nationalists turned against the Tudeh, and the opportunity for national economic and social transformation passed.

World War II loosened the hold of the Western powers on their colonies, protectorates, and mandates. The defeat of France in 1940 and the quarrels of the Vichy French and the Free French in North Africa weakened the French, and nationalist movements grew in Algeria, Morocco, and Tunisia. In 1941 the British defeat of the Vichy French in Lebanon and Syria brought about the end of the French mandate, but De Gaulle's Free French tried to hold on in both countries for several years longer. However, in 1946, finding little support from the indigenous peoples, the French finally evacuated both Lebanon and Syria, and these countries became independent states.

In 1946 Britain recognized the "independence" of Transjordan, and soon after, its Amir Abdullah proclaimed himself king. However, Britain still retained the right to keep bases, to station its forces in the country, and to supervise the Arab Legion. In 1948 the British made still more concessions but retained two military bases and continued to pay subsidies. The following year Transjordan changed its name to Jordan.

The most persistently explosive situation in the Middle East was the intransigent hatred of Arabs and Jews. It had become evident by 1947 that the two peoples could not live peacefully together in Palestine. That year the United Nations voted to divide Palestine into an Arab state and a Jewish state, a decision violently opposed by the Arabs. The following year there were around 1,320,000 Arabs in Palestine and the Jewish population had climbed to around 640,000. (A great part of the immigrants were European Jews displaced by the war.) In 1948, following Britain's termination of its mandate and the proclaiming of the state of Israel, Arab armies from Egypt, Lebanon, Syria, Iraq, and Jordan invaded Palestine to eradicate Israel. A war between Arabs and Israelis ensued (1948-1949). The war was characterized by fanaticism, cruelty, and massacres of civilian populations. The Israelis, already taking firm grip on their new state, which was to make it the most progressive in the Middle East, were better organized and their armies fought much more effectively than the Arabs. A series of armistices were signed in 1949 which left Israel in possession of over three-fourths of Palestine territory. Of that left to the Arabs, Jordan occupied the central eastern part of Palestine, and Egypt the Gaza strip.

Through the years the Arabs and Jews could make no peace and the boundaries were left as they were at the time of the armistices, which substantially recognized the territorial dispositions resulting from the war operations. Through the years, too, there would be repeated border clashes, commando raids by both sides on the villages of the other, and numerous massacres. The establishment of Israel resulted in the displacement of around 70 per cent of the Arab population there, whom the Israeli government refused to readmit. Thereafter, almost 1 million Arab refugees lived precariously year after year along the borders and in the Arab-occupied parts of Palestine. After the establishment of Israel as an independent state Jewish immigration assumed even larger proportions, and in the first three months of Israel's existence around 500,000 immigrants entered the country.

It was out of the Egyptian revolution of 1952 that the forces of

Arab nationalism and social reform would at last find their leader. This Egyptian revolution had long been germinating. The Wafd movement had spent its force. It had failed to gain full independence for Egypt, had little appeal to the new generation because of its inability to develop a program of economic and social reform, had frittered away much energy in fruitless conflicts with the monarchy over questions of limiting the royal power, had failed to curb King Farouk's extravagance and graft, and its own leaders had become involved in the prevailing corruption. The standard of living of the peasants and the urban workers had been falling. Egyptian pride had been wounded by the defeats inflicted by little Israel. The Communist and Socialist parties had been growing some, but the Moslem Brotherhood, a reactionary right-wing mass movement representing militant Islam and demanding resistance to Westernization and a return to a theocratic state, had become the most powerful political movement in Egypt with supporters from Morocco to Iraq. However, it was the Society of Free Officers, a secret organization within the Egyptian Army, led nominally by General Mohammad Naguib but in reality by Lt. Colonel Gamal Abdul Nasser, which engineered the revolution, an entirely different one from that contemplated by the Moslem Brotherhood.

The Free Officers, through their control of the army, seized power in 1952 and deposed King Farouk; in 1953 they proclaimed the republic; and in 1954 Nasser displaced Naguib as premier and national leader. Naguib wanted to establish a free parliamentary democracy, but Nasser and his following insisted that a consolidated and decisive government was necessary to achieve sweeping reform. A tight centralized government was ultimately established with major power in the President. The National Union was organized to give the government systematic contact with the masses and guide popular support. The new leadership proclaimed as its goals complete national independence, modernization, industrialization, and economic and social reform.

By the terms of the Anglo-Egyptian treaty of 1953, Britain agreed to evacuate the Sudan and to allow the Sudanese to determine for themselves whether they would federate with Egypt or become independent. By the terms of the Anglo-Egyptian treaty of 1954, Britian gave up her last footholds in Egypt and agreed to evacuate her huge fortifications in the Suez Canal Zone and withdraw all her troops. Egypt was at last free. However, the privately owned Suez Canal Company would continue to operate the Canal in territory "an integral part of Egypt," and the Convention of 1888 guaranteeing freedom of navigation in the Canal was reaffirmed.

These stirring events in the most important of Arab states were hailed throughout the Arab world, and Arab nationalists believed that in Nasser they had found their symbol of authentic nationalism, basic reform, and social change.

Oil and the Suez Canal were the two most vital specific interests of the West in the Middle East, and it was Iran's nationalist revolution of 1951-1953 which for the first time seriously challenged the West's monopolization of Middle Eastern oil. Backed by the National Front, a coalition of many groups and parties, including the Tudeh, Premier Mohammad Mossadegh in 1951 confiscated and nationalized the Anglo-Iranian Oil Company. In defiance of the Shah, Mossadegh thus embarked on a thoroughgoing economic and social revolution. Backed by the army, the British, and the Americans, the Shah was able to depose Mossadegh and break the revolution. The oil properties remained technically nationalized, but in reality little was changed, for in 1954 an international consortium took over the properties for production, refining, and distribution. The shares in the consortium were divided as follows: 40 per cent for the British Petroleum Company (formerly the Anglo-Iranian Oil Company), 40 per cent for fourteen American oil companies, 14 per cent for the Royal Dutch Shell, and 6 per cent for the Compagnie Française des Petroles. Profits were to be divided equally between the consortium and the Iranian government, and the consortium promised increasingly to train and use Iranian engineers, technicians, and managers. Thus the Iranians profited by the new arrangements, the British lost their monopoly, and the American companies gained enormously at British expense. But the national revolution which might have provided the popular base for modernizing and reforming the backward Iranian society was aborted.

In the postwar years it was the American companies which made the greatest inroads into Middle Eastern oil. American and British companies controlled most of the Persian Gulf oil, but as between the British and the Americans, the Americans by the mid-1950's had 100 per cent of the Saudi Arabian oil, 50 per cent of the Kuwait oil, about 25 per cent of the Iraq Petroleum Company, and 40 per cent of the consortium operating in Iran. British companies owned 50 per cent of Kuwait oil, about 25 per cent of the Iraq Petroleum Company, 100 per cent in three other companies operating in Iraq, and 40 per cent of the international consortium in Iran.

Middle Eastern nationalists, realizing that they could not yet eject the foreigners and that they still lacked the technical facilities to produce, refine, and distribute the oil by themselves, had three aims: to get as high royalties as they could (by the mid-1950's the usual pattern was to divide profits on a fifty-fifty basis, which represented a real gain for the local governments over earlier practice); to win agreements requiring the oil companies to employ a larger and larger number of local people in technical and managing capacities (thus increasing local employment and preparing for the day when the indigenous peoples could effectively operate the properties); and to pressure the local national governments to channel the oil royalties into socially progressive services—roads, schools, public health, land reform, irrigation, hydroelectric plants, and so forth. In Saudi Arabia, Kuwait, Bahrain, and Qatar, there was no distinction between the finances of the state and the ruling family. By the mid-1950's over 90 per cent of Saudi Arabian income came from oil. In the government budget "the royal household" got twice what was spent on education, four times what was spent on public health, nearly five times what was spent on public works, and more than twelve times what was spent on agriculture. Over 1 billion dollars of the Sheikh of Kuwait's savings were invested in Britain and represented one of the mainstays of the sterling area. In Iran a large part of the oil revenues were spent on the army and on the secret police, over 50,000 strong. Only in Iraq did some considerable part of the oil royalties go into development projects.

In southern and southeastern Asia, as we have seen, where the Western empires had been direct, truly vast, and in some cases dated back three hundred years, the Western retreat from imperialism had been rather swift and clearcut. But in the Middle East, where Western imperialism had been less complete and generally of shorter historical duration, the retreat was procrastinating and tortuous; it had been going on in an ambiguous and rearguard manner since World War I. Why were the Western powers clinging to their holdings in the Moslem world more tenaciously than to those in southern and southeast Asia?

For one thing the Middle East was closer to Europe physically, and the Middle East, especially the Suez Canal, was considered to be the West's gateway to the East, where the West still had much commerce, despite the retreat from imperialism. Did the Egyptians, for instance, have the technical facilities to handle the enormous commerce which went through the Suez Canal? The French possessions in North Africa were physically close to France, Algeria was a department of France itself, and over a million Franchmen made their homes in Algeria. These Frenchmen looked to France to save them from the "instability" of "native rule." (Western countries were finding it difficult to disengage themselves in colonies where there were large numbers of the ruling power's nationals living as citizens.)

Again, the European empires in the Far East had been pretty well shattered by the Japanese conquests, but in the Middle East the Western powers had largely maintained the *status quo* during World War II, and they experienced nothing as distruptive there as the Japanese conquests in southeast Asia. The Europeans were not quite sure just how popularly based the Middle Eastern movements for genuine national independence were. Europeans had been impressed by the mass support of the early Kuomintang and of the India Congress party, but the Middle Eastern movements had no mass parties analogous to these. Europeans were at first inclined to think that the nationalist movements in the Middle East represented merely old ruling families or only small parties led by agitators, demagogues, and power-hungry politicians. But at last they were learning that the nationalist movements in the Middle East and in North Africa no less than the Far Asian ones did indeed express mass aspirations. However, no matter how wide the popular base, nationalist opposition to the Westerners in the relatively small countries of North Africa and the Middle East seemed more easy to "manage" than that in countries like China, India, and Indonesia with their vast territories and huge populations. Then, too, Western refusal to yield to nationalist demands in Middle Eastern and North African countries seemed less likely to turn nationalist movements into Communist ones, for there were fewer Communists in Moslem lands than in the Far East and southern Asia.

Finally, Middle Eastern oil had become a vital necessity to the Western industrial societies; and did the Middle Eastern populations have the engineers, technicians, and managers who could maintain the flow of oil to the West? The oil companies and their business allies were among the most powerful pressure groups in the United States, Britain, and France, and these exerted an effective influence on Western opinion and on Western governments, not merely to maintain the West's oil holdings in the Middle East but to extend them.

There was some friction among the Western powers themselves. The French blamed the British for forcing them to give way in Lebanon and Syria. The British, not without some resentment, saw the Americans gradually take over the commitments which were formerly theirs but which the British no longer had the strength to maintain—in Greece, in Turkey, in Iran, and even in faraway Saudi Arabia, where in 1947 the British military mission had withdrawn and American officers undertook the training of the Saudi army. By the early 1950's the British position in Jordan and Iraq was becoming more and more untenable. The British could scarcely be expected to welcome the American oil "monopoly" in Saudi Arabia and Bahrain and the encroachments by American oil companies on their former preserves of Kuwait and Iran. Some Britons observed that while the Americans piously talked about the evils of colonialism they capitalized on their very anti-imperialist pretensions to pick up imperialist advantages for themselves. Stalin saw in all this the inevitable working out of the Leninist thesis that the rival capitalist imperialisms would eventually destroy themselves and pave the way for Communism.

The Middle East, then, was an area of many new, poor, and unstable nations. In most of them the development of nationalism itself was only in its formative stages. All had within themselves many diverse groups. Iraq, for instance, contained a large Kurdish minority and smaller minorities of Armenians, Assyrians, Yazidis, Lurs, Turkmen, and Mandeans. There was a disturbing sectarian division between Sunni and Shia Moslems. Syria contained Druses,

Alawi, Kurds, Armenians, Circassians, Assyrians, Turks, and Greek Orthodox Christians. In Lebanon the differences between Maronite Christians, Sunni Moslems, Shia Moslems, Greek Orthodox Christians, and the Druses were so significant that they constituted the basis of a sectarian politics and a sectarian administrative structure of government.

Throughout the whole area (except in Israel) there was a grinding poverty and urgent need of agrarian reform, irrigation projects, and hydroelectric developments. The great potentialities of the Jordan, the Tigris-Euphrates, and the Nile were still largely undeveloped. There were semi-nomadic tribes, and a peasantry just emerging from hard semi-feudal conditions. In the cities a wide gap existed between landowners, industrialists, and rich merchants on the one hand and small shopkeepers, artisans, workers, and the chronically unemployed on the other.

Middle Eastern nationalism, like the new nationalism in other economically underdeveloped regions, had democratic aspirations, but actual democratic practices would be difficult to operate among peoples with little experience in self-government, much illiteracy, considerable leftovers of feudal class structures, and governments compelled to undertake a wide range of urgent economic and social changes. The two mass parties which appeared in the Middle East—the Tudeh and the Moslem Brotherhood—were fanatical and extremist, the one leftist and the other rightist. The multiple bloc parties which seemed democratic were generally expressions of feudal lords, pashas, religious hierarchy, and rich merchants; they usually had regional bases from which local notables manipulated the votes of peasants and workers; the issues they raised rarely related to the country's real problems, for the political struggle was really one of the distribution of government offices and of political patronage and power. The Communist party was small but well organized in most Middle Eastern countries. The Syrian Social National party sought to achieve democratic socialism, and it had a large following, but it was evident that because of the multiplicity of parties it would not be able to achieve the power necessary to make the economic breakthrough to industrialism and work a social transformation of the country.

The National Union of Nasser, like the Kemalist experience in

Turkey which preceded it, was frankly a one-party dictatorship designed to accomplish revolutionary objectives. The military *coup d'état* and army control as the means to achieve the political, economic, and social goals of an anti-imperialist revolution was first used in the Middle East—by Kemal and Nasser—but there were already signs that the military *coup d'état* would be increasingly used in the Middle East and elsewhere not only by the social revolutionaries but also by the feudal, reactionary right.

Another political device more and more being used in this century of rising mass expectations was the organized city mob, the staging of huge street demonstrations, to be turned on and off as directed. This was a technique in evidence not only in Teheran, Baghdad, Damascus, and Cairo but also in Tokyo, Seoul, Havana, Caracas, Lima, and Buenos Aires.

There were numerous rivalries among the various Arab countries. King Ibn Saud and his successor King Saud were leaders in the Wahhabi Moslem sect, and this together with the medieval character of their country kept them somewhat apart from the Arabs outside the Arabian peninsula. The house of Saud was the traditional enemy of the Hashimites, whose representatives sat on the thrones of Jordan and Iraq. In much of the Arab world to the west and among many Arabs in Jordan and Iraq themselves it was felt that these two Hashimite kingdoms were too socially conservative in their domestic policies and that they were still too much dependent on Britain. At one time or another, Jordan, Iraq, and Syria had ambitions to put together the countries of the whole Fertile Crescent into one nation, and whenever this showed itself there was alarm in other Arab nations.

Following the rise of Nasser, the pan-Arabs looked to Egypt to put the Arab countries together in a single nation or at least a federation. Many felt, too, that under Nasser's leadership the economic and social transformation would come much faster. Pro-Nasser and anti-Nasser Arabs politically contested inside the various Arab nations. The basic question for the future appeared to be this: Would Arab nationalism continue to express itself through many individual nations or would it ultimately result in the development of one large Arab federation? If federation were to develop, would it also include the countries of North Africa west of Egypt?

In the Cold War which developed between the Communist and Western powers after World War II, it often appeared to Americans that the Arabs were more favorably disposed to Russia than to the West. There could be no doubt that the Arabs had grievances against the West. The Arabs felt that their chief enemy was Western imperialism and they directed their chief energies against it. Also, the Arabs held the United States and Britain responsible for the establishment of Israel. On the other hand, Russia had identified itself less clearly with Israel, had never held any colonies or protectorates or oil in the Arab world, and Russian leaders made much of their anti-colonialism, their friendship for the anti-imperialist revolutions, and their lack of racism. In Turkey and Iran, however, the situation was quite different, for these two countries had had a long historical experience with Russian imperialism. The strong hold of Islam on Middle Eastern peoples, Arabs and non-Arabs, seemed to make them peculiarly resistant to Communist doctrine.

It would take the Americans a long time to realize that the Arab peoples were not much interested in the conflict between East and West, that they were inclined to say "a plague on both your houses," that they were primarily concerned with cutting the last links of Western imperialism and concentrating on their own problems and development.

However, the instability of the new nations, the immensity of their problems, the West's stubborn clinging to its last vestiges of imperialism, the implacable hatred of Arabs for Jews, and the proximity of Russia to the area—all of these factors created a volatile and highly explosive situation in the Middle East.

The Anti-Imperialist Revolutions in Africa

In Africa, the least developed of all the continents, nationalists were also astir in the decade following the war. The bright young African nationalists who in the 1930's had studied at the Sorbonne, Cambridge, Edinburgh, Columbia, and Howard, who had imbibed the "isms" at the London School of Economics, and who had watched with passionate concern the ups and downs of Gandhi's civil disobedience campaign in India, were now at work in their homelands recruiting still younger bright young men, agitating among workers and peasants and even tribal chiefs, and organizing nationalist parties. They hoped that the imperial powers, weak and weary from war, busy with reconstruction and basic reforms at home, and with leftists now in powerful positions in London and Paris, would not resist profound colonial reform, self-government, and even eventual independence of the African colonies.

In the Anglo-Egyptian Sudan, the task was to induce the British to depart and then decide whether to federate with Egypt or "go it alone." In the cities, where the Cairo newspapers were read and there was much familiarity with Arab nationalism, the prevailing sentiment was for federation with Egypt, but in the rural areas the preponderant opinion was for Sudanese independence. In Somalia, a United Nations trust and formerly an Italian colony, the nationalist movement was well advanced and demanded an independent Somalia incorporating the Somali people not only of the trust territory but also of French Somaliland, British Somaliland, eastern Ethiopia, and northern Kenya.

On the other side of the continent, in British West Africa— Black Africa—impressive nationalist movements were making great headway in Sierra Leone, the Gold Coast (later Ghana), and Nigeria. In this area the white population was negligible in numbers, there was not much of a color bar, relations between Europeans and Africans were amicable, and the white settlers were not numerous enough to demand that the British stay indefinitely in order to preserve them from "the instability of native rule." The British Labour party was in power in London, and the African nationalists were immensely encouraged by the liberal way the Attlee ministry was liquidating the British empire in India, Pakistan, Burma, and Ceylon.

West Africa had solid reasons for its optimism because in 1948 and 1949 the Labour government embarked on a policy of "creative abdication," of a systematic liquidating of colonial rule in Africa by adopting policies and timetables involving phased stages of self-government and then independence. "The only way to train people for self-government is to let them govern" became the watchword in Whitehall. Even British Conservatives saw the handwriting on the wall, felt that independence could not be permanently delayed, and that the British stake in the African colonies was not worth the sacrifices and money involved in waging a procrastinating delaying action. Increasingly it was felt better to leave with African good will and a continuation into a post-colonial period of commerce and intercourse, with former colonies becoming members of the British Commonwealth, than to leave with animosity and the cutting off of all ties. So while the Labourites took the lead, the Conservatives followed suit, and with the British the problem was how to prepare the Africans for meeting the responsibilities of independence and keeping the governmental, legal, administrative, and technical services going once the governing power had withdrawn.

Britain proceeded to provide a wide franchise in Sierra Leone, the Gold Coast, and Nigeria and to encourage African participation in local and colony-wide government. Colonial assemblies became "Houses of Commons in Black Miniature." British officials listened to eloquent speeches in which African members quoted Burke and Fox, Patrick Henry and Thomas Jefferson. African politicians increasingly sat in local councils and in cabinets of colonial governors.

In West Africa, Britain's policy of creative abdication confronted its toughest situation in Nigeria, the most populous country in all Africa, and one of its most heterogeneous. At mid-century the population of Nigeria was around 32 million. (However, only about 12,000 of this was European, which meant that the intransigent white minority opposing Britain's ultimate withdrawal could pretty well be ignored.) Nigeria contained around 250 different tribes and an infinite variety of indigenous languages. Moreover, the country was divided into three natural geographical sections—east, west, and north—and the remote north was the largest, the most populous, the most backward, and contained around 10 million Moslems. Nevertheless, the Nigerian nationalists seemed to be succeeding, with difficulty, in welding most of the tribal chiefs and the three sections into an all-Nigeria movement. The British established three Houses of Assembly, one for each section, and a federal House of Representatives, all chosen by a combination of direct primaries and electoral colleges. The membership in all these legislative assemblies was overwhelmingly Nigerian.

In the Gold Coast, by mid-century, the nationalist party of Kwame Nkrumah, the Convention People's party, was thoroughly organized in all parts of the country, was integrating tribal chiefs into the movement, and had developed party techniques and a party mystique which included party colors, salutes, slogans, uniformed brigades, loud-speakers, and decorated automobile caravans. In 1951, when a self-governing constitution went into effect, the party was already in the midst of a civil disobedience campaign. Nkrumah was clapped into jail, but when his party overwhelmingly won the first national election in Gold Coast history, the colonial governor pardoned him and made him "Leader of Government Business" in the Legislative Assembly. In 1952 Nkrumah became prime minister and he and his ministers worked closely with the British officials in conducting government affairs and in preparing the way for the time when the Gold Coast as Ghana would be the first all-Negro colony to become independent and a member of the British Commonwealth. (Liberia and Ethiopia had not been European colonies, and the Union of South Africa had become a dominion in the British Commonwealth under white leadership.)

As African nationalism grew, those imperial powers and elements within Africa opposed to it increased their vigilance and their oppressive measures. In the Union of South Africa, the dominant white minority carried segregation of the races to extreme lengths, increasingly tightened apartheid, became more and more oppressive in its treatment of its Indian and Pakistani populations, talked of seceding from the British Commonwealth, and defied the United Nations in South West Africa, which theoretically it held in trust under that organization, by applying apartheid to the majority African population there and by treating it little different from its own territory.

In her vast empire in Angola and Mozambique, Portugal turned her back on all reforms and met the rising threat of African nationalism with implacable hostility. Education for Africans was virtually non-existent, colonial government was an authoritarian police state, and the economy was based on a corrupt and brutal system of forced labor which was virtually slavery. Portugal prided herself that there was no color bar, for segregation at law did not exist and there was an absence of the racial bigotry prevailing in the Union of South Africa; but the vast economic and social differences which separated Europeans from Africans constituted segregation in practice. In an attempt to strengthen her hold on the colonies, Portugal in 1951 officially exorcised colonialism and made Angola and Mozambique integral and organic parts of Portugal itself. But this legerdemain fooled nobody.

In the Belgian Congo, colonial rule was not as oppressive as it was in the Portuguese colonies, but the Belgians, too, obstinately refused to come to terms with the rising tide of African nationalism. They neglected education, positively made it a policy to keep advanced and technical education from the Congolese, would have nothing to do with such measures as elections and assemblies, and ruled the colony in a thoroughly paternal fashion. The Belgians prided themselves that the Congo had no perceptible nationalist movement. They believed that without education there would be no Congolese demands for elections and self-government and that without these there would be no formidable nationalist movement. Although forced labor existed it was declining in economic importance. As the Congo developed economically, which it did under the thrifty Belgians, the standard of living rose gradually—and there was the rub. Rising standards of living brought Congolese demands for education and self-government. In the province of Katanga the Union Minière du Haut Katanga was developing huge mining operations and extracting increasing amounts of copper, cobalt, zinc, platinum, tungsten, columbium, cadmium, silver, and other valuable minerals. The Union Minière was a powerful part of the Société Générale, a gigantic combination of financial and industrial power which played a dominant economic role not only in the Congo but in Belgium itself.

The British were having their greatest difficulties in East Africa, in the territories of Southern Rhodesia, Northern Rhodesia, Nyasaland, Tanganyika, Kenya, and Uganda. These bordered on the Union of South Africa and the unprogressive Portuguese and Belgian colonies. There were sizable European minorities in the Rhodesias and Kenya who vowed they would never be ruled by local governments dominated by Africans. Some of the whites were migrants from the Union of South Africa and carried with them the racial intolerance of that country. In the Rhodesias there were powerful British and other European mining interests which pressured for a continuation of British rule. Yet British statesmen felt that African nationalism in these areas could not be ignored and that Africans here, as in West Africa, should be prepared for self-government and eventual independence. In an attempt to bridge the views of Europeans and Africans, and possibly to prepare against the day when the Union of South Africa would leave the Commonwealth, Britain experimented with the Central African Federation, composed of Southern Rhodesia, Nyasaland, and Northern Rhodesia. The Africans in these countries pointed out that the franchise was still so restricted that the Federation was dominated by the whites, a relatively small minority, while the whites claimed that Britain was preparing for a too-rapid extension of the franchise and full racial partnership.

In the early 1950's Kenya, which was overwhelmingly African but had a sizable European minority which maintained the color bar and for decades had been encroaching on the best agricultural lands, experienced the fiercest of racial uprisings. For a time a secret African society, the Mau Mau, murdered and massacred both whites and blacks (those who refused to join the Mau Mau or were too closely identified with the whites) and subjected the country to a state of terror. Although the Mau Mau was finally suppressed, it had demonstrated what a desperate African majority might do elsewhere. Friends of African nationalism took this to mean that the whites would have to come to terms with African nationalism. Intransigent whites saw in it arguments for following the lead of the Union of South Africa and keeping the Africans in strict submission.

However, African nationalism steadily gained ground in East Africa and the long-time policies of London seemed to encourage creative abdication in this area as well as in West Africa. Africans in the Rhodesias and in Nyasaland pressed for a dissolution of the Federation, and for independence for their respective countries; and Africans in Tanganyika, Kenya, and Uganda set their faces against any federation of their own lands. However, nationalists in East Africa divided into two groups. Although both groups wanted national independence for the individual countries, one favored ejecting the whites entirely and proclaimed the doctrine of "Africa for the Africans," but the other group conceded that the whites had a place in African countries provided they were willing to accept in good faith the rule of the African majority.

Sometimes African nationalism was divided between those who would return to the old ways and those who would press ahead to the new. An example of this was in Uganda, where the chiefs had not yet been assimilated into the modern nationalist movement and where there was considerable traditionalist sentiment for restoring the authority of the Kabaka of Baganda. The nationalist party, the Uganda National Congress, increasing in strength, was determined to move on to democratization and an independent and modern national state.

The French, unlike the Portuguese and the Belgians, were fully alive to the modern democratic and nationalist forces rising in Africa. At the same time, they adopted policies and methods in French West Africa and in French Equatorial Africa quite different from the British. The British were preparing for self-government and eventual independence, but the French were determined to make of their African colonials good Frenchmen and to assimilate them to French culture. Instead of maintaining a color bar, Frenchmen and colonials were encouraged to associate with one another, and more and more schools stressing the French language and culture were built for the colonials. The French Constitution of 1946, which established the Fourth Republic, provided for the French Union. The French colonies in Negro Africa became overseas territories within the Union and were allowed to elect local councils and mayors and colonial assemblies. Each territory also sent representatives to the French Chamber of Deputies, the Senate, and the Council of the Republic in Paris. Those elected were largely Africans. Even the political parties of metropolitan France appeared in some of the colonies, and the colonial deputies in Paris associated themselves with the various French parties. However, these measures did not arrest the growth of African nationalism in the French colonies. In effect they were preparing Africans to conduct their own affairs once independence was achieved. But they were inculcating a respect for French culture which might stand France in good stead if and when the colonies severed their political ties with France.

A Madagascar revolt in 1947 of Malagasy nationalists, which was ruthlessly suppressed by the French at the cost of around 80,000 patriot lives (according to the charges of the Malagasy nationalists), was a grim warning that African nationalism could not long be stayed.

How much of an appeal would Communism have for the proliferating nationalist movements in Africa? Nobody knew for
sure, but despite the fact that many African nationalist leaders
had been exposed to Marxism in European universities, Communism did not seem to be playing any considerable part outside
the French colonies, and even there it appeared to be not so much
indigenous as a propitiation of the powerful French Communist
party. The industrial proletariat was small in Africa. Unlike Asia
and the Middle East, Africa was free of a landed feudalism. In
all parts of the continent, and to a marked degree in West Africa,
the peasants owned small plots of land. Political independence was
a concept much easier to grasp than Marxism. There was a disposition to regard Communism as a *white* movement, and most
people were suspicious of it for that reason. There was a strong
tendency to pin all hopes on political freedom and national independence.

However, in the French colonies Communism was getting more
of a play than elsewhere. In the late 1940's the Communists were
not only the largest single party in France but they were participants in the French government and held seats in the French
Cabinet. This made a strong impression on African politicians in
the French colonies, and in the French Chamber of Deputies they
often associated themselves with the Communists and maintained
working relationships with French Communist leaders, for there
was no telling to what extent the French Communists would be
in a position to determine the future of their homelands. For
instance, the party of Sékou Touré in Guinea and that of Félix
Houphouet-Boigny in the Ivory Coast were busy organizing
workers and peasants on a somewhat class basis and both Touré
and Houphouet-Boigny were on good terms with the Communist
leaders in France. Were the Communist party in France to continue to grow and to increase its participation in the French government, and certainly if the Communists were to come to power
in France, the impact on France's African colonies would be
enormous. And from the French colonies that influence would
spread to the British, Belgian, and Portuguese colonies. It was
plain therefore that despite the limited appeal of Marxism for
most of the early African nationalist leaders, the spread of Communism in Western Europe would have marked and perhaps
decisive repercussions on African nationalist movements.

In any event troublesome days seemed to lie ahead. By taking an intransigent stand against progressive, democratic, and nationalist movements, the Portuguese and the Belgians might be heading for bloody years in the future. Even the British government in East Africa found it increasingly difficult to steer a course between the demands of the white settlers and the aspirations of the African nationalists. Prolonged and hideous race wars in South Africa, in the Rhodesias, and in Kenya were a distinct possibility. And prolonged wars of African liberation would have grave implications for international relations and would open the way to serious Communist penetration in Africa.

But even should the independence of the African states come peacefully the problems would still be enormous. Nationalism was even less mature in Africa than it was in Asia and the Middle East. For the most part, the new African states would have to contend with more numerous tribal and linguistic diversities; transportation and communications were even more primitive than they were in Asia and the Middle East; and the other makings of the modern administrative state were scantier. Africans had either no experience with voting, elections, and assemblies (as in the Portuguese and Belgian colonies) or such experience was of shorter duration than in Asia and the Middle East. In the formative years of national independence and democracy the African states would have to be even more dependent on patriarchal and paternalistic methods and on the mystiques of party and personal leadership.

Finally, African leaders were probably too extravagant in the good things they promised would flow from national independence. The people were not only expecting national independence but along with it a higher standard of living and the services of the welfare state. But for fulfillment these required an increase in real wealth and in the communications, transportation, accumulated capital, and technical services upon which real wealth depended. Nationalist leaders in Asia were seriously debating the pros and cons of Communism, for they were acutely aware of the difficulties which beset a pre-industrial society attempting to make the breakthrough to modernity and industrialism, and they realized that Communism, drastic as it was, did throw light on how to meet some of these difficulties. There was something disturbing in the fact that the African leaders did not seem concerned enough about the enormity of the economic difficulties which lay ahead of them. However, unlike the Asian countries, African countries had relatively small populations and much unoccupied land and waste space. Frontier conditions might allow them to pursue a more leisurely path to industrialism. Nevertheless, frontier economies which specialized in the production of only one or two raw materials did not provide the wealth to maintain high living standards for the masses and extensive welfare services.

In the immediate postwar years, then, large questions loomed for Africa. Would the African countries achieve their independence without bloody wars and hideous racial strife? With independence once achieved, would they be able to cope successfully with the tremendous political and economic problems which would confront them, and if not, would nationalist revolutions then be followed by totalitarian ones?

Anti-Colonialism in Latin America

Although most of the Latin American countries had been independent nations for a century and a quarter or more, by the middle of the twentieth century they still remained largely colonial economies which specialized in the production of foodstuffs and raw materials for the advanced industrial countries. In one way or another segments of the population in all these countries were now in revolt against colonial conditions and demanding industrialization, balanced economies, and rising living standards. All of this expressed itself in an intensified nationalism.

What were the basic difficulties in Latin America? Why was this vast area which had been opened to European settlement over four hundred years ago still economically underdeveloped?

Some of the difficulties inhered in geography. While Latin America had much natural wealth and scenic beauty, it also had more of its share of swamps and jungles, almost impenetrable mountain barriers, and desolate desert wastes. It had much mineral wealth but lacked the coal and iron so basic to the nineteenth-century industrial revolutions. Except for the La Plata region, it was not blessed with large stretches of rich agricultural lands. For instance in Mexico the natural crop lands were confined to less than 8 per cent of the country's land surface, and even this was not fertile or level or well-watered. There had never been enough corn in Mexico—there was not enough corn in Aztec times; there was not enough corn at the mid-twentieth century.

At mid-century each of the Latin American countries was still tied economically to specialized production of one or two raw materials. These raw materials were dumped on an unprotected world market and were subject to violent fluctuations in price. When prices of commodities in which a particular country specialized sagged, the entire economy and government budget suffered disastrously. In Cuba these commodities were sugar and tobacco. In the Dominican Republic they were sugar and coffee. In Haiti they were coffee and sisal. In Guatemala, Honduras, and Costa Rica they were coffee and bananas. In El Salvador and Nicaragua they were coffee and cotton. In Panama they were bananas and cacao. In Ecuador they were bananas and coffee. In Colombia they were coffee and petroleum. In Brazil they were coffee and cacao. In Chile they were copper and nitrates. In Venezuela the decisive commodity was oil. In Bolivia it was tin. In Uruguay it was wool.

The system of agriculture and landholding was feudal. Land ownership was concentrated in the hands of a few old families. Large estates were worked by *peons* or *inquilinos*, by peasants or tenants, for a mere subsistence living. Often the same faithful peasant families worked on the same estates generation after generation. The big estate had a different name in the various countries. In Argentina it was the *estancia*, in Brazil the *fazenda*, in Chile the *fundo*, and in many places the *hacienda*. Actually, the big estate differed little from the colonial *encomienda*, or for that matter from the Roman *latifundium*. The big-estate system was the basis of a social-caste structure, and it was notoriously inefficient and often did not produce enough food for the population. Traditionalism, inertia, and low labor costs discouraged scientific and machine methods in agriculture. For instance, the *fundo* system in central Chile, the most fertile area in the nation, was so backward that each year Chile had to import food. Chile had six times the amount of productive soil as Switzerland, but produced less than half as much per capita. During the early decades of the twentieth century, large corporations, usually foreign and very often American, particularly in the Caribbean and Central American countries, established a new type of big estate. This was the commercial plantation or ranch, corporate-owned, which hired day laborers at the prevailing low wage scale. In many parts of Latin America, Indians still worked in primitive fashion the exhausted village lands to eke out the barest subsistence. Meantime, large areas of more fertile lands in South America, particularly in Bolivia, Paraguay, Brazil, and Colombia, still remained unoccupied waste space because of social inertia and the lack of planning, communications, technical skills, and capital.

Most of Latin America had a class sytem inherited from sixteenth- and seventeenth-century Spain. The big landowners were at the top of the social pyramid. Very often they were less concerned with agriculture than with the ostentatious living and the social prestige large land ownership conferred. They were often absent from their estates for long periods of time, frequently had homes in the capital city and even Paris, and not infrequently, in addition to perpetuating old-fashioned agricultural methods, let large parts of their lands lie idle. The landed aristocracy supplied most of those who went into the professions, commerce, banking, the army, the higher clergy, and politics. These constituted the small ruling elite. The middle class, growing throughout the nineteenth and twentieth centuries, was still relatively small. The mass of people were workers and peasants who lived in poverty. The caste system was made even more pointed by the fact that the elite was largely white (or "whitish"), for the most part descendants of the old colonial creole families, while in Central America and the northern and western countries of South America the mass of people were Indians and *mestizos* (a mixture of white and Indian). Race differences did not produce the caste system, they only accentuated it, for the class stratification existed in countries which were almost entirely white, as in Argentina.

Latin America's ruling class had less sense of *noblesse oblige* than the ruling classes in the older, more traditional, and more racially homogeneous countries of Europe. The ruling elite did little for its poor, had throughout the decades crushed or reduced the mavericks from its own ranks who sought to ameliorate social conditions, shamelessly used public office for personal enrichment, refused to bear its share of taxation and saddled most of the tax burden on the poorer elements of the population, spent a large part of its income on personal pleasure and display, and instead of investing its money at home very often stashed it away in foreign banks in fear of domestic instability and revolution.

Although Latin American countries had republics, written constitutions, popular suffrage, constitutional civil liberties, and even the system of separation of powers and checks and balances of the United States Constitution, in practice they had little genuine democracy. The ruling elite monopolized the government and the political offices; party battles were mostly sham battles between the ins and the outs, between different factions of the same ruling class, for place, position, and power. Local notables coerced and manipulated the voters of their districts, and bribery, vote stealing, and fraudulent election returns were common. If things threatened to get out of hand and elitist control was really challenged, the army was usually called in to restore "order."

The contest between the various factions of the elite were tame compared to the frequent seizures of dictatorial power by some *caudillo*—a "grand personality," a fiery orator, a florid demagogue, or more commonly a shrewd military man—who appeared as a deliverer either to make changes or to preserve the *status quo*. Whatever the forces which brought him to power, the *caudillo* usually wound up liquidating his personal political enemies, ruthlessly suppressing democratic procedures and civil liberties, and enormously enriching himself, his family, and his friends—but leaving essentially intact the privileges of the elite. The prevalence of the *caudillo* came largely out of the persistence of the authoritarian tradition of Spain and a need on occasion to break through the barriers of the elite to get a modicum of change or to rescue the elite from a modicum of change. Latin American democratic *forms* came out of the rather superficial enthusiasm for the Enlightenment during the revolutions for national independence, but these forms had never become assimilated to basic Latin American thought and reality. The great Bolívar sensed this when near the close of his life he wrote: "America is ungovernable. Those who have served the revolution have plowed the sea."

The intellectual tradition, too, was contributing to the difficulties the Latin Americans were having in adjusting to the modern world. Latin American intellectuals were the products of Spanish scholasticism. They were steeped in linguistics, syntax, dialectics, and abstractions. They often mistook words for realities. Most of the members of the ruling class got a classical or theological or legal education, and the emphasis was on pure logic and the theoretical ideas of traditional thinkers divorced from actual social conditions. All too few of the elite went in for scientific and technical educations. And the rest of the population got little education of any kind. The relative lack of scientific and pragmatic thought contributed to inertia and backwardness.

However, it should not be assumed that no progress had been made in Latin America. There had been periods in some of the countries when their political battles had been real ones and not make-believe. There had been revolutions which had helped some. There were times when even Indians had come to power; the two most respected presidents in Mexican history—Juárez and Cardenas—had risen from the squalor of Indian villages. During the previous century, and particularly during the previous decades, wealth had increased, technical facilities had expanded some, the middle classes had widened, education and other services had spread, and some reforms were made through the party contests of democracy and not through revolution, military *coup d'état,* or dictatorship. But in the main the hard and heavy hand of the past lay on these lands, and by mid-century the most formidable attacks on the *status quo* in Latin American history were under way.

Despite the ceremonial talk about the common destinies of the peoples of the Western Hemisphere, and the shared blessings of representative government and democratic ideals, and so forth, there never had been any real rapport between Anglo-Americans and Latin Americans. Anglo-American culture was derived from the British Isles and the European countries of the North Atlantic, and it was Protestant, commercial, middle-class, prosaic, and prudent. Latin American culture was derived from Spain, Portugal, and Rome, and it was Catholic, non-commercial, caste-ridden, humanistic, colorful, and passionate.

Latin Americans had never had any marked sympathies for the Monroe Doctrine. Although one of the declared purposes of that Doctrine was to protect Latin Americans from European intervention, the Doctrine had never been based on the cooperation of all the Western Hemisphere republics but only on the unilateral fiat of the United States. Nor had it protected Latin Americans from the power they feared most, "the colossus of the North," for the United States had annexed much of Mexico in the nineteenth century and had penetrated large parts of the Caribbean area in the first decades of the twentieth century.

Economically, there were problems. American and Argentine beef and wheat had always competed in world markets. By mid-century the greater part of Latin America's exports were going to the United States and the greater part of its imports were coming from the United States. Any shift in American trade and tariff policies had immediate effects on Latin American economies. By mid-century, too, American investors and corporations owned vast plantations, ranches, sugar refineries, oil refineries, pipelines, public utilities, and mineral wealth in Latin American countries. Latin Americans rarely gave American investors credit for the benefits their enterprises conferred—the economic development of their countries, the widening of job opportunities, the increase in technical know-how, the rather enlightened welfare programs of some American corporations. Instead, Latin Americans frequently charged that American investors and corporations siphoned off Latin American wealth to the United States and further unbalanced local economies by encouraging them further in the direction of extractive, mining, and agricultural enterprises and neglecting their diversification and industrialization. They further charged that American concerns exerted undue influence on Latin American ruling classes and governments and, in their insistence on a favorable investment climate and in their opposition to government controls and taxes, backed conservatives and reactionaries, dodged their share of taxes, and pressured against the adoption of government welfare programs.

One of the earliest of the twentieth century's anti-imperialist revolutions took place in Mexico from 1910 to 1940. This revolution was in part directed against the foreign concessionaires, but in much greater part it was a furious uprising of Indian and *mestizo* peons and laborers against the white-dominated feudal-clerical society inherited from Spanish colonial days. During the course of that revolution, peonage was abolished; the *haciendas* were broken up and land distributed to the *ejido* communities (shared agriculture by cooperatives or Indian villages) and to small farmers; irrigation works and hydroelectric plants were built; the Church was stripped of her landed wealth and even her temples of worship and excluded from taking part in public education; thousands of public schools were erected to educate children and provide recreation, health centers, and vocational guidance for the communities; subsoil mineral wealth was vested in the nation and the oil properties expropriated and nationalized; much social legislation was enacted and labor guaranteed the right to organize, bargain collectively, and strike; and industrialization was encouraged. There had been compromises; some of the promises had not been fulfilled; and because of her poor soil, her still very limited industrialization, and her explosive population growth, Mexico continued to be a land of widespread poverty. But the break with the past had been drastic, the way had been opened for a modern society, and the Mexican Revolution and its Constitution of 1917 were exerting a powerful influence on the mid-century revolutionary movements in Latin America.

That one of the great "capitalist" and "imperialist" powers (with a democratic tradition) could itself work a Latin American revolution was demonstrated in the remarkable changes which began in Puerto Rico in the 1940's. Under the leadership of American Governor Rexford Guy Tugwell, a specialist in government planning, and Muñoz Marín, leader of the dominant Popular Democratic party in Puerto Rico, heroic measures were adopted which greatly changed Puerto Rican life. Puerto Ricans called these exciting years "Operation Bootstrap." Land holdings of corporations were limited to five hundred acres and a Land Authority bought the land in excess of that amount and leased it to small farmers or cooperatives of rural laborers. The Agricultural Development Company was organized to help diversify agriculture, discover the commercial possibility of new kinds of crops, and lend scientific and technical aid. Livestock and dairying, garden truck, different kinds of tobacco, and the production of pineapples, grapefruit, and coconuts were encouraged. The Economic Development Administration was created to give technical advice and tax exemptions to new manufacturing enterprises, and under its stimulation hundreds of new factories producing a great variety of products were established both by the government and private business. Sometimes the government developed a new industry and then sold it to private enterprise. The Puerto Rican

Development Bank was founded to finance new government-owned and private-owned industries. The Water Resources Authority developed irrigation projects on the southern coast, built hydroelectric plants for industrial expansion, and extended electricity to farm communities. The Planning, Urbanization, and Zoning Board built schools, clinics, hospitals, recreation centers, and public housing projects. A momentum of change was thus initiated which continued on, and Puerto Rico became a showcase of how great social adjustments and higher living standards could be achieved in an underdeveloped society, with an explosive population growth, by using democratic methods. The record of Americans in Puerto Rico, where they had political responsibilities, was much better than it was in Cuba, where they enjoyed immense economic advantages but were charged with no political, social, or educational responsibilities.

In 1945, at the close of the war, Latin America was seething with discontent. The high war prices paid for raw materials had given the masses some taste of a better life, but this prosperity was soon virtually canceled out by the inflation which set in, and after the war the fall in world prices for raw materials threatened economic disaster in many countries. Almost everywhere revolutionary forces of one kind or another were on the move, and the elite was fighting back, sometimes ferociously. Communists sought to turn internal strife to their advantage.

In Venezuela, the forces valiantly striving to bring democracy to that country had elected in 1947 a gifted and idealistic president, but the ruling classes, taking alarm, deposed him and established the rule of a military *junta* which was followed by the dictatorship of Pérez Jiménez, who sent his democratic and labor opponents to concentration camps and the torture chambers, while inflation ran riot and the unprecedented flow of oil revenues financed a program of gaudy public works.

In Colombia, the contest between the old and the new assumed a clear-cut form in the political battles between Laureano Gómez, admirer of Hitler, friend of Franco, and defender of the clerical-authoritarian tradition of Spain, and Jorge Eliécer Gaitán, utopian socialist with some Communist support. When Gaitán was assassinated in 1948, the country was plunged into a decade of civil war during which partisan raids, ambushes, pillages, and massacres took at least 200,000 lives. To maintain the old order, the most intransigent of the old ruling class imposed first the brutal dictatorship of Gómez and then the sadistic tyranny of Rojas Pinilla.

Prospects for democracy looked fairly bright in Ecuador for a time, when an enlightened landowner, Galo Plaza Lasso, was elected to the presidency in 1948 to succeed the semi-fascist Velasco Ibarra. Galo Plaza encouraged land reform, improved methods in agriculture, and industrialization, but the ruling hierarchy managed to return Velasco Ibarra to the presidency in 1952, and in 1956 to elect as president Camilo Ponce Enriquez, a clerical rightist.

In Peru, the forces of basic reform found a leader in Haya de la Torre and his *aprista* party, which espoused a program which combined the agrarian reforms of the Mexican revolution and European socialism. *Aprista* support made possible the election of José Luis Bustamante to the presidency in 1945, and *aprista* leaders were active in his administration. The ruling elite took alarm, and in 1948 backed the military *coup d'état* of General Manuel Odría, who ruled as dictator and then as president and suppressed the *apristas*. As one observer put it: "Odría restored the order and balance that the forty most influential families of Lima have been aiming for under the most varied forms of dictatorship."

Many believed that Chile was headed for a national transformation by way of the democratic process. From 1938 to 1952 a coalition of progressive parties and groups known as the Popular Front was in power. Although the parties composing this coalition shifted from time to time, the parties forming the basic support for the Popular Front came from the Radicals, the Socialists, and the Chilean Federation of Labor. The Communists sometimes supported it and sometimes opposed it. During the decades of Popular Front rule social reforms were made and social services widened, but its greatest achievement was the establishment of Fomento, a government development corporation, to provide credit, capital, technicians, and technical know-how to industry, mining, agriculture, and fishing. The aid went mostly to private enterprise, but government capital and initiative built many hydroelectric plants and the Huachipato steel mill. Chile thus embarked on a planned and mixed economy under democratic auspices. How-

ever, even after the long rule of the Popular Front, land concentration remained, the old-fashioned methods of the *fundo*
generally persisted, there were grave tax inequities, and widespread poverty and malnutrition continued. By 1950 it seemed
clear that no real economic breakthrough had been achieved. The
Communist party was growing. There was popular agitation
against the foreign corporations which controlled the copper
and nitrate mines. The old families and vested interests breathed
somewhat easier with the election to the presidency in 1952 of
Carlos Ibáñez del Campo, a former Chilean dictator.

The most sensational attempts at quick industrialization and
advances in living standards were made in Argentina under Juan
Domingo Perón, who from 1943 to 1955 was dictator. Perón
smashed the old conservative oligarchy of big landowners, bankers,
industrialists, high clergy, and army by detaching the Church
and the army, winning them to his side, and combining them
with his basic labor union support. Perón practiced a kind of
national socialism. Freedom of the press and civil liberties were
ruthlessly suppressed. From the profits of a government monoply
on foreign trade he bought the British-owned railroads and took
over the telephone system, some grain elevators, some port installations, and other public utilties. He planned the government
construction of many huge hydroelectric plants. Labor unions
were favored, wages were steadily raised, and social services extended. But the government projects were uneconomically managed, industrial expansion was inadequately financed, the debts
piled high, inflation set in, foreign capital was scared off, and—
most important—grain growers and stockmen, denied fair prices,
curtailed production of Argentina's chief exports. Following the
death of his glamorously popular wife and his break with the
Church, Perón's popularity declined, he was deposed by army
leaders, and the old ruling elements attempted a return to orthodox economic policies. But Peronism continued popular in Argentina, and there were influential Peronists in all Latin American
countries who felt that it afforded an example their own countries
might well follow.

In Brazil, the dictatorship of Getulio Vargas (1930-1945) had
already anticipated some of the Perón policies and techniques.
Vargas used government to hasten industrialization, and he pro-

vided better medical care, more housing, and higher wages. Vargas fell from power in 1945, but his appeal to both Peronists and Communists and to "the shirtless ones" in general restored him to power in 1950. Ambitious plans for industrialization were balked by corruption, overspending, mounting debts, and inflation.

In Bolivia, a combination of organized tin workers, leftists, Peronists, and Communists, under the leadership of Víctor Paz Estenssoro, in 1943 temporarily broke the rule of the old order, but the president they seated was lynched by a manipulated mob, and the conservatives returned to power. However, in 1952 the revolutionary party of Paz and Juan Lechín, the organizer of the tin workers, was strong enough to capture the presidency for Paz. That same year Paz nationalized the properties of the three big "tin monopolies"—the Patiño company, the Hochschild, and the Aramayo—and large amounts of land were taken from the *haciendas* and restored to the Indian villages or distributed to small farmers. It looked as though Bolivia, one of the most backward of Latin American countries, had embarked on a genuine revolution.

Nearer the United States, in the Caribbean and Central American areas, the forces of revolt and reaction, so much in evidence in South America, were likewise in conflict. In the Dominican Republic, Rafael Leonidas Trujillo Molina maintained a savage right-wing dictatorship. In Cuba, Fulgencio Batista returned to power in 1952 and his government became increasingly right-wing, oppressive, and corrupt. In Guatemala, the leftists came to power in 1945, adopted a constitution similar to the revolutionary Mexican constitution of 1917, prepared to expropriate unused land and distribute it to small holders, threatened to curtail the activities of the United Fruit Company, and increasingly showed signs of Communist infiltration. Honduras continued to manifest its usual political instability. In El Salvador the grip of the old ruling families was slipping and the elite was compelled more and more to rely on the military to maintain its power. Nicaragua was ruled by Anastasio Somoza, a strong dictator who maintained the *status quo*. Among Caribbean and Central American countries, only Costa Rica seemed committed to democratic reform.

From a survey of conditions in Latin America in the immediate postwar years, two conclusions clearly emerged. One was that in general the ruling classes were stubbornly setting their faces against the basic reforms increasingly demanded by the people, that few indeed among those accustomed to rule would espouse the cause of democratic gradualism. The other was that among those who wanted to press ahead to rapid industrialization, economic and social reforms, and extensive welfare services there was little realization of the enormous difficulties ahead. The tragedy of both Perón and Vargas was not so much in their dictatorships (bad as these were) as in their leading their peoples to believe they could enjoy high wages, much better living standards, and greatly extended social services without the increase in real wealth which alone would make these things possible. Attempts to enjoy the good things of an advanced economy before actually achieving that economy could lead only to debts, inflation, bankruptcy, and the blighting of popular expectations. The most alarming thing about Latin Americans was their refusal to recognize that planning, work, saving, and great sacrifice would be necessary to achieve the breakthrough to industrialism and economic modernity, no matter the "ideology" or "system" employed.

The Staggering Problems of World Leadership

This, then, was the crisis world which confronted America at the time she came to international leadership: two great powers broken and their societies in confusion; many countries in the world devastated and hungry; traditional international trading patterns shattered; the collapse of what had remained of the old multiple balance of power; the swift rise to colossal influence of the Soviet Union, now become the most important power in both Europe and Asia and riding a world revolutionary movement; revolutions of indigenous peoples in Asia, the Middle East, Africa, and Latin America to oust political and economic imperialism and uproot their old feudal societies; and an explosive population growth in progress everywhere. The problems were staggering, and the great power of the West called on to give world leadership to meet them was without a tradition of international participation, let alone leadership, and in the past had actively resisted assuming that leadership.

[3]

WERE AMERICANS
PREPARED FOR
WORLD LEADERSHIP?

HOW WELL prepared were Americans to meet the problems they confronted in their new world leadership? Americans had both weakness and strength.

A Pessimistic View of American Leadership

Americans had never experienced any sustained exercise of power on a world scale. They had not been in the habit of maintaining great military strength as an instrument of diplomatic and political influence. They had a positive tradition against "entangling alliances" with foreign powers. Many Americans believed that power politics was something peculiar to the blood feuds and perverse selfishness of Europeans. These felt that Americans should either reform international relations or retire from them. Most Americans seldom noticed the redundancy in their term "power politics"; it rarely occurred to them that all politics involved power.

In the world at large many Americans were in the habit of thinking of international relations in terms of law, contract, moral principles, ideal systems, cosmic creeds. Even as late as 1943 the speeches of Secretary of State Cordell Hull were mixtures of legalisms and moral platitudes. Although in dealing with power questions in the Western Hemisphere Americans had been realistic (*that* was another matter, for it was within their experience), their approach to world politics tended to be idealistic.

Americans conceived an international collective-security system in terms of eighteenth-century rationalism and the compact theory of government out of which their own Constitution had come. (Their Constitution had worked in fact largely because functional groups, in response to social and economic conditions, had crossed state and sectional boundaries to make it work.) Americans thought that they could sit down and write a charter literally creating a new international organization which would work exactly as it ought to work. (If it did not, Americans, in self-righteousness, could retire.) It would take the Americans some time to realize that in its transitional stages an international organization would need to be supplemented by balance-of-power alliances and spheres of influence, and that even if and when it reached maturity, it would not eliminate power conflicts between nations, groups, classes, and ideologies but would merely provide legal and political machinery through which these could be resolved peacefully, just as the power conflicts of sections, groups, classes, and ideologies within nations had long been resolved.

That international relations, whether inside or outside an international organization, involved hard bargains in which there had to be both give and take, and in which Americans would have to give as well as receive, was something the Americans would need to learn through prolonged experience in dealing with power combinations with as much strength as themselves. (In the Western Hemisphere, Americans had dealt only with lesser American powers or faraway European powers which had regarded questions in the Western Hemisphere as secondary.) The British knew that international relations required give and take, and even the Canadians seemed to realize this through their long association with Britain in world politics. That a nation might wage a war in which the total power situation in the world made it the part of wisdom not to win was to many Americans fantastic. (During the Korean War, Britons often said: "We British have been defeated by Afghans, Baluchi, Boers, Zulus, and Kaffirs, but this Korean experience is something new to you Americans. You are finding that there are wars which larger power considerations forbid you to win.")

Again, Americans would experience difficulty in understanding twentieth-century social politics and the need to supplement power politics with wise social politics. Twentieth-century revolutions, unlike nineteenth-century revolutions, tended to collectivism, to vastly widened economic and social activities by government. Americans understood the nineteenth-century revolutions because these confirmed their own liberal experience and tradition, but little in the American experience shed light on the contemporary collectivist revolutions. Americans had made a phenomenal success of their own economic system, and it was hard for them to understand that the North American conditions which had made this possible for them could not be duplicated in other continents. The Americans were the least communal of peoples. Their historical experience lacked the guilds, the communal agricultural villages, and the cognate families of foreign peoples. Americans were the product of frontier conditions. Throughout much of American history most Americans had lived scattered over great distances, their farmsteads widely separated. Even in the twentieth century their population was relatively small, their man-land ratio low. Americans were not only the least communal of peoples, they were also the least gregarious. They did not mingle in the streets and cafés like foreign peoples, and in the twentieth century the automobile, the drive-in, and television made them even less gregarious than they had been.

Americans had carried laissez-faire capitalism to an extreme—and a success—unknown elsewhere; their moral ethic was particularistic Protestantism; their political philosophy was the individualism of John Locke. Even America's "underprivileged," the wage-workers and the Negroes, for the most part shared enough in the national prosperity and had sufficient middle-class attitudes to make their understanding of Socialist, still more of Communist, revolutions difficult. It had not taken the Americans long to assimilate the New Deal into their Lockean tradition, and relatively few Americans consciously acknowledged the collectivism which had crept into their own system. The New Deal was thought of not in terms of the "isms," but in terms of specific, pragmatic problem solving.

Americans had had little experience in ideological class politics either at home or abroad. They enjoyed a remarkable consensus on social and political values—on the essential goodness of a liberal capitalist, democratic, middle-class society. Almost all Americans thought of themselves as middle class. Americans were the nation of "monolithic liberalism." They had no feudal or aristocratic right, no Marxist left. Politically they had only a center, but within the framework of that liberal center their geographical sections, functional groups, and political parties vigorously contested over the distribution of the national income. Americans had little patience with the political extremism of right and left abroad because they had little understanding of the historical and contemporary conditions out of which such extremism emerged.

Since their own experience threw so little light on the "isms," on ideological conflict, on the various kinds of collectivist revolutions abroad, Americans would have to learn of these through vicarious thinking and social imagination, rare in any people and especially difficult for Americans because of their lack of knowledge of European and world history, their limited international experience, and the stupendous success they had made of their own system.

American understanding of the problems of foreign peoples would not be made any easier by the proliferation of articles and books by American intellectuals during the late 1940's and the 1950's which emphasized the differences between the American and foreign societies, the uniqueness of the American experience. What these writers kept saying was that the gap between the American and foreign societies was unbridgeable, that the American system was unexportable (by 1960 this would have become a cliché), and that there was something gratuitous and patronizing, if not insulting, in rich America presuming to lecture impoverished societies, let alone to reform them. Most of this was the usual national ethnocentrism dressed up in sophisticated garb, much of it merely a refurbishing of Charles A. Beard's latter-day doctrine of "the uniqueness of the American Republic," which Beard made the basis of his isolationism. (Most of these "New Conservatives" professed to be opposed to the Beard school of American history and they seemed not to realize how much of Beard's doctrine they had absorbed.)

As we have noted, in many ways the American experience *was* unique, but this harping on those aspects of our society which differentiated it from other societies, to the exclusion of those aspects it shared with other societies, was defeatist; it gave Americans the feeling that no amount of understanding could surmount the divergencies and make possible cooperation with other societies to realistic ends.

Again, Americans were among the most race-conscious people in the world. Even when they tried to hide this, their effusiveness in the presence of non-whites was telltale. At home, white Americans had dominated their non-white minorities, not adjusted to them; white Americans had dealt with Negro and Indian minorities in the dominantly white American environment, and these minorities had had to adjust to white standards or die. Yet Americans were now called to the world leadership at a time the colonial peoples of the world, most of them non-white, were everywhere in revolution, and racism or the lack of it would be an important factor in the contest of the Communist and the non-Communist worlds for the support of the non-white peoples.

Strange as it may seem, the British, who had been the world's leading colonial power, in many ways understood the economic and social aspects of the twentieth-century revolutions better than the Americans. The British had behind them the tradition of the medieval corporative community, the ideals of the closely integrated society typified by Richard Hooker's philosophy and strong in the Conservative party, the socialism of the British Labour party, their own movement toward moderate socialism, their long experience in colonial countries which extended in a personal way into almost every British family, and a cultural relativism, even agnosticism, born of centuries of dealing with Asians and Africans in their indigenous cultural environments. Although there was racial snobbery in the British, they had had to come to terms with innumerable non-white peoples in these peoples' own bailiwicks, where British compromise and adjustment were the price of survival. The racial experience of white Americans had been largely confined to the United States, which the whites considered *their* land and where they had clearly dominated.

The lack of understanding of basic economic, social, and political currents abroad might affect American foreign policies in several crucial ways. It might cause Americans to fail to distinguish between the totalitarianism of Fascism and the totalitarianism of Communism, which were superficially alike but fundamentally different in philosophy and aims; between the various kinds of rightism and the various kinds of leftism; between Communism, socialism, and social democracy. It might lead them seriously to underestimate the indigenous collectivism in the anti-imperialist revolutions, the pragmatic necessity for governments in underdeveloped societies to initiate industrial revolutions; to minimize the strength of the non-Communist left abroad and to miss the opportunity of using social democracy and socialism to check Communism. Even if Americans should see the importance of encouraging social democracy abroad, they might reject such a course as a "betrayal" of free enterprise. (Actually, in backing the non-Communist left in certain situations abroad Americans would merely be recognizing in a realistic way that they could not duplicate elsewhere the historical conditions which had made free enterprise so successful in America.) Again, a lack of understanding of the social realities in the outside world might lead Americans to back feudal elements, rightist dictatorships, and neo-Fascist movements abroad (because these were most vociferous in their anti-Communist professions), to seek to erect a kind of twentieth-century neo-Metternich system, which would alienate the much more powerful democratic and social-democratic forces in the world. Finally, the failure of Americans to realize the large ingredient of nationalism in Communist revolutions and movements abroad (as these had actually developed, distinguished from the way earlier Communist prophets had predicted and hoped they would develop) might result in persuading Americans that every Communist advance was necessarily an advance of Soviet power and in America's underrating the possibility of exploiting Communist nationalism to split the international Communist front and to restore, if not a multiple balance of power, at least a less dangerous and more flexible power situation in the world.

Because Americans thought of democracy almost exclusively in terms of popular elections, universal suffrage, political parties, and representative assemblies, they might be misled into thinking that some political systems abroad which were in fact democratic or leading to democracy were undemocratic, that some abroad which were in fact undemocratic were democratic. It would be necessary to see through the forms to the realities. In many under-developed countries two-party or multiple-party systems which appeared to be democratic were frequently merely the instru-ments of a few politicians and local notables; the issues of vital interest to the people were not raised; politics was merely a game of the elite for personal power and prestige; the voters were controlled, manipulated, and bribed by the local magnates. On the other hand, there were some countries in which only one party had any effective power but that party expressed mass aspirations and was being used by the leaders to train the people in the practices of democracy. (The Congress party in India was such a party.) Among peoples without democratic experi-ence a degree of enlightened paternalism was often required. It would be easy to make the mistaken judgment that Nasser's "Presidential democracy," Ayoub's "basic democracy," and Sukarno's "guided democracy" were mere window-dressing for dictatorship. Even army coups in backward countries might be rightist or leftist or social-democratic depending on the particu-lar factions and leaders in the army which engineered them. In a country still without working democratic machinery and mores, the army, drawn from all parts and classes of the country, might reflect the various elements and points of view of the popula-tion, and seizure of power by an army faction bent on popular and social reform might be the only way at the time for demo-cratic mass aspirations to express themselves effectively. In the absence of democratic machinery and opposing mass parties, popular opinion was often expressed by methods unfamiliar to Americans. Americans would have to take care lest they mistake rightist governments for popular ones, popular governments for rightist or dictatorial ones.

In the field of international trade, if the Americans insisted on a too literal return to the free and multilateral trading practices which prevailed before World War I they would alienate both the old economic nationalists (mercantilists) and the new social planners committed to controlled economies. If they pressed too strongly for a "favorable investment climate" for private capital abroad and opposed international agreements to stabilize the world prices of raw materials, they would earn the resentment of the underdeveloped countries. If at the same time they reserved high tariffs for themselves (in response to their own mercantilists) and dumped abroad their agricultural surpluses (the incidental result of their own national economic planning about which they said little), they might work economic injury abroad, create confusion, and leave themselves open to charges of inconsistency and even hypocrisy.

The United States was the nation par excellence of functional pressure groups—religious, ethnic, national-origin, social, economic, business, occupational. These operated on the most sensitive spots in government, political parties, and opinion making. It was certain that the German-Americans and Irish-Americans would continue to pressure against anything "pro-British"; the Zionists to lobby for Israel; the Polish-Americans, Czech-Americans, and Hungarian-Americans to agitate for the liberation of the Soviet satellites in Eastern Europe; and all manner of businesses to maneuver for trading and foreign policies favorable to themselves. In this cacophony of clashing groups, would it be possible to hammer out a rational foreign policy that took into account the broad and long-time interest of the entire nation? During the debate over the League of Nations, opponents of the League often made the point that America, because of its heterogeneous ethnic and national-origin groups, could not play an active part in "foreign politics" without impairing its harmony at home.

America's rise marked an epoch in world politics; for the first time a nation committed to democracy in the conduct of foreign policy took over the leadership. Hitherto, foreign policy had always been the province of a small elite. Despite its parliamentary system, British foreign policy had been in the hands of a tight little in-group with common education, training, and values. Soviet foreign policy was monopolized by those at the top of the Communist party hierarchy. Even among many Americans it was admitted that democracy might not work as well in foreign affairs as it did in domestic affairs, for in domestic affairs people depended on their personal experience but in foreign affairs they had to depend on hearsay and secondhand information. Now, America was not only a democracy but a free-wheeling, boisterous, egalitarian one in which all kinds of opinion, uninformed and informed, made their weight felt and in which there was little tradition of a professional foreign service and even less respect for it. Moreover, America's government of separation of powers and its blurred, heterogeneous, and decentralized political parties might make the formulation of foreign policy, especially where decisiveness and dispatch were required, extremely difficult.

However, most Americans did not expect that "the people" or the Gallup poll would actually create foreign policy—that would be for the leaders—but they took for granted that without popular understanding and consent no foreign policy could long be sustained. Would American leaders really take the complicated issues of world politics and foreign policy to the people, would they raise and explain the real issues; or would they follow the apparently easier path of over-simplifying, disseminating half-truths and myths, reducing foreign policy to a few popular stereotypes? If they pursued this seemingly easier path, would they thus circumscribe their own flexibility and future freedom of action by becoming the captives of the popular stereotypes they themselves had fostered?

Would Americans find effective leadership in their presidents? Great leadership was rare in any country at any time, and the methods of nominating and electing American presidents certainly were not conducive to producing consistently able or even competent leadership. Most American presidents had been ordinary and a few had been abject failures. But Americans had a folk myth which held that great crisis always produced the leader to measure up to it—as evidenced by Washington, Lincoln, Wilson, and Franklin D. Roosevelt. The strong probability was that this reassuring expectancy would be sorely strained if crisis followed crisis decade after decade. Some discerning Americans were haunted by Walter Bagehot's irreverent remark, apropos of the way Americans elected their presidents, that success in a lottery was no argument for lotteries.

The importance of propaganda and psychological warfare in international relations was something Americans might have difficulty learning, but on the other hand if their foreign policies hit snags, they might tend to put too much store by it. Political propaganda, of course, became a high art only in the hands of the creative politician with insights into social forces and historical trends. Wilson, Lenin, Hitler, F.D.R., and Churchill were conspicuous examples of effective practitioners of this art. But the Americans were likely to think of propaganda on the one hand in terms of mere skills, techniques, devices, gimmicks, and tricks or on the other in terms of moral absolutes. To be effective, it was necessary that propaganda take a relativistic approach in harmony with social and historical realities of time and place. It was precisely in this area—in understanding the deeper social and historical forces at work in Europe, Asia, the Middle East, Africa, and Latin America—that the Americans were likely to experience their most baffling difficulties.

An Optimistic View of American Leadership

However, we must beware of distortion, of falling into the caricature attributed to Bismarck that "God takes care of drunks, little children, and the United States of America." The young republic had survived in a world of monarchical enemies, it had lived to become the world leader. If the Americans had weaknesses, they also had great sources of strength.

It was an exaggeration to say that the Americans were devoid of international experience. The early leaders of the nation had lived for years as subjects of the British empire and they were familiar with the intricacies of British balance-of-power politics on the European continent and of Britain's world imperialism. As responsible statesmen in the first years of the republic, American leaders had been forced to grapple with the tough ideological and power problems of the French Revolutionary and Napoleonic wars. After 1898 the nation had again played some considerable part on the world stage, and for a few years under Wilson it had stood at the very vortex of world affairs. In 1945 Americans were seriously taking to heart their mistakes following World

War I, and they were attempting to avoid them. After all, America was an offspring of Europe and of Western civilization and Americans knew something of European and world history, though of course not as much as those peoples who had been at the center of international politics for centuries.

Americans had wealth, technological power, unrivaled productive capacity, administrative and technical efficiency, individual inventiveness, and practical sense. In these respects they resembled the ancient Romans. Moreover, the attributes of practical efficiency and inventiveness were no monopoly of an elite; they were truly national characteristics diffused throughout the American population.

Again, the United States was a satisfied power; it had no territorial ambitions. Americans had long enjoyed a territorial and economic amplitude which made them generous in a large-handed way and contemptuous of petty territorial grasping and economic penny-pinching. American prosperity had been built on exploiting a rich internal market and while a capitalist system in much of the rest of the world would undoubtedly benefit the American economy and fit in with American habits of doing business, it would be difficult to convince Americans that their essential prosperity depended on advantages, markets, and investments abroad. Americans would not likely make their foreign policy pivot on political or even economic imperialism abroad, at least in the historic sense, although they might possibly pursue policies of economic nationalism, strong in the American tradition, and other policies ill adapted to a creditor nation in a way that would hurt their friends abroad and slow the development of an international world.

It was not likely that American foreign policy would be dominated by pressure groups, important as these were in America's domestic politics. In the past some specific measures in foreign policy had plainly been the result of group pressures, but none of America's major foreign policies had been adopted primarily in this fashion. All of the great foreign policy decisions of the past—Washington's Proclamation of Neutrality, the Louisiana Purchase, the War of 1812, the Florida Purchase, the Monroe Doctrine, the annexation of Texas, the Mexican War, the Mexican Cession, the Spanish-American War, the acquisition of the Philippines, the building of the Panama Canal, penetration into the Caribbean, participation in World War I, the rejection of the League of Nations, the Good Neighbor Policy, Lend-Lease, participation in World War II—had represented something vastly more than the sum total of group pressures. Adoption of the Marshall Plan in the early postwar years would indicate that larger considerations of the national interest were in the main still determining America's leading foreign policies.

Americans possessed an ideology which still had a magic attraction for peoples in a revolutionary age—the Declaration of Independence and the dictum that all men are created equal. This was revolutionary doctrine in 1776 and it was revolutionary doctrine in the mid-twentieth century. Of course there was discrepancy between ideal and fact, between mystique and reality (as there was also in Communist doctrine, as there has been in all ideologies), but the American creed had played a large part in American history (the anti-slavery crusade was only one of its many manifestations) and it was still playing its part as evidenced by the contemporary national urge to eliminate racism. Despite the New Conservative intellectuals who labored to prove that the American Revolution was not much of a revolution or no revolution at all ("a conservative restoration" was what some called it) and that in America "equality" at best had meant only an approximate equality of opportunity to amass property and beget status, the Declaration was still a powerful motive force in American life, and twentieth-century revolutionary leaders in Asia and Africa were quoting Thomas Jefferson, Tom Paine, Abraham Lincoln, and Walt Whitman.

Another important element in the American creed was the self-determination of nations. This would put salutary restraints on the use of America's enormous power. It would also appeal to the anti-imperialist revolutions, the most important political movement at mid-century. National self-determination seemed much more in harmony with the actual historical trend of the twentieth century than the Communist ideal of an international proletarian society, for as the century progressed it appeared increasingly clear that the world was moving not to monolithism but to a new pluralism of many emerging national societies with mixed economies. By identifying itself with this new pluralism the United States would be putting itself on the side of what was apparently the dominant historical trend. Those who were urging the United States "to grow up," and "to learn the uses of power" (that is power in its most literal and naked sense, military power and military alliances), while correct in their belief that many Americans needed to shed some of their earlier innocence, were themselves unrealistic when they advocated a monistic "power" approach, conceived ideology to be incompatible with "power," overlooked the tremendous force of crusading ideas in history ("crusade" was a dirty word with these "realists"), and ignored the fact that ideas and ideals had always been among the most telling elements of power. The United States had never been so appealing—and powerful—as when Woodrow Wilson and F.D.R. stood before the world as crusaders for liberty, democracy, and national self-determination.

Perhaps the most common characteristic of Americans was their practicality and pragmatism, their problem-solving rather than theoretical approach to situations. They would tend strongly to see problems in the underdeveloped societies not in terms of the "isms" but in terms of public schools, public health, roads, soil erosion, experimenting with new crops and industries, training technicians for particular jobs, and so forth. They would need no particular doctrine to motivate them or determine the answers; rather the answers would be derived from the concrete situations. But before putting forth great exertions the Americans would have to be convinced that their own welfare and interests were involved. Once convinced on this score, the Americans would likely tackle the practicalities and not be over-concerned whether the end result in a given country was "modified free enterprise," "social democracy," or even "socialism."

In one sense all the revolutions among the underdeveloped peoples, even the Communist ones, were American revolutions. The great urge in all of them was to achieve advanced machine technology and the mass production, distribution, and consumption of goods and services; and in these industrial techniques the Americans were the models. Even in Russia, in the late 1920's and early 1930's, when the Soviet Union was feverishly industrializing, American technicians were avidly sought and American methods were eagerly imitated, and in actual practice Henry

Ford was more of a hero than Marx. Americans were fortunate in that the revolutions of the twentieth century pivoted around the very technological, managerial, and organizational skills at which they were past masters. But again, whether the Americans would be aroused to put their skills and experience to the service of foreign peoples would depend upon whether they saw the relevance to American interests. Perhaps they would not be fully aroused until the Russians, who at mid-century were fast developing a pool of skills and experience of their own, sparked a Soviet-American competition in the sharing of industrial know-how with the underdeveloped peoples.

To proponents of *Realpolitik* the legal and moral approach to world politics was an American weakness, but this was a weakness only if the legalists and moralists made their approach a single-track one and became as monistic as the advocates of the military and power-alliance approach. True, the American emphasis in the 1920's and 1930's on such merely verbal formulas as "the outlawry of war" and the Stimson doctrine of "non-recognition" had something of the pathological in it, was a rationalization of a bad conscience for running away from concrete international responsibilities. But over-all, the interest of twentieth-century American statesmen in the Hague Court, arbitration treaties, the League of Nations, and the United Nations were manifestations of both a good heart and a good head, for by 1945 the revolution in the technology of war had proceeded in such a way as to make war not only "total" but "totally total" and threatened to render it obsolete as a method of settling international difficulties. At mid-century a foreign policy which did not take into account both traditional *Realpolitik* and the new attempts to institutionalize international relations through world-wide legal and political organizations would be unrealistic.

The charge that the Americans had no sense of the shrewd uses of diplomacy and military power was highly exaggerated. Where they were convinced of the relevance of power to their own interests, Americans had made adroit use of both diplomacy and arms. In the Western Hemisphere, particularly in North America, the Americans had early developed a remarkably keen "power sense." The astute (and sometimes ruthless) achievements of Benjamin Franklin, Thomas Jefferson, John Quincy

Adams, James K. Polk, William H. Seward, James G. Blaine, William McKinley, and Theodore Roosevelt in carving out American power and influence in the Western Hemisphere would match the most successful maneuvers and manipulations of a Talleyrand or a Bismarck. The roster of distinguished military practitioners graduated from West Point in the nineteenth and twentieth centuries would compare not unfavorably with the rosters of the leading British, French, and German war colleges. True, the Americans had fumbled in Asia, particularly in China, since their entry into world politics following the Spanish-American War, and their flight from power responsibilities following World War I was notorious. But this had not meant that they did not understand how to use power; rather it had meant that they had not yet been persuaded that the uses and exertions of power on a world stage were vital to their interests. When once convinced that they had a permanent stake in the world at large as great as their stake in the Americas, there was little in the record to indicate that Americans would not operate on the world stage with as much sense for power realities as they had always operated in the Western Hemisphere and as they had operated during the war years of 1917-1918 and 1941-1945.

However, because Americans were told so frequently by foreigners and fellow Americans that they had no "power sense" they might in compensation emphasize sheer power too much, power in its most literal and naked sense, military force and military alliances, and pay too little attention to the other factors in international relations. And thus through distortion Americans might in fact become unrealistic, as unrealistic as the "realistic" Germans had been.

Americans, too, in the first decades of their leadership, in the first flush of their realization that they had a permanent stake in world affairs, might compensate for their past lack of sustained international participation by over-doing, by attempting too much in too many areas of the world, by failing to fashion the priorities cogently and to relate them in a discriminating way to their interests and capabilities. Sometimes it took decades (in the case of Rome much longer) for the most influential powers of the past to discover the workable limits of world leadership. Some never discovered them.

No doubt Americans would have a difficult time learning the basic nature of international relations: that they are everlasting and that they are pluralistic, that they involve the use of many approaches and factors all operating at the same time, and that the *emphasis* must shift from approach to approach and from factor to factor depending upon the circumstances. But this is something all peoples have had difficulty understanding, and few indeed of the practitioners of world politics have had the resiliency to grasp it fully and operate with top effectiveness. But there is a comforting aspect to international relations: if one side makes its blunders and fails to exploit its opportunities, so also does the other side, and not infrequently the success of a foreign policy depends less on its positive qualities than on the errors of the opposition.

American Opinion and American Foreign Policy

In the postwar years, American opinion with respect to foreign policy tended to break down into several roughly differentiated groupings. What were these?

First there were the idealistic or doctrinaire internationalists who still conceived of international organization in terms of completed or near-perfect systems. The World Federalists represented this view, and so also did those who would abolish the big-five veto in the United Nations and in other drastic ways so revolutionize the organization as to imperil its very existence. This group was a declining one.

Second, there were the Wallaceites, the followers of former Vice-President Henry A. Wallace, who strongly favored the United Nations as chartered at San Francisco and were reluctant to believe that the wartime American-Soviet collaboration could not continue into the postwar world and form the basis for the realization of the Allied war aims. They felt that the Soviet Union was not as aggressive as it was made out to be, that it would continue to cooperate with the Western Allies if the West recognized the Soviet sphere in Eastern Europe and otherwise showed that it had no intention of "encircling" the Soviet Union. Some Wallaceites favored turning the "know-how" of the atomic bomb over to the United Nations in the hopes that this would prevent a nuclear arms race between the United States and the Soviet Union. The Wallaceites were suspicious of Churchill's policies in

Greece and Eastern Europe and critical of his "Iron Curtain" speech at Fulton, Missouri. They maintained that the only alternative to cooperation with the Soviet Union was a global contest with the Communists and the restoration of the power of America's late enemies, Germany and Japan. They claimed this would be a reversal of Roosevelt policies, a miscarriage of Allied victory, and a temptation to America to back the imperialist and neo-Fascist elements in the world. The Wallaceites made a valiant attempt to maintain an American-Russian partnership, but the attempted cooperation (1945-1947) proved increasingly difficult because of Communist suspicions and intransigence, and when in 1947 America decisively shifted its foreign policy to containment of Communism and acceptance of Cold War, the Wallaceites rapidly dwindled in numbers and influence. Most of them joined the large fourth group described below as the cooperationists, and they constituted a wing in that group which welcomed any thaw in the Cold War and stood ready, should the international opportunities offer, to take a lead toward American-Soviet peaceful but competitive coexistence.

Third, there were the unilateralists, who inclined to think that America could still go it alone, could follow the policy Senator Robert A. Taft described as that of "the free hand." The unilateralists fell roughly into two groups: the isolationists and the crypto-imperialists.

The isolationists in turn were composed of two wings: the pacifists and the nationalists. The pacifists came largely from the evangelical and pietistic Protestant sects, and many of them hovered between isolationism and doctinaire internationalism. The career of William Jennings Bryan had reflected this hesitation between isolationist pacifism and platonic internationalism.

The isolationist nationalists believed that America's peculiar geographical position still gave it relative immunity from the world's troubles and that the power and ideological conflicts among the European and Asian countries would so embroil them as to lead to Eurasian balances and counterbalances, leaving the United States in a relatively safe position. These views were exemplified in the writings of Charles A. Beard, which still carried weight with a diminishing number of Americans. Sometimes the nationalist and the pacifist seemed to merge, as in Herbert Hoover.

Hoover's concept of a "defense perimeter" and a "Western Hemisphere bastion" may have had in it a measure of lingering Quakerism. Senator William E. Borah, a powerful isolationist in the authentic tradition, died during the war, but Senator William Langer of North Dakota and Senator Henrik Shipstead of Minnesota, both redolent of the Populist, anti-imperialist isolationism of 1900, lived on to cast the two votes in the United States Senate against American entry into the United Nations.

The other branch of the unilateralists, the crypto-imperialists, were the spiritual heirs of Albert J. Beveridge and William Randolph Hearst. The crypto-imperialists were represented by General Douglas MacArthur and Senators Joseph McCarthy and William Knowland and later by Senator Barry Goldwater. They were "Asia Firsters" and gave priority to Asia over Europe. They believed that America's allies did not give sufficient support to American ideas and American foreign policy and that the United States, because of its wealth, power, and responsibility, ought to go ahead with bold pro–Chiang Kai-shek policies of its own in Asia, even at the cost of separation from its allies and alienation of neutralist opinion. They were not reconciled to the permanency of the Red revolution in China, and they believed that China could still be redeemed from the Communists. Many of them chafed under the policy of merely containing Communism, and these tended to favor some sort of Communist "rollback." This wing was inclined to take a doctrinaire view of free enterprise and yet clung to mercantilist trade policies.

The isolationist-nationalists and the crypto-imperialists, both unilateralists, were suspicious of Britain; both found much support from the Americans of German and Irish descent; and both looked upon American economic aid abroad as "globaloney" and "Afghanistanism." Isolationist-nationalists were a declining group, but the crypto-imperialists were strong in the country and might gain greater strength in the future, particularly if the Cold War dragged on for years and American opinion, in a mood of frustration, veered toward "decisive action."

Fourth, there were the cooperationists, the numerically strongest of the groups and the one which initiated most of American foreign policy after 1945. The cooperationists believed in developing American foreign policy in close consultation and concert with other governments. After 1947 most of them believed in the policy of containment of Communism. Their approach was pragmatic: they would cooperate with friendly countries both inside the United Nations and through a series of power-politics alliances. The cooperationists refused to compartmentalize the world; they tended to view all aspects of foreign policy as an integrated whole. If they gave priority to Western Europe it was because they felt that this area, next to the United States itself, contributed most to the power of the West and that its loss would be an irretrievable disaster to the non-Communist cause everywhere in the world. But they also saw that if southeast Asia fell to the Communists, Japan, a deficit area needing Asian trade, would be cut off from the continent and face permanent economic dislocation. What would happen then to the defense-perimeter strategy based on Japan and the other Pacific islands?

The cooperationists clearly predominated in the Democratic party, and they were represented in the Republican party by the majority Vandenberg-Willkie-Dewey-Eisenhower wing. Although the cooperationists largely formulated postwar American foreign policy, there were times when they had to yield to other views. There was some yielding to nationalist views in trade policies, and much yielding in China policy to the crypto-imperialists.

By about 1950 the cooperationists tended to divide into two groups, representing a somewhat different emphasis in policy. One group stressed the sheer power phase of the world situation. Members of this group insisted that America should make use of allies, whatever their ideology, who had effective power and were willing to use it. In this view, an alliance with Chiang, President Rhee of South Korea, and Franco Spain should take precedence over winning the friendship of power-weak countries like India, Burma, and Indonesia; the alliance with Britain and France should take precedence over winning the friendship of the weak and "erratic" Arab states. The other wing insisted that while military alliances were important, particularly with the Western European powers, so also were ideology, the good will of the mass populations of the rising new nations, and the integrity of collective security in the United Nations. This wing tended to move more in its thinking to the Asian-African bloc and to resist even Britain and France when these powers clung to their vestiges of imperialism or violated collective-security principles. Moreover, this wing, which included many of the old Wallaceites but also more numerous liberal and social-democratic elements which had never been Wallaceites, welcomed international opportunities which might allow a thaw in the Cold War and the emergence of a peaceful but competitive coexistence of the Communist and non-Communist worlds. This wing also emphasized playing social politics abroad, using the democratic left to defeat the Communists, and giving economic aid to the underdeveloped countries.

What was the attitude of America's powerful business community toward international affairs? The cooperationists were strong among those businessmen who represented international banking and gigantic industries like steel, automobiles, electrical equipment, those more and more interested in foreign markets, who looked with increasing favor on a real revolution in America's tariff policies. The center of this group was New York. The nationalists were strong among those whose markets were almost exclusively in the United States. Their center was Chicago. If events should push the nationalists toward imperialism, that imperialism likely would be neo-mercantilistic.

In the critical years when America was assuming the international leadership, cooperationists within the Democratic and Republican parties developed a bipartisan support for American foreign policy. Senator Arthur H. Vandenberg took the lead among the Republicans in establishing a bridge between Republican and Democratic cooperationists. Bipartisan support of foreign policy did not extend to China, but it was most effective with respect to the United Nations and Europe. Some internationally-minded Americans were suspicious of this bipartisan alliance. They feared it would result in a lack of vigorous debate about foreign policy and would require the Democrats to yield too often to the Republicans, who in turn would find it expedient for party purposes to coddle the right-wing, unilateralist elements of their party. (The Democrats also had an unilateralist wing in their party, but it was not as strong as the unilateralist wing of the Republican party.) Defenders, pointing to Wilson's experience, argued that some compromise was the price the cooperationists would have to pay for an internationalist foreign policy.

That some nationalistic attitudes persisted in American opinion and American policy should not be surprising, because national interest was still the pivot of a nation's foreign policy. It would be a long time before Americans or any other nationals agreed that what was good for the world was also always and necessarily good for their particular country. Nor was it unusual for a country taking the lead in international politics to intersperse parochial and seemingly archaic and inconsistent measures among its international policies. Many a Roman of Augustan times carried into his world imperialism Catoesque misgivings and throwbacks, and in many ways the British carried their "insularity" and their "little England" attitudes into their nineteenth-century world policies. It was naive to think that American isolationist and unilateralist attitudes would disappear. They would, of course, continue to affect Americans and American policies for a long time to come. Even some cooperationists were nationalists in trade policies, and many cooperationists would have misgivings about this or that of the policies they supported.

Would the Americans, new to the leadership, quail before the difficulties? Americans had envisaged a democratic, disarmed, and peaceful postwar world. Instead, that world was a crisis world of extraordinary perplexity. Moreover, the crisis was likely to continue for years. Would the Americans, unaccustomed to indefinite crisis and frustration, seek short cuts like a preventive war, the dropping of their atomic bomb, or improvised anti-Soviet revolts among the satellite peoples? (The last-named would be popular with certain American minorities.) Or would Americans scuttle and run? Would they return to their own Western Hemisphere bastion? After all, they had no tradition of world leadership and they had done just that in 1919, when the world situation was less trying.

De Tocqueville had observed more than a century earlier that America once it had made up its mind brooked no nonconformity and no further discussion; but, De Tocqueville also observed, America sometimes changed its mind with equal decisiveness.

Would the Americans see the world crisis through? Would they dare do otherwise? How successful would their leadership be?

[4]

THE PERIOD OF
ATTEMPTED
COOPERATION
(1945-1947)

FOR NEARLY two years after V-J Day most Americans clung to the concept of world peace and security through international cooperation. Although they were learning to play world power politics and relied on exclusive possession of the atomic bomb for temporary protection, Americans continued to think of the United Nations as the beginning of an effective collective-security system. The actual record of the first two years was both encouraging and chilling.

The United Nations: Progress and Disillusionment

The various branches of the United Nations and its specialized agencies were organized, and in the light of the later bitter conflicts in the United Nations this was no small accomplishment. There was even agreement in some areas where disagreement might have been expected. The Soviet Union joined the United

States in favoring American soil as the site for the permanent home of the United Nations. Also, the Soviet Union was in substantial agreement with the United States' taking over the Marshalls, the Carolines, and the Marianas as strategic-area trusteeships to be governed as an integral part of the United States.

But from the first there were serious disagreements. The Soviet Union failed to join UNESCO and some other United Nations agencies. Russia and India objected to the trusteeship system, which looked to them like the old imperialism dressed in a new terminology. India proposed that trusteeships be administered not by separate powers but jointly by the whole United Nations organization itself. The United States, over Russian objections, favored widening the Assembly's powers of participation and led the fight to create the Little Assembly, which was designed to continue the influence of the Assembly (and of the smaller powers) the year round. Russia early began using her big-power veto repeatedly and in a frivolous way, and in the controversy over the Soviet-sponsored regime in Iranian Azerbaijan in 1946 sought to exercise the veto in even a procedural dispute by walking out. However, through practice it became established that abstention by a permanent member did not constitute a veto, that even in the area where vetoing might legally be done (in substantive matters) it had to be done expressly.

Disagreements early developed over admitting new members, and the universality of the United Nations was impaired, for the United States and the Soviet Union each disliked admitting states they regarded as satellites of the other. Even as late as 1954 such states as Finland, Rumania, Bulgaria, Hungary, Italy, Portugal, Ireland, and Japan were not members of the United Nations because of the big-power conflict.

What brought keen disappointment to believers in collective security was the failure to implement Articles 43 and 45 of the Charter, which provided that member states set aside armed forces for the use of the Security Council. The Charter contemplated that the major portion of United Nations forces would be made available by the five permanent members. The United States, backed by Britain, France, and Nationalist China, recommended "comparable" contributions from the big five, in view of the differences in size of the armed forces of the permanent members.

But Russia insisted that the military contributions be equal. Within the first year of the United Nations' existence it became plain that United Nations security forces had little chance of ever being created, and that if they were, they would be largely token forces. Clearly the Russians feared an international police force acting as an agency of an organization in which they were in the minority.

The most important disagreement was over the control of atomic weapons. In 1946 the General Assembly set up the International Atomic Energy Commission. Bernard Baruch was the American representative on the Commission, Gromyko the Russian. The Commission endorsed the Baruch Plan, drawn largely from the Acheson-Lilienthal report. The Baruch Plan would establish an International Atomic Development Authority which would have an absolute monopoly on world supplies and mining of uranium and thorium. It would have its own stockpile of fissionable materials and it would sell these in denatured form for commercial use. National governments and individuals would be licensed to carry on safe activities, and these would be subject to the Authority's rigid inspection system. Individuals as well as governments would be punished as criminals if they carried on prohibited activities. But how would the nations protect themselves from a nation which took over the Authority's plants within its borders? Safety would lie in the widespread geographical distribution of the plants, and the Authority would use the plants in the other countries to manufacture such a preponderance of atomic weapons as to bring the offending nation to book. Violators could not escape punishment by using the veto, for in atomic matters the veto was to be abolished. The United States was to disclose its information and its atomic facilities were to be transferred to the Authority only by gradual stages. After the Authority was well established and the system of international control effective, the manufacture of atomic bombs would be forbidden and all existing stocks destroyed.

The Soviet Union rejected the Baruch Plan and instead proposed destroying all stockpiles of atomic bombs immediately, outlawing all atomic weapons by international convention prior to the setting up of a system of control, putting enforcement in the hands of the Security Council, and retaining the veto on punishment of violators. Thus the Soviet Union, which at the time did not have the bomb, sought at one blow to destroy the American superiority, and the United States was asked to throw away its advantage before a system of inspection and sure punishment of violators could be worked out—indeed, without any assurance that it ever would be worked out.

However, it is easy to see the reasons for the Soviet position. Under the Baruch Plan, the United States would retain its stockpiles during the whole period of transition while other countries would be bound by international agreement to do nothing to secure atomic secrets for themselves. Agents of the Atomic Authority would inspect Soviet territory, and the Soviet Union was extremely skittish about international inspection on its territory. If accused of violations, the Soviet Union, shorn of the veto, would be tried before an international body in which it would be in a distinct minority. Because of its minority position and its Communist system, the Soviet Union feared it might not be awarded its share of atomic plants, or might not be able to buy from the Authority its share of denatured fissionable materials; and thus the Soviet Union would be fatally handicapped in the development of economic production. If atomic energy became vital in industrial production, the Soviet Union might be staking its whole economic future on the decisions of an international body dominated by unfriendly nations. The very peculiarity of its system impelled the Soviet Union to reject the plan, which was about as fair and foolproof as could be devised under the circumstances.

The Soviet Union made shrewd propaganda use of its own plan. Even to many Americans, particularly the followers of Henry A. Wallace, the Soviet plan was appealing. Its call for the immediate destruction and outlawing of atomic weapons was concrete and easily understandable. Its plan of fitting atomic control into the already existing framework of the Security Council seemed logical and consistent. And it accompanied its plan for the control of atomic energy with a drive for general disarmament, linking together the control of conventional and atomic armaments.

The United States countered by insisting that security must come before disarmament, that this involved not only control, inspection, and punishment but also finding solutions to the tremendous issues posed by the peace settlement, and that the linking together of conventional and atomic armaments was likely to submerge the deadly serious business of finding a method of effective atomic control. The American position prevailed when the Council set up a Commission for Conventional Armaments separate from the Atomic Energy Commission.

Peace and Stability Through Enlightened Trade Policies

In the field of international trade cooperation the Truman administration took a bold lead, expanding the policies of Cordell Hull. In effect it sought to stay the world trend of the 1920's and 1930's toward nationalistic trade restrictions (neo-mercantilism) and to restore with some modifications a nineteenth-century world of international capitalism—a world of multilateral trade, with lower tariffs, convertibility of currencies, and easy balance-of-payment arrangements, a world virtually without import and export controls, quotas, blocked currencies, international cartels, and intergovernmental commodity agreements. In spearheading such a program the Americans ran into stupendous difficulties. "Temporary" and "transitional" exceptions continually had to be made to meet the "abnormal" conditions produced by war and its aftermath and later by rearmament. The most pressing of the "temporary' difficulties was the enormous dollar gap between American exports and imports.

During 1946 American shipments of food and supplies and American shipping services were so much in excess of foreign imports and services to the United States that at the year's end foreigners owed Americans more than 8 billion dollars. More than 3 billion dollars of this deficit was made up by temporary and exceptional extensions of Lend-Lease, other government grants, gifts through private organizations, and UNRRA, the international organization largely financed by the United States which undertook to feed civilians in the war-stricken areas. This still left foreigners owing more than 5 billion dollars. Foreigners paid for more than 2 billion dollars of this, partly in gold but mostly out of their dollar balances or by selling American investments and securities. But this still left a dollar gap of 3 billion dollars, which was met by credits from the Export-Import Bank, Lend-Lease credits, surplus-property credits, and an advance to Britain of 600 million dollars on her six-year-to-run 3.75-billion-dollar loan from the United States government which had been agreed to in December 1945.

This 1946 dollar gap revealed a more deep-seated situation than had been supposed and showed how badly the old multilateral trading pattern had been shattered. The negligible part played by private capital in meeting the dollar-gap problem of 1946 was significant, and the huge government loan to Britain and the rapidity with which it was used foreshadowed the necessity for the Marshall Plan.

The dollar-gap problem was intensified by a number of elements: the precipitant cutting off (in August 1945) of Lend-Lease; the abandonment of American price and other controls, thus making American exports to Europe spiral in price; the American scuttling, in 1946, of UNRRA, at the very height of the world food crisis; the fact that Europeans had already liquidated many of their American investments during the war; the drastic decline of European shipping and the phenomenal increase in American shipping. (In 1939 Americans owned only about 14 per cent of the world's merchant fleet, but at the end of the war Americans owned 60 per cent of it; moreover, the United States government, contrary to the principles it professed, continued to subsidize this swollen fleet, and the Merchant Ship Sales Act of 1946 favored American purchasers over foreign.)

Both Bretton Woods institutions, the International Monetary Fund and the International Bank for Reconstruction and Development (the World Bank), were inadequate to meet the dollar-gap crisis. The Fund had no authority to use its resources for relief, reconstruction, or armaments, or to meet a large or sustained outflow of capital on the part of a member. Instead, it was limited to giving temporary assistance in financing balance-of-payment deficits on current account for monetary stabilization operations. The World Bank, which had been expected to play a large part in financing reconstruction and development, was delayed in getting started and pursued extremely cautious policies because its own bond issues had to be floated in the private securities markets of the United States. More useful in financing foreign reconstruction and development was the Export-Import Bank, a United States government agency which in 1946 had a lending capacity of 3.5 billion dollars. However, reflecting the nationalistic outlook of the American Congress, goods purchased with Export-Import Bank loans had to be bought in the United States, insured there, and transported in American ships. There were some exceptions permitted, but it was paradoxical that loans made to bridge the dollar gap should themselves be saddled with provisions which were partially self-defeating. In 1947 this bank curtailed loans for reconstruction purposes.

In the summer of 1947, under American leadership, an international conference at Geneva negotiated mutual tariff reductions and resulted in the General Agreement on Tariffs and Trade. Delegates from the United States had behind them the authority of the President, who under the Reciprocal Trade Agreements Act of 1945 had the power to cut American tariff rates to 50 per cent of the rates in effect on January 1, 1945, instead of 50 per cent of the Smoot-Hawley rates.

At Geneva the United States got and gave many tariff concessions, and the United Kingdom and the Dominions reduced or eliminated some of the preferences accorded to each other. It has been estimated that the Geneva negotiations resulted in cutting the average American tariff rate from about 25 per cent of the value of goods imported into the United States to about 20 per cent, representing around a one-fifth reduction in rates.

However, American rates still remained high; many rates were not reduced at all; the whole system of collecting American customs continued needlessly complex, confusing, and difficult for the importer; and Germany, Japan, Italy, and the countries behind the Iron Curtain (except Czechoslovakia, for a time) were not parties to the Geneva agreements. Moreover, the reduction of rates on certain agricultural products like wheat, potatoes, meat, milk, and butter meant little in practice because these items were protected by quotas which limited their entries at the lower rate or any rate. Again, internal regulations and subsidies sometimes impaired the effects of low tariff rates. For instance, crude rubber was on the United States free list, but government regulations required that domestic synthetic rubber be mixed with the natural rubber in the manufacture of automobile tires and some other rubber products.

In the very midst of the Geneva negotiations the fragile basis of America's international economic policy was demonstrated in a dramatic way when Congress passed a bill allowing the Secretary of Agriculture to impose "fees" on wool imports up to 50 per cent of their value. The conference was saved when Truman vetoed this bill. The precarious nature of American economic policy abroad was again demonstrated when early in 1948 a Republican Congress renewed the Reciprocal Trade Agreements Act for only one year and enjoined the Tariff Commission, apart from all other government agencies interested in trade policies, to advise the President when his tariff reduction on any item reached the "peril point." The sole criterion the Tariff Commission was to apply was the threat to domestic interests, a throwback to the old cost-of-production formula. In 1949 the act was renewed for two years without the "peril point" provision; but in 1951 the "peril point" provision was revived when the act was again renewed for another two years.

In the fall of 1947, again under American leadership, an international conference at Havana put the finishing touches to a charter for an International Trade Organization. Members of this organization bound themselves to multilateral trading practices and set up machinery to see that these obligations were carried out. The ITO was to be connected with the United Nations Economic and Social Council. The charter was the longest and most comprehensive international trading agreement in history, and it represented the functional approach to international federation, the project-by-project method.

Members bound themselves to negotiate mutual tariff concessions; to forgo the use of export subsidies, quotas, and other quantitative restrictions; to limit preferential agreements; to refrain from giving non-members more favorable treatment than members and from acquiring legally exclusive markets in non-member countries; to desist from restrictive business practices and intergovernmental commodity agreements likely to become producer-controlled and price-fixing government cartels; to maintain convertibility of currencies. The ITO was to determine whether a member had lived up to its obligations, and it was required to give its approval to the invoking of escape clauses. Examples of escape clauses were the use of tariffs and quotas to develop infant industries and the employment of intergovernmental commodity agreements where the commodity in question was about to become a "burdensome surplus" or was characterized by widespread unemployment. The United States obtained the right to subsidize agricultural exports, under certain conditions, without ITO approval, and at American urging intergovernmental commodity agreements affecting stockpiles of strategic materials were exempted.

The United States had wished to write an international investment code into the ITO charter, a code which among other things would have guaranteed the mobility of assets and earnings, equality of treatment for national and foreign capital, and compensation in the event of nationalization. However, the underdeveloped countries rejected this, and the best the United States could get was a provision making it mandatory for a member country to negotiate with any other member that requested negotiation with a view to reaching agreement on the terms of foreign investment. It was plain that the underdeveloped countries did not believe that under existing conditions private investors would or could furnish enough capital to finance industrial revolutions in their countries; what they wanted was large capital investments in the way of long-time intergovernmental loans on easy terms. The emerging countries were already suggesting an international agency, financed by the governments of the advanced countries, to make such loans. On the other hand, the United States insisted that all that was necessary was a healthy investment climate to stimulate the flow of private capital.

Even in the United States, where ITO principles were most highly regarded, the charter ran into widespread opposition. Economic planners, strong in the Department of Agriculture and among some farm organizations, were suspicious of ITO's antisubsidy features and its strictures against intergovernmental commodity agreements. Indeed, many features of the Food and Agriculture Organization, of the proposed world food board of 1947, and of the International Wheat Agreement of 1949, favored by many farm organizations, appeared to run counter to ITO principles. Free enterprisers disliked the ITO's many escape clauses and its failure to provide an investment code. Economic nationalists, powerful with American public opinion and in Congress, were repelled by its international control of domestic matters. Already many advanced countries had moved to pervasively controlled economies; indeed, by 1947 no country, not even the United States, had a free economy in the 1914 sense. Both old mercantilists like Empire traders and new social planners were suspicious of ITO. And in underdeveloped countries, attracted both to old-fashioned mercantilist "stimulation" and to new-fashioned social planning as means of developing their own industrial revolutions, there was much opposition. The continued dollar gap and imbalance in world trade portended a longer period of abnormal conditions than ITO architects cared to admit. Year after year the ITO remained buried in committees without Congressional approval, a continuing reminder that even in the United States there was persistent opposition to reviving the old world of free and multilateral trade.

Regional Security: The Inter-American System

Another expression of America's attempted cooperation was evidenced in the relation of the United States to the twenty Latin American republics to the south. Out of the Good Neighbor policy of the 1930's was emerging an inter-American security system. In the years prior to World War II the United States had reversed its protectorate policies. American Marines had been withdrawn first from the Dominican Republic, then from Nicaragua, and finally from Haiti. Treaty rights which allowed the United States to intervene in Cuba and Panama were relinquished. The United States had lent Mexico the money with which that country indemnified (in part) American owners for the loss of oil properties which Mexico had nationalized. Reciprocal trade treaties had been negotiated with Latin American countries. Vast loans had been made to enable Latin American countries to survive the challenge of the Axis powers.

Gradually, in a series of inter-American conferences, the Monroe Doctrine had been transformed from a unilateral to a multilateral policy. At Montevideo (1933) the United States had solemnly promised not to intervene in the internal affairs of any Latin American state. At Buenos Aires (1936) and at Lima (1938) the American republics had promised to consult in the event of a threat to the security or territorial integrity of any American state. At Havana (1940) it was agreed that an attack on any American state by a non-American power would be deemed an act of aggression against all American states. And at Mexico City (the Act of Chapultepec, 1945) the American collective-security system was extended to include all acts of aggression against American states whether from outside or within the hemisphere. In case of aggression the American republics agreed to consult together on applying sanctions such as the rupture of diplomatic relations, economic coercion, and the use of armed force. Thus from the doctrine of non-intervention the American republics moved to the doctrine of collective intervention.

The Act of Chapultepec was a war measure, an executive agreement entered into by the President. Since it would lapse after the end of the war, there was much agitation to make it a permanent part of the inter-American system. However, there were some doubts. Would not collective intervention amount in fact to intervention by the most powerful member, the United States? Most Latin Americans seemed willing to take that chance. Would not such a regional system conflict with the jurisdiction of the United Nations? No, because inter-American action was to be taken only until the Security Council acted to restore peace.

The Chapultepec principle became permanent policy when at the Rio de Janeiro conference of August 1947 the American states agreed to act together in the event of aggression from a non-American or an American power. Under the treaty all would have not only the right but the obligation to assist an American state if attacked. Collective action would involve breaking diplomatic relations, imposing economic sanctions, and using force, and it would be applied when two-thirds of the American states voted that an aggression had taken place. (In a conflict between two American states, the parties to the dispute were to be excluded from voting.) "Aggression" would be what the American republics, by a two-thirds vote, defined as such in each particular case as it arose. However, no state would be forced to furnish armed forces without its consent, a proviso made necessary in order to get ratification by the United States Senate. The security zone to which the treaty would apply included the Western Hemisphere from the North Pole to the South Pole; thus Canada and Greenland, but not Hawaii, were covered. Although protected, neither Canada nor Greenland was a member of the inter-American system.

At the Bogotá conference of March 1948 the whole inter-American system, which had been growing piecemeal since the 1880's, was integrated and its branches and agencies formally organized and given a permanent constitutional status. Henceforth the organization was to be called the Organization of American States, a regional agency within the United Nations.

What were the reasons for this development of a Good Neighbor policy? In the early 1930's, in response to the Depression, the chief motive was the capture of Latin American markets; in the late 1930's and early 1940's, anxiety over Axis penetration was primary; after 1945 the Soviet threat and Peronist movements became the important considerations.

Occupation of Japan: From Reform to Anti-Communism

In one sense the American occupation of Japan well exemplified the spirit which animated the Allied peoples during the war years, the spirit of fundamental social reform. During the first years of the occupation the United States carried out a far-reaching program of social change in the belief that non-democratic elements in a society cause war and democratic elements make for peace. In another sense the American occupation of Japan represented a repudiation of the high resolves of the war years. The expectations of international cooperation miscarried, and the occupation came near to being the unilateral responsibility of the United States, almost as unilateral as the Russian occupation of the Balkans. There were times when this virtually one-country occupation of Japan irked the British, the Australians, and the Chinese, both Nationalist and Communist, almost as much as it irked the Russians.

The United States government working through the State-War-Navy Coordinating Committee determined the basic directives, although in fact General MacArthur, with the title of Supreme Commander for the Allied Powers, was given wide latitude. In theory, MacArthur and the United States government were somewhat limited by the Allied Far Eastern Advisory Commission sitting in Washington and the Allied Council sitting in Tokyo, but these bodies actually exercised little influence on the evolution of events and policies.

The terms of the Japanese occupation and peace settlement were outlined in the Cairo Declaration, the Potsdam agreement, and the stipulations of the surrender. Japan was to be stripped of all her conquests made since 1895, she was to lose all territories beyond her four home islands, and she was to suffer occupation of her home territory, dissolution of her armed forces, elimination from authority of all responsible for Japanese aggressions, and payment of reparation in kind.

The changes ordered during the first months of the occupation were breath-taking. War criminals were ordered arrested and tried; military societies were dissolved; all military drill was abolished; thousands of leaders identified with the prewar and war regimes were barred from holding office; war production was prohibited; Japan's gold and silver assets were seized; all exports and imports were forbidden without authorization; the largest banks and all concerns which had been financing war production and colonization were closed; the secret police was swept away; the home ministry was stripped of most of its centralized powers and the police system was decentralized and democratized; the end of press censorship was decreed; freedom of press, speech, assembly, and religion was proclaimed; racial and religious discrimination was prohibited; education was decentralized and the teaching profession purged; textbooks in the schools were revamped to stress the evils of a militaristic society and the virtues of a liberal-democratic one; equal opportunity in education was emphasized; women were urged to become active in civic and business affairs and to get an education; free labor unions were encouraged.

A fundamental question was what to do with the Emperor. Was he not the very center of the old order which had produced an imperialistic Japan? Liberals and leftists throughout the world, and many even in Japan, felt that abolition of the monarchy was indispensable to a regenerated Japan. But in the end, largely because of fear of Communist revolution, the view prevailed that the institutions of monarchy and Shinto should be used though not supported. However, no doubt was left in the Japanese mind that the authority of the Emperor and his government was subject to the Supreme Commander, and in December 1945 the Emperor in an imperial rescript repudiated the doctrine of his own divinity. About the same time Shinto was divorced from state support and compulsory adherence to that religion forbidden.

A political revolution was produced by the adoption of a new constitution and the enactment of a series of laws under it. Sovereignty was declared to rest with the people. Many civil liberties, a long list of fundamental rights and freedoms, were guaranteed. Armaments were banned and Japan renounced war forever. (The Americans later repented of this.) The Emperor became a constitutional figurehead. The Premier and his cabinet were made responsible to a two-house Diet. Women were granted the suffrage. Local government was drastically revised; prefectures, cities, and towns were given wide local autonomy; the old neighborhood associations, which had been controlled by local bosses in alliance with the old centralized home ministry, were broken up.

An onslaught was made on the zaibatsu, the great family trusts which controlled a large part of Japanese finance, industry, and transportation. They were heavily taxed and their wartime claims against the government were disallowed. By the end of 1947 nearly seventy holding companies had been dissolved and a government commission had impounded the assets and secured control of more than four thousand zaibatsu subsidiaries. It was planned to sell these assets to cooperatives, trade unions, and small and moderate-sized business firms. However, after 1947 American attitudes were to change and most of these assets were never sold as planned.

Armament and aircraft factories were shut down entirely. Japan's chemical, light-metals, and heavy industries were to be reduced to the 1928-1932 level; later this was changed to the 1930-1934 level. The industrial equipment used for production above this level was to be shipped to Allied countries as war reparations. Thus in one stroke the problems of reparations and industrial disarmament would be solved. By late 1947 the equipment of about nine hundred Japanese factories had been designated for removal to Allied countries as reparations. However, since American attitudes changed after 1947, the bulk of this industrial equipment never actually left the country.

Drastic agrarian reform was undertaken, and it was planned to purchase 5 million acres of land and to transform about 80 per cent of Japan's landless or small-holder peasants into independent farmers. Local commissions were set up to purchase land from landlords and to sell it on easy and long terms to peasants. By the end of 1947 nearly 3.5 million acres had been acquired by the commissions and more than ½ million acres had been resold to peasants.

The spring of 1947 represented the high-water mark of liberal reform in Japan. In the elections of April, the Social Democrats won a plurality in both houses of the Diet. Tetsu Katayama, who adhered to the democratic socialism of the British Labour party, became premier. The victory of the Social Democrats, who nosed out Japan's two old conservative parties, was due to support from trade unions, peasants, and small businessmen. Inflation and the conservative government's unpopular methods of rice collection were the winning issues. The Katayama government abolished the home ministry, attacked the old bureaucracy and began a reorganization of the civil service, and attempted effective nationalization of the coal industry. Since the Katayama government had only a plurality in the Diet, it depended on conservative votes to stay in office. When Katayama failed to stabilize prices or devise an adequate system of rice collection, he fell from power in February 1948.

With Katayama's fall the era of reform came to an end. After that a reaction set in and American policy changed direction. American purpose in Japan shifted from democratization to the building of a strong anti-Communist bastion in Asia. There were many reason for this shift: the crystallizing of the East-West conflict; increasing alarm over the spread of Communism on the continent of Asia, particularly in China; widespread feeling among American conservatives and businessmen that American policy in Japan had been too radical; the growing desire of American businessmen to find markets and investments in Japan; the slowness of Japan's economic recovery; the mounting cost of the occupation to American taxpayers; the belief that democratic reform had gone far enough to make certain a peaceful Japan.

The years 1945-1947 revealed that Americans, if properly motivated, had more capacity for social politics than was commonly supposed, and the day would come, several years later, when many Japanese would look back on these achievements in fundamental reform and the American contribution to them with some feeling of bewilderment.

The Steady Trend to National Independence in Asia

The high resolves of the Allied peoples characteristic of the war years continued in Asia somewhat longer than in Europe. The withdrawal of Britain from the major part of her empire (India,

Pakistan, Ceylon, and Burma) displayed wisdom and realistic insight into the dominant trend of the times. These events were followed with wide popular approval in the United States.

Americans little realized the strength of social-democratic ideas among Nehru's followers and the wide appeal of socialist doctrines to all the important factions in Burma, where the governing coalition, the Anti-Fascist People's Freedom League, was composed of Social Democrats, Socialists, and nationalistic Communists and shared some of the attitudes of Mao Tse-tung. In 1948 the new government of Burma nationalized a considerable amount of British properties, but it was not radical enough for the Trotskyite Communists and the pro-Soviet Communists, who gave it considerable trouble throughout the country. Burma slowly achieved greater stability under the leadership of U Nu, a Buddhist mystic and strong believer in the democratic socialism of the British Labour party. In Malaya the British resisted independence on the ground that the nationalist movement was immature and had insufficient popular support. From 1948 to 1960 the Communists waged a fierce guerrilla war in Malaya, but the growing nationalist movement there had conservative leadership and supported the British in gradually overcoming the Communists. After the peak of the emergency had passed the British granted independence to Malaya in 1957.

In both Indonesia and Indochina there was a three-way conflict between nationalists, Communists who wanted both national independence and Communism, and vested interests who rallied to the European governing powers. The situation in Indonesia became less troubled after the Dutch withdrew in 1949, but there was instability, and the country's leading nationalist, Achmed Sukarno, a democratic Socialist, maneuvered his way among the army, the conservative Moslems, and the Communists and sometimes was in alliance with the last. In Indochina conditions steadily became more chaotic, and Vietnam's Bao Dai, supported by the French within the framework of the French Union, was increasingly pressed by both the more extreme nationalists and Ho Chi Minh's Communists. The French stubbornly clung on and soon found themselves bogged down in a nasty war with both Vietnamese nationalists and Communists. French resistance to Vietnam independence drove many nationalists into the Communist camp.

The United States made its own contribution to the anti-imperialist trend by proclaiming, on July 4, 1946, the independence of the Philippines. Since 1934 the Philippines had been a "commonwealth," a transition stage to independence. However, the United States did not retire from certain responsibilities or from all participation in Philippine affairs. The American government threw its weight behind President Manuel Roxas, who had served in the Japanese puppet government in the Philippines and was a right-wing Nationalist. Roxas obtained military equipment from Americans with which to fight the Hukbalahap, a left-wing peasant movement, said to be Communist-oriented, which demanded drastic agrarian reforms.

The United States retained eleven army bases and four naval bases in the Philippines. Specific quotas of Philippine sugar, tobacco, cordage, and rice were to be admitted to the United States duty-free for a period of eight years. This provision was attacked both in the United States and the Philippines as a further stimulus to the vested interests, both Filipino and American, which had monopolized the Philippine export trade, and as a discouragement to diversification and a better standard of living for the Philippine people. The Filipinos were also required to guarantee to American citizens a position of absolute equality with Philippine citizens in the development of the country's natural resources, a requirement which forced the Filipinos to amend their new constitution.

From Mediation to Anti-Communism in China

During the two years following the war, Americans made serious attempts to understand the Chinese Revolution and to bring Nationalists and Communists together. The weakness of the middle way was the most serious handicap postwar American policy had to face in China.

After the Japanese capitulated there was a race between the Nationalist government and the Communists to receive the actual surrender of the Japanese troops and to acquire their arms. The United States flew its armed forces into many parts of China to forestall the Communists and to facilitate surrender to the Nationalists. American forces also held certain lines of communication open to the Nationalist troops. After V-J Day, Lend-Lease continued for the Nationalist government and in one form or another more than 1 billion dollars in American aid and equipment was extended to Chiang Kai-shek during the year and a half after the Japanese surrender. The Communists denounced the American "intervention," but the Americans replied that they were merely helping the lawful Chinese government to wind up the war against the common Japanese enemy. Meantime a large number of American journalists, voicing the feelings of many of the career diplomats in the American and other embassies in China, reported to the American public that Chiang's government was increasingly corrupt, reactionary, and inept, that disastrous inflation threatened, and that the Chinese Communists had been the more effective fighters against the Japanese and that they were the more sincere friends of basic reform.

In December 1945 the American government declared its purpose to work for a truce and a provisional government in China representing the Kuomintang, the Communists, and intermediate liberal-leftist groups. At the Moscow conference of the same month the Russians promised to work for the same policy, and both the United States and Russia agreed to an early withdrawal of American and Russian troops from China. In January 1946 General Marshall was sent to China to mediate between the Nationalist government and Mao's Communists. A truce was arranged, but the ensuing negotiations broke down because of the depth of the mutual distrust, the reluctance of the Communists to integrate their army into the Nationalist army, and the growing belief of the Communists that conditions favored their winning all China in the near future. As American troops remained in China after the disarming of the Japanese, the Communists began to question the impartiality of American mediation. When the civil war was resumed, Marshall blamed both sides for the failure of the negotiations.

Chiang went ahead with plans for government reform, promised the end of Kuomintang one-party rule, and convoked a national assembly which included some representatives of the Social Democrats and the Young China Party. This national assembly wrote a new constitution which was to go into effect in December 1947 and which promised the end of Kuomintang domination. Meantime Communist armies were winning more and more Chinese territory.

What was the attitude of the Soviet Union toward the enlarging civil war in China? For the most part it was cautious and not far out of harmony with the Yalta agreement and the Soviet-Chinese alliance of August 1945. Russian troops occupied Manchuria after Russia's declaration of war against Japan. At Dairen and Port Arthur the Russians assumed the privileges accorded them at Yalta, but nothing was done about organizing a joint corporation for the operation of the Manchurian railroads. In the spring of 1946, Russian armies evacuated Manchuria, but Russian troops remained at Port Arthur and Dairen, and the port of Dairen remained closed to American and world commerce contrary to the Yalta agreement. In two ways the Russians helped Chinese Communists: they made little or no effort to see that Japanese surrenders were made to the lawful Nationalist government forces, and they allowed Japanese arms and equipment to fall into the hands of the Communists. Still, the Russians were circumspect and seem to have given little direct aid to the Communists. And as it turned out, their removal of enormous amounts of Manchurian machinery and industrial equipment to Russia actually "cheated" the Chinese Communists of much industrial production they well might have used after they came into control of Manchuria.

Throughout 1947 and 1948 the Communists continued to make territorial gains in China. At the same time American policy became virtually one of watchful waiting. At the beginning of the year 1947, Marshall's mission was terminated and American troops were withdrawn. American financial aid, for both economic and military purposes, declined. American technicians and military advisers continued on. American officers trained Chiang's combat troops. Formosa was developed as a training center. General Wedemeyer, sent to China to investigate conditions, reported that military force alone would not eliminate Communism, that domestic reforms were indispensable, that deeds and not words were necessary. However, Wedemeyer abandoned the Marshall policy of trying to bring both sides together and urged speedy economic aid and military supplies for Chiang's government. Senator Vandenberg, Governor Dewey, and other leading Republicans called for increased aid to Chiang, thereby emphasizing that the administration's stand on China was no part of the bipartisan foreign policy. The Luce publications and the Scripps-Howard chain argued for energetic policies in support of Chiang. Increasingly it was claimed that Chinese Communism was not indigenous, that it was part and parcel of Soviet imperialism, that victory for the Chinese Communists would be victory for an international Communist conspiracy bent on world domination.

The administration, however, refused to be convinced. It had decided that Europe was the more critical theater and that large-scale aid should go there. Also, it was pointed out by people in and out of the administration that even a billion-dollar grant to Chiang would be woefully inadequate to bolster his disorganized armies, inflation-ridden economy, and demoralized administration. It was argued that much American equipment would certainly be captured by the Communists and turned against Chiang's own armies. Probably only full-scale participation by American air and ground forces in China could turn the tide, and no responsible American had proposed sending American armies into China. Moreover, American armed intervention might alienate the non-Communist masses in Asia and might lead to Russian intervention on the other side. It was contended that even a Chiang victory with large-scale American help probably would not at that late hour result in a unified and democratic China.

In late 1947 and early 1948 Congress took the initiative from the administration. The Foreign Assistance Act of April 1948 earmarked 463 million dollars for Chiang's China, 125 million dollars for military aid and 338 million dollars for economic aid. By this time the Chinese Communists controlled about one-fourth of China's territory and about one-third of China's population. The aid thus given to Chiang amounted to a declaration that the United States was now definitely committed to his side. It was overt intervention, but on a scale so small as to have little effect on the outcome. Nevertheless, the United States had now moved from mediation and non-involvement to open support of Chiang's war against the Communists. On the other hand, about the same time the Russians, more and more alienated by the Marshall Plan, increased their direct aid, hitherto negligible, to the Chinese Communists.

Korea: Portent of Things to Come

The future failure of Soviet-Western cooperation was most clearly foreshadowed in Korea, where even in the days immediately following the war there was little pretense of agreement between Americans and Russians.

Although the Cairo Declaration had promised Korea, governed by Japan since 1910, freedom and independence, the Potsdam conference made a military decision to divide the country "temporarily" at the 38th parallel, the north to be administered by the Russian army, the south by the American. Ostensibly this was done to facilitate the disarming of the Japanese in Korea, although Russian opposition to United States occupation of northern Korea, which would have brought the Americans to the very frontier of the Soviet Union itself, doubtless entered into the decision.

North Korea was the more industrialized; South Korea was the nation's rice basket and contained two-thirds of the population. During the several years following the war, economic conditions in South Korea were critical due to the poor rice crops, the influx of some 3 million repatriates and refugees, and the inability to get chemical fertilizer from North Korea and grain from Manchuria. When the Americans were unable to provide rice for export to the northern zone the Russians cut off the export of fuel, electric power, and industrial equipment to the southern zone. Even feeble attempts at bizonal agreements on transportation, postal service, and the movement of individuals across the dividing line came to a halt.

Although at the end of the war there were more than fifty political parties in Korea, public opinion for the most part was divided between the extreme left and the extreme right. The strength of the extreme right lay in its uncompromising demands for immediate independence for the whole country, its influence in the police, and its support by landlords and other propertied elements. In South Korea the extreme right was led by Syngman Rhee and Kim Koo. The extreme left, Communist-dominated, drew its strength from those who wanted the parceling of the large estates among the peasants, the liquidation of those who had collaborated most closely with the Japanese, and the distribution of the large landed and industrial properties owned by the Japanese. As Japanese rule collapsed, parties of the left, largely Communist-dominated, set up a People's Republic, which had Russian support in the North.

In the South, where the People's Republic was the nearest thing to a functioning government when the American troops arrived, the Americans refused to recognize any native government. The Americans set up a military government and declared their intention gradually to Koreanize the administration. Some American authorities advised the use of middle-of-the-road leaders like Lyuh Woon Hyung and Kimm Kiusic; but in Korea, as in China, the moderate social-democratic position had little popular support. Little by little the conservative elements under Rhee came into the lead, at first with American encouragement, then with American misgivings, and finally with American acquiescence. Conservative elements repeatedly won the elections provided by the military government. The South Korean Labor (Communist) party attacked the military government, organized strikes and riots, and frequently boycotted elections.

At the close of 1945, Americans and Russians had agreed tentatively on a plan which would have put Korea under a provisional trusteeship held jointly by the United States, the Soviet Union, Britain, and Nationalist China. This plan was accepted by the Korean Communists but violently opposed by Rhee and his extremely nationalist right-wing following, who would settle for nothing less than immediate independence for all Korea. The United States finally jettisoned the trusteeship plan, and from time to time called for free elections to select a national assembly. This led to endless bickering. Should the elections be all-Korean elections or separate elections in each zone? Should the northern zone, with one-third of the population, have equal representation with the more populous southern zone? What parties should be allowed to participate? The Russians insisted on excluding "reactionary, anti-democratic parties," the very parties which were closest to the United States authorities. The Americans countered by accusing the Russians of permitting only Communist-dominated parties to participate in politics. Repeatedly the Russians fell back on the argument that the proper way to unify Korea had been established in the Moscow agreement of 1945, the essence of which was the joint four-power trusteeship plan. The Russians complained that the Americans had repudiated this agreement.

Finally, in the fall of 1947, the United States took the Korean problem to the General Assembly of the United Nations. The Soviet government objected and called for the withdrawal of all occupying troops by the end of the year, thus, it was argued, giving the Korean people the opportunity to determine their own government. This proposal seems to have met with widespread approval, even in South Korea. The Americans feared such a solution would lead to civil war in Korea, a war in which the Communists would have advantages they would not have in relatively free and honest elections. In November 1947 the United Nations Assembly called for free elections throughout all Korea to select a national assembly. The national assembly was to provide civilian government for the whole country. A United Nations temporary commission on Korea was established to observe these elections. The Soviet government bitterly resented international supervision in its zone and regarded the United Nations action as intrusion by an international puppet of the United States. The commission was denied access to the Soviet zone. With the consent of the interim committee of the General Assembly, the commission went ahead with elections in South Korea alone. The elections, held on May 10, 1948, resulted in a right-wing victory. The national assembly thus elected adopted a liberal-democratic constitution for the Republic of Korea and elected Rhee president. The People's Republic in the North rebuffed all overtures from the Republic of Korea. In June 1949 the United States withdrew its troops from South Korea, leaving the South Koreans with only a lightly armed native constabulary with which to defend the new republic.

By early 1948 it was apparent that the partition of Korea was likely to continue indefinitely. As had so often happened to small countries in the past, Korean unity and independence were being sacrificed to power politics. The United States feared an independent Korea dominated by the Communists. The Soviet Union feared an independent Korea dominated by American and anti-Communist influence. Each preferred partition to the possibility of a united Korea allied to the other side.

Europe: The Breakdown of Four-Power Collaboration

In Europe, the first storm warning was in Greece, where late in 1944 British troops took part in a civil war, ejected the EAM, Communist-dominated wing of the underground, and set up a right-wing government under a regency which prepared for the return of the King. Moscow did not protest, for the Russians had agreed with the British, in October 1944, that in return for a free hand in Rumania, Bulgaria, and Hungary, they would allow the British a free hand in Greece. (Later, Britain claimed that Yalta superseded the agreement as to the three former Axis satellites.) Churchill regarded Greece as strategically vital in the eastern Mediterranean. Nevertheless, American opinion was shocked at British sphere-of-influence politics in Greece, at the ruthless treatment of left-wing war allies (EAM), and at British connivance with some Greek politicians who had collaborated with the Germans. Many of the former EAM took up arms and in northern Greece carried on systematic guerrilla war against the government. In Italy, however, the Russians did protest. They claimed that as the Allies moved up the peninsula they collaborated with Fascists, and they demurred when Britain and America made all of the important decisions of the Allied Control Commission there.

In Poland, Czechoslovakia, and the Balkans north of Greece, however, the shoe was on the other foot, and the Russians dominated the Allied Control Commissions. The United States and Britain complained bitterly that the Russians were violating Yalta, that the Communists dominated the provisional governments, that only token representation from democratic, peasant, and Socialist parties was admitted to these governments, and that free elections were not being held. Whatever may be said of British and American conduct in their spheres in Greece and Italy, at least before 1946 was out relatively free elections were held in both countries to determine the nature of their future governments. In Italy the King was voted out; in Greece the King was voted in.

Russian dominance in the Balkans and British-American dominance in the Mediterranean showed unmistakably that genuine joint control was a fiction, that definite spheres of influence would prevail, and that a cooperative peace treaty to settle anything would be very difficult. However, the grand alliance did succeed in making peace treaties with Finland, Rumania, Hungary, Bulgaria, and Italy. It took over a year of hard bargaining, but at last it was achieved in early 1947. There was endless wrangling in the process—over territorial changes, Trieste, the Italian colonies, disarmament, reparations, and even whether the lesser allies should be consulted, which ones, and to what extent. In general, Russia opposed participation by the lesser powers and the United States favored it.

Russia dominated the territorial settlements in Eastern Europe and in the Balkans north of Greece, and extended her own boundaries. Among other decisions, Rumania retained Transylvania over Hungarian protests and ceded southern Dobruja to Bulgaria. But in the Mediterranean area the views of the Western powers tended to prevail. Italy ceded the Dodecanese to Greece but retained the southern Tirol in the face of Austrian claims. Italy ceded eastern Venezia Giulia and Istria to Yugoslavia, but Italian and Yugoslav claims to Trieste were most heatedly contested. The Western allies feared that Trieste, if awarded to Tito's Yugoslavia, then in alliance with Russia, would become a Soviet naval base. In the end, Trieste was made a free territory under the United Nations, which was to choose a governor. "Temporarily" British and American troops were assigned to patrol Trieste's Zone A, Yugoslav troops to patrol Zone B. For years this provisional arrangement stood and no governor was selected.

Ethiopia's independence was proclaimed anew, but the future of Italy's other colonies produced much contention. The Russians, to counter Western demands for a voice in Eastern Europe, put in a claim to administer the Italian colonies. Finally it was merely agreed that Italy was to surrender her colonies and that if a decision as to their disposition could not be reached within a year, the United Nations should decide their future. Later the United Nations Assembly provided for the independence of Libya, Italian administration of Somaliland as a trusteeship, and Eritrea's federation with Ethiopia.

Limits were set to the military establishments of the five defeated nations. The upper limit for the Italian army was to be 250,000 men. Reparations were also written into the treaties. The

Italian obligation was fixed at 360 million dollars, a victory for Russia and some smaller powers and a defeat for the United States, which feared it would have to compensate Italy for the economic drain reparation payments would entail.

While these negotiations with respect to Eastern Europe and the eastern Mediterranean were going on, the Russians were attempting to consolidate their hold on Iranian Azerbaijan. They also sent a note to Turkey in August 1946 demanding a new regime for the Straits "solely under the competence of Turkey and the Black Sea powers" and joint defense of the Straits by Turkey and Russia. This meant Russian bases on Turkish soil. The Turks refused to negotiate and mobilized their army. Their stiff resistance prevented an international crisis. In December 1946 tensions over Iran also relaxed when the Soviet-sponsored regime in Azerbaijan, unpopular with the people, collapsed and the Russians made no attempt to restore it.

Repeated attempts to make a peace treaty with Austria failed completely because of conflicts between Russia and the Western powers. Year after year Austria, like Germany, was split by the line dividing Eastern and Western Europe. In theory, Austria was not an enemy state but a liberated country. Nevertheless, it was divided into four zones of occupation, although a single Austrian government ruled, with limitations, in all four zones. The Russians did not set up a separate political government in their zone but frequently vetoed Austrian laws there. (The Russians did less vetoing as time passed.) Relatively free elections revealed that Austrians continued to vote as they had done before Nazi domination: the rural areas were largely conservative and clerical, and Vienna was strongly Social Democratic. Even in the Soviet zone the Communists were weak and the labor unions were in the hands of the Social Democrats.

A minor obstacle to a peace treaty was the Yugoslav claim to Carinthia, which Russia supported. The major obstacle involved a prior agreement that the Russians should take as German reparations all of the German assets they found in their Austrian zone of occupation. Britain and the United States claimed that "German assets" meant only those owned by Germans before *Anschluss;* Russia claimed in addition all property taken over by the Nazis after *Anschluss,* much of which the Nazis had seized or paid for inadequately. Under their definition the Russians claimed about 750 million dollars in property, including all or part ownership of about three hundred factories, all the oil reserves, 75 per cent of Danubian shipping, and even banks, joint-stock companies, urban real estate, and farmsteads. The Russians also demanded extraterritorial rights in connection with these assets. The Western powers felt that this would maim Austria economically and virtually destroy her independence.

The Russians profited by the stalemate: in the early years of occupation they sent goods and equipment back to Russia, and through the years they were enabled to keep an army within striking distance of Italy and Trieste and to station troops in Hungary and Rumania in order to guard the Red Army's lines of communication. When the Western powers repeatedly urged renewal of negotiations, the Russians pleaded additional excuses and eventually contended that there could be no Austrian treaty until the government of the Free Territory of Trieste was set up in accordance with the peace treaty.

Austrian leaders boldly committed their country to the West, and participated in the Marshall Plan in the face of Russian opposition. At best, the economic future of Austria appeared bleak: for political reasons it would never be allowed to join Germany, and neither the Western powers nor its own people would allow it to join the Soviet sphere. After a few years the Russians themselves made no further effort to integrate their Austrian zone into their Eastern orbit. Vienna remained a head without a body, and Austria failed really to integrate into either world.

The Problem of Germany

It was Germany that was crucial for the future balance of power, and with respect to Germany there was at first some agreement. Germany was divided into four zones of occupation. The Russians got the agricultural East, the Americans the mountainous South, the British the industrial Ruhr and commercial Hamburg, the French the Rhineland. Berlin, surrounded by the Russian zone, was itself divided into four zones. An Allied Control Council, consisting of the four zone commanders, was set up to coordinate certain policies in all zones.

Germany was to be treated as a single economic unit. There were to be central administrative agencies for transport, communications, finance, industry, foreign trade. There were to be common Allied policies on these and on matters of currency and banking, production, wages and prices, and reparations.

Cartels and all excessive economic concentrations were to be eliminated. Industries producing armaments, aircraft, seagoing ships, aluminum, synthetic gasoline, and ball bearings were to be prohibited, and production of other metals and chemicals was to be restricted to peacetime needs. Germany was to be allowed a steel capacity of 7.5 million tons a year and a production of 5.8 million tons. (Germany's production was 18 million tons in 1929.) In general, Germany was to be allowed an industrial capacity somewhat below 55 per cent of the 1938 level. (It was estimated that this would give the Germans a standard of living approximating Depression years.) Industrial capital equipment which would produce in excess of this was to be distributed as reparations. The Soviet and Polish share would be taken from the Soviet zone in Germany, the shares of the other allies from the Western zones. In addition, Russia would get 25 per cent of the equipment removed from the Western zones, receiving 10 per cent without payment, and paying for 15 per cent in food and other products from the East.

There was easier agreement on other matters: destruction of the Nazi party, removal of all Nazi influence from German life, punishment of war criminals, disarmament, disbandment of all armed forces, abolition of the General Staff, destruction of all military equipment and of all war-serving industries.

The Western powers agreed to Polish annexation of most of East Prussia (thus eliminating the Corridor) and of Upper Silesia, and to Russian administration of the northern part of East Prussia, including the city of Königsberg. However, Poland's occupation of eastern Germany up to the Oder and the western Neisse was another matter; and while the United States and Britain acquiesced, they reserved final judgment for the peace conference. Both feared that Polish annexation of this area would poison German-Polish relations permanently, inflame German nationalism, make Poland dependent on Russia, and render difficult the feeding of the German nation.

Economic cooperation was the first to break down and after that eventually came the breakdown of all other forms of cooperation. The Russians paid little heed to the basic policy that Germany should be administered as an economic unit. The commander in the Soviet zone repeatedly vetoed economic measures agreed to by a majority of the Allied Control Council. The Russians took as reparations both capital equipment and currently produced goods, in defiance of the Council. They failed to make deliveries of food to the Western zones. At the same time, they put their reparations bill at 10 billion dollars, which the Western powers considered too high, complained that they were not getting their share of dismantled equipment from the Western zones, and demanded reparations out of current production, to which the Western powers had never agreed. The Western powers pointed out that the Russians had failed to make their deliveries, that German production was even below the level allowed by the Control Council, that the costs of German imports and of the occupation were a first charge and had priority over reparation payments, that these costs exceeded what the Western powers themselves were getting as reparations, and that any payment to Russia out of current production would in fact come from American taxpayers.

By the middle of 1946 the chief problem seemed to be not how to keep German production down but how to increase it. Germans were producing even below the levels planned by the victors, and the Germans were on a bare subsistence diet. Dangerous bottlenecks existed in coal and transport. Germany was still the industrial center of Europe, and Europe's recovery revolved around German coal and German industry. Perhaps the relocation of German factories in France, Belgium, and Czechoslovakia would redistribute industrial power in Europe; but the obstacles were stupendous, and even the value of those factories already transplanted to new locations was seen to have been greatly overestimated. How long could recovery be postponed to work so revolutionary a transformation? Would American and British taxpayers consent to pour money indefinitely into an impoverished Germany? Americans and Britons began to reappraise their whole policy toward Germany, dismantling slowed down, and fewer factories were removed.

There was never any mistake about the French program toward Germany. It pleaded for severing the Saar, the Rhineland, and the Ruhr from Germany. France would annex the Saar, the Rhineland would become a separate state under permanent French occupation, and the Ruhr would be placed under an international regime with its industries largely in French, Belgian, and Dutch hands. The remainder of Germany would become a highly decentralized confederation, like the Germanic Bund after 1815. German economy and armaments would remain under control and inspection of the victorious powers. Many dismantled German factories would be relocated in France, for it was "as easy to ship German coal to Lorraine as Lorraine ore to Germany." The French tried to keep Russia and the Western powers together on Germany, and many Frenchmen feared that General Lucius Clay's policies were heading toward a revived German industry with much of the same old crowd in control.

In the Eastern zone, the Russians encouraged the Communist-dominated Socialist Unity party, moved toward one-party government, and nationalized some of the industries. In the territories taken from Germany, the Poles distributed land to the peasants and destroyed the old Junker class. Many German farmers and peasants fled from Polish-administered territories and their places were taken by Polish peasants. The Russian reparations policy and support of Polish expansion into German territory were intensely unpopular with the Germans. On the other hand, Russian encouragement of centralized government on the pattern of the Weimar republic (in the hope, the Western powers believed, that it could be used by Communists to get control of all Germany), and insistence that the Ruhr, the Rhineland, and the Saar be retained by Germany were popular with the Germans. However, the Russians were primarily interested in reparations and in a Germany that could no longer menace the Slavic world, and as a means to these ends they favored joint four-power control of the Ruhr industries. The French did not like the Russian stand on the Saar. The United States and Britain were opposed to the Russians having a hand in the Ruhr, and killed the proposition by countering with a plan for four-power control of Upper Silesian industries.

The British shared the American view that the truncating of Germany would stimulate intransigent German nationalism and prevent economic recovery. They also agreed with the Americans that European recovery depended on German recovery and that German production would have to be stimulated to do better than it was doing in 1946. However, the British shared the French fears with respect to American softness toward Germany's old industrialists. The British Labour government encouraged the Social Democrats and made plans to nationalize the Ruhr industries and some other industries in the British zone.

In the American zone, administration was gradually transferred to German officials, first on the local, then on the land (state) level. Literally thousands of Americans—military personnel and civilians—participated in democratization programs. The Americans minimized economic controls and encouraged free-enterprise policies. They got on best with the Catholic parties, the remnants of the old Center party and the rising Christian Democratic party. During 1946 official American long-range policy for all Germany was declared to be re-examination of the Oder-Neisse line, retention by Germany of the Rhineland and the Ruhr, sympathy for French aspirations in the Saar, eventual political unification of Germany as a decentralized federal state under a democratic constitution, economic unity for Germany as contemplated at Potsdam, and revision upward of the levels of economic production.

To the charges that American policy in Germany was soft, the Americans replied with a draft treaty on the disarmament and demilitarization of Germany in which the United States promised to share responsibilty for Germany's future up to twenty-five years (and even forty years if the other powers wished) and to join the other powers in limiting Germany's war potential and in maintaining inspection teams to enforce these limitations. This indeed—a definite commitment to remain in Europe for a generation—would have been a revolutionary step in American foreign policy, but both the Russians and the French were cold to the plan. The Russians apparently hoped that within a few years the Americans would withdraw from Europe. The French hoped for something more—a mutual assistance pact—and were skeptical of any paper arrangement that posed as a substitute for the permanent maiming of Germany economically and for the actual redistribution of industrial power in Europe.

Failure to agree on implementing the Potsdam decisions giving

Germany economic unity was made clear at the Moscow conference in the spring of 1947. This conference marked the parting of the ways. Anticipating failure, the Americans and British had agreed earlier (January 1947) to an economic merger of their zones. This agreement involved pooling resources, allocating supplies according to need, common food rations, and a common export-import program. From time to time additional activities were included. Attempts were made to draw the French into the arrangements and convert bizonia into trizonia. However, it was not until the spring of 1948, at the time of the Marshall Plan and the dropping of the Communists from the French government, that the French agreed, and then it was not to trizonia but to the establishment of a provisional West German federal government including the French zone. In order to secure French cooperation the Americans and British consented to the Saar's incorporation into the French economy, larger coal allocations to France, and the establishment of an international authority (the United States, Britain, France, Germany, and the Benelux nations) to exercise some control over Ruhr industries, primarily to allocate coal and steel as between German consumption and export. Even so, the decision to establish a West German government and encourage German industrial recovery was unpopular in France.

The merger of the American and British zones in 1947 had momentous consequences. The British, under American pressure, jettisoned their plans to nationalize the Ruhr industries, and increasingly free-enterprise policies prevailed. Even more important, this merger indicated a willingness to recognize two Germanies and two Europes. However, the Western powers were cautious. At first they emphasized that the merger was merely economic and not political. Then after political merger took place they emphasized that the division of Germany was only temporary. Care had to be taken lest German national feeling be inflamed. The division of Germany, deplored by all Germans, was particularly galling to the Social Democrats, who accused their political opponents of acquiescing in a divided Germany in the hopes of coming to power in a predominantly conservative, Catholic West Germany.

For years both the United States and Russia would talk bravely of unifying Germany, but neither really meant it. Both still feared that the German problem had not been solved, that a reunited Germany would be dangerous to peace. (Nationalistic, racist, militarist, and authoritarian traditions persisted; many Germans resented not Hitler but Hitler's failure; by 1950 scores of neo-Nazi parties swarmed in the Western zone.) Although there were many neutralists in Germany, both powers feared that if they left Germany, the whole would fall to the other side, putting the balance of power in grave peril. The Russians preferred not to withdraw—perhaps in the state of Eastern European opinion they dared not withdraw—their enormous military salient from the center of Europe. As had so often happened in the past, Germany, in the heart of Europe, was split nationally and ideologically by the rival forces of the time. The powers would continue to write propaganda notes urging a united Germany, but each time their proposals would founder on the question of what constituted proper inspection of free elections.

1947: The Year of Decision

In the spring of 1947 the foreign policy of the United States decisively shifted direction. The organization of a Western zone in Germany independently of Russia acknowledged a split Europe. The far more dramatic enunciation of the Truman Doctrine with respect to Greece and Turkey proclaimed the policy of containing Communism. The latter was a revolutionary landmark in American policy, for the United States acknowledged a sphere of influence in the faraway Middle East where it had never had even the traditional though amorphous interest it had had in China; a sphere of influence, too, that was in no way connected with American responsibilities for liquidating affairs in the defeated countries.

In a somewhat shrill message to Congress in March 1947 Truman asked for 400 million dollars for military and economic aid to Greece and Turkey, the dispatch of military supplies, and the sending of civilian and military missions to supervise aid and to help train the Greek and Turkish armies. In the background was the Soviet threat to the Straits, and the EAM guerrilla war, aided by Communist Albania, Yugoslavia, and Bulgaria, against the Greek government. The eastern Mediterranean was considered of vital strategic importance. The situation was no more critical than it had been for months, but the new element was the decision of the over-extended British to withdraw from Greece. The crisis tone of the Truman message indicated that officials felt that the American people needed a jolt to arouse them to support so revolutionary a departure.

At first the reaction was one of shock. Liberals and leftists in Europe disliked the language, spirit, and arguments of the message. They felt it committed America to a crusade against Communism, to a twentieth-century neo-Metternich system. At home the Wallaceites thought it presaged war, the old isolationists were outraged, and many internationalists were indignant that the United Nations had been bypassed. Everywhere it was anxiously asked: "Does this mean opposition to Communism everywhere in the world and eventually a third world war?" American opinion rallied when it was made clear that the Americans were merely taking over in a limited area responsibilities that the British could no longer afford to carry. Friends of the United Nations were pacified when the Vandenberg Amendment promised that the aid program would cease whenever the United Nations itself decided that its own capacity to take effective action in this critical area made the continuance of American aid unnecessary. The bill passed both houses of Congress by large majorities. The bulk of the opposition came from Midwest Republicans, representing the persistence of isolationist sentiment.

In Europe, then, the acceptance of two worlds came in the spring of 1947. The turn in Asia came a year later: in Japan, with the fall of Katayama in February 1948 and the restoration to power of Japan's shopworn prewar politicians; in Korea, with the United Nations decision, likewise in February, to go ahead with elections in South Korea independently of the People's Republic in the North; and in China, when the Foreign Assistance Act of April 1948 officially committed the United States to Chiang's war against the Communists. The Cold War had arrived. Henceforth the chief energy of the United States in foreign affairs would be directed toward building the economic and military defenses of the "free world."

[5]

CONTAINMENT
AND COLD WAR

BEGINNING IN 1947 the United States entered on a foreign policy
of containment deliberately designed to check the expansion of
Communism. In its early years this policy involved bolstering
the economy of Western Europe, giving pledges of military
support to nations which seemed threatened by Communist aggression, building a series of military alliances, and in Korea
actually fighting a shooting war of considerable proportions.

Large-Scale Economic Aid to Europe: The Marshall Plan

In 1947 foreigners, on balance, owed the United States 11.3
billion dollars for goods and services. Most of the goods and
services were going to Europe, which desperately needed food,
feed, fertilizer, fuel, and modernized equipment. As the world
stood in 1947, much of these would have to continue to come
from the United States. But how could Europeans get dollars?
Their own production for export was down and the United
States would not need or take an equivalent in European goods
and services even if produced. (The United States, unlike Britain
when she was the creditor nation, was a large producer of both
raw materials and manufactured goods.) Private credit was not
available. Large government loans would complicate the dollar

gap and make Europeans dependent on the United States indefinitely. Increasingly it was felt that the American government should make European credits available in the United States, Canada, and elsewhere in the form of enormous grants and thus allow Europe to increase vastly its agricultural and industrial production within a short time, restore its intra-European trade, become big exporters again to all parts of the world, and within a few years "normalize" the international trading situation. Otherwise the crisis would drag on for decades. Such a program would insure American prosperity, and in the event Russia and Eastern Europe declined to participate it would strengthen the Western world to meet the continuing threat of Communist expansion.

Before such a grand scale of economic aid was voted for Europe, however, the United States insisted that the European countries produce a joint (and not a country-by-country) plan for European recovery and that the plan emphasize permanent economic cooperation among the participating countries themselves. Accordingly, European nations formed the Organization for European Economic Cooperation (OEEC) and presented a plan asking for around 22 billion dollars over a four-year period during which European countries, dovetailing their economies as never before, would strive to reach certain production goals in agriculture, fuel, power, transport, merchant fleets, and modernization of equipment. For instance, coal production was the important item in Britain, food in France and Italy. The United States government would furnish the credits in the form of grants, not loans. The United States would be the source of much of the goods and equipment and would furnish technicians and managerial assistance to help Europeans modernize their agricultural and industrial production. Europeans would create and maintain internal financial stability, plan national production goals on an intra-European basis, and begin work on permanent intra-European economic cooperation. Even before the Marshall Plan was voted by Congress, the three Benelux countries had organized a customs union, and other customs unions were being negotiated by the Scandinavian countries, by France and Italy, and by Greece and Turkey.

To begin with, the Marshall Plan offer was made to Russia and Eastern Europe as well as to Western Europe. Indeed, Western governments would not have accepted without the offer to

Russia, for Europeans did not want a split Europe, and the majority of West European peoples either felt friendly to Russia or feared to antagonize her. But Russia refused to join, and following her example the Eastern European countries (even Finland and Czechoslovakia, which were economically oriented to the West) also refused. The plan required the participating countries to furnish statistics as to their economic conditions and it allowed the United States to exercise some control over their internal budgets. The Russians found this intolerable for themselves and for their satellites. Moreover, such a plan would mean less Russian control in her own orbit, and the stabilizing of the European economy on a capitalist basis with the United States in a dominant position. Finally, the whole plan envisaged a restoration of the relatively free and multilateral trading pattern of the pre-1914 period, and the Russian system would have difficulty fitting itself into such a pattern.

As the Marshall Plan was taking shape, during the latter part of 1947 and the first part of 1948, the Russians met the challenge by further pushing the economic integration of their own orbit. Each of the Russian satellites had its own two-, three-, or five-year plan, and these were speeded up, which meant increased activity in reconstruction, land reform, mechanization of agriculture, nationalizing of industry. The extent of nationalization differed from country to country, as did the extent of direct Soviet participation. In some countries some industries were nationalized as joint enterprises, such as the Soviet-Hungarian and Soviet-Rumanian companies in banking, transportation, timber, and oil. Trade between the satellites and with Russia was encouraged, although trade with the West was not prohibited. Increased Communist activity in the East in response to the Marshall challenge resulted in the establishment of the Cominform in the fall of 1947, and the Communist coup in Czechoslovakia in February 1948. Communist seizure of power in Czechoslovakia made a deep impression on the West, for while it was known that the Communist party had been the first party in that country since 1946, it was also clear that Communists were far from being a majority.

However, the Russians may have pushed their satellites too importunately, for in the spring of 1948 came the dramatic and highly important break with Tito. Tito was excluded from the Cominform, and Yugoslavia took herself out of the Soviet orbit. The deviation of Yugoslavia may be explained by a number of factors. Yugoslavia did not border on Russia; it faced the Adriatic and the West and had open lines of communication with the outside. It did not feel the need of protection from Germany as Poland and Czechoslovakia did. Its leader was a great figure in his own right and had come to power largely without Russia's help. Land in Yugoslavia for the most part was not held by feudal landlords but by small-holding and individualistic peasants who would resent collectivization and too literal an application of Soviet methods to agriculture. Tito himself declared that Communism should be adapted to national needs, conditions, and cultures. The defection of Tito was a sensation; it showed that the Communist international front might be split and a more multiple balance of power established; it suggested that Mao in large and populous China might be no mere puppet of the Kremlin. The British Foreign Office was especially impressed by the possibilities of Titoism. Stalinist Communists feared the spread of Titoism, and the followers of Gomulka in Poland, Kostov and Petkov in Bulgaria, and Nagy in Hungary were closely watched.

On the whole European front the lines were drawn for a bitter fight over the Marshall Plan. Communists withdrew from the French and Italian governments and intensified their political war against non-Communists. A bitter campaign against America was launched and everywhere appeared the slogan "Marshall aid means martial aid." Serious strikes occurred in all parts of non-Soviet Europe. In Greece the government enacted an anti-strike law providing for the death penalty. The Marshall Plan split the French labor unions and a minority seceded from the Communist-dominated CGT to form Jouhaux's Force Ouvrière. Russia and the West clashed head on in Germany and Italy. In Germany the Russians showed their resentment over the Marshall Plan and over the West's rebuilding of West Germany by attempting to force the Western powers out of Berlin. The result was a blockade of West Berlin beginning in the spring of 1948, in which the Soviet military government refused to permit American and British supply trains to pass through the Soviet zone of Germany. (The subsequent successful American-British airlift relief during which American and British planes delivered 2,343,315 tons of food and coal to West Berlin caused the Russians to abandon the blockade in September 1949.) In Italy, the conflict reached a climax in the April 18, 1948 elections, in which the Communist–Nenni Socialist alliance bade fair to capture the country. On the eve of the election Russia came out for the return of Italy's colonies. The United States and Britain countered with the declaration that the Free Territory of Trieste would be returned to Italy. Equally persuasive, on April 3 President Truman signed the recently enacted Marshall Plan in time to influence the Italian election. De Gasperi's Christian Democrats won in a hard-fought contest.

The battle over the Marshall Plan and the contests which came out of it in late 1947 and early 1948 constituted the crucial postwar conflict for Western Europe. Communism in Western Europe was contained, and the Marshall Plan promised even better conditions designed to keep it in check.

At home the Republicans were divided over the European Recovery Program. Senator Taft faced both ways, and Senator Wherry led a fight against it. However, as the program increasingly appeared as a plan to check Communism, as well as a constructive measure to stabilize the world economy, conservatives and Republicans fell in behind the ERP. The Czechoslovak coup and the imminence of the Italian elections melted much of the opposition.

As finally approved, 4 billion dollars as a grant and 1 billion dollars as a loan were provided for European economic aid for a twelve-month period. The Economic Cooperation Administration was set up as an agency independent of the State Department to administer the program.

Among internationally-minded Americans there were some disappointments and misgivings: the cut from 22 billion dollars to 17 billion dollars as the total contemplated for the four years; the cut from 6.8 billion dollars for fifteen months to 5 billion dollars for twelve months; the fact that one-fifth of this was a loan and not a grant; the subsidy-to-American-agriculture feature which encouraged the ECA to get rid of domestic agricultural surpluses; the guarantee of the convertibility into dollars of private American investments in the participating countries; the requirement that the participating nations help furnish stockpiles of strategic materials for the United States; the provision that half of all ERP cargoes shipped from the United States be carried on American vessels (whose rates were higher than those of European carriers); the eligibility of Spain for inclusion in the program; the belief that West Germany was given a preferential place in the program (it was granted more than the OEEC recommended) and that General Clay was more interested in German recovery than in Germany's integration into the European economy.

The participating ERP countries, in the order of their inclusion in the program, were France, Ireland, Italy, Denmark, Austria, Belgium, Greece, the Netherlands, Iceland, Luxembourg, Norway, Sweden, Turkey, Britain, West Germany, Portugal, Trieste.

The Results of ERP in Action

The ERP worked mainly in four ways. First, the ECA operated as a financial agency providing government funds for the purchase of goods, most of which moved through private trade channels in the United States. Food, feed, fertilizer, and fuel for current consumption were the main items during the first months of the program; but later, raw materials and equipment for production took first place. Second, the ECA authorized "offshore" purchases in foreign countries, especially in Canada and Latin America. This saved scarce American materials, helped non-European countries, and prepared the way for the re-establishment of multilateral international trade. Third, each participating government was required to set up counterpart funds into which it paid in its own currency what it had received for the ERP goods when it sold them to its own people. (The ECA could draw on up to 5 per cent of these funds for administrative expenses and to help pay for strategic materials for the United States.) The participating government, with ECA approval, used these funds where they could best improve recovery and financial stability. In Italy counterpart funds were used mainly on public-works reconstruction programs, in France for debt retirement but mainly for capital investment, and in Britain for debt retirement to check inflation. Fourth, the ECA and the OEEC encouraged convertibility of currencies and intra-European trade, which was boosted by setting up the Intra-European Payments and Cooperation Agreements under which European creditor countries on a bilateral basis made grants of drawing rights to their European debtors and received matching dollar aid from the ECA. After 1950 an improved system was set up, the European Payments Union, which provided multilateral cancellation of trading debits and credits and made each country a net debtor or creditor of the whole group rather than of individual members. After the end of the year a creditor nation received ECA grants to close the trade gap.

The Marshall Plan was the chief way the American capitalist system made its impact felt in Europe. The ECA discouraged European exchange controls, import quotas, tariffs, cartels. American administrators of ECA and American businessmen, who went to Europe in the Marshall Plan years to advise European governments and businessmen, encouraged free and competitive capitalism and the streamlined methods of American business. Frequently they took an even more active part against socialist measures and Socialist parties than against cartels. Many were discouraged that they did not make a more permanent impression and complained of the radicalism of European labor, of the feudal mentality of European businessmen, and of the practice of doing away with one control and then substituting another, for instance, of doing away with an import quota and then getting the same results by a high tariff or an international cartel arrangement.

In 1947 the dollar gap had been more than 11 billion dollars, but in 1948 this had been narrowed to 6.3 billion dollars. In spite of the ECA goods going to Europe, our foreign exports had fallen almost 2 billion dollars and our imports had increased by nearly 1.5 billion dollars. Industrial production in the ERP countries was up 14 per cent, agricultural production up 20 per cent. Europe was importing less, exporting more, and "paying" for much of its imports by ERP grants. This meant cumulative gains for the next years. The funds applied by ECA the first year amounted to about 5 per cent of the national income of the participating countries as a group, but that 5 per cent produced a much greater gain than was proportionate, because it provided the scarce equipment which helped ease bottlenecks. In 1949 Congress authorized 4.28 billion dollars for another year of ERP.

However, the ERP was only one factor in increasing recovery. By the spring of 1950 Europe had had five years of peace and her economic bottlenecks were fewer. Germany, the industrial center of Europe, was beginning to recover. By the fall of 1948 the June 1949 production goals of ERP had already been met in West Germany. More than to anything else, recovery in Germany was due to re-establishing ordinary economic incentives by withdrawing the old depreciated currency and establishing a more stabilized one. (This drastic treatment of inflation, although a cruel blow to holders of the old currency, in the long run was probably preferable to prolonged and progressive deterioration of the currency such as occurred in France.)

It must be remembered that official figures of European recovery did not tell the whole story. Europe's population was higher than before the war, in some areas acute shortages persisted, inflation continued, and the gap between wages and prices was wide. The social reforms promised in the war years mostly failed to materialize, and in some countries the premature lifting of price, rent, and social controls caused distress. Even in 1953 the mass of Europeans still looked back to 1938, even to 1914, as better days. It was not until the late 1950's that the new European economic cooperation, the lowering and eliminating of intra-European tariff barriers, the curtailing of cartels, the new equipment, the new managerial and mass production-distribution techniques, and the recapture of world markets would combine to produce an unprecedented mass consumer prosperity in Europe.

Late 1949 and 1950 saw a steady narrowing of the dollar gap. Balance of payments seemed nearing an equilibrium. The first year of rearmament and the Korean crisis caused the United States to buy enormous stockpiles of strategic and scarce raw materials, much of this in the sterling area. But by 1951 the dollar gap was widening again. Rearmament had produced inflation and rising prices in the United States, American exports were more costly, and Europe was buying more goods for its own rearmament program and producing less of exportable goods. In 1951, the cost to Europe of its worsening terms of trade was estimated at 2 billion dollars a year. Congress was increasingly reluctant to give economic aid, and the emphasis shifted more each year to military aid and military-end items. (At the close of the fiscal year in

1953, foreign military aid for the year amounted to about 4.4 billion dollars and all other aid to almost 2.6 billion dollars. Western Europe and dependent areas received 3.5 billion dollars in military aid and 1.7 billion dollars for other assistance.) Meanwhile, the ERP had become the Mutual Defense Assistance Program and then the Mutual Security Program. The ECA had become the Mutual Security Agency. Even that portion appropriated for economic aid was called "defense support."

By 1952 Western European production increases were leveling. In that year the trend began in an opposite direction and for the first time since 1947 there was an over-all decline of West European industrial production. But increased industrial production was only part of the problem. Where would West Europe find markets for increased production? Experts were predicting that a huge dollar gap would become chronic. By the end of 1953 the dollar gap was running around 5 billion dollars a year. The cry arose, "Trade, not aid!" But there seemed little likelihood that the United States would further reduce its tariffs to any extent. William H. Draper, Jr., saw real danger of a "perhaps disastrous fissure between the economies of Europe and America." And Western Europeans were having difficulty recapturing old markets in East Europe and Asia.

The Drive to European Union

The OEEC represented the most ambitious intra-European cooperation yet undertaken, and it spurred action toward West European union. In 1947 Britain and France in the Treaty of Dunkirk had made a hard and fast military alliance. In 1948 Britain, France, and the three Benelux countries, in the Treaty of Brussels, formed the Western Union, pledged economic and cultural cooperation, and mutually bound one another automatically to come to the aid of any member that should be attacked in its European territory by any power. On May 5, 1949, in the Statute of London, ten nations set up the Council of Europe with its seat at Strasbourg: the three Scandinavian countries, the three Benelux countries, Britain, France, Italy, and Ireland. Later six others were added: West Germany, Iceland, Greece, Turkey, Austria, and Cyprus.

The purposes of the Council of Europe were to achieve the

benefits of greater economic, political, and cultural cooperation; to check Communism; to fit Germany with safety into the larger life of Europe; and to represent a third force in world affairs. Three organs were established: the Secretariat; the Committee of Ministers, consisting of the foreign or special minister of each member; and the Consultative Assembly, where representation was based roughly on population. The Consultative Assembly had wide scope for discussion, and since its delegates usually represented the *avant-garde* of European union, it often came in conflict with the more conservative Committee of Ministers. Delegates to the Assembly were drawn from the home parliaments, but the custom grew up of sending representatives of all the major domestic parties, and these were seated not in lumped national groups but alphabetically as individuals. For instance, during the second year's session Churchill sat between a Belgian and an Italian delegate and De Valera found himself seated between two British delegates. This practice was closer to a national parliament than to an international organization: national delegations split; political groups in one country made alliances with similar groups in other countries against dissimilar groups in their own country; De Valera, when out of office, often differed on the floor from his fellow Irish delegates, and Churchill debated a fellow British delegate, Hugh Dalton, and the two frequently voted on opposite sides of questions. (This, more than the formal arrangements, is the most likely way a body which begins as a collection of out-groups may become an in-group, a developing state. This was what made the American Constitution work: state delegations in Congress did not vote *en bloc* in relation to other delegations, but all delegations split, and groups in each delegation joined groups in other delegations against groups in their own delegations.) However, this was only a tendency, and delegates still lined up frequently in national blocs.

The Council of Europe operated as a clearinghouse of ideas. In the early 1950's the chief questions before the Assembly involved an examination of the various ways to attain more effective European cooperation. Should cooperation be intergovernmental, federal, or functional? The intergovernmentalists wanted to keep cooperation on a government-to-government basis as represented by the European Payments Union. The federalists wanted to build a federal state at once with wide supranational powers and with an assembly elected by popular suffrage. The functionalists wanted to create supranational activities in just one area at a time—a slow approach to federalism, project by project. (The Schuman Plan, the European Defense Community, and the proposed pools for agriculture, transport, and development of African colonies were examples of the functional approach.) The federalists were strong in the French and Italian delegations. The intergovernmentalists were strong in the Scandinavian and British delegations. In general, the Scandinavians feared too close a union with the rest of Europe. There were a number of reasons for this: their more or less isolationist tradition; their Protestantism as opposed to Catholic predominance in West Germany, Belgium, France, and Italy; their lack of a Communist problem at home; their standard of living, higher than that of the rest of the continent; their fear for their national economic and social controls. Britain took a predominantly intergovernmental and anti-federalist view for many of the same reasons. The Labour party was committed to nationalization, national planning, and national controls. Again, Britain had strong ties with Commonwealth countries and the sterling bloc, and these might be jeopardized by over-close continental commitments. Perhaps most important, the convertibility crisis of 1947, the devaluation crisis of 1949, and the trading crisis of 1951 underscored for the British that convertibility meant a rush for dollars and British bankruptcy, and that Britain, uniquely dependent upon foreign trade, would have to maintain as best it could freedom of action over any revaluation of its currency and over import and export controls.

Gradually a middle-of-the-road functionalist approach prevailed, and a compromise was worked out: it would not be necessary for all members of the Council of Europe to join a specific supranational authority set up to coordinate a single activity. Thus Britain could remain a member of the Council of Europe and yet not join the Schuman Plan, which both British Conservatives and Labourites opposed. (It was Conservative Harold Macmillan who said, "The British people will never hand over to a supranational authority the right to close British pits and steelworks.") However, the federalists did not give up working to create a general West European Assembly based on popular election.

The first notable triumph of the project-to-project approach was the Schuman Plan, or European Coal and Steel Community, in which six nations—France, West Germany, Italy, and the three Benelux countries (Belgium, the Netherlands, and Luxembourg)—sought to create a common market for coal, iron, and steel, a supranational community within which capital, goods, labor, and transportation involving these products would move freely across national boundaries. Lorraine iron ore would be obtainable in Germany and other participating countries at the same price as in France; Ruhr coal would be obtainable in France and other participating countries at the same price as in Germany; steel would be available to users in all participating countries at the same price. This would be accomplished by eliminating within the Community the customs duties, quotas, export and import licenses, discriminating freight rates, price differentials, and restrictive cartel agreements with respect to coal, iron, steel, and iron and steel products. Labor, too, would become more mobile. Armed with his labor card and his Community passport, the coal miner and steel worker would move easily across national boundaries, and the Community would help pay his transportation and resettlement expenses. The Community would also act as a new social agency in the coal and steel industry with control over its housing, health, and other welfare measures.

The executive body of the Community was the High Authority, whose nine representatives—two each from France, West Germany, and Italy, and one each from the Benelux countries—were to be chosen by the respective national governments. However, once elected, the Authority was made independent of the national governments; it was given the power to finance itself through a Community tax imposed directly on coal and steel enterprises. Moreover, it could inspect the books of coal, iron, and steel companies for business infractions and incorrect tax payments. The High Authority was flanked by a Council of Ministers, chosen by the respective governments of the member states of the Community, designed to balance the supranational arrangements with national restraints. On most questions the Council of Ministers had only to be consulted before the High Authority took action, but on some questions its approval was required before executive action became binding. The Authority was made accountable to the Common Assembly, whose members were chosen by the parliaments of the member states. (Often the same people who were members of the Common Assembly were also members of the Consultative Assembly of the Council of Europe.) The Assembly, through its plenary sessions and its standing committees, was continuously to review the work of the Authority. By a two-thirds vote it could oust the members of the High Authority and thus compel a change of executive personnel and policy. From the start the Assembly operated as a genuine supranational body, and its members did not vote in national blocs but as individuals on the basis of the right, left, and center in European politics. There was also a Consultative Committee to represent management, labor, and consumer groups. Finally, there was a Court of Justice to interpret the treaty establishing the Community and whose judgments, which superseded those of the national courts of the member states, were binding on individuals, business firms, labor unions, the national governments, the High Authority, and other organs of the Community.

The Community became a reality in August 1952 with its "capital" in the city of Luxembourg. Jean Monnet, who had done much of its planning, became President of the High Authority. Paul-Henri Spaak, a prominent Socialist politician of Belgium, became President of the Assembly. By mid-1954 nearly all customs duties on coal, iron, and steel had been abolished, double-pricing had been discarded, many discriminatory freight rates had been eliminated, a vigorous anti-cartel program was under way, about 40 per cent more coal and steel was being shipped across national boundaries, a genuine Community transportation system was in the making, and soon the Community's EUROP freight cars were moving freely across national frontiers. The Community was hailed as a triumph for the functional approach, and Robert Schuman, the French Foreign Minister for whom the Plan was named, declared: "Europe will not be built in one stroke, nor as one finished edifice. It will be built by means of concrete achievements, which provide a practical basis for solidarity."

However, the economic gains expected to come from the ECSC and its use as the basis of a future political unification of Europe were not the only considerations in the minds of the statesmen who had formulated the Community. National considerations, immediate and long run, also played a part. For West Germany, membership in the Community meant ending her isolation and achieving equal status with her former enemies; it was a step toward recovering her sovereignty and inclusion in the West's political and military alliances. Despite the prominence of French statesmen in establishing the Community, many Frenchmen were still reluctant to cooperate with the Germans. Would not the Community help the Germans, with their larger population and their great industrial and technical skills, to forge ahead of the French, and would not the Community come ultimately to be "dominated" by the Germans? But pro-Community French leaders argued that once France, which possessed Europe's largest iron deposits, got equal access to Ruhr coal French industry would hum; and that instead of Germany dominating the Community, the other five nations would find in the ECSC an instrument for integrating Germany's heavy industries into the general European economy, that the German economy would be so interwoven with the European that any future war between Germany and France would become not only unthinkable but impossible.

Gradually more and more Frenchmen took this view and they came to see additional advantages in a functional integration of Western Europe: increasing continental (and French) influence in the counsels of the Western powers, and decreasing continental (and French) dependence on the "Anglo-Saxons," toward whom the French had ambivalent feelings (they particularly resented the fact that British influence carried so much more weight in Washington than the French); creating a "third force" in world affairs; providing a hedge against the day Americans might "abandon" Europe and retreat into isolation (this was an obsession with some Frenchmen, among them Charles de Gaulle, at the time out of politics); enhancing Western Europe's economic prosperity and thereby weakening the appeal of Communism in France and Italy and providing a stronger barrier against the Soviet Union; enlarging the opportunities of the French colonies, particularly the African ones (the French would attempt to work their African colonies into the future Common Market); and winning compensation for additional losses of French colonies by extensifying markets in Europe.

Indeed, the ECSC proved to be the beginning of a general *rapprochement* between France and Germany which developed through the following years. During the late 1950's a diplomatic revolution would occur, the traditional French-British cooperation in international politics would give way to a new French-German cooperation, and the Paris-Bonn axis would become an important reality in European affairs. However, before this would be achieved there would be many doubts, hesitations, backslidings, French-German crises, and much more experience with the ECSC and other European supranational organizations in which Germans and Frenchmen cooperated.

The immediate effect of the ECSC was to suggest to some French leaders a similar device to lessen the dangers of German rearmament—a supranational authority in European defense matters, the European Defense Community, to be linked to the North Atlantic Treaty Organization. We have carried the story of the growing economic integration of Western Europe through 1954. In large part the movement to West European union came originally out of the cooperation demanded by the OEEC which in turn came out of the Marshall Plan. We must now go back to the year 1948, for that same year which saw the birth of the Marshall Plan also saw the birth of the North Atlantic Treaty Organization.

The North Atlantic Treaty Organization

In the spring of 1948, while tensions caused by the hostile Communist reaction to the Marshall Plan, the Communist coup in Czechoslovakia, and the Soviet blockade of West Berlin were at their height, President Truman called for American rearmament. Americans were asking: "Is ERP enough? Are we about to restore German and European industry only to see it fall into the hands of the Russians? To what extent should we provide arms for Western Europe? Should we give West Europe a guarantee of American armed intervention in the event of a Russian attack?" It was generally agreed that only large grants and something like Lend-Lease would provide West Europe with sufficient arms to withstand attack. In June the United States Senate in the Vandenberg Resolution went on record as favoring association of the United States with regional and other collective arrangements based on continuous and effective self-help. This was regarded as an invitation to a North Atlantic alliance.

Russian military power was indeed impressive, and had the Russians chosen to attack in Europe they would have met with only token resistance. All that would have opposed a Russian advance in the West were half a dozen American, British, and French divisions in Germany. On the other hand, the Russians alone were believed to have from 175 to 200 divisions and their satellites from 60 to 70 divisions. A "people's police" was believed to be training some 50,000 East Germans. The Americans had a vast superiority in atomic weapons, even after the Russians exploded an atom bomb in 1949, but American military planning had not yet been adjusted to the nuclear revolution in war, for many good reasons Americans recoiled from putting their chief reliance on atomic weapons, and it was doubtful if atomic weapons alone could win a war should Russia overrun Europe.

North Atlantic pact negotiations continued from July 1948 to the final signing in April 1949. The treaty contemplated the maximum of defense exertions on the part of each member, aid and supplies from the United States, joint service commands, and a permanent organization which ultimately involved a North Atlantic Council, a Secretary-General, an International Staff, a Military Committee consisting of the chiefs of staff of NATO members, and various regional planning groups. The twelve parties to the treaty were: the United States, Canada, Britain, France, Italy, the three Benelux countries, Iceland, Norway, Denmark, and semi-Fascist Portugal. Later Greece and Turkey were admitted. The adherence of West Germany at this time was out of the question. Sweden and Switzerland preferred to maintain their traditional neutral positions. Ireland, claiming that she could not honestly participate in Western defense as long as Ulster was a part of the United Kingdom, refused to join. Franco's Spain, said to have twenty-two divisions, could not be admitted for ideological reasons, but a series of bilateral economic and military agreements between that country and the United States ultimately brought Spain into the Atlantic system. Yugoslavia, too, with about thirty divisions, was excluded for ideological reasons and because of the Trieste conflict with Italy. However, Yugoslavia likewise came in through the back door by a series of agreements between Tito and the United States, between Tito and Britain, and between Tito and France—all of them tentative.

There still was a dangerous flank in the Middle East, where Russia by making a thrust to Suez might cut the West's communication with the East and seize the Middle Eastern oil fields upon which Europe depended. Nevertheless, the Arab states refused to associate themselves in a Middle Eastern command when this was later proposed. These states refused to think of themselves as committed to the West; they were interested in freeing themselves from "Western imperialism" and in modernizing their agriculture and industry. Egypt was concerned with getting the British out of Suez and the Sudan. The Arab countries keenly resented the part played by the United States in establishing a Jewish state in Israel.

The rearmament program and NATO did not go unchallenged. The Russians told the world that the alliance was aggressive, was aimed at rearming Germany and starting a third world war, and would bring atomic bases to the very doorstep of the Soviet Union. Non-Communist leftist groups in Western Europe, notably the Bevanite wing of the British Labour party, claimed that the rearmament program was the result of a superficial analysis of the international situation; that the world was not immediately endangered by Russia; that the Russians were still too weak from the wounds inflicted by the late war to start another; that the peoples of both Eastern and Western Europe were primarily concerned with recuperation; and that by putting first emphasis on arms the Americans (who had come out of the war unscathed, had not seen a bomb dropped on their homeland, and had more productive power than before the war) would exacerbate tensions and divert the West from long-time basic reforms which alone could win the ultimate victory over Communism. The Bevanites claimed that the surest way to check Communism was for the West to finance a huge capital development fund for use in the underdeveloped countries. The Bevanites had wide support among non-Communist leftist and neutralist groups in Europe.

Even among many Europeans convinced that the West was in great danger from Soviet aggression there were misgivings. Would not a Western power-politics alliance and rearmament split Europe irrevocably into East and West? Would it not invite the very attack it feared? Could the European economies, barely recovering from the late war, survive a formidable rearmament program? Did the Americans understand that even modest rearmament in West Europe would involve grave personal hardships for Europeans? The average yearly income in the United States was around $1800, but the average yearly income in West Europe was only around $600. (And the gap between wages and prices was wide in most continental countries.) The Americans could divert from 15 to 20 per cent of their national income to rearmament and still the average American would live well; he would merely forgo some luxuries. But for Western Europe any substantial diversion of national income to rearmament meant that the people would have less food, less clothing, and less housing— and they already had little enough. Finally, many friends of the United Nations asked anxiously if NATO really squared with the letter and spirit of the United Nations Charter, in spite of the invoking of Articles 51 and 52 in defense of the alliance's legality.

Just how far did the United States commit itself to sending its own armed forces to Europe in the event of an attack on any of the NATO members? After all, only Congress could declare war, and the sensibilities of the Senate had to be considered. The formula agreed upon was something short of an actual pledge of direct military assistance; yet for the United States it constituted a revolution in foreign policy. The United States promised "to assist the Party or Parties so attacked by taking forthwith, individually and in concert with the other Parties, such action as it deems necessary, including the use of armed force, to restore and maintain the security of the North Atlantic area." This satisfied for the time being, because the United States had troops in Germany, Austria, and Trieste; but European fears were not allayed. These fears were seriously aroused when the United States Senate in April 1951 approved the administration's plan to send four additional divisions of ground forces to Western Europe but specifically resolved that no more be sent without further Congressional approval. This was a victory for the Taft-Wherry view, and it served notice to the world that the Senate disputed the administration position that no Congressional authorization was required to send reinforcements to Europe. Many Europeans asked anxiously: "Will the United States leave us in the lurch after having encouraged NATO and induced us to rearm?" A fundamental conflict of views developed: the Americans wanted the Germans to bear a large part of European defense, but this could not be done without large German rearmament, which alarmed Europeans, particularly the French. As the years passed it became clear that the Europeans would be satisfied with nothing less than assurances that large American ground forces would be kept in Europe as protection from both the Russians and the Germans, but the Americans were unwilling (and perhaps unable under their Constitution) to give these assurances. Every subsequent crisis in NATO and the European Defense Community went back to this fundamental cleavage.

The United States pressed its allies hard, especially after the beginning of the Korean War. In 1950 Britain raised its conscription period to two years, announced plans for spending 4.7 billion pounds within three years, and planned to form three new divisions at once. At about the same time France announced plans to re-equip and modernize five standing army divisions and to raise fifteen completely new divisions. The Americans suggested that the Germans supply ten divisions. In 1951 NATO set as its goal armed forces of 1.29 million men in Europe by the end of 1953. By the end of 1951 the actual strength of NATO was augmented with the arrival in Germany of four additional American divisions and two additional British divisions.

However, the United States did not keep to its own rearmament timetable. In September 1951 the Administration modified the pace of the program in order to lessen the strain on the national economy, and by the fall of 1952 the value of military-aid shipments to West Europe since the beginning of the rearmament program in 1949 totaled only around 2.6 billion dollars out of the 11 billion dollars which had been allocated to the Defense Department. Congress continued to cut "defense support" (economic aid). In late 1951 Churchill slowed the British program, and the French had only three modernized divisions. The French attributed their serious lag to the Indochina War and inflationary pressures at home.

The Peace Contract with Germany and the Problem of German Rearmament

Increasingly the United States looked to Germany to bolster the military strength of the NATO world. But other Europeans resisted, especially the French. And the Germans themselves had yet to be convinced. The Germans were war-weary. With more than a touch of malice they recalled that they had already fought a war against Soviet Communism; why should they have to do it again? They taunted the West for disarming them and dismantling their factories. The Social Democrats feared a restoration of the old militarism. The neo-Nazis demanded an independent German army if Germans were going to be called upon to fight. Who would protect Germany in the interval before effective rearmament? Was the German homeland to bear the brunt of another war with the East? A defense on the Rhine would do Germany no good, and were the Allies ready for even that? Would not an alliance with the West result in a permanent partition of Germany? However, the fear of Russia was very real in Germany, and perhaps an alliance with the West would lead eventually to winning back not only East Germany but also the lost provinces in Poland and East Prussia. Anyway, many Germans were receptive, provided they were granted equal rights with the other Western nations. Increasingly the Germans used rearmament as a *quid pro quo* for the restoration of their economy and their sovereignty. The revival of Germany came first, the defense against the Russians was secondary.

More and more concessions were made to the Germans. In June 1948 the promise of a constituent assembly had been made and the French were mollified by the promise of an International Ruhr Authority. In April 1949, about the time that the NATO treaty was signed, it was announced that 159 of the 381 German factories marked for dismantling and relocation outside Germany would be left in Germany, but that the manufacture of certain products useful in war would continue to be prohibited or strictly limited. It was also announced that the International Ruhr Authority would be set up at the same time the provisional German government was established. In May the Bonn assembly adopted a federal constitution for West Germany and the three Western zones were fused under the new government, but the Allies, under the terms of an occupation statute, retained control over foreign affairs, foreign trade and exchange, Ruhr industries through the Ruhr Authority, the level of industry, reparations, disarmament and demilitarization, and protection of the occupation forces. The American government cooperated closely with Adenauer's Christian Democratic government and during 1950 and 1951 pressed on Britain and France additional concessions to Germany: the establishment of a German ministry of foreign affairs, the lifting of many restrictions on shipbuilding and steel, and various steps toward termination of the occupation and restoration of German sovereignty. The Americans were particularly eager for German rearmament and for ten divisions under German commanders working under the auspices of NATO. As in Japan, the Americans were now less and less interested in punishing and reforming their former enemies, more and more interested in securing them as effective allies against the Communists.

The French had repeatedly retreated from their various proposals to curb Germany, but they were determined to mitigate as best they could the dangers of German rearmament. The Schuman Plan and the functional approach to European federation suggested the idea of a European defense community in which German military units would be so distributed within a multinational army as to make them incapable of operating as a separate force. French proposals for a European defense community were embodied in the so-called Pleven Plan which contemplated a supranational European defense ministry to administer a multinational European army. The basic military units would be small teams of around 3000 men each, and the teams of several nations would be grouped into divisions.

Both the NATO authorities and the Germans were cool to the Pleven Plan. They feared that a polyglot army composed of such small fighting units would be ineffective. NATO authorities, with American approval, tentatively decided on a German army of twelve divisions, nine infantry, and three armored. Each would have a peacetime strength of 15,000 men and a wartime strength of 18,000. This is what the Germans had asked for. However, events in Germany in the spring of 1951 gave Americans pause. Neo-Nazi parties were proliferating and made impressive showings in the German elections. The Germans were grumbling over the costs of the occupation. The Bonn government itself took a high tone and declared that Germany had unsatisfied territorial claims not only to the lost eastern provinces but to the Saar and to certain frontier areas in Belgium and the Netherlands! Meantime France went ahead with her plan for a European defense community, and representatives of France, West Germany, Italy, Belgium, and Luxembourg began discussions. France let it be known she would agree to 6000-man teams with three teams to a division and with no division embracing more than two teams of the same nationality.

The climax of the postwar settlement in the West appeared to come with the European Defense Community Treaty and the Peace Contract with the Federal Republic of Germany, both signed the same week in May 1952.

The EDC consisted of West Germany, France, Italy, and the three Benelux countries. Any armed aggression against a member state would be considered an attack on all the member states and resisted by them. European defense forces would take the place of national forces, which were strictly limited. The European defense forces would consist of contingents placed at the disposal of the EDC by the member states. Recruitment would be largely a matter for the individual countries. The basic national unit would be the equivalent of an infantry division and would have a strength varying from 13,000 to 15,600 men. (Armored units would be smaller, air units smaller still.) Basic units from different nationalities would be combined into army corps. Integration not at the division level (of the once-proposed combat teams) but at the higher corps level was a victory for the United States and Germany and a defeat for France. The command and general staff would also be integrated from different nationalities. (The supreme command would be in NATO.) A common training, organization, equipment, and uniform would be provided. Bases and training camps would be held in common on an "infrastructure" basis. It was hoped that a Community land force of forty-three divisions would be available by the end of 1953.

The Peace Contract with West Germany restored the territory's sovereignty with some limitations. The Allied powers reserved the right to station forces in Germany to protect the West, to maintain their special position in Berlin, and in the event of a threat to stability which the Republic or EDC could not handle, to proclaim a state of emergency and restore order. The Allies also reserved for future determination the question of German unity and of Germany's permanent frontiers. As a share toward national defense the Federal Republic promised to make a yearly contribution to EDC and to the support of Allied forces in Germany. The Allies virtually gave up all reparations and all control over German industry. Control of coal and steel would end with ratification of the ECSC. Hereafter the West German government would be free to nullify most of the reforms undertaken by the Allies up to that time. The Contract did not even attempt to control Germany's war potential or her armaments. However, in order not to appear to discriminate against Germany, these matters were covered in the EDC treaty, and all defense production was placed under the authority of the EDC itself with the definite understanding that the Community would not allow the production of chemical, biological, or atomic weapons, long-range missiles, military aircraft, or heavy warships in "strategically exposed" areas. Chancellor Adenauer declared Germany to be an area to which these prohibitions applied. The Peace Contract was not to come into effect until the EDC treaty was ratified and went into force. By the end of 1953 only Germany had fully ratified EDC.

During 1952 and 1953 Adenauer's position in Germany improved. His government benefited in public opinion by German economic revival. Growing opposition in East Germany to the Russian occupation impressed the West Germans and made them friendlier to the Western orientation. Neutralism declined. The neo-Nazi groups moved closer to Adenauer as they increasingly felt that the way to win East Germany and the lost provinces in East Prussia and Poland was by an alliance with the West. The Social Democrats continued hostile to EDC, were alarmed at the threat of a militaristic revival in Germany and of a restoration to power of the old military clique, feared both a permanent partition of Germany and an attempt to win back the East by force, and pointed to the growing influence of the old industrialists, the wide gap between wages and prices, the social distress produced by a free-enterprise economy, the tax policies which favored business over social welfare, the boldness of certain interests in demanding sale to private enterprise of industries long nationalized, the moves to sow dissension between Catholic and Protestant wage earners, and the revival of guild and cartel practices. However, the popularity of Adenauer resulted in German ratification of EDC.

In France the trend was the other way. De Gaullists denounced EDC as a scandalous plan to liquidate the French army and to give Germany and Italy control over French internal affairs. Leftists feared a neo-Nazi revival in Germany. Most Frenchmen feared German rearmament and doubted whether EDC would be a sufficient curb on the Germans. Frenchmen wanted further exploration of East-West relations by negotiation, and especially a more definite promise of adequate American military forces in Europe to check both Russia and Germany. Ratification dragged in France, and it was apparent that even if it were won by a narrow victory the French would be in little condition for effective participation. The French seemed to be playing for time. When they opposed the rearming of Germany within NATO they emphasized the danger of an independent German army; now in opposing EDC they emphasized the danger of liquidating the French army.

NATO was subjected to its gravest crisis when on August 30, 1954, the French Assembly refused to ratify EDC. In the French Assembly, the extreme left and the extreme right, the Communists and the Gaullist nationalists, united to defeat this project. Except for MRP, which favored ratification, the other French parties were split about evenly over the question. The feelings of the French were summarized by Édouard Herriot, the "Grand Old Man" of French politics, when he asserted that West Germany would be able to leave EDC when East and West Germany were reunited, and then France, without her own army, would be left in the lurch.

The EDC failed for three reasons, and the United States, in its haste to rearm the Germans, had minimized all three. First, it over-emphasized the degree of supranationalism for which the West Europeans were prepared. By that time the French were willing to experiment with a project in economic supranationalism with the Germans (ECSC), but they were not willing to do so in military matters, even though it was some of their own leaders who had initiated EDC. Second, EDC envisaged the power structure in terms of an unprecedented French-German cooperation in international affairs in place of the traditional French-British cooperation. Much more experience in ECSC and other supranational economic communities would be required before the traditional French-British partnership in international affairs would give way to a French-German partnership. Third, EDC took no account of the effect on the military arrangements should Germany be reunited, an eventuality which at that time appeared more likely than it would later. The substitute arrangements adopted to take the place of the EDC covered the first two difficulties.

The collapse of the EDC caused consternation in the West. What formula, what way, could be devised to make the rearming of West Germany acceptable to France? At the height of the crisis, Britain came forward with a definite continental commitment the like of which it had never made before in its long history of active participation in world politics. Britain promised to keep certain contingents of British forces (four divisions and a tactical air force) on the Continent as long as its allies in Western Europe wanted them. Britain definitely committed itself in advance to the defense of the Continent. This was a commitment more definite and far-reaching than Britain's NATO commitment. It was one that the leader of the West, the United States, was not willing or able under its constitutional processes to make. This British pledge was what France had been looking for. It committed Britain not only to the defense of Western Europe against Russia, but also—and more important to many Frenchmen and Belgians —to the defense of Western Europe against a rearmed Germany, the very Germany the West was rearming, the very Germany which was about to be taken into full alliance.

Britain made its historic commitment on October 3, and on October 23 the Paris pact was announced. According to the terms of this pact, the Federal Republic of Germany (West Germany) was to get full sovereignty, except for such forces as the United States, Britain, and France, with German consent, elected to keep in Germany to guard the peace. (Britain was committed by the pledge of October 3 to keep troops there if its Western European allies wanted them; but the United States, except for the vague terms of NATO, was not nearly so committed to keep troops there.) These nations would also continue to occupy West Berlin until the unification of Germany. The Brussels Treaty Organization was to be expanded into the Western European Union, with Germany and Italy joining the original members, Britain,

France, and the Benelux countries. The original Western Union of the Brussels Treaty (1948) had been an organization of very little scope, but the expanded Western European Union was to have important powers. It was only with the consent of a majority of the member nations of the WEU that Britain, according to its pledge, could withdraw its troops from the Continent or diminish their strength below that originally agreed upon. West Germany was to contribute to NATO through WEU a maximum of twelve divisions and France fourteen, as previously provided by EDC. German rearmament was to be limited to these twelve divisions. Military contributions to NATO by members of WEU could not be increased over the original maximums without the unanimous consent of members of the Union. (This was a device to keep a curb on German rearmament.) West Germany was to be admitted to NATO, and German armies, like the armies of other NATO members, would be under the Supreme Allied Commander of the European division of NATO (SACEUR). The authority of SACEUR to move and base forces, standardize and integrate these, and coordinate logistics was increased. (Again, this was a device to tighten the hold of NATO over the German divisions, to keep German armies under restraint.) However, nothing comparable to the EDC "scrambling" of armies was possible under the new arrangements. West Germany was not to manufacture atomic, biological, chemical, or related weapons. This was to be enforced through WEU. West Germany was not to make guided missiles without the approval of WEU and NATO. West Germany promised never to use force to get German reunification or modification of present boundaries.

At the time the Paris accords and protocols were concluded, the United States, Britain, and France made a public declaration setting forth (1) that they recognized West Germany as the only German government freely and legitimately constituted and entitled to speak for the German people in international affairs; (2) that an attack on West Berlin while under Allied protection would be an attack on all three powers; (3) that German unification must be achieved by peaceful means and final determination of German boundaries must await the permanent peace settlement.

These complicated arrangements of September and October 1954 restoring West Germany to sovereignty, admitting her to

NATO, and establishing an effective WEU were among the most curious in history. Their main purpose was to strengthen the West against Russia by providing a way for West Germany to rearm and join NATO. But at the same time they sought to restrain this new ally through WEU, which not only bound Britain more closely to the Continent as a check on Germany, but also contained ingenious institutional devices for curbing Germany.

Rounding Out the Military Alliances in Europe and the Middle East

During 1953 and 1954, the United States strengthened its military position in southeastern Europe. An agreement was reached with Greece which provided for the joint American-Greek development and use of certain airfields and naval facilities in that country in accordance "with approved NATO plans." In August 1954 a Balkan alliance of Turkey, Greece, and Yugoslavia was completed. An armed aggression against one or more of the parties was to be regarded as an aggression against all three and all parties were to provide assistance "individually or collectively." Although it was stated that the rights and obligations of Greece and Turkey under NATO were in no way affected, it was difficult to see how NATO could avoid involvement if Yugoslavia were attacked and Greece and Turkey went to its assistance. Yugoslavia, on the other hand, was under no obligation to do more than consult its allies in case some other NATO country was attacked. However, Yugoslavia was thus brought closer to NATO, and American aid to Yugoslavia was increased.

In addition, Italy and Yugoslavia developed better relations as a result of the settlement, at long last, of the thorny Trieste dispute. In October 1954 the United States, Britain, Italy, and Yugoslavia agreed that, except for a minor territorial adjustment favorable to Yugoslavia, Italy was to have Zone A, Yugoslavia Zone B, and the Anglo-American military forces were to be withdrawn. Italy promised to maintain Trieste as a free port, and both Italy and Yugoslavia promised to respect ethnic minorities. Thus, by late 1954, from Norway through Turkey an unbroken Western defense barrier had been set up, with Yugoslavia, however, its weakest link.

The United States also sponsored formation of the Baghdad pact by Britain, Turkey, Iran, Iraq, and Pakistan. The process of linking this chain covered two years of diplomatic activities, but the final link was forged in February 1955 with the agreement between Turkey and Iraq. The five nations set up the Middle Eastern Treaty Organization, and the United States increased military aid to Turkey and channeled military aid to Iran and Pakistan while Britain increased military aid to Iraq. Thus by early 1955 multilateral military alliances defended most of the northern tier countries of the Middle East from (and including) Turkey to the borders of India. (Afghanistan was the exception.) In April 1956 the United States joined the Baghdad pact in all but name, establishing military and economic liaisons with METO and agreeing to pay a share of the expenses of the permanent secretariat.

It was doubtful if much was gained by the Baghdad pact, and a high price was certainly paid for it. Turkey, a traditionally able military nation, was already an ally in NATO. Pakistan was an ally in the South East Asia Treaty Organization. A bilateral military agreement had existed between the United States and Iran since 1947. The inclusion of Iraq in METO produced hostile feelings among the Arabs. Iraq's fellow members in the Arab League keenly resented her "apostasy," even though the Iraq government insisted there was no incompatibility in belonging to both METO and the Arab League, and even though METO repeatedly assured the Arab League that METO was not aimed at the Arabs. Throughout the Arab world, Iraq's joining METO was viewed as additional evidence that her Hashimite dynasty was a puppet of Britain. Anti-imperialist (but non-Communist) nationalists who wanted to overthrow existing governments in the Middle East regarded the Baghdad pact as an instrument of the *status quo* to be used against "internal subversion." They were convinced that METO was designed primarily to prevent national revolutions and change. Indeed, the Baghdad pact contributed notably to the tensions in the Arab world which were to lead to the acute Middle Eastern crises of 1956 and 1958, to be discussed later. Finally, India vehemently protested military aid to Pakistan as an intrusion of Western military alliances into the very heart of Asia and as likely to strengthen Pakistan in its controversy with India over Kashmir.

Somewhat on the sidelines, the United States in September 1953 concluded a bilateral agreement with Spain in which the United

States was to construct or modernize certain airfields and naval facilities in that country, in return for which Spain would receive large American economic and military assistance grants each year. All such facilities were to be open to joint use by both Spanish and American forces, but would remain under Spanish flag and command. America's European allies did not like this arrangement. They disliked Franco's fascism and anything which increased Franco's power. Britain feared the growth of Spanish prestige would engender Spanish demands for the return of Gibraltar. But mostly it was feared that this arrangement portended a "new look" in America's military strategy, a growing emphasis on American air and naval power and nuclear weapons as an alternative to the dependence on localized ground forces which loomed so large in the defense planning of Western Europe proper. America's allies feared American aggressiveness, but they feared much more any indication of an American retreat to a defense perimeter which would include the periphery but not the heart of Europe.

Problems of Security in the Far East

In Asia the trend was less reassuring to Americans than in Europe. The Communists had captured China in 1949 and Chiang's government had fled to Formosa. Britain and many European and Asian governments recognized the Red regime. The United States refused. Americans professed to see in the victory of Mao an extension of Soviet Communism, and they feared admission of Red China to the United Nations would strengthen the Communist bloc and give Russia an ally on the Security Council. Americans increasingly demanded measures to check Communism in Asia. What was the good of checking Communism in Europe and letting it expand in Asia, they asked. The Truman administration argued that nothing short of an American army in China could have checked Mao and that no leading Americans had gone so far as to propose such large-scale intervention; that the middle way had been wanting in popular support in China; that it was more important to cope immediately with the threat in Europe than with that in Asia, for West Europe was an area of modern technology, heavy industry, mechanized agriculture, scientists, technicians, and skilled workers, but that it would take a generation to develop such war potentials in Asia. The Republicans were not committed to a bipartisan approach in Asia and they made the most of the administration's weakness there. There was even a disposition on the part of right-wing Republicans and nationalist extremists to blame the fall of China on Communists and spies in the American State Department! An organized campaign of vilification was directed against Secretary of State Dean Acheson. The American public seemed more and more impressed.

While many Americans thought that the administration was not anti-Communist enough in Asia, many in Britain, India, and other Commonwealth countries felt that it was too anti-Communist. The latter favored both the recognition of Mao and admission of Red China to the United Nations. They pointed out that the Red government was the government in fact. They intimated that it was an improvement over Chiang's government and a clearer expression of Chinese opinion. A middle way would have been preferable, but such a way had no adequate support in China. Why should Western threats literally force the Reds into the arms of Russia? Would it not be better to encourage them to follow an independent course in international relations, for were they not nationalists as well as Communists and would they not eventually resent the Russian position in Manchuria and the Liaotung peninsula? Besides, the masses of Asians, of non-Communist Asians, were watching the Western powers. China was a test case. The West could either recognize the revolution or try to overthrow it by force. There was no other alternative. Would the Western powers refuse to recognize this expression of an Asian people just because the Westerners did not like it or thought they might lose financially by it? Would the Westerners do worse and support Chiang, who had become the symbol of feudal counter-revolution in the eyes of most Asians, of most non-Communist Asians? Would the Western powers use Chiang's anti-Communism to reimpose the old imperialism-feudalism on Asia? Would not using Chiang as an instrument in a war to overthrow the revolution alienate the mass of Asians from the West and put the West in an impossible position in Asia for decades to come?

American policy toward China was just the opposite of American policy toward Yugoslavia. Tito's deviation was encouraged, but Mao was treated as a mere puppet of Moscow. The effects of American policy were also the opposite in each case. The gulf between Belgrade and Moscow continued to widen, but the link between Peiping and Moscow necessarily grew stronger. In early 1950 Mao went to Moscow and signed the Sino-Soviet treaty of friendship and alliance. Russia gave China long-term credits and Russia gained recognition of her existing rights in Manchurian railroads and at Port Arthur and Dairen. Later, joint Sino-Soviet companies were organized to develop China's civil aviation, to run the Manchurian Changchun Railroad, and to undertake mining operations in Sinkiang.

British policy in Asia was twofold. (Hong Kong had relatively little to do with it, for Britain's trade with China through Hong Kong was piddling and actually stood a better chance under Chiang than under the Communists. The British, who voluntarily withdrew from India, would hardly descend to pivot their whole Asian policy on Hong Kong!) First, the British sought to wean Chinese Communists away from the Russians on national grounds and also to keep the pipelines of information between Asian countries like India and China open so that the Chinese, when they ran up against conditions which differed from the Russian experience (the peasant problem would be different in China from what it was in Russia), might be influenced to modify their programs under the impact of broader Asian advice and experience. Second, where the Communists had not won, the British hoped to develop a vast program of social reform which would convince Asians that under non-Communism both bread and freedom could be attained in this generation. The British pointed out that until now Communism had been checked in Asia by Westerners, not Asians: in Indonesia by the Dutch, in Indochina by the French, in Malaya by the British, in Korea by the Americans. If Asians could be convinced that there was a better way than Communism to achieve agricultural reform and industrialization, the time would come when they themselves would stand up and check Communism, argued the British.

In line with this approach the British Commonwealth governments made public in November 1950 their ambitious Colombo Plan for southern and southeast Asia, a six-year development program covering India, Pakistan, Malaya, Singapore, North Borneo, and Sarawak. The plan envisaged the spending of 5.2 billion dollars in technical assistance and capital investment for improvements in transport, communications, agriculture, mining, and industry. The chief emphasis was on capital investment. India would absorb about 70 per cent of the funds. British financial participation was to be mainly in the form of released sterling balances held on behalf of the participants and beneficiaries. It was hoped that the United States would participate directly, perhaps for as much as 2 billion dollars. In any event, American policies with respect to Britain and the Commonwealth countries would largely determine their abilities to go ahead with the program.

The Americans had their own program for underdeveloped peoples, the Point Four program announced in President Truman's 1949 inaugural and implemented by the Act for International Development in June 1950 and subsequent legislation. The first year only 34.5 million dollars was allocated to the program. More than 12 million dollars of this went to the United Nations technical assistance program. (The United Nations finally got contributions from other countries which brought its budget for this program to more than 20 million dollars.) More than 10 million dollars went to Latin America, 5 million dollars to the Middle East, and only 2 million dollars to the Far East. This program was a keen disappointment to the underdeveloped peoples. It was small in amount and concentrated on technical assistance rather than on the more important capital-investment programs. Technical assistance appealed to the American Congress because it involved less money and much of that money would go to American technicians. Most important, the American Congress believed that capital investment was a matter for private enterprise and that primarily what was needed was a "healthy investment climate" abroad to attract private capital.

Friends of the program hoped that it would develop into something much more significant, that it might even be combined with the Colombo program; but even when Point Four got into its stride in 1951-1952, it was clearly inadequate. In a world-wide program of foreign military and economic aid involving around 7.4 billion dollars, Asia, Africa, and the Western Hemisphere were allocated less than 1.4 billion dollars, most of which went for military assistance; only 418 million dollars went for economic aid of all kinds, including Point Four's technical assistance. (The 190-million-dollar emergency food loan to India and some lending by the Export-Import Bank were additional.) Only 237 million dollars in economic aid went to Asia and the Pacific, to be spread over India, Pakistan, Burma, Indonesia, Indochina, Thailand, the Philippines, and Formosa. Congress was always generous with Formosa and the Philippines. Of the 160 million dollars for the Near East and Africa, 100 million dollars went to Israel and to Arab and Jewish refugee relief in Palestine. Only around 21 million dollars was left for the twenty Latin American republics. Increasingly Congress put the emphasis on foreign armament programs. Economic assistance, which had been largely concentrated in Europe, declined; technical assistance lagged; and capital-investment programs were ignored.

Japan and the Beginning of the American Military Alliance System in Asia

If the United States faltered in social politics, the Korean War spurred it on to specific achievement in Pacific power politics. The treaty with Japan, signed at San Francisco the first week in September 1951, was not only a peace treaty with a fallen foe but also the foundation for a system of defense-perimeter alliances in the Pacific. Friends called the treaty generous, critics called it soft. It marked the transformation of Japan from United States enemy to United States ally. The treaty was popular in the United States because it aimed at checking Communism in Asia and seemed to score against the Soviet Union and Red China. Japan's victims in southeast Asia were disappointed because reparations were not provided. Australia, New Zealand, the Philippines, and other sufferers from Japanese aggression were reconciled to this treaty, which put no limits on Japan's war potential, only because a series of accompanying bilateral and trilateral pacts laid the foundation for a security system in the Pacific. A few in America and many in Britain and Canada questioned the long-time wisdom of an Asian settlement which did not include Russia, China, India, or Burma.

By the terms of the treaty Japan surrendered all her territories (and all rights and interests in China) except her four main islands.

However, the treaty did not designate the countries to which the surrendered territories were to go. This got around acknowledging Russian sovereignty over the Kuriles and southern Sakhalin and determining which of the two contesting Chinese governments was to have sovereignty over Formosa and the Pescadores Islands. Later, under some American pressure, Japan chose Nationalist China as the state with which to conclude a formal peace. Japan recognized United States jurisdiction over the Ryukyu Islands (including Okinawa) and the Bonins, and consented to any future United Nations trusteeship in these islands under American administration. No limitations were placed upon the Japanese economy, war potential, or armaments. The Japanese were free to repeal the reforms of the occupation. Reparations were virtually renounced, although the settlement postponed reparations for later bilateral negotiations between Japan and any signatory which still claimed them.

A separate United States-Japanese Security Treaty allowed the United States to maintain land, air, and sea forces in and about Japan to maintain international peace and (at the request of the Japanese government) to suppress large-scale internal disturbances instigated by a foreign power. Later Japan promised that Japanese facilities would be available for United Nations members in any United Nations action in the Far East. That same year (1951), the Tripartite Security Treaty of the United States, Australia, and New Zealand (ANZUS) declared an armed attack in the Pacific area on any of the parties would be dangerous to each of them and each would meet the common danger in accordance with its "constitutional processes." This was even less definite as a promise of future American action than the language of NATO. A United States-Philippine Mutual Defense Treaty (1952) paralleled in essentials the ANZUS treaty. The most solid advantages of these three treaties consisted in American rights to station armed forces in Japan and in the confirmation of an immense American sphere of influence from the northern tip of Hokkaido to the southernmost Philippines, Carolines, and Marshalls..

In the United States-Japanese Security Treaty, Japan promised to make a beginning toward providing for its own defense. Despite constitutional limitations, Japan, by 1954, possessed a "national self-defense force" of 110,000 men. The Japanese were reluctant to rearm further, but in consideration of larger American economic and military aid, they signed, in 1954, a Mutual Defense Assistance Agreement promising to increase their self-defense force. It was also understood that the Japanese would work toward repealing their constitutional prohibition on rearmament and after repeal was accomplished would undertake rearmament on a wider scale. However, the Japanese insisted that they would not undertake any military obligations other than those of self-defense, that their forces would not be sent out of the country, and that their defense build-up would not proceed fast enough to threaten their economic and political stability. There was to be a progressive withdrawal of American forces as the Japanese forces grew strong enough to defend the country.

There were still many qualms about the future of Japan. Would it resume its former cutthroat trading practices in the world markets? Would the occupation reforms become assimilated to Japanese life? More and more of Japan's old guard politicians were rehabilitated and resumed public life. The "depurges" ran close to 100,000. The police system had again become centralized. Land reform, economic decentralization, and postwar labor, educational, and civil-liberties legislation were under attack. Even Japan's conservative American friends were anxious lest Japan yield to economic pressures for markets and for iron ore, coking coal, and other minerals and enter into trade relations with Communist China. Also they were annoyed at Japan's reluctance to rearm. Japan, like Germany, was playing coy. There was considerable irony in a situation in which Japan could use the American-inspired constitutional provision renouncing arms forever as bargaining power *vis-à-vis* those very Americans. Just how badly did the Americans want the provision modified, and just how much would the Americans pay for its modification?

Japan, like Germany, had in the late nineteenth century come fresh from feudalism to industrialism. Unlike the "commercial revolution" countries of Britain, France, the Netherlands, Scandinavia, and the United States, where industrialism had emerged slowly out of three centuries of commercialism, the industrialism of Japan and Germany had rested on a feudal base, a fact which reflected itself in the deferential attitudes of a hierarchal society. Just how much of an impression had the impact of defeat and occupation made on the basic social structures of Japan and Germany? By the middle of the twentieth century it was clear that all parts of the non-Communist world were moving toward varying degrees of mixed economy, neither completely capitalist nor completely socialist. But it was not yet clear whether those mixed economies would be democratic or non-democratic. The influence of Japan and Germany would still be important in determining the future of democracy in the non-Communist world.

The Korean War and Fissures in the Non-Soviet World

The Korean War which opened in June 1950 let loose tortuous forces that were both constructive and destructive, and future events had yet to demonstrate which were the stronger. The war may have diverted pressure from southeast Asia, prevented a third world war, and set an epochal precedent for collective security. On the other hand, it seriously divided the Western world, and by creating a situation which made it more difficult for the United States to recognize the Chinese Revolution may have prepared the way for another world war.

At the time of the attack forty-three governments in the United Nations still recognized the Nationalist government of China, which had charged in the United Nations that Russia was unduly interfering in Chinese affairs. The Red Chinese government bitterly resented not being accepted by the United Nations as China's effective government, and for months Russia had boycotted sessions of the United Nations Security Council to underscore its disapproval of this "discrimination" against China. On the other hand, sixteen governments in the United Nations had already recognized the Mao regime in China, including Britain and India; and both the British and the Indians believed that Mao might be induced to take a more independent course in international relations, even eventually perhaps to become another Tito. It was generally believed in world diplomatic circles that even if Mao turned out to be no Tito, at least relations between China and Russia would be those of near equals.

Why did the North Koreans make their sudden attack on South Korea? The West does not yet have the answer. We do not know whether the initiative came from Russia, from China, from North Korea itself, or from a combination of these. (The Russians at the close of 1948 had announced the withdrawal of their forces from Korea and the end of the occupation.) Did the Russians want to prevent for all times the possibility of a unified Korea under Rhee, the existence of an anti-Communist all-Korean government, backed by the West, whose authority would extend to their very borders, within easy distance of Vladivostok? Did the Russians believe that a Korean war would result in easy victory and enhanced prestige for Communism in the East to compensate for Communism's losing ground in Europe? Were the Chinese made apprehensive by their failure to gain recognition from more governments and to be admitted to the United Nations? Writing as late as December 1953 in *Foreign Affairs*, former Prime Minister Attlee expressed the feeling prevalent at the time of the attack not only in his own party but in nearly all political groups in Britain that the Korean War might never have been started had Mao's government been recognized and Red China admitted to the United Nations. Attlee referred to the fact that face is of great importance in Asia and that refusal to recognize the actual Chinese government was regarded by the Chinese Communists as an insulting affront. Did the Communists, reading American reports that the United States did not regard Korea as strategically important, that it was not included in the American defense perimeter, believe that the Americans would offer no resistance, would evacuate what apparently they had decided was not worth holding? Was the Korean thrust only part of a planned general Communist offensive in Asia, an offensive which later had to be curtailed elsewhere because of unexpected resistance in Korea?

Whatever the cause, the North Koreans suddenly struck on June 25 and thrust south of the 38th parallel. The same day, with Russia still absent in protest against the barring of Communist China, the United Nations Security Council called on the North Koreans to withdraw forthwith. President Truman ordered American forces to go to the aid of the South Koreans. On June 30 an American air force was ordered to bomb military targets in North Korea. About the same time the Security Council called on member states of the United Nations to furnish assistance to the Republic of Korea. This time the Council was divided: Egypt and India abstained and Yugoslavia opposed. The actual response was not as great as the United States had hoped, but in time nine-teen nations responded with military assistance and twenty-one others with non-military assistance. The bulk of the fighting force was composed of South Koreans and Americans, but ground forces in considerable numbers were furnished by Britain, Australia, New Zealand, Canada, the Philippines, Thailand, and Turkey. President Truman designated General MacArthur to be United Nations commander in Korea, increased aid to the French in Indochina, ordered American reinforcements to the Philippines, and neutralized Formosa by commanding the Seventh Fleet to prevent any Communist attack on that sanctuary of Chiang and the Nationalist forces.

America's energetic action was widely supported in the United States, for most Americans felt either that the third world war was actually at hand or that the only way to stop it was by decisive measures which showed dictators that this time there would be no appeasement. The rest of the Western world, too, in general approved these early collective-security measures, but the action of the United States with respect to Formosa raised serious doubts. Was this intervention on the side of Chiang and against Communist China? Did the United States intend to make Formosa a part of its defense perimeter without regard to the interests of Red China and without the consent of other governments? When in July MacArthur personally went to Formosa for conversations with Chiang the doubts increased. Meantime the Russians had returned to the United Nations and were boldly claiming that the North Koreans had entered the war merely to repulse an unprovoked attack by South Koreans. They branded American action in Formosa an aggression against Communist China. Red China's stake in the crisis was recognized by the Security Council when it voted, over the protests of only the United States, Nationalist China, and Cuba, to invite a representative of Mao's government to the United Nations to voice China's position in the conflict. China's long frontier with North Korea, Manchuria's dependence on hydroelectric installations just south of the Yalu River, and Red China's charge of American intervention on behalf of Chiang gave Red China a vital interest in the crisis, reasoned the Council. When the Assembly met, India led a move to replace Nationalist China with Communist China as

China's official representative in the Assembly. (Each branch of the United Nations judges for itself what government is entitled to represent a member state.) The United States battled hard and eventually defeated this move, but the motion received the support of Britain, the Netherlands, Sweden, Burma, India, Pakistan, Israel, and Afghanistan. France, Canada, and the Arab states abstained.

The United Nations went ahead and announced its ultimate program as a "unified, independent, democratic Korea." Britain introduced this resolution. Only the members of the Soviet bloc opposed. India, Yugoslavia, and the five Arab states abstained. When on October 23 the United Nations forces, then steadily advancing, crossed the 38th parallel, this resolution became the basis for United Nations action north of the parallel. President Rhee claimed that all that was necessary to put the resolution into effect was to extend his government to North Korea, and General MacArthur reputedly shared that view. The crossing of the parallel caused little adverse comment at the time, but the Indian delegation announced that it viewed this action with greatest misgivings. Later, many Asians and some Europeans claimed that by this act the United Nations itself became an aggressor.

Meantime China showed increased activity: Chinese army units penetrated Tibet, China reportedly increased aid to the Vietminh Communists in Indochina, and Chinese troops mobilized on the North Korean border. Some Chinese "volunteer" divisions were said to have appeared in Korea a few days after the United Nations' crossing of the parallel. The very day the special Red Chinese delegation arrived at the United Nations to air China's views of the crisis, MacArthur began a full-scale offensive and declared against a privileged sanctuary beyond the Yalu for the Communist aggressors. The Red Chinese delegation to the United Nations declared Mao's terms to be withdrawal of all United Nations forces from Korea, withdrawal of all American forces from Formosa, and admission of Red China to the United Nations. As MacArthur advanced north he encountered more and more Chinese "volunteers," and his offensive bogged down.

The new crisis produced by full-scale Chinese intervention brought apprehension and divided counsels. It came about the time of the 1950 Congressional elections in which Republicans and nationalists had gained much ground. Those who resented the war itself and those who thought the war had been fought without decision and energy while playing "footsie" with the Communists all united against the administration. There was talk of a naval blockade of China, of air action in China itself, even of dropping the atom bomb. America's allies became alarmed and Prime Minister Attlee flew to Washington to get assurances that the bomb would not be used without consultation with Britain and other interested governments.

Meantime the Chinese, reinforced by the million and a quarter men massed on the border, mounted a full-scale counter-offensive and pushed south. Britain, India, and various Asian and Arab states sought to arrange a cease-fire and appealed to the Chinese not to cross the 38th parallel. The Chinese refused, crossed the parallel, and moved deep into the Republic of Korea. There were times when it was feared that United Nations forces might be driven from the peninsula. In the United States criticism mounted higher. Herbert Hoover, Joseph P. Kennedy, and others intimated that our allies had let us down, that the United States should retire to its Western Hemisphere bastion. In January 1951, MacArthur, with reinforcements, turned the tide and United Nations forces moved back in the direction of the 38th parallel.

In February the United Nations branded Red China an aggressor. The American Congress by unanimous vote of both houses had insisted that the United Nations take this action. Britain had refused to sponsor this move in the United Nations. In the final vote the five members of the Soviet bloc, India, and Burma opposed, and seven other Asian and Arab states, Sweden, and Yugoslavia abstained. As MacArthur moved north, new questions arose. Should the United Nations forces again cross the 38th parallel? For how complete a victory should the United Nations command aim? The administration wanted to propose to the enemy that the war stop where it had begun, at the 38th parallel, and that the outstanding issues be settled by negotiation. If this were refused, then MacArthur would be instructed to tell the enemy that the United Nations would be compelled to resume the conflict. MacArthur demurred at "burdening" the Korean negotiations with such "extraneous matters" as Formosa and a seat in the United Nations for Red China. He favored negotiating on the narrower issue of the Korean question, and if this failed then he proposed to widen the war, blockade the China coast, bomb supply bases in China, and utilize Chinese Nationalist troops, perhaps on the China mainland itself. If this were not done, he favored evacuating Korea. Because MacArthur was inclined to substitute his own objectives for United Nations objectives and to go over the heads of the United Nations, the President, and the Chiefs of Staff, he was, on the advice of the Chiefs of Staff, dismissed by Truman from his commands. Civilian control of the military itself appeared at stake. MacArthur was dismissed on April 10, one week after the victorious United Nations troops had recrossed the parallel.

At MacArthur's dismissal, the smoldering tensions inside the United States and between the United States and its allies exploded. MacArthur's critics claimed that he was heading toward a continental invasion of China with Chiang's troops; that such a reactionary war would be far more formidable than he realized and would alienate even most of the non-Communists in China and in Asia; that such a war would be regarded by Asians as a revival of Western imperialism on a grand scale; that Russia, gathering strength as America and the West, still unprepared for a large war, bogged in this vast war in the heart of Asia, would be free to strike in Europe. It would be the wrong war, against the wrong enemy, at the wrong time, and at the wrong place. Even if it did not lead to world war it would be a tremendous undertaking in itself, an undertaking which might put the West in an untenable position with Asians for decades to come. And besides, was not large-scale war avoidable? Were there not forces already operating which might ultimately overcome the crisis peacefully to the eventual advantage of the West? American critics of MacArthur emphasized the West's growing rearmament, how as the West moved from situations of weakness to situations of strength the chances of eventual large-scale war would diminish. Europeans emphasized the growth of social democracy as a check to Communism and the growth of nationalism within the Communist bloc as a movement which probably would separate Communist countries from one another and eventually restore a multiple balance of power. Would not the West still be confronted with the problems of the underdeveloped peoples even after it had won a vast war with them, it was asked.

MacArthur replied that in war there was no substitute for victory, especially in Asia where face meant so much. A long-drawn-out "small" war or a series of such wars would be more costly than a decisive blow against China. (American casualties of dead, wounded, or captured in Korea totaled around 140,000 by 1953.) MacArthur claimed that there was little chance of Russia entering the war on the side of China, that Russia had few dispositions in the Far East and scant rail connections with it. On the question of a possible Russian attack in Europe while America was engaged in Asia, MacArthur was not so sure.

The debate brought to the surface a curious similarity of views of MacArthurites and Bevanites, of American nationalists and European neutralists, with respect to one aspect of the international situation. Both agreed that Russia and China were not so close as generally believed. For the MacArthurites this meant that China could be knocked out with relative ease. For the Bevanites and neutralists it meant that the Communist international front was not as solid as supposed, that the security of the West was not imperiled to the degree made out by the exponents of rapid rearmament. Then why the haste, why the anxiety, why the hysteria, they asked.

MacArthur's dismissal did not change America's Far Eastern policy. In May the United Nations, under American prodding, voted economic sanctions against China. The American Congress, again unanimously in both houses, had insisted that the United Nations take this action. Congress also voted to cut off economic aid to any country which exported strategic goods to Communist countries. In June a military stalemate settled over the front, with United Nations forces holding a line which curved northeastward above the 38th parallel almost to Kosong. Then on June 22 the Russians unexpectedly suggested an armistice and the withdrawal of both forces from a neutral zone along the 38th parallel. Why did the Communists show a disposition to end the war? Was it the conviction they could not win in Korea? Was it because the drain was too great on Red China, deeply involved in agrarian reform and industrialization at home? Was it because the Communists believed they could expand more easily elsewhere—in Indochina, for instance?

Negotiations for an armistice began on July 10, 1951, but an armistice was not signed until July 26, 1953. The armistice never ripened into a definitive peace settlement, and the Korean "peace conference" held at Geneva (April 26–June 15, 1954) was a complete failure. Korea remained partitioned, another example of the stalemate between the East and the West. Here, too, the *status quo*, highly unstable and dangerous, could not be upset without war, but neither could the situation be thought of as a permanent solution. There were constant rumors and charges that North Korea was violating the Korean armistice terms and building up its armed forces behind the armistice lines. In his turn, President Rhee chafed under the armistice terms, which he felt betrayed the cause of Korean unification. Rhee repeatedly threatened to go it alone, even if this meant renewal of the war, in an attempt to unify all Korea under his government.

In order to stabilize the situation, the United States entered into a Mutual Defense Treaty with the Republic of Korea, which was ratified by both countries in January 1954. Under its terms the United States pledged to go to the military aid of South Korea in the event of an external armed attack against territory recognized by the United States as lawfully under the administration of the Republic of Korea. The treaty would not apply in case South Korea itself initiated an attack. Thus the treaty was aimed at deterring North Korea from attacking South Korea and also at restraining Rhee from attacking North Korea.

United States China Policy

The problem of Red China remained the pivotal one in Asia. China under the Communists was emerging as a modernized, an industrialized, a unified, and a highly nationally conscious state. "The sleeping giant," the world's most populous country, was asleep no more. Here was a potential of tremendous strength, and for the time, at least, this aroused giant was backed by the Soviet Union in the Moscow-Peiping Axis. Red China had intervened in Korea; it was supplying Communist armed bands in Vietnam, Laos, and Cambodia; it had sent troops into certain areas of northern Burma under the pretext of rectifying frontiers; it had asserted its sovereignty over Tibet; its influence was penetrating Nepal; it had taken the lead in the Communist movements in Asia; and among the large Chinese populations in Indochina, Thailand, Malaya, Singapore, the Philippines, and Indonesia it had many ardent supporters. However, Red China was just at the beginning of its industrialization, it faced Herculean problems of internal development, and it would take decades before its technological revolution would manifest itself in an effective national strength at all comparable to that of the United States or even to that of the Soviet Union.

The United States still refused to recognize the government of Red China and it opposed its admission to the United Nations. It still recognized Chiang Kai-shek's government in Formosa as the legal Chinese government, and the United Nations still recognized Chiang's representatives in the world organization as the representatives of the legal China. However, more and more countries were recognizing the Communist government as the legal government, and the United Nations was constrained to refuse Red China admission largely because of American insistence. Increasingly, the rest of the world felt that the United States was making a mistake and that it was only a question of time until Red China would be admitted.

Those who felt that the United States was making a mistake in its intransigence toward Red China argued that the Communist government was the government in fact of all mainland China and that in the end the Communist government would have to be recognized or overthrown, and obviously it could be overthrown only by a full-scale war. It was pointed out that the mass of non-Communist Asians, imbued with the spirit of the anti-imperialist revolutions, were irritated by America's support of Chiang, who had come to be regarded by most Asians as a symbol of reaction. Were not the Americans revealing the old Western attitudes of imperialism when they refused to recognize a successful anti-imperialist revolution in China just because it had gone all the way to Communism, and were not the Chinese the best judges of what was good for them? How could the big international problems in Asia ever be tackled realistically without direct conversations with the government which actually controlled China? Was not the American attitude literally forcing China into the arms of Russia, instead of encouraging China to take international positions independently of Russia? Were not the Americans building up a Chinese hostility toward themselves which might become traditional and needlessly embitter relations for decades to come?

On the other hand, the American State Department felt that its position with respect to Red China was a sound one, at least for the immediate future, and that it had the support of most Americans. The Red Chinese, during the Korean War, had flagrantly violated many of the conventions and moralities of international conduct and had never accounted for thousands of United Nations prisoners, many of whom were Americans. It was expedient to keep the Red Chinese guessing, not to help them with moral or material support. It was expedient, too, to keep Western technicians and capital goods out of China. Why should China build its Communist revolution and its technological might with the aid of the West? Why not slow this revolution down by keeping Western engineers and Western machinery out of China? If China must get an industrial revolution by way of drastic Communism, let it get its aid from Russia, which of necessity would be limited because the Russians still needed most of their technicians and capital goods at home. Why not keep the large Chinese populations in southeast Asia divided by sustaining Chiang on Formosa, for were Chiang's government to disappear from Formosa, then all the Chinese scattered throughout the Pacific islands and southeast Asia would gravitate to the Chinese Communists, and these Chinese in foreign countries would operate as subversive forces in innumerable Pacific and Asian communities. Finally, why not hold back formal recognition of the Chinese Reds as long as possible, thereby raising American bargaining power to such a pitch that the Reds would be willing to make large concessions to get the recognition they craved for the sake of prestige and face?

The most sensitive trouble spot in Red Chinese–American relations was in the Formosa Straits. The United States protected Chiang's government in Formosa (Taiwan) and the Pescadores Islands as the Republic of China, the legal government of China. Chiang also held the islands just off the mainland of China, the so-called offshore islands, the most important of which were the Quemoy Islands, Matsu, and the Tachens. These offshore islands were juridically a part of the mainland, but Formosa and the Pescadores had not belonged to mainland China since 1895, and when Japan officially and permanently surrendered them in 1951, the treaty did not designate the power to which they were to go. Later, Japan had made its peace treaty with Chiang's government and not with the Communist government, and thereby had recognized the Republic of China as the ruling power over them. Red China claimed Formosa and the Pescadores in the name of the people of mainland China, who had helped win the war against Japan, and also because these islands were peopled by Chinese. However, the juridical claim of mainland China to the offshore islands was much stronger.

During the Korean War, Truman's order to the Seventh Fleet had prevented Chiang and the Communists from attacking each other. In the early days of his administration, Eisenhower had "unleashed" Chiang for an attack on the mainland, but since the United States showed no inclination to support such an attack, Chiang made no serious move to make one, although Chiang's air force sometimes attacked the mainland, using its occupied offshore islands as bases. However, the United States continued its support of Chiang's government in Formosa in order to keep the Red Chinese guessing and diverted from other areas and to keep the Chinese populations scattered through southeast Asia divided, and especially because the United States regarded Formosa and the Pescadores as parts of its defense perimeter and was determined that these should not fall into unfriendly hands.

At the close of 1954, a Mutual Defense Treaty was signed between the United States and Chiang's government in which each party recognized an armed attack in the West Pacific area directed against the territories of either of the parties as dangerous to its own peace and safety and pledged each to meet the common danger in accordance with its constitutional processes. The offshore islands along the mainland coast, held by Chiang, were not included in the agreement. At the same time, Chiang's government obligated itself to take no forcible action or even to strengthen its own forces in the offshore islands without prior agreement of the United States. As in the treaty with Rhee, the agreement thus had a twofold purpose—to deter the Reds from attacking Chiang and to prevent Chiang from undertaking any military ventures on his own. In other words, Chiang, who had been "unleashed," was now leashed again.

Since the treaty did not cover the offshore islands, the Chinese Reds were left in uncertainty how far they could extend their military moves there. In January 1955, the Chinese Communists made concerted air attacks on the Tachens in apparent preparation for a full-scale invasion. Congress, in response to the President's request, granted the President emergency powers to use the United States armed forces to protect Formosa and the Pescadores and to assist Chiang in deploying and consolidating his forces. The Seventh Fleet helped Chiang evacuate his forces from the Tachens. Just what action the United States would take if the Communists attacked Quemoy and Matsu was left in doubt, and official American pronouncements through the years continued to be Delphic. However, the Chinese Reds, perhaps deterred by the Congressional grant of emergency authority to the President, made no further attacks at that time. America's allies, who had been particularly jittery throughout January lest an attack on Quemoy or Matsu lead to a full-scale war, now relaxed. The British had made it plain that they did not consider Quemoy or Matsu vital to the defense of Formosa and that certainly they were not worth a war. Fears of a "preventive war" waged by the United States through Chiang to recover the Chinese mainland and of a Red Chinese attack on Formosa receded.

It now appeared that the United States stood in a position to protect the *status quo*, that it favored a *modus vivendi* in which the Chinese Reds would keep what they had, Chiang would keep what he had, and neither would attack the other. This seemed to be a tacit admission by the United States that the Communists governed mainland China and would be left undisturbed there.

Projecting our story a bit into the future, in late August 1958 the Chinese Communists again threatened large-scale operations against Matsu and the Quemoy group. Heavy bombardments occurred during the next two months. The reasons for the attack appear to have been various: an expectation that the crisis over Iraq, Lebanon, and Jordan in the Middle East would not die down as rapidly as it did and that the Americans would be preoccupied with that crisis; the attempt to whip up Chinese patriotism during the initial steps in the organization of the communes; the belief that the United Nations Assembly, soon to meet, might be influenced to admit mainland China to the United Nations; and indignation and fear over the hasty concentration of one-third of

Chiang Kai-shek's best troops on the offshore islands. During the crisis the United States assembled in the Formosa area the most powerful air-naval striking force in its history; United States naval units furnished escorts to Nationalist China's convoys to Quemoy; and the Nationalist aircraft, equipped with American "Sidewinder" missiles, proved themselves more than a match for the Communist MIG-17 fighters which increasingly appeared over the Straits. Khrushchev demanded the recall of the American fleet from the Formosa Straits. America's European allies were alarmed and again insisted that Quemoy and Matsu were not worth a war. Segments of American opinion were most critical of American policy. Why, it was asked, had not the Nationalists been encouraged to reduce rather than increase their forces on the offshore islands during the years of quiet?

During October both sides made conciliatory gestures. Secretary of State Dulles observed that the United States had no absolute commitment to defend Quemoy and Matsu and hinted that if a cease-fire were arranged the Nationalist forces on the offshore islands would be thinned out. About the same time, the Chinese Communists switched from force to political propaganda tactics and appeals for fifth-column subversion among Chiang's followers. Defense Minister Peng, in a broadcast beamed to Formosa, declared that Dulles' recent statements showed that the Americans would ultimately desert Chiang, that all Chinese patriots should unite against "the American imperialists." Peng announced an unilateral cease-fire, provided the Americans refrained from escort operations. After a flying visit from Secretary Dulles, Chiang made a pronouncement which seemed for the first time to put the Generalissimo on record as renouncing the use of force to recover the mainland. Peng now beamed another broadcast to Formosa in which he teasingly promised that the Chinese Communists, in the absence of American escort operations, would in the future lay off any bombing of the Quemoy port and airfield on all even dates of the months, so that the Nationalist-held offshore islands could continue to lay in their needed supplies! Thus the grave crisis of the preceding two months ended on a note of mockery. But Secretary Dulles still refused to clarify whether the United States would or would not intervene directly to protect Quemoy and Matsu in the event of a concentrated Communist attack.

Crisis in Indochina

During 1953 and 1954, the situation in Indochina was critical. Throughout 1953, the forces of Ho Chi Minh, the Communist leader, steadily gained strength in northern Vietnam and even invaded Laos; and during the first half of 1954 the Communists penetrated as far south as Cambodia, and laid siege to Dienbienphu, the French concentration in North Vietnam. The Chinese Communists were giving aid to the Minh Communists, but not as much aid as the United States was giving to South Vietnam and the French. The French were plainly weary of the war. French Union casualties by the end of 1953 were around 158,000, around 60,000 in killed and missing. To the French, the war was an open sore which contributed to inflation and discord at home, increased French fears of German revival, enhanced French opposition to EDC, and weakened France in its attempts to hold French North Africa, which was regarded as more vital to France than Indochina. In 1953 the Americans gave 785 million dollars in military aid to the French, and by the following year they were shouldering three-fourths of the costs of the Indochina War. They were eager to take over the training of the South Vietnamese troops.

French will to resist collapsed in May 1954 with the capitulation of Dienbienphu. Mendès-France became Premier of France in June, vowing to bring the war in Indochina to a conclusion by direct negotiations with the Communists. The Americans had made peace with the Communists in Korea. How then could they complain when the French followed a similar course in Indochina? The French claimed that the Indochina War was far more of a drain on France than the Korean War had been on the United States. Would the United States intervene alone to save the situation? Was this a case for "massive retaliation" with nuclear weapons?

It soon became clear that the United States would not intervene alone. However, the United States sent feelers to Britain and France suggesting that the big three join in continuing the war. It also suggested that a military alliance of the big three together with Australia, New Zealand, the Philippines, and Thailand be formed to check Communists in southeast Asia. But Britain was opposed to any action which would widen the war in Indochina;

it felt that a settlement should be made which reflected the actual power situation there; and it maintained that the Communist movement in Indochina was more indigenous than it was Chinese- or Russian-inspired. By now, French opinion was committed to a settlement. Asian neutrals, led by Nehru, also insisted on a settlement. As a matter of fact, the Americans, who had borne the brunt of the Korean War and were glad to get out of it, would not have welcomed "another Korea" in southeast Asia (unless the brunt of the actual fighting were done by the French and the South Vietnamese), and they finally acquiesced in a disagreeable settlement they found to be inevitable.

Consequently, in July 1954, the French, backed by the British and with the United States standing more or less as an observer, made peace with Ho Chi Minh. The settlements coming out of the July negotiations were in essence that Cambodia and Laos were to become independent, the French Union forces were to be withdrawn from their territories, and the Communist insurgents were also to be withdrawn or to be disarmed and disbanded. Vietnam was to be partitioned at "the waist," approximately at the seventeenth parallel. North of that line, Ho Chi Minh was to have control. A new "people's democracy" or "people's republic" was established there with the Communists in control. The Americans came to call this territory Vietminh. It had a population of about 12.75 million and its capital was at Hanoi. South of the line was what was left of Vietnam. This truncated Vietnam had a population of 9.3 million and its capital was at Saigon. General elections were to be held in July 1956 both north and south of the line, under international supervision, to determine the permanent future of the country. These elections were never held.

President Eisenhower refused to call the settlement "another Munich" or "appeasement" and declared it would go far toward stabilizing the area. However, the United States was determined that no more Communist gains be made in southeast Asia. The United States had at last learned that backing colonialism was no way to win in Asia. Americans more and more realized that if earlier they had insisted the French get out of this area, the Communists would not have been able to capture so much of the Vietnamese nationalist, anti-colonial, anti-French sentiment. Henceforth the Americans increasingly used their influence and their aid to back nationalist sentiment in South Vietnam, Laos, and Cambodia, and to liquidate French interests in these areas.

In South Vietnam, the United States backed nationalist Ngo Dinh Diem against the French puppet, Bao Dai, Vietnam's nominal ruler. Bao was deposed and Ngo came to power pledged to give Vietnam genuine national independence. The Americans now took over from the French the training of the Vietnamese army. The United States began channeling all its aid directly to the national governments of Laos, Cambodia, and South Vietnam, and not through the French. American aid to South Vietnam alone in 1955 totaled around 500 million dollars, and by 1956 this whole area, including South Vietnam, Laos, Cambodia, and Thailand, had superseded Korea as the chief beneficiary of American aid in Asia. The purpose of much of the aid given to South Vietnam, Cambodia, and Laos was not only to check the Communists directly but also to check them indirectly by insuring that the governments would reflect the national sentiments of their peoples against all attempts by France to hang on to its interests in this area. Even so, Cambodia manifested strong signs of neutralism, and there was a danger that Asians would see in American activities in this area merely the supplanting of French influence by American influence. Americans would have to walk warily lest they be regarded as "the new Western imperialists."

The Network of American Military Alliances

As a result of the Communist victory in Vietminh and the continuing threat of Communism to other parts of southeast Asia, the United States initiated a comprehensive military alliance which went much farther than the defense-perimeter concept of its prior Asian treaties. It sponsored the Manila Conference of September 1954 which set up the South East Asia Treaty Organization. SEATO sought to protect from Communist aggression the general area of southeast Asia and the southwest Pacific. The territories of the Asian members of the organization, together with Cambodia, Laos, and South Vietnam, were specifically included in the area to be protected. Hong Kong, Formosa, and all territories to the north were excluded from SEATO's protection. (Many of these areas were covered by other treaties.) Participants in SEATO were the United States, Britain, France, Australia, New Zealand, the Philippines, Thailand, and Pakistan. However, India, Burma, Ceylon, and Indonesia refused to join and regarded SEATO as aggravating tensions in the area rather than relieving them. Each signatory recognized that aggression by means of armed attack in the designated area would threaten its own peace and safety and agreed to act in that event to meet the common danger in accordance with its constitutional processes. In case of a threat to political independence by means other than armed attack (subversion), the parties were to consult immediately in order to agree on measures to be taken for the common defense. The parties promised "to strengthen their free institutions" by cooperating in economic measures and technical assistance. SEATO represented the indefinite type of commitment like ANZUS rather than the more definite obligations and more institutionalized organization of NATO.

SEATO brought little additional military strength to bear on this part of the world; the chief military responsibility would still have to be borne by the United States; supporting military strength would come from countries which in all likelihood would provide it without any additional treaty and were already in formal military alliance with the United States through other treaties. The principal Asian countries refused to join SEATO and resented this intrusion of "Western military alliances" into the heart of Asia. Laos and Cambodia, not parties to the treaty, were sensitive about being included within its protected area, for was this not a violation of their neutrality? Asians pointed out that by emphasizing the dangers of internal subversion the treaty was in effect preserving the internal *status quo*. For instance, would South Vietnam or Thailand be allowed to have any revolutions at all, even democratic non-Communist ones?

A decade after the close of World War II, America's containment policy had encircled the Communist powers with a network of military alliances: NATO, the Balkan League, METO, SEATO, ANZUS, and bilateral treaties with Spain, Japan, South Korea, Formosa, the Philippines, and other countries. The United States was also allied to all the Latin American countries through the Organization of American States (a general regional security association and not a military alliance) and if anything took their support too much for granted. NATO was by all odds the most important of the alliances, although the NATO nations, including the United States, continued to have difficulties assembling the armed forces in Germany and Western Europe that most American military planners thought adequate for Europe's minimum safety.

By 1955 the world had become divided three ways: the Communist powers, led by the Soviet Union; the West and its allies scattered all over the world, led by the United States; and most of the emergent nations of the old colonial areas, which were attempting to stay out of the big-power conflict and remain neutral.

American policy was under attack in neutral and even some Allied quarters for putting too much emphasis on the military factor in international affairs and minimizing the other factors. The Americans seemed to back away from negotiations with the Russians. Many Europeans said in effect: "You Americans claimed we needed to rearm in order to get strong, that only through strength could we negotiate successfully. But the more we arm the more you resist negotiation. And so after all, does not an armaments race mean what it has always meant in the past—war?" It was also thought that the United States was overlooking the possibility of splitting the Communist powers, was failing to exploit the nationalism of Communist countries, particularly in its China policy. Again, it was felt that the United States did not sufficiently respect the sentiments of the neutral nations, that it went too far in attempting to pressure them into becoming military allies. The most widespread criticism of American policy went something like this: "There may never be a military showdown at all. The future of the world may depend upon attitudes in the emerging nations, which may determine the balance of power as between the Communist bloc and the Western bloc. Whether these nations are won for the West or lost to it will largely depend on the West's understanding the problems of the underdeveloped peoples, giving these peoples adequate economic aid and technical assistance in developing their economies, playing effective social politics, using the revolutionary aspirations of social democracy to defeat the more drastic revolutionary goals of Communism."

Most of America's critics did not condemn the use of military alliances to check Communism, but they believed that these alone were not enough, that mere military alliances would fall short of their objective unless supplemented by wise diplomacy and constructive, large-scale economic and social measures.

Even some American military planners believed that more of America's military spending should go to the development of nuclear weapons and guided missiles and less to subsidizing the armed forces of America's military allies and supplying them with the conventional military equipment they felt was fast becoming obsolete.

Breach in the Free World at America's Own Doorstep: The Guatemala Incident

By 1954 the Arbenz government in Guatemala appeared to be moving from leftism (basic agrarian reforms and discriminations against the United Fruit Company) to outright connection with the Communist powers. At the Tenth Inter-American Conference, held at Caracas in March, the United States secured the adoption of a resolution declaring that "the domination or control of the political institutions of any American state by the international Communist movement" would be "a threat to the sovereignty and political independence of the American states." By May it appeared that the Arbenz government was beginning to function as a true Communist spearhead. When the United States refused to sell Guatemala arms, the Arbenz government obtained two thousand tons of arms and ammunition from Czechoslovakia. The United States promtly authorized compensatory arms shipments to Honduras and Nicaragua. In June, Guatemalan rebels, using arms from Honduras and Nicaragua and bases in those countries, crossed into Guatemala, were joined by Guatemalans hostile to Arbenz, and overthrew the Arbenz government. Arbenz fled, by way of Mexico, to Czechoslovakia. Some Latin Americans regarded the actions of the United States as unauthorized intervention in the affairs of a sovereign state, but the United States claimed that Arbenz had been overthrown by the Guatemalans themselves and that any aid given them by any outsiders was designed to rescue Guatemala's national sovereignty from a foreign, non-American intervention representing a system alien to the Western Hemisphere.

The new Guatemalan government repealed many of the measures of Arbenz, including the discriminations against the

United Fruit Company. In extending economic aid to the new government, the United States made an exception to its general rule in Latin America at that time and extended grants not only for technical assistance but also for long-range capital-development projects. However, successive Guatemalan governments proved oppressive, incompetent, corrupt, erratic, and unpopular.

The Guatemalan episode was a reminder to the United States that not only in Asia and the Middle East but also at its very back door there existed the instability and political extremes of left and right which at mid-century almost always characterized impoverished and underdeveloped countries.

[6]

DEADLOCK

Post-Stalin Thaw

The year 1953 marked the beginning of a somewhat new direction in world politics. That year the Soviet Union detonated a hydrogen bomb. (This was one year after the United States had tested its hydrogen bomb and four years after the Soviet Union had developed an atom bomb.) In 1953, too, Stalin died and a new Soviet leadership began experimenting with a somewhat new approach to world politics. In that year, also, Dwight D. Eisenhower became President of the United States and took a "new look" at American foreign policy. The new President scarcely ever used the term "Cold War" and in time it became apparent that he did not regard direct negotiations with the Russians as "appeasement" or portending "another Munich." Eisenhower's enormous prestige and the fact that he was a Republican allowed him to ease American policy into a new world climate without being charged with "pro-Communism."

The "new era" beginning in 1953 was given a variety of names: nuclear stalemate, *pax atomica*, peaceful coexistence, competitive coexistence.

Now, it must not be supposed that the somewhat different turn to world affairs after 1953 eliminated the ideological and power conflict between the United States and the Soviet Union.

By no means. That conflict continued, and crisis situation followed crisis situation. However, there was a new spirit abroad and a growing feeling that the points of conflict would have to be made to yield to peaceful solutions, or if not to solutions, then at least to tolerable compromises and piecemeal accommodations. Both sides shied away from pressing situations to the point of big war or even of "little" and "limited" war such as the one in Korea.

Following Stalin's death a "collective leadership" of Communist bigwigs took over the direction of Soviet affairs. G. M. Malenkov became premier and was an advocate of more consumer goods at home and of a less hard line abroad. Molotov, L. M. Kaganovich, and some others stood for an essentially Stalinist line at home and abroad. Nikita Khrushchev, one of the most complex and resilient figures the Communist world had produced, and N. A. Bulganin favored a middle course—a somewhat less hard line at home and abroad but a continued emphasis on the development of heavy industry. From 1953 to 1955 there was a maneuvering for position by all three groups, and the cooperation of the Khrushchev group and the Malenkov group allowed a more relaxed approach at home and abroad. But in 1955 Khrushchev cooperated with the old Stalinists to oust Malenkov and make Bulganin premier. However, Malenkov retained high government posts. From 1955 to 1957 Bulganin as premier and Khrushchev as first secretary of the Communist party ruled as a kind of diarchy with Bulganin the front man and Khrushchev the driver. In 1957, in a struggle for power between Khrushchev and the old Stalinists, now aided by Malenkov, Khrushchev emerged the victor. Molotov, Malenkov, Kaganovich, and others were removed from their high party and government posts, but they were not personally liquidated and there was no drastic general purge as there would have been in Stalin's time. The new rulers were bent on demonstrating to the world that the Soviet political system had "matured." In 1958 Khrushchev emerged as premier and after that, although he never exercised the degree of power Stalin had exercised and was required to defend his policies in party committees, there was no doubt who was at the helm.

From the time of Stalin's death the ruling clique emphasized a return to the "Leninist principles" of "collective leadership." Stalin was subtly downgraded, and in 1956 at the twentieth congress of the Soviet Communist party, Stalin and "the cult of personality" were spectacularly denounced by Khrushchev. The late dictator was described as one who had made great contributions to the building of socialism in the early years of his rule but who had degenerated into a cruel personal tyrant and subverted the aims of communism. A de-Stalinization campaign was begun and it increased with intensity with the years. Stalin's statues and busts were toppled from their pedestals, Soviet history books were rewritten, and later Stalin's body was removed from the Lenin mausoleum on Red Square and placed in a more modest grave along the Kremlin wall. Great risks were run in so suddenly converting the infallible leader and popular idol of the Communist world into a mere mortal who had erred grievously.

In part the de-Stalinization drive was an expression of the personal abhorrence of the new rulers for a despotism which they had served and to which many owed their careers but which had destroyed many of their Bolshevik comrades, often personally humiliated them, and kept them in mortal terror of their own lives. In part it was an acknowledgment that the Soviet system itself could not long survive so great a concentration of personal power which had grown inflexible and been guilty of some serious mistakes. In part it was a sincere attempt to go back to the more flexible intra-party methods of Lenin's time. And in part it was "good politics" intended to impress the Russians and the outside world that the tyranny of Stalin was personal and not a part of the Communist system. Communists believed that even their own liquidation was justified if it would help the "cause," and the time had now come for Stalin to suffer liquidation for the good of Communism. Stalin was fortunate; his liquidation was posthumous, that of his victims had often been by execution. No attempt was made to explain how such a bloody dictatorship could have developed within the Communist system or whether the Leninist principle of "democratic centralism" did not naturally lend itself to such a development. The whole Stalinist dictatorship was put down to a mere accident of history. However, it was now clear to the most ardent of Communists that their system and their leaders were not infallible, and many Marxist theorists inside and outside of Russia (but mostly outside) pressed for a more searching and dialectical examination of the phenomenon of Stalinism.

After the death of Stalin, Russia's top leaders were no longer men of mystery secluded in the Kremlin. Like the Soviet leaders of Lenin's time, Khrushchev, Bulganin, A. I. Mikoyan, and others were seen often in public, rode through crowded city streets in open cars, addressed huge mass meetings. Khrushchev, like an American politician, seemed especially to enjoy the rough-and-tumble of popular crowds. The security police was curbed some; L. P. Beria, who had been head of Stalin's secret police, was dismissed and executed; a broader, but still severely limited, freedom of expression in intellectual, artistic, and literary matters was allowed; there was a perceptible increase in consumer goods; a wider latitude was permitted workers in factories and collectives and there was relaxing of the rules with respect to absenteeism and changing jobs; a minimum wage law was announced and social security benefits increased. Although Khrushchev favored continuing the pace of collectivization of agriculture and the emphasis on heavy industry, significant changes were made in industrial management. In the interest of efficiency and the morale of managers, engineers, and technicians, industrial management was in many ways decentralized and wider latitude in decision making given to those responsible for production in mines, mills, and factories.

Khrushchev was particularly desirous of easing the Soviet relations with the satellites and healing the breach with Tito. He wanted to bring Yugoslavia back into the Soviet orbit. In 1955 Khrushchev went to Belgrade and publicly apologized for the Stalinist policies which had led to the rift. Khrushchev said in effect that the Soviet way of "building socialism" was not the only way, that there were "separate roads to socialism." The following year Tito visited the Soviet Union and was given a great popular reception wherever he went. During the Tito visit the Soviet leaders again assented to Tito's broad ideological view and agreed "that the path of socialist development differs in various countries and conditions, that the multiplicity of forms of socialist development tends to strengthen socialism, and . . . that any tendency of imposing one's opinion on the ways and forms of socialist development is alien to both. . . ." In 1956 the Communist Information Bureau (Cominform), which had been organized by Communist parties in eight European countries and had waged a bitter fight on "Titoism," was abolished. In some of the satellite countries (notably Poland and Hungary) national (Titoist) Communist leaders came out of hiding or were released from the jails to resume careers in their Communist parties. Those who had been executed were now publicly "rehabilitated." The Soviet Union recognized the "sovereignty" of the East German Democratic Republic and withdrew some of its troops from that area. However, there was no real relaxation of the military and economic ties between the satellites and Moscow, and Tito, while somewhat closer to the Soviet Union than he had been at any time since 1948, remained a neutralist and never restored Yugoslavia to the Soviet orbit.

The Soviet Union increased economic aid to Red China and in 1955 surrendered its naval base at Port Arthur. With respect to its non-Communist neighbors, the U.S.S.R. extended diplomatic recognition to the Federal Republic of West Germany, sought to "normalize" its relations with Turkey, and relinquished its naval and military base at Porkkala to Finland. Moscow now boasted that it no longer held any military bases on the soil of other nations.

Khrushchev proclaimed that war between the Communist camp and the "imperialist powers" was not inevitable; indeed, that changed conditions and nuclear weapons now made such a war unthinkable. He proposed a *modus vivendi* for the capitalist and Communist camps, a peaceful and competitive coexistence. The Soviet leader made it clear that the Communists would continue to seek to convert the world to their system, that Communists would give up this aim only "when shrimps learned to whistle." But Khrushchev argued that Communists would come to power peacefully in many countries, that there were many roads to socialism, that capitalist and Communist countries should vie in proving the merits of their respective systems in a world contest in economic productivity and social well-being. Time, he asserted, would prove to the peoples of the world the superiority of the Communist system.

Increasingly the Soviet Union gave economic aid and technical assistance to underdeveloped countries. The Russians envisaged this as an important aspect of their competition with the capitalist countries. The Soviet Union emphasized that "no strings" were attached to its economic aid, that recipients need not become allies of the Soviet Union, that the neutralist position of the non-Communist states would be respected. Moreover, in a way most convenient to underdeveloped countries, the Soviet Union's aid often took the form of trade-aid agreements in which the Russians sent technical assistance and machinery and other capital goods in exchange for the agricultural surpluses of the recipient nations. The U.S.S.R. chose most shrewdly the projects for which it gave aid—projects which were spectacular, impressed the popular mind, and allowed a large number of technicians to enter the recipient country. Very often for much less money the Soviet Union got more good will than the United States with its larger expenditures. To emphasize that the Soviet Union was now rich enough to compete with the United States in economic aid and was in the market for "customers," Khrushchev and Bulganin in 1955 made a barnstorming trip through India, Burma, and Afghanistan and not only negotiated with governments but addressed huge throngs of people. The bouncing Khruschev enjoyed his appearances before these peasant audiences in which he endorsed the aspirations of the anti-imperialist revolutions, promised aid for economic development, and jibed at "the Wall Street capitalists" and "the imperialist warmongers" in the earthy and salty manner of a Gene Talmadge or a Huey Long.

The Iron Curtain was lifted a bit and there were East-West exchanges of scientists, technicians, journalists, artists, musicians, factory managers, farm administrators, and tourists. From Russia came mostly official delegations, from the United States to Russia went not only official delegations but many individual tourists. Russian leaders, particularly Khrushchev, dropped in on diplomatic parties, talked freely to foreign journalists, were readily available to visiting Western notabilities, particularly American. Top Russian leaders increasingly visited Western nations, and Khrushchev and Bulganin while on a tour of Britain publicly debated Nye Bevan and other British Labour party leaders. Later, trade minister Mikoyan, visiting the United States, publicly aired East-West differences with American business and labor leaders. Khrushchev appeared on American television networks in which he took his case directly to the Americans, and in 1959, the ebullient Soviet leader, after official conferences at the White House and Camp David with President Eisenhower, made many public appearances in the United States and complained that his itinerary allowed him to talk only to important people, select groups, and banquets and gave him no opportunity to visit with the people and harangue the multitudes. Khrushchev avidly pursued the scheduling of summit conferences of the top leaders of the Soviet Union, the United States, Britain, and France with a view to settling outstanding East-West differences. It was not clear to Westerners whether Khrushchev genuinely wanted *rapprochement* with the West or was primarily interested in using such conferences as a world propaganda stage.

In the early post-Stalinist years the Soviet government announced cuts in the numerical strength of its conventional armed forces, though this was done more in response to a "new look" at military strategy induced by the development of nuclear weapons than for purposes of *rapprochement;* and it was never clear in the West just how far these announced cuts were actually carried into effect. However, there was no doubt of the relaxation of tensions in the United Nations when in late 1955 the Soviet Union agreed to a package deal whereby a deadlock of many years was broken and twelve non-Communist states were admitted to United Nations membership in return for the admission of four Communist states.

The three most important achievements which came out of the early post-Stalinist thaw were the armistice in Korea in 1953, the end of the war in Indochina and the compromise settlement there in 1954, and the peace treaty with Austria.

It was ironic that the Soviet Union, which for ten years had held out against a sensible peace for Austria, should finally get the credit for sponsoring the negotiations which at last, in May 1955, led to the generous and definitive peace treaty with that country. Austria was re-established as a sovereign, an independent, and a democratic state, within the borders existing before the *Anschluss* of 1938. It was stipulated that Austria was to be neutralized, that it was to join in no military alliances against any of the victorious allies of World War II (neither against the West nor against the East), and that it was to permit no foreign military bases on its soil. After the ratification of the treaty, the Allied occupation ended, and thus the Soviet withdrew from its farthest point of penetration into Central Europe. The Russians meant this treaty to be both a warning and a promise to Germany. The Russians, in effect, were saying to the West Germans: "You see, Austria did not join either side, and now Austria is unified and freed from all foreign occupation. If you West Germans had remained neutral, if you had not joined the West, you, too, might have been reunited with your fellow nationals in the East and your soil cleared of foreign occupation. You West Germans had better reconsider your alliance with the Western powers and your rearmament program, if you want to achieve national reunification."

The climactic event of this "new era" occurred at the famous Meeting at the Summit in Geneva, in July 1955, when the top leaders of the Soviet Union, the United States, Britain, and France came face to face with one another. In the course of this conference, President Eisenhower turned to Bulganin and said for the whole world to hear: "The United States will never take part in an aggressive war." Bulganin replied: "Mr. President, we believe that statement." Here indeed was a momentous exchange. For years, the leaders of the Soviet Union had been proclaiming to their own people and to the world that "the American capitalist warmongers" were bent on waging an aggressive imperialist war to destroy the Soviet Union and Communism, and yet here was Russia's top leader saying out loud in the presence of the whole world that the Soviet leaders now believed in the peaceful intentions of the United States.

What were the motives behind and the causes of the post-Stalinist shift in Soviet policy, both at home and abroad?

The ruthlessness and drive of revolutions tend with time to slow down, and perhaps the Russian Revolution would be no exception to this general rule. We have already discussed the reasons for the de-Stalinization campaign and alluded to the fact that Russia's industrial revolution had spawned hundreds of thousands of engineers, technicians, directors, managers, and university-trained personnel who, while loyal to the Communist system, resented the activities of the secret police and wanted more personal and intellectual freedoms and a wider latitude of decision-making in their own jobs. The Soviet government could no longer ignore the pressures of these new classes. However, the process of liberalization would have to be a slow one, with tentative advances and then some frightened reversals, for if liberalization proceeded either too rapidly or too slowly there would be danger of a social explosion. At the very best, it would take at least a generation for accumulating accommodations to work a substantial modification of the Soviet Union's police state and dictatorship, personal or collective.

Perhaps the most important reason for the relative relaxation was that Russia was now pretty well over the industrial hump, the historical breakthrough to industrialism had been achieved. (Years ago Walter Duranty, the New York *Times* correspondent in Moscow in the early years of Bolshevik rule, predicted that there would be no relenting of dictatorship until Russian steel production began to approximate that of the United States.) Moreover, eight years had now elapsed since the end of the war and Russia had repaired much of its frightful damage. About one-third of the wealth of Russia had been destroyed in the war, yet Russia had achieved sufficient industrial momentum to retrieve the enormous losses in less than a decade. This, rather than the death of Stalin, explained the decision to increase somewhat the amount of consumer goods. It was Malenkov, who was closest to Stalin, who wanted to increase the volume of consumer goods still more. Russia's industrial strength also explained the new emphasis on Soviet aid to the underdeveloped peoples. Indeed, the determination to do this was largely made in 1952 at the nineteenth congress of the Soviet Communist party, still under the domination of Stalin. Stalin's successors merely implemented, accelerated, and widened a decision already made before Stalin's death.

In shifting its position with respect to the Western powers, the post-Stalinist leadership was merely accommodating itself to facts. No strong Communist party had developed in West Germany. Communist parties in France and Italy, so formidable in the immediate postwar years, had failed to grow as expected. Stimulated by Marshall Plan aid, Western Europe had experienced a remarkable postwar economic recovery. American capitalism was booming in 1953, and the postwar economic depression predicted by Soviet economists for the United States showed no signs of developing. Neither was there any evidence that the "Western imperialist powers" would tear themselves to pieces in mutually destructive imperialist rivalries and wars, as Stalin to the very end proclaimed they would do. (Even the Suez crisis would produce only a temporary rift in the Western alliance.) Instead, the Western powers were bound together in military alliances, they had successfully rearmed, and they were in a position to face the Soviet Union from the vantage point of a new strength. In a sense, the shift in Soviet foreign policy was a tribute to the continuing prosperity of the American economic system and the success of American foreign policy in Europe.

Now that Russia was surrounded by Communist countries and satellites and at last had its own hydrogen bombs and other advanced nuclear developments, the Russians, too, believed that they could negotiate from the vantage point of a new national security. The Hungarian Revolution would shake this new Russian confidence some, but only slightly and briefly.

A recognition of the revolution in the technology of war caused by the nuclear weapons was probably the most important reason for the Soviet Union's new departure. The Russians, like human beings everywhere, were frightened by the awesome prospects of nuclear war. Perhaps more than most peoples they were impressed by these because in World War II, according to various estimates, the Russians had lost in killed alone from 20 to 30 million individuals. More, the Soviet Union was becoming less and less a "have not" country, and by 1953 it had colossal industrial developments. The very thought of the destruction of these, built at so much human sacrifice and the supreme pride of Communist achievement, was a nightmare.

Significantly, the Soviet theoreticians had come to the conclusion that in a nuclear war there could be no victor, that capitalism and Communism would both be destroyed. Soviet military experts agreed with General Nikolai A. Talensky that "an aggressor could not hope to survive, even in the event of a surprise attack," and that "it was impossible to use weapons for the solution of political tasks as has been the case in the course of thousands of years." The Marxists began revising their doctrine about the inevitability of war between the capitalist countries and the Communist countries. They believed, now the Soviet Union had nuclear weapons and was so strong scientifically, technologically, and industrially that it could replace them in the event disarmament agreements broke down, that the capitalist powers would realize that they could not overthrow Communism by force and that the two systems would have to test their strength in other forms of competition. For Lenin and Stalin, "peaceful coexistence" was a temporary, tactical doctrine required during that passing interlude in history when both systems were in being prior to the inevitable climactic military clash. But with Khrushchev, peaceful and competitive coexistence became a long-time, strategic doctrine necessary to the interest of the Soviet Union and the eventual peaceful triumph of Communism. As we shall see later, not all Marxists agreed with this analysis, which became official Soviet doctrine under Khrushchev, and there would be years of bitter debate in the Communist world over the acceptance of this tenet of permanent peaceful coexistence.

Another motive was behind the coexistence drive. In 1959 Khrushchev announced that the Soviet Union—alone—would move from "the socialist stage," in which citizens were remunerated in accordance with their work, to "the communist stage," in which there would be economic plenty and citizens would be rewarded not according to their work but to their needs. "Economic plenty," in the communist sense, would not be the riot of consumer goods of the American economy but simply satisfying essential consumer needs by Soviet standards. The urge to reach American productivity (but not the plethora of American luxuries), to prove to the world the merits of the Soviet system, and to enter "the communist stage" of human development seemed to be the overriding goals of the Soviet leadership. However, the achieving of these goals would inevitably be slowed down unless the U.S.S.R. could divert much of the capital accumulations and labor used in producing armaments to producing electric and nuclear power plants, industrial and agricultural equipment, scientific research for peaceful purposes, consumer goods, and social services. But the Russians, like the Americans, felt they could not afford to disarm unilaterally; they, like the Americans, were saddled with huge armaments until the international tensions were ended or appreciably reduced and arms-control or disarmament agreements made.

Despite the post-Stalinist thaw, the Cold War continued. The Russians feared America's military alliances, the threats to the

Soviet "defense area" in Eastern Europe, the rearming of the West Germans, the ring of bases in countries bordering on the Soviet Union. The Americans feared the Communist system and its police state, the use of Communist parties as Soviet fifth columns, the fomenting of totalitarian revolution even in lands remote from the Soviet Union. Americans were also anxious about the repeated obstacles the Russians placed in the way of a world order based on law, their ruthless and nasty tactics, and their Delphic ambiguity which made it agonizingly difficult to know when to believe them and when not to believe them.

The new Soviet flexibility posed a new challenge to American leadership. It was not long before many Western Europeans, whose standard of living suffered more from the rearmament program than the standard of living of Americans, were saying: "Now that the Soviet threat is diminishing, why should we continue to bear the burdens of heavy armaments and military alliances?" Soon demands arose that the military features of NATO be diminished and its economic and social features enlarged. Some of the Socialists and social democrats of Western Europe were impressed by the new Russian slogan that there were many roads to socialism and that the Soviet brand was not the only brand. Was it not a bit safer now for Communists and Socialists to cooperate? As a result of the increased Soviet economic aid and technical assistance to underdeveloped peoples, the bargaining power of these peoples was enhanced and they were better able to play one side off against the other. At the same time the Communists continued to proclaim that Communism was the surest and most self-reliant way for an underdeveloped society to get an industrial revolution in a hurry. In addition to the shrewd ways the Russians had of giving their economic aid (already mentioned) the personality equation also loomed as a new difficulty for America. Many of the Russian representatives abroad were of peasant origin, and when they soft-pedaled their conspiratorial roles and their doctrinaire Marxist attitudes and exploited their earthy characteristics they could be very attractive personalities to the peasant peoples of the backward countries. On the other hand, American representatives abroad reflected a wealthier society and middle-class attitudes. Very often they appeared as patronizing do-gooders or as pallid functionaries or as too smooth salesmen with chamber-of-commerce and Madison Avenue techniques. As the contest for the friendship of the underdeveloped peoples intensified, the final outcome might well turn as much on manners as on substance.

The Ups and Downs of American-Soviet Relations

Although the power and ideological conflict between the East and the West was constant and continued after 1953, there were periods of relative intensity and of relative accommodation. For the sake of clarity it might be well to point out the roughly demarcated periods into which the postwar years fell. This would also show how even during periods of relative good feeling there were also many difficulties, and how the various situations, scattered as they were throughout the world, usually converged and operated not separately or successively but interdependently and simultaneously.

The period from 1945 to 1947 was one of attempted cooperation, although even in this period there were the breakdown of the Yalta agreements, the accumulating difficulties over administering Germany, the civil war in China, the civil war in Greece, the Russian maneuvers in northern Iran, the Russian claim to a voice in the Turkish Straits, the differences over the Baruch Plan, Winston Churchill's Iron Curtain Speech, and so forth.

The period from 1947 to 1953 was that covered by the first years of acknowledged Cold War and the building of two worlds, the period which saw the Truman Doctrine, the overt division of Germany, the shift from reform to anti-Communism in Japan, the Communist coup in Czechoslovakia, the Marshall Plan, the defection of Tito, the Berlin blockade, the building of NATO, the triumph of the Communist revolution in China, and the hot war in Korea.

The period from 1953 to 1956 was the period of the post-Stalin thaw, but it was also the period during which NATO was expanded with the WEU treaties and Germany brought into the alliance and rearmed, the Indochina war continued for a time, SEATO and METO alliances were built by Secretary of State Dulles, the first grave crisis over Quemoy and Matsu occurred, and the leftist revolution in Guatemala was liquidated.

Despite the fact that the Soviet Union and the United States saw eye to eye for a short time in the Suez crisis, the period from 1956 to 1958 was one of hardening of American-Soviet relations during which the Russians suppressed the Hungarian Revolution, Nasser and Khrushchev reached the high peak of their cooperation in the Middle East, the crisis over Iraq, Lebanon, and Jordan occurred, and the second grave crisis in the Formosa Straits took place.

The period from 1958 to 1960 was one which witnessed the highest hopes for *rapprochement,* when Khrushchev, following the illness and death of Secretary Dulles, made his great pitch for the Paris summit to inaugurate an East-West *rapprochement,* when the Soviet premier toured the United States and made with President Eisenhower the agreements of Camp David; but it was also the period when Khrushchev made his demands for settlement of the Berlin and German questions and indicated that such settlement was the prerequisite of *rapprochement* and agreements on armaments.

If the period of 1958-1960 was that of Khrushchev's "soft sell," the one after it was the period of Khrushchev's "hard sell." The U-2 incident and the torpedoing of the Paris summit conference ushered in a time during which Khrushchev, while still maintaining that he wanted *rapprochement,* took a more belligerent line. These were the years of renewed Berlin crisis, the step-up of the guerrilla war in South Vietnam, the crisis in Laos, in the Congo, and in Cuba.

At the end of 1962, there was a mellowing on the part of Khrushchev, produced by a number of causes: the realization of how near Russia and the United States had come to nuclear war over Cuba in October, and a new determination to escape such crises in the future; the Red Chinese attack on India; the widening rift between Russia and China. During December 1962 and January 1963, it probably would have been easier to initiate the beginnings of Soviet-American *rapprochement* than at any time since the commencement of the Cold War. But De Gaulle's disruptive force within the Western alliance, ruthlessly revealed in January and February 1963, caused some stiffening in the Soviet leadership.

Again it should be emphasized that those charged with the

formulation of American foreign policy were confronted with many simultaneously operating and interrelated situations and cross-currents in all parts of the world every day in the year.

America's New Look at Military Strategy

When the Eisenhower administration came to power in 1953, it undertook a reappraisal of America's vast military commitments and came to the conclusion that there must be some change in America's over-all strategy. It was assumed that the international crisis would go on indefinitely and that America would have to maintain vast armaments and military forces for a long time to come. For the long pull, the administration felt that the United States was militarily over-extended. There was general recognition that the United States could not go back to pre-Korean days, when in early 1950 Congress debated whether the defense budget should go to 16 billion dollars, but it was also felt that defense budgets in the 60-billion or even 50-billion-dollar brackets were excessive. Was it not just as important to maintain a sound economy as it was to be adequately prepared militarily? And a sound economy, it was argued, could not be maintained with defense spending continuing at the 1953 levels and with so much of America's manpower absorbed in military pursuits. Super-taxation must yield to more moderate taxation, the budget must be trimmed and real attempts made to balance it, and an all-out effort made to halt inflation. If this involved some "disengagements," the risks taken would be more than compensated for by the strengthening of the American economy. In short, American military strategy and commitments must be adjusted in such a way that these could be maintained over the years, over the decades if need be, without wounding the American economy.

Had not the development of nuclear weapons reached the point where these could be relied on to a much greater extent, relieving America of maintaining so many of the old conventional armaments and weapons and such large ground forces? Bombers that could fly around the world without landing or refueling, long-range jet bombers, guided missiles, and intercontinental ballistic missiles were being developed, and would not these free the Americans from having to maintain so many bases abroad and even from the necessity of maintaining as large an air force as formerly?

President Eisenhower's defense budgets reflected some of this new thinking. Even President Truman's later-year budgets had cut defense spending from around 61 billion dollars in 1951-1952 to around 52 billion dollars in 1952-1953. As outgoing President, Truman had recommended a defense budget of around 41 billion dollars for 1953-1954. The Eisenhower administration, however, cut this to around 35 billion dollars. Much of this progressive trimming was the result first of the diminished fighting and then of the end of the fighting in Korea. But some of it represented shifts in long-time strategy and commitments. For 1954-1955, Eisenhower proposed a defense budget of around 34 billion dollars and cuts in the military forces from 3.218 million to 3 million. For 1955-1956, the defense budget was again around 34 billion dollars and the President recommended further cuts in the military forces from 3 million to 2.85 million. In June 1956, however, Congress, feeling that the administration was going too far in defense economies, insisted on a larger air force budget and passed a total defense budget of nearly 35 billion dollars.

The administration did not shrink from the implications of this new look for military strategy. In January 1955, Secretary of State Dulles declared that the National Security Council had taken a basic decision "to depend primarily upon a great capacity to retaliate instantly by means and at places of our choosing." This came to be known as "massive retaliation" by atomic weapons.

This new strategy stirred the gravest misgivings both in the United States and among America's allies. Who would do the choosing as to when and where a hydrogen bomb was to be used? Would America's allies be consulted? How about humanitarian considerations? Was every little war to be turned into a nuclear holocaust? Would not world opinion be alienated? (In May 1956, the United States announced that in a test at Bikini, the United States had proved that the hydrogen bomb could be dropped from a jet bomber on any chosen target, and that it was estimated that such a blast in a populated area would flatten nearly all buildings within six miles from the blast and do heavy damage within a radius of twelve miles. After this announcement, the fears of hydrogen bomb warfare increased.) Specifically, where were high-powered nuclear weapons, presumably even hydrogen bombs, to be used in retaliation? For instance, in the war in Vietnam, did the American government propose to use a hydrogen bomb in the Vietnam jungle? If so, how effective would it be on a non-industrial people fighting a guerrilla war and living on the country? Would the United States implement its assumption that the fighting in Vietminh was made possible by Chinese and Russian encouragement and supplies, and if so, would the United States bomb Chinese cities, even Russian cities? Moreover, did not the whole world know that Russia now had the hydrogen bomb, and would not "retaliation" lead to "counter-retaliation"?

The new American doctrine raised the most articulate alarms in Europe. Would not the European countries with American air bases be the first targets of Russian nuclear reprisals? But if "massive retaliation" were found actually to be impracticable, after Americans had based their strategy and preparations on it, would the United States be sufficiently prepared in ground forces and conventional weapons to fight the little local wars that neither side dared turn into big ones? If no longer able to wage the local wars effectively, would not the West be "nibbled away" by them not only in Europe but in the brushfire wars of Asia? And would not the impairment of America's conventional weapons and ground forces invite a Russian attack on Germany and Western Europe by conventional weapons and ground forces? Then how was America, its conventional weapons and ground forces neglected, to liberate Western Europe? By dropping hydrogen bombs on the Russian-occupied territories of its allies and slaughtering allied populations in attempting to "liberate" them? Would America's new concentration on nuclear weapons lead to America's abandonment of its European allies and bases, since these would no longer be so necessary for the defense of America if America were to abandon the old concepts of war for the nuclear concepts? Either way, the West Europeans, particularly the West Germans, were frightened by America's new nuclear strategy— if America used nuclear weapons on Russia, they would be the first victims of a Russian retaliation of like kind; if America found it impracticable to use the methods of full-scale nuclear war, then a Russian attack would be invited and the West Europeans likewise would be the first victims, this time of Russia's vast superiority in conventional weapons and ground forces, which America, in emphasizing nuclear war, had neglected. Conceivably, the new strategy might protect the United States, but it certainly would not "protect" Western Europe. Later, when there was greater awareness of the dangers from radioactive fallout, Europeans wondered whether an all-out nuclear attack on Russia by the United States would not have serious fallout consequences in European countries outside Russia.

The Dulles doctrine of massive retaliation was subjected to much intellectual as well as practical criticism. It was argued that massive retaliation came out of the American doctrine of "the just war," and that, too, came in for critical analysis. The "just war" doctrine, in its pure form, held that the right to employ force in international affairs was limited to the contingency of a prior armed aggression. Did not this doctrine over-simplify the differences between preventive and defensive war? Might not a preventive war be defensive in every sense save for the initially "aggressive" act of resorting to armed force, and might not the state made the object of the preventive use of force wage a war that was anything but defensive except for the fact that it did not literally initiate the armed conflict? Did not the doctrine of defensive war assume that "the first blow" would not be decisive, and was that assumption warranted when the powers had nuclear weapons? Were there not aggressions as dangerous and unjust as overt armed aggression—subversion and satellitism, for instance? When a nation went to war in response to aggression should it limit itself to repelling the immediate danger or should it go ahead and fight a war of unconditional surrender to remove the danger? It seemed that the American doctrine held that once war came it should be expanded to the broadest of objectives.

Out of this doctrine of a defensive and just war had come the doctrine of deterrence of aggression by the ever-present threat of massive retaliation. This doctrine presupposed for its success a united and determined national will always ready to sustain the threat of massive annihilation regardless of the intrinsic value of the place or places attacked. It was based on the sanguine expectation that it would succeed, that it would actually banish force from history.

What if this continuing threat of massive retaliation should in fact fail to deter? Then the literal annihilation of an aggressor might readily be justified as a defensive measure. All that was necessary was that the act of annihilation be attended by a defensive purpose! Defense for whom? For the nation with the power to inflict the massive retaliation. In the final analysis, then, the massive retaliation would be justified by the nation that employed it on the ground that national survival or even national security was an absolute value transcending moral judgment or that that particular nation embodied transcendent moral values necessary to all mankind.

But what if the policy of deterrence through the continuing threat of massive retaliation should prove to be an unqualified success? What if by this process force were really banned from international relations? What if even "indirect aggression" and "subversion" were prevented in this way? Would this be a desirable world order? Would it be a just peace? Would it not corrupt the purposes it allegedly was designed to serve? Would it not freeze the *status quo* and prevent even desirable change? Would it not be a peace resting on force, coercion, and in the final analysis on the unilateral fiat of the power with nuclear superiority? (One of the ablest critiques of "the just war" doctrine was written by Professor Robert W. Tucker, and his and other critiques caused much discussion among American publicists.)

To allay these alarms, the Eisenhower administration stated its military aims more explicitly. Dulles explained that the American emphasis on nuclear weapons did not mean full-scale nuclear war, that the Americans merely planned to make more use of smaller nuclear weapons pinpointed to limited objectives. There would be no neglect of conventional weapons and ground forces. There would be no abandonment of bases abroad or of America's allies. What the United States was aiming at was somewhat more emphasis on the new instruments and weapons. However, the old, too, would be maintained and a better balance of old and new arrived at, in harmony with the new technological realities. Somewhat later, after the United States had developed a nuclear second strike capacity, President Eisenhower announced that the United States would never strike the first blow in a nuclear war.

American nationalists liked the new look. Economy-minded

Byrd Democrats and Taft Republicans liked it. Even America's cooperationists were not too displeased, because in practice it worked out not as a revolution but only as a new and moderate balancing of all the military factors. Moreover, the Eisenhower administration maintained an international foreign policy in cooperation with the allies. Even some neutralists in Europe were not too displeased. These thought they saw in the new look's military cutbacks some moderating of American aggressiveness, an abandonment of any idea of a preventive war, and perhaps a new emphasis on the non-military elements in meeting the challenge of Communism. If the new look could satisfy Taftites and Bevanites, as well as cooperationists, it would indeed be a political feat of no mean proportions.

Actually, in one important respect, America's European allies had taken premature alarm. Operational intercontinental guided missiles were still some years away, but by the mid-1950's it appeared that intermediate missiles would be a reality by 1957 or 1958. Intermediate missiles could be fired at the heart of the Soviet Union from American bases in Europe, but they could not be fired from the Western Hemisphere. Thus, for some time to come, the United States would have a new and an additional need for bases in Europe.

The United States was not the only power which adjusted its military strategy to nuclear weapons and missiles. The Soviet Union announced cuts in its ground forces, although it continued to enjoy a heavy preponderance in ground forces and conventional weapons in Europe. In 1957, Britain took a "new look" at its military situation and announced a drastic reduction in conventional arms and military and naval forces. Henceforth Britain would rely more on its own developing nuclear weapons and primarily on the American nuclear deterrent.

In the closing years of the Eisenhower administration there was much criticism of the Eisenhower defense policies. It was charged that the urge to economy had weakened America's defense position. It was claimed that in emphasizing the nuclear deterrent the ability of the United States to fight conventional wars had been seriously impaired. It was said that failure to maintain adequate ground forces had resulted in too few American forces in Europe and encouraged America's allies to neglect their own ground-

force contributions to NATO. America's lack of units trained
to fight guerrilla wars also caused criticism. Mainly, however, the
complaints were directed at the alleged inadequacy of the nuclear
deterrent, the allowing of the Russians "to get ahead" in missiles
and in the exploration of outer space. These criticisms bulked
large in Senator John F. Kennedy's campaign for the presidency.
On the other hand, President Eisenhower maintained that the
bomber force of the United States Strategic Air Command, supplemented by the Polaris missile-carrying submarines, represented
a fully adequate deterrent force, and that America's missile and
space programs had not been neglected.

American missile developments during the Eisenhower administration were greater than realized at the time. The truth was
that the missile gap in favor of the Russians was largely a fiction.
The Russians boasted having operational intercontinental missiles
in 1958 and 1959. American intelligence experts apparently mistook Soviet capacity for building ICBM's for actual production.
While the Russians got their big missiles on an operational basis
before the United States, production faltered because the heavy
manufacturing costs put too much strain on the Soviet economy.
Instead of concentrating on intercontinental missiles, the Soviets
concentrated on the production of less costly intermediate missiles. As a result, by 1962, according to reliable estimates, the
Russians had more intermediate missiles than the West, but the
West had more intercontinental missiles than the Russians. The
chief intercontinental missile of the West was the American
Atlas, which was liquid-fueled and required a fixed site for launch-
ing. The Americans might have produced far more first-generation missiles, both intercontinental and intermediate, but they
were waiting until the second-generation missiles, which were to
be solid-fueled and mobile, became operational before going into
fuller production. However, the Eisenhower administration went
ahead with preparations to make effective use, should the need
arise, of the first-generation missiles. Bases for nuclear-armed intermediate-range missiles were even set up in Europe—for Thors
in Britain, and for Jupiters in Italy and Turkey. Some of these
reached operational status in early 1960, the nuclear warheads remaining in tight American custody. In the meantime, the Eisenhower administration concentrated successfully on the develop-

ment of the Polaris missile, intermediate in range and carried and fired by submarines. The great advantages of the Polaris submarine were its undersurface mobility and the fact that it carried the solid-fuel Polaris missile. The Eisenhower administration also paid great attention to the development of the Air Force's Minuteman, which eventually emerged as an intercontinental solid-fuel missile with a speed of 15,000 miles per hour and a range of over 6,300 miles, capable of being launched in seconds (since it would not have to be fueled), storable in underground silos, and mobile, able to be moved by truck, railway, and barge and therefore less vulnerable to surprise attack. The Minuteman did not become operational until after Eisenhower left office.

During its first two years, the Kennedy administration expanded America's defense policies. The defense budget of Eisenhower's last year, 1960-1961, was close to 40 billion dollars. The defense budget of Kennedy's first year, 1961-1962, was upped to 44.66 billion dollars. The Strategic Air Command extended its airborne alert capacity. The Kennedy administration expanded the program for Polaris submarines and for missiles, particularly the new solid-fuel missiles. During 1961 and 1962, there was an increase in the number of Polaris submarines available for combat, the number of first-generation Atlases went up significantly, and the Titan and the Minuteman seemed well on the way to operational development. To decrease the chance of accidental nuclear war, the warning systems were improved and the nuclear deterrent forces were put under tight control.

In late 1961, to allay fears in the United States that Russia was "ahead" in the arms race, Deputy Secretary of Defense Roswell L. Gilpatric, with the blessings of the Kennedy administration, declared publicly: "Our defenses are so deployed and protected that a sneak attack could not effectively disarm us. . . . In short, we have a second strike capacity which is at least as extensive as what the Soviets can deliver by striking first. Therefore we are confident that the Soviets will not provoke a major nuclear conflict." This statement was particularly significant because both Presidents Eisenhower and Kennedy had proclaimed that the United States would never strike the first blow in a nuclear war. Incidentally, Gilpatric's statement was a tacit admission by the Kennedy administration that the Eisenhower administration had not been remiss in American defense, for obviously the Kennedy administration could not claim the credit for so strong an American defense position after having been in office so short a time.

By 1963 the defense policies of Robert S. McNamara, President Kennedy's Secretary of Defense, were clearly in evidence. McNamara believed in a balanced defense strategy emphasizing both conventional and nuclear arms. The Army's combat divisions were boosted from eleven to sixteen, the tactical wings of the Air Force from sixteen to twenty-one, and the Marine Corps from 85,000 men to 100,000 men. For guerrilla activity, the Army's Special Force was tripled to 5,600 men. Through improved air lift, United States troops would be able to move much more rapidly to the world's trouble spots.

McNamara was also determined to build NATO's ground forces from their 1962 strength of twenty-four divisions to the long-sought thirty divisions. (In 1963 there were around 400,000 American troops stationed in Europe.) McNamara pointed out that an all-out Soviet attack in Europe, even if such an attack were limited to non-nuclear means, would require the use of tactical nuclear weapons and eventually perhaps strategic nuclear weapons as well, unless NATO's ground forces were strong enough to cope with the Soviet attack. Both President Kennedy and Secretary McNamara lost no opportunity to persuade the Western European allies to meet their ground-force quotas.

By 1963 it was estimated that the United States had around 50,000 nuclear warheads and bombs, theoretically enough nuclear concentration to wipe out the Soviet Union many times over. (Actual effectiveness would depend on the ever-improving delivery systems.) By that year, too, nine Polaris submarines, each carrying sixteen missiles that could be fired from beneath the sea and with ranges from 1,380 to 1,725 miles, patrolled the North Atlantic. The aim was to have at least thirty Polaris submarines by 1966, forty-one by 1967, with A-3 models with a range of 2,875 miles. By 1963, too, a year ahead of schedule, Minuteman missiles were operational and protected in hidden underground silos in Montana. It was expected that by 1966, approximately 950 Minutemen would be ready to fire. The intermediate Polaris and the intercontinental Minuteman had become the chief reliance in American nuclear strategy, and American land bases in Europe were becoming less important. McNamara reportedly believed that manned bombers would be obsolescent by the early 1970's.

In the spring of 1963 the United States began dismantling its intermediate missile bases in Britain, Italy, and Turkey, with a view to substituting Polaris submarines for the immobile, vulnerable Thors and Jupiters, which had come to be regarded as "sitting duck" targets for the enemy. To compensate for the removal of the 60 Thor missiles from Britain at least eight Polaris submarines would be operating out of Holy Loch, Scotland, each carrying 16 missiles. To replace the 30 Jupiters in Italy and the 15 Jupiters in Turkey, the United States planned to deploy, by the end of 1963, possibly six Polaris submarines in Mediterranean waters with a total firepower of ninety-six Polaris missiles.

There were charges that the Kennedy administration had made a "deal" with Khrushchev, that the United States was dismantling its missile bases in Italy and Turkey in return for Khrushchev's removal of Soviet intermediate missiles from Cuba and his acceptance of on-site inspection in a prospective treaty banning nuclear testing. The Kennedy administration denied that there was any connection between these events. It insisted that the decision to dismantle American missile bases in Italy and Turkey had been taken independently and on purely strategic grounds. This answer pleased those American who thought that any bargaining with the Russians was "dishonorable." On the other hand, those Americans who were "power politics"-minded wondered why the Kennedy administration had not held out for *quid pro quo*s in return for America's retirement from the Italian and Turkish bases, even though that retirement had been already planned.

The Nuclear Revolution in War

Just how far advanced were nuclear weapons and missile systems and their diffusion among the nations in the early 1960's? These had not proceeded as far as the general public supposed; the public imagination usually ran a few years ahead of the actualities. In 1962 both Russian and American missile forces were small, and the main striking power of both countries was still in their bombers, which had steadily improved in speed, range, and altitude but had limited capability with respect to massive annihilation of peoples. The popular image of massive annihilations as a possible consequence of war would be a more likely reality for the middle and late 1960's if countervailing defenses were not developed.

By 1963 both the United States and the Soviet Union were believed to have a nuclear second-strike capacity, that is, the ability to survive a first nuclear attack and deliver a devastating counter-blow. By the middle and late 1960's, missiles—short range, intermediate, and intercontinental—would supplant bombers as the chief striking power of the United States and the Soviet Union. It was authoritatively estimated that by 1966 the number of American manned-bombers would fall from an approximate high of 1,600 in 1963 to an approximate 700; that on the other hand the number of Polaris missiles would increase from over 140 in 1963 to an approximate 500 in 1966; and the number of intercontinental missiles (Atlas, Titan, and Minuteman) from an approximate 200 in 1963 to an approximate 1,100 in 1966.

"Gigatons" of 1000 megatons and "begatons" of even greater force were sometimes spoken of as possibilities for the 1970's. (The Soviets in late 1961 exploded a bomb which for all practical purposes had the force of 100 megatons, that is, of 100 million tons of TNT.) Perhaps by the 1980's Herman Kahn's anticipated "near-doomsday" machine, a device or set of devices which when exploded in place would destroy all unprotected life on a continent and, in addition, have major world-wide effects, would be a reality.

The diffusion of nuclear weapons among the nations was not as rapid as it was feared it would be. Britain's development of nuclear weapons was most limited, and France was finding it more difficult and expensive to become a diversified nuclear power than her leaders had anticipated. Red China was still working on the technology of ordinary atomic and nuclear bombs. No nation had made a cobalt bomb. Neither Japan nor India had nuclear-weapons programs. After the French achieved a nuclear explosion it was thought the West Germans, the Italians, and perhaps the Swedes and the Swiss would make a pitch for atomic weapons. However, the West Germans were limited by treaties in this matter, and the other countries showed little inclination to adopt nuclear-weapons programs.

But nuclear technologists pointed out that as the making of

nuclear weapons and missiles became less expensive (some were even talking in terms of a "suitcase" bomb) the proliferation of nuclear powers, some with relatively large nuclear arsenals and some with small ones, probably in the 1970's, more certainly in the 1980's, would become a terrifying reality, unless international agreements abolishing or severely limiting nuclear weapons were made. Once nuclear weapons spread, it would of course be infinitely more difficult to make international agreements controlling them. Unless there was complete abolition of all nuclear devices the late-comers and the small powers which had the weapons would then be asked to accept a reduction in their current capability rather than simply to abstain from acquiring weapons. (This was one of the reasons the Chinese Communists opposed Khrushchev's drive for summit conferences and international agreements; the Chinese wanted no agreements until they had their own nuclear weapons and could get in on the bargaining.)

A world of many nuclear powers would be even more terrifying than the present one. The possibilities of war through mechanical or human error, false alarm, or unauthorized behavior would be enormously increased. Opportunities for anonymous mischief-making would multiply. If a nation were attacked by a Polaris-type submarine, how would it know which of the many nations was responsible? Would not a small nation be tempted through subterfuge attacks to set off a war between two large powers for purposes of its own? What would become of the nuclear deterrent? If aggressors could not be identified with accuracy how could they be restrained by threat of nuclear retaliation? If "suitcase" bombs became a reality, what would prevent rebels, guerrillas, and terrorists from acquiring them? The world was still a long way from such a nightmare situation (indeed, this was much farther off than the public imagination had it), but some such grotesque anarchy might well develop in future decades unless international controls were made and enforced.

What would nuclear weapons do to the future of war as a science and an institution? One group held that by the time of World War I and World War II, technology had already made war total, and now the nuclear revolution had made war "totally total" and therefore obsolete. They argued that now the world would have to develop international institutions that would provide for the settlement of disputes among the nations by peaceful legal and political methods. The other school disagreed vigorously. These argued that even should international organization eventually develop to the point of effectively controlling and even eliminating war that there would be a considerable time lapse before this could take place, and in the meantime how would nations in unyielding conflict maintain their vital interests and basic concepts of justice except in the last resort by force? What the nuclear revolution had done, this group maintained, was to widen the kinds of wars available. Efforts should be made to wage "limited" wars, "controlled" wars; nations should return to the old concepts of "measured warfare." It was pointed out that until the world wars of the twentieth century, the conduct of war had always been guided, graded, and hedged about by the prudent regulations of the science of war itself. To this group, the nuclear revolution had not abolished war but created a situation demanding that war be conducted in a more rigidly precise and discriminating way.

There was much discussion of the kinds of war now available and of the ways these should be fought. It was pointed out that nuclear weapons did not mean "all-out" war, "spasm war," wars of annihilation, indiscriminate strikes by each side on the bases and cities of the other. Every attempt should be made to limit war as to area and the kinds of weapons used. Most wars could and probably would still be fought with conventional arms and ground forces. Not to be prepared to fight such wars, to put sole reliance in nuclear weapons, the use of which could be justified only in a last resort, was to put the nation and its interests in an untenable and fatal position. This, it was contended, was the trouble with the massive retaliation doctrine; in its concentration on nuclear weapons it was likely to denude the nation of its conventional arms and leave it unprepared to fight small-scale conventional wars.

But how about the lesser nuclear weapons, the tactical ones suitable for battlefield purposes, and the smaller rockets which could be fitted with either conventional or nuclear weapons? All of them were far more destructive than the high-explosive weapons of World War I and World War II. Where did tactical nuclear weapons leave off and strategic ones begin? Would not a weapon which was "tactical" in an Asian jungle become "strategic" when used in highly populous Europe? Just how destructive in the scale of tactical weapons could one go before the other side brought in still more destructive ones, and then the plainly strategic ones?

If the war became general, waged in various parts of the world, could it still be kept "limited" as to weapons? The advocates of guided, graded, and measured warfare thought that it could and that indeed it would. The result would be calculatedly controlled general nuclear war—controlled targets and methods, controlled force and counterforce, controlled retaliation, a nuclear tit for a nuclear tat, graded strategic escalation. The first strike would probably be at a restricted and minor military or industrial target, with care not to kill civilians unnecessarily, using low kiloton bombs rather than multi-megaton bombs, and air bursts rather than ground bursts. (It is the ground bursts that produce the "local" fallout which threatens people hundreds of miles from the explosion.) Then the other side would strike at a slightly more important target of the attacking country. Presumably a pause would follow for appraisal and negotiations. Each side would say: "Have you had enough?" If there was no urge to fruitful negotiation, the war would go on. The party which had struck the first blow would then attack a more important target. The other party would retaliate by striking a still more important target, or include a wider area of kill than the immediate target, or use a low megaton bomb, or use ground bursts, or a combination of some or all of these. The other side would answer in kind, or step up the target, or the other elements of the attack, or both. Again there might be a pause for appraisal and negotiation. If there was still no agreement, the war of tit-for-tat would proceed, finally to a city for a city, with or without warning, with more ground bursts, with bombs of greater megaton strength. And so on.

Opponents of nuclear war and of maintaining an elaborate arsenal of nuclear weapons expressed alarm that the proponents of nuclear weapons did not take into sufficient account in both beginning and waging nuclear war the possibility of technical and human mistakes somewhere along the line in the network of warning, command, and control systems. Proponents answered that these were questions of efficiency in techniques, that while the possibility of error could not be ruled out entirely, the technical systems could be made almost air-tight in their reliability, and that both the leading nuclear powers would have to develop procedures in which neither side was under any necessity to make rushed decisions.

Proponents of limited local war and controlled general war ran up against their most serious difficulties in the political and social obstacles. Skeptics pointed out that the non-total and controlled wars of the seventeenth, eighteenth, and nineteenth centuries, which incidentally were never as "controlled" as some thought, were conducted in an age when decisions were made by an elite, few people were involved directly in war, the theaters of war were usually remote, and the rise and fall in the fortunes of the belligerents, because of lack of mass communications, were not followed closely or immediately by the public. But in the mid-twentieth century, decisions were subject to immediate mass response, even in non-democratic countries, and the decision makers and the elites had a much less free hand; all people regarded themselves as direct participants in war; and mass communications brought war to an aroused public every minute of the day. The proponents of limited, measured warfare envisaged a rational and mechanical conduct of war which would be difficult if not impossible to practice in twentieth-century mass societies. Total war was the product not merely of the technological revolution in war but in everything else, and the social impact of that revolution could not be escaped.

Nevertheless, proponents and opponents aside, the mid-twentieth-century situation was entirely without precedent. After all, both the Korean War and the Indochina War had been local and limited wars in the sense envisaged by the adherents of controlled war, although it was important to note that in neither of these cases had the main contenders in the world contest faced each other in hot war. But what of a local war in which the principal rivals were directly involved? What would happen if one of them was losing the local, limited war? Would not the one losing it begin using the deadlier weapons? Would not the war become a general one? Would there be enough rationality to allow the waging of a controlled general nuclear war? What if in a tit-for-tat nuclear war one side was losing more of its strategic sites, missiles, and weapons than the other? Would not decision makers, pressured by mounting mass hysteria, become more indiscriminate in their strikes against the other side until the war cascaded into a spasm war? One could not be sure of the answers. Nuclear weapons had confronted man with a situation entirely unprecedented. Mass emotions on both sides might be held in check by the individual fear of death. On the other hand mass pressures might be exerted for all-out slaughter, for a war of annihilation. If a mutually controlled general nuclear war between the United States and the U.S.S.R. degenerated into a spasm war on both sides, then no matter the outcome—whether stalemate or "victory" for one side—an odd result might well be that those areas in the world which had escaped with less death and destruction would forge ahead of both the United States and the Soviet Union and walk away with what prize was left to be had.

Increasingly in the early 1960's the emphasis of decision makers, game theorists, policy analysts, and military experts in the United States was on proving that a general nuclear war was (1) fightable and (2) survivable. It was stressed that Americans would have to get used to looking at the possibility of nuclear war in a practical way and not flee from reality. The contest for survival might hang on the steadiness of the population's nerves and its informed preparation to face the supreme nuclear test. It was said again and again that general nuclear war, even spasm war, was not doomsday, did not mean the end of the human race or of America.

The estimates of the number of American survivors of a general nuclear war waged in the middle or late 1960's varied with the length of the war fought, whether there were warnings, what kinds of civil defense precautions were available, what the targets of the attacks were (whether military and industrial or cities, whether limited or over-kills), how many megatons were used, whether ground bursts or air bursts were employed. In short, the number of survivors would depend on whether the war was a low-geared controlled one, a high-geared controlled one, or a spasm war of a day or a few hours in which all the buttons were pushed on the one side and then minutes later all the buttons were

pushed on the other side, raining missiles of death and destruction in both directions. American casualties might be 10 million
or 30 million or 50 million or 70 million or even 100 million, depending on the nature of the war fought.

In a short controlled nuclear war perhaps there would be no
more casualties than the Germans or the Russians suffered in
World War II. The depth of the traumatic reactions and the
number of deformed babies likely to be born after the war were
difficult to measure. Perhaps, said the "survivalists," there would
be no more horrible personal experiences or emotional disturbances than were suffered by the Russian, German, Polish, and
Japanese survivors of World War II. Admittedly living and health
standards would be low for maybe as long as a decade, perhaps
as low as in the poor and underdeveloped countries, but life
would go on, and the remarkable technological know-how which
made possible the nuclear destruction would also allow for a
remarkable physical and economic recovery, just as population
growth and recovery were phenomenal in Germany and Russia
after World War II. The modern technology which had the
capacity to destroy also had the power to rebuild. It was also
suggested that America's value system would come through a
nuclear war with little change. Illustrative of the statements of
the survivalists, but emphatically not typical, was the following
assertion of Clare Boothe Luce in *McCall's* magazine for January
1962: "I hold with those who believe that a few million Americans
are bound to survive the most horrendous holocaust and that they
will rebuild civilization out of the worst imaginable ruins. And
if their children are born with two heads, so much the better. Our
generation, on the record, has not done too well with one."

However, most biologists and geneticists were inclined to believe that the survivalists minimized the biologic and genetic
damage of nuclear war; most psychiatrists, that they underrated
the psychological trauma; most economists, that they exaggerated
the ease of economic recovery; and most political scientists and
sociologists were skeptical that the American political and social
system could survive a nuclear war. The amount of regimentation required to keep society from complete disintegration would
be enormous. In the expressions of all the survivalists there was a
tacit surrender of Western civilization's ideal of the individual; all

the emphasis was on the survival of society, nation, and collectivity, none on the survival of the individual. Could a value system which had at its center the dignity and worth of each individual, the supreme importance of individual personality and life, survive among a people who witnessed the killing of 30 or 50 million of its citizens in a day or a week?

Speculation aside, one profoundly important trend was discernible and it was difficult to attribute it to anything else than the nuclear revolution in war. That trend was the increased determination of the big powers to keep out of war. Despite the intense power and ideological conflict and a world-wide revolutionary turbulence unprecedented in history, there had been no third world war. The big powers shied away from both big wars and little wars. The little wars in Korea and Indochina *were* limited wars, and they did not spread. Since then even the little wars were avoided (as in the Middle East, in South Vietnam, in the Congo, in Cuba), or cut short (as in Laos). There was brinkmanship (Berlin, Quemoy and Matsu) but not war. Crises were prudently pressed and not allowed to proceed to the point of no return. Perhaps the world *was* in the age of the *pax atomica*. But if it was, unfortunately there was still little evidence that peace was going to be internationally institutionalized. The mushroom cloud hung hauntingly over the lives of all men.

Outer Space: The Second Age of Discovery and Exploration

Concentration on rockets and missiles had allowed the U.S.S.R. to make breath-taking breakthroughs in outer space exploration. In 1957 the Russians launched two artificial earth satellites into outer space, Sputnik I and Sputnik II, the latter carrying a dog. In 1958 they launched into outer space the 2925-pound Sputnik III. In 1959 they launched a cosmic rocket, Lunik I, which went into permanent orbit around the sun as "the first artificial planet." That same year they launched a second cosmic rocket, Lunik II, which made contact with the moon, and a third, Lunik III, was launched with "an automatic planetary station" designed to circle the moon, and a photograph of the hidden side of the moon was released. In 1960 they placed in orbit a space ship carrying a dummy man; later that year a space ship, with a cargo of two dogs and other animals, which was later returned to earth; and still later a 5-ton space ship, carrying two dogs and other animals, which burned out. The climax came in 1961, when Vostok I carried a human passenger into space, and Vostok II carried an astronaut through seventeen orbits around the earth. In 1962 Vostok III carried a human passenger through sixty-four orbits (four days) and Vostok IV a passenger through forty-eight orbits (three days) with both ships in orbit at the same time and communicating with each other.

The American outer-space achievements were far less spectacular and they often appeared anticlimactic, for they usually followed some flashy Russian feat and American satellites were far smaller in size, but for precision and range of scientific exploration they were remarkable. In 1958 and 1959 the United States placed in orbit its various Explorers and Vanguards, ranging from around 3 to 31 pounds in weight. In 1960 the Americans placed in orbit many highly valuable weather, navigation, communications, and missile defense alarm satellites. In 1961 the United States successfully carried out two different manned space flights. In 1962 the United States orbited one astronaut three times around the earth, another three times, and another six times. That same year the United States exploded a nuclear test some 260 miles above the earth, the first invasion of the fringes of outer space by a thermonuclear device. Also that same year, in lofting Telstar into the heavens, the United States raised the curtain on intercontinental television and opened a whole new epoch in the art of communications. Telstar was the product of Bell Laboratories and thus was an example of how private industry and government could work together in the American system to make breakthroughs in space.

However, the Russian space achievements captured the imagination of the world more than the American. Even Americans were grudgingly impressed. In concentrating on space achievements which were both spectacular and for apparently peaceful purposes (though they could be used for both peaceful and nuclear-war purposes), the Russians won repeated propaganda advantages. The Russians successfully pioneered dazzling space ventures because of the scientific bent of their system, the fact that they deliberately set aside a large slice of their budget and much of their research for the space field, and specifically because they invested in solid-fuel rockets earlier than the Americans and thus acquired a heavier booster capability sooner. Both the U.S.S.R. and the United States were in an exciting race to be the first to land a man on the moon.

Not since Christopher Columbus, not since the first age of discovery and exploration in the late fifteenth and early sixteenth centuries, had the space range of human endeavor been so prodigiously widened. Then it was connecting the whole of the earth for the first time, now it was the universe itself. The first age of discovery and exploration had led to a great imperialist rivalry among the leading nations to appropriate for themselves large parts of the earth. The imperialism begun in that age was just now closing. Would the second age of discovery and exploration lead to greater cooperation among the nations, a new internationalism? Or would it, like the first, lead to a new imperialism, a new race to grab space and "territory," an intensification of the rivalry and conflict among the nations?

Fencing over the International Control of Armaments

The story of the attempts of the United States and the U.S.S.R. to reach agreements on disarmament or arms-control in any form was tedious and dreary. As the story unfolded the impression grew that these powers were engaged in a mere game of shadow boxing, that they were more intent upon putting the other side in the wrong and winning propaganda advantages than they were in finding any accommodation to the most stupendous problem of this or any age—escape from cataclysmic war. However, this impression was not entirely true.

With an eye to world opinion, the Russians usually took the initiative and presented large and sweeping plans which demanded immediate action. The Americans were usually cast in the role of careful, cautious analysts insisting that arms limitations be linked with political settlements, that one phase of arms limitation be connected with the others, and that there be adequate international inspection and control to make sure that one side did not cheat on the other. The Russians frequently seemed to be saying: "The way to disarm is to disarm, the way to begin is to begin." The Americans often seemed to be saying: "But we must go slow about something as vital as this, we must take care that we do not create more problems than we solve; agreements which are violated and backfire will exacerbate our difficulties and tensions and those that clandestinely allow an upsetting of the arms balance are an actual invitation to attack by the power which has benefited by cheating." However, the Soviet tactics often made the Russians appear to be crusaders for peace, while the United States tactics frequently made the Americans appear to be indulging in dilatory and defeatist practices. Most of the "plans" usually had some built-in national advantage for the side which presented them, even when this advantage was incidental to the larger aim of achieving some arms control.

Officially, the Russians had long espoused total disarmament, the immediate outlawing of all nuclear weapons, and the destruction of all stockpiles of such weapons as prerequisite to negotiating about other phases of disarmament. However, in 1955, after they had their own stockpile of atomic and hydrogen weapons, the Russians receded from their previous demands for a total ban on atomic weapons as a condition precedent to further discussion and announced a plan in which the total ban on nuclear weapons and testing would become effective with the final stage of a phased reduction in all armaments, conventional and nuclear. Russian plans repeatedly emphasized the importance of the withdrawal of foreign troops from countries in Central Europe and the elimination of all military bases of one country on the soil of another. (The Russians wanted to get Americans troops out of Germany and to remove the American bases in countries bordering on the Soviet Union; their own withdrawal of Soviet troops from countries in Eastern and Central Europe would still leave their armies physically close to these countries.) The negotiations during 1955 and 1956, over the Russian proposals for phased reductions in all armaments to be climaxed by the prohibition of all nuclear weapons and testing at the final phase, foundered on questions of international inspection and control.

During the mid-1950's the United States concentrated on some mutual assurances against surprise nuclear attacks. President Eisenhower's "open skies" proposal was a plan for mutual aerial inspection in which both sides would be allowed to fly over the territory of the other and take photographs. The Russians contended that this was a mere pretext for getting target intelligence. Had the Russians agreed to this plan President Eisenhower might have found much hostility in the United States to such reconnaisance flights by Russians over American territory. Even attempts to work out "open skies" agreements limited to a zone in Europe proved fruitless.

By 1957 the Russians were emphasizing the importance of suspending all testing of nuclear detonations. They maintained that if agreements could not be made on other aspects of arms control at least an agreement could be reached on banning the testing of nuclear weapons, and that such an agreement on this one phase of the problem would slow down the arms race and prevent the nuclear fallout which was hazardous to the health of people everywhere. The Russians specifically proposed that nuclear explosions be suspended for two or three years and that an international control system be set up to insure that the suspension was observed. The Russians found much world support for their plan. The United States countered with a proposal of a trial suspension of ten months which would be an integral part of a first-stage disarmament agreement providing, among other things, for a reduction in armed forces and armaments, acceptance of an "open skies" inspection zone, and a freeze on the production of fissionable material for weapon purposes. In contrast to the destruction of the existing stocks of nuclear weapons such a freeze on new production was believed to be susceptible to effective international inspection and control. From the American point of view the latter provision was particularly advantageous, for it would prevent any increase in the Soviet nuclear stockpile (which was not as large as the American) beyond its current dimensions, and it would prevent any additional countries from entering the nuclear arms race.

These stiff American counter-proposals killed the Russian proposal, but in any event even without them the Russian plan would probably have foundered on the precise methods of international inspection and control to prevent clandestine tests. However, Harold E. Stassen, the President's special adviser on disarmament, thought the Soviet plan was worth serious negotiation and favored breaking the American package in order to explore the test-ban proposal independently of other questions. Stassen was vigorously opposed by Lewis E. Strauss, chairman of the Atomic Energy Commission, and others, and as a result Stassen resigned his position in early 1958. The Russians won a propaganda victory, for in the course of the discussions it appeared to the outside world that the American Atomic Energy Commission, the Defense Department, and large segments of Congress were alarmed at even America's guarded counter-proposals. It also seemed that the United States was minimizing the hazards of nuclear testing to public health, as indicated by statements of Dr. Edward Teller and others. A group of distinguished American scientists told President Eisenhower that they were steadily decreasing the fallout from nuclear testing and that given "four or five years" they would produce "an absolutely clean bomb."

When in 1958 Khrushchev became premier of the Soviet Union (in addition to being first secretary of the Communist party) one of his first official acts was to announce on March 31 that since international agreement on banning nuclear testing had failed to materialize, the U.S.S.R. would henceforth unilaterally discontinue all types of atomic and hydrogen weapon testing. However, if the United States and Britain went ahead with nuclear testing, then the U.S.S.R. reserved the right to resume its own testing. At that time the Soviet Union had just completed an intensive series of tests. Khrushchev thus won great propaganda advantages and really sacrificed nothing, since if the Americans and British went ahead with their planned testing, the U.S.S.R. could resume its own testing and blame it on the Americans. Khrushchev still urged the necessity of suspending nuclear testing by international agreements, but it was clear that there would probably be insuperable obstacles to accomplishing these because the Russians let it be known that such agreements really required no international machinery for verification and control, since any violations would be immediately registered by seismic and other detective devices throughout the world.

As for the larger question of general disarmament or at least reductions in armaments, the Russians increasingly objected to the five-power subcommittee of the United Nations Disarmament Commission, which had conducted the previous discussions. This subcommittee was composed of representatives from the United States, Britain, France, Canada, and the U.S.S.R., and the Russians claimed it was obviously "stacked" against them four to one. In 1957 the Russians demanded that the Commission itself be widened to include all members of the United Nations, and in 1958, to please the Soviet Union, the United Nations expanded its Disarmament Commission on an *ad hoc* basis for 1959 to include all members of the world organization. Still the U.S.S.R. was not satisfied and demanded "parity." Accordingly in 1959 a ten-nation committee was established, composed of five Western nations (the United States, Britain, France, Italy, and Canada) and five Communist nations (the Soviet Union, Poland, Czechoslovakia, Bulgaria, and Rumania) to work outside the United Nations but to report to its Disarmament Commission. For a time this group wrestled with proposals for general disarmament or limitations on armaments. At the same time a tripartite conference of the three nuclear powers—the United States, Britain, and the U.S.S.R. —intensively discussed the problems connected with international agreements banning the testing of nuclear weapons. In a sense this arrangement was a victory for the Soviet Union, since it divorced the question of nuclear testing from the general problem of limitation of armaments.

In September 1959 Khrushchev appeared before the United Nations Assembly and put forward a plan for universal and complete disarmament to be achieved in stages over a four-year period. The plan envisaged not merely the restriction but the elimination of both the weapons of mass destruction and all warmaking potential, limiting each nation after the final stage to only the contingents required for internal security purposes. The plan contained the usual Soviet demands for a denuclearized zone in Central Europe and the liquidation of military bases on foreign territories. It also called for a complete system of international inspection and control, including aerial observation and photography. Would the different stages of control be put into effect before or after the corresponding phases of the disarmament program were carried out? The West considered this question vital. Khrushchev declared that he would accept "any kind of inspection" if the West would accept the principle of total disarmament. But of course it was one thing to make such a sweeping statement and another thing to agree to the specific details of inspection. The West remained skeptical of Khrushchev's total, across-the-board disarmament, nuclear and conventional, and would not agree even to the idea of total disarmament in advance of details on an inspection system. But Khrushchev expressed a willingness to accept partial disarmament steps if the Western powers refused to accept his full program. Khrushchev's plan was transmitted to the new ten-nation committee on disarmament.

At the ten-nation conference opening in Geneva in March 1960, the United States proposed a plan not of total disarmament but of "progressive, general, and balanced reductions in national military forces," safeguards against surprise attacks and against the promiscuous spread of nuclear weapons, and a system of inspection and control to be established before the reduction in armaments. The United States plan envisaged a time when an international armed force would take the place of national armed forces. The conflict at Geneva turned on the degree of disarmament and the measures of inspection and control. The Soviet Union said: "Disarmament before inspection." The United States said: "Inspection before disarmament." The Soviet Union called the American plan "control without disarmament" and a system of licensed espionage. The Americans said in effect: "We want to witness not only the bonfire but also the assembly line before and after the bonfire." At one stage of the proceedings the Soviet demanded that all the nuclear powers solemnly declare that they would not be the first to use nuclear weapons. The collapse of the Paris summit conference in May killed what small prospects of success had remained for the Geneva meeting.

After the torpedoing of the summit conference and the deadlock at Geneva, Khrushchev asked that the matter of disarmament be referred to the United Nations Assembly. The United States instead took the question to the United Nations Disarmament Commission, which recommended a resumption of negotiations, presumably by the ten-nation committee. In another speech before the United Nations Assembly in the fall of 1960, Khrushchev again pressed for his disarmament plan, slightly modified, and called for the addition of five neutral states to the ten-nation committee, which in effect would have established his "troika" machinery in the disarmament discussions. The United States opposed this, for it felt such an arrangement would make agreement even more difficult and feared that the neutral nations underrated the importance of adequate enforcement machinery in disarmament agreements. During the interval between disarmament meetings, negotiations continued between John J. McCloy for the United States and V. A. Zorin for the Soviet Union. But the stalemate persisted. The United States continued to insist that inspection and control should be applied not only to the armaments that a state gave up but also to those that it retained. The Soviet Union construed this as a control over armaments and the antithesis of disarmament. That the United States was preparing to take even more interest in disarmament discussions in the future was evidenced in 1961 when Congress at last established the United States Arms Control and Disarmament Agency, under the direction of the Secretary of State, to conduct long-range disarmament studies.

In September 1961, President Kennedy presented his own disarmament plan to the United Nations Assembly. He called for general and complete disarmament through three balanced and safeguarded stages to give no state a military advantage over the other, with a United Nations Peace Force eventually to take the place of national armed forces. His plan provided for a reduction of nuclear weapons and delivery systems in the first stage of disarmament as well as for a prohibition of the transfer of nuclear weapons, information, and material to countries not having them, which would obviously deny nuclear weapons to such states as West Germany and Communist China. The Kennedy plan did not make any suggestions about how to break the deadlock on the question of inspection and control. In a series of resolutions on disarmament passed by the United Nations Assembly in 1961, the majority in that body seemed to be closer to the Soviet view on inspection and control than to the American view. With the prior agreement of the United States and the U.S.S.R. the United Nations Assembly's Political Committee set up an eighteen-nation disarmament committee which included the five Communist and the five Western countries of the prior committee and added eight neutral states—India, Mexico, the United Arab Republic, Brazil, Burma, Ethiopia, Nigeria, and Sweden. This committee was scheduled to meet in the spring of 1962 to consider not only general disarmament but also the question of a nuclear test ban (the tripartite conference on the banning of nuclear testing adjourned in January 1962 without coming to any agreement), and thus for the first time in four years the same body would explore both questions.

While the discussions on general disarmament had been proceeding off and on for four years, other aspects of arms control had been explored. In 1958, the Soviet Union, apparently alarmed over the flight of American bombers carrying nuclear weapons in the Arctic area close to its borders, finally agreed to participate in an East-West technical discussion on methods of safeguarding against surprise attacks. However, these talks got nowhere. That same year the United Nations Scientific Committee on the Effects of Atomic Radiation, which included Eastern as well as Western scientists, filed a report which indicated that the United States had been too optimistic about the effects of fallout. The report specifically referred to fallout from nuclear weapons tests as a major source of harmful radiation.

The most encouraging development came that same year when the United States and the U.S.S.R. agreed to sponsor the Conference of Experts to Study the Possibility of Detecting Violations of a Possible Agreement on Suspension of Nuclear Tests, although Khrushchev still insisted that international machinery for detection was unnecessary in the light of the scientific devices available in every advanced country for detecting detonations in any part of the world. The conference of experts, composed of scientists from Communist and non-Communist countries, exhibited an unusual freedom from political considerations and actually agreed that an effective international control system was entirely feasible. The conference report estimated that the controls it proposed would be 90 per cent reliable in detecting nuclear explosions of a force as small as one kiloton under water or in the atmosphere up to a height of 30 miles, and nuclear explosions of a force of five kilotons or more under the surface of the earth.

Accordingly, the United States, the U.S.S.R., and Britain agreed to hold a tripartite conference at Geneva beginning October 31, 1958, to attempt to work out an agreement on the permanent banning of nuclear-weapons tests. In August, President Eisenhower made the historic announcement that the United States would withhold further testing of atomic and hydrogen weapons for a year, beginning at the start of the Geneva negotiations, provided testing was not resumed by the Soviet Union during that period, and further that the suspension of tests by the United States was subject to further extension for subsequent one-year periods if a satisfactory inspection system was in operation. Britain made a similar announcement. However, the United States and Britain proceeded with their plans for a series of nuclear tests, which were completed by the October 31 deadline. On August 30 Khrushchev declared that in view of the American and British tests the Soviet Union was no longer bound by its unilateral declaration of March 31 and would resume testing. Thus the three nuclear powers engaged in intensive last-minute testing before the convening of the test-ban conference. By October 31 it was estimated that since the era of atomic-weapon tests the United States had set off some 132 atomic explosions to 21 for Britain and 53 for the Soviet Union. However, it was believed that the Soviet Union set off two relatively low-yield nuclear devices in southern Russia the first week in November. After that there were no more tests by the nuclear powers during the voluntary moratorium.

The tripartite Geneva conference on the banning of nuclear testing came closer to agreement than any of the other conferences on armaments control. It actually wrote eighteen sections of a draft treaty and two annexes. The chief difficulties revolved around whether the decisions of the Control Commission were to be made by unanimous vote, as the Soviets insisted, or by majority vote, as the West wanted; the number of veto-free inspections to be imposed on a country; the number of foreigners in an international corps to be stationed at control posts in a country and the scope of their operations; and whether mobile inspection teams should be stationed at control posts. However, progress was made, and the Russians finally agreed to four or five foreigners with operational responsibilities at each control post, an unprecedented concession for them.

But the atmosphere of the conference changed for the worse in 1959, in the main, it seemed, because the Americans had some second thoughts about the feasibility of detecting high-altitude and underground explosions. Their high-altitude Argus explosions, conducted before the convening of the conference, went completely undetected in Moscow; and their Hardtack underground explosions, which also took place before the test moratorium, indicated that it might not be possible to distinguish underground nuclear explosions of less than 19 kilotons from earthquakes. Thus the findings of the experts and the findings of the tests had a "detectable" discrepancy in underground explosions of from 5 to 19 kilotons. The United States was impressed with the difficulties of monitoring underground, high-altitude, and outer-space tests. President Eisenhower suggested to Khrushchev that because of the difficulties of detecting such tests, perhaps the test ban ought to apply only to tests in the atmosphere. In the midst of the conference the Americans asked for experts from both sides to examine the new data on underground explosions. The Russians complied, but from that time they appeared to lose interest in the conference. The Russians, who felt that the various national systems of detection made international machinery unnecessary anyway, now seemed to feel that the Americans were using dilatory tactics, attempting to undermine confidence in the control systems already agreed on. Some American observers, too, felt that the United States was exaggerating the importance of developing infallible detection systems.

From that time on the conference went from bad to worse. The collapse of the summit conference in May 1960 made matters even more difficult. In early 1961, with the conference still dragging on, the Russians moved to replace the Chief Executive Officer of the seven-nation Control Commission, already agreed on, with the *troika*, an administrative council made up of one representative from the Communist states, one from the West, and one from the neutrals. The Soviet announcement on August 31, 1961, that the U.S.S.R. would break the voluntary moratorium, would resume nuclear explosions the next day, brought consternation to the Western camp. In November the Russians, having conducted their own important tests, in effect moved that most of the work of the conference be scrapped and that the nuclear powers agree to a draft treaty providing for an immediate cessation of nuclear testing in the atmosphere, in outer space, under the water, and underground; and that instead of international inspection the parties use their national systems of detecting nuclear explosions. This was completely unacceptable to the West, and the conference limped to a final adjournment in January 1962.

Meantime attention shifted to the new series of nuclear-weapons tests. In the fall of 1961 the Soviet Union conducted over forty nuclear explosions in the air. One blast had a force equivalent to about 100 megatons, and one weapon was exploded 100 miles above the earth, presumably in an attempt to create a missile defense system. Some experts believed the Russians had made some progress toward the development of an anti-missile warhead. Study of debris of Soviet explosions revealed progress toward reducing the weight of both weapons and missiles with no sacrifice of explosive force, thus permitting greater target accuracy.

On September 5, 1961, President Kennedy authorized resumption of underground testing by the United States, and on March 2, 1962, the President announced that the United States would conduct a series of tests in the atmosphere, with great care to keep fallout to a minimum. In his March announcement the President asserted that the United States would never again offer an uninspected moratorium but that it would cancel its planned tests if agreement on a test-ban treaty, with effective controls, could be reached at Geneva. The purpose of the atmospheric tests conducted in the spring and summer of 1962 was to determine the effectiveness of the existing nuclear weapons, measure the explosive force of weapons in relation to weight, and explore the defense potential of high-altitude nuclear blasts with particular reference to developing American anti-missiles and rendering ineffective enemy anti-missiles or interceptors that some day might be developed.

The Soviet Union was severely criticized around the world because it had broken the moratorium and because of the large amount of radioactive fallout from its tests. However, the Americans were disappointed that some of the leading neutral nations were not as emphatic in their disapproval of Soviet conduct as had been expected. The United States was criticized for following suit. Some pointed out that the United States was still far ahead in the number of its nuclear-weapons tests and was believed to enjoy an over-all nuclear superiority. These critics felt that it would have been wise of the United States to forgo another round of tests, appeal to world opinion, and through popular world pressures and some concessions attempt to persuade the Soviet Union to enter test-ban agreements with reasonable inspection and controls—more than the Soviet Union had yet been willing to accept but less than the United States had hitherto demanded. American opinion and American scientists were divided on the decision to resume testing. Leading American scientists like Hans Bethe and Leonard Reiffel welcomed the tests. But Ralph E. Lapp asserted that the Kennedy decision was motivated by political considerations and that from a technical point of view the new tests would not affect the balance of power between the Soviet Union and the United States. And the *Bulletin of the Atomic Scientists* declared that if nuclear weapons were needed only for the purpose of inflicting retaliatory damage on the enemy, then present weapons were certainly more than adequate.

In March 1962 a panel of economists officially reported to the United States Arms Control and Disarmament Agency that annual military expenditures by all the nations were about 120 billion dollars, or 9 per cent of all the world's goods and services. About 85 per cent of the total was spent by seven countries: the United States, the Soviet Union, Britain, West Germany, France, Canada, and Red China. Armies numbered about 20 million men, and around 30 million people worked in defense-related industries. Military expenditures by all the nations equaled at least two-thirds of the total annual income of all the underdeveloped countries. If only "a fraction" of the international defense budget was diverted to economic aid to needy nations, it would result in "a marked increase in the rate of growth of real income in the poorer parts of the world."

Also in March 1962 the eighteen-nation conference on disarmament, under United Nations sponsorship, got under way at Geneva. It was to consider both a nuclear-weapon test ban and general disarmament. The United States presented the Kennedy plan with more details and some modifications. The plan envisaged three stages of arms reduction, eventually eliminating national armies altogether. The first two stages would last three years each; no time limit was set for the third and last stage, during which a United Nations Peace Force would gradually take over all military power in the world except for minor law enforcement units each nation would need to maintain internal order. During the first stage—the first three years—there would be a 30 per cent cut in conventional weapons and in nuclear bomb carriers including rockets. Successive stages in the reduction of armaments would be supervised by a United Nations agency ultimately responsible to the Security Council. There were specific provisions for inspection and control, but to meet Russia's fears of espionage in the guise of inspectors, the plan introduced a new concept of zonal inspection or sampling, geographical spot checks which would discourage treaty violations without maintaining permanent control centers and constant surveillance. (These applied to the proposed treaty on general disarmament, not to a test-ban treaty.)

With respect to renewed attempts to secure a test-ban treaty, the Kennedy administration went beyond any American concessions in the past. During 1962 it presented a draft treaty which called for a halt to testing in atmosphere, space, and under water, and which contained no policing provisions at all. As to underground explosions, the American delegation at Geneva suggested that if the Russians agreed to on-site inspections by international teams the United States might be willing to reduce the number of annual inspections from the previously proposed minimum of twelve. If the Russians accepted on-site inspections, the United States would also consider drastically modifying its demands for monitoring posts on Soviet soil from nineteen to eight and agree to have them manned by Soviet nationals, provided they were checked by international observers. By the end of 1962 it seemed that the Kennedy administration had still not made enough concessions to satisfy the Russians. However, it now appeared to the world that the Russians were the obstructionists, and in this matter the Americans had at last put the Russians on the defensive.

Perhaps the new concessions by the Americans reflected a feeling (a possible result of their late tests) that their nuclear position was now unassailable. It might be that the Americans were now more concerned with cutting off the number of the members of the nuclear club than they were with the possibility of Russian cheating.

During December 1962 and early 1963, the negotiations with respect to underground tests took on new life. The United States now put less emphasis on the Soviet-manned monitoring stations and was inclined to drop the demand for international observers to check them. It put more emphasis on the automatic, unmanned seismic detection stations, the so-called "black boxes," and proposed at least twelve of these on Russian soil. Khrushchev suggested that he might accept three. To investigate suspicious tremors, the United States still insisted on on-site inspections by international teams but indicated a willingness to reduce the number of such inspections each year from twelve to eight. Khrushchev, at last, suggested he might accept three. The United States had earlier demanded that international inspectors be allowed to check the territory within an 800 square kilometer area of a suspected clandestine test site, but now offered to shrink this area to 500 kilometers. At the same time the United States agreed to permit each inspected country to exclude sensitive defense installations from areas subject to inspection. The prime reason for the progressive concessions by the United States was the belief held in Washington that because of the improvements in United States detection capability in recent years, the chances of the Soviet Union conducting a series of tests which would remain undetected were "vanishingly small."

There was an element of multilateral power politics in the negotiations. The Russians might be seeking to widen the differences between the United States and France, for De Gaulle would resent an international test ban while he was still in the early stages of developing his nuclear force. On the other hand, the United States might be using the negotiations to deepen the rift between Russia and Red China, for the Chinese would certainly be hostile to a test ban before they had achieved their own nuclear arsenal. Viewed from another angle, the Sino-Soviet rift freed Khrushchev from having to consider Chinese interests, and it made the United States less fearful that Chinese territory would be used by the Russians to cheat on a test-ban agreement. Even if the United States and the Soviet Union succeeded in hammering out agreements, the further questions of whether China and France would consent to become parties to them still remained, but such agreements and controls would make it much more difficult for China and France to proceed with their plans for building independent nuclear forces.

Negotiations over disarmament were not merely a game, not merely contrivances to embarrass the other side or gain hidden advantages, although to be sure there was much of this. There were also genuine fears of nuclear war on both sides and desires to escape some of the crushing economic burdens of armaments. The differences in approach of the United States and the U.S.S.R.

were frequently honest and rooted in objective and psychological conditions.

The Russian reluctance to accept international inspection within the borders of the U.S.S.R. and the demand for "parity" or a *troika* arrangement in international machinery seemed obstinate, or worse—evidence of a shabby intention to cheat on agreements. But Russian apprehensions were explicable. The Communists sincerely feared "the capitalists" and their apparent refusal to really accept Communist rule where it existed. They believed "the bourgeoisie" and "the imperialists" still regarded them as pariahs. Communist countries were in a minority in the United Nations and in other international organizations and they feared decisions taken by a majority vote. Psychologically, as Communists, the Russians found it hard to submit their country to inspection by "the capitalists." The Soviet system was a closed one, and the Russians were loath to expose its backwardness and repressions to outsiders. Some close observers of Soviet affairs suggested that perhaps the Russians did not have as strong a nuclear arsenal as was generally supposed, that while strong in some areas they might be weaker in other areas than the world believed. According to this view, the Russians prudently did not want to expose their shortcomings. If indeed the Russians had fewer important strategic military installations than outsiders supposed, then it became even more necessary to hide those "targets" they did have. The Russians appeared to be sincere when they argued that the various national systems for detecting nuclear explosions in any part of the world were adequate to prevent cheating on agreements, and if this was of doubtful validity when the Russians first argued it, the fact was that every year the devices for detecting detonations were becoming more precise and sensitive and making less and less necessary an international detection system. James J. Wadsworth, President Eisenhower's chief disarmament negotiator, indicated that in his belief the Russians were not resisting international inspection in order to cheat on the agreements, that the Russian government had every intention of living up to any agreement it made covering tests or the larger area of disarmament; but after the Soviet's sneak missiles in Cuba most Americans were even less convinced of the honesty of the Russians.

There was a fundamental difference in the Russian and American approach to the question of what to do about armaments. Officially, the Soviet Union over and again plugged for complete disarmament in a relatively short time. The Americans preferred "arms control," a limitation on armaments. This would hopefully minimize the risk of war, and at the same time, according to Thomas C. Schelling and Morton H. Halperin, constitute an "enlargement of the scope of our military strategy." The Russians said repeatedly that a total commitment to complete disarmament would dispel their fears of the capitalist countries and overcome their reluctance to international inspection.

On the other hand, the Americans, too, seemed more honest in their approach than they were often given credit for. The Americans felt they were dealing with no ordinary diplomatic opponent but with adversaries with an entirely different set of values from theirs. Americans could not very well dispel the notion that they were dealing with revolutionaries and conspirators. And many Americans asked this question: "Now, why would the Russians sincerely want to eliminate nuclear weapons, and more than that —all armaments? How could the Russians hold the satellite countries if there was complete disarmament? Has it not been the fear of nuclear war that has prevented a third world war, a war involving the liberation of the satellite countries?" (The Russians probably concluded that with complete disarmament they would no longer have to fear wars of liberation waged by the West, and that the local police forces and domestic military contingents, under Communist control, would keep the satellites in line.)

The Americans wrestled with the larger problem of international relations more profoundly than did the Russians—the problem of how in the last resort to vindicate concepts of justice and settle the ultimate disputes of nations if force were banished from international affairs before international political and legal machinery was developed to take its place. The various American plans for nuclear-weapons test bans, limitations on national armaments, and general disarmament emphasized international machinery and anticipated some of the problems of world government. (There were military analysts and game theorists who felt we might actually be nearer genuine world government—not merely an evolving United Nations—than most people realized, that even a short, controlled nuclear war might wreak such havoc as to sound the death knell of the old system of sovereign national states almost overnight.) Finally, there seemed little doubt that the Kennedy administration was going further than its predecessors in making concessions to Russian fears in order to get a test-ban treaty and beginning disarmament agreements.

The chances for agreement were still not promising. The record of the disarmament negotiations of the 1950's and 1960's reads chillingly like that of the "peace conferences" prior to World War I and like that of the League of Nations disarmament discussions of the 1920's and 1930's. The nuclear revolution had apparently not changed the traditional behavior of human societies. As always, men wanted peace, provided they could have it "their" way, without sacrificing some other things they apparently wanted more. But against the background of the cataclysmic weapons, the dialogue between the antagonists seemed more puerile than usual, a grotesque caricature of the human situation.

Meantime members of a new generation, who knew only the nuclear age into which they had been born, were growing up. They were being habituated to the neo-morality which could contemplate slaughters of whole societies with equanimity; to the neo-rationalism which encouraged analysts, decision makers, and game theorists to make their "models" and their "scenarios" in terms of killing 50 million or 100 million or 150 million people, more or less, depending on this or that situation; to the new esthetics which saw beauty in the grace and symmetry of the missile, in the pure white mushroom cloud floating toward the heavens, suddenly shot through with sun rays, producing a riotously gorgeous kaleidoscope of colors; to the new religion with its Gothic rockets and its galaxy of Moloch-devouring pagan deities—Atlas, Titan, Jupiter, Thor, and Saturn. The new generation was being conditioned to regard all this not as lunacy but as "normalcy."

The Chief Stumbling Block: Berlin and Germany

The chief obstacles to a *modus vivendi* between East and West, a trial acceptance at least of peaceful coexistence, were the questions of Berlin and Germany. Even eighteen years after the end of the war, Germany remained partitioned, the four victors occupied Berlin, and no peace had been made. If some settlement could be achieved with respect to Germany it was believed that the Cold War would ease all along the line and that there would be a better chance to make a treaty banning nuclear-weapons testing and a start on arms limitations and possibly disarmament.

It will be recalled that the four-power occupation of Germany had met with such obstructions that the Western powers had gone their own way and created West Germany, and that Russia had followed suit and created East Germany. At the same time in Berlin cooperation of the American, British, and French with the Russians had also virtually come to an end. It was with difficulty that sufficient intercourse between East and West Berlin had been maintained to allow a viable city.

In a sense there were not two but three "Germanies." There was the Federal Republic, or West Germany, with a population by 1963 of around 55 million, a highly industrialized country with a Catholic majority. There was the German Democratic Republic in East Germany which by 1963 had a population of around 17 million, an agrarian country with a Protestant majority but with industrial cities like Berlin, Leipzig, and Dresden, which in the pre-Hitler days had been bastions of the Social Democratic party. And there was the Germany of the "stolen" or "lost" provinces, the German territory taken by Russia and Poland at the end of the war. There were many West Germans who believed not only that East and West Germany should be reunited but also that East Prussia, the other former German territory beyond the Oder-Neisse line, and even Silesia (now Polish and Czechoslovak) and the Sudetenland (now Czechoslovak) should on ethnic and historic grounds be united into one Germany. Russians, Poles, and Czechoslovaks opposed a reunited Germany not only because of its strength and general potential threat but also because they feared it would seek to regain the former German territories now held by the Slavic countries. The Russians exploited these Polish and Czech fears.

West Berlin was 110 miles within the East German zone—a Western island in a Communist sea. The Western Allies maintained military forces of 11,000 men in West Berlin—4,000 Americans and 7,000 British and French. West Berlin's population of around 2.25 million looked to the West to protect it from being engulfed by the Communists. The Communist regime in East Germany was most unpopular. Open rebellion flared in 1953. Nearly 3 million

East German refugees had fled to West Germany in the postwar years.

During the early postwar years the Russians had entertained some hopes of a revival of a strong Communist party in West Germany. But the Nazi regime had pretty well liquidated the Communist activists; German armies in Russia had been impressed with the backwardness of life in the Soviet Union; and the insatiable demands of the Russians for reparations in goods and machinery after the war had further embittered the Germans toward the Russians. It was soon clear to the Russians that there was no possibility of controlling Germany through a German Communist party and that a reunited Germany would be Western-oriented, not Eastern-oriented. Moreover, some students of Communist affairs felt that the Russians were not interested in building a unified Germany, Communist or otherwise; that a unified Communist Germany would have been almost as dangerous to Russia as a unified non-Communist one; that it would have taken the lead in the Communist world away from Russia, that it would have been far more troublesome than Communist China had been. These observers maintained that the Russians early realized that a divided and demilitarized Germany was the only "safe" one for Russian security. In 1959 Khrushchev openly stated that despite professions to the contrary, "no one" really wanted German reunification.

On the other hand, the official Western position had consistently favored the reunification of Germany. Western plans envisaged a national plebiscite in both zones, a free election in which the Germans themselves would decide whether they would be reunited and on what terms. It was generally assumed in the West that they would vote for reunification. But the West and the Russians could not agree on what constituted "free elections" and the machinery to supervise them, and the Russians used this disagreement to prevent any elections from taking place. The West officially favored a referendum on the ground of democratic national self-determination and in the belief that a resurgent German nationalism would some day arise and produce serious trouble to the peace of Europe and the world if its legitimate aspirations were not fulfilled. The West also believed that a unified Germany would be pro-Western and anti-Communist.

By 1958 the Russians were pressing for a German settlement on their terms. They believed that after thirteen years it was time for the victors in the war to accept "the realities" as they then existed and write definitive treaties of peace with both German governments. By that time the Russians had become accustomed to using East German resources and East German scientists and technicians. East Germany's economy had been integrated into the Soviet orbit, and East Germany was a member of the Communist Countries' Council on Economic Mutual Assistance (Comecon), the East's nearest equivalent to the West's developing Common Market. Members of a new generation had risen in East Germany, and some of them were sincere Communists. Certain East German politicians and leaders in other fields had cast their lot with the Communist government, had a vested interest in the survival of East Germany as a separate entity, and the Russians felt they could not let these people down, even if the Soviet government was disposed to surrender East Germany, which of course it was not. The Russians felt they had been moderately successful in integrating East Germany into their sphere in a way they would never have been able to integrate the whole of Germany.

But the main reason the Russians wanted peace treaties signed by all the victorious allies of World War II and the two German governments was that the Russians wanted to liquidate the West German army, and if not to liquidate it at least to ensure that it was never allowed nuclear weapons, and they were prepared to wage shrewd diplomatic war to see that such provisions were written into the treaties. True, the West had tacitly recognized East Germany and the other satellites as part of the Russian orbit, particularly when the Western Allies had declined to intervene in 1953 in behalf of the rebellious East Germans and in 1956 in behalf of the Hungarian revolutionaries. But the Russians felt the existing situation would be uncertain and unstable and would be constantly jeopardized by West German agitation to "redeem the lost provinces of the East" unless definitive peace treaties were written. With the Russians, too, it was a matter of prestige. They felt that the West did not recognize their actual power position, and Khrushchev remarked at various times that the West wanted to treat the Russians as "schoolboys," as "poor relations." Khrushchev was thinking in terms of traditional power politics, the practice in the past of the leading powers of either going to war to change a power situation they did not like or frankly recognizing and stabilizing it.

The Russians envisaged peace treaties, signed by the victors of the war with the two German governments, which would recognize "the socialist order" in East Germany and also the existing western boundaries of the Soviet Union, Czechoslovakia, and Poland, which would legalize the Polish-East German border at the Oder-Neisse line. If Germany were to achieve any kind of unification at all it would come through negotiations by the two German governments themselves. The Russians conceded that at some later date this might take the form of a "federation" between East and West Germany. In any event, West Germany would withdraw from NATO. The boundaries of the two Germanies would be guaranteed by an all-European security system in which NATO and the Warsaw Pact countries would conclude non-aggression and mutual assistance treaties to protect the two Germanies and their neighbors against aggression. The Russians also favored some such arrangement as was formulated in the Rapacki Plan, put forward by the Polish Foreign Minister in 1957 and 1958, which would establish a "denuclearized zone" in Central Europe, incuding West Germany, East Germany, Poland, and Czechoslovakia, in which nuclear weapons would not be manufactured or maintained and which would be guaranteed against nuclear attacks by outside powers. The Rapacki Plan was a form of "disengagement," and there were other similar plans, one in particular by George F. Kennan, who had originally been one of the makers of the American policy of containment.

With respect to West Berlin, the Russians wanted the Western Allies to give up their military occupation, and in return the Russians would surrender their military occupation of East Berlin. The Russians maintained that the existing arrangements went back to the Potsdam Agreement, which the Russians claimed was now obsolete since all of its other arrangements had long since been superseded by others. Khrushchev suggested that West Berlin be made a "free city," separated from both East and West Germany, neutralized, demilitarized, and barred from carrying on "subversive" activities against its Communist neighbors. The Soviet premier suggested further that this "free city" be protected by the presence of token contingents of the four big powers, including the Soviet Union, and by a United Nations guarantee of its freedom and independence. If token contingents from the big powers were unsatisfactory, then Khrushchev said that token forces from the smaller powers, East and West, might be employed. Khrushchev did not categorically rule out the idea of the whole city of Berlin, East and West, becoming a free city, as was suggested by Senator Mike Mansfield, and the Soviet leader was reported as having informally hinted at this as a possible solution, to the violent dismay of Walter Ulbricht, the Communist leader of East Germany.

What were Khrushchev's motives? Khrushchev knew that the Western powers would not consent to West Berlin's being incorporated into East Germany, and even if its incorporation were possible, the Soviet premier might not have welcomed the addition of a large number of Social Democrats, regarding them as "indigestible," as potential trouble-makers within the East German state. But Khrushchev did want to make sure that West Berlin was no longer thought of as the capital of a future reunited Germany, that it was no longer maintained as a symbolic rallying point for such an eventuality in the future, and in addition that it did not become a part of West Germany. Khrushchev also wanted to weaken West Berlin's capacity to "show up" the inferiority of living standards in East Germany. West Berlin as a "showcase" of Western capitalism was bad enough, but the Russians wanted to make certain that its "propaganda" broadcasts to Communist Europe were discontinued too.

To prod the Western Allies into giving up their military occupation of the three sectors of West Berlin, Khrushchev threatened to terminate the big-four agreements with respect to Berlin, to turn over all the functions exercised by the Russians in Berlin to the East German government, and so far as the Russians were concerned give that government complete control over the land, water, and air space of Berlin. If the Allies wanted to provide for the freedom and viability of West Berlin, the continued presence of Allied forces there, and their free access to that city, they would thereafter have to negotiate with the East German government, which would force them to recognize that government. If the Western powers "browbeat" the East German government, they would have the Soviet Union and the Warsaw Pact powers to reckon with. However, the Western powers knew that Khrushchev did not like Ulbricht, a diehard Stalinist, and that he would be most reluctant to give Ulbricht unrestricted power to interfere with the access to West Berlin, for Ulbricht might use that power in the most sensitive spot of the Cold War to embroil the Soviet Union with the West or blackmail the U.S.S.R. into giving East Germany more economic or political support.

Meantime, the Western powers insisted on the agreements on Berlin which had existed since 1945 and maintained that the question of Berlin would be finally settled when Germany was unified through free elections and Berlin again became the capital of a reunited country. The indications were that if a treaty were signed with a united German government that the Western powers would accept the present western boundaries of the Soviet Union, Czechoslovakia, and Poland, including the Oder-Neisse line. Even President de Gaulle, who usually held out rigidly against making any concessions to the Russians, was on public record as favoring the Oder-Neisse boundary. And the Western powers had declared repeatedly that after the unification of Germany they would be willing to give friendly consideration to a multilateral non-aggression and mutual assistance pact which would pledge the parties to go to the aid of any country which suffered aggression from a reunited Germany.

However, as was frequently pointed out, especially by such British periodicals as the *Economist*, the *Manchester Guardian*, and the *New Statesman*, the Western powers carefully refrained from asking the Russians the decisive question: Will you agree to free elections and the reunification of Germany if that country is required to leave NATO and is permanently denuclearized, demilitarized, and neutralized? These were the only conditions upon which the Russians might conceivably have consented to the reunification of Germany. Had the question of neutralizing Germany ever been negotiated it would have had to have been defined, and there would have been much discussion about whether neutral status meant refraining not only from military alliances but also from joining exclusive international and supranational economic arangements like ECSC and the European Common Market. But since, after the formation of NATO, the neutralization of

Germany was ruled out by the West, this question was not clarified. In short, the Western powers never took the gamble. They refused to consider sacrificing German participation in NATO for the reunification of Germany. By 1958 any chance of reunification of Germany, even on a basis of German neutralization, had passed, for the time, and the Russians were pressing for other solutions.

It was in the fall of 1958 that Khrushchev announced categorically that the time had come to end the four-power status of Berlin, that the Soviet Union would participate in the existing arrangements only six months longer, and that if the U.S.S.R. and the three Western Allies could not within that time negotiate agreements among themselves as to the future status of Berlin, the Soviet Union would surrender its rights in Berlin to the East German government and from then on the Western powers would have to negotiate with that government, for the U.S.S.R. would be out of the Berlin situation entirely, except that it would stand behind the East German government if the Western powers resorted to force or a violation of its frontiers.

By the end of 1958, then, the Western powers were confronted with two propositions, neither of which they liked. The Rapacki Plan of disengagement and a denuclearized zone in Central Europe, put forth earlier in the year, would disrupt NATO's "forward strategy," which by now was fundamentally based on the use of some nuclear weapons, without providing adequate security against the Communist superiority in conventional military forces. Now Khrushchev's demand that the Western powers give up their military occupation of West Berlin raised the possibility of having to do business with the East German government and of various kinds of harassments by that government, all the way from protests to the full-scale blockade of West Berlin by land and air. Such a blockade might be limited to the Western military forces or it might extend to the civilian population of West Berlin as well. Now that the Soviet Union was stronger than it was in 1948 and had its own nuclear arsenal, an airlift, such as the West successfully employed at that time, might not be tolerated as it was earlier. In any military contest with conventional forces in the Berlin area, the West would still be far inferior in numbers to the forces the Warsaw Pact powers could command. The truth was that the West's defense *did* depend on the nuclear deterrent and the use of nuclear weapons, and the question would be whether the West would resort to so awesome an expedient and thus convert a conflict into a nuclear war.

To Khrushchev's categorical demands about West Berlin, the Western powers replied that they would not be pushed out, that they would stand on their legal rights, and that these rights did not depend merely on the Potsdam agreement, as Khrushchev contended, but also on precisely defined military agreements made prior to Potsdam, and that if the Potsdam agreement were indeed dead, then what right did Poland have to the former German territories up to the Oder-Neisse line, which depended exclusively on the Potsdam agreement? (After this, Khrushchev made no more mention of the Potsdam agreement being a dead letter.) The Western powers further declared that while they were willing to negotiate over Berlin within the framework of the larger question of the future of Germany, they would not negotiate under threats, menace, deadlines, and ultimatums.

As the diplomatic duel unfolded and as Khrushchev over and again postponed his deadlines, there was considerable sympathy in neutral countries and even among segments of opinion in the Allied countries for Khrushchev's contention that the arrangements of fifteen years ago no longer squared with the realities, that new arrangements in fact should be negotiated. Many neutralist leaders said in effect: "Why are the Western powers so agitated about this question? All that Khrushchev appears to be asking is that after fifteen years the victors of the war sit down and try to negotiate a peace treaty. Why don't the Western powers come up with some ideas of their own, why do they merely sit tight on their legal rights? Why do they always allow themselves to be put on the defensive? This creates a situation in which mere face-saving looms too large." There were some differences of opinion among Allied peoples and governments about the future of Berlin and Germany, and this added to the difficulties of the Western powers in meeting the Soviet challenge.

During the early months of 1959 the situation was clarified some. The Russians denied that they had delivered an ultimatum, that there was any fixed deadline, but they insisted that they were deeply serious about getting negotiations on Berlin started. It soon became plain, particularly during the visit of Deputy Premier Mikoyan to the United States early in 1959, that Khrushchev, despite his emphasis on Berlin, was really seeking a summit conference which would deal with Berlin, the larger question of Germany, a ban on nuclear-weapons testing, and disarmament. That Khrushchev's campaign was having an effect was evidenced when even Secretary Dulles publicly observed that free elections might not be the only way of reunifying Germany, as the West had hitherto insisted. President Eisenhower expressed a willingness to participate in a summit conference provided a prior meeting of the foreign ministers of the big four indicated that there was sufficient flexibility in the Soviet position to afford some real prospect of agreement at the summit.

At the Geneva meeting of the foreign ministers of the United States, the U.S.S.R., Britain, and France in the spring of 1959, the whole question of Berlin and Germany was again thrashed out. The Western powers suggested that the whole city of Berlin, East and West, be separated from East Germany and become an entity in itself, under the continued occupation of the four powers, until the coming into force of an all-German peace treaty. They also reiterated their position that Germany be reunified through free elections. They made no offer that a unified Germany be required to renounce membership in NATO and become neutralized. As on previous occasions they maintained that a reunited Germany would have to decide for itself whether it would or would not have membership in NATO. But the Western powers did make some concessions. They indicated they were willing to make agreements curbing propaganda activities of both the East and the West in Berlin and to consider a limitation of armaments, under effective inspection and control, in an agreed area in Central Europe, with the understanding that this would have to have the consent of the future all-German government. This was the nearest approach in the Cold War years to some meeting of minds of East and West on the German question. However, Foreign Minister Gromyko, speaking for the Soviet Union, rejected the Western package plan and again threatened that his government would make a separate peace with the East German government if within eighteen months the big four had not made an agreement ending their military occupation of Berlin.

Although the fruits of the Geneva conference scarcely satisfied President Eisenhower's prerequisite for a summit meeting, by late summer the President had apparently decided to bypass the conference of foreign ministers and consent to a summit meeting provided his personal talks with Khrushchev, during the latter's forthcoming visit to the United States, were satisfactory. The two leaders met in Washington and Camp David in September 1959 and agreed to the scheduling of a summit conference in Paris for May 1960 to negotiate about Berlin, Germany, the banning of nuclear-weapons tests, and the limitation and reduction of armaments under effective inspection and control. Khrushchev assured the President that while negotiations over Berlin should not be postponed indefinitely there would be no fixed time limit on them. During the following months "the spirit of Camp David" prevailed, relations between the United States and the U.S.S.R. were the most amicable of the whole postwar period, and the world looked forward with keen anticipation to the forthcoming summit conference.

Even so, the prospects for actual agreement on the larger questions at the summit did not appear bright, and even Khrushchev gave the impression that he would be satisfied with merely some interim solution on Berlin. In the months before the conference was scheduled to open, Secretary of State Herter and Under Secretary of State Dillon made speeches indicating a "hard" approach to Berlin by the United States delegation. Khrushchev replied truculently. It may be that these speeches, together with other accumulating evidence that the Western powers would stand firm at Paris, convinced Khrushchev that little or nothing would be gained by him at the conference. Nevertheless, Khrushchev professed to believe that the conciliatory spirit of President Eisenhower would make the conference fruitful.

And then came the sensational blow-up of the conference. On May 1, just two weeks before the conference was to convene at Paris, an American U-2 photo-reconnaissance plane was shot down from the skies in the heart of the Soviet Union. The plane had taken off from Pakistan and was to have landed in Norway. Khrushchev angrily asserted that the United States was attempting to "wreck" the conference by committing aggressive acts. At first the United States announced that the plane was on a weather research mission in the Middle East and that if in fact it had entered the Soviet Union such intrusion was accidental. But thereafter Khrushchev revealed that the pilot himself had been captured and had admitted having been engaged in a photo-reconnaissance mission and that the plane had been found to have "espionage equipment." Then the United States conceded the substantial truth of this version, and more, admitted that the United States for several years had been carrying on extensive aerial surveillance of the Soviet Union by unarmed aircraft "normally of a peripheral character but on occasion by penetration." Neutral and even Allied opinion was shocked by these activities of the United States, which were contrary to international law and certainly extraordinary in actual practice. Even many Americans who agreed that such flights were prudent safeguards against surprise attack were exasperated that such flights had been allowed to continue in the weeks prior to the summit conference. Khrushchev gave the President an "out" by declaring that he did not believe the President himself could have known of such flights, but the President cut the ground from under him by taking personal responsibility for the flights, though it appeared that he had not authorized this particular one. Moreover, the President justified these flights (and thus intimated that they would be continued) by saying that distasteful as such intelligence-gathering activities might be, the safety of the free world made them indispensable.

Although the Russians themselves were in the habit of resorting to all sorts of trickery and deceit in order to get access to the secrets of their opponents, these events caused a sensation in the Soviet Union. Were the Soviet defenses so poor that an American plane could penetrate to the heart of the Soviet Union before being shot down? Why had not such planes been shot down before? How much did the Americans know about Soviet strategic areas? Did the Americans know where Soviet missiles lay hidden, thus upsetting the present balance of terror and even betokening the possibility of an American pre-emptive strike? So this was why the Americans had always pressed for "open skies," "mutual aerial inspection," and "spying" controls over disarmament agreements! Khrushchev's own political prestige was at stake at home. Stalinists inside and outside the Soviet Union and the Communist Chinese were now in a position to say with persuasiveness: "We always knew Khrushchev's policies of relaxing tensions were dangerous. This is what comes of a naive following of the peaceful coexistence line. Now we are more convinced than ever that it is impossible to do business with the imperialist warmongers."

Accordingly, when the Paris conference opened in mid-May, Khrushchev was in a rage, actual or simulated. In the presence of the world press gathered at Paris and in the conference itself he screamed like a fishwife. He would not allow the conference to proceed unless President Eisenhower would publicly apologize. The President conducted himself with dignity during the whole ordeal, but refused to humiliate himself and his country by apologizing. Thus the conference was torpedoed. It may be that even before the U-2 incident Khrushchev was convinced by the tenor of American and Western policy statements that the summit conference would fail to make any meaningful agreements, and that he took the U-2 furor as a pretext for breaking up the conference.

Even in the days just preceding the opening of the conference the United States seemed to continue to make blunders. President Eisenhower had planned to announce the suspension of the U-2 flights as soon as the conference convened, and he did make such an announcement at Paris. But many critics wondered why this statement had not been made earlier. And the peoples in other countries wondered why on the night of May 15-16, on the very eve of the opening of the conference, Secretary of Defense Gates in Paris ordered a world-wide alert of the American military forces. A short time later the Russians also made valuable propaganda out of their shooting down of an American Air Force RB-47 in the Barents Sea, allegedly close to Soviet territory.

However, after the collapse of the summit, Khrushchev still pressed for peaceful coexistence. From Paris he went to East Berlin and announced that he was still not ready to carry out his oft-repeated threat to make a separate peace treaty with East Germany, that he would wait "a little longer" and hoped for another summit meeting to take place when Eisenhower's successor had taken office. At a meeting of Communist leaders at Bucharest in June, Khrushchev vigorously defended his peaceful coexistence thesis in the face of opposition from the Stalinists and the Chinese Communists. In the fall Khrushchev attended in person the United Nations Assembly meeting, and a group of leaders from the neutral nations attempted to get Eisenhower and Khrushchev together for a conference. Khrushchev seemed willing, even eager, for such a meeting, but when President Eisenhower declined, Khrushchev did also. About the same time, Khrushchev and Prime Minister Macmillan, who was also attending the Assembly meetings, got together and agreed to promote another summit meeting of the big four to take place after the election of a new American president.

Those who felt that agreement could be reached with the Russians by mutual concessions used many arguments. Those with a flexible approach wondered if the Americans, in using such terms as "appeasement" and "another Munich," were not failing to distinguish Communism from Nazism. These argued that while both were totalitarian, they were markedly different. Nazism was an improvised, nihilistic, supernationalistic, and militaristic movement which frankly proclaimed imperialist expansion by military means. Communism was a movement with over one hundred years of history behind it, was based on a thoughtful philosophy, and theoretically at least had humanitarian aims. It was claimed that while Communism was aggressive in a social revolutionary sense, it was less so in a military sense than generally was supposed. When the Communists spoke of the inevitable war with the capitalist countries it was in the belief that it was the capitalist countries which would be the military aggressors. In theory, Marxism-Leninism did not advocate the expansion of Communism by aggressive or evangelistic war, but it did advocate helping indigenous revolutionary forces when the "objective conditions," social and economic, within a country made this realistic. The Soviet Union was not only the head of a social revolutionary movement but it was also a national state. Its hegemony over the European satellites could be interpreted as fulfilling traditional Russian national aims, intensified by the feeling that Communist Russia was encircled by "aggressive" capitalist countries, for a defense zone on Russian borders. When at the end of the war the balance of power had collapsed in this area, the temptation to build friendly governments in Eastern Europe was too great to resist, but even so the old Russian sovereignty over Finland and Poland was not re-established. But the satellite countries aside, where had the Russians been militarily aggressive? They had got out of northern Iran. They had pressed their claims to a voice in the Turkish Straits but had backed down. Communist revolution in China was largely an indigenous one. The one act of overt military aggression was in Korea, which like the European satellites was on Russian borders; and the Communists, like the Americans, took great pains to restrict the Korean War. Many Europeans felt that the Americans exaggerated the military aggressiveness of Communism and underestimated its economic and social aggressiveness. Hitler through pressures of naked military aggression had taken Austria, the Sudetenland, the rest of Czechoslovakia, the Corridor, Danzig, Memel, and Poland within seventeen months, whereas it was pointed out the Russians at the end of seventeen years were still waiting to reach an agreement on West Berlin, an island in their sphere. Khrushchev had been asking for a Berlin settlement since 1958 and had repeatedly postponed his "deadlines."

It was also pointed out that the Russians were not asking for any territory in a neutral area or in the Western sphere—which if they were, would of course have to be resisted even at the chance of all-out nuclear war. They were not, for instance, asking for Helsinki or Vienna in neutral territory or for Hamburg or Munich in the Western orbit. They were not even asking for West Berlin, located well within their own orbit. They were asking for a neutralization of West Berlin, a formal recognition of their actual position in Eastern Europe, and, if they could get them, peace treaties with both East Germany and West Germany which they hoped would require West Germany to withdraw from NATO in return for the withdrawal of East Germany, Poland, and Czechoslovakia from the Warsaw Pact, and result in the establishment of a denuclearized zone in Central Europe and perhaps an all-European security system. However, the general belief was that the Russians would settle for a change in the status of West Berlin and a legal recognition of East Germany and of the present western boundaries of the Soviet Union, Czechoslovakia, and Poland—in short for mutual recognition of the two spheres rather than mutual withdrawal from them. Those in the West who favored the flexible approach hoped that a relaxation of tensions following the mutual recognition of spheres would later lead to a denuclearized zone in Central Europe which would cut across both spheres, an arrangement made either separately from or as part of a general agreement on arms limitation.

Many doubted that a free city in West Berlin would be really viable, but David Riesman, speaking for those who believed that a mutual accord was urgently necessary, made fruitful suggestions about how this might be done. According to Riesman, once the West Berliners realized that their city was not to become the spearhead of a crusade against Communism, and that their hope of becoming the capital of a reunited Germany was unrealistic and part of a dangerous mystique, their energies would flow into making their city a still greater cultural, educational, and commercial center. The city's industrial development could be further enhanced by Allied as well as West German assistance. The Free University might be expanded to become a sort of European university, even more cosmopolitan and influential than at present. It might be possible, in agreement with the Russians, to locate in Berlin one or another international agency, moved there from New York or Paris or Geneva or Vienna. "It might become desirable to create in West Berlin a tribunal of neutrals not unsatisfactory to the Russians or the West, whose main duty it would be to hear complaints and develop in effect a common law of distinctions between the anti-Communist talk and writing natural to the West and the incitements aimed not at strengthening the West but in weakening the East. In turn, of course, the Communists could be assured freedom for *their* propaganda in West Berlin— precious little good it will do them."

It was argued that certain advantages might flow from a legal as distinguished from a mere tacit recognition of the situation in Eastern Europe. If the East Germans or the Russians threatened any of the Western rights guaranteed in the agreements—such as impairing in any way the Western access to Berlin—then the West in turn might withdraw its recognition of East Germany or of the Oder-Neisse line. These would be negative advantages, but there might also be important positive ones. As the *Economist* of London observed, formal recognition of the situation in Eastern Europe might lead to a lowering of barriers between East and West, more intercourse between East and West Germany, a relaxing of tensions not only among the great powers but especially in the satellite countries. The *Economist* emphasized that any settlement made with the Russians would not be a complete or final one, that it would be only a first step toward *rapprochement*, that if successful other steps would follow, that conciliation would have to proceed in stages, that the end result might be some form of unification of Germany itself.

Would the West Germans be seriously disaffected by the miscarriage or even the indefinite postponement of German reunification? It was predicted that although the German politicians would naturally be expected to continue to give much lip-service to German reunification, the West German people would probably not be overly concerned. The West Germans seemed to like very well their present situation—participation in NATO and particularly their economic integration into Western Europe and their mass-consumer prosperity. For the present at least German nationalism did not seem to be to the fore, and the leading party in West Germany, the Christian Democratic, was a Catholic party with conflicting emotional ties to the old Charlemagne Europe and to the later German nation.

Those inclined to a settlement on the basis of a virtual mutual recognition of the two spheres of influence in Europe, with perhaps some modification through a limited denuclearized zone in Central Europe, were hopeful that such an accord would lead to enough relaxing of tensions to allow a treaty banning the testing of nuclear weapons and making a beginning in reduction and limitation of armaments.

Those who resisted negotiations or favored a "hard" line in the negotiating relied on numerous arguments. They stressed the legal rights of the Western powers in West Berlin and that these should certainly not be weakened in the face of Communist threats. They emphasized that the diplomatic duel was not with ordinary opponents but with ones who had a different set of values, were bent on fomenting revolution by any means at their disposal, and were aggressive in every sense—in economic and social warfare, in propaganda, in military action. If indeed these opponents had been "moderate" in their actual military aggressions it was because the West had the power and the inflexibility to withstand them, and yielding now would be appeasement, another Munich, which would whet the appetites of the aggressors for still more gains at the expense of the free world. Despite

Khrushchev's blandishments and his peaceful coexistence line, had he not consented in late 1962 to the secret and sly building of Soviet intermediate missile bases in Cuba with the apparent intention of suddenly and ruthlessly blackmailing the United States into giving way on Berlin?

Americans were pledged to defend West Berlin, and if the people of that city were abandoned, which would be cruel enough in itself, how would America's other allies ever be able to trust America again? What, then, would become of NATO? Berlin was not only important in its own right, but even more important, it was the symbol of the future reunification of Germany and was being held in trust as its capital. To recognize East Germany and to abandon West Berlin, or even to weaken the Western position there, would be giving up even the *idea* of a reunified Germany. Then what would happen to morale in West Germany? The West Germans had been told for years that the surest way to obtain future reunification was to be strong, trust the Western Allies, and remain faithful to NATO obligations. Would not the patent failure of this policy bring disillusionment? Would not the Germans move away from the West, toward neutralism, toward even an understanding with the Russians? If German reunification was indefinitely and apparently permanently blocked, would there not be a dangerous resurgence of German nationalism which would play East and West off against each other in the interest of a new German chauvinism? If Berlin lost its hope of becoming the capital of a reunified Germany or even of becoming a part of the Federal Republic and decade after decade was surrounded by Communist East Germany, would it not lose its viability and gradually be seduced into the Communist camp?

Why were not the Russians willing to let well enough alone? The West was not pressing the Russians into an immediate reunification of Germany. The West had tacitly recognized the present Russian position in East Germany and the other Eastern satellites. Why the pressure on the West for a formal recognition? Sometimes it was wiser to leave a situation in an ill-defined but roughly workable way.

Why the haste? Why all this hysterical talk about the "danger" of West Germany? As President Kennedy pointed out in the interview he gave to the editor of *Izvestia*, it was not West Germany which was endangering the peace. The only powers really able to threaten the world with military conquest were the United States and the Soviet Union. West Germany had a relatively small army and no nuclear capacity of its own, and the President added that he would be extremely reluctant to see West Germany acquire such a capacity. President Kennedy in his disarmament speech before the United Nations Assembly gave assurances of his willingness to enter into agreements with the Soviet Union and other nuclear powers to insure that nuclear weapons and know-how were not given to other countries—which in practical terms meant that the Russians would withhold nuclear weapons from the Red Chinese and the Americans would withhold them from the West Germans. And, argued those who were skeptical of a definitive settlement of the Berlin and German questions, if the Russians wanted treaties banning nuclear-weapons testing and making a start on disarmament, they could do this without insisting on a prior legalizing of the situation in Eastern Europe, a situation the West seemed perfectly willing to let alone but found embarrassing to formalize.

Governments and peoples in the Western countries differed somewhat in their approach to the Berlin and German questions. Most of the British leaders, Conservative as well as Labour, not only favored negotiating but were inclined to a settlement which, temporarily at least, would relinquish the Allied demand for the reunification of Germany through free elections and would seek to stabilize Eastern and Central Europe through an essential recognition of the existing situation there, with some change in the status of Berlin which would not mean Western withdrawal. Some British leaders favored going beyond this to accept some form of disengagement involving a limited denuclearized zone in Central Europe. (American policy makers opposed a denuclearized zone in the belief that the Russians, because of their proximity and superiority in conventional forces, would then have the advantage.)

In France, President de Gaulle was against negotiations with the Russians on the grounds that the West should not negotiate under duress and that no agreements were likely to come out of the deliberations. To observers who probed beneath the surface it appeared that De Gaulle wanted to keep Germany divided but in view of his alliance with Chancellor Adenauer could not avow such a view, that therefore he did not want to negotiate on the subject at all. If nothing was done, the *de facto* partition of Germany was likely to continue anyway.

In Germany, Adenauer, too, opposed negotiating, and officially he put his opposition on the ground that any big-four conference was likely to result in a weakening of the Western position on Germany. It certainly would not result in German reunification but on the other hand might make changes in the status of Berlin and recognize East Germany and the Oder-Neisse line. He feared an American-Soviet "deal" behind Bonn's back. But many surmised that Adenauer, like De Gaulle, rather liked the present arrangement in Germany, and in the absence of agreements among the big four such an arrangement would probably continue. It was recalled that Adenauer was emotionally oriented to the old Catholic Germany, that in the 1920's he had reportedly sympathized with the Rhenish separatist movement, and that the pre-eminence of his Christian Democratic party was based on Catholic voters, who had a majority in West Germany but not in Germany as a whole. It was Adenauer's inflexibility toward negotiations which had cost him his losses in the West German elections of 1961. He was able to stay on as Chancellor only because his Christian Democrats made a coalition with the Free Democrats, a businessman's party which favored a more flexible economic and political relationship with the Communist world. As the price of coalition, the Free Democrats demanded the head of Foreign Minister Brentano and the appointment of Gerhard Schroeder to take Brentano's place. Schroeder was more favorable to negotiations, and he kept a suspicious eye on the aging Chancellor. The Social Democrats, the second party in West Germany, made significant gains in the 1961 elections with Mayor Willy Brandt of West Berlin as their leader. The Social Democrats in pre-Hitler days had drawn much strength from Protestant East Germany and they were the most flexible of the West German parties in their approach to the Soviet Union. They argued that relaxing of tensions, *rapprochement*, and the eventual reunification of Germany would require repeated negotiations, piecemeal accommodations, and successive stages of development.

There were, then, roughly three views in the West: one which wanted the present situation to continue through a "prudent" and pragmatic non-action; one which sought to legalize and stabilize the present situation (with some change in the status of Berlin) in the hope of easing tensions and getting on with a nuclear-test ban and disarmament agreements; and one which held out for assurances of the reunification of Germany through free elections. Public opinion polls in both France and Germany revealed that the peoples of both these countries were more favorable to negotiations than were their heads of state. The willingness to negotiate did not mean a yielding to Russian views but a desire to find some basis for mutual concessions and accommodations. In the United States there was some difference of opinion as to the proper approach, but in the day-to-day dealings among the Allied powers, the United States usually took a position somewhere between the leniency of the British and the inflexibility of De Gaulle and Adenauer.

However, during 1961 and 1962, in their approaches to each other, both the American and the Russian governments were in a dangerous contest of nerves, each seeking to convince the other that it had the willingness to fight, with nuclear weapons if need be, if pressed too far. Provocation was piled on provocation. Both were caught in a vicious cycle.

The Russians said that the Americans must join in a German settlement. The Americans replied that they would not be pushed around. Khrushchev threatened to make a treaty with Ulbricht surrendering Russian rights of occupation in Berlin. The Americans reacted as though this would be a calamity. In the spring of 1961, Khrushchev and Kennedy exchanged sharp words over Castro's Cuba, the Cuban expedition failed, and the Communist build-up in Cuba continued.

At Vienna in June, Khrushchev impressed on Kennedy personally and in an *aide-mémoire* the urgency of making a German settlement. In contrast to previous Soviet plans, Khrushchev did not insist on the immediate withdrawal of West Germany from NATO and he did not even insist that the Western powers recognize the East German government; but he did insist that he was going to make peace with that government, with or without the West, that the occupation regime in West Berlin would thereby be terminated, and that if the Western powers wanted to remain in the city and have access to it they would have to negotiate with the government of East Germany.

Kennedy returned home, called up reserves, and exhorted the nation to build bomb shelters. In August, Ulbricht built a wall of concrete and barbed wire between East and West Berlin, and incidents multiplied. The Americans increased their counter-force capacity and their Polaris deterrent. The Russians broke the truce on nuclear-weapons testing and in September began their atmospheric explosions. The Americans resumed under-ground testing. The Russian tests continued. The Americans, in the spring of 1962, resumed tests in the atmosphere. Then the Russians began another round of tests, which were followed by more American tests, which were followed by still more Russian tests. Then Khrushchev built his sneak missile bases in Cuba and the Americans reacted sharply.

The tensions mounted while the contestants only ran the harder. As Riesman observed, one does not break out of a circle by moving faster within it.

[7]

THE WORLD
OF THE NEUTRALS

The Attitudes of the Neutrals

The postwar era was one not of two worlds but of three: the American-bloc countries, the Soviet-bloc countries, and the neutrals. Most of the emergent nations in Asia, the Middle East, and Africa were neutral, refused to line up with either of the power blocs. However, a few of the underdeveloped countries were definitely aligned: Outer Mongolia, North Korea, and North Vietnam with the Sino-Soviet bloc; and South Korea, Formosa, the Philippines, Thailand, Pakistan, Iran, and Turkey with the American bloc. South Vietnam, although neutralized by the international agreements which brought her independence in 1954, was in reality an American ally. But inside the underdeveloped countries allied to the United States there was much anti-colonial sentiment and some neutralist opinion. The United States also regarded the members of the Organization of American States as allies, but on so-called anti-colonial matters they often lined up with the Afro-Asian neutrals, and one of them, Cuba, had gone over to the Communist bloc. Among the avowed neutrals there were various shades of neutralism; some of them inclined to the West, some to the East, but frequently Americans tended to think that certain neutralist nations were more inclined to the East than they were in fact.

It was the large number of neutrals which prevented the world from being bipolarized. The most populous and important of the emergent nations were neutral. Pakistan was the only major new nation that was willing to become an American military ally. As the number of new and neutral nations increased, the trend to depolarization was accentuated.

Only Communist states were in alliance with the Communist bloc, and there were few of these. The remarkable fact was that despite the appeal of Communist economics as a means for an underdeveloped country to get an industrial revolution in a hurry, after about two decades of anti-imperialist revolutions, which by 1963 had brought independence to almost all of the old European colonies, only one former European colony—North Vietnam—had embraced Communism. China had never been a European colony; in the late stages of Western imperialism it had been divided into economic spheres of influence and been exploited economically by the various Western powers, but political rule had not been established. The European powers had escaped governmental, legal, educational, and social responsibilities, and no European culture had penetrated any part of China the way British culture, for instance, had penetrated India. North Korea, too, had never been a European colony. Neither had Outer Mongolia. Cuba, if indeed it could be considered a Communist society, had not been a European colony for several generations.

But while the new nations recently emerged from political colonialism had up to the present successfully resisted Communism, most of them were extremely sensitive about their new independence, insisted on being free in fact as well as in name, resented intensely any apparent attempts from the outside to control their actions. Although they sought economic aid from both the United States and the Soviet Union, their foreign policies were not for sale. Most of them insisted on pursuing a neutralist course. They believed that each power bloc exaggerated the danger from the other, that both were responsible for the Cold War tensions. They disliked the police state and satellitism of

Communism. But they associated the West with colonialism and were busy eradicating the last traces of it. They wanted to escape the burdens of military alliances, wanted to concentrate their energies and what wealth they had in developing their own economies. They believed that testing of nuclear weapons and threats to plunge the world into nuclear destruction showed a callous disregard for the welfare of other peoples. Most important, they deplored the billions spent by both sides on the arms race and had rather a sense of outrage when they contemplated how a small fraction of those billions, if diverted as capital for their economic development, would allow them to conquer their mass poverty.

The United States and the Political Aspect of the Anti-Imperialist Revolutions

The former colonial peoples and those still struggling against colonialism liked America's revolutionary tradition and its doctrine of national self-determination. They applauded the United States record in Puerto Rico and Hawaii, the granting of independence to the Philippines, and the friendly pressures the United States had exerted on Britain to get out of India and on the Dutch to get out of Indonesia. They were profoundly impressed with America's stand against Britain and France in the Suez crisis of 1956.

But they were repelled by racism in the United States and underestimated the recent strides taken to overcome it. They were highly critical when the United States inclined to support its allies Britain and France in colonial matters. They condemned the way the United States, because of its fear of the spread of Communism, had urged the French to remain in Indochina, thereby, in their opinion, allowing the Communists to identify themselves with Vietnamese nationalism and preparing the way, ironically enough, for the Communist takeover in North Vietnam. They were antagonized when time after time the United States either lined up with France or abstained from voting when resolutions condemning the French war in Algeria were before the United Nations.

The United States had a difficult time trying to make the new nations realize that while it sympathized with the national aspirations of the colonial peoples it could not afford to alienate its European allies. Indeed, the United States had a difficult time steering a course between the interests of its European allies and the aspirations of the colonial peoples, and the middle position it often pursued only resulted in irritating both.

The new states, too, expected the United States to support their claims to "unredeemed" national territory and they were put out when they did not get that support. Tunisia expected America to back its claims to Bizerte air base, Indonesia its claims to Dutch New Guinea (West Irian), and both India and Pakistan to their conflicting claims in Kashmir. When India, in the name of anti-imperialism, seized the Portuguese enclaves of Goa, Damão, and Diu on its western coast, it was "hurt" when the United States charged that India had violated the United Nations Charter. (Nehru's high-handed actions in Kashmir and Goa served to remind Americans that after all the Indian Prime Minister was not primarily a philosopher but a politician, and sometimes a shrewd one.)

The Kennedy administration vastly pleased the Afro-Asian nations when Assistant Secretary of State for African Affairs G. Mennen Williams, while touring Africa, publicly endorsed the principle of "Africa for the Africans," and the President backed him up by observing, "I don't know who else Africa could be for." The Kennedy administration also took a more decided stand with the anti-imperialists in the United Nations. The United States in both the Security Council and the Assembly separated itself from its European allies to admonish Portugal for its oppressive policies in Angola. The United States also became more friendly to criticism by the United Nations of the Union of South Africa's apartheid racial policies and its discriminations against persons of Indian and Pakistani origins in South Africa, and it actually voted to condemn South Africa's administration of the mandated territory of South West Africa. Cynics explained all this in terms of the administration's solicitude for Negro votes in the United States and to the fact that now that Britain and France had relinquished most of their colonies in Africa the United States could well afford to brave the displeasure of little Portugal and the Union of South Africa and take a more vigorous anti-colonial stand in Africa. Be that as it may, America's more vigorous anti-colonialism was warmly applauded in Asia, the Middle East, and Africa.

The United States and the Economic and Social Aspects of the Anti-Imperialist Revolutions

The Americans understood the political aspects of the anti-colonial revolutions better than their economic and social aspirations. Even as late as 1963 few Americans believed that the future of the world more likely would be determined by constructive economic and social measures in the underdeveloped countries than by armaments and military alliances. Americans, who had more wealth and technological and organizational know-how than any other people in the world, were slow to rise to Khrushchev's challenge of competitive coexistence, slow to share adequately their capital and skills to help the world's peoples fulfill their revolution of rising expectations.

Even in matters of international trade there was much criticism of American policies. The United States, the chief creditor nation in the world, was in an anomalous position. Unlike Britain, the chief creditor nation of the past, the United States was not only an industrial nation but also a leading producer of foodstuffs and raw materials, which meant that it took less of such products from the rest of the world than was often expected and that it was also in competition with raw-materials-producing nations for world markets. Moreover, the United States, despite its reciprocal tariff agreements, still had many tariffs, and not infrequently, to protect its own producers, resorted to quota limitations on the import of raw materials. Then, too, the reciprocal tariff reductions were always subject to "peril point" upping, when the President, on the advice of the Tariff Commission, decided that higher tariffs were necessary to protect American producers. Again, the United States, the defender of the free market in the United Nations, in the Organization of American States, and in numerous international economic conferences, decisively opposed international agreements to stabilize the world prices of raw materials, and then if any of its own producer groups were hurt compensated them by domestic subsidies. It seemed to foreigners that the United States was for economic nationalism (neo-mercantilism) when this served its interest, but that at the same time it preached the international free market for others. Moreover, the United States sometimes dumped its own agricultural surpluses on the world market in such a way as to injure countries which specialized in producing one or two agricultural commodities. As we shall see later, the United States began taking a more favorable attitude toward international commodity agreements in the late 1950's, in the later days of the Eisenhower administration, particularly with respect to Latin American products, and that the Kennedy administration moved to a drastic liberalization of American trade policies.

But the decisive need of the underdeveloped countries was for foreign capital. The United States insisted that these countries should look primarily to foreign private capital for their modernization, mechanization, and industrialization. Many Americans believed that government grants and easy loans to the governments of the new nations were "socialistic," a betrayal of free enterprise. Again, in the United Nations, in the Organization of American States, and in numerous international conferences, the United States emphasized the importance of a favorable investment climate in the underdeveloped countries. The United States often criticized these countries for their "anti-business" tax policies, their regulations and controls of foreign business firms. But to the underdeveloped countries such preachments smacked of interference in their own affairs, and they pointed out that the business practices of foreign corporations in their countries were often a species of "economic colonialism" in that they frequently developed those industries that brought the greatest and most immediate profits and neglected those which would diversify, balance, and rationally develop the economies of underdeveloped societies. Besides, they insisted that foreign private capital was simply not available in sufficient amounts to do the job of transforming their pre-industrial economies into industrial ones, and the actual statistics bore them out.

For instance, as of the end of 1955 there was a little over 19 billion dollars in direct private American investments abroad, and of this around 6.5 billion dollars was invested in Canada, about 6.5 billion in Latin America, about 3 billion in Western Europe. This left only around 3 billion spread thinly over all Asia, the

Middle East, and Africa. In terms of strictly long-term capital, the facts were even less encouraging. In the years 1953-1954 Americans invested only about 500 million dollars (net) annually of private long-term capital in independent underdeveloped countries, and 60 per cent of that went into Latin America, most of it in direct investment aimed primarily at opening up sources of minerals—especially petroleum, iron ore, and copper—for export, and toward establishment of branch plants. There had been extremely little portfolio investment by Americans in the underdeveloped countries since World War II. In these countries there was still danger of further revolution and of expropriation; there were restrictions in many countries on the full withdrawal of profits; and most important, the immediate needs of the emergent societies were for harbors, roads, communications, social and educational services (what the economist calls the infrastructure), which were basic to future economic growth but produced little or no profits. The private investor wanted profits, and he avoided the long-haul risks and put his money in going countries and concerns.

Even when the Americans became convinced of the importance of extending economic aid to the underdeveloped peoples, they still resisted putting the emphasis on the basic need—investment capital by way of intergovernmental grants and loans—and instead emphasized technical assistance, the sending of American technicians to train indigenous technicians. This cost less, gave jobs to American specialists, and did not involve a "betrayal" of free enterprise. President Truman's Point Four program and the American sponsorship of the United Nations Expanded Program of Technical Assistance, beginning in 1949, were examples of this early stress on technical assistance. Americans moved much more slowly to supplying capital for basic developments. The British, in their Colombo Program for southern Asia, saw the need of intergovernmental grants and easy loans for capital development earlier than the Americans.

The Economics of Foreign Aid

It was during the most active Marshall Plan years (1948-1951) that the United States first carried out a systematic program of economic aid; one, too, which involved supplying capital equipment. (From 1946 to 1955 America's total economic aid to Western Europe was around 33 billion dollars.) But with the Korean War, American foreign aid shifted from the economic to the military and military-end items and for several years thereafter it showed the influence of that war. For the fiscal year 1953 American foreign aid was 4.4 billion dollars for military assistance and 2 billion for economic assistance; and in fiscal 1954 it was 3.5 billion for military assistance and 1.7 billion for economic assistance. Military assistance was used to buy arms and military equipment for America's military allies. Moreover, over half of what was called economic assistance went for the defense support of America's military allies, for over-all measures which allowed them to sustain military forces. For fiscal 1956, as Americans moved farther away from the Korean War, foreign aid in the Mutual Security appropriation fell to around 2.8 billion dollars, with about 1 billion for military assistance, around 1 billion for defense support, and less than 800 million dollars for economic aid. The breakdown for economic aid was roughly 263 million dollars for capital development assistance: 151 million for Asia, 73 million for the Middle East and Africa, 39 million for the Western Hemisphere. The President was given 100 million dollars for use in economic aid where he thought it was most needed. Technical assistance got 127.5 million, the United Nations Technical Assistance Program 24 million, and various international economic programs and agencies the rest of the economic-aid appropriation.

In the mid-1950's the dollar gap in world trade continued to be an important argument for the retaining of the foreign-aid program. Balances of payments were still running heavily in favor of the United States and against the rest of the world. In the mid-1950's, America's commercial exports and export equivalents were around 21 billion dollars a year; America's commercial imports and import equivalents were around 16 billion dollars a year. The dollar gap was thus about 5 billion dollars a year. This was in considerable measure covered each year by United States grants in foreign military assistance and economic aid. In other words, foreigners were able to get enough gold and dollar holdings to continue to do business in the United States and the dollar areas largely because of American military and economic grants abroad.

(Although a net private capital outflow each year helped too.) Abroad during these years there was a constant scamper to get dollars, dollar holdings were precarious, and foreign governments, including the British, could not allow their currencies free convertibility into dollars, which in turn necessitated government controls of many kinds. All foreign governments, those of the advanced countries and those of the underdeveloped countries, were uneasy as they faced the decline in America's foreign aid.

In the mid-1950's, then, America's total foreign aid was declining, most of it was still going to military assistance and defense support, and the chief recipients were America's military allies.

During this period, Secretary of State Dulles was of the opinion that neutralism was "immoral," and he sought to use economic aid as a means of inducing the uncommitted peoples to tie themselves closely to the West. Moreover, the United States took the attitude that if a country received economic aid from the Soviet Union it ought not to be given aid by the United States. (It was argued that Soviet technicians, administering economic aid by the Soviet Union, would penetrate the country and act as agents of Communist subversion.) But neutral countries resented America's attempt to use economic aid to link them more closely to the West and to prevent their taking aid from the Soviet Union. They regarded this as an attempt to dictate their policies. Many American critics of this policy asked: "Is this not a short-sighted policy? If the Soviet Union gives aid to a non-Communist government will not that non-Communist government be given credit for any economic improvements which follow, and will not this likely help fortify the non-Communist government against its domestic Communists? As non-Communists, we ought actually to welcome any economic aid to a non-Communist country that will better its economic life." One of the reasons the United States backed out of its promise to help Nasser build the Aswan Dam was the persistence of rumors that the Soviet Union was also to lend financial help to this project. The Dulles insistence that Egypt must forgo Soviet aid if it were to receive American aid contributed to the sparking of the Suez crisis of 1956.

In the spring of 1957, the State Department, the President's Citizen Advisers on the Mutual Security Program (the so-called Fairless Commission), the International Development Advisory

Board (headed by Eric Johnston), and two closely parallel studies prepared by the University of Chicago and the Massachusetts Institute of Technology all made recommendations covering America's future economic-aid program. While these reports differed in detail and in several instances were contradictory, in the main they agreed on the following recommendations: (1) that military assistance be divorced from the foreign-aid program and that military-assistance funds be transferred from the Mutual Security budget to the Defense Department budget, so that henceforth this part of the program would be labeled exactly what it was, a military program and not an economic program; (2) that the defense-support program be continued as "economic aid" and remain under the management of the International Cooperation Administration, because while the bolstering of the general economies of America's military allies was military it was also economic and often called for long-time economic programs; (3) that capital-development programs be given far more emphasis than in the past; (4) that economic aid for capital-development projects be given to neutrals as well as to allies (here the Fairless Commission differed, recommending priority for allies); and (5) that the President be delegated considerable flexibility and discretion in allocating funds for capital development and be allowed to make commitments for projects requiring some years to plan and execute.

The University of Chicago and M.I.T. studies estimated that the underdeveloped countries would need to invest annually about 14 to 15 per cent of their national income in capital development to bring a 3 to 4 per cent annual increase in per capita income. But these countries, the authors contended, could not invest more than 9 to 10 per cent of their income without resorting to totalitarian forced savings or crushing taxation. Since the total income of the underdeveloped countries in Asia, the Middle East, and Africa was approximately 110 billion dollars in 1955, the gap was of the order of 4.5 billion dollars. The industrialized nations of the West probably would balk at putting up that much. To do so would probably be self-defeating because of the limited absorptive capacity of many of the underdeveloped nations. Therefore these reports suggested additional investment from all sources—the national governments of the West, the international organizations, private capital—of 2.5 to 3.5 billion dollars a year. Of this they proposed that the United States government put up about 1.5 billion. This would be over 1 billion dollars more than was appropriated by Congress for the 1956-1957 fiscal year for capital development and technical assistance in Asia, the Middle East, and Africa. The two criteria for allocating aid to any country would be its absorptive capacity and the productivity of the proposed projects. Thus there would be no question of "equitable" allocation as between countries nor would there be any attempt at equalizing the per capita income of all the underdeveloped countries.

Responding to these various studies and to its own studies, the State Department recommended the establishment of an Economic Development Fund, within the International Cooperation Administration, which would be an agency of the United States similar to the Export-Import Bank. This Fund would make long-time loans (not grants) for capital-development projects in the emergent societies at low interest rates. (Up to this time most economic aid had been outright grants.) According to C. Douglas Dillon, Deputy Under Secretary of State for Economic Affairs, this Economic Development Fund would not compete with the World Bank, the Export-Import Bank, or with private capital. It would make no loans unless assurances had been received that the projects could not obtain financing either from other public institutions or from private sources. The Fund would differ from the World Bank in that projects would not necessarily have to develop the foreign exchange required for prompt repayment in dollars. Loans would be repayable largely in the currency of the borrowing country. For instance, a loan to India might be repayable in rupees. But repayment in local currency would not rule out possible eventual repayment in dollars. If the Fund made a loan to an underdeveloped country repayable in local currency over a period of fifteen or twenty years, after this loan had been repaid the money might well be loaned again to the same government with the reasonable hope that the economic situation in that country would have so improved that it would be possible for this second loan to be repaid at least partly in dollars. Secretary Dulles said that in his view the loans by the Fund might eventually amount to some 750 million dollars a year, thus paring the figures said by the Chicago and M.I.T. reports to be desirable but upping considerably the figures Congress had been in the habit of allocating for capital-development projects.

These recommendations began to bear fruit in the budget for the fiscal year 1958, which authorized the establishment of the Development Loan Fund or revolving credit plan for providing investment capital for meritorious long-time development projects which did not qualify for loans from existing institutions. Congress appropriated 500 million dollars to get the Fund started. The budget for fiscal 1959 provided for 1.5 billion dollars for military assistance, 750 million for defense support, and slightly over 1 billion for the various aspects of economic aid, including the Development Loan Fund, which was continued. Thus economic aid was creeping up on military aid. For the fiscal year 1960, military aid was 1.3 billion, defense support less than 700 million. The Development Loan Fund was granted 550 million, other economic and capital development activities 245 million, and technical assistance 150 million. For fiscal 1961, economic aid was 1.3 billion dollars, including defense support, with 550 million for the Loan Fund. In addition, Congress authorized 600 million dollars of aid for Latin America, but actual appropriations were left to the future.

The Kennedy administration made significant advances in foreign-aid programs. In 1962, 1.6 billion dollars went for military aid and 2.3 billion for economic aid, including defense support, with 1.1 billion for capital development lending. The rest of that earmarked for non-defense economic aid went for technical assistance, the Peace Corps, the Inter-American Bank, and other international agencies and activities. All of the government's foreign economic-aid activities were grouped together into a new, semi-independent State Department bureau to be known as the Agency for International Development. Congress authorized a five-year, 6-billion-dollar long-term lending program. However, Congress balked at allowing the President to finance this through annual installments of Treasury advances and insisted that the money be sought through annual Congressional appropriations in the usual way.

Thus from 1957 to 1962 the United States moved to greater emphasis on foreign economic aid, and to a realization that capital-development programs were the most significant aspects of economic aid. Moreover, the direct aid programs of the United States government did not tell the whole story, for the Export-Import Bank (an American government agency, not an international one), the International Bank for Reconstruction and Development, the International Development Association, and other international institutions were steadily expanded and increased their lending to underdeveloped countries; and sometimes funds from several of these institutions and from the Development Loan Fund were pooled to support given development projects in underdeveloped countries. Again, the United States often made bilateral agreements with underdeveloped countries in which the United States sold them surplus agricultural commodities (which the American government had on hand as a result of its domestic agricultural program) for payments in their domestic currencies, which were loaned back to them for their internal development programs.

For instance, it was estimated that in the year 1961 America's total foreign *economic* aid amounted to 4.389 billion dollars. This figure was arrived at by adding together all of the government's regular economic aid, the contributions it made to international agencies (which in turn gave aid), and the sums involved in all its surplus commodity agreements. In the Far East the largest recipients of economic aid were America's military allies, South Korea, Formosa, and South Vietnam. In southern Asia the largest recipients were India and Pakistan, but neutral India got more than twice as much as ally Pakistan. In the Middle East the largest recipient was neutral Egypt, followed by allies Turkey and Iran. In Europe, the largest recipients were rightist and allied Spain and leftist and neutralist Yugoslavia. Thus the United States had learned to use its economic aid in a broad and eclectic way.

Indeed, economic aid had come to be handled in a much more sophisticated manner than formerly. Neutrals were regularly given economic aid along with the military allies; aid was given without strings attached; and neutrals which got large credits from the Soviet government often got even larger credits from the United States. The philosophy behind foreign aid had come to be to keep the neutral countries from going to the other side, to convince them that the American system was strong enough to help them solve their problems, to enhance the welfare of the underdeveloped peoples themselves, and to benefit the world economy, including the economies of the advanced industrial countries, which profited as *effective* economic wants were multiplied.

But just about the time Americans had become more mature in their approach to foreign aid, a new obstacle arose in the behavior of the American economy itself. There was growing concern about the repeated recessions in the economy and about the slackening rate of economic growth in the United States, especially in the light of the rate of growth in other economies, particularly that of the Soviet Union. The rate of annual American growth had fallen close to 2 per cent while the over-all rate of Soviet expansion had been running in the late 1950's to about 9.5 per cent annually. The Soviet Union, with a gross national product less than half that of the United States, was investing more new capital in new plants and machinery than was the United States. The capitalist economies of West Germany, Japan, and even Mexico were showing rates of growth comparable to that of the Soviet Union.

An alarming danger signal was the deficit in the international balance of payments running against the United States. By 1958 there was "a dollar gap in reverse," America's non-military exports fell from 19.3 billion dollars in 1957 to 16.3 billion in 1958 and 1959. (Western Europe and Japan were increasing their world trade.) American imports for 1957 were 13.3 billion, for 1958, 12.8 billion, and for 1959, 15.2 billion. Thus by 1959 America's non-military exports only slightly exceeded its imports. Because of this narrow gap between exports and imports, America's military and economic aid abroad, along with some other factors, produced a balance-of-payments deficit against the United States of 3.6 billion dollars in 1958, of 3.8 billion in 1959, of 3.8 billion again in 1960, of 2.4 billion in 1961, and apparently of over 1.5 billion in 1962. Thus since 1958 there had been an annual net outflow of gold and dollars from the United States, and America's gold supply was shrinking at the rate of 6.5 per cent annually.

As a consequence there were new demands for cutting foreign military and economic aid and a new insistence that foreign loans and credits be spent in the United States, that recipients of American aid buy their arms and machinery in this country. Instead of emphasizing the flow of American capital abroad, there were increasing calls for measures to keep American capital at home and attract foreign capital to this country. (As one wag put it, the shoe was now on the other foot, and Americans needed British, German, and Japanese capital to develop "the underdeveloped areas" in Wisconsin, Ohio, and New Jersey.) It was agreed that an American depression would be fatal to the free world, that recurring American recessions presented a serious problem, and that the rate of American economic growth would have to be stepped up. But there were great differences of opinion about how this was to be done. Suggestions ranged from expanding social services, widening the public sector of the economy, tax reforms to stimulate venture capital, and high interest rates at home to keep American capital from flowing abroad and to encourage foreign investments in the United States. There were some who even hinted that the diversion of such prodigious amounts of capital to armaments each year was the root of the scarcity of capital. (The need for armaments was the obstacle to the tax cuts many felt were necessary to give the economy the stimulation it required.)

At the same time Americans were also warned that to increase their own rate of economic expansion at the cost of cutting off capital to the underdeveloped societies would only widen the gap between the rich nations and the poor nations and push the impoverished societies to Communism. When the first alarm wore off it was generally agreed that the United States would have to increase the rate of its own economic growth and at the same time continue its program of economic aid to the underdeveloped areas. More and more it was thought that this would require an increase in American trade abroad and in world trade generally. This gave added importance to the Common Market in Europe and to President Kennedy's trade program designed to do business with it, which will be discussed in another connection.

A new look was taken at various aspects of foreign economic aid. There was a new "buy American" insistence, but it was discovered that about three-fourths of economic aid had always been spent in the United States. (However, critics pointed out that the one-fourth spent abroad was just about the amount of the 1961 balance-of-payments deficit.) Critics of foreign aid also demanded to know just how much of the capital of the underdeveloped peoples themselves was going into their economic development programs, and in reply India's new Five-Year Plan (1961-1966) was cited as envisaging a total investment of 25 billion dollars, only 5.5 billion dollars of which was to come from external sources, the share pledged by the United States over the five-year period being around 2.2 billion dollars.

Americans became more emphatic in their contention that the other non-Communist advanced industrial countries should lend more economic assistance to the emergent nations. It was felt that West Germany and Japan had been particularly remiss. One of the reasons the United States Senate in 1961 ratified American entry into the Organization for Economic Cooperation and Development (an international agency, dedicated to "fair trade" practices, which the Senate was finally persuaded would not unduly limit the autonomy of the United States in trade matters) was its "burden sharing" features, the opportunities it afforded to institutionalize a kind of international consortium to lend economic aid to the less advanced societies. Within this new organization the United States took the position that each industrial country should set aside 1 per cent of its gross national product for aid purposes, thus producing an aggregate of some 7.5 billion dollars each year, in comparison with the annual average of 4.2 billion dollars (plus 2.7 billion in private investment and loans) during the 1956-1959 period.

Despite the pessimism about the performance of the American economy, America's gross national product reached a record high of 521.3 billion dollars in 1961, and the United States' contribution to foreign economic aid would just about reach 1 per cent of its gross national product in 1962, if the use of argricultural surpluses in foreign aid were included. In the light of the voluminous criticisms of American foreign policy and poor economic-aid showing of many of the non-Communist industrial countries, this American achievement was impressive.

However, by late 1962, balance-of-payment difficulties and other factors produced a reaction against foreign aid, and the President's request for 4.9 billion dollars for 1963 foreign aid—military assistance, defense support, and economic assistance

—was slashed in the actual Congressional appropriation to little more than 3.9 billion. The President feared that the Peace Corps, the Alliance for Progress, and America's long-term commitments under the Loan Fund would have to be cut back. Aid to Poland and Yugoslavia, except for agricultural commodity agreements, was prohibited. Whether this represented a temporary or permanent slowing up of foreign aid was not clear.

The Enormous Difficulties in Administering Foreign Aid

There were all sorts of headaches in picking the recipients of foreign aid. Care had to be taken that in helping one country other countries were not offended. Measures had to be taken to ensure that American goods and projects in one country were not so used as to harm another country. Some countries complained that the United States, through its bilateral commodity agreements, "dumped" its agricultural surpluses in a way that pre-empted their markets and depressed world prices. For instance, Egypt was not happy about America's "dumping" of cotton, Burma about rice, and Canada and Argentina about wheat. Again, America's military allies were sometimes incensed that neutralist countries got more American aid than they did. It was a sore point with ally Pakistan that neutralist India got more than twice as much economic aid. America's military allies asked in effect: "Why should a country take on the risks of a military alliance with the United States while other countries which do not assume these risks get better treatment than America's allies?"

It was difficult to explain to allies that some countries, although neutralist, were of more strategic importance in the context of competing systems than were some of America's allies. India received large economic aid because next to China it was the most populous of the underdeveloped countries and was a testing ground of democracy's ability to compete with totalitarian systems in industrializing large underdeveloped societies in a short time. Egypt had economic priority in the Middle East because it was the most populous of the Arab countries and had the greatest influence with the others. Yugoslavia, which was neutralist, and Poland, a member of the Communist bloc, received economic aid because this was a means of encouraging Communist countries to become more independent of Moscow.

The nature of the indigenous governments had to be taken into most serious consideration in selecting the receipients and the amounts granted. Did the indigenous government mean business about raising the living standards of its people? Was it reasonably honest and efficient, so that the aid would not be frittered away in corruption and incompetency? Would the money be spent on genuinely wealth-increasing activities that would actually serve the welfare and the aspirations of the masses? Care had to be taken that the aid did not go to strengthen right-wing dictatorships and the feudal elements which would use it not to satisfy popular expectations but to deny them and perpetuate the old order. Those who cried anti-Communism the loudest were often the very ones who would pursue policies that would discredit democracy and ultimately bring Communism rather than check it. However, the United States had some military allies that most of the world considered rightist—Franco Spain, South Korea, Formosa, South Vietnam, Thailand, and Iran—and it gave them military and economic aid because of their strategic military value.

Once the recipients had been selected, there were all sorts of practical and immediate difficulties: choosing and giving priority to the kind of projects most likely to benefit a particular country at a particular time; taking care that the new projects and the means used to achieve them did not violate the felt needs and mores of the country; discovering the precise amounts of capital a country could profitably absorb in a given time; finding ways to maintain agricultural production while taking labor away from the villages for industrial construction; insuring the various kinds of technical assistance that would facilitate and conserve the capital developments being made.

The kind of American specialists sent to the underdeveloped countries to guide their early projects and train indigenous specialists and technicians was most important. Mere technicians would not do the job. What was needed were specialists *plus*— persons who were thoroughly at home in their specialties but who also had a sense of social diversity and popular feeling, were able to appreciate the histories, cultures, and aspirations of the indigenous peoples with whom they worked, were friendly, earthy, practical, inventive, spontaneous, and willing to share the hardships of the country in which they worked. There was considerable criticism that the American specialists and technicians sent abroad, while competent enough in their work, were otherwise wooden and parochial, that they tended to live like many of the characters in *The Ugly American*, isolated and aloof from the people of the country to which they were assigned. As a result, greater attention came to be given to finding American personnel who understood the social and political implications of their technical jobs.

The Peace Corps, established in 1961, was designed to use thousands of young Americans in underdeveloped countries in a way that would help those countries meet their critical need for skilled and semi-skilled technicians and workers and dispel some of the grosser misconceptions about Americans. Members of the Peace Corps worked side by side with indigenous people in public health measures, road building, and agricultural and industrial projects, taught their skills while working on their jobs, and lived in the villages and neighborhoods of the local people, sharing their way of life. They also brought back to America more realistic conceptions of peoples abroad.

Economic Aid in Action: Would It Succeed?

By the early 1960's there was feverish economic activity in most of the underdeveloped countries. Some were merely at the planning stage, exploring and mapping their resources and needs. Others were building the infrastructure—port facilities, roads, communications, schools, and the training of technicians. Others had already made considerable advances in modernizing and mechanizing their communications, transportation, and agriculture, and had built power dams and hydroelectric plants to control floods, to irrigate, and to provide power for agriculture and industry. Still others were moving on to the building of steel mills and some other heavy industry. Travel in a country like India in the early 1960's was a moving experience; the old and the new had not yet been integrated; modern roads, up-to-date school buildings, antiseptic hospitals, hydroelectric developments, and new industrial plants were mingled with the primitive villages, the teeming bazaars, and the squalor and superstition of centuries. The per capita income was still not much above 60 dollars a year.

Asia and the whole world were watching the contest in quick industrialization between Red China and India, both heroically attempting to make the breakthrough to industrialism and modernity, one by way of Communism and the other by way of democracy. Each was experiencing enormous difficulties, but it was generally felt that China, with all its oppressions and setbacks, was probably farther along the road to industrialism than India. There was uneasiness over the fact that not a single one of the new nations using democratic methods was yet on a sure road to industrialism.

Some suggested that the United States ought to concentrate all of its economic aid on only three or four big countries—for instance, India, Egypt, Nigeria, and Brazil—to prove once and for all that democratic methods could achieve the historic leap to industrialism. But this would result in much resentment among the neglected countries, and the United States did not dare adopt such a program, appealing though it was.

A new pluralism seemed to be developing in the world as the many new societies emerged and adopted fluid and mixed economies—pragmatic combinations of indigenous collectivism (for instance, the communal villages transformed into farm cooperatives), state enterprise, private enterprise, and welfarism, varying in proportions from country to country.

The most disturbing thing about the underdeveloped countries was that many of them were already among the most densely populated in the world—for instance, China, India and Egypt—and that they were among the most fast-growing peoples today. The world was experiencing a population explosion, and its 1960 population of 2.8 billion was expected to rise to 6 or 7 billion by the end of the next four decades. India, which in 1960 had a population of over 400 million, was growing by over 7 million a year, and its population was expected to go to over 800 million by the year 2000. China, which in 1960 had over 600 million, was increasing by about 15 million a year and by the year 2000 was expected to have a population of more than 1 billion. In 1900 there were two Asians for every European, but by the year 2000 there would probably be four Asians to one European. In Mexico and some other Latin American countries, the rate of growth was even higher than it was in India and China. By the year 2000 there probably would be two Latin Americans to one North American. As medicine and public health measures spread among the underdeveloped peoples their death rates declined and their infant mortality was cut drastically, but they still had the blind breeding which characterizes agrarian, pre-industrial societies.

Thus the economic gains in the underdeveloped areas were being offset by the population increases; the advances in economic production were being wiped out by the larger number of people to be fed, clothed, and housed. The gap between the rich nations and the poor nations threatened to grow wider rather than narrower. The job ahead was not merely to raise living standards but to raise them in the face of sensational upswings in the populations, for family standard-of-living consciousness (which puts brakes on births) would develop very slowly, and birth control practices ran counter to centuries-old mores and religious attitudes. And the Communists boasted (seriously and not merely as propaganda) that their system was so efficient that it did not require birth control, that population growth was not a problem to those societies which adopted Communism.

Politics Among the Neutrals

The neutralists insisted that they were not a bloc or even a third force, that they intended to organize in a military way neither against the Soviet Union nor against the West. They deplored military alliances and balance-of-power combinations and they avowed that these increased the tensions and the likelihood of wars. They denounced the armaments race and called for a ban on nuclear-weapons testing. They declared that they intended to hold aloof from both sides, mediate between them, and explore the "real ways" to peace. Undoubtedly the greatest intellectual and moral leader among them was Prime Minister Nehru of India, who enunciated the principles of neutralism over and over again, and whose opinions often carried weight in all parts of the world because of their moral fervor. Next to Nehru, the most prominent neutralists were President Nasser of Egypt, President Tito of Yugoslavia, President Sukarno of Indonesia, and President Nkrumah of Ghana.

Nehru often used the conferences of the Colombo powers (India, Burma, Pakistan, Ceylon, Malaya, and Indonesia, all of them neutralist except Pakistan) to expound neutralist views. The meetings of the Arab League (Egypt, Syria, Lebanon, Iraq, Jordan, Saudi Arabia, Yemen, Sudan, Libya, Tunisia, Morocco, and later Kuwait and Algeria) were also sounding boards for neutralist sentiment. The get-togethers of the Casablanca powers (Ghana, Guinea, Mali, Morocco, and Egypt) had since 1961 also become occasions for expressing a "positive neutralism."

Over the years, Nehru concentrated the basic principles of neutralism into the "five principles." In 1954, these were formally written into an agreement between India and Communist China, in which India recognized the sovereignty of China over Tibet. These principles were: (1) mutual respect for each other's territorial integrity and sovereignty, (2) mutual non-aggression, (3) mutual non-interference in each other's internal affairs, (4) equality and mutual benefit, and (5) peaceful coexistence. Skeptics wondered just how sincerely Red China believed in these principles and suggested that Nehru's approach to international politics was moralistic rather than realistic.

The event which first dramatically focused attention on the important part the new nations were playing in world politics was the Bandung conference, held in Indonesia in the spring of 1955, when the delegates of twenty-nine Asian and African nations, representing the old colonial peoples, the non-white peoples, got together to formulate and express their views on international affairs. The conference was initiated by Nehru and the Colombo powers. South Korea, North Korea, and Chiang's Formosa were not invited. The Soviet Union, with more of its territory in Asia than in Europe, angled for an invitation, but did not receive one. Red China, however, was invited, and its chief delegate, Premier Chou En-lai, became the most conspicuous representative at the conference, and among other things he used it as an opportunity to indicate that Communist China was willing to negotiate with the United States over the tensions in the Formosa Straits.

However, the conference was not allowed to become a sounding board for Communism or even for an unadulterated neutralism, because the Philippines, Thailand, Pakistan, Iran, and Turkey vigorously maintained the reality of the Communist threat and the need to meet it by military preparations and alliances. Japan played a curious role somewhere between the committed countries and the uncommitted countries. But the uncommitted countries were in the majority and their views prevailed in most of the resolutions adopted by the conference, but in watered-down versions. The conference urged independence and self-determination for all peoples, membership for all nations in the United Nations, human rights, the rights of Arab refugees in Palestine and territorial revisions there, disarmament, prohibition of nuclear weapons, economic cooperation, and economic aid from the advanced industrial countries to the underdeveloped countries, preferably through international and not national agencies. An attempt to get a resolution denouncing satellitism as an evil equal to colonialism failed, but a resolution was finally passed condemning "colonialism in all its manifestations." All in all, the conference was a striking illustration of how far the old colonial peoples had come in independence and influence during the past decade.

Another important occasion for the enunciation of neutralist principles was at the Brioni (Yugoslavia) conference of July 1956 when Tito, Nehru, and Nasser called for the application of the Bandung principles to world problems, admission of Red China to the United Nations, and national independence for Algeria. Sometimes neutralism was expressed in more vigorous fashion, as when Nasser declared in November of the same year that Egypt would never become "a stooge or satellite or pawn or hireling of anybody," and that Egypt would remain free of all foreign ideologies "such as Marxism, fascism, racism, colonialism, imperialism, and atheism, all of which, incidentally, are European in origin."

Still another significant conference of the anti-colonial countries took place at Belgrade in September 1961. It was attended by the heads of state of twenty-five of the neutralist governments. Unlike the Bandung conference, which was a meeting of the Asian and African nations, those aligned and those non-aligned, this conference was confined to the non-aligned in all parts of the world. Even Cuba attended, since it was not a member of the Moscow-Peiping Axis or of the Warsaw Pact and was technically regarded as being non-aligned. The Belgrade conference officially called for "prompt elimination of every vestige of colonial influence." France was explicitly called on to retire from military bases in Tunisia, and the United States from its naval base at Guantánamo. During the discussions there was heated denunciation of France's war in Algeria, apartheid in the Union of South Africa, and Belgium's "neo-colonialism" in the Congo. At one point Nehru gently warned his younger colleagues against dwelling too much on the evils of the colonial past.

The conference recommended "a more appropriate structure" for the Secretariat of the United Nations, bearing in mind equitable regional distribution, and establishment of additional memberships in the United Nations Security Council and the United Nations Economic and Social Council. Those states which had recognized Communist China joined in urging that Mao's government be admitted to the United Nations. The delegates issued a solemn "Statement on the Danger of War and Appeal for Peace," which entreated President Kennedy and Premier Khrushchev "to make most immediate and direct approaches to each other to avert the imminent conflict and establish peace." The United States and the Soviet Union were equally blamed for failing to arrive at a nuclear-test ban and nuclear disarmament. In the United States there was much disappointment when the conference failed to officially condemn the Soviet Union for its breaking the truce on nuclear testing.

Even the increasing aggressiveness of Communist China in southern Asia did little to shake Nehru's neutralism and his faith in the five principles. The Chinese Communists violated Burma's frontiers repeatedly and claimed territory which Burma regarded as Burmese. In 1959, the Chinese Communists, who in 1950 had taken *de facto* control of Tibet (over which Manchu China had exercised a loose suzerainty), tightened their grip on the country and began extending their political and economic system to Tibetan tribal society. Mounting resistance led to Chinese suppressions. The Dalai Lama, the spiritual and temporal ruler of this Buddhist theocracy, fled to India. The Chinese put down the Tibetan revolt with an iron hand and thousands of Tibetan refugees fled to Nepal, Bhutan, Sikkim, and India.

Even more serious from the Indian point of view, the Chinese made encroachments on Indian territory and buffer countries in the Himalayas. By 1959 the Chinese were putting pressures on Nepal (an independent country), on Sikkim (an Indian protectorate), and on Bhutan (a semi-Indian protectorate), and they were laying claim to 32,000 square miles of India's Northeast Frontier

Agency and 6000 square miles in the Ladakh province of Kashmir. The Communist Chinese (and the Nationalist Chinese, too) refused to recognize the British McMahon Line as the legal Chinese-Indian boundary. The Chinese even built a military road through a corner of Ladakh. In 1959 the Chinese made two military incursions into the Northeast Frontier Agency, and later that year Chinese and Indian armed patrols clashed at Hot Springs in Ladakh.

At the same time the Chinese were antagonizing the Indonesians by claiming a measure of control over the activities of the large Chinese minority in Indonesia. The Indonesians retaliated by tightening their restrictions on the Chinese minority, but President Sukarno did not abate his neutralist position. Chinese border disputes with Nepal were settled by treaties in 1960 and 1961, while frontier controversies between China and Burma were resolved by a treaty ratified in 1961.

However, Chinese differences with India continued, and in 1960 and 1961 the Chinese established three new outposts in Indian-claimed territory. Nehru made vigorous protests to China, but he did not recede from his neutralism, and each year India continued to sponsor Communist China's admission to the United Nations. It was not until the formidable Red Chinese attacks along the Himalayan border in late 1962 that India at last made large-scale preparations for defense, asked for American and British military equipment, and Nehru, somewhat shaken, rallied India to brace itself to meet its gravest crisis since independence. The Americans prepared, if need be, to give India the same kind of help they were giving South Vietnam.

Those who were disturbed by the impact of neutralism on world politics were apprehensive that the great increase in the number of independent African states would add to the West's difficulties. By 1963 there were thirty-two such states. The majority of these had become independent during 1960—"the year of Africa"—and since. Although the increase in the number of new African states had swelled the ranks of the neutrals, it had not added much to an assertive neutralism. Only Ghana's Nkrumah regularly added his voice to the Nehru-Sukarno-Nasser-Tito pronouncements. The Casablanca countries asserted a "positive neutralism," but there were only five of these, and two, Ghana and Egypt, were already well known for their neutralist position. However, it was significant that Nasser was not only playing the leading role in Arab politics but also a prominent one in African politics and sometimes acted as liaison between the Asian and African nations. Algeria at last attained its independence in 1962, and its leader, Ben Bella, was attracted to the Nasser leadership in both Arab and African affairs.

However, most of the African states, while neutralist, were most moderate in their views and were oriented to the West. Britain and France had liquidated their empires in Negro Africa in an orderly and peaceful way. "Creative abdication" had worked, and the new nations had gained first self-government and then, shortly after that, independence in accordance with smoothly running time tables. The fierce racial strife and bloody wars of liberation, which some in the late 1940's had predicted, had fortunately been avoided.

Few of the new nations of Negro Africa had cut all of their ties to the old colonial powers. Ghana, Nigeria, Sierra Leone, Tanganyika, and Uganda were members of the British Commonwealth. Six of France's former colonies—Gabon, Chad, the Central African Republic, the Congo Republic (with its capital at Brazzaville, as distinguished from the Republic of the Congo with its capital at Léopoldville), Senegal, and Malagasy—had chosen to remain in the French Community. Another eight—the Ivory Coast, Upper Volta, Niger (not to be confused with Nigeria), Dahomey, Mauritania, Mali, Togo, and Cameroon—retained close ties to France through bilateral treaties. Only Guinea, under the leadership of Sékou Touré, had cut all its ties to France. All of the former colonies of France in Negro Africa, with the exceptions of Guinea, Togo, and Mali, belonged to the so-called Brazzaville combination, cooperated closely in economic and cultural matters, and enjoyed distinct economic advantages because of their associate membership in the European Common Market. The Ivory Coast, Upper Volta, Niger, and Dahomey were also tied even more closely together in the Council of the Entente.

The Brazzaville nations and the Council of the Entente were neutralist but oriented to the West. President Bourguiba of Tunisia, President Houphouet-Boigny of the Ivory Coast, President Tubman of Liberia, Prime Minister Balewa of Nigeria, and Tanganyika's Julius Nyerere were democratic gradualists in philosophy and distinctly friendly to the West. Even Tom Mboya, leader of the independence movement in Kenya, who proclaimed "Africa for the Africans," seemed to be moderating his extremism, and the two most ardent of Africa's revolutionaries, Kenneth Kaunda of Northern Rhodesia and Joshua Nkomo of Southern Rhodesia, were followers of Gandhi and not of Marx. Even Ghana's Nkrumah, who next to Touré was suspected of an over-friendliness with the Communist bloc, cooperated with Britain in the British Commonwealth and, like Nehru in India, had never suggested withdrawing from membership in the Commonwealth; and it appeared that the long flirtation of Touré with Marxism was coming to an end.

Responses to neutralism varied widely. Some regarded neutralism as immoral for not seeing the immorality in Communism, and as being all the more immoral because it disguised its immorality in the loftiest of moral tones. Some regarded it as dangerously innocent and naive, as a Trojan horse making Communist subversion easier. Some welcomed it as a brake on a bipolarized world, as a trend to a less dangerous world of de-polarization and multidiplomacy. Some saw it as a portent of the future, for if indeed the world was entering the dawn of the *pax atomica*, we would all, in time, be "neutralist." But whatever one's view of neutralism, there was no denying that it was an important element in the world, not only in the uncommitted countries themselves, but also in all the underdeveloped countries. In addition, neutralism had an attraction for liberal, socialist, and labor parties in Europe, which generally felt that the way to check Communism was not in more military preparation, which had been stressed too much, but in economic measures, which had not been stressed enough. And even in America, the utterances of Nehru warmed many liberals.

However, Red China's aggressive attack in 1962 on India, which had been China's good friend, seemed to weaken neutralism somewhat and strengthen the West. This jolting new evidence of Communist ruthlessness, which Nehru, out of his early intellectual flirtation with Marxism back in the 1920's, had always minimized, caused him to have some second thoughts, and this belligerence of China and Nehru's reaction to it had a marked influence on the most "positive" of the neutralists. However, the neutral world regarded Russia, not China, as the authentic voice of Communism.

Misjudging the Importance of Neutralism: The Crisis in Laos

While the Communists contributed more than their share to the trouble spots, crisis situations, and brinkmanship in the world, sometimes the West contributed to these by its refusal to relinquish vestiges of the old imperialism, its failure to understand the vitality of neutralism, and its attempt to push nations which wanted to remain neutral into the anti-Communist camp. However, whenever the West made such misjudgments, the Communists were ready and eager to exploit them to their own advantage. The crisis in Laos, which had been building up since 1954 and reached a pitch from 1958 to 1962, was one intensified in part by America's failure to understand the strength of neutralist sentiment.

As a result of the Geneva conference of 1954 Vietnam had been partitioned and Laos and Cambodia made independent and neutral states. An International Control Commission, consisting of representatives of Canada, India, and Poland, was set up by the Geneva conference to see that the French evacuated the country and all foreign military personnel were withdrawn, and that the Communist Pathet Lao armies (mostly Laotians but with infiltrations from North Vietnam and Communist China) gave up their control of two Laotian provinces on the northeastern border of the country and were disbanded or integrated with the national Laotian army. From the very first the United States was suspicious of the Commission because it was feared that the Polish and Indian representatives would be "soft" on the Communists.

Despite the popular appeal the Communists were making to the peasants, it appeared that most Laotians genuinely wanted neutrality. Indeed, the strategic position of their little country of around 2.5 million people, with Cambodia on the south, Thailand on the west, Burma on the northwest, Communist China on the north, and Vietminh and South Vietnam on the east, made neutrality a necessity not only for internal peace but also for peace in southeast Asia and possibly the world.

From 1955 to 1957, Prince Souvanna Phouma, who was premier and a dedicated neutralist, and the International Control Commission were busy negotiating with the Pathet Lao Communist armies and political leaders. By 1957 the Pathet Lao armies had been demobilized (although at least two evaded demobilization), the national government had taken over at least nominal control of the two Pathet Lao provinces, and Pathet Lao leaders had been admitted into the government. In 1958, the International Control Commission, its work apparently done, was disbanded. But in the election that year the Pathet Lao group and other leftists, led by Prince Souphanouvong, half-brother of Souvanna Phouma, won a substantial victory. Souvanna Phouma, disappointed at the apparent failure of his neutralist policy, resigned.

Complicated dickering among the politicians (and perhaps United States encouragement) led to formation of an anti-Communist government under Phoui Sananikone, which excluded leftists and neutralists. Prince Souphanouvong was put under detention. It looked as though the government was headed for rightest extremism, and the Soviet Union and Communist China, together with some other governments, called for a revival of the International Control Commission. The United States opposed this and gave military credits and supplies to the right-wing government and sent officers to train the royal Laotian army, which succeeded in defeating the two Pathet Lao armies which had evaded demobilization; one was captured and the other escaped to Vietminh. New Pathet Lao armies were recruited, and the Soviet Union, Communist China, and Vietminh increased their aid to these contingents. At the same time the United States stepped up its military aid to the anti-Communist government. Phoui Sananikone resigned to make way for the temporary imposition of military government pending the election of 1960, which was so managed as to give the right-wing a strong majority. Anti-Communist General Phoumi Nosavan became defense minister and the leading spirit in the government.

But late that year, leftist and neutralist elements in the Laotian army, led by paratroop captain Kong Le, disclaiming any Communist connections, overthrew the rightist government, and Souvanna Phouma returned to power and again sought to integrate the Pathet Lao elements into the national life. Anti-Communist Prince Boun Oum and Phoumi Nosavan set up a rival government at Savannakhet on the Mekong. Thailand, under the leadership of rightist Marshal Sarit Thanarat, urged the United States to give full-scale support to the rightist Boun Oum–Nosavan government. On the other hand, Britain and France welcomed the second opportunity to establish a neutralist government in Laos and urged sole support for the Souvanna Phouma government at the nation's political capital at Vientiane. At this juncture the United States decided to give military support to both sides, but Souvanna Phouma complained that the bulk of it went to the "rebel" right-wing government at Savannakhet. But a military coup at Luang Prabang gave this seat of the royal residence to Boun Oum and Phoumi Nosavan. The mounting difficulties, too great for Souvanna Phouma, caused him to resign the premiership for a second time and flee to Cambodia.

The United States now gave its full support to the right-wing governments, and Boun Oum and Phoumi Nosavan captured Vientiane and became the "legal" government. The Soviet Union continued to recognize Souvanna Phouma. The Pathet Lao increased its activities, the Viet Cong Communists in South Vietnam became more active, and Soviet, Chinese, and Vietminh aid for the Pathet Lao mounted. In late 1960 and early 1961 the civil war intensified and the chances of ultimate Communist victory in Laos increased. There were complaints in Washington of Boun Oum's weak leadership, of "the easy-going, Buddhist, lotus-eating, comic-opera royal Laotian army." The Soviet Union threatened to intervene directly unless American "intervention" ceased.

Thus when the Kennedy administration came to office it was confronted with a serious Asian crisis. France and Britain vetoed use of SEATO. The United States was apprehensive about taking the crisis to the United Nations because of the strength of the Afro-Asian bloc and the prevalence of neutralist sentiment there. Should the United States, then, intervene directly and get itself bogged in "another Korea," a jungle guerrilla war? Opinion in the United States seemed ready to make a stand in South Vietnam and Thailand but not in Laos.

At this juncture, Britain, as co-chairman with Russia of the Geneva conference of 1954, proposed to the Soviet government that there be a cease-fire in Laos supervised by a reconvened International Control Commission, that as soon as the effectiveness of the cease-fire had been confirmed that the Geneva conference, with a few added members, be reconvened in order to seek a permanent settlement on the basis of a Laotian government of national unity representing all factions. The Soviet Union agreed, but took a tantalizing long time in implementing the negotiating machinery, and in the meantime the Pathet Lao advanced within a short distance of Vientiane. At one stage of the negotiations the United States sent marines to Thailand, so great was the fear in that country of a Communist victory in neighboring Laos. For more than a year, from May 1961 to the summer of 1962, the negotiations proceeded at Geneva while the International Control Commission kept verifying the cease-fire (which was broken intermittently) and the three rival political factions in Laos haggled over an agreement.

In the final settlement, the Laotian government pledged itself to remain neutral. The United States, Britain, France, the Soviet Union, Communist China, and the other eight conference powers pledged themselves to respect Laotian neutrality, sovereignty, and independence. They formally recognized Laos' desire not to be protected by any military alliance, including SEATO. Except for a small French military mission, all foreign military personnel were to be withdrawn from the kingdom, such withdrawal to be supervised by the Canadian-Indian-Polish International Control Commission for Laos. (It was estimated that the United States had 800 military advisers and technicians in Laos and that there were around 10,000 officers and troops from Communist North Vietnam.) The Commission was also to maintain a check on the borders to prevent re-entry of foreign forces and armaments. The agreement between Laos' three political factions provided that neutralist Souvanna Phouma was to become premier, and anti-Communist Phoumi Nosavan and Pathet Lao's Prince Souphanouvong were to become deputy premiers. The ministries of defense, foreign affairs, and interior were to be held by neutralist followers of Souvanna Phouma, but all decisions related to these departments would have to have the unanimous consent of the three chiefs of the factions. The integration of the armed forces of the factions was left to the Laotian government, although the

United States felt strongly that this was a matter which should have been settled on the international level.

Thus after eight years the United States was back where it was originally—with the same neutralist premier, the same neutralist program, and the same International Control Commission, whose decisions, as before, would have to be unanimous, thereby allowing Poland to exercise a "Soviet" veto over the work of the Commission. In some ways the United States was in a less advantageous position than before, because the SEATO protocol protecting Laos had been repudiated by a conference of all the great powers, and the Communists were entrenched in Laos' neutralist government.

With favorable prospects of Communist victory in Laos, why did the Soviet Union sponsor a compromise settlement? There seemed to be a mixture of motives: fear of getting involved in a nasty "brushfire" war, which might expand into a general war (the Soviet Union always succeeded in staying out of these "little" wars, including the Korean War and the Indochina War); a belief that the arrangements in Laos would over-all be more favorable to the Communist powers than to the West; the feeling that long-range conditions in southeast Asia were working for the Communists and that it would not be wise to interfere with their ultimate ripening by arousing the Americans to maintain large forces in South Vietnam, Thailand, and perhaps Malaya; a genuine desire for a settlement of Berlin and a *rapprochement* with the West, which would certainly become impossible if the United States and the Soviet Union engaged in a shooting war in Laos.

The Laos crisis revealed the weakness of SEATO. It also showed that out of fear of nuclear war both the United States and the Soviet Union were shying away not only from the big war but also from the little "limited" wars which might spread and become the big one.

Misjudging the Strength of Anti-Imperialism and Neutralism: The Middle East

Tensions in the Middle East were kept at a high level by the never-ending feud of Arabs and Israelis, which manifested itself most conspicuously in the miserable plight of the nearly 1 million Arab refugees and the repeated and bloody border raids conducted by both Israelis and Arabs. Arab-Israeli animosity was so great that it prevented the consummation of the Jordan River Valley project, which would have distributed much-needed water to Israel, Jordan, and Syria and would have been mostly financed by American economic aid. However, the most dangerous international tensions in the Middle East came from other sources: the failure of Britain and France to relinquish some of their old imperialist responsibilities and advantages at a pace commensurate with the growing strength of anti-imperialism; the reluctance of the United States, as in Laos, to recognize neutralism, the American disposition to over-pressure the Middle Eastern nations to take a Western position in world affairs; and the propensity of the Soviet Union to fish in troubled waters.

In 1955, when Iraq joined the Baghdad pact and became an ally in METO, other Arab states denounced this as a Western plot to undermine Arab neutralism and to split the Arab League. Most Arabs took this as additional evidence that Iraq's Hashimite dynasty was in reality only a British puppet. And when in 1956 efforts were made to bring Jordan into the Baghdad pact the popular resistance in that country was so great that the proposal not only failed but led to King Hussein's expelling the long-time British Commander of the Arab Legion, General John B. Glubb, together with most of the other senior British officers. It was against this background of mounting tensions that the Suez crisis of 1956 occurred, which in essence was an attempt by Britain and France to hold on to old concessions by force of arms, a method quite suited to the ethos of the 1880's and the 1890's but clearly an anachronism in the middle of the twentieth century.

What were the origins of the Suez crisis? In June 1956, in accordance with the Anglo-Egyptian agreement of 1954, Britain withdrew from her huge military bases in the Suez Canal Zone. The United States regarded this as a most favorable step in improving Western relations with the Arab states. About the same time there was an intensification of the Arab-Israel border raids. Egypt and Syria were purchasing arms from Czechoslovakia, with Soviet approval, although an added attraction for Egypt was the fact that this involved barter deals in which Egypt paid with surplus cotton and rice. Appeals by Israel for increased arms from the United States were denied on the grounds that Israel seemed to be ahead in the Arab-Israeli arms race, that France was furnishing Israel arms, and that the United States did not want to contribute to an acceleration of the arms race.

Along with these events, Nasser was negotiating with the Western powers for a loan with which to start building a billion-dollar power dam along the Nile at Aswan. The United States contemplated an initial loan of 56 million dollars, Britain one of 14 million, and the International Bank one of 200 million. Egypt felt that it had assurances of these loans. There were rumors the Soviet Union would extend loans to help build the dam. American sources warned Egypt against taking a loan from the Soviet Union, that to take Soviet aid would jeopardize American aid; but in the meantime the Soviet offers, if indeed they were ever officially made, did not materialize. Then on July 19 the United States withdrew its offer and on July 23 the International Bank did likewise. It was explained that the Egyptian economy was already obligated too heavily to pay for the dam.

On July 26, Nasser announced a decree vesting ownership of the Suez Canal in the Egyptian government (the profits from the Canal to be used to build the Aswan Dam), and promising that the private company which owned and operated the Canal, whose shares were held mostly by French and British investors and the British government, would be reimbursed. The next day, Egypt seized the offices of the Company and declared martial law in the Canal Zone. (This was just a little over a month after the British had withdrawn!)

Britain and France, fearing that Egypt did not possess the technical skills necessary to run the Canal, that the company's shareholders would not actually or adequately be reimbursed, and that Egypt might not be relied on to maintain the Convention of 1888 requiring that the Canal be open to the ships of all nations on equal terms (it was revealed that Egypt was high-handedly preventing Israeli ships from using the Canal), demanded that the Canal be internationalized. Nasser and the anti-colonial nations called this "collective colonialism," and Nehru declared that Egypt's sovereignty in the Canal was without question. A large number of the nations whose nationals were the main users of the Canal organized a Suez Canal Users Association, which was to promote the safe operation of the Canal and hold all tolls pending final settlement. Egypt rejected this arrangement. When most of the Western pilots departed, Egypt astonished the world by maintaining efficient navigation through the Canal, and this went far to dispel the notion that Egypt was incapable of operating the Canal.

On October 13, the United Nations Security Council approved the basic principles for operating the Canal, no matter who "owned" it. These were: (1) free and open transit through the Canal without overt or covert political or technical discrimination; (2) respect for the sovereignty of Egypt; (3) insulation of the Canal's operation from politics; (4) agreement between Egypt and the users on fixing of tolls and charges; (5) allotment of a fair proportion of the dues for Canal development; and (6) settlement of disputes and unresolved affairs between Egypt and the Canal Company by arbitration. Egypt accepted these six principles, but Britain and France failed to get specific implementing machinery either from Egypt or by international agreement.

Taking advantage of Egypt's conflict with Britain and France over the Canal and Russia's grave troubles in Hungary, and smarting under Egyptian border raids and Egypt's refusal to allow Israeli ships to pass through the Canal, Israel, on October 29, suddenly attacked Egypt in force to wipe out commando bases in the Sinai peninsula, and pushed to within 25 miles of the Canal. On October 30, Britain and France sent a joint ultimatum to Israel and Egypt demanding that they stop fighting and confine their forces to positions 10 miles from the Canal. Egypt was asked to accept temporary occupation of Port Said, Ismailia, Suez, and key points along the Canal to safeguard operation. Israel agreed, but Egypt rejected the ultimatum. Then, on October 31, Britain and France struck at Egypt, ostensibly to protect the Canal but in reality to force Nasser to denationalize the Canal and perhaps even overthrow Nasser altogether, since his growing stature as leader of the anti-imperialist forces in the Middle East threatened their positions in many ways. Britain and France landed troops and bombed Egyptian airfields. The attack resulted in the British capture of Port Said and put the Israelis within 10 miles of the Canal.

The week of October 31–November 6 was one of confusion. The Suez Canal was blocked by Egyptian sabotage, oil pipelines were destroyed by Syrian saboteurs, tankers had to begin making the long trip around the Cape of Good Hope, and oil was hurriedly rationed in Western Europe.

Whether the British and French acted in prior agreement with Israel is still disputed, but it is clear that all three acted without prior consultation with the United States. Insult was added to injury (or injury to insult) in that the attacks came just one week prior to the presidential election in which President Eisenhower had stressed his role as international peacemaker.

The aggressive action by Britain and France was condemned around the world; the new nations of Asia and Africa were outraged by this "new imperialism"; British and French influence in the Arab countries almost vanished; the Soviet Union threatened to send "volunteers" to protect Egypt and then asked the United States to join with it in using American-Soviet air forces and naval units to stop aggression against Egypt; the relations between the United States and its chief allies were severely strained; NATO was put in jeopardy; the British Commonwealth was temporarily torn with internal dissension, with opinion in the Commonwealth preponderantly opposed to Britain's action; and inside Britain itself public opinion was bitterly divided.

On October 30 the United States sponsored a resolution in the Security Council for an immediate cease-fire, withdrawal of Israeli troops to the Israeli-Egyptian Armistice limits, and no help to aggressors by any United Nations members. A somewhat similar resolution was introduced by the Soviet Union. On both resolutions, the United States was compelled to vote with the Soviet Union against its own allies. Britain and France vetoed both the United States and the Soviet resolutions. As usual, because of the veto in the Security Council, the dispute had to be transferred to the General Assembly, which was called into emergency session on November 1. Here, during the first week in November, the United States backed winning resolutions asking the belligerents to agree to an immediate cease-fire and for the immediate withdrawal of Israeli, British, and French troops from Egyptian soil. Britain was particularly dissatisfied because it was thought the United States might at least have supported a gradual withdrawal. The United States supported the approved Canadian resolution calling for an emergency United Nations force to maintain and supervise the cease-fire. This force was to be composed of troops drawn from the smaller powers, and it was stipulated that none was to be drawn from the five powers with permanent seats on the Security Council. The voting in the Assembly showed that Israel, Britain, and France were clearly isolated in United Nations and world opinion, with only Australia and New Zealand coming to their occasional support.

The United Nations undertook two specific duties: to police the troubled area with its emergency international force and to make immediate arrangements to clear the Suez Canal. United Nations forces, drawn from Scandinavian and other small countries, began arriving on November 15, and as these forces were augmented, Israeli, British, and French troops progressively withdrew.

It will always be a moot question just how much the attacking nations were influenced in their withdrawal by United Nations action. Undoubtedly, the United Nations provided a convenient place for the mobilization and expression of world opinion; and by being able to utilize United Nations forces and agencies rather than the national forces and agencies of the United States and the Soviet Union, the world may have been spared Soviet and American intervention in the troubled area and subsequent clashes by these big powers in this area. In any event, the use of United Nations agencies was safer, more impartial, and more inclusive than the use of the national agencies of the big powers would have been. Nevertheless, the most decisive pressure on Britain and France to withdraw came from American opposition to their military activities and from the fact that Britain and France needed American credits and Western Hemisphere oil to carry them through the economic crisis their actions had precipitated.

American opinion was somewhat divided over American policy during this first crisis. A minority felt that America's joining the Soviet Union against its old and trusted British and French allies was a fantastic misalliance, which would weaken the Western alliances and the West's position in the Middle East and the world and strengthen the Soviet Union. Moreover, these Americans felt that American action would complicate rather than solve the immediate problems of the Suez and of Arab-Israeli relations and that it did not take into account America's past actions which had helped bring on the crisis—America's urging of Britain to evacuate the Suez Zone military bases, America's abrupt withdrawal of its promises to help Egypt build a dam at Aswan, America's failure to develop a clear and constructive policy with respect to the Suez Canal, and America's wishy-washy position with respect to Arab-Israeli boundaries and the long-continued Arab-Israeli border raids and massacres. There was also a feeling that American policy was too much influenced by the interests of American oil companies, which did not wish to offend Arab countries where their oil holdings and pipelines were located.

On the other hand, the majority of Americans seem to have supported the Eisenhower administration in this first crisis. A variety of elements went into the making of this majority. There were those who welcomed the opportunity to increase the prestige of the United Nations. There were many Americans who still felt uneasy about "power politics," and these felt better when international relations were based on collective-security measures rather than partisan alliances. Even among those realistic Americans who realized that "power politics" was still the most basic factor in international relations, there were those who welcomed some "give" in bipolarization and evidence of a return to a more flexible multidiplomacy. Almost all Americans were agreed that once the crisis was upon the world, no matter how the blame for producing it was shared, the United States had no other recourse but to condemn aggression. If the United States condoned aggression when aggression was committed by its allies, how could it condemn aggression when aggression was committed by its foes? There simply could not be two standards of aggression, one for Communists and another for non-Communists, one for Asians and Africans and another for Western Europeans and Americans. A few American publicists pointed out that American action in halting aggression probably saved from sabotage oil pipelines in the Middle East, and therefore that Americans had saved Britain and France from an even greater economic crisis. Some Americans welcomed the opportunity to show the world and the Arabs in particular that America was not pro-Zionist, that it could act impartially in a conflict between Arabs and Israelis. More important, many Americans were pleased to have the chance to side forthrightly with the Asian-African bloc, to square

American policies with America's own tradition of anti-colonialism and self-determination for all peoples. These Americans, of course, would not have created a crisis just to do this, but since the crisis was upon them, many felt that it gave the United States the opportunity to bid for anti-colonial and neutralist support, to counter the Communist appeals to the non-aligned peoples, and to dramatize for the benefit of still-doubtful Americans the importance of economic-aid programs for underdeveloped areas.

Then there were the "hate-Britain" elements in the American population which welcomed this chance to give a twist to the British lion's tail. And there were those, not among the professional Anglophobes, who derived a certain psychological satisfaction in having America pull Britain back from war. For over a decade Americans had heard that the British were more "mature" in international affairs than the Americans, that it was the British who had restrained "the American warmongers" in China and elsewhere. Now it was the Americans who were proving themselves more "mature" and more in rapport with world trends and opinion; it was the Americans who were holding back Britain from "the brink." (In fairness, it should be pointed out that the British themselves were divided on the Suez crisis, that the most trenchant criticisms of Prime Minister Eden's policies were coming from British Labour, Liberal, and even Conservative leaders and periodicals.)

Another crisis developed in January 1957, when the Israelis, who had withdrawn their forces from deep within Egyptian territory, halted in their withdrawal at the Gaza strip and dug themselves in along this 25-mile stretch of territory, refusing to comply further with United Nations demands for Israel's complete withdrawal from Egyptian territory. The Asian-African bloc demanded United Nations sanctions against Israel if Israel persisted in defying the United Nations. American opinion became more sharply divided over this crisis than over the first. President Eisenhower insisted that, in addition to the justness of the United Nations demand, the prestige of the United States and of the United Nations was committed to Israel's compliance. Could a nation commit aggression and then hold on to the fruits of its aggression literally to force acceptance of its demands?

But many Americans rallied to the support of Israel. Some believed that Israel, having complied substantially with United Nations demands, should hold on to the Gaza strip until Egypt gave real assurances that Egyptian raids on Israeli territory would cease and that Israeli ships would be allowed to use the Canal. Others were uncomfortable that the United States continued to line up with the Soviet Union against Britain and France. The doctrinaire internationalists, with a conception of a near-perfect and already fully completed collective-security system in mind, and the nationalists, whose hostility to the Communists was most intense, united in demanding that sanctions not be voted against Israel unless sanctions were also voted against Russia for aggressions in Hungary.

However, sanctions against Israel were not voted, and they were not required, for in mid-March the intensity of the Egyptian crisis abated when Israeli troops evacuated Gaza and Egypt's Gulf of Aqaba coast and allowed United Nations Emergency Force troops to move in. But Israel still clung to a little triangle in the Negev desert known as El Auja. El Auja was a demilitarized zone, a 19-mile area barred to the armed forces of both Israel and Egypt by the 1949 Armistice terms because of its strategic location as a meeting place of desert trails. In violation of Article VIII of the Armistice, the Israelis, in 1953, had set up a farm settlement in El Auja and in 1955 installed troops in the zone. Because of Israeli occupation of El Auja, Egypt, upon the clearing and the reopening of the Canal in April, continued to bar Israeli ships from the Gulf of Aqaba and the Canal.

As a result of the Suez crisis, British and French influence in the Middle East was sharply reduced and the Middle Eastern Baghdad pact members ostracized their ally Britain for a time, even refused to attend meetings where British representatives were present. Secretary of State Dulles believed that a dangerous power vacuum existed in the Middle East. Just as the withdrawal of British responsibilities in Greece had led to the Truman Doctrine, so now Dulles proposed an Eisenhower Doctrine in which the United States would guarantee stability in the Middle East. Accordingly, in early 1957, Congress authorized the President to employ the armed forces of the United States as he deemed necessary to secure and protect the territorial integrity and political independence of any nation or group of nations in the general area of the Middle East which requested such aid against overt armed intervention from any nation controlled by international Communism and to lend economic and military assistance to Middle Eastern nations desiring it. Two hundred million dollars in Mutual Security funds were earmarked for the Middle East for the year 1957. During the debate in the Senate over the Eisenhower Doctrine, Senator William F. Knowland, the administration leader in the Senate, asserted that the Doctrine was designed to prevent both direct armed aggression and indirect subversion.

The Eisenhower Doctrine met with mixed reactions abroad. In Britain and France, smarting under the Suez rebuke, there were many who resented the American talk about the decline of their prestige and power in the Middle East, and they acidly maintained that there would have been no decline of Allied strength in that area had the United States supported its European allies in the Suez crisis. The American take-over in the Middle East, coming on the heels of the international oil consortium in Iran (1954) in which the American oil interests had enormously increased their shares in Iranian oil at the expense of the British, persuaded some Britons that the Americans were determined to replace the British as the first power in that whole area.

Among the Middle Eastern countries themselves there were vast differences of opinion about the Eisenhower Doctrine. The Baghdad powers, particularly Turkey and Iran on the borders of the Soviet Union, warmly welcomed it. The pro-Western governments in Lebanon and Iraq officially accepted aid under the Doctrine, but they were the only members of the Arab League to do so. In Egypt and Syria and among ardent Arab nationalists everywhere there was intense opposition. They were still eager for American economic aid but they wanted no strings attached and did not relish being "pushed" into becoming military allies of the West. These resented the American talk about a power vacuum. Had not the indigenous governments filled the void left by the departure of the imperialists? Were the indigenous governments so weak that they needed "a new imperialist protector"? Was not the real purpose of the Eisenhower Doctrine to divide the Arabs and set Arab state against Arab state? Where was the Communist aggression of which the Americans spoke?

Was not the Eisenhower Doctrine designed to maintain the economic and social *status quo*, to be used in such a way as to brand all social revolutionary movements indiscriminately as "Communist" and "subversive"?

In Jordan, popular resistance to internal conservative elements and the Eisenhower Doctrine almost cost King Hussein his throne. As a warning, the United States in April 1957 dispatched its Sixth Fleet to the eastern Mediterranean and stepped up economic and military assistance grants to Hussein's government. It was carefully explained that the aid funds came from the regular appropriations for foreign aid and would not require Jordan's acceptance of the Eisenhower Doctrine.

In Syria, the Eisenhower Doctrine helped push opinion in a leftist, anti-Western direction. For a time it was feared Syria would abandon the neutrals and join the Communist bloc. It was charged that the Syrian government was supplying arms to leftist, Communist, and pan-Arab rebels in Lebanon, Iraq, and Jordan. In August and September, emergency deliveries of American military equipment were rushed to these three countries, and the Sixth Fleet was again dispatched to the eastern Mediterranean. Khrushchev took great delight in further fanning the flames of international crisis by charging in October 1957 that Turkey, with United States backing, was planning an armed attack on Syria with the objective of overthrowing the Syrian government. The crisis abated when it became clear that there was nothing to the Khrushchev charges.

The leftist, pan-Arab government in Syria, mistrusting its ability to carry out broad social reforms in Syria alone and fearing a conservative reaction within the country, early in 1958 initiated a startling event—nothing less than the complete union of Syria and Egypt. The United Arab Republic was proclaimed on February 1, 1958. Egypt and Syria were merged, with Nasser as President and the capital at Cairo. This was a signal triumph for pan-Arabism and tremendously accelerated the drive of the militant pan-Arab movement in other countries for union or at least federation under Nasser. Yemen, because of its quarrel with the British Aden Protectorate, became associated with the United Arab Republic in a looser combination called the United Arab States.

Nasser seems to have had serious doubts about the merger. Syria, which historically had been a leader in the Fertile Crescent, often opposed to Egypt, was not even territorially contiguous to Egypt. One of the reasons which induced Nasser to go through with the union was his desire to curb the leftism of the Syrian pan-Arabs, his determination that pan-Arabism not be infiltrated by the Communists. In filling the cabinet positions of the United Arab Republic, Nasser took care to bypass the more radically minded Syrian politicians and military men, the very ones who had initiated the merger, and to fill the posts allotted to the Syrians with moderates. Thus paradoxically it was Nasser (and not Dulles) who prevented the development of perhaps a real Soviet satellite in the Middle East. The Eisenhower Doctrine did not win any American allies; neither did it push the Arabs to the Communist side; what it did was to strengthen Nasser's pan-Arab movement.

Nasser took his great triumph in stride. He curbed his domestic Communists and signed the international agreement providing payment to the shareholders of the old Suez Canal Company; and the United States in turn resumed economic aid to Nasser's government.

The union of Syria and Egypt had immediate repercussions in the Arab world. The pan-Arab Nasserites went on the offensive everywhere. In self-defense the governments of young King Faisal II of Iraq and young King Hussein I of Jordan, two Hashimite cousins, formed the Arab Union, a confederation in which both countries retained their sovereignty. King Saud of Saudi Arabia thought it politic to go into retirement, and he delegated his duties to Crown Prince Faisal, his brother, who was not identified with anti-Nasserism as was Saud. By May 1958 a formidable rebellion had broken out in Lebanon composed of leftists, pan-Arabs, Moslems generally, and neutralists who were aroused by the government's endorsement of the Eisenhower Doctrine, its pro-Western policies, its Christian Maronite and non-Moslem orientation, and the intention of President Camille Chamoun to retain office beyond his stipulated term. By June a large part of Lebanon territory was in the hands of the rebels. The army commander, General Fuad Shihab, popularly respected and not identified with the rebellion, neglected to push the campaign against the rebels, for he felt there was something in their grievances and believed that a political compromise could be worked out. It was increasingly charged that the rebels were being supplied arms by Nasserites across the border in Syria, and that Nasser was in league with the rebels to overthrow the Lebanon government. The United Nations dispatched observers to Lebanon's frontiers.

But it was in Iraq that the West received its most serious blow. Iraq had not only endorsed the Eisenhower Doctrine but was a member of the Baghdad pact. For years opposition had been building up against the Hashimite dynasty, its pro-British and pro-Western policies, its corruption, its alliance with the feudal landlords, its failure to provide social services. On July 14, 1958, an army coup, led by Abdul Karim Kassim, overthrew the government, massacred the king, the crown prince, and the premier, jailed hundreds of leaders of the old regime, and proclaimed a republic with Kassim as premier. The new government had the backing of neutralists, pan-Arab Nasserites, and Communists. This staggering news caused consternation in Washington and London. Would the Communists take over the Iraq revolution? Would Iraq join the United Arab Republic? Would the Iraq revolution spread to Jordan? Would it give the rebels an outside push to victory in Lebanon?

On July 15 over 14,000 American Marines were dispatched to Lebanon and a few days later British army units were airlifted to Jordan to protect Hussein's government. The Soviet Union threatened intervention to get the American and British forces out of the Middle East. Nasser flew to Moscow to assure himself of Soviet support in the event that American and British moves were not confined to Lebanon and Jordan but assumed the character of an anti-Nasser crusade in Iraq and in the United Arab Republic itself. But he also urged Khrushchev to avoid any drastic step, to wait on developments before taking any action. Nasser did not want Soviet intervention in the Middle East any more than he wanted Western intervention. American emissaries sent to Iraq received the strong impression from Kassim that his new regime would not foster Communism or pro-Nasserism in the Middle East. As a result, in October American Marines were withdrawn from Lebanon and British forces from Jordan. The

United Nations continued to maintain a team of observers in Lebanon and stationed some observers in Jordan.

An internal pacification took place in Lebanon by an agreement among the political factions. President Chamoun gave up his intention of remaining in office. General Shihab became president, a neutralist became premier, and the new government withdrew Lebanon's acceptance of Eisenhower Doctrine military aid. Kassim's government in Iraq withdrew from the Arab Union with Jordan, from the Baghdad pact, and from military and other commitments made by the late government under the Eisenhower Doctrine. The seat of the Baghdad pact alliance was moved to Turkey, and the name of the alliance changed from METO to CENTO (Central Treaty Organization).

Thus within two years the United States dissipated much of the Arab and neutralist good will it had won during the Suez crisis. By attempting in its Eisenhower Doctrine to induce the neutral Arab states to become military allies, the United States precipitated events which merged Syria and Egypt into the United Arab Republic, converted Lebanon from an ally into a neutral, transformed Iraq from a Western military ally into a neutral with a distinct anti-Western flavor, immobilized King Saud, and isolated Jordan.

In Iraq, Kassim had difficulty pursuing a purely national course. During 1959 he shrewdly eliminated the influential pro-Nasser leaders among his followers. In order to do this, he had to use the Communists, and for a time this made for warm Iraq relations with Moscow, acrimonious relations with Nasser, and chilly relations between Nasser and Khrushchev. However, by 1960, Kassim's pro-national and neutral policies had gained sufficient strength for him to break with the Communists. This in turn brought Khrushchev and Nasser closer, and the Soviet Union, which had already undertaken a large part of the financing of the first stage of the Aswan Dam, committed itself to a large part of the financing of the second stage. Kassim's checking of Nasserism in Iraq had repercussions elsewhere. The Nasser tide began receding. King Saud resumed his duties in Saudi Arabia, announced a neutralist course, and declared that the Americans would be required to leave their air base at Dhahran in 1962 because of their "partiality for so-called Israel."

American inactivity in the Middle East appeared to bear more favorable fruit than American activity. In September 1961 a Syrian army coup seized control of Damascus and other centers and took Syria out of the United Arab Republic. There were a number of reasons for this secession. Syrians had never had cordial relations with the Egyptians. They had always thought of themselves as the center of the Fertile Crescent and of the Fertile Crescent as the center of the Arab world. Syrians resented the number of Egyptian administrators and soldiers in their country. The commercial and propertied classes were bitterly opposed to Nasser's "Arab Socialism"—nationalization of banks, land reform, limitation of the size of landholdings, graduated income taxes, and so forth. The coup of September was nationalist and conservative. A conservative but neutralist government was formed, and Syria resumed its seat in the United Nations and was readmitted to the Arab League. Egypt officially retained the name of United Arab Republic.

Nasser reacted to his Syrian defeat by intensifying his reform and socialist program within Egypt and giving it a bigger propaganda play outside Egypt than his pan-Arabism. He increasingly emphasized the difference between the "progressive" Arab states and the "feudal" ones. He took little interest in the movements in Muscat and Oman and in Kuwait for independence from British tutelage, because these territories were feudal. He severed Egypt's connection with Yemen in "the United Arab States" on the grounds that Yemen was a tradition-bound principality.

In the fall of 1962, a Yemenite follower of Nasser, General Abdullah Sallal, led a revolution which overthrew the old despotic monarchy and proclaimed the Yemen Arab Republic. There were revolutionary repercussions in Britain's Aden, in Muscat and Oman, in Kuwait, in Saudi Arabia, and in Jordan. As revolutionary ferment spread to the regions rich in oil and threatened the kings, sultans, emirs, imams, and sheikhs, Americans and Britons were concerned for the future of the West's oil concessions. The kings of Saudi Arabia and Jordan vowed to overthrow the Yemen Republic; but the tides of change were moving over the Arabian peninsula, a last bastion of medieval Islam, and they would be difficult to check.

Early in 1963, military coups brought to power social revolutionaries and pan-Arabs in the two most important countries of the Fertile Crescent, Iraq and Syria. In February a bloody army revolt in Iraq overthrew Kassim and caused him to be executed. Kassim had developed into a "lone wolf" and a "mad tyrant." He had broken with the Communists and the Nasserites; he had no dependable following; he failed to provide agrarian and social reform; his claims to Kuwait alienated the other Arab states; he had on his hands a formidable revolt of Kurdish tribesmen. Iraq's new leader, Abdul Salam Aref, backed by the Baath, a pan-Arab, social-democratic party, played down the army and the cult of personality. In March a virtually bloodless army coup brought the Baath party to power in Syria. The new premier, Salah El-Bitar, also emphasized civilian rule. The slogan of the Baath party in both Iraq and Syria was "Unity, Freedom, Socialism." The Baath leaders were drawn to Nasser's revolutionary reforms—nationalization of banks and some industry, modernization of agriculture, the breakup of the big estates and the distribution of land to the peasants, more equitable tax systems, public schools, river and hydroelectric developments, birth control—and proposed to undertake similar programs in Iraq and Syria. They were also drawn to Nasser's pan-Arabism, but wanted Arab federation rather than unification of all Arab states in one nation. Nasser agreed and declared the previous mistake of Egyptian-Syrian amalgamation would not be repeated. The Baath also believed in free elections, free speech, and free press, and were somewhat skeptical of Nasser's dictatorship.

In mid-April, Egypt, Syria, and Iraq announced the formation of a new United Arab Republic with its capital at Cairo. Egypt dropped its name of United Arab Republic and again took the name of Egypt. The federal government in Cairo became responsible for defense, foreign affairs, and economic cooperation, while lesser matters were left to the individual state governments. Other Arab states were invited to join the new federation.

Nasser's socialism had proved as attractive as his pan-Arabism. Egypt was on the way to becoming, next to Israel, the most up-to-date country in the Middle East, and it now appeared that the Egyptian reforms would be applied in Syria and Iraq. The revolutions in Syria and Iraq encouraged social-revolutionary and pan-Arab movements in other Arab countries; Sallal's revolution in

Yemen was strengthened; the kings of backward, feudal Jordan and Saudi Arabia were in great peril and drew closer together despite the old dynastic quarrel which had previously kept them apart; and Israel was apprehensive over the increasing cooperation of the Arab states and the growing power of Nasser.

Although the usual complaints about the monopolization of Middle Eastern oil by the Western imperialists continued, Middle Eastern oil did much to smooth the relations of that region with the West. It was the royalties paid to Middle Eastern governments by Western companies for oil concessions which met government budgets and supplied the extremely limited government services in Saudi Arabia and Kuwait and the considerably larger ones in Iraq and Iran. The development of new oil regions in the Sahara and the drive of the Soviet Union to market its oil in Western Europe at lower than world prices threatened to diminish profits and royalties from Persian Gulf oil and to pose new problems for the West in the Middle East.

"Neo-Colonialism": The Crisis in the Congo

The crisis in the Republic of the Congo in the early 1960's illustrated the reluctance of a European power to surrender the substance of colonialism after giving up its form, the depth of feeling about this neo-colonialism, and the services of the United Nations in moderating extremes and acting as a buffer between the East and the West.

The Congo gained its independence from Belgium on June 30, 1960, but because the Belgians had kept education and democratic institutions from the Congolese the latter were ill-prepared for the responsibilities of statehood. President Joseph Kasavubu and Premier Patrice Lumumba were political enemies and temperamental opposites. Kasavubu was a conservative and believed in a federal type of government for the Congo. Lumumba was a leftist and a neutralist and believed in a centralized government. He was also an emotionalist and frequently appealed to extreme nationalism and racism.

Independence was a signal for renewed tribal wars and a loosening of individual inhibitions. Scarcely a week had passed before the military police revolted and the central government lost control of the situation. Albert Kalonji set up an insubstantial independent government in Kasai province. The large province of Katanga, seat of rich copper and other mines, seceded and formed a separate government under the leadership of shrewd and ruthless Moïse Tshombé. Its capital was at Élisabethville. Katanga's mining properties were owned and controlled by the Union Minière du Haut Katanga, a key subsidiary of the Société Générale, the most formidable agglutination of financial and industrial power in Belgium, in which there was considerable British capital. Belgian administrators and technicians had remained in Katanga to service the Union Minière, and after the secession, Belgian civil servants who had been stationed in the Congo became employees of the Katanga government. Belgian, French, Rhodesian, and other soldiers of fortune constituted Katanga's military mercenaries. The Katanga secession was thought to be largely the work of the Union Minière, and its financial support was Katanga's chief source of revenue. Anti-colonial forces everywhere denounced the whole business as "a perfidious Belgian neo-colonialism."

After the mutiny of the Congolese police, the dangers to life and property became so serious that Belgian military forces re-entered the country to restore order. In mid-July Premier Lumumba called on the United Nations to repel Belgian "aggression." He expected that organization to curb his unruly forces, expel the Belgians, restore Katanga to the central government, and unify the country under his leadership. A United Nations Security Council resolution was passed authorizing the Secretary General to provide the Congo with such military assistance as might be necessary until Congolese forces could do the job, and called on Belgium to withdraw its troops "from the Republic of the Congo," which included Katanga. The United States supported this move in order to rescue the Congo from chaos and prevent an unilateral intervention by the Soviet Union, which would have produced a grave international crisis. The anti-imperialist countries supported it in order to achieve the larger purposes Lumumba had in mind. Accordingly, the United Nations assembled an emergency military force which eventually reached around 20,000 in number and included contingents from thirteen neutralist nations. The United Nations also undertook to supply administrative and technical services to the Congo government in order that public health and other necessary activities would not completely break down.

As United Nations forces gradually took over, the Belgians promised to withdraw their troops but insisted on retaining them in Katanga and in three of their old military bases which a Belgian-Congo treaty, never ratified, allowed them to keep. After much negotiating, the Belgians finally consented to withdraw their forces from Katanga and the three bases, but they were permitted to retain an operational staff of technicians in the bases. For a time Tshombé refused to allow United Nations forces in Katanga, but finally consented when Secretary-General Hammarskjold assured him that entry was merely for the purpose of supervising the withdrawal of the Belgian forces and that the United Nations would keep "hands off" the political quarrel between him and the central government.

This promise of Hammarskjold not to use the United Nations to restore Katanga to the central government raised the ire of the Communist bloc and some of the most ardent of the anti-colonial neutralist states. These looked upon Hammarskjold's conduct as a surrender to Belgium's "aggressive subversion" in the Congo. They demanded that the United Nations forces be used to bring Katanga and Tshombé to book. The Soviet Union hinted at unilateral intervention and threatened to send "volunteers" to the Congo to help Lumumba recover Katanga. Soviet and Czech technicians, military equipment, and aircraft moved into the Congo. Thus the unilateral intervention that the United States feared and the United Nations operation was designed to prevent now appeared imminent.

At this juncture, in September, President Kasavubu dismissed Lumumba as premier. The Communist bloc and many neutralist nations declared that only Parliament could dismiss a prime minister and that Lumumba was still premier. It looked as though the central authority itself would have two rival governments, with the nations taking sides with one or the other. To prevent the delivery of military equipment not designed for the United Nations forces, United Nations officials closed down Congo airports, and they threatened to disarm some of the Congolese forces. The pro-Lumumba bloc in the United Nations angrily interpreted this as Hammarskjold support of Kasavubu against Lumumba. Civil war between Lumumba and Kasavubu supporters was narrowly averted when Congolese "strong man" Colonel Joseph

Mobutu took over, established military rule, closed the Soviet and Czechoslovak missions, and dismissed President Nkrumah's personal representative. After much wrangling, the United Nations Assembly gave Secretary Hammarskjold's conduct of affairs in the Congo a strong vote of confidence.

The Communist bloc and the most aggressive of the neutrals were again stirred up when Rajeshwar Dayal of India, Hammarskjold's personal representative in the Congo, reported that Mobutu was quietly allowing Belgians to take up official positions in the Congo, that over two thousand had recently returned. And a battle royal was staged in the United Nations Assembly when both Kasavubu and Lumumba delegations arrived at the United Nations, each claiming to represent the Congo. The United States now openly came out for Kasavubu, and his delegation was seated after a bitter debate and a vote in which there were many abstentions. On this occasion the moderate neutrals either abstained or lined up with the West.

Meantime, Lumumba's followers were assembling at Stanleyville and preparing to launch a revolt against the Kasavubu-Mobutu government. On his way to Stanleyville to take over the leadership, Lumumba was captured, and President Kasavubu inexplicably turned Lumumba over to Tshombé. After maltreatment, Lumumba was killed, and some reports said that the deed was committed in the presence of Tshombé himself (February 1961). The followers of Lumumba then organized a government at Stanleyville with Antoine Gizenga at its head. The Communist bloc and the more aggressive of the anti-colonial neutrals claimed that the Gizenga government, as the successor of Lumumba, was the legal one in the Congo.

The murder of Lumumba stirred his supporters around the world. The Soviet Union demanded the dismissal of Hammarskjold, the arrest of Tshombé and Mobutu, the dispersal of their armed forces, the roundup of all Belgian personnel, the recognition of Gizenga, and the liquidation of the United Nations operation. Again the Soviet Union threatened unilateral action. Egypt, Guinea, Morocco, and Indonesia withdrew their contingents from the United Nations military force, but India came forward with an offer of combat troops to help fill the void. (Even among the positive neutrals there were differences of opinion at various stages of the Congo crisis.) The Communist bloc and many of the neutral states refused to make further contributions to the financial support of the United Nations forces in the Congo, as did Belgium, Portugal, and France, which had opposed the United Nations operation from the beginning. At this juncture the United States came to the financial rescue of the United Nations forces.

In the late winter and the spring of 1961 the United Nations Security Council and the Assembly gave the Secretary-General new instructions with respect to United Nations operations in the Congo. Mr. Hammarskjold was to work to prevent civil war between the factions, to urge the convening of the Congolese Parliament and a political settlement, to prevent Congolese armed forces from interfering with political life, and to remove all Belgian and other foreign military and paramilitary personnel and administrators and all mercenaries. To prevent an outbreak of civil war the United Nations was to use force if necessary. It was clear that the Kennedy administration, through its representatives in the United Nations, was now moving toward a Congo policy more pleasing to the Afro-Asian bloc.

The political situation in the Congo clarified somewhat. A conference of Congolese leaders resulted in the selection of Cyrille Adoula as premier. He seemed to be the ablest of the Congolese politicians yet to appear, and in politics he was a neutralist. Many of the nations which distrusted Kasavubu and Mobutu had respect for Adoula. Gizenga, who attended the conference, became first vice-premier. However, he went back to Stanleyville and his dissident movement was not absorbed, but Gizenga failed to gain ground. Belgium was again asked to withdraw all personnel from the Congo and replied that what Belgians remained in the Congo and Katanga were there on their own responsibility and had no official connection with Belgium. Tshombé still remained the stumbling block. He refused to dismiss the Belgians or any other of his foreign personnel and held on to his foreign mercenaries. In September United Nations forces in Katanga began taking military measures to force Tshombé's compliance. Stiff fighting between United Nations and Katanga forces followed. It was when Hammarskjold was on his way to meet Tshombé to negotiate a cease-fire that the Secretary-

General met his death in a plane crash. A cease-fire was later arranged.

But United Nations representatives in New York pressed for strong measures against Tshombé. A new Security Council resolution called for the use of force, if necessary, to get rid of the Katanga mercenaries and other unauthorized personnel. U Thant, Acting Secretary-General, moved to implement this, and Tshombé called for a war to the death. Fighting took place in December 1961 in which the United Nations forces at first met with reverses. The United States lent an emergency airlift to United Nations troops. United Nations forces fought their way back to Elisabethville, and a "hold-fire" was ordered by U Thant on condition that Tshombé meet Adoula to iron out their differences.

Negotiations between Adoula and Tshombé dragged on through 1962. Negotiations revolved around a compromise in which Katanga would dismiss all its armed forces, the Congo would become a federal state with large autonomy for the provinces, and Katanga would split half of its revenues with the central government. (Many feared that federalism would mean a revival of local tribalism.) But Tshombé proved a slippery negotiator and after making concessions he repeatedly wiggled out of them. U Thant, with the apparent backing of the United States, attempted to line up support for United Nations economic pressures on Katanga, perhaps even a boycott. The British government openly opposed such a move. Dr. Conor Cruise O'Brien, former United Nations political chief in Katanga, charged that the British were impeding United Nations efforts for Congo unity and that the commercial interests controlling Katanga would never come to terms with the central Congo government except under the heaviest pressures. The future effectiveness of any United Nations military measures in Katanga depended upon the success of a United Nations bond issue, a large part of which the United States agreed to underwrite.

Meanwhile, certain elements in the United States had become critical of American and United Nations policy in the Congo. These claimed that Tshombé had maintained law and order in Katanga; that he was the only genuine anti-Communist leader in the Congo; that he was favorable to private business interests;

that it was one thing for the United States to yield to anti-imperialism and neutralism when this was necessary but quite another thing for the United States to take the lead for the aggressive anti-imperialists and neutralists; that Tshombé represented self-determination in Katanga; and that the United Nations Charter did not allow that organization to impose an internal political settlement, and emphatically not by force of arms.

Supporters of American policy countered that there was foreign subversion and aggression in the Congo; that the elimination of the foreign subversive elements had been the original mandate of the United Nations when it intervened in the Congo, with American (and Eisenhower administration) backing; that the central Congo government was gathering greater effectiveness and respect with time and United Nations support; that to turn back now would revive the Lumumba and Gizenga groups, the suspicions of the Afro-Asian countries, and the threat of unilateral Soviet intervention; that the United Nations operation in the Congo had prevented such unilateral intervention and the direct and dangerous confrontation of East and West in the heart of Africa.

Events in the Congo reached a dramatic climax in December of 1962 and January of 1963. By the end of 1962, U Thant, who had been elected Secretary-General and who was an anti-colonial himself, determined to carry out the long-delayed Security Council and General Assembly mandates which called on the Secretary-General to use force if necessary to get rid of the Katanga mercenaries and other unauthorized personnel. His reasons were many: the impairment of United Nations prestige by the continued flouting of its authority; the mounting costs of maintaining the United Nations force in the Congo, which threatened United Nations bankruptcy; new discords in the central government of the Congo, as evidenced by a rebellious Parliament and a restless army; the fear that if the Katanga crisis was not resolved there would be a Soviet-backed leftist take-over in the Congo (the Congo Parliament had recently voted for the release of Gizenga); the failure to induce those countries which had the most trade with Katanga to put an economic boycott on the recalcitrant province.

Therefore, with the backing of the United States, Thant began a build-up of United Nations military strength in Katanga. The United States armed services stepped up their supplies of trucks, armored cars, and transport planes to the United Nations force. As the United Nations build-up grew, undisciplined Katanga mercenaries became belligerent, got out of hand, and a series of trigger-happy incidents in December provided the United Nations force with the excuse it wanted to crack down and take over the province. The last week in December and the first weeks in January, United Nations forces clamped a tight hold on Elisabethville and fanned out through the province, capturing control of the chief transportation lines and the population centers. Jadotville, seat of many of the Union Minière's mining operations, was occupied, despite the pleas of Belgian and British officials and officers of the Union Minière and the Bank of Katanga to halt United Nations troops and resume negotiations with Tshombé. At this juncture, too, officials of the Union Minière and the Bank of Katanga flew to Leopoldville to persuade the central government to resume negotiations by promising that henceforth the central government would get a share of the Katanga revenues. White leaders in Kenya, the Rhodesias, and the Union of South Africa hoped that Tshombé would put up a stiff resistance—the strange spectacle of an African Negro becoming a hero to the most intransigent white minorities in Africa.

But Tshombé, his weakness exposed at last, bounced around like an India rubber ball. One day he would flee to Southern Rhodesia, the next day he would brazenly reappear in Elisabethville; one moment he was breathing defiance, the next moment he was all for conciliation; once he actually led United Nations forces to their objective, but he finally made a rally at Kolwezi, where he threatened to blow up the huge dams and the copper and cobalt mines of the Union Minière in an all-out gesture of defiance. In the end he yielded to the pleas of Union Minière and Bank of Katanga officials, and late in January he grandly announced the end of the secession. In February Tshombé fled to Paris and exile.

Even before Tshombé made his announcement, the secession had indeed been ended. The future of Congo federalism and of the Katanga revenues would be decided not through negotiations with Tshombé and Katanga but by all the provinces of the Congo nation. Central government officials and United Nations technicians and administrators poured into Elisabethville, and the mercenaries and Katanga officials made haste to make their peace with the central government. The Congo and its two hundred tribes still faced enormous problems for the future.

The United Nations victory in the Congo represented the triumph of the United States and its Afro-Asian allies. The Soviet Union, hoping to exploit a continuing Congo chaos to precipitate a left-wing coup and achieve "real Lumumbaism," opposed the United Nations operation. Spain and Portugal, holding tenaciously to their African colonies, and Britain, France, and Belgium, whose citizens had large investments in the Union Minière, likewise opposed the operation. United Nations victory in the Congo was a defeat for neo-colonialism, which sought to continue its economic advantages by severing from the Congo a rich province which could be "managed." United Nations victory, too, probably prevented a leftist take-over in the Congo, possibly a Soviet beachhead, which might have resulted in a new and larger civil war and a direct confrontation of the Soviet Union and the United States. Finally, United Nations victory resulted in increased prestige for the world organization and in enhanced respect for it and the United States among the former colonial peoples. On the other hand, the Katanga operation produced much bitterness toward the United States among certain powerful business groups in Western Europe.

Thus, by 1963 the United States had come a long way in its understanding of the new nationalism and of neutralism. Instead of using its immense prestige and power to induce new nations to become its allies, it was—in both Laos and the Congo—using that prestige and power to allow new nations to maintain their national integrity, as they conceived it, and their neutralism.

Neutralism and the West

As we approached the mid-sixties the anti-imperialist revolutions, which had been at flood tide since the close of World War II, had just about accomplished the political independence of the colonial peoples. There were a few such revolutions to come, notably in the Portuguese African colonies, but in the main these revolutions—at least their fight-for-independence phase—had already passed into history. These had indeed been epoch-making, for they represented the drawing to a close of one of world history's major imperialisms—the European imperialism which had begun with the age of discovery and exploration at the end of the fifteenth century.

Despite the attraction of Communist economies for the under-developed societies, only one of the former European colonies in Asia, the Middle East, and Africa had gone Communist—little Vietminh. Not only had the former colonies not gone Communist, but most of them, despite their revolutions against the Western powers, had retained close ties with the West. Thus far this represented a miscarriage of Leninism, which had held that the colonial peoples, because of their economic exploitation by Western imperialism and their hatred of the foreign capitalists, would establish a Communist system and join an international proletarian society.

The former colonial peoples still had grievances against the Western powers, particularly their holding on to various im-perialist vestiges in the new nations—enclaves and patches of nationally unredeemed territories, military bases, oil and other economic concessions, and trading privileges for their nationals. But many of these traces of the old imperialism were of mutual benefit to the former colony and the old imperial power, and those that were not were bound to pass away. Again, the former colonial peoples disliked white racism, the big-power contest, the arms race, nuclear-weapons testing, and the billions poured into armaments, some of which might otherwise have gone to the underdeveloped peoples for their economic development.

Why had the former colonial peoples thus far resisted Com-munism and remained essentially friendly to the West? There were a number of reasons: fear of the police state and satellitism; the economic aid granted by the United States and other Western powers, which promised to help transform their pre-industrial economies into industrial ones within a reasonable time and in a less painful way than the Communist way; the emergence of fluid and mixed economies in the new societies, economies which even when they had many collectivist features were much nearer to Western economies than to Communist ones; the cultural impact left by the West on the indigenous peoples as a result of the long years of imperial rule; the fact that most of the leaders of the new nations had Western educations and were Western-oriented; the persistence, because of years of habit and the productivity of the West, of more trade and intercourse with the West than with the Communist countries; the miscarriage of the Marxist revolution in Western Europe, which left Communism with insufficient prestige and too few Western carriers to win the colonies and the former colonies.

However, the story was not yet finished, and the anti-imperialist revolutions might still pass through a second phase and move to Communism. The truth was that not a single underdeveloped country had made the historic breakthrough to industrialism by using democratic methods, although Russia had made that breakthrough by using Communist methods and China *appeared* to be making it by using similar totalitarian methods. If the mixed economies currently developing in most of the new societies should fail to carry them over the hump to industrialism they might well eventually turn to Communism.

Not a single one of them had yet achieved assured stability either, and nationalist but feudal governments and reactionary military dictatorships, by frustrating mass aspirations, might pave the way for ultimate Communist take-overs. But the signs here did not necessarily bode ill for the West, for even among the many military coups which had occurred in the new societies, few had as yet been right-wing in their orientation. Military seizure of power by Ibrahim Abboud in the Sudan, by Chung Hee Park in South Korea, and by Sarit Thanarat in Thailand appeared to be rightist; but the military coups of Ayub Khan in Pakistan and Ne Win in Burma were centrist and stabilizing; while most of the others, following the original Kemalist inspiration, were leftist or leftish—those of Nasser, Kassim, Sallal, Aref, Kong Le, and Gürsel, which in varying ways sought to fulfill popular and basic reforms. (In February of 1963, General Ne Win's centrist government in Burma moved sharply to the left, and Ne Win announced a far-reaching program of industrial nationalization and agrarian collectivization.)

Many Americans misjudged the trend up to this time in the new societies. They tended to think of the new societies as pro-Soviet and anti-Western. Why? Because their economies were not free-enterprise economies but mixed economies with some collectivist features; because they were neutralist in politics; and because they often lined up with the Communist bloc, or more accurately the Communist bloc often lined up with them, on the remaining anti-colonial issues in world politics. This thinking of the new societies as pro-Communist was a serious misjudgment, because on balance they were far closer to the West than to the Communist countries. One basic fact stood out: The former colonial peoples had given the West a second chance. At last this basic fact was becoming clear, even to Americans.

And yet as 1963 advanced it became doubtful whether the West would effectively avail itself of that second chance. The United States seemed to be backing away from its foreign aid program, and the other industrial countries did not seem disposed to shoulder their share of responsibilities for economic aid. In March of 1963, President Kennedy's special committee investigating America's foreign aid program, headed by General Lucius Clay, recommended that the United States reduce the number of countries receiving American aid, cut its annual foreign-aid program of the 1962-1963 level of 3.9 billion dollars by half a billion dollars, encourage the Western European countries to bear most of the aid burden in Africa, discourage aid to projects of foreign governments which competed with private enterprise, and work to stimulate a flow of private capital abroad. The committee's recommendations, which were a throwback to earlier American attitudes, collided with President Kennedy's 1964 proposed foreign aid program, which had called for 4.9 billion dollars. This report revealed a growing disillusionment in the United States with foreign aid programs, which in turn reflected growing Western skepticism about the ability of many of the new countries to manage their own affairs effectively (the reactionary ebb following the anti-imperialist flow, the inevitable disappointment which follows revolutionary advances), the increasing Western confidence that most of the new nations were now safe from a Communist tide anyway, and the hard facts of America's balance-of-payments difficulties. And so, just as it appeared that the West had won its battle to save most of the new nations from Communism, a weakening of economic aid and of the conviction that social politics was an indispensable part of Western policy threatened to undo the West's achievements, eventually bring a new Communist challenge to the emerging nations in Asia, the Middle East, and Africa, and again throw the future commitment of the underdeveloped societies into grave doubt.

[8]

DEPOLARIZATION
IN THE WEST:
THE DECLINE OF
WASHINGTON

The Weakness and Strength of NATO

In the late 1940's and early 1950's the United States was clearly
the arbiter of the non-Communist world. But by the late 1950's
and early 1960's even America's closest European allies no longer
deferred to Washington as they once had. Each was exercising a
degree of independence which would have been impossible in the
earlier postwar years, and sometimes that independence together
with America's lack of sympathetic understanding of it endangered allied unity and the common effort to withstand the drives
of the Soviet Union. However, from the American point of view
the most comforting aspect of the world situation was that Moscow, too, no longer commanded the authority it once did in the
Communist bloc.

It now seemed clear that the bipolarized world so much in
evidence in the late 1940's had yielded to a degree of depolariza-

tion, that the long-time trend, if not toward a genuine multiple balance of power, was at least toward a more plural and polycentric world. Washington's relative decline of influence in the Western bloc, Moscow's relative decline of influence in the Communist bloc, and the multiplication of neutralist states all pointed in the direction of a world more politically diversified.

There were a number of reasons why London, Paris, Bonn, and Rome did not follow Washington as closely as they did during the early postwar years. Western European nations no longer depended on the United States economically; they had recovered from the war, and they were enjoying a mass consumer-goods prosperity unprecedented in European history. The sense of urgency about the Communist danger had declined. There had been no overt, direct Communist aggression comparable to that in Korea since 1950. There had been no Communist expansion in Europe since the Czechoslovak coup of 1948. The defection of Yugoslavia and Albania had actually cut down the size of the territory in the Soviet orbit. Communist parties had declined in influence in France and Italy, the two countries in which they had been a postwar threat. The rift between Russia and China was now obvious. Some Europeans wondered if the Americans did not exaggerate the Communist danger, and if the danger was indeed exaggerated, then there was no reason why Europeans should tie themselves so closely to the United States.

But most Europeans agreed that the Communist danger was still very real, and they pointed to China's attack on India and Russia's missiles in Cuba. However, these divided into three schools of thought, all of which implied a larger independence on the part of Europeans. One point of view was that the Americans for the sake of their own security would have to stay in Europe to protect it from Communist aggression, and in that case the Americans needed the Europeans as much as the Europeans needed the Americans, and consequently there was no need for Europeans to defer to the United States. Another school of opinion maintained that, since the defense of the West was now seen to be a matter of many decades to come and increasingly involved nuclear weapons, the United States should take its European allies into closer confidence, share with them on a plane of greater equality its nuclear arsenal and its nuclear know-how, and give them more voice in nuclear developments and decisions concerning the actual use of nuclear weapons. A third school of thought held that, as intercontinental missiles came into operational use, the United States would have less need for European allies and bases and might gradually abandon Europe and concentrate its defenses in North America. To prepare for such a contingency Europeans owed it to themselves to increasingly develop their own nuclear weapons and missiles independently of the United States.

The personality and policies of the powerful and strong-willed French President, Charles de Gaulle, also raised problems for the Western alliance. As we shall see, along many fronts his influence was a divisive one, and he came more or less in conflict not only with American views but with the views of some of his fellow Europeans and fellow Frenchmen.

Let us survey some of the differences between the United States and its various allies and among the various European allies themselves.

Little Portugal, whose Azores were sites of American bases integrated into the framework of NATO, resented the American position in the United Nations in support of Angola. Spain, where the United States had important air and naval bases, was sensitive about its non-inclusion in NATO, and as a holder of scattered possessions in Africa and a close friend of Portugal, did not relish America's support in the United Nations of anti-colonialism in Africa. Belgium smarted under its loss of the Congo and the United Nations' attempt to restore Katanga to the central Congolese government. Powerful business interests in most of the Western European countries, with investments and connections in Belgium's influential Société Générale, also bristled at the policy of the United States and the United Nations in Katanga. In its guarded anti-colonialism the United States at one time or another had stepped on the imperialist toes of the Dutch, the French, and the British. The French were particularly resentful because the United States had not vigorously upheld French policy in Algeria but instead had played a rather "gum-shoe" game every time the Algerian question had come before the United Nations.

In Denmark and Norway there was uneasiness over the new

Baltic Approaches Command within NATO's Northern European Command area. But if the Danes and Norwegians did not especially look forward to having to share with West Germany the tighter defense cooperation demanded of them, they liked even less the thought of being overrun by the Soviet Union.

Although Italy had been most cooperative within NATO, the still large Communist and pro-Communist vote in that country aroused some doubt in American minds about whether Italy's multi-party alliances might not some day bring into power a neutralist government there. However, that possibility seemed to be receding since the majority Socialists under Nenni had broken away from their long-time collaboration with the Communist party and had made an electoral combination with Italy's largest party, the Christian Democrats. Without the support of the Nenni Socialists, the Communists were reduced to winning about one-fourth of the Italian voters.

However, it was in France, West Germany, and Britain that the future vitality and effectiveness of America's Western alliance system largely depended.

In 1958, Charles de Gaulle, France's most powerful political figure of the twentieth century, became first premier and then president. A new Constitution was adopted, the Fourth Republic gave way to the Fifth Republic, the power of the executive was greatly increased and that of the legislative assembly greatly decreased, and France's parties and multi-party system declined in influence. De Gaulle's personality and policies made for both a new unity and a new divisiveness in the Western alliance. His coming to and remaining in power at a crucial time and his prolonged, cautious, and effective maneuvering in the face of right-wing intransigence in France, of bitter opposition on the part of the French settlers in Algeria, and of treasonable and terroristic activities of a portion of the French army itself, all bent on keeping Algeria French at all cost, eventually brought independence to Algeria and probably saved France from a bitter civil war between right and left. Had such a civil war come to France, violent ideological conflict might have erupted in a number of other countries, European and non-European, the ideological conflict between East and West would have been critically intensified, and even world war, all-out nuclear war, might well have resulted. De Gaulle's service to France and to the world had been beyond price.

On the other hand, in a lower key, De Gaulle was a divisive force within the Western alliance. Among other things, he took a most independent course toward NATO. He was offended that the United States consulted Britain more often and intimately than France, and early in his presidency he suggested a kind of three-power directorate (the United States, Britain, and France) for NATO. When this did not materialize, he moved to closer collaboration with Chancellor Adenauer.

France served notice in 1959 that it would retain under its control that portion of its navy (about one-third of it) that had been designated for NATO in case of war. De Gaulle resisted an integrated NATO air and naval defense and for a time even an integrated air-warning system. About this same time France also announced that it would no longer allow NATO (in this case the United States) to stockpile nuclear weapons on its territory. This necessitated the transferring of around two hundred United States bombers to less strategic bases in West Germany and Britain. France also had to be omitted for the time from agreements the United States made with some other NATO powers concerning training their NATO forces in the use of tactical nuclear weapons. (The United States retained possession of the nuclear warheads and the technical information and know-how of production.)

In 1959 and 1960 the United States successfully negotiated with Britain, Italy, and Turkey about setting up squadrons of nuclear-armed intermediate-range missiles in those countries. (These were in answer to the Soviet Union's long-range missiles and boasted intercontinental missiles.) By 1960 it appeared that this would be no stop-gap arrangement but an important element in the Western deterrent for some time to come. In any event and under all the arrangements the nuclear warheads would remain in American custody. The arrangement with Britain required a joint decision of the American and the British governments before the missiles could be fired. The arrangements with Italy and Turkey provided that the missiles would not be fired except on agreement between the individual government in question and NATO headquarters. France had been a country favored for the location of some of these missile squadrons, but France flatly refused to accept any arrangement which would subordinate the discharge of missiles from its territory to agreement with NATO headquarters. With the detonation of two French atomic devices in the Sahara (February and April 1960), France became an atomic power and threatened to develop its own nuclear striking force independently of the United States and NATO.

What were the reasons behind De Gaulle's attitude? The French president was inspired with the French nationalistic sense of "*la gloire*," of France's great past. He felt that his country had too often been slighted in making the big NATO decisions, and he was determined to command greater participation by France in those decisions. De Gaulle also resented the American refusal to give France atomic information or help her develop her own atomic weapons. He believed the United States hugged too tightly its atomic information and weapons and in effect monopolized the decisions about how and when atomic weapons should be used. He feared the United States might make the decision to use atomic weapons without due regard to the interests of the country from whose territory they were fired. He also feared the opposite, that the United States might refuse to use its nuclear weapons when continentals thought they ought to be used, or worse, that the United States and even Britain might some day abandon Europe, leaving the Continent with no nuclear defenses of its own.

It is difficult to resist the conclusion that De Gaulle had developed an anti-"Anglo-Saxon" bias. This bias seemed to be based on the belief that the United States and Britain used the continental countries or abandoned them, depending on American or British needs of the time. (This view about "the Anglo-Saxons" was not without historical foundation, but all nations were motivated by national interest, and since 1870 the national interest of "the Anglo-Saxon" powers had been on the side of France, not against her.) Subconsciously De Gaulle appeared to nurse and exaggerate the slights he felt he had endured during World War II, when his Free French movement was the "poor relations" ally of Britain and the United States, and President Roosevelt, sensitive to De Gaulle's enormous egocentricity and mystical nationalism, was wisecracking about the French general's being "a twentieth-century Joan of Arc."

De Gaulle received little support from the other NATO partners, not even Adenauer, in his independent stand. Sometimes his actions seemed to them capricious and quixotic. The rest of Europe was not about to trade American security for French "security." As one prominent Belgian leader remarked: "Does De Gaulle think the Continent can defend itself with bows and arrows?" Europeans were apprehensive that De Gaulle's eccentricities would invite the very American withdrawal the French President professed to fear.

However, De Gaulle never pressed his independence to the point of disloyalty to the NATO alliance. His many brushes with the United States and NATO were generally construed to be motivated not only by desires to increase the power and prestige of France but also to arouse the Americans to the need of giving their European allies a greater voice in the use and control of the tightly held American nuclear materials and know-how. If this was De Gaulle's aim, then he would have plenty of European, especially West German, support; but Europeans would still quarrel with the tactics he used to accomplish it.

The relations of the United States with the West Germany it had done so much to create and foster were on the whole friendly. West Germany was the chief continental pillar of NATO. The West Germans were enjoying an unprecedented mass-consumer prosperity. Since the future of Germany still depended so much on American policy there was naturally a good bit of grumbling about that policy. When the Americans negotiated with the Russians, the Germans said: "The Americans will make concessions at our expense." When the Americans did not negotiate with the Russians, the Germans said: "But how can we make even a beginning toward reunification if there are no negotiations with the Russians?" There was a widening feeling in Germany that Chancellor Adenauer, while ostensibly opposing American negotiations with the Russians for fear that too many concessions would be made to them, actually opposed negotiations for the same deep and unavowed purpose that De Gaulle opposed them: to maintain the division of Germany. (Adenauer, "an old Rhenish separatist," derived his support from the Catholic voters who predominated in West Germany.) Nevertheless, it would be difficult for West Germans to accept a formal treaty which put down in black and white a recognition of "the reality" of the two Germanies and the loss of old German territories beyond the Oder-Neisse line, and there was apprehension that the Americans would move in the direction of British policy and seek *rapprochement* with the Russians at the "expense" of Germany.

The West Germans were unhappy about their military situation within NATO. They contributed from seven to nine divisions to NATO forces, more than any of the other NATO members, including the Americans, but their contingents were not equipped with even tactical nuclear weapons. The Germans felt that any army not so equipped was fatally handicapped in any contest with the nuclear-equipped Russian armies. The Americans were the only forces in NATO so equipped. The delivery systems for tactical nuclear weapons were made available to German and other NATO armies, and the Americans trained the German army, as they did the armies of other NATO partners (even the French, after De Gaulle gave in on this matter), in the use of tactical nuclear weapons, but the nuclear warheads themselves were kept under tight American custody. However, the British and the French were now developing their own nuclear weapons, but the Germans were not allowed, under the WEU treaties, to develop such weapons. The West Germans insisted that there should be no discrimination among allies in the availability of nuclear weapons.

Increasingly the West Germans felt that the WEU treaties should be revised to allow them to have their own nuclear weapons or that at least the Americans should share custody of the tactical nuclear weapons with the non-American armies of NATO, including the German, which might be called upon to use them in combat. The West Germans also favored a multilateral medium-range ballistic missile force which would operate under NATO. The Americans regarded the repeal of the ban on Germany's having its own nuclear-weapon program as clearly inadmissible, and the United States still held off from implementing the requests for a collective nuclear deterrent force under NATO and the sharing of the tactical nuclear warheads with the national contingents assigned to NATO. It was quite under-standable why the United States was reluctant to disseminate nuclear weapons and why in the case of the Germans the United States had to be particularly careful because of the fears of Germany's neighbors in the West and the alacrity with which Khrushchev would make propaganda about "America's arming the Nazi criminals with nuclear weapons."

The United States, in turn, felt that the Bonn government, considering Germany's decided economic prosperity, did not contribute enough financially to the mutual defense costs and the economic-aid programs for the underdeveloped peoples.

America's relations with Britain were characterized by numer-ous irritations, but the United States and Britain remained staunch friends, and America's other partners were sometimes jealous of Britain as America's "favorite" ally.

British Tories were furious at America's vigorous espousal of the cause of Egypt in the Suez crisis and irked by American "encroachment" on the old British oil monopoly in Iran, the "dis-placement" by the United States of Britain in the Middle East, and America's "anti-Katanga" policy in the Congo. British liberals, socialists, Labourites, as well as a good many Conservatives, took a "soft" line on Red China; on southeast Asia; on keeping British NATO forces on the Continent up to full strength; on the pos-sibility of fruitful summit conferences; on Berlin, East Germany, and even Central European disengagement and the Rapacki plan; and on the urgency of nuclear-test ban and arms-limitation agree-ments. The United States steered a middle course between the opposition of Adenauer and De Gaulle to negotiations with the Russians and the somewhat eager willingness of the British to negotiate.

On the other hand, the British government fell in with Ameri-ca's military strategy, allowed British bases for America's nuclear-armed bombers and nuclear-armed intermediate-range missiles, and concluded an agreement whereby the United States was granted a Polaris submarine support base at Holy Loch in the Firth of Clyde, despite the fears among all classes of Britons that their country might be inviting destruction as a result of American actions unauthorized by the British government (in the case of the Polaris base the United States government was to "consult" with the British government before any American action) and despite the angry demonstrations of Britain's numerous advocates of unilateral nuclear disarmament, led by Bertrand Russell.

NATO was still far from fulfilling its original purpose of providing a shield of large ground forces of the Western powers in Central Europe as a protection against the Soviet strength in Eastern Europe. The Soviet Union and its satellites still had a great superiority in ground forces. Some of the Soviet divisions were provided with tactical, battlefield nuclear weapons. Since the formation of the NATO shield force, the goal had been thirty divisions of the Western Allies in Central Europe. Even as late as 1961 there were only twenty-one such divisions. The French had withdrawn divisions for the war in Algeria. In the closing days of the Eisenhower administration it was hinted that the United States might reduce its forces in Germany. Numerically the American forces were second only to the German, and the only ones equipped with nuclear weapons. The United States itself had never maintained the number of NATO ground forces originally intended, largely because of the "new look" military policy adopted in the early years of the Eisenhower administration, which put the emphasis on the nuclear deterrent. However, the United States prodded its allies to fill their original ground-force quotas, on the assumption, never bluntly stated, that if the United States provided the nuclear deterrent its allies should at least contribute their full share to the conventional forces.

The Kennedy administration felt that the Eisenhower administration had put too much stress on the nuclear deterrent, that it was high time to increase the NATO ground forces. This seemed required to convince Khrushchev that the Western Allies meant to preserve their rights and commitments in Berlin and to enhance NATO's ability to conduct military operations, if these became necessary, without immediate resort to anything beyond the smaller battlefield nuclear weapons and perhaps without having to resort to the strategic cataclysmic weapons at all. America's allies, particularly the Germans, continued to insist on the importance of their forces being equipped with the tactical, battlefield nuclear weapons, that their merely having training in the use of such weapons and possession of their delivery systems were not enough.

To emphasize the importance of building up ground forces and as a spur to its allies to step up their own ground forces, the United States in 1961 announced that it would send an additional 40,000 men to Germany, which would bring the American Seventh Army and other combat and support units committed to NATO to around 290,000 men. The United States also announced that it would dispatch 3400 men to the European theater to operate the new short-range missiles. France, with two divisions operating under NATO, reported that it would bring back two divisions from Algeria to rejoin its NATO forces. West Germany was in the process of increasing the number of its NATO divisions from seven to nine. Great Britain, with 51,000 troops in Germany and still short its quota, promised to send an anti-aircraft regiment and a guided-missiles regiment to its Army of the Rhine. Canada, Belgium, and the Netherlands were well along toward filling their quotas.

In the closing days of the Eisenhower administration, Secretary of State Christian A. Herter announced that the United States "conceived" a plan of a multilateral, medium-range missile force under NATO which would consist of five Polaris submarines with eighty missiles to be given to NATO by 1963 and one hundred additional Polaris or Pershing missiles, also for deployment at sea, which would be sold to NATO. In 1961, President Kennedy, without reference to the Herter plan, declared that the United States would commit to NATO five Polaris atomic-missile submarines, and in the future still more, subject to agreed NATO guidelines as to their control and use; beyond this, that the United States was looking to an eventual NATO atomic seaborne force which would be truly multilateral in ownership and control, *once NATO's non-nuclear goals had been achieved.* It was clear that the United States was still reluctant to commit nuclear weapons to NATO, and that in the meantime it was using promises of eventual nuclear weapons for NATO, under multilateral control, as inducements to America's allies to reach and maintain their full quotas of ground forces under NATO. Chancellor Adenauer kept the problem to the fore by announcing from time to time that it was particularly important to have a nuclear deterrent under NATO that was not dependent on American authority.

Toward a New Center of Power:
Western European Integration

The movement toward Western European economic integration, begun with the European Coal and Steel Community, was marching steadily forward. In 1957 two other Communities, the European Atomic Energy Community (Euratom) and the European Economic Community (the Common Market) were established. The conflicts of opinion over the Common Market revealed some differences among the Six (the countries which belonged to European Coal and Steel Community, Euratom, and the Common Market) and between the Six and the Seven (those countries which in 1959 organized the European Free Trade Association). In this sense the development of common economic institutions was evocative of some painful adjustment making. If the end result was an economically integrated and politically federated Western Europe, then it would constitute an enormous step toward depolarization, for Western Europe would become an influential power center equal to the United States and the Soviet Union. (A fourth such center was probably emerging in China.) But of course in another sense the trend to an economically integrated and politically federated Western Europe, if carried to success, would represent a tremendous triumph over the separate and often conflicting European nationalisms which in the twentieth century had brought the Western world to near ruin.

The establishment of Euratom by the treaty of Rome (March 1957) had for its purpose the pooling of scientific and economic resources in West Germany, France, Italy, and the three Benelux countries to develop atomic energy for peaceful purposes. It was felt that the economy of Western Europe was too much dependent on Middle Eastern oil, which was subject to the uncertainties of Middle Eastern and world politics and placed a heavy burden on the balance of payments of European countries. It was hoped to fill the energy gap of the future with atomic power. Euratom sought to encourage, finance, and centralize atomic research and development, place fissionable materials under the direction of a single agency, and locate and supervise nuclear power plants in a safe, economical, and equitable way. The political organization of Euratom followed closely that of the

ECSC. The executive power was placed in a Commission (called in ECSC the High Authority). There was a Council of Ministers to represent the respective governments. And the existing Assembly, now renamed the European Assembly, and the Court of Justice of the ECSC were also to serve Euratom.

At the time the Euratom treaty was signed in Rome, the Six signed an even more important treaty setting up the European Economic Community or the Common Market. This represented a tight customs union. Its objective was a completely free-trade internal market. All import duties, export duties, and industrial quotas among the Six were to be abolished gradually. By January 1, 1962, at the end of the first stage, internal tariffs on each product would be cut at least 25 per cent and all export duties and quotas terminated. At the end of the second stage, in 1966, the cuts on each item would total at least 50 per cent. By 1970 all tariffs among the Six would come to an end and all goods would move freely from country to country. As the internal customs fell, new common external customs rates would take the place of the many national rates. The external tariffs of each of the Six would then be the same. The first step toward creating a common external tariff system was to be taken by the end of 1961.

But the Common Market went far beyond a mere customs union. By the end of the third stage, capital investments and labor would move across the national frontiers as freely as goods and commodities. As in the ECSC there were to be rules of fair competition, and practices which inhibited the flow of trade were to be subjected to anti-cartel measures. The Community would have common policies for transport, foreign trade, and even agriculture. The Community, then, would ultimately invade policy areas in such matters as cartels and agricultural stabilization, hitherto considered far more "domestic" than matters of tariff and trade. Much of the French Community in Africa and France's former African colonies which so desired were made associate members of the Common Market, which would facilitate their access to that Market and provide some assistance in their economic development.

The executive of the Common Market was placed in a Commission, and there would be a Council of Ministers representing the respective national governments, which would have wider decision-making power than the Council of Ministers of ECSC or of Euratom. Until the beginning of the third stage, decisions would have to be unanimous, but after that time decisions would be by a qualified majority vote, which would virtually abolish the national veto. At the beginning of the third stage, then, the movement toward a uniform tariff structure would become practically irreversible. The same European Assembly and Court of Justice which served the ECSC and Euratom would also serve the European Economic Community.

By May 1960 so much progress had been made in lowering internal tariffs that the Six decided to accelerate their goals. All quotas on industrial products would be eliminated by the end of 1961 instead of 1970 as originally planned, and by the end of 1961 internal tariffs would be lowered at least 40 per cent instead of 25 per cent. However, the Market delayed entering the second stage for a time because of the discontent of the French and the Dutch, who produced agricultural surpluses, over the fact that the agricultural part of the program was not moving as fast as the industrial. The Germans were resisting common measures which in effect would mean larger markets for French and Dutch agriculture and lower prices for West Germany's already subsidized farmers. Questions concerning the future of grain prices and the financing of price-support arrangements and farm subsidies within the Common Market caused considerable difficulty. But what was impressive was that with the many possibilities for economic conflict among the Six the progress was as great as it was.

Great Britain, which did not join ECSC or Euratom and which traditionally held aloof from too close association with the Continent, chose not to join the Common Market. The most important reason for her non-participation was her commitments to the nations of the British Commonwealth, which enjoyed preferential tariff treatment in British markets. Membership in the Common Market would have meant that eventually Britain would have to take the products of the countries of the Common Market on a free-trade basis, no matter how much this injured the Commonwealth countries, and that she would have to enforce the external tariffs of the Common Market against the Commonwealth nations. On the other hand, formation of the Common

Market meant that British trade would be shut out of the most populous countries on the Continent or at best have to compete with Community producers in their market at a distinct disadvantage. Other non-member countries in Europe faced the same difficulties.

Accordingly, "the Outer Seven"—Britain, Sweden, Norway, Denmark, Austria, Switzerland, and Portugal—in 1959 organized the European Free Trade Association in which those nations undertook to reduce and eventually abolish as among themselves all tariffs on non-agricultural products. Each country would still continue to have its own external tariffs with respect to non-member countries. This allowed Britain to continue to give preferences to the Commonwealth nations, for they were largely exporters of agricultural products which would not be affected by the EFTA agreements, and it also allowed Britain in her external tariffs to continue to give the goods of the Commonwealth countries a favorable position. However, those members of EFTA which specialized in agricultural produce, like Denmark, felt that the EFTA's confining of internal tariff cuts and eliminations to industrial products gave Britain, an industrial country, the better part of the deal.

But as the Common Market developed it became increasingly clear that membership in EFTA was no substitute for membership in the Common Market, which contained the most populous nations of Western Europe. Access to the markets of those nations would become increasingly difficult as their internal tariffs went down and they maintained common tariffs against non-members. Accordingly, in July 1961 the British government announced that it would make a revolutionary break with its traditional policy and seek admission to the Common Market. Thereafter Denmark and Norway also announced that they would apply for membership. But Sweden, Switzerland, and Austria took the position that if they joined the Common Market they would forfeit their status as political neutrals. Indeed, the Soviet Union warned Austria that its entry into the Common Market would be a violation of the Austrian peace treaty. About the same time Britain announced her intention to seek entry into the Common Market, Ireland and Spain announced a like intention.

Opposition within Britain to that country's joining the Common Market was formidable and came from many sources. There was a nostalgia for Britain's great past, a reluctance to break with Commonwealth and traditional world ties to become permanently and more closely associated with Europe. There was fear among some businessmen and those Conservative politicians who reflected their views that the restrictive policies of certain large business enterprises and the tight-knit British trade associations would suffer from the EEC's anti-cartel policies. A left-wing element in the Labour party was apprehensive that Britain's socialist controls, nationalized industries, and wage scales might suffer interference from the continental supranational agencies.

The most effective opposition argument was that Britain was turning her back on her partners in the EFTA and especially the members of the British Commonwealth. Canada, Australia, and New Zealand complained that Britain was "selling them out," that they would suffer serious economic injury. Nehru argued that Britain's entry into the Common Market represented a further bipolarization of the world, that as the Common Market became more and more effective the Eastern European nations, including Poland and Yugoslavia, because of loss of Western European markets, would be forced into a closer collaboration with the Soviet Union. Ghana's representative declared that his country did not want to become an associate member of the Common Market, even if such membership were offered, because EEC was another club of the rich nations and associate membership was just another form of neo-colonialism.

Defenders of Britain's entry into the Market argued that Britain must look to her own interests, that "Britain was an independent nation, too," that the bonds that held the Commonwealth together were largely sentimental and less and less economic, that while Britain gave preferences to Commonwealth countries in British markets the Commonwealth countries in turn took far less of British goods than formerly, that Britain as a member of the Common Market would be in a position to promote the interests of Commonwealth countries inside that Market.

On the Continent, the leaders of the functionalist or supranational approach to European unity had been well satisfied with the evolution of the three Communities—the ECSC, Euratom, and the EEC. They regarded themselves as the vanguard of the emerging "Europe of the peoples," as opposed to "the Europe of the national states" or "the Europe of the bosses." They looked forward to the time—not long distant, they felt—when the functions of the three Communities would be merged into one organization, when the activities carried on at Brussels, Luxembourg, and Strasbourg would be concentrated in one capital city or Federal District, when the High Authority of ECSC and the Commissions of Euratom and the Common Market would be combined into a single executive, and when the European Assembly, instead of being elected by the various national legislatures, would be elected directly by universal suffrage.

Most of the functionalists favored the admission of Britain because this would enormously strengthen the Market, add a large number of buyers and sellers; and besides, how could there be an integrated Western Europe without Great Britain?

On the other hand, some had their doubts. These recalled how in the past Britain had always favored the intergovernmental approach and opposed the functionalist approach. Britain was not a member of the other two supranational Communities. Would not the admission of Britain, still with many world-wide ties, make the emerging new Europe too unwieldy, endanger its European character, make impossible the development of a truly European consciousness? Britain was European, yet it was not European. Was there not a danger that the Common Market would become not a unified entity but merely a grand bazaar for bargaining over reciprocal tariff concessions with nations around the world, a mere fulcrum for world-wide free trade?

But if all this represented a real threat from without, a new challenge from within appeared by way of "a new splendid intransigence" from President Charles de Gaulle, and this gave Britain's membership a different aspect and converted many who otherwise might have been opponents of Britain's entry into British supporters.

For some time President de Gaulle had let it be known that he regarded the expectation that Western Europe would achieve political unity through the slow development of functional, supranational economic institutions as "utopian." Only the states, he maintained, were valid, legitimate, and capable of achievement; any Europe aside from the states was a compound of "myths, stories and parades." De Gaulle was well satisfied with the existing geographical grouping, for the Six represented the heart of Europe, the authentic Europe, essentially Catholic Europe, the Europe of the Charlemagne tradition. What he envisaged was a stronger political collaboration of the governments of the Six, the formation of intergovernmental political, economic, and social secretariats dependent on their national governments; unlike the agencies of the developing supranational Communities, these secretariats would have little authority of their own. De Gaulle conceived an intergovernmentally unified Six, politically strong enough to become independent of NATO and "the Anglo-Saxons," guided by the Paris-Bonn Axis, with its own nuclear deterrent (that is, a French deterrent, since France was the only one of the Six which was developing nuclear weapons of its own).

De Gaulle personally and assiduously cultivated Adenauer, and that "old Rhenish separatist" was not without some sympathy for De Gaulle's grand conception of a revival of "the old, true Europe." However, the Germans had mixed feelings about De Gaulle's courtship of Adenauer. After being pariahs for so many years they were flattered by being wooed by anyone, particularly their old enemy offering them absolution. But they were inclined to be reticent and skeptical about this so-called Paris-Bonn Axis and wondered about its practicality.

In July 1961, De Gaulle, backed by Adenauer, persuaded the Six to set up the Fouchet committee to work out a plan for political collaboration. The Fouchet committee proposed that the Six make a political treaty providing for the pursuit of common foreign policies, defense, and economic and cultural matters. These would be achieved through regular meetings bringing together ministers of the member governments.

To the functionalists and supranationalists, still strong in France itself, De Gaulle's "grand design" seemed a threat to their European Communities and to their organic approach to European unity. But even though De Gaulle never proposed taking France out of the Communities or ever avowed wanting to impair their concrete work (he only publicly held that they would not bring political unity to Europe), and even though his attitude did not undermine their development, it was increasingly feared by many in the Netherlands, Belgium, and Italy that the burgeoning Paris-Bonn Axis might upset the political balance within the Six. As a result, many elements within "Little Europe" which might have had misgivings about admitting Britain and widening the Common Market membership now welcomed the prospect of Britain's entry as a makeweight to the De Gaulle–Adenauer alliance.

Various other groups pushed for British membership. Socialists throughout Europe embraced the opportunity for closer relations with Britain and the Scandinavian countries as an offset to the supposed influence of the Catholic Church. This had an effect on the Fanfani government in Italy which was wooing the Nenni Socialists into making an alliance with the Christian Democrats. Those West Germans who began to see in the De Gaulle–Adenauer hard line on Berlin and on negotiations with the Russians a bar to eventual German unification welcomed British entry as a brake on the De Gaulle–Adenauer combination. Foreign Minister Gerhard Schroeder was reported to be of this opinion and for this reason. Some non-Communist newspapers in Western Europe reported that even the Russians, although keeping up a steady drumfire against any strengthening of the Common Market, actually welcomed Britain as a balance to De Gaulle and Adenauer and an encouragement to eventual successful negotiations over East Germany and Berlin and more liberal trade policies between the Common Market and the Eastern satellites. (Like France, the Eastern satellites had agricultural surpluses, and their products would likely get into the Market on liberal terms only after overcoming French opposition.)

The United States strongly favored Britain's joining the Common Market because it believed that the Market would be strengthened thereby and given a more outgoing orientation, that Britain as a member would throw its support to liberal trading policies favorable to the United States, the British Commonwealth nations, the underdeveloped countries, and the neutrals like Sweden, Switzerland, and Austria, which could not or would not enter the Market. The United States also welcomed any development which would weaken the De Gaulle–Adenauer collaboration and curb De Gaulle's disposition to operate independently of NATO.

In April 1962, at a meeting of the foreign ministers of the Six to consider the Fouchet treaty, the representatives from Belgium and the Netherlands held up the De Gaulle plan for a political combination of Common Market states. Paul-Henri Spaak, Belgium's foreign minister and a strong functionalist, explained his position this way: "I think, as before, that it is necessary to create a supranational Europe. But I also think that . . . if we must accept a European organization as vague as the one proposed [by De Gaulle], then the operation will be more acceptable with Great Britain than without her."

Negotiations by the Six continued around the so-called Fanfani compromise. This accepted De Gaulle's "Europe of the States." But it included amendments which protected NATO and the three developing economic Communities and provided that after three years (when De Gaulle and Adenauer would perhaps have left office) the whole question of Europe's political character would be reconsidered. Finally, Britain, after joining the Common Market, would be invited to sign the political treaty.

During 1961 and 1962, for over a year, the hard bargaining went on in Brussels to determine whether Britain would be admitted to the Common Market and on what terms. There was general agreement that in the end Britain would be admitted, but the bargaining was interminable and the price of admission high. De Gaulle and Adenauer showed little enthusiasm for Britain's entry, and they continued their political conversations in an apparent attempt to make the political treaty of the Six a *fait accompli* before Britain became a member of the EEC. The negotiations at Brussels were most complex, for Britain was bargaining not only for herself but seeking assurances of liberal trade policies by the Common Market for the Commonwealth countries and her partners in the EFTA, particularly the neutrals like Sweden, Switzerland, and Austria. The French were the hardest bargainers, for in addition to De Gaulle's aversion for "the Anglo-Saxons," France produced agricultural surpluses, and Britain's proposals to liberalize the Market's policies with respect to the agricultural Commonwealth nations frequently ran head-on into the interest of the French in preserving a large part of the Community's markets for their own agricultural products.

The negotiations proceeded on the proposition that until 1970 Britain would maintain her tariff preferences for the Commonwealth countries, which would however taper off gradually during that period. After 1970 the Commonwealth countries would be in the same category as other "third countries" such as the United States and Argentina, and all preferences would be confined to members of the Common Market. The negotiations, then, revolved around the British preferences to be allowed the Commonwealth countries until 1970, the stages of "phase out" of those preferences, and what assurances might be given the Commonwealth countries as to their prospects for liberal treatment by the Common Market after 1970. With respect to the treatment of Commonwealth products until 1970, the most tedious negotiations went on concerning the tea of India, Pakistan, and Ceylon, the cereals of Canada and Australia, the meat and butter of New Zealand, and so forth. With respect to Commonwealth products after 1970, the British sought to get guarantees that the foodstuffs of Canada, Australia, and New Zealand would continue to be bought in tolerable quantities in the European market. The Six replied with unanimity that no such guarantees could be given, but it was finally agreed that the Common Market would follow policies making for "reasonable" agricultural prices and would initiate world-wide negotiations for international agreements to stabilize agricultural commodity markets. If world agreements were not reached, the enlarged Community would consult with those countries willing to reach them, and particularly with the Commonwealth countries, to make special arrangements.

The general review of agricultural policy brought to the fore by Britain's application for membership revealed another sharp conflict over agricultural policy within the Six themselves. Illustrative of the cross-currents of world politics, this involved another collision between the French and the Germans similar to the one which early in 1962 delayed for a time the Market's moving on to its second stage. The French exported agricultural products but imported little of them. The Germans imported large quantities of agricultural products but exported little of them. The Rome treaty provided that the Community might undertake and finance agricultural export subsidies, price-support arrangements, and structural improvements in Community agriculture to prevent surpluses from arising. These would be financed by Community funds, which accumulated largely out of levies raised on imports from the outside world. The French pointed out that the Germans, as the heaviest importers of foodstuffs in the EEC, received the bulk of the levies on imported foodstuffs. After 1970 all levies held for the Community reverted to the national governments the year after the budget year in which they were not spent. The spending of Community funds for agricultural export subsidies, agricultural price supports, and so forth were among those decisions which even after 1970 required a unanimous vote of the Council of Ministers on recommendation of the Economic Commission. The French, with evidence that the Germans did not propose to use "their" accumulating levies "to subsidize French agriculture," demanded assurances that the Germans would not veto the use of Community funds for agricultural support measures. In short, before the French agreed to some of the British proposals for liberalizing Commonwealth agricultural imports into the Common Market, they wanted guarantees that the Germans would not stand in the way of the Community's taking and paying for measures to stabilize and subsidize the agriculture of Common Market countries.

In the belief that Britain's entry into the Common Market was assured, the United States in 1962 revolutionized its own trade policies. It was clear that the old trade-agreement type of law, which had become customary since Cordell Hull's reciprocal trade legislation in 1934, would no longer meet the demands of the world situation. In the future, trade legislation would have to cover a longer period of time, include a larger number of negotiable items, permit more drastic slashes in rates, give the President the authority to negotiate with the EEC and other developing common markets in "across-the-board" bargaining rather than in individual items, and surrender the American practice of unilaterally rescinding cuts according to a "peril point" formula. Some notable Americans like Dean Acheson, Christian Herter, and William L. Clayton advocated virtual membership in the Common Market as a step toward an Atlantic Community. But the Kennedy administration moved instead for an enormously liberalized trade-agreement act.

The Reciprocal Trade Agreements Act or Trade Expansion Act of 1962 authorized the President to reduce existing tariffs as much as 50 per cent and to eliminate them entirely on goods in which the United States and the Common Market together constituted 80 per cent of world trade. The Common Market and other countries, of course, would have to make like concessions in return. The "peril point" practice was abolished. An adjustment assistance program provided federal payments of up to $62 a week for a full year to workers made jobless because of import competition. It also made available federal loans, technical assistance, and some tax concessions for industries suffering from the increases in competitive imports.

Although platoons of protectionists paraded before Senate and House committees in intense opposition to the bill, the new departure was taken with little debate and surprising consensus. Thus with little stir did the United States abandon its protective tariff policy which had prevailed since the Civil War but which had been undergoing erosion since the reciprocal trade program of the mid-1930's.

Despite the many national controls over a broadening variety of economic matters in most countries, the world seemed headed for an era of the widest international free trade since the 1840's and 1850's, when Manchester economics was dominant, Britain was abolishing the last of its old mercantilistic restrictions, and the United States was under the low-tariff Walker Act. The protective tariff systems in vogue in the late nineteenth and early twentieth centuries in most industrial countries and the nationalist, autarchic, neo-mercantilist practices so pervasive in the period between the two world wars seemed to be dying. This was an amazing revival of liberalism, which had to fight the old mercantilism on the one hand and adjust to the new national social controls and international commodity agreements on the other, and it was, among other things, a delayed and positive response to the Communist challenge.

The contrast in the United States between the climate of opinion on world trading matters in the late 1940's and in the early

1960's was striking. In the late 1940's the United States was encouraging freer world trade and particularly intra-European economic cooperation but was actually most guarded in liberalizing its own trade policies; in the beginning 1960's the initiative in liberalizing European and even world trade policies came not from Washington but from Europe, and Washington was responding to European leadership. Even though, as we shall soon see, some of this met a ruthless Gaullist rebuff, it still appeared likely that in the long run autarchic forces in the Common Market would not prevail, that in the end the trend to liberalize world trade would continue.

Although the opposition within Britain to that nation's joining the Common Market was formidable and all the obstacles set up by the Six had not yet been hurdled, it appeared reasonably certain as late as the fall of 1962 that Britain would become a member of the Common Market. However, there remained a disposition in the United States to see only the achievements of the Common Market and not its internal difficulties. The economic integration of Western Europe was still not assured, and its political unity was even less so. The road ahead would still be arduous. Just how much of the difficulty was caused by the highly personal policies of De Gaulle would be hard to determine until after he left office. But the importance of the De Gaulle personality was again a reminder of the impact of the largely adventitious and imponderable factor of charismatic leadership in human affairs.

Gaullist Crisis in the Western Alliance

In the winter of 1962-1963, President de Gaulle vetoed Britain's entry into the Common Market and made it quite clear that what he wanted was not a tripartite directorate for NATO or a multilateral NATO nuclear force but his own *force de frappe*, his own independent nuclear "deterrent." This action produced a dramatic crisis for the Western alliance which would have repercussions for years to come.

De Gaulle had been increasingly critical of the Kennedy-McNamara policy in NATO of "controlled response" to a possible Soviet attack in Europe. Did not this virtually tell the Soviets that the worst they need to expect from an attack in Europe was a conventional counter attack? And did not this destroy the most essential factor of the American deterrent—its credibility? Now that the Russians were rapidly building a second strike capacity, would the Americans ever be willing to expand a conventional ground war in Europe into a nuclear war, thus inviting a counter nuclear attack by the Russians and the destruction of American cities, in a war which up to the time had been confined to Europe? On the other hand, De Gaulle was impressed with the willingness of the Americans to threaten nuclear war in a situation in which they were immediately and closely concerned, as illustrated by the Cuban crisis of October. This Cuban crisis also underscored for De Gaulle the high effectiveness of nuclear diplomacy for a nuclear power which dared play it. De Gaulle was more convinced than ever that a country without its own nuclear force was no "power" at all. The Nassau agreement of December 1962 between President Kennedy and Prime Minister Macmillan also had a marked influence on De Gaulle. In this agreement, Britain, under pressure from the United States, reluctantly gave up the arrangement whereby the United States was to furnish Britain at cost with the American Air Force's Skybolt missile, which was to have carried British nuclear warheads and been fired from British bombers (and thus have constituted the basis for Britain's own nuclear deterrent) and instead would receive Polaris missiles which would be used by Britain's prospective submarine fleet and be committed to a NATO nuclear force except when Britain's "supreme national interest supervened." De Gaulle was reported to believe that Britain had been "double-crossed" by the United States, that under duress Britain had really surrendered its own independent nuclear force. De Gaulle seemed to resent the fact that the British, instead of reacting to the American "rebuff" by cooperating more closely with France in nuclear matters, had elected to continue their "special connection" with the United States. Some observers believe that it was at this point that De Gaulle decided to switch from delaying tactics to outright veto of Britain's entry into the Common Market.

By the winter of 1962-1963 President de Gaulle was in a much strengthened position. The war in Algeria had come to an end. In late October of 1962 De Gaulle had won a national referendum, which declared in favor of electing the French President by popular vote rather than by just 80,000 local officials. (De Gaulle was stronger among the people than among the politicians and the parties.) The tenaciously held prejudice of republican France against a strong executive, a possible man on horseback—a repetition of Bonaparte and Louis Napoleon or a McMahon and Boulanger threat—was at last overcome. De Gaulle had won out over most of the newspapers, the farm associations, the labor unions, the politicians, and the old-line political parties. A few weeks later, in November, De Gaulle gained another decisive victory when in the parliamentary elections his personal party won a majority in the National Assembly, something which had eluded every other party in French history. Most of the other parties were smashed, although the Communist party managed to retain considerable strength. Dozens of France's most prominent political leaders of the past were swept out of office. Not since Napoleon III had a ruler of France wielded so much personal power.

On January 14, 1963, De Gaulle held an audience for the benefit of the world press, and with éclat he declared that Britain should be kept out of the Common Market, and that France had no interest in joining the Nassau agreement or in a NATO nuclear force and would pursue its own national nuclear "deterrent." Britain, declared De Gaulle, was not "a good European," and would not fit harmoniously into a continental system.

The third week in January, Adenauer journeyed to Paris and on January 21 a special Franco-West German alliance was signed. The treaty had been in the making for several months. The Fouchet commission's project of "a Europe of the states," which had finally been shelved by Benelux and Italian reluctance to move forward to a political consummation until after Britain's inclusion in the Common Market, was now by-passed in favor of a special alliance between West Germany and France. This version had the advantage that the British could not get into the scheme whether they got into the Common Market or not. The treaty of alliance provided for regular meetings at all levels, ranging from at least twice-yearly encounters between the heads of state to monthly meetings of high officials from all the ministries except the economic ones. Military cooperation was to involve closer ties between the French and German chiefs of staff, combined maneuvers, the exchange of officers and of units, and the joint development and production of weapons. (Government spokesmen in Paris pointed out that nuclear collaboration was excluded by other treaties.) The treaty recommended that the parties should seek analogous positions in NATO and the European Economic Community. For Chancellor Adenauer, the signing of the treaty must have seemed a consummation of the vision of a life time. In 1919, after World War I, and again after World War II, Adenauer had maintained that Franco-German reconciliation should be the first law of European politics. For his efforts in behalf of such a reconciliation he had been bitterly termed "a separatist." Now, in 1963, as his life goal came to apparent fruition, there was, in the words of the *Economist*, much that was bitter and tragic, for Franco-German amity was coming about in a way which identified it with De Gaulle's campaign to drive American and British influence altogether out of continental Europe. It was not an innocent display of international brotherhood but "a move in a Gaullist game—the game, even in 1963, of straight power politics."

The last week in January of 1963, on the heels of the Paris-Bonn treaty of alliance, the French, by insisting that Britain's application for membership in the Common Market be shelved indefinitely for future study by the Six, finally succeeded in ending the Brussels negotiations. All of the five other members favored continuing the negotiations, but France was adamant, and her veto, under the terms of the Rome treaty, stuck. However, it was felt that the months of negotiation and the agreements hammered out with the British had not been altogether wasted, that many of the decisions tentatively made would be applicable at a later date when Britain, under more "normal circumstances," would again apply for membership.

It would be a mistake to assume that De Gaulle was alone in his opposition to Britain's admission, that he was indulging a mere personal whim. A number of elements supported De Gaulle: those who wanted the European Community to be truly European and not world-oriented; industrialists in France, West Germany, Belgium, and Italy who did not want to compete with British manufacturers on equal terms within the Common Market and who feared that American capital might invest more heavily in Britain in order to get the free trade benefits within the Common Market; French farmers and West German farmers who wanted Common

Market external tariffs which would penalize American, Commonwealth, and Latin American produce in favor of French and German produce; those West Germans who feared that numerous concessions to the agricultural Commonwealth countries would create a situation in which Common Market funds would have to be used for Common Market agricultural stabilization, with French agriculture the chief beneficiary.

However, in many quarters within the Common Market, there was grave disappointment at Britain's exclusion. Numerous industrial and agricultural groups had looked forward to free access to British markets. Eurocrats feared that the bad feeling engendered by the French veto would retard the whole movement to European economic and political coordination. Labor unions, Socialists, and liberal democratic elements were apprehensive about De Gaulle's authoritarian concepts and feared their spread to other countries in Western Europe. Italy, the Netherlands, Belgium, and Luxembourg deplored the revival of "big power" politics and were deeply concerned that Britain was not to be a member of the European Community and not to be in a position to act as a counterweight to France and Germany.

Nevertheless, the exclusion of Britain was not likely to prevent the continued economic growth of the Common Market. None of the Six was likely to secede. The truth was that the Common Market had become a howling success. In 1962 the Common Market poured 80 million tons of steel compared to the United States' 98 million; it was the world's second largest producer of automobiles; it was first in world imports, second only to the United States in exports. The economies of the Common Market countries were growing at the rate of 5 per cent annually compared to the 2.3 per cent of the United States.

However, the Gaullist methods and drive to power were likely to slow down the economic integration of the Common Market. The essence of the Community's methods had been compromise and mutual concession, with no member running roughshod over the interests of another. De Gaulle had violated all of this; he had set dangerous precedents; he had in effect invited other members to operate in similar fashion. The trend to political supranationalism would almost certainly be arrested, and there was small hope that in the immediate future a common executive for ECSC, Euratom, and the Common Market would be established, or a popularly elected European Assembly created, or a Community capital founded to centralize the work carried on at Strasbourg, Luxembourg, and Brussels.

What was the real attitude of the West Germans toward the Gaullist policies? The Franco-West German treaty was welcomed by a majority of the three parties in the Bundestag as being an agreement between two nations which did not at all prejudice Germany's relations with the rest of the world. They argued that the treaty did not constitute a West German choice between France on the one hand and Britain and America on the other. The West Germans fully realized that they were dependent on the United States for military defense, that De Gaulle's nuclear force was less than two per cent of the nuclear striking power of the United States and in fact was no deterrent at all, that the Russians knew that De Gaulle's obsolescent bombers, in the face of the Soviet's advanced nuclear and missile technology, would not get through to discharge a single nuclear warhead. The Germans did not take seriously De Gaulle's reputed belief that Khrushchev would hand over East Germany in return for the recognition of the Oder-Neisse line. (And De Gaulle himself probably did not believe this, or want it; it was a sop to the Germans, the feeding of a hope that De Gaulle knew would come to nothing, thus leaving intact the *status quo*, the partition of Germany.) What reason would Khrushchev have for doing for De Gaulle what he had steadfastly refused to do for anybody else?

Why did the West Germans play along with De Gaulle? There were a number of motives and elements involved. There were those like Adenauer with a deep but unavowed emotional attachment to the old Charlemagne tradition, to Catholic Little Europe. There was the satisfaction of being courted, as an equal, after the many years of semi-ostracism. There was Bonn's dissatisfaction with Washington at not being consulted as often as it had been in Dulles' day. There was the feeling that if West Germany went along with De Gaulle, the latter would not revive his drive for an American-British-French directorate of NATO, which would leave Germany in an inferior position. There was the urge to play France and the United States off against each other for German support, thereby increasing West Germany's bargaining power to secure a genuinely multilateral NATO nuclear deterrent (for since West Germany was debarred by treaties from having its own nuclear weapons, the next best thing was a NATO deterrent in the administration of which the Germans would have a large voice), and to diminish the possibility of a "deal" by the United States and Russia at the "expense" of Germany. (Thus the Germans were using De Gaulle, who doubtless wished to keep Germany partitioned by making no agreement at all, in order to prevent the United States and Britain from consenting to a formalization of that partition by agreement.) There was the hope in some quarters that West Germany might get access to nuclear weapons or at least the opportunity to develop nuclear military technology through close Franco-German military collaboration. Again, there was an inner confidence that in the end it would be Germany and not France that would dominate Little Europe. Finally, there were the economic interests which thought they stood more to gain from a more restricted Common Market than from a more extensive one. These economic forces seemed to be as strong as those which thought they would gain more from a wider Common Market. This was the reason why Adenauer did not forthrightly oppose De Gaulle's veto of Britain's admission to the Common Market (as Britons and Americans expected and hoped he would do) and why no German political leader came forward to challenge vigorously Adenauer's Janus-faced course.

The Russians naturally welcomed rifts in the Western alliance and any slowing down of economic and political integration in Western Europe. They saw the differences among the Western Allies as confirmation of the Leninist thesis that "the capitalist-imperialist countries" would tear themselves to pieces in their mutual rivalries and conflicts. However, the dominant reaction in Moscow was a different one. The Soviets saw De Gaulle as "an adventurer" who had "delusions about taming German militarism with traps." The Russians feared the eventual take-over of the Paris-Bonn Axis by the Germans, the whetting of German "ravanchism," the "arming of Hitler generals with atomic weapons." The Russians dismissed De Gaulle's "grand design" of an eventual European order reaching to the Urals (an idea De Gaulle got from his intellectual mentor, André Malraux, who believed that aggressive China would eventually push Rusisa to *rapprochement* with

Western Europe) as grandiose nonsense. Doubtless the Russians believed that if such Chinese developments took place they would need to be countered by *rapprochement* not with a Gaullist Europe but with the United States, the seat of effective nuclear power.

Nevertheless, in the short run, as long as De Gaulle was in office, the Soviet Union on occasion could be counted on to attempt to play France and the United States off against each other just as West Germany was doing. And since it was in Russia's power, and in her power alone, to permit the reunification of Germany, the time might conceivably come when Russia would play its trump card and win Germany against both France and the United States (and the West generally), although that was not at all probable in the forseeable future. Incidentally, European wiseacres in power politics believed that the United States, by constantly advertising its inflexibility and intransigence with respect to Russia, was throwing away its own trump card—that is, letting West Germany and France understand that in fact it had a decisive capacity, if it chose to use it, to play one ally off against another, and Russia off against Western Europe or any country in Western Europe. Some of this indicated that multidiplomacy had in fact returned, and all of it indicated that the habit of thought of the old multiple balance of power had not died.

For Britain, rejection by the Common Market represented a serious economic setback. The British had counted on an increase in continental markets and a consequent enhanced flow of American and other foreign capital investments into Britain to stimulate their rate of economic growth, which lagged behind that of the Common Market countries. To counter the blow, Britain would need to bargain shrewdly with the Common Market as an outsider; encourage American, Commonwealth, and world trade; perhaps even lower its own barriers to trade in unilateral fashion; reactivate the Outer Seven; and increase the economy and efficiency of its own production.

For the Kennedy administration, Gaullism posed the gravest perplexities. The setback to European unity was a shock to Americans. The United States had counted on British membership in the Common Market not only to widen Europe's markets but to provide outward-looking leadership that would help liberalize Common Market trade policies with the United States, Commonwealth countries, and Latin America. Much of the Trade Agreements Act of 1962 had been written with this in mind, and the United States had looked hopefully to expanded American and world trade to stimulate its rate of economic growth, ease its balance-of-payments difficulties, and provide an economic surplus for increased Western aid to the underdeveloped countries. But instead of the prospect of increasingly liberalized world trade, the United States feared it now faced the prospect of a Common Market which at least temporarily threatened economic autarchy rather than extended economic cooperation. America's agricultural markets in continental Europe seemed in particular to be immediately threatened; and De Gaulle was moving to policies which would limit American capital investments in France, possibly in other Common Market countries. De Gaulle's Europe, too, looked more and more like a white man's club, with a French-speaking African adjunct, which if it did not actually pursue policies of neo-colonialism would prefer to keep its new wealth to itself rather than sharing it.

It appeared to Americans that De Gaulle was wilfully stimulating national selfishness and power politics in its worst sense, drawing the United States into a tug of war with France for the friendship of West Germany, and encouraging not only West Germany but other European countries to demand more from the United States. (In early 1963 Spain suddenly raised the ante for American bases.) Worst of all, it seemed that Europeans were losing sight of the Communist threat and increasingly operating as though it did not exist.

Despite their own defeat, the British advised the Americans not to withdraw petulantly from the struggle and asked their friends in the Common Market not to waste their strength in retaliatory gestures but instead to wage a holding operation and keep steadily in mind the ultimate goal of an Atlantic Community in which Western Europe and America would be equal partners and not, as De Gaulle appeared to see them, as competitors in a world power market. Meantime, the United States should press ahead with the new tariff-slashing provisions of the 1962 Trade Agreements Act or Trade Expansion Act and negotiate freer trade arrangements with the British and with the Common Market. If

Britain had got into the Common Market that Act would have allowed the President a wide range of items on which to bargain for deep tariff cuts, as much as 50 per cent on all items and complete abolition of duties on goods for which the United States and the European Economic Community together were responsible for 80 per cent of world trade. With Britain out, the 50 per cent cut still applied, but the chance of total elimination of duties virtually disappeared. In early 1963 a bill was introduced in the United States Congress to extend the range of items on which the President would be empowered to negotiate for a total abolition of tariffs even with Britain outside the Common Market. Armed with this power, it would be difficult for De Gaulle to keep closed the tariff door, especially after 1966, when the third stage of the Common Market would come into operation and voting procedures would no longer allow France alone to block tariff cuts favored by the other five members.

The United States was faced squarely with giving its allies a larger voice in the control of nuclear weapons. It was clear that America could no longer virtually direct the Western alliance, that the views of Western Europeans would have to be given more weight. Concretely and for the immediate future this involved greater sharing of the control of nuclear weapons and decisions affecting them. The United States was still reluctant to disseminate nuclear weapons, and there was a tacit agreement with the Soviet Union that the United States would not supply West Germany with such weapons and Russia would not supply China with them. The rational way out of the difficulty was for the United States, Britain, France, and the Soviet Union to make international agreements outlawing or rigidly controlling nuclear weapons. But such a rational solution did not appear to be in the offing, and meantime France would cooperate even less effectively with the Western alliance, and West Germany would slow down fulfilling its commitments, unless the United States loosened its hold on its nuclear monopoly. Accordingly, early in 1963 the Kennedy administration proposed expanding and making more explicit the Nassau agreement. The American plan envisaged both a NATO Nuclear Force (NNF) and a sea-borne Multilateral Nuclear Force (MLF).

NNF would be made up of strategic nuclear forces which the United States and Britain would assign to NATO's Supreme

Allied Commander for Europe. The British would assign their bomber command, the United States three Polaris submarines. Britain and the United States would transfer rights over the fire-power of these forces to NATO's Supreme Allied Commander for Europe, who would have first call on their services. The British would continue to own the planes and the Americans the submarines. They would be manned and serviced by officers and men of the British and United States forces. The British could withdraw their bombers and the Americans their submarines any time either country believed its supreme national interests made this necessary. France agreed to cooperate but not to throw any of its national nuclear force into the NATO pool.

MLF vessels and missiles would be internationally owned, either by NATO or by a consortium of the NATO members contributing to it. Polaris missiles would be mounted, eight or less to a ship, on twenty-five or more surface vessels, which would be more vulnerable but less costly than submarines. The crews would lose their identities as Americans, British, Germans, Italians, or whatever, to become members of the NATO Legion with distinctive uniforms and flag. The United States would expect the European members of the force to pay more than half of the initial and continuing costs of the fleet. Any participant, including the United States, would have the right to veto a firing order.

Difficult problems involving the sharing of costs of the MLF force and the nature of the control over it continued. The West Germans proposed eventual abandonment of unanimity, that is the veto, including the American veto, in favor of majority rule in the multilateral deterrent's controlling committee, but they did not ask for majority control right away. If the West German proposal were adopted, what was envisaged by the United States as a deterrent of additional national deterrents, governed by a United States veto, would escape from the United States veto, but not from the United States influence. The West Germans again proposed that the United States should equip all its NATO allies, including West Germany, with tactical atomic weapons if it issued such weapons to its own troops. All of these plans, projects, and discussions about multilateral nuclear forces illustrated vividly that in the future the United States would have to share more of the nuclear decisions with its allies than it had done in the past.

In the meantime, in the spring of 1963, the United States withdrew its Jupiter missiles from Turkey and Italy and instead began deploying three Polaris submarines, presumably the starter for the projected NATO nuclear force, in Mediterranean waters. But the United States discovered that its allies were not at all eager to furnish bases for the Polaris submarines. The Italians held off from furnishing bases, and Spain demanded membership in NATO as a condition for any granting of Rota as a Polaris base. The United States was forced to fall back on using the Holy Loch base in Scotland as the overseas maintenance point for the Mediterranean group. (About this same time, even America's good ally, Canada, gave the United States defense headaches when the Diefenbaker government, after having accepted American-made defense weapons, the Bomarc-B missiles and the F101 jet interceptors, hesitated to take the nuclear warheads, under American custody and control, without which the carriers would operate at far less effectiveness. This issue produced a political crisis and a Canadian national election in which anti-Americanism played a part, but a close vote resulted in a defeat for Diefenbaker and the elevation to the premiership of Lester Pearson, a creative leader in world affairs.)

There seemed to be several views in Western Europe with respect to the nuclear deterrent. The French favored an independent national deterrent. The West Germans strongly pressed for a genuinely multilateral NATO deterrent. It was the attitude of France and West Germany which produced the crisis in the Western alliance. The British seemed inclined to give up their own independent nuclear deterrent; they trusted the American deterrent and were willing to cooperate fully in a multilateral NATO deterrent. Most Europeans disagreed with De Gaulle. They felt that the American nuclear arsenal was indeed a deterrent, and that if in fact it failed to deter, the Americans would if necessary use it in a counterattack in defense of Europe. It would be difficult to frighten Europeans with even the bugbear of an American return to isolation. An increasing number of Europeans suspected that even if the United States retreated to its Western Hemisphere bastion that America's nuclear power would continue to deter the Russians, and if not, that in the event of a Russian attack in Europe the Americans would probably employ their nuclear arsenal against the Soviet Union. Perhaps even deeper was the feeling in Europe that the peak of the twentieth century's crisis had been passed, that for a number of reasons—the nuclear deterrent was just one of them—there was less and less likelihood of a Communist attack anywhere in Europe. This enveloping feeling was most frustrating to Americans and it increased the difficulties of impressing on Europeans their responsibility for assuming a fair share of the sacrifices and costs of the West's defense.

America's difficulties with its Western allies underscored the fact that the postwar's bipolarization had been greatly impaired, that depolarization had progressed so far as to produce if not a multiple balance of power at least a vigorous multidiplomacy. During its full-scale participation in world politics—during World War I, World War II, and the height of the Cold War—the United States in the final analysis could almost always rely on a common danger and a common enemy to weld its allies together and induce those allies to defer to American leadership. But now for the first time, the United States was faced with "normality" in world politics, with all its flux, shifts, instability of combinations, conflicting cross currents within alliances, even byplays among members of opposing alliances. The United States had never before been forced to operate fully in the give-and-take of hard diplomacy and power politics, but in the future its ability to operate successfully in this fashion would be an acid test of its world leadership.

Troubles Among America's Allies in the Middle and Far East

Among America's military allies in the Middle and Far East there were difficulties. In Turkey, which never wavered in its loyalty to the Western alliances, a military coup in 1960 led by General Cemal Gürsel ousted the government of President Celâl Bayar and Premier Adnan Menderes and their conservative Democratic party. That party had ruled in an increasingly authoritarian manner and threatened to eliminate the opposition Republican People's party, the old party of Mustafa Kemal, which tended to push industrialization through state enterprises more vigorously than did the Democratic party. Gürsel became president, and former President Ismet Inönü, leader of the Republican People's party, backed by an uneasy two-party coalition, became premier. To those sensitive to the charge that most of the governments with which the United States was allied in the Middle and the Far East were conservative and authoritarian, it was hoped that the new Turkish government would develop democratic practices and recover the momentum of economic and social reform of the Kemalist era.

The weakest link in America's chain of military allies along the northern tier of the Middle East was Iran, with its backward semi-feudal society. The Shah was valiantly attempting to introduce basic economic and social reforms, but since the foundation of his own support and of the two major political parties which were allowed to operate came from the landed aristocracy and the big city merchants, there seemed little chance that the reforms would take place. Thus far the Shah's reforms had been merely token ones. The supporters of the old National Front of Mossadegh and of the old Tudeh party were working underground, and there was the ever-present possibility that a leftist revolution would occur and take Iran out of her alliance with the West and make her neutral. The Shah's ministers tended to lay the blame for all their troubles on the alleged inadequacy of American military and economic aid.

Afghanistan constituted a breach in the West's wall of military alliances from Turkey to Pakistan. The West had never been able to convert Afghanistan into a military ally. Indeed, that country adhered to a neutral position and received substantial economic aid from both the United States and the Soviet Union. But the Soviet Union gave more aid, gave it in a more spectacular way, and purchased many of Afghanistan's commodity surpluses. Besides, Khrushchev endorsed Afghanistan's claim to the Pushtu territory in neighboring Pakistan, but the United States could not afford to do this because Pakistan was its military ally.

Pakistan, like Turkey and Iran, was a member of CENTO, but in addition it was a member of SEATO. America's military and economic aid to Pakistan was equivalent to about 40 per cent of the Pakistani budget. But Pakistan was extremely poor, its social structure anachronistic, and in East Pakistan there were constant government upheavals. Pakistan was a bifurcated state, with its eastern province and its western provinces separated by the huge bulk of India. India-Pakistani relations were embittered by refugee problems, rancorous Hindu-Moslem animosities, the dispute over the Indus River waters, and conflicting claims to Kashmir.

A military coup by General Ayub Khan in October 1958 ousted the Pakistani civilian government, annulled the constitution, and dissolved the political parties. A little later General Ayub became president and proclaimed his intention to build democracy gradually from the grassroots and introduce basic land reforms. The United States was relieved when this summary military revolution turned out to be a stabilizing force committed to "basic democracy" and agrarian reforms. In 1960 the International Bank completed negotiations with India and Pakistan for the development of the Indus River Basin for hydroelectric and irrigation purposes at a cost of 1 billion dollars, the United States to contribute 280 million dollars in grants and loans. Nevertheless, Ayub was dissatisfied with the United States on a number of counts. The U-2 plane of Francis G. Powers had taken off from Pakistani territory and caused Pakistan much embarrassment. The United States refused to back Pakistan's position in Pushtu or its claim to Kashmir. Most important, Ayub was irritated that India, a neutral, annually got more than twice the American economic aid that Pakistan, a military ally, received. In 1961, Pakistan for the first time accepted some economic aid from the Soviet Union.

Of all America's allies the largest recipients of direct American military and economic aid were Chiang Kai-shek's Republic of China (Formosa or Taiwan and the Pescadores Islands) and Syngman Rhee's Republic of Korea (South Korea). Yet these two governments were also the most authoritarian non-Communist governments in the Far East. It was therefore an occasion for much American embarrassment when Thailand, one of the three Asian members of SEATO, became an authoritarian military state under Marshal Sarit Thanarat. The Marshal installed himself in supreme power in September 1957, and in October 1958 he abolished the constitution, declared martial law, and assumed personal control. Marshal Sarit Thanarat declared that the threat of Communism forced him to take over the government, but many observers believed that the real reason for his action was the growth in influence of Thailand's National Assembly and the fact that its hand-picked members were gradually being replaced by more self-assertive elected ones.

The course of events in South Korea was also discouraging. In the presidential election of 1960, President Rhee's opponent died a month before the poll, and the opposition to Rhee's increasingly police-state methods concentrated on re-electing Vice-President John M. Chang. Chang was defeated four to one in an election characterized by widespread fraud, intimidation, and violence. The resulting furor forced Rhee to resign and flee the country (April 1960). Special elections resulted in an anti-Rhee victory and Chang became premier. He abandoned Rhee's ambition to "march north" and by force unite North and South Korea. Chang sought for democratic reforms and attempted to curb the ramifying corruption, but in May 1961 he was deposed by a right-wing military junta headed by young General Chung Hee Park. Premier Chang and his cabinet were jailed for several months on the preposterous charges of encouraging the Communists. Park suppressed the politicians, waged a war on corruption, and curbed newspapers and university faculties and students even more rigorously than Rhee had done. The United States had opposed this military coup but later acquiesced in it. It seemed strange that in a showdown the United States had so little effective influence in a country which owed its very existence to a large expenditure of American lives and to impressive and continuing American military and economic support.

The United States was not even able always to control the situation in the country which came nearest to being an American puppet than any other. In May 1957 a wave of anti-American sentiment swept over Formosa, and in spite of Chiang Kai-shek's tight police methods, anti-American mobs in Taipei wrecked the American Embassy, the American Information building, and police headquarters, and injured a number of Americans.

Relations with Japan, America's most important ally in the Far East, were on the whole satisfactory but characterized by growing Japanese independence. Japan had experienced a remarkable economic recovery and even Peiping's petulant breaking off of all Chinese-Japanese trade relations in 1958 did not harm Japan as much as was expected. Japan's trade with the United States and most Western European countries continued to increase. The Japanese resented the "voluntary" limitation on their export of textiles, electrical goods, and tuna to the United States, which Japan imposed at Washington's request. Great Britain and other Western nations put restrictions on imports from Japan, which the Japanese felt was a violation of their rights as participants in the General Agreement on Tariffs and Trade (GATT). Japan retaliated by imposing restraints on American and other foreign goods. The United States in turn was sensitive about this and likewise believed that Japan was shirking her share of economic assistance to the underdeveloped countries. Nevertheless, the United States had become Japan's largest foreign market, and Japan, next to Canada, had become America's largest foreign market.

The most serious difficulty involved the continuance of the American-Japanese Security Treaty of 1951. In 1958 the United States removed all of its combat ground forces from Japan, for Japan's own modest defense force had grown considerably. (The Japanese government had not been able to muster the necessary two-thirds parliamentary majority to abrogate the Japanese constitutional provision in which Japan had renounced the maintenance of land, sea, and air forces. Japan's "defense force" was a questionable and inadequate circumvention of this provision.) The Security Treaty of 1951 allowed the United States a virtually free hand in disposing of its land, air, and sea forces in and about Japan as a contribution to Japanese and Far Eastern security. Neutralists in Japan, led by the large Socialist party and by leftist labor, teacher, and student organizations, carried on a campaign to terminate the treaty altogether, bar the introduction of atomic weapons into Japan, and require the United States to withdraw from Okinawa and other Ryukyu and Bonin Islands, which the United States retained under its direct control.

The Security Treaty was renegotiated in 1960 and some concessions were made to Japanese sentiments. Henceforth the United States would consult the Japanese government about any major changes in the deployment and equipment of its forces in that country as well as any use of American bases in Japan for combat operations. This meant, among other things, that Japan would have to be consulted before the United States undertook to introduce atomic weapons into the country or made use of its Japanese bases in repelling an attack on Formosa. But Japanese neutralists pointed out that there was no express statement of how far the United States would be obliged to abide by Japan's opinion once the consultations had taken place. Neutralist agitation against renewal of the treaty reached such a pitch and street mobs and demonstrations became so ominous that at the very last minute President Eisenhower was asked by the Japanese government to postpone his imminent visit to Tokyo. Nevertheless, the treaty was finally ratified in June 1960.

Despite these leftist demonstrations, Japanese opinion seemed to be moving to the right. Over the protests of the teachers' organizations, education was again becoming centralized and a new emphasis placed on "moral education" and patriotism. Women were being discouraged from entering the universities and public life. Wage scales remained pitifully low. There was a renewed emphasis on Shintoism. A movement was on foot to restore the Emperor to the headship of religion and to amend the Constitution to make the Emperor again sovereign and not merely a symbol. The Emperor had resumed the old practice of going to the shrine at Ise to report his activities to his ancestors. The Black Dragon Society, advocating larger armed forces and a restoration of the Imperial status, was openly re-established. Increasingly the progressive forces were rallying around the slogan: "Don't change one word of the MacArthur Constitution." Conservatives replied that they were not changing the MacArthur Constitution but merely adjusting it to the spirit of the Japanese genius.

The middle way seemed to be losing ground. The Democratic Socialist party was virtually dead and the large Socialist party was slowly losing electoral strength. Extreme rightist and extreme leftist forces were growing. On the right there was a proliferation of fringe organizations appealing to religious and patriotic fanaticism. On the left the Communist party reported a doubling of membership during 1961-1962.

All of this was not immediately alarming. It might represent merely a natural reaction to the breath-taking changes of the MacArthur days. On the other hand, it might indicate that not even yet had Japan escaped the long arm of her feudal past.

The behavior of the Philippines revealed the same tendencies which manifested themselves elsewhere—the difficulties of industrializing underdeveloped societies and the urge of small nations to be less dependent on the big powers in world politics. However, the Philippine Republic remained loyal to its American alliance. The death in 1957 in a plane crash of President Ramón Magsaysay, young, magnetic, dynamic, social-democratic, and fearlessly honest, was a tragedy to the Philippines and to the democratic cause in Asia. The administration of his successor, Carlos P. Garcia, was characterized by the usual tax evasion, corruption, and favoritism. Soon the Filipinos were experiencing the same difficulties as contemporary Latin Americans, the consequences of the refusal to bear the sacrifices required to pay for the capital and machinery of industrialization—dangerous inflation and balance-of-payment problems. President Garcia finally adopted an austerity program of limiting imports and fighting inflation.

American economic aid was generous, but the Filipinos did not think it was enough. A number of Filipinos, believing that the American-Philippine trade agreement, the preferential tariff treatment by each country to the products of the other, was harmful to the Philippines, supported a "Filipino First" movement. (Actually the tariff preferences were gradually being eliminated through the years and would end in 1974 unless a new agreement was made.) Other grievances of the Filipinos were the inactivity of SEATO, the failure to expand its economic and social activities, the growing belief that Britain and France were a drag on the organization and ought to drop out, the widespread feeling that Japan, the late enemy, was the most favored American ally in the Far East. There was, however, some tendency for the Philippine government itself to move closer to Japan in economic matters.

In 1959 an issue which had caused considerable American-Filipino friction was removed when the Bases Agreement of 1947 was superseded by a new agreement in which the United States withdrew from many of its bases and military reservations and thereafter would confine itself to only four major bases in the Philippines. Moreover, there would be increased consultations with the Philippine government over the operational use of these bases. This curtailment of American bases in the Philippines was part of a world-wide policy of the United States to gradually reduce the number of its foreign ground-force and air bases in favor of greater concentration on missiles.

In the Philippine presidential election of 1961, Diosdado Macapagal, who was opposed by the administration candidate, was elected president. This was a tribute to the vitality of democracy in the Philippines. Macapagal was in the social-democratic tradition of Magsaysay.

In the early 1960's the most serious crisis in an allied country was in South Vietnam (the Republic of Vietnam). Technically, Vietnam was not an ally, for along with North Vietnam (the Democratic Republic of Vietnam or Vietminh), Laos, and Cambodia it had been neutralized by the Geneva conference of 1954. However, the guerrilla war between Communists and non-Communists in South Vietnam had never entirely ceased, and the International Commission for Supervision and Control in Vietnam was even less effective than its counterpart in Laos. Since 1954 the United States had converted South Vietnam into a military ally and by late 1962 had poured nearly 2.5 billion dollars of military and economic aid into that country. To the Communist and neutralist complaints that it was violating the 1954 settlement, the United States replied that although it had indeed joined the other powers in guaranteeing that settlement, it was the conspicuous violation of the agreement by the Communists, particularly Vietminh and Red China, which had forced the Americans to take action.

The Viet Cong guerrillas spearheaded the Communist drive in South Vietnam. They were largely an indigenous peasant organization. Wherever they operated they lived on the local peasantry. If the villagers were unsympathetic they terrorized them. Their most extensive stronghold was in the south, in the Mekong delta region along the Cambodian border. In 1961 the Viet Cong established new strongholds in the northern areas closer to Vietminh, from which they received much support. The Communists of Laos, growing stronger in 1960 and early 1961 (before the Laotian peace settlement of 1962), also lent support to the Viet Cong.

South Vietnam's President, Ngo Dinh Diem, like Syngman Rhee and Chiang Kai-shek, was a strong-willed man with whom it was difficult to deal. His rule was authoritarian, and many non-Communist Vietnamese criticized his government for tolerating widespread corruption and being too much of a family affair. He showed little interest in the peasants and resisted economic and social reforms. Yet no other leader of Ngo's ability had appeared to challenge him. In November 1960 Ngo narrowly escaped both assassination and removal from office by dissatisfied military elements in his own army. In April 1961 he was reelected in spite of the efforts of the Communists and democratic leftists to unseat him.

As the Viet Cong gained ground in 1961, the Kennedy administration wanted to help South Vietnam more effectively. Overt American military intervention was considered. Elements in the United States opposed to American military intervention in Laos were not opposed to such intervention in South Vietnam if it seemed necessary to save that country from the Communists. But President Ngo, always sensitive about American pressures on his government, told Vice-President Lyndon B. Johnson, who had been sent by President Kennedy to survey the situation, that he did not want American combat forces but only an increase in economic and military assistance. Later Ngo informed General Maxwell D. Taylor that he would be glad to have American troops for logistics and communications purposes only. Still later he apparently welcomed additional American military help.

By late 1962 the United States had boosted its military advisers and technicians in Vietnam to more than 10,000 men and was spending 1 million dollars a day to beat the Viet Cong. It was arming and training 130,000 members of the Vietnam Civil Guard and Defense Corps and the augmented Vietnam regular army of 200,000 men. The emphasis was on training for guerrilla warfare, on which a segment of the American armed forces had been belatedly specializing. Much use was made of helicopters armed with machine guns and rockets. A vast strategic hamlet program was under way. Its aim was to concentrate the rural population in fortified villages, thus depriving the Viet Cong guerrillas of the supplies and shelter they had long exacted from the peasants. Although the Viet Cong repeatedly attacked these strategic hamlets they had been unable to subdue any of them. The strategic hamlet program was giving the peasants their first experience in self-government. Bolstered by United States economic aid, the experiment had also brought teachers, doctors, and agricultural advisers to remote areas. One top Vietnam official observed that a social revolution was taking place, that a whole new scale of values was being acquired by the peasants.

Without doubt the war against the Viet Cong was at last going much better. Ngo's troops were no longer on the defensive; for the first time the Vietnam army was making major offensive sweeps against the Viet Cong. But there were still grave difficulties. The relocation of peasants in the strategic hamlets was resented by many of them, and undoubtedly normal agricultural activities and productivity in some areas had been seriously impaired. The Viet Cong was still strong enough to cut off rice and rubber shipments from large parts of the interior. Vietnam's gold and foreign exchange reserves dipped dangerously. Ngo was still in no mood to relax his authoritarian rule and resented American suggestions that he undertake programs of permanent economic and social reform.

Aside from Thailand's abandonment of its experiment with democracy when Marshal Sarit Thanarat became dictator, conditions in southeastern Asia were looking up for the Western democracies. As we have seen, the war against the Communists was going better in South Vietnam. Peace was made in Laos in 1962. In Malaya the twelve-year war with the Communist insurgents, beginning back in 1948, had been won, and the state of emergency was ended in 1961. Malaya, under the able leadership of Premier Tengku Abdul Rahman, had become an independent nation within the British Commonwealth in 1957, and Singapore, despite its large Chinese, Communist, and left-wing population, had voted in a popular referendum in 1962 to join the Federation of Malaysia. In late 1963 North Borneo, Sarawak, and Brunei would complete their federation with Malaya and Singapore, and then the Federation of Malaysia would form a 1600-mile crescent around the South China Sea. Malaya was neutralist (although oriented to the West) and not a member of the West's system of military alliances.

However, events in southeast Asia in 1963 emphasized the continuing instability of that area. The war in South Vietnam took a turn for the worse after the Viet Cong learned how to decoy and ambush helicopter landings. The tenuous truce in Laos was repeatedly violated and the Communists seemed gaining in strength. It was felt in some informed quarters that the United States had waited too long to back a neutralist government in Laos and that it had never found the personnel and program to reach the mass of peasants in Vietnam and Laos. And the consummation of the Malaysian Federation was troubled by a revolt in Brunei, the claim of the Philippines to North Borneo, and the ambitions of Indonesia for all three of the northern Borneo territories—Sarawak, Brunei, and North Borneo. This in turn threatened discord among the Philippines, Indonesia, and the new Federation of Malaysia.

Latin America at the Time of the Castro Revolution

In addition to some difficulties with its allies in Europe and Asia, the United States was increasingly under fire in Latin America. The Castro revolution in Cuba was not only a formidable challenge in itself but combined with the combustible economic and social ferment throughout Latin America it might well undermine American influence in much of the Western Hemisphere. Never in all its history had the United States been so embattled in its own bailiwick.

In most of Latin America the rising expectations of the masses were in conflict with the old order, and the traditional oligarchies were being spectacularly challenged. It was increasingly hazardous to flout openly the popular aspirations. There were fewer old-fashioned right-wing military dictatorships, and those that appeared were usually shorter lived than they had been in the nineteenth and early twentieth centuries. Even the conservatives had to go through the motions of promising reforms. There was still the old habit of elevating "grand personalities," but now the *caudillo* was more likely to come from the ranks of politicians on-the-make than from the great landowners or the generals. But the old elites still knew how to manage and control elections; when they lost to popular parties they still had all sorts of ways of sabotaging popular administrations; and not infrequently elections resulting in popular victories were subverted or even countermanded by the military.

The magic panacea of democratic, leftist, Peronist, and even some right-wing parties was now industrialization. For democratic parties industrialization meant a wider middle class, for leftist parties a more extensive welfare state, and for rightists the chance to develop a plutocracy. Lavish promises to bring the benefits of industrialization in a hurry were now the basis of great mass movements which sometimes combined some rightist elements with pervasive labor and leftist elements, as did Peronism.

Now, capitalist economies and socialist economies had very definite but different ways of accumulating capital, and both systems understood that this involved saving and sacrifice. A mixed economy like India, too, took into account the difficulties of capital accumulation, and there was a general understanding that there was no easy path to capital accumulation and that to make the historic breakthrough to industrialism involved heroic measures. But in Latin America there was the curious notion that the "take-off" to industrialism could be achieved without much pain, that the benefits of industrialism could be enjoyed prematurely and the costs postponed indefinitely. The mass movements which had supported Vargas in Brazil and Perón in Argentina were particularly infected with this virus, but at least such movements represented popular aspirations and were concerned that the benefits of industrialism were not confined to an elite but were spread instead throughout the whole population, including particularly "the shirtless ones."

Where conservatives and rightists spearheaded industrialization there was more regard for the orthodox capitalist ways of accumulating capital, but rightists were intent on guiding industrialization in such a way that the old aristocracies were converted into new plutocracies, that the traditional class system was not impaired but instead fortified, as it had been when Japan industrialized in the nineteenth century. But in the twentieth century it was much more difficult to direct an industrial revolution on such class lines, and many rightists, for instance those in Paraguay and most of the big landowners in Argentina, Chile, and Peru, tended to oppose industrialization itself for fear that it would inevitably undermine their privileges.

There was, then, a great danger that the mass of people, frustrated in their expectations by the repeated failures of such movements as Peronism to bring industrialism in a quick and easy way and by the dilatory tactics of rightists opposing industrialization or attempting to convert it into a class plutocracy, would eventually turn to Communism or extremist upheavals of indigenous variety.

From the point of view of democratic gradualism, slow and steady economic progress and developing stability, the Latin American countries which stood out were little Costa Rica; Mexico, which had made basic reforms during its long revolution from 1910 to 1940; and Puerto Rico, which had been undergoing fundamental economic and social changes since its Operation Bootstrap beginning in the early 1940's.

In Colombia and Venezuela the late 1950's and early 1960's had brought changes for the better. In Colombia, President Alberto Lleras Camargo with great tact presided over an uneasy political truce after a conflict between rightists and leftists which for almost a decade (1948-1957) had torn the country asunder in bloody civil war, although Colombia's rich still felt so insecure that they continued to keep millions of dollars in Swiss banks—enough money, it was said, to capitalize Colombia's industrial revolution without foreign aid. In Venezuela, the corrupt and brutal right-wing dictatorship of Pérez Jiménez (1952-1958) had given way to the social-democratic regime of President Rómulo Betancourt, who undertook land reform, the breaking up of large estates, the distribution of land to poor farmers, the mechanization of agriculture, the building of hydroelectric and irrigation projects—and with prudent concern that the country not incur debts beyond its capacity to pay them. However, Betancourt was still beset by the inflation inherited from Pérez and by bitter opposition from both right and left.

But elsewhere the situation was less encouraging. In Cuba, Fulgencio Batista was in the midst of his second dictatorship. His first (1934-1944) had been mild and characterized by progressive measures, but his second (1952-1959) was corrupt, reactionary, cruel, and terroristic. In Haiti, the most hopeless land in Latin America where three hundred people to the square mile sought to eke out a living on the exhausted soil, François Duvalier was tightening his dictatorship. In the Dominican Republic, Rafael Trujillo still maintained his savage tyranny. Guatemala was ruled by an erratic right-wing dictatorship, and in Honduras, the most backward land in Central America, the government was even more erratic. In El Salvador, the grip of the ruling families was loosening, and in 1960 a conservative president was ousted by a left-wing military junta, which was succeeded by another military junta, less leftist, a few months later. In Nicaragua, the younger Somoza continued the right-wing dictatorship of his father. In the Panama election of 1960, Roberto F. Chiari, representing those elements of the oligarchy hostile to the United States, was elected president.

In South America, Ecuador was characterized by instability. The reform President Galo Plaza had been followed by a clerical rightist, who was followed in 1960 by the volatile and opportunistic Velasco Ibarra. In Peru, the oligarchy was increasingly threatened by the growing popularity of the social-democratic *apristas*. In Bolivia, the part-Peronist and part-leftist movement of President Paz Estensoro was in power and had discovered that nationalizing the tin mines and some land reform were not enough to put that impoverished country on the road to economic stability. In Chile, the conservatives were back in power and carrying on an anti-inflation austerity program to pay for the industrialization measures undertaken by the long rule of the Popular Front (1938-1952). Demands for land and tax reforms were increasing, the *fundo* system was not providing the food necessary to sustain the country's growing population, the austerity program was unpopular, and leftists and Communists were gaining. In Paraguay, the antiquated landed-clerical oligarchy continued to rule in nineteenth-century fashion, and General Alfredo Stroessner operated as an old-fashioned military dictator. Even in stable social-democratic Uruguay, where the welfare state had been extended beyond the economic ability of the nation to sustain it and where the crash of wool prices had brought near financial collapse, the conservative Nationalists in 1958 came to power for the first time in Uruguay's modern history.

In Argentina, President Arturo Frondizi was valiantly attempting through austerity measures to pay the debts and control the inflation produced by Perón's headlong plunge into industrialization and reckless extension of social services without regard for the nation's ability to finance them. In Brazil, President Juscelino Kubitschek (1956-1960) flatly refused to undertake an austerity program to pay for the industrialization measures and the expanded social services of the prior decade, and the result was galloping inflation.

Most Latin American countries were floundering. The conditions that had brought them to this pass were clearly evident in 1945, when the United States came to the world leadership. Americans had closed their eyes to the real situation in Latin America. Now they were to be rudely awakened.

Fidel and Fidelismo

The Castro revolution, which took over Cuba from Batista on New Year's Day, 1959, had long been in the making. On July 26, 1953, a small band of about 150 youths, led by Fidel Castro, a law student and son of a rich sugar planter, attacked the army barracks at Santiago. More than half were killed, but Castro and his brother Raul escaped. With the hope of putting a stop to the bloody reprisals which followed, the Castro brothers gave themselves up, were sentenced to prison, later amnestied, and fled to Mexico to plot a new revolt. Late in 1956, Castro's force landed on the southeastern coast, most of them were mowed down, but Fidel and Raul with a dozen followers escaped to the jungles of the Sierra Maestra where for two years they held out against Batista's armed might. Their guerrilla band grew to a sizable force of bearded youths who lived on the country and raided plantations. Raul established another rebel stronghold in northeastern Oriente province, and a revolutionary network spread throughout Cuba. When most Cubans in 1958 boycotted Batista's elections the dictator saw the handwriting on the wall and fled the country. Castro was hailed as a deliverer.

It was soon clear that this was to be no ordinary Latin American revolution. Castro refused the presidency, but became dictator with the title of prime minister. Castro made a clean sweep in all government and military agencies. Over seven hundred Batista officials faced firing squads. Thousands of Batista's aides were jailed. Elections and civil liberties were dispensed with. The press was muzzled. A new revolutionary press appeared. Castro charged that Batista had plundered the nation of 200 million dollars. Scrupulous honesty was demanded of all in the revolutionary government, and Castro preached national moral regeneration.

Castro tackled agrarian reform as the nation's chief problem. Three-fourths of the nation's land had been concentrated into large plantations and ranches, and much land had been left unused. Much of this was in the hands of American corporations.

The United Fruit Company alone owned 270,000 acres. The revolutionary government established the National Institute of Agrarian Reform, which took over the large holdings of sugar, tobacco, and cattle lands. Compensation was promised the owners. Each landless peasant was to be allotted around 66 acres of land. However, nothing was done toward paying the owners; and the peasants, instead of receiving individual plots of land, were put to work on large cooperative farms managed by the Institute. Schools and clinics were established in the villages, and heroic efforts were made to train technicians.

Banks, public utilities, mining companies, and some other industries were nationalized. Even some hotel and country club properties were taken over. Strict controls over wages, prices, and rents were established in the interest of the workers. Castro's chief wrath was vented on "the pro-Batista American imperialists" but the properties of other foreign and of Cuban companies were not spared.

At first the American government tried to get along with Castro. A friendly ambassador was sent to Havana. In a series of public pronouncements the United States made clear that it had nothing but good will for the Cuban people and recognized their right to undertake such economic, social, and political reforms as they wished, subject only to the fulfillment of Cuba's normal obligations under international law.

But the United States government also made it plain that it was disturbed by the Cuban government's repeated violations of the legal and legitimate interests of the United States and its citizens and by Castro's vilification of America before the Cuban people and the world. Scores and scores of times during 1959 and 1960 the United States filed protests with Havana over the Cuban government's successive arrests and expulsions of American citizens, expropriations of property of Americans (aggregating over 1 billion dollars), and propaganda attacks against the United States.

The United States was troubled by the incoming reports that the Cuban government was encouraging revolutionary movements in other Latin American countries and by the increasing prominence of Communists within the Castro government. As Castro's former aides broke with him and fled to the United States they reported that the Castro revolution was no longer an indigenous one, that it was being taken over by the Communists.

During 1960 the attitude of the American government stiffened. The United States cut off the sale of arms and planes to Cuba and put pressures on its allies to do likewise. What remained of American economic aid to Cuba was terminated. In July, President Eisenhower took the decisive step of suspending, except for a token allotment, Cuba's American sugar quota. Up to this time Cuban sugar had enjoyed a preferential treatment in the American market. Little by little America's import and export trade with Cuba in other items was interdicted.

Castro charged that the United States had instituted an economic blockade against him, that it was using its base at Guantánamo to foment counter-revolution, that it was planning to employ Cuban refugees in an attack on Cuba, and that Florida airfields were being used by anti-Castro Cuban exiles as bases for leaflet raids and arms drops to counter-revolutionaries in Cuba. (This latter charge seems to have been true.) In July 1960, Cuba appealed to the United Nations for protection against "the repeated threats, harassments, intrigues, reprisals, and aggressive acts perpetrated against Cuba by the United States government." In bypassing the Organization of American States, Cuba was making an appeal to the Communist bloc and the neutrals outside the hemisphere.

During 1960 Cuba moved rapidly to increase its intercourse with the Communist countries. Diplomatic relations were resumed with the Soviet Union and established with Communist China. The Soviet Union and even Communist China extended substantial credits to Cuba and undertook to supply that country with technicians for industrial developments. There were also important trade agreements, most of which involved barter arrangements. For instance, Cuba took machinery and crude oil from Russia and Russia took Cuban sugar. When in May 1960 foreign oil companies still operating in Cuba refused to refine Russian oil, their properties were seized. Following the American suspension of the Cuban sugar quota, Khrushchev declared that the Soviet Union would help the Cuban people defeat the American "economic blockade" and would offer military protection in the case of an American attack. "The rockets will fly" was the popular interpretation of Khrushchev's remarks. (Later Khrushchev emphasized that actually he had used the term "figuratively," that his remarks were meant "in the symbolic sense.") A few days later, Khrushchev asserted that the Monroe Doctrine had "outlived its time" and "should be buried as every dead body is." President Eisenhower replied that in recent years, through the development of the Organization of American States, the Monroe Doctrine had undergone an important extension but that it had not entirely lost its unilateral character, that in the case of necessity the United States would operate unilaterally to protect its interests in the Western Hemisphere.

Leftist exiles from other Latin American countries flocked to Havana. The Cuban government was repeatedly accused of training exiles for insurrectionary invasions of their respective countries and of fomenting revolutionary movements inside a number of nations. It was hard to distinguish the activities of the Castro government from the extra-governmental activities of Castro's followers. In 1959 a series of complaints were filed against the Castro government. In April, Panama reported that insurrectionaries from Cuba had landed on her soil and had been captured. For a time the United States provided a naval and air patrol of Panamanian waters under the authority of the OAS. In June, Nicaragua charged that it was threatened by three groups of armed men which had set sail from Cuba. That same month the Dominican Republic claimed that it had been invaded on two different occasions and that the invaders had been virtually annihilated. The Dominican government blamed both the Castro government and the Betancourt government in Venezuela. In August, President Duvalier reported an abortive invasion from Cuba. Investigations by the OAS into all of these cases were inconclusive. In November, Panamanian nationalist mobs, not instigated by *Fidelistas* but exploited by them, rioted, attempted to invade the Canal Zone, and were beaten back with heavy casualties. Their cry was: "Panama has as much right to its Canal as Egypt has to Suez."

During 1960 the troubles continued. In El Salvador, a military-civilian junta, said to be Castro-infiltrated, ousted conservative President José Maria Lemus, and took over the government. Both Nicaragua and Guatemala experienced short-lived revolts alleged to have been Castro- and Communist-inspired. At the same time, the United States, without consultation with the OAS, instituted a naval patrol of Guatemalan and Nicaraguan Caribbean waters. Haiti again complained of *Fidelista* and Communist infiltration. In November, leftist mobs rioted in Caracas and attempted to set up a Castro-like government in Venezuela. Nationalist agitation in Panama against the United States continued, and in 1960 the United States agreed to allow a limited display of the Panamanian flag in the Canal Zone. There was even some talk in the United States of turning the Canal over to international control, but this found no favor in official quarters. In 1961, Panama demanded an increase in the annual royalty paid by the United States for the Canal Zone.

The activities of the Castro followers were not confined to the Caribbean area. Indeed, no country in Latin America was without its *Fidelista* elements. In Ecuador, President Velasco Ibarra flirted with them and they were said to be behind the renewal of an old quarrel with Peru over a boundary dispute. (Peru's government was taking an anti-Castro stand.) The eleventh Inter-American conference, scheduled to meet in Quito in 1960, was indefinitely postponed for fear of Castro and Communist demonstrations. *Fidelista* elements were strong among the tin workers of Bolivia and were said to be behind repeated street demonstrations in La Paz. Castro sympathizers were reported to be growing rapidly in Brazil's impoverished northeastern areas. In British Guiana, the party of Dr. Cheddi Jagan, a Marxist, was forging into the lead.

But all the activities in this intensifying ideological conflict were not on the side of the leftists. The Trujillo government in the Dominican Republic was active on the side of the rightists. Cuba repeatedly complained of Dominican aggressions, and in June 1960 President Betancourt of Venezuela narrowly escaped assassination from a bomb explosion which he claimed had been engineered by "the bloody hand" of Trujillo. Thus Betancourt was sorely besieged from both the left and the right.

At a meeting of the American Foreign Ministers at San José in August 1960 the American states agreed to a collective break in diplomatic relations with the Dominican Republic and an arms embargo. In January 1961 the Council of the OAS voted an extension of the embargo to include petroleum and trucks. It was expected that the United States would cut the Dominican Republic's import sugar quota, but instead, after the United States suspended Cuba's quota, a large part of the Cuban allotment, under the rigid formula set by Congress, went to the Dominican Republic. This outraged much Latin American opinion. On the other hand, the United States attempted at San José to get some collective action against Cuba, but the larger Latin American countries, apparently responding to opinion in their countries, resisted any concrete action. The United States had to be satisfied with a reaffirmation of general Inter-American principles such as non-intervention and rejection of totalitarianism.

American-Cuban relations increasingly deteriorated in the closing weeks of the Eisenhower administration. In January, Cuba peremptorily informed the United States that its embassy in Havana would be limited to eleven people and that all other embassy personnel must leave the country within forty-eight hours. President Eisenhower replied by ordering the immediate severance of all diplomatic and consular relations with Cuba.

Opinion in America was aroused by the Cuban situation more than it had been by any crisis of the postwar world, and the whole country was expectantly awaiting President Kennedy's Cuban policy. Americans were in a mood to *do* something. To them what happened in the Congo or Laos or even Berlin was not as important as Cuba, at their very doorstep. President Kennedy was confronted with the fact that the OAS was not likely to do anything, that in all probability it would not even take the collective measures it had taken against the Dominican Republic. In the light of all the circumstances surrounding the Cuban situation, it was plain that America's treaty obligations under the OAS and under the United Nations forbade direct United States military intervention. President Kennedy renounced direct United States action and declared that the main issue in Cuba was not between the United States and Cuba but among the Cubans themselves.

What the United States could not do directly it might be able to do indirectly. There was the precedent of Guatemala in 1954 when the United States in effect had used Guatemalan refugees and rebels to liquidate the Communist-oriented regime of Arbenz. The Eisenhower administration had been moving to a similar handling of the Cuban situation, and Cuban exiles had been undergoing military training in Nicaragua, Guatemala, and isolated places in the southern United States under the auspices of the Central Intelligence Agency. These activities continued under President Kennedy and the political activities of the Cuban exiles were coordinated through the Cuban Revolutionary Council, which was established in March of 1961. The Council was headed by José Miro Cardona, who had been Castro's first prime minister, and included a wide variety of political groupings from right to left. The faction headed by Manuel Ray, which claimed the largest following and the most sensitive contacts with the anti-Castro underground in Cuba, favored most of the economic and social reforms of the Castro regime but opposed totalitarianism and Communist ties.

On April 15 came the electric news that three military air bases in Cuba had been attacked by B-26 bombers which bore the insignia of the Cuban Air Force. Washington claimed that these were piloted by deserters from Castro's Air Force and might be the first steps in a general Cuban uprising. This was the version given to the United Nations by Ambassador Adlai E. Stevenson, who had not been informed by his own government of the real situation. Later it was learned that the planes had come from Guatemala and were part of a squadron of sixteen bombers which were to have destroyed Cuban military aircraft on the ground prior to the invasion by Cuban exiles.

In the meantime around 2,000 armed Cuban exiles were transported from Guatemala and Nicaragua to Vieques Island, off Puerto Rico. From there United States naval vessels escorted them to within a short distance of the actual Cuban landing place in the Bahía de Cochinos. From that point, the invaders were on their own. United States air support and naval artillery support were denied them, for Washington was determined to avoid direct American involvement in the military operations.

Just before dawn, on April 17, the invaders made a landing on the southern coast of Las Villas province. After two days of fighting in which there were heavy losses, the beachhead was abandoned. Some 1240 survivors were captured. The attackers simply had no chance against the Cuban Air Force, the guns and tanks of the Cuban army, and Castro's revolutionary militia. There was no rising of the Cuban people.

Following this disaster the United States was condemned around the world. The Communists had a propaganda field day. The neutrals were shocked. Latin Americans were outraged. In Western Europe, among America's staunchest allies, American prestige fell precipitately and the immense popularity of America's new young President plummeted. Was European security in the hands of impetuous and irresponsible leadership?

In the United Nations Assembly a Mexican-sponsored resolution demanding the immediate cessation of military operations against Cuba and asking the countries involved to deny any assistance to the attackers won a majority vote but not a two-thirds vote. But the Assembly did pass a resolution appealing to all United Nations members to take action to remove existing tensions. Thus for the first time, and against United States opposition, the United Nations brushed aside the contention that inter-American affairs were essentially the business of the OAS rather than of the United Nations.

Most galling to Americans were the boasts of Castro and Khrushchev that the United States had been driven to use indirect methods because its fear of Russia made a direct attack too risky. Khrushchev badgered the Americans, declared that they could not "take it," that a containment policy in reverse made them lose their heads, that the mere thought of a Soviet base in Cuba (which in fact did not exist and was not planned, according to Khrushchev) drove the United States to take rash actions which the Soviet Union, with numerous American military bases in countries along its borders, had always abstained from taking.

Some specialists in international relations took this occasion to observe that for a nation to give military aid to irresponsible hands for attacks on neighboring countries was in effect a cruder and more primitive threat to the international order and the world community than direct military aggression and the subtler art of internal subversion.

Americans felt that the whole affair had been grossly mismanaged. What irked them was not the attack but the fact that it had failed. It was believed that this was the type of operation which could be justified only if it succeeded. Why was the invasion allowed to proceed after it had been ascertained (as seemingly it had been ascertained) that the B-26 bomber attacks of April 15 had not seriously impaired Cuba's air strength? Why was United

States air support and naval artillery support denied the invaders? Since official American support for the entire affair was too notorious to hide, why jeopardize the whole operation for the sake of maintaining a fiction that fooled nobody?

At bottom the failure was a political one. It was premised on the wholly false belief that Castro had lost the support of his people and that there would be a mass uprising. The truth was that Castro at that time still had the overwhelming support of the mass of Cubans. Americans were too much influenced by the views of the well-to-do and middle-class Cuban exiles. A reading of the leading South American, European, and Asian newspapers, many of them with correspondents in Havana, for the months prior to the invasion must leave in any mind with political insight the conclusion that Castro had popular Cuban support. Reports from America's Central Intelligence Agency were apparently otherwise, but such reports were only one of many sources of information. (Undercover agents rarely have political insights of the highest order; their dossiers must be examined but should never be conclusive.) Responsibility could not be shunted off to the intelligence service or the technicians; this was the sort of situation which called for the coordination, the perceptive evaluation, and the experienced hunches of top political leaders. Senator J. William Fulbright, Chairman of the United States Senate Foreign Relations Committee, seems to have been one of the President's few advisers who relied on his political insights and advised against an attack on Cuba at that time in any form.

However, even had there been a large underground in Cuba, the United States was not prepared to make use of it effectively, for at the time of the invasion Manuel Ray and his associates, who seem to have had the best contacts with what popular underground there was, were deliberately isolated and denied radio facilities, while the more conservative and reactionary forces within the Cuban Revolutionary Council were favored.

In the light of American political ineptitude during the whole affair, it may be that the failure to lend air support was a blessing. For had the invaders actually made a successful landing and found little popular support, the United States would have had to continue to feed them reinforcements, and finally the United States would have been committed to large-scale military conquest of the island. This ugly affair might have dragged on for weeks, with the whole world looking on with increasing revulsion. And after the conquest had been made, the United States would have been faced with controlling a hostile and sullen population. Thus the agony of Cuba might have become comparable in world opinion to the agony of Hungary.

It would seem that it would have been wiser to have waited, to have worked more vigorously to have the OAS declare collective sanctions against Cuba, and in any event to have allowed time for growing economic deterioration and resentment over Communist methods to produce widespread popular disillusionment inside Cuba. True, internal uprisings against a police state are extremely difficult, but outside help, to be effective and democratic, must wait until a situation has ripened for popular revolution.

The invasion fiasco had important repercussions inside Cuba. Castro increased the curbs on the Catholic Church; brought the education system under tight state control; quickened the rate of socialization; merged the 26th of July Movement and the Popular Socialist (Communist) party into the Integrated Revolutionary Organization, the only party permitted; and late in the year publicly announced that he had long been a Marxist, that from the very beginning, despite his profession of democracy, he had intended to steer Cuba to proletarian dictatorship.

In the United States the Kennedy administration determined to work for collective sanctions by the OAS against Cuba and for large-scale economic aid and basic reforms in Latin America to the end that democracy would prove its superiority over Communism as a way of providing material and spiritual satisfactions for the masses.

Although the chief work of the Inter-American Economic and Social conference at Punta del Este, Uruguay, in August 1961, was the laying of the groundwork of the Alliance for Progress, the United States hoped to get, if not sanctions, at least a conference expression of disapproval of the Castro government's repudiation of the democratic principles of the OAS. The declaration which finally emerged was platitudinous and free of anti-Cuban overtones. The representatives of the big three, Brazil, Argentina, and Mexico, along with the representatives of Chile, Bolivia, and Ecuador, apparently in response to bitterly divided opinion in their countries, refused to support any move which subjected Cuba to inter-American discipline.

However, at the gathering of the foreign ministers of the OAS, again at Punta del Este, early in 1962, a resolution was adopted declaring that the present government of Cuba, in officially identifying itself with Marxism-Leninism, had created an "incompatibility" which excluded that government from participation in the inter-American system. But Brazil, Argentina, Mexico, Chile, Bolivia, and Ecuador abstained from voting. The result was achieved by the support of the United States and thirteen Latin American countries, most of them the smaller ones. Of perhaps greater immediate practical importance was the vote of twenty Latin American nations to exclude Cuba from the Inter-American Defense Board, and the vote of sixteen not only to suspend arms trade with Cuba but to instruct the OAS Council to study the desirability of extending the suspension to other items. At long last it looked as though the OAS was moving to economic sanctions against Cuba.

Nevertheless, the Americans seemed still to be on the defensive in their own hemisphere. In 1961, Cheddi Jagan, a Marxist, won the premiership of British Guiana and promised to make his country independent of Great Britain. That same year the abortive West Indies Federation collapsed, and in 1962 Jamaica and Trinidad, untried nations with restless populations, became independent countries. In the process of British withdrawal, the United States had agreed to give up 80 per cent of the leased areas for bases which it had obtained from Britain in 1941, but made arrangements to retain its naval station at Chaguaramas in Trinidad.

Americans seemed to be living in a strange new hemisphere: the retreat from the West Indian bases; an international conference of neutrals suggesting that they get out of Guantánamo; nationalists in Panama clamoring for the Canal; Canada refusing America's pressing invitation to join the inter-American system and Canadians blandly intimating that Canada should remain in a position to "mediate" between the United States and its Latin American neighbors; President Sukarno telling the Latin Americans that they should join the Asian-African group; and President de Gaulle (reviving the grandiose vision of Napoleon III?) proferring a Franco–Latin American alignment. The bipolarized world of 1945 had indeed become the depolarized world of the 1960's.

And then in the fall of 1962 American prestige shot up, as the result of the second Cuban crisis, which more than repaired the damage of the first one.

For months the concern of Americans about Russian penetration of Cuba had been mounting. There were repeated rumors that the Russians were sending offensive arms to Castro and turning Cuba into a military satellite. The extensive popular discussion of the Monroe Doctrine showed that the old cardinal tenet of America's traditional foreign policy was still a powerful popular mystique, that Americans little realized how their active participation in affairs in all parts of the globe had robbed the Doctrine of its original relevance (without, of course, impairing the Western Hemisphere's importance as an American defense zone) and the extent to which the defense of the Western Hemisphere had become the multilateral responsibility of all the nations of the hemisphere and not that of the United States alone. President Kennedy repeatedly assured the nation that the Russians had not supplied the Cubans with offensive weapons, and Khrushchev and Gromyko had told the President that they had no intention of doing so.

But during October 1962, as the result of American aerial reconnaissance it was learned that the Russians were hurriedly and stealthily building intermediate missile bases in Cuba and delivering missiles which could strike cities as far away as Mexico City and Washington. Unlike the American missile bases in Britain, Italy, and Turkey, which had been erected only after well-publicized negotiations with the nations concerned, these Russian bases were being built without even the knowledge of the Cuban people.

As a result of this alarming information, the President on October 22 proclaimed an American naval and air blockade of Cuba to halt the delivery of further missiles. At that same time he announced that any nuclear missile launched from Cuba against any nation in the Western Hemisphere would be regarded as an attack by the Soviet Union on the United States requiring a full retaliatory response upon the Soviet Union. In the light of Khrushchev's previous bellicose warnings that Soviet missiles "would fly" in defense of Cuba, the nation braced itself for any eventuality, and many Americans were confident that attempts to stop Soviet vessels would result in warlike incidents at sea.

But Khrushchev realized that he had been caught red-handed in a situation far more compromising than the American U-2 flight over Russia, that he was indeed in a most embarrassing and untenable position. The Russians had no notion of appearing to the world as ready to provoke a war for the "right" to send offensive weapons to a nation not remotely in their defense area. Most Russian ships turned back; others submitted to search by American naval units. On October 28, Khrushchev promised to dismantle the bases, withdraw the missiles and other offensive equipment, and submit to international inspection in Cuba, and Kennedy promised that if these conditions were carried out there would not be an American invasion of Cuba.

The American victory was a resounding one. Castro's faith in the Russians was undermined. Many of Castro's followers opined that it would have been better to have pursued a neutralist course like Nasser and not to have entered the Communist camp at all. Castro's position among the Cuban people was weakened. The Red Chinese publicly denounced Khrushchev's backdown, and the breach between the two Communist partners was widened. Latin Americans were finally impressed with the danger Castro posed to their own security, and the Organization of American States unanimously backed the American blockade of Cuba. President Kennedy emerged as a strong leader, and the United States appeared to most of the world as a resolute nation willing to risk nuclear war over a position that was not only morally right but which unquestionably involved its own defense area, a nation which had used power prudently and had called into play no more force than was needed.

Although the Russians attempted to repair the damage to themselves by posing as defenders of the peace willing to make ready concessions to secure it and by emphasizing the existence of American missile bases in Turkey, Khrushchev's image as an exponent of peace was tarnished, and his sly and reckless activities in Cuba together with Red China's formidable attack on India at about the same time made a bad impression on the neutral world. But instead of all this healing the breach between China and

Russia it only intensified it, for the Stalinists and the Maoists now claimed that Khrushchev was not only an untrustworthy Marxist but a bungler to boot. Khrushchev was robbed of his plan to black-mail the United States into making concessions on West Berlin and Germany by threats of missiles fired from Cuba. And the weak-ness of the Soviets in the missile race was revealed, for despite their boasts of intercontinental missiles, it was now seen that they had so few of them that they were attempting to overcome their own missile gap by building intermediate missile bases in Cuba.

This second Cuban crisis underscored the importance of Presi-dent Eisenhower's "open skies" plan as a safeguard against surprise attack, a proposal which had never rated the priority it deserved. This affair also served to reveal that Khrushchev's fear of nuclear war was not simulated, for his personal communications to the President at the pitch of the tension apparently were highly and genuinely emotional on the subject.

However, in the period following their triumph, the Americans suffered some let-down. Although the Russians dismantled their bases and shipped many missiles back to Russia, Castro refused on-site inspection by the United Nations and other international agencies; some Soviet bombers perhaps still remained in Cuba; negotiations involving inspection and verification were protracted; and Castro remained in power in Cuba, a continuing invitation to further Russian penetration and an active fomenter of social revo-lution in Latin America.

The Alliance for Progress: An Experiment in "Controlled Revolution"

What were the basic reasons for the ferment in Latin America? As we have seen earlier, many of the causes of the unrest had their origins deep in the past: economies based primarily on the production and export of a single commodity; concentration of land ownership; a social and sometimes racial caste system inherited from Spanish and Portuguese colonial days; backward agricultural production; the need of essentially agricultural societies to import even food; a ruling class largely without a sense of *noblesse oblige* or civic consciousness; an inequitable tax structure which favored the rich and bore down on the poor. To these historic difficulties new ones were added: the decline in the late 1950's and early 1960's in the world prices of coffee, cotton, wool, petroleum, tin, and other metals; heavy importations of capital goods for industrialization; the refusal to provide the education, technical training, communications, and transportation upon which permanent industrialization depends; the inclination to enjoy high wages and other advantages of industrialization before the actual increase in wealth would justify them; inflation; insufficient export exchanges and deepening balance-of-payments deficits; galloping population increases.

There was a strong tendency for the Latin American masses to blame their difficulties on "the Yanqui imperialists." It was easy for agitators to denounce American corporations owning sugar, tobacco, coffee, and banana plantations in the Caribbean and in Central America; petroleum fields and refineries in Venezuela and Colombia; and mines of copper and other metals in Peru and Chile. American firms were accused of siphoning off the profits and wealth of Latin American countries to the United States, of withholding land and resources from current use for future development, of exploiting labor, of circumventing the regulations of the governments of the countries in which they did business, of meddling in the politics of these countries—even when American concerns (as was not infrequently the case) paid higher than prevailing wages and provided more welfare services for their workers than did local employers.

When Latin American countries with deficits in their international balance of payments sought loans from the United States Export-Import Bank or from the International Monetary Fund (in which the United States had a large voice) with which to meet their payments, the United States insisted that such countries, as a prerequisite for getting the loans, balance their budgets, curtail imports, limit consumption, adopt effective measures against inflation, go on austerity programs. (An austerity program was the way a country caught up its payments on its imports of capital goods for the preceding years.) These orthodox economic procedures hit the mass of people hardest, for they meant declining wages and lowered consumption for them. Although the United States tried to hide behind the International Monetary Fund, Americans were blamed nonetheless. The United States also usually advised the Latin American governments to plug their tax loopholes, make the rich pay their fair share of the taxes, undertake land reform and diversification and intensification of agriculture; but this part of the advice was rarely taken, for such measures were not prerequisites for getting the loans. American admonitions about reforms were platonic, but the austerity programs were real.

Latin American governments and peoples had grievances against United States trade policies. The Latin Americans wanted international agreements to stabilize the prices of raw materials on an unprotected and fluctuating world market, but the United States had consistently opposed these in the interest of the free market. The Latin Americans pointed out that, despite this American doctrine of free trade, the Americans seldom hesitated to clamp down on Latin American imports to the United States when American domestic producers of oil, metals, and commodities were endangered by low prices and competition from Latin American sources.

The loudest complaint of the Latin American governments in recent years had been the refusal of the American government to make extensive grants and easy loans to Latin American governments for capital development projects. Latin American countries pointed out that the United States had been much more generous with economic aid, both for technical assistance and capital developments, in Europe, Asia, and the Middle East than it had in Latin America. (The United States had considered these former areas the first lines of defense against Communism, felt that Latin America was remote from the main path of Communist advance.) What particularly rankled was that the United States now thought it was all right for countries outside the Western Hemisphere to get aid from both the Soviet Union and the United States, and thereby increase their bargaining power by playing one side off against the other, whereas Latin American countries were denounced for betraying the Inter-American system if they sought aid from the Communist powers. Latin Americans said: "If India and Egypt can take aid from both sides, why can't we? If we are not to be allowed to take aid from the Soviet Union, then the United States is under a special obligation to supply us with adequate aid." Despite American objections, by 1959 some Latin American governments were actively seeking Soviet aid, and in 1960 the United States found itself in competition with the Soviet Union over large-scale economic aid to Bolivia.

Year after year, the Latin Americans had clamored for a United Nations capital-development fund which would lend aid to underdeveloped countries for projects which could not qualify for loans from the Export-Import Bank, the International Bank, or other established agencies. Again, the Latin Americans had repeatedly asked for an Inter-American development bank within the framework of the Organization of American States. But the United States had invariably taken the decisive action which had scuttled plans for both a United Nations development fund and an Inter-American development bank. The United States claimed that it was already doing all that it could with its own economic aid programs and its contributions to the International Bank, the International Monetary Fund, the United Nations Technical Assistance Program, and other going agencies. Besides, maintained the United States, the major funds for capital developments should come from private capital. Latin Americans replied that American private capital was inadequate, that mostly it had gone into oil and metals and therefore further unbalanced their economies, that the aid from the United States government, small compared with that given to other continents, had been mostly for technical assistance and not for capital development projects.

During its last two years the Eisenhower administration made very significant shifts in America's economic policies in Latin America. Indeed, the Eisenhower administration may be said to have anticipated and laid the earliest foundations for President Kennedy's Alliance for Progress. The reasons for this important new departure were the crash in the world prices of many of the commodities in which Latin America specialized, the revelation of Latin American feeling toward the United States as dramatically exposed by the popular demonstrations against Vice-President Nixon during his "good-will" tour of Latin America in 1958, and the challenge posed by Castro.

The United States reversed its position on international commodity agreements. In 1959 it encouraged fifteen Latin American coffee-producing countries to make an agreement to limit coffee exports by the participating countries to specified quotas for the following year. Portuguese and French territories in Africa also joined this agreement.

Later, the United States also undertook to help the Latin

American countries get the same trading concessions in the European Common Market that the African associate members of the Market enjoyed. Latin Americans were justifiably afraid that the African producers of coffee, cocoa, sisal, and tropical fruits, which Latin America also produced, would henceforth have advantages in the European market over the Latin Americans unless the United States supported the latter by using its great bargaining power on many fronts. In coming to the support of the Latin Americans in this matter, the United States was not reversing itself but was being consistent in its current policy of widening free trade.

Of like purport was United States encouragement of the Latin American Free Trade Area, which was negotiated in 1960 and went into effect in 1961. Eight nations—Argentina, Brazil, Chile, Uruguay, Paraguay, Peru, Colombia, and Mexico—undertook gradually, over a period of twelve years, to eliminate customs duties among themselves. The United States also backed the Central American Economic Integration Treaty, which included Guatemala, El Salvador, and Nicaragua and went into effect in 1961. It was expected that Honduras and perhaps Costa Rica would also join. This plan envisaged an elimination of tariffs among the participating nations, development of a common market, and other economic cooperation. The United States pledged 10 million dollars of support to the Central American Bank for Economic Integration.

As in the case of international commodity agreements, the United States began reversing itself on the availability of easy loans by public international agencies for capital developments in Latin America. In 1960, with decisive United States support, the Inter-American Development Bank was established with an eventual lending capacity of 1 billion dollars—850 million dollars for regular loans and another 150 million for "soft" loans. The United States pledged itself to contribute 450 million dollars over a period of years. In 1960 the United States extended to Peru 53 million dollars of credit for land improvement and low-cost housing projects. Later that year President Eisenhower took the momentous step of asking Congress for 600 million dollars for Latin America over and above the regular aid program. Chile was to get 100 million dollars for earthquake rehabilitation while 500 million dollars were for capital development projects and programs "designed to contribute to opportunities for a better way of life for the individual citizens of the countries of Latin America." The following year President Kennedy asked Congress to go through with this Eisenhower recommendation, and he made it the basis of America's first-year contribution to the Alliance for Progress.

At the Inter-American Economic and Social conference at Punta del Este, Uruguay, in the late summer of 1961, President Kennedy's Alliance for Progress program was drawn up and subscribed to by all the representatives except those from Cuba. This program envisaged that during the next ten years each of the Latin American states would expand economically at about the rate of 5 per cent a year on the average. While most of the capital for this expansion would come from the Latin Americans themselves, it was estimated that about 20 billion dollars of capital would be supplied by outside sources over the ten-year period. These outside funds would come from the United States government, from the Export-Import Bank, from international agencies like the International Bank and the Inter-American Development Bank, and from private American, European, and Japanese capital. But most of the outside funds would come from public sources. For the year 1961-1962 the United States government provided a ½-billion-dollar Inter-American Fund for Social Progress. Of this amount, 394 million dollars would be administered by the Inter-American Bank as a trust agent of the United States and would be for loans on flexible terms for improved land use, land settlement, housing, water supply, public health and sanitation, and so forth. Another 100 million dollars would be administered directly by the United States government, and the other six million would go to the economic and social work of the Organization of American States. The United States also set up a special emergency fund of 150 million dollars for short-term aid. It was announced at Punta del Este that the United States would continue to support "workable" international commodity agreements and was contemplating joining the International Tin Agreement, and that the United States would continue its efforts for fair treatment by the European Common Market for Latin American exports.

However, the Latin American countries in their turn were expected to do certain things. In order to be eligible for easy-term development loans from the United States and the international agencies, each Latin American country would have to set up long-term economic planning, undertake much economic self-help, and assure that the benefits achieved would be distributed to the population as a whole. Tax reform, land reform, educational expansion, public health, housing developments, slum clearance, urban planning, and so forth were listed as areas requiring action. Before public funds would become available, each nation would have to submit blueprints of national planning for the approval of either a panel of experts of the Inter-American Bank or a review board unconnected with the Bank. What was being attempted was "limited or controlled revolution."

The Latin American countries were slow to submit their blueprints. They tended to ask for the emergency loans, which did not require concrete planning. There was much opposition to going through with the domestic reforms required, especially among the ruling elites. Both conservatives and leftists were critical. Conservatives cried: "You Americans are fostering leftist revolution. You are abandoning those who were your strong friends to court the leftists. You are inviting us politely into your home to commit suicide." The Communists, the followers of Castro, and some other leftists shouted: "You Yanquis are attempting to take us Latin Americans over on a pretext of idealism. You are using the Alliance for Progress to usurp our sovereignty. You are talking about reform, but you don't mean it. In the long run the money will go again to the *ricos* [the rich men]." The United States was making its appeal to the liberal, democratic center, and in few Latin American countries was this element in control.

The first year of the Alliance for Progress brought both successes and disappointments. There were favorable omens in Mexico and Costa Rica. In El Salvador, a president was elected in late 1961 pledged to full support of Alliance for Progress reforms. Colombia and Venezuela genuinely attempted to translate the Alliance for Progress into concrete terms, but in Venezuela President Betancourt's social-democratic government was hard pressed from both the left and the right. In Bolivia, President Paz Estenssoro reoriented his original revolutionary movement along more moderate lines, and the end of a serious mine strike in mid-1961 gave him an opportunity to plan a reorganization of the tin industry and take other constructive economic and social measures which would qualify Bolivia for substantial Alliance for Progress aid. Events in the Dominican Republic were most encouraging to the forces of democracy. The hated Trujillo was assassinated in May 1961, and after attempts of his puppet President Joaquin Balaguer to hold on and an abortive plot of Trujillo's two brothers to re-establish the dictatorship (at which point the United States "intervened" and dispatched naval units to Dominican waters, to the applause rather than the condemnation of most Latin Americans), the democratic forces prevailed. Balaguer withdrew, and a seven-man council of state headed by President Rafael Bonnelly promised reconstruction of the country on a democratic basis and cooperation with the Alliance for Progress. Subsequently, in a free election, Juan Bosch was elected president. Bosch, like Betancourt of Venezuela, Muñoz Marín of Puerto Rico, and José Figueres of Costa Rica, was a dedicated believer in the democratic middle way. The social-democratic *apristas* were gaining strength in Peru. In Chile the Christian Democrats, social reformers in the liberal Catholic tradition, were mushrooming.

But the disappointments seemed to outweigh the successes. In Brazil, President Jânio Quadros, who had adopted an austerity program to curb inflation but moved Brazil in the direction of a neutralist foreign policy, suddenly resigned the presidency in 1961, some said because he did not like the prospect of unpopularity produced by the austerity program, others because he did not feel confident enough to proceed with basic reforms. His leftist vice-president, João Goulart, was allowed to assume the presidency only on condition that he share the duties of that office with a prime minister. With divided government, Brazil was not in a position to proceed with fundamental reforms. In Argentina, President Frondizi's austerity and orthodox economic policies were increasingly unpopular, and congressional and gubernational elections in 1962 brought impressive gains for the Peronists. Army leaders, disturbed that Frondizi had allowed free elections at all, removed the president from office and installed a puppet president who canceled the election returns and refused to let the Peronists take office. The resulting stalemate gave Argentina no opportunity to enact basic reforms. In both Brazil and Argentina it was all the governments could do to carry on from day to day.

In Ecuador, that artful old demagogue, President Velasco Ibarra, after flirting with *Fidelista* elements, came out for tax reforms consistent with Alliance for Progress objectives. Such legerdemain riled both the right and the left and in 1961 Velasco Ibarra was deposed by the armed forces, supported by the street crowds. This Ecuadorian revolution was thought to illustrate the difficulties in the path of Latin American officials who sought to enact the domestic reforms contemplated by the Alliance for Progress. In the 1962 presidential election in Peru, Haya de la Torre, leader of the social-democratic *apristas,* ran first in a field of three, but he did not get the necessary popular majority. Rather than let the election go to Congress, an army junta seized power and annulled the election returns. For a time President Kennedy canceled all American aid to Peru.

Skeptics were predicting that, because of the complicated political situation in most Latin American countries and the strength of the old elites, the Alliance for Progress reforms would not be made; that Latin America was headed not for the liberal democratic center but for Castro-like extremism on the one hand and rightist extremism on the other. However, here and there the Alliance for Progress was making headway. The victories for the democratic middle way were rarely spectacular, but it was possible that enough reforms would be made, now in this country and now in that, to break the grip of the old order gradually and in democratic fashion translate the rising expectations of the masses into solid satisfactions.

Paradoxically, it may turn out that Castro was the instrument not of drastic but of moderate revolution in Latin America. His revolution pushed the United States into underwriting a vast program of social reform in Latin America. By proclaiming himself a Communist he threw away his magic symbolism as leader of indigenous Latin American revolution, checked the growth of his following, and may have paved the way for basic reforms and revolutions of milder nature.

[9]

DEPOLARIZATION
IN THE EAST:
THE DECLINE OF
MOSCOW

THE COMMUNIST world, like the non-Communist world, had undergone a process of depolarization. Just as the influence of the United States in the non-Communist world was not as strong as it had been in the late 1940's, so even Moscow was experiencing increasing difficulty in leading the Communist world. In the case of the Communist countries this was more significant than in the free world, for the latter did not attempt to operate on a monolithic principle, but Marxism-Leninism emphasized that class and party would cooperate across national boundaries to unite Communists and Communist countries.

The Miscarriage of Marxist Prophecy

As we have seen, the Marxist expectation of a general European Communist revolution at the end of World War I and again at the end of World War II did not materialize. The only advanced industrial country which had gone Communist was Czechoslovakia, won in 1948 by a coup and the threat of hovering Russian armies. The only former European colony which had gone Communist was little Vietminh. Since 1954 no additional territorial gains had been made by the Communists except in Cuba and some Himalaya border areas occupied by the Red Chinese. Communists debated whether the Cuban Revolution was really Marxist, and besides the permanency of that revolution was in much doubt.

Not only had Communism failed to make the territorial gains its votaries had predicted but even where it had been established it was not operating as its prophets had said it would. It had not resulted in an international proletarian society. The international proletarian society was a myth. Nor was Communism an empire controlled from a single center. It was soon evident that China was too large and populous a nation to be ruled as a Russian puppet. The defection of Tito's Yugoslavia showed that the Russians could not always manage even their European satellites. And increasingly it was clear that Communist governments did not invariably see eye to eye in international politics, that they did not always present a solid phalanx to the non-Communist world.

Everywhere Communism had appeared it had taken a national form. Communist countries differed from one another in history, cultures, conditions, circumstances, interests, stages of revolutionary development, and degrees of Marxist "orthodoxy" or "revisionism." In Russia and China, Communism represented genuinely indigenous national revolutions. In the Eastern European satellites it had been largely imposed by Russia, backed by Russian armies of occupation. In North Korea and Vietminh, Communist governments represented both indigenous revolutions and outside pressure. Maoist Communism was different from Soviet Communism, and Titoist Communism was different from both. The Russian Revolution was in a more mature stage of development than the Chinese, and the Chinese in a more mature stage of development than the North Korean or the Vietminh. In short, it was becoming increasingly clear that history in fact was disposing of Communism in a way far different from what the Marxist dialecticians had prophesied.

Nevertheless, Communist countries did operate more closely together than non-Communist countries. They were motivated by a common view of economics, history, and class struggle, by the belief that industrialism made inevitable a collectivist form of society, and by a sense of being ostracized by the outside world. And the Communist parties in non-Communist countries still looked to the established Communist governments for guidance. When a country first became Communist, especially if it were a backward one, it was dependent on the older Communist countries for economic and technical help and military support.

But when a Communist government became more stabilized and less dependent on outside support, there was a tendency to follow a more independent national line. Moreover, as Communism spread geographically and as it made more contacts with the world at large, there was less sense of isolation and there were also competing centers of influence. In the 1930's, Moscow's influence on external Communist parties was greater than it was in the 1960's. Three centers of Communist influence had developed: Moscow, Peiping, and Belgrade. And in a sense Warsaw was a fourth center of attraction, for Gomulka's ability to pursue for Poland a milder totalitarianism and a semi-independent position within the Soviet orbit was not without its impact on the thinking of Communists in other Communist countries and non-Communist countries.

The actual historical experience with a number of established Communist countries was still too short and limited to allow reliable predictions about how the Communist countries would react to a crisis which involved the survival of Communism itself in one or more of them. As we shall see, the crisis in Hungary threw some light on this question. It was probable that in the face of such a crisis ideological bonds would tighten and produce close cooperation among Communist countries, but much would depend on the circumstances and the cross-currents of the particular crisis. At least those charged with the making of foreign policy in non-Communist countries would still operate at their peril if they minimized the importance of international Communist ties.

The actual narrative of how Communist countries had operated in world politics during the decade following Stalin's death served to clarify both the divisive and the unifying forces within the Communist world.

Divisive and Unifying Forces in Eastern Europe

Among the Eastern European satellites, Russian influence was more persuasive in some than in others. In Rumania and Bulgaria —Slavic, always Eastern-oriented, with traditionally lower standards of living than the other satellites (except Albania), with Greek Orthodox rather than Roman Catholic traditions, and owing their very origin as independent nations to Russia (to the nineteenth-century struggle of Russia against Turkey)—there was more indigenous friendliness to Russia than in the other satellites. Poland and Czechoslovakia, although Slavic, were more Western-oriented than Rumania and Bulgaria, had Roman Catholic traditions, and were held to the Soviet orbit in part by fear of a reunited and resurgent Germany. Western travelers and observers in Rumania, Bulgaria, Poland, and even Czechoslovakia tended to agree that public opinion in these countries was favorable to the socialization of industry, and to a limited degree to the socialization of agriculture, particularly if agricultural cooperatives were favored over the Soviet type of agricultural collectives. But hostility centered on Soviet interference, on political dictatorship, and on the police state.

Next to East Germany, the opposition to Communism itself, pro-Soviet or Titoist, was strongest in Hungary. Hungary was not Slavic but Magyar. Hungary traditionally had enjoyed higher standards of living than any of the other satellites except East Germany and possibly Czechoslovakia. Hungarian nationalism was strong and was historically centered in its aristocratic landholding class, the magnates. Hungarians were Roman Catholics. Hungary had been no "subject nationality" in the old Hapsburg empire but an equal partner with the Germans in governing Slavic subjects. Hungarians did not fear a revived Germany, indeed Hungary had been a willing and seemingly "equal" ally of Germany both in World War I and in World War II. In Hungary, the national Communists were stronger than the pro-Soviet Communists, and the non-Communists were stronger than both. Indeed, the majority of Hungarians if left to their own devices probably would not adopt even socialism, even "green socialism," but a more "bourgeois" system, like their neighbor and old partner in empire, Austria, although on this point observers disagreed.

Even as early as the late 1940's, public opinion in most of the satellite countries tended to divide three ways: the pro-Soviet, Stalinist Communists; the national or Titoist Communists; and the Socialists. In free elections most of them would probably have voted for a nationally independent, democratic socialism.

Until 1953 the leaders and government heads in the satellite countries were pro-Soviet, Stalinist Communists. The defection of Tito's Yugoslavia in 1948 had caused purges of budding Titoists elsewhere. Some were executed, some imprisoned, some went underground. Wladyslaw Gomulka in Poland and János Kádár in Hungary suffered imprisonment. But the atmosphere changed following the death of Stalin, the adoption of the Khrushchev doctrine of "many roads to socialism," and the Soviet apologies to Tito. This shift loosened the restraints from Moscow and lent strength to the Titoist Communists. The new Soviet leaders realized they were taking great chances, but they felt that the friendlier relations which they expected would flow from the liberalized policies justified the risks. Titoist Communist leaders reappeared and found followings. Gomulka and Kádár again became political leaders. Titoists who had been executed were now publicly "rehabilitated."

There was in all the satellites, to greater or lesser degree, a conflict within the Communist ranks for control of party and government. In some countries the contest was muted and compromised. In others it was sensational, as when Tito himself took a personal hand in getting his ideological enemy, Mátyás Rákosi, the Stalinist dictator of Hungary, removed as first secretary of the Hungarian Communist party. In all the satellites there was restlessness in the Communist party as readjustments were made to the de-Stalinization policies. There were increasing demands for greater national autonomy, wider personal freedoms, a slowdown or abandonment of collectivization of agriculture, less pressures on labor in the rapid industrialization programs. Communists were divided on how far they could go in satisfying these demands without endangering the hold of Communism itself.

Also, a factor often overlooked, in the first years of Communist enthusiasm in the satellites (at least among the Communists), there had been much misplanning of resources. The drive to industrialization had been too importunate. Heavy industry had been lavishly planned, and then some of the plants were found to be without adequate raw materials and hence unproductive. Half-finished factories were symbols of planning that had gone wrong in a most expensive way. (Over-all, however, subsequent increased industrial production in the satellites was impressive.)

By the middle 1950's the satellite peoples were experiencing that adverse reaction to the sacrifices required by rapid industrialization which usually comes in that period after the first years of enthusiasm and before the breakthrough to industrialism and its attendant benefits has been attained. (It will be recalled that it is the boast of the Communists that their disciplinary drives can carry a people through this critical period and that other systems of rapid industrialization will fail at this point. Candid Communists say that the critical period in Russia was the 1930's, in the satellite countries the middle and late 1950's, and that in China it would be the 1960's.)

Communist parties in non-Communist countries were also stirred by the new de-Stalinization policies. Many of their leaders were not satisfied with the Moscow explanations of the phenomenon of Stalinism, thought they were superficial, and asked for an interpretation not in terms of personality and the accidents of history but in terms "of a profound Marxist analysis."

The first big crisis within the post-Stalinist Communist world came in Poland. The Poles, Communist and non-Communist, had no desire to go back on the Warsaw pact, least of all at the time the West Germans were joining NATO and being rearmed. They looked upon Russia as their only strong protector against a revived Germany, which they feared would wage "a war of revenge" to recapture the German territories taken by Poland at the end of the war. In all their long history of being overrun by cruel conquerors, the Poles had never experienced anything even approaching the ferocity and meditated savagery of the Nazis. It would take generations for this to fade from Polish memories. But most Poles were not Communists, and if their situation with respect to Russia was such that Communism was inevitable, then they favored a more nationalist Communist regime. The Poles were a highly nationalist people. Even the Polish Communists resented the influence of the Russian armed forces stationed in Poland and of the Soviet officers within the Polish military establishment, and many of them felt that collectivization of agriculture was a mistake, that the Polish peasant could be made to respond favorably to farmers' cooperatives but not to collective farms. Many workers felt that industrialization was too rapid, that too much was being required of them. The intellectuals wanted more freedom of research and expression. The Polish masses, devout Catholics, were repelled by the restrictions on the Church.

Wladyslaw Gomulka now came forward as the leader of the national Communists. Gomulka wanted to curb the Soviet military, and he stood for a Communism which took greater account of Poland's own culture and needs, for Polish autonomy within the Communist world. In June 1956, workers and citizens of Poznań rioted, and the Communist government in power suppressed the riots ruthlessly. This sparked the general discontent, and dissent became much bolder. Pressures from the Polish Communists themselves forced the Communist government to give those arrested in the Poznań riots a fair and open trial. Their testimony, which was published throughout the nation, gave in detail the miserable economic and social conditions which had produced the demonstrations.

The pitch of the crisis was reached on October 19, when the Central Committee of the Polish Communist party met to elect Gomulka first secretary. The big brass from the Kremlin— Khrushchev, Molotov, Mikoyan, Kaganovich, and others—flew to Warsaw and suddenly descended on the meeting. But at this moment of supreme decision the Polish Communists stood firm, and the Russians backed down. Gomulka was elected. He later went to Moscow and worked out an agreement which in substance provided that Soviet officers in the Polish army would be withdrawn, and Poland would enjoy a wider latitude in other matters than heretofore. On the other hand, there was no doubt that Gomulka would continue a Communist regime and the close ties of the Warsaw pact and Soviet-Polish economic collaboration. For Poland a new period of "restrained freedom" set in, and across a building at the University of Warsaw was unfurled the banner: "Long Live Friendship with the Soviet Union on the Principles of Equality." Polish intellectual life, under the stimulation of conflicting Catholic and Marxist philosophies, began experiencing a remarkably creative ferment.

Developments in Poland called forth a clarification of American policy in Eastern Europe. Polish-American communities in Buffalo, Cleveland, Chicago, and other industrial cities were thrilled at the news from Poland, and many wondered if the time had not come to take advantage of the obvious popular discontent "to liberate the satellites." During the Presidential campaign of 1952, candidate Eisenhower and John Foster Dulles had in their speeches given encouragement to liberation movements and "rollbacks" in Eastern Europe. (Organizations and committees to pressure the American government to pursue policies to liberate the "captive peoples," in which were included even the Ukrainians, were active in most of America's large cities in the North, not only during the campaign but afterward.) When Americans spoke of liberating the captive peoples they still thought in terms of ousting the Communists, not in terms of encouraging national Communism as a first step in the process of restoring ultimate national independence.

When Tito had made his break from Moscow, it was the British foreign office which had first pointed out the possibility of using Titoism to divide the Communist world and restore national independence to the satellites. The United States government had gradually accepted the British view, and Tito had become a regular recipient of American aid, but Congress kept a jaundiced eye on him and threatened to cut off aid any time Tito seemed to be getting too close to Moscow. But the administration always interpreted Tito's moves as neutralist, even when he sided with Moscow, as he not infrequently did, and American aid continued.

Now in Poland the American government was confronted with another manifestation of national Communism. Secretary Dulles used the opportunity to be more specific about American policy in Eastern Europe. He warned that American military intervention could "precipitate a world war which could wipe out the Polish people." For outsiders to try to hurry the process of Poland's recovery of independence, he said, was the last thing the Polish people wanted. Washington at last seemed willing to accept and publicize the view that Communist governments in the satellites were not always obstacles to national independence, that they might instead become vehicles toward it. Later, the American government each year extended some economic aid to Gomulka's government, but not as much or as consistently as it did to Tito, who was neutralist and not an ally of Russia, as Poland continued to be.

A few days after the crisis in Poland came the revolt in Hungary. On October 23 there were peaceful demonstrations in Budapest for the withdrawal of Soviet troops, punishment of Rákosi, and dismissal of remaining Stalinists. The Hungarian security police fired on the demonstrators, thus contributing to revolutionary urges. On October 24, a national Communist, Imre Nagy, became premier and Kádár became party chief. This elevation to power of national Communists had the approval of most Hungarian Communists and the blessings of Tito and Gomulka. But the changes announced did not go far enough to meet popular demands. Most Hungarians were not willing to accept a settlement similar to that in Poland. Demonstrations sponsored by Socialists and other groups, in which young people took the lead, increased. A general strike spread to most of the country. Instead of standing firm for a national Communist government, Nagy increasingly made concessions to the non-Communists. Representatives from some of Hungary's prewar parties, denounced by most Communists as "bourgeois" and "counter-revolutionary," were admitted to the government. Cardinal Mindszenty was restored to freedom after years of Communist imprisonment. The demonstrators demanded Hungary's withdrawal from the Warsaw pact and the Soviet orbit. At this juncture Moscow seemed still willing to compromise and on October 30 announced a grand plan for autonomy in satellite Europe, "a great commonwealth of socialist nations."

The Soviet declaration failed to end the demonstrations and strikes. On November 1, Premier Nagy renounced the Warsaw pact and declared Hungary's neutrality. Moscow decided on big-scale military action and the Hungarian Communists closed ranks against Nagy. Kádár, another national Communist, became premier. On November 4, Soviet divisions, augmented to 200,000 troops and 5000 tanks, opened a violent assault on Budapest to restore it to submission.

The Russians claimed that the Hungarian rebellion was "Fascist," and instigated by the feudal, aristocratic, and bourgeois elements which had maintained the right-wing Horthy dictatorship in Hungary in the years between the two world wars. The truth was that the revolution was led by Socialists and young Hungarian idealists. But "Fascist" aside, the Russians felt that they could not afford to allow another of the satellites to break away as Tito had done, that Hungarian secession would jeopardize their whole set-up in Eastern Europe. They probably honestly believed that a Hungarian government outside the Soviet orbit would be not only non-Communist but anti-Russian and a danger to their defense area. The Russians were probably prepared to allow another Gomulka Poland, but not another Tito Yugoslavia, and they envisaged Hungary as going far beyond Tito, certainly to non-Communism and probably to anti-Communism. It was most significant that while both Tito and Gomulka had encouraged a national Communist regime in Hungary, they now supported Russia's military suppression of the Hungarian revolution. National Communism was one thing, but ousting Communism altogether was quite another. Communist China, too, strongly disapproved of Nagy's deviationist measures and wholeheartedly supported the Russian intervention to crush "the counter-revolution."

The Hungarian patriots, with no heavy weapons, put up a heroic fight. Throughout November and December the strikes continued and spread, there was bloody fighting in the city streets and guerrilla war in the countryside. Most difficult for the Kádár regime to deal with were the strikes and the pervasive passive resistance which paralyzed economic life. But little by little the back of the revolution was broken. Nagy, who had fled to the Yugoslav embassy, was kidnapped from in front of the embassy, spirited to Rumania, and later executed. Cardinal Mindszenty became a virtual prisoner in the American legation. More than 150,000 Hungarian refugees poured into Austria, several thousand into Yugoslavia. Kádár continued in office as a "national" Communist, but all opportunity to reconstruct Hungary on the Gomulka model had been lost.

Among the Hungarian patriots there was much bitterness toward the United States. Why had not the Americans intervened for freedom? Had they not promised to help liberation movements? But even before the Hungarian rebellion, Secretary Dulles, in his comments on the Polish crisis, had made it clear that the United States would not intervene in Eastern Europe, and during the bloody days in Budapest the American policy of non-intervention was underscored. The United States realized that military intervention in an area regarded by the Russians as their defense zone would mean a world war. The Americans were now reaping in the outraged indignation of the patriots the fruits of their rather reckless talk about liberating the captive peoples and rolling back the Communists. At this time President Eisenhower took pains to point out that the United States had always encouraged the captive peoples to maintain their spirit of freedom and not to lose hope but had never urged any kind of open rebellion by a defenseless populace against a force over which it could not possibly prevail. But to ardent patriots on the spot this distinction between encouragement and inducement appeared not only abstract but deceitful.

The ferocity of the Russian suppression of the Hungarian rebellion was condemned around the world, the neutralists were shocked, and many of those intellectuals in Western Europe hitherto favorably disposed to Communism drew back. The reaction would have been even more decided had not the Hungarian crisis come just at the time the world was denouncing the British and the French for their attack on Egypt. The United Nations Assembly, immersed in the Suez crisis, overwhelmingly voted for resolutions calling for an end of the Soviet intervention in Hungary and the withdrawal of Soviet troops, affirming Hungary's right to responsible government, and providing the stationing of United Nations observers in that country. The Hungarian government refused to allow the United Nations observers to enter Hungary. The Soviet government ignored these United Nations resolutions and the similar ones passed in succeeding years.

In this time of troubles for the Soviet Union, Communist China played a mediating role. In December the Chinese Communist Politburo issued an important statement declaring in effect that Comrade Tito had gone too far; that the attacks on Stalinism should be tempered, for while Comrade Stalin's errors had been grave they took second place to his achievements; and that "great nation chauvinism" should not impair equality among Communist parties. This latter point was regarded as support for Gomulka's position *vis-à-vis* the Soviet Union. In January 1957, Premier Chou En-lai journeyed to Moscow, apparently in support of Gomulka. He then visited Warsaw, where he seems to have advised Gomulka that "separate roads to socialism" must be a practical matter and tempered with "proletarian internationalism." Proceeding to Budapest, he threw his support behind the Kádár regime.

What the Chinese seemed to be saying was that both Stalinism and Gomulkaism were authentic brands of Marxism. After all, the Chinese had been the first to pursue a revolutionary development virtually independent of Moscow, and Mao had always emphasized "a flexible and creative" application of Marxist doctrine to specific national conditions. To the Chinese, Nagy had deserted Marxism, and Tito had become a disruptive force within Marxism, but Gomulka's position was an example of that Marxist flexibility which Mao had always claimed for China. On the other hand, it appeared that the Chinese believed that anti-Stalinism, if carried too far, would not only impair Marxist international solidarity but foreclose Stalinism itself as one of the roads to socialism, the road the Russians themselves had followed, the road which in their internal economic developments (ruthlessly rapid industrialization) the Chinese seemed now to be traveling. (Later that year, when Mao attempted to combine in China ruthless industrialization with wider freedom of expression, he found such a combination impossible. Following Mao's famous speech, in which he said, "Let a hundred flowers bloom, let a hundred schools of thought contend," there was such an outburst of unorthodox opinion that Mao had to backtrack and urge "a rectification campaign" to ferret out "the poisonous weeds.")

In January 1957, in the freest election ever held in a Communist country, Gomulka's Communist-dominated National Front, backed even by the Roman Catholic hierarchy, won an overwhelming victory. This strengthened Gomulka's position for dealing with the Soviet Union and enabled him to offer steady resistance to both those Polish Communists who wanted to return to Stalinism and those Poles who advocated even more Polish national independence and personal freedom. Gomulka's National Front was characterized as "an alliance of the Cardinal and the Comrade" with the Comrade clearly in the driver's seat. Gomulka's government allowed a rather wide latitude of intellectual expression, eased some of the restrictions on the Church, and shifted agricultural policy from collectives to cooperatives.

For the immediate future it did not appear that other Communist countries would succeed in breaking away from the Communist bloc and operating in the independent fashion of Tito. For the time being, at least, Gomulka rather than Tito would be the example most often emulated by national Communists. But Gomulkaism required walking a tight rope. The problem of Gomulka was to be sufficiently Communist to satisfy the Soviet Union and the Polish Stalinists and to implement his own sincere Communist objectives and yet sufficiently national to retain the support of the Polish non-Communists. There was always the danger that too much anti-Sovietism would become anti-Communism.

The disturbances within the satellites during 1956 had repercussions in Moscow. Molotov, Kaganovich, Malenkov, Shepilov, and others felt that Khrushchev's policies at home and abroad were too flexible. They believed he was carrying de-Stalinization too far and dangerously encouraging national Communism, and that his decentralization of the management of Soviet industry was unwise. They thought Khrushchev a pragmatist rather than a true Marxist. Khrushchev's often repeated expression, "One cell dies and another takes its place," was regarded by them as illustrative not of shrewd adjustment to changing conditions but of sheer opportunism.

The intra-party conflict came to a head in June 1957 at a meeting of the party's Central Committee. Khrushchev won, and his opponents, instead of being liquidated as they would have been in Stalin's days, were removed from their party and high government posts and given minor places. From that time Khrushchev was more firmly in the saddle and soon afterward he displaced Bulganin as premier. After his victory, Khrushchev assured Tito that their old understanding about "separate roads to socialism" was still in effect. In the fall, Marshal Zhukov was dismissed as defense minister on the grounds that he had attempted to curtail the work of party organs within the armed forces. (The enemies within the Communist world have been too rigid "doctrinaire dogmatism," too liberal "revisionism and deviationism," and "Bonapartism," the danger that the military would take over the Communist Revolution as they did the French Revolution.)

The troubles of 1956 also called forth new plans for some central directing and coordinating agency for the Communist movement to replace the old Communist Information Bureau, but these had to be abandoned because of the vigorous opposition of Gomulka, backed by Communist leaders from Western Europe, notably Palmiro Togliatti of Italy. However, there was a renewed emphasis on coordinating the economic planning of the Soviet Union and the Eastern European satellites through the Council of Economic Mutual Assistance.

Even anti-Stalinist Communists were concerned about Tito. There was increasing feeling in the Communist world that Tito had carried his "deviationism" too far, had become "the tool of the capitalists and the imperialists." There were pressures on Khrushchev to modify his "soft" policy toward the Yugoslav leader. The pressures were particularly strong from the Chinese, who in 1958 were at the beginning of their second Five-Year Plan, their "great leap forward," the most drastic pace of industrialization ever yet attempted by any people. Consequently, Khrushchev shifted his ground with respect to Tito. The Communist parties of Russia, China, and the satellites boycotted the 1958 Congress of the Yugoslav Communist party, and the Soviet Union cut off economic aid to Yugoslavia for the next five years. The United States took advantage of this to increase its own economic aid to Yugoslavia, although most of this was in surplus agricultural commodities. On the other hand, American economic aid to Poland never reached the proportions which Gomulka hoped for, and remained more moderate than aid to Yugoslavia. The bulk of it was also in surplus agricultural commodities. Poland's relations with the Soviet Union and the other satellites were stabilized, and Poland received much aid from Russia for its industrialization program. The difficulties of hammering out the respective jurisdictions of Church and State in Poland resulted in much mutual irritation.

In Hungary Kádár attempted to rebuild his image as a national Communist. He replaced many Communist managers with non-Communist Hungarian technicians, arguing that "political reliability and technical competence are two different things." In 1962 the Central Committee of the Hungarian Communist party expelled from the party twenty-five top Stalinists, including Rákosi and Ernö Gerö, for "factionalism" and crimes committed during the Stalinist era.

The limits of Russian pressure were underscored when, despite the Soviet Union's marked hostility to the European Common Market, the Italian and Belgian Communists officially endorsed the Market, and Poland, with 20 per cent of her trade with the six

Common Market countries and Britain, conducted trade negotiations with it.

The Rift Between Russia and China

A far more portentous development than anything that had yet taken place in the Communist world was the growing breach between the Soviet and the Communist Chinese leaders. From the beginning, Mao had insisted on "different roads to socialism" and the Chinese had pursued their developments in their own way. But Soviet economic aid and technicians had accelerated China's industrialization, and, among other things, American opposition and the unavailablity of American loans and technicians had forced the Chinese to close cooperation and alliance with the Russians.

But around 1958 differences between the two powers became increasingly visible, and they grew. That year the Chinese replaced collectives, cooperatives, and individual peasant households with people's communes, military-type organizations whose members, male and female, would live together in barracks, eat in common mess halls, and be available for any work, industrial as well as agricultural, assigned them by directors. About 90 per cent of the country's people found themselves members of these communes. The Russian leaders did not think much of these and said publicly that they had experimented with them in a small way and that they had not worked. Chinese leaders took offense at this publicly expressed disapproval. More important, the Chinese felt that the Russians did not back them strongly enough in their demands for Formosa, and they especially resented the failure of the Russians to help them in their nuclear-weapons program or supply them with the smaller atomic weapons or even anything as modern as the Sidewinder air-to-air missiles which the United States was providing the air force of Chiang Kai-shek. What hurt even more was the reduction in the amount of Soviet economic aid to China. In agreements made in 1959, covering the next nine years, the Russians promised only about one-half the aid they had furnished during the previous nine-year period. Soviet aid was to be paid for by deliveries of Chinese commodities.

For their part, the Chinese publicly disagreed with the Soviet Union's increasing practice of giving "indiscriminate" aid to non-Communist countries, with Khrushchev's harping on anti-Stalinism, and with his peaceful-coexistence approach and pursuit of summit conferences. Khrushchev was irritated when in the late summer of 1959, just before his visit to President Eisenhower in Washington, the Chinese poured cold water on his *rapprochement*-with-the-West campaign and created provocative incidents in their border disputes with India. Immediately after his return from the United States Khrushchev visited Peiping and lectured the Chinese on the advantages of peaceful coexistence and the dangers of "predatory wars" and attempts to "test the stability of the capitalist system by force." The Chinese gave Khrushchev a chilly reception and at no time during Khrushchev's stay did Mao make any statement at all.

During 1960, 1961, and 1962 the conflict deepened. Chinese leaders and publications insisted that Khrushchev's anti-Stalinist campaign and his conciliatory approach to the West were non-Marxist, that ultimate war with the "capitalists and imperialists" was inevitable. Both sides sought allies among Communists and Communist parties of other countries. Marked differences of opinion on these issues existed inside all of the Communist parties (except perhaps the Chinese party), but Khrushchev succeeded in carrying the Communist parties of the Soviet Union and most of the satellites with him. Both the Soviet Union and China vied with each other in winning support by promises of economic aid to Outer Mongolia, North Korea, and Vietminh. (Although the Chinese needed Russian aid, they found the means to spare aid for Communist countries in Asia. When one studies the foreign-aid programs of all the countries in some detail he is struck by the amount of aid given by poor countries to poorer ones.) Outer Mongolia lined up with Russia, but North Korea and Vietminh attempted to dodge the issues by remaining silent. North Korea finally sided with China. Little Albania, because of its hatred of Yugoslavia, remained firmly Stalinist and aligned itself with China. Russia cut off aid to Albania and refused to invite representatives of the Albanian party to the big Communist gathering in Moscow in the fall of 1961.

At this conclave, where speaker after speaker castigated both dogmatism (Stalinism) and revisionism (Titoism), a ringing declaration on the primacy of peaceful coexistence was adopted. The gathering stepped up the anti-Stalinist campaign. (Shortly after the conference Stalin's body was removed from the Lenin-Stalin tomb on Red Square.) Khrushchev and others, instead of assailing China directly, denounced little Albania for its failure to follow the de-Stalinization line. Premier Chou En-lai took the floor in defense of Albania and then abruptly left Moscow while the congress still had more than a week to run. Following the conference, Russia and most of the satellites cut off diplomatic relations with Albania, but China responded by extending aid to Albania and sending Chinese technicians to replace the departing Russians.

Of more practical significance than these ideological thrusts and counterthrusts was Russia's withdrawal during 1960 and 1961 of hundreds of Soviet technicians from China, at the very time that country was in economic difficulties because of floods, droughts, agricultural failures, and the lagging of its five-year plan. The Russians also took the lead in 1961 and 1962 in arranging the cease-fire and compromise settlement in Laos.

What explained these differences between the Russians and the Chinese? For one thing, each had had a different cultural and historical experience. The Chinese were Oriental, while the Russian society was Western in its background, the product of the Christian Greek Orthodox tradition. Russia's old ruling classes and its intellectuals were heavily affected in the eighteenth and nineteenth centuries by German and French influences, and the intellectuals by the French Enlightenment. During most of the nineteenth century Chinese-Russian relations were not harmonious. Czarist Russia's most aggressive imperialism was at the expense of the Chinese—Russia's taking of the north bank of the Amur and the Maritime Province in 1860, Russian penetration into Manchuria in the 1890's, the clash of Russian-Chinese interests in Sinkiang and Outer Mongolia. After 1945 there was some Russian-Chinese rivalry in this same general area, particularly in Sinkiang, Outer Mongolia, and North Korea.

The Communists came to power in China with little help from the Russians. Mao Tse-tung, the Lenin of the Chinese Revolution, was remarkably independent of Moscow and gave Marxism an unusually flexible interpretation. "A revolution," observed Mao, "wanders where it can, retreats before superior forces, advances where it has room." The Chinese Revolution took a different course from the Russian in a number of ways: the seizure of power was done with an almost complete dependence on the peasantry and not on the proletariat; the use of "technological dualism," employing high labor ratios in rural areas and on public works and high capital ratios in key industrial sectors; the establishment of people's communes, thus making labor readily available for both agriculture and industry; the allowing of multi-class and non-Communist political organizations to exist, while maintaining undisputed leadership in the Communist party; the muting of ideological conflict within the Communist party, the long and continuous tenure of the top leaders and the absence of purges, liquidations, and bloody violence among them. In other ways, too, the Chinese had been flexible: their attempts to "let a hundred flowers bloom" and their backing up on this; their use of communes and their pragmatic modification of them; their denunciation of Malthusian fears of over-population as being un-Marxist (in failing to recognize the value-begetting quality of human labor and the ability of a rationally planned society to assimilate a large population) and at the same time their encouragement of the use of contraceptive devices.

While China's going its own way had caused some irritation in Moscow, that phase of Russian-Chinese relations now belonged to the past, and after 1955 it was the Russians who were flexible and accused the Chinese of inflexibility and dogmatism. The shift had occurred because of a change in "objective conditions," to use a Marxist phrase. The Chinese were in the crucial stages of their Herculean industrialization program. They wanted more economic aid from Russia. While the Chinese themselves gave some economic aid to non-Communist countries (Nepal, Cambodia, Ceylon, Indonesia, Algeria among them), most of their economic aid went to Communist countries such as North Korea, Vietminh, Outer Mongolia, Albania, Cuba. They were irritated that so much Soviet aid went to non-Communist countries and exasperated that now they were in the critical stages of their own industrialization the Russians gave them not more aid but less aid than formerly. The Chinese deplored the emphasis given to the de-Stalinization campaign. They themselves had preached and practiced "many roads to socialism" long before this became Soviet doctrine, but the Chinese did not want to eliminate

Stalinism as one of those roads. They were now in the Stalinist stage themselves. To the Chinese it seemed gratuitous for the Russians, in part for propaganda purposes in the West, to denounce the methods they themselves had used. True, Stalin had made mistakes, but the Chinese insisted that much of the ruthlessness of Stalinism had come out of "objective conditions," Russia's need at that time to collectivize the peasants and squeeze capital out of agriculture for rapid industrialization. What was most galling to the Chinese Communists, still desperately poor, was the cooling of revolutionary ardor in Russia with the growing affluence and "bourgeoisization" of Soviet society.

The Chinese disliked summit conferences because they were not included in them. They were afraid that Khrushchev, in his negotiations with the West, would make a deal at the expense of China. They were suspicious of arms limitations agreements because they were not convinced that war with "the imperialist powers" could be avoided. The Chinese believed that Khrushchev woefully underestimated the aggressiveness and intransigence of the Americans and that they understood this better than Khrushchev because they had fought the Americans in Korea, felt their military might in the Formosa Straits, and had been the "victims" of American "hatred" at the United Nations and at every international conference. Besides, if there were to be arms limitations, the freezing at some level of the military strength of the nations, then the Chinese wanted these postponed until they had nuclear weapons and therefore the bargaining power to win for themselves a quota of armaments comparable to the other powers.

The Chinese resented Khrushchev's lecturing them on "predatory wars," for they claimed that they had refrained from "liberating" the offshore islands, Formosa, and the Pescadores by force; that they had offered the Americans a peace pact of mutual nonaggression to make the Pacific a nuclear-free area; that they had kept the Geneva agreements of 1954 neutralizing Laos more faithfully than the Americans; that they had agreed to the 1962 settlement in Laos; that they had peacefully settled their quarrels with Nepal, Burma, and Indonesia. True, they had given indirect military aid to local Communists where control was uncertain and where there appeared to be possibilities of Communist victory, as in Vietnam and Laos—but so had the Russians. True, too, the Chinese had clashed with the Indians along the Himalayan border, but this was because all Chinese, including the Nationalist Chinese, refused to recognize the British McMahon Line as the legal Chinese-Indian boundary. This, argued the Chinese, was a national and not an ideological matter, and they pointed out that they had not followed up their victories with a penetration into India, which their military superiority over India would have allowed them to have done. Besides, argued the Chinese, if one did not "swallow" the Indian view of the McMahon Line, the Indians had been provocative in the border areas, and the Chinese had merely countered their "provocations." (Incidentally, this Chinese contention was not without some support in high diplomatic and military quarters in the West.)

The Russians seemed uneasy about their Chinese neighbor with its population explosion, its growing technological strength, and the certainty that within a few years it would have nuclear weapons. Despite floods, droughts, scarcities, and laggings in their five-year plans, the Chinese appeared on the way to the industrial breakthrough. The Russians would have to share leadership in the Communist world with China. The Russian-Chinese border stretched interminably, Siberia was still relatively lightly populated, and in the future would crowded China covet some of Siberia's open spaces? The immediate source of Khrushchev's apprehension about the Chinese was their "dogmatism" in not evaluating the impact of the nuclear revolution in war on world politics and history, their refusal to adjust Marxist doctrine to the world's new realities, their harping on the inevitability of war with the capitalist powers in an age when if Communism were going to win at all it would have to be by peaceful means.

In the fall of 1962 the differences between Russia and China reached a new pitch of acrimony. The Chinese proclaimed that Khrushchev's back-down in Cuba was "another Munich." Even before the Cuban crisis the Chinese had stepped up their military attacks along India's Himalayan border, in part, the Russians believed, to embarrass Khrushchev's drive for peaceful coexistence and his friendly policy toward India. After the Cuban crisis, perhaps to further advertise to the Communist world that they were the true leaders of a militant Marxism and Khrushchev an apostate to it, the Chinese extended their war against India. (At least this was the way it looked to Soviet leaders.) Maoism seemed to be making a strong impact throughout the Communist world; in late 1962 the Bulgarian Communist party went through an upheaval and many Maoists were purged.

Nehru professed to believe that the arms and military planes contracted for before the Chinese attack would be delivered to India by the Soviet Union. Khrushchev was in a dilemma: to send arms to India in the altered circumstances would be a betrayal of his ally; not to send them would alienate the neutrals and undermine his drive for peaceful coexistence. Nehru was consistent: he appeared blandly to assume that just as India got economic aid from both the West and the Soviet Union, so even during its war of self-defense, his country, neutral as between the United States and the Soviet Union, would get arms from both. The crisis was dramatic in its larger historical implications: in Stalin's time it was China which appeared more flexible and possibly the weak link in the Communist world; now it was the Chinese who were the more aggressive and the Russians the more conciliatory; Nehru attempted to use his own uncomfortable situation to prove the reality of diversity within the Communist bloc, to support his contention that the world was moving in the direction of depolarization, pluralism, neutralism, and eventual peace.

In late 1962 and January of 1963, the quarrel between Russia and China reached a still higher pitch of public acrimony. China's attack on India was denounced by Soviet leaders as "dangerous adventurism," and the Soviet Union finally confirmed the sale of MIG jet fighters, which might be used against invading Red Chinese troops, to India. At the conference of the Italian Communist party in Rome, Red China was denounced by name, "for when we Communists want to say China we don't have to say Albania." Tito was welcomed in Moscow and trade and aid arrangements were negotiated between Russia and Yugoslavia. Khrushchev publicly ridiculed the Red Chinese for stopping their war on India and declared that the Chinese comrades, too, perhaps had discovered that imperialism's "paper tiger" had nuclear teeth. At a January meeting in East Berlin of Communist parties from many countries, Khrushchev announced that the "success" of the Berlin Wall rendered the problem of West Berlin less important than it had been, that West Berlin was not worth a war, that those who called America a paper tiger should be reminded that the Americans had 40,000 atomic and nuclear warheads. Even Ulbricht was for the first time conciliatory in his public remarks about the

Berlin question. Yugoslav delegates were pointedly welcomed to the gathering, and when China's delegates attacked revisionist Yugoslavia, they were howled down. (It was in these months, during the "afterglow" of the Russian backdown in Cuba and the heightened intensity of the Russian-Chinese rift, that Khrushchev was most conciliatory about Berlin and made his offer to Kennedy to accept on-site inspection in a test-ban treaty. After January, when the Gaullist rift in the Western alliance widened, Khrushchev appeared somewhat cooler in his conciliatory approach to the West.)

While the conflict within the Communist world over the implications for Marxist doctrine of the nuclear revolution in war appeared to be one between Khrushchev and Mao, between Russia and China, it actually cut across almost all the Communist parties, including the Soviet party. It might even result in toppling Khrushchev's leadership in Russia, for while Khrushchev's conciliatory approach to the West had paid some dividends—Kennedy's allowing Khrushchev to save face after his Cuban backdown and some moderation of relations between the Communist countries and the Vatican—it had not brought a settlement of the German and Berlin questions, still less of the situation in the Formosa Straits, and Khrushchev as yet had few actual successes with which to persuade doubting "orthodox" Marxists. The Khrushchev policies had slowed down the Communist "momentum" in southeast Asia, too, and Asian Communists seemed more and more to line up with Mao. But even if Khrushchev should fall from power, this probably would be followed not by less but by more conflict inside the Communist world, for the basic question of how the Communist powers should approach the non-Communist powers in this age of cataclysmic nuclear weapons would not down.

However, it was still too early to say whether the divisive or the unifying forces within the Marxist world were the stronger. It should be emphasized that Marxism gave both the Russians and the Chinese a common way of viewing history, society, and world politics. The Marxists themselves knew that Marxist theory was broad enough to leave room for all sorts of actions. The distinction between China and the Soviet Union was whether to emphasize this or that element in the package of Marxist tactics which the leaders of both countries theoretically approved. Moreover, as the Chinese Revolution grew older, as the rigors of early industrialization and collectivization subsided and China passed over the industrial hump, and as China's managers, engineers, technicians, and professional people proliferated, then that revolution, like the Russian before it, would likely grow more moderate, and the current Sino-Russian differences about tactics would likely recede. And looking into the long future, Marxism itself might become so devitalized by revisionism on revisionism as to render it merely mythological and ritualistic and no longer a guide to driving practical action. But this view, increasingly held in the West, that Marxism had largely become an historical instrument for the rapid industrializing of backward countries which, when industrialized, would develop some kind of variant middle-class society, might seriously underestimate the potential of totalitarian elites to perpetuate their power structures and the depth of conviction of uniformly educated populations that collectivism indeed represented a superior way of life.

Significance of the Rifts in the Communist World

There was no longer any doubt that the Communist world was not only polynational but polycentric. There were forces at work to divide it and to unite it. Whether a major international crisis would increase the division or the unity of the Communist world would depend on the circumstances of the particular crisis; in the multiplicity of interests which involved any state, some Communist countries might find the Communist attraction the most binding of their interests and others might not. A world war or a situation involving the survival of Communism itself would probably find the Communist countries acting together, just as Mao, Gomulka, and Tito supported Khrushchev in suppressing the Hungarian uprising. But the rift between China and Russia had by 1963 reached such proportions as to cast some doubt on even that.

American policy had done little to exploit the divisive elements in the Communist world. What little it had done, as in giving aid to Tito, had modestly contributed to encourage Yugoslav independence. In the early days of the Chinese revolution the United States, by giving some economic and technical aid, might have rendered the Chinese more independent of Moscow. Since 1955, and particularly since 1959, the United States, by a tentatively friendly nod now and then, might have added persuasiveness in the Communist world to Khrushchev's doctrine of peaceful coexistence as a general principle or goal. However, Khrushchev had little to show for his efforts.

Americans had tended to treat the Communist world as much more monolithic than it was in fact. As Professor Howard Zinn pointed out, Americans insisted on thinking of the Communists as invariably intransigent. "When their words are moderate we are suspicious, and when they are tough we believe them. When their deeds are nasty, we note them. When they make a concilia-tory move, we say they don't mean it and point to Marxist theory. We switch from believing statements to believing prac-tice, depending on which is politically expedient for us." Some Americans actually suspected that the resounding conflict in the Communist world between the Stalinists and the anti-Stalinists, between the Chinese and the Russians, was merely a gigantic hoax perpetrated to deceive the West. In molding a realistic American foreign policy it was just as important to understand the divisive forces in the Communist world as it was to understand the unifying forces, and more important to understand the actual historical evolution than Marxist theory.

The Limits of Big-Power Influence

Since 1945 both the United States and the Soviet Union had built an awesome arsenal of nuclear weapons. In physical power they stood in a class by themselves. But since the Korean War both powers had increasingly recoiled from pressing situations which might lead to war, big or little, unlimited or limited. And ironically enough, as the armaments had swelled, the influence of Washington in the non-Communist world and of Moscow in the Communist world had declined. Nothing better illustrated the limits of sheer physical power.

A world war or a crisis which seriously threatened to become this would probably revive bipolarization, but in such an event it appeared that the Western world would be more unified than the Communist one, except in the unlikely (though possible) con-tingency that Western leadership had become right-wing, reactionary, and "Fascist," and the conflict thus assumed the apocalyptic character of Marxist prophecy.

[10]

E PLURIBUS UNUM

Nationalism, Regionalism, and Internationalism

Not since the days when the Aegean and Mediterranean worlds were dotted with little self-governing city societies were there so many independent states as there were in the 1960's. The twentieth century had indeed become the century of national self-determination. If there was no longer a multiple balance of power there was certainly a multiplicity in the international "system." Indeed, many of the new nations owed their existence to the disintegration of the larger political units upon which the old balance of power had depended. And in most of the new states, nationalism was no ordinary political phenomenon but a secular religion.

On the other hand, never had independent states shown so ready a disposition to voluntarily cooperate and even federate with one another as did the nations of the latter half of the twentieth century. This trend was being literally forced on the nations by the technological revolution which was eliminating distance and producing increasingly accelerated interdependence and by the fragmenting of the world into so many small political units.

Nations were more and more cooperating on both a regional and an international basis. Among the regional organizations were the well-known Organization of American States, the European Coal and Steel Community, Euratom, the European Economic Community, the European Free Trade Association, the Council of Europe, the Western European Union, Eastern Europe's Council of Economic Mutual Assistance, the Arab League, the Colombo Plan countries. Among the many lesser known were the Union of African States (Ghana, Guinea, and Mali), the Council of the Entente, the Brazzaville Conference group, the Casablanca Conference group, the Latin American Free Trade Area, the Central American Economic Integration area. The many regional organizations differed from one another in kind and degree of cooperation, but they all evidenced unmistakably the urge to unite to tackle common problems.

On top of the nations and the regional associations were the United Nations, its many international agencies, and other international organizations.

The Political Evolution of the United Nations

One of the most significant developments after World War II was the evolution of the United Nations. The United Nations began in 1945 with a membership of fifty-one. For the first ten years of the United Nations' existence its growth in membership was very slow. For several years a deadlock existed over the admission of new member states. In the Security Council, the Soviet Union vetoed the proposed non-Communst states, while the United States vetoed the proposed Communist states. In December 1955 the long impasse was at last broken and sixteen new members were admitted in an omnibus deal which involved concessions on both sides. The sixteen new members, which brought the total membership of the United Nations to seventy-six, were the Communist states of Albania, Bulgaria, Hungary, and Rumania, and the non-Communist states of Austria, Cambodia, Ceylon, Finland, Ireland, Italy, Jordan, Laos, Libya, Nepal, Portugal, and Spain. The Communist state of Outer Mongolia failed to be admitted, which led the Soviet Union to veto the admission of Japan. The admission of the new Communist members boosted the Communist bloc's votes to nine. In November 1956 the Sudan, Morocco, and Tunisia were admitted to membership; and in December, Japan, with Russia committed to Japanese admission as a result of the agreement between the Soviet Union and Japan earlier in the year, became a member. Within the year, then, the membership of the United Nations climbed from sixty to eighty, and thus that organization came nearer the universality to which its supporters aspired.

After 1953, debates in the General Assembly reflected less the East-West conflict and more the differences of opinion on colonialism and economic aid to the underdeveloped peoples. Another significant trend after 1953 was the increasing tendency, still limited, however, of the Communist members to join the specialized technical agencies of the United Nations. In the past, the work of these agencies had generally been confined to the non-Communist members. Increased Communist participation was most marked in the International Labor Organization and in UNESCO. However, this resulted in a backward step, a step away from the cause of true internationalism, when a constitutional amendment was adopted which required that henceforth UNESCO's twenty-two-man Executive Board would serve in a governmental rather than a personal capacity. This would establish in UNESCO the practice common to most international bodies and prevent individual representatives from multilaterally breaking away from the restraints of their national governments and power blocs to form functional combinations representing international points of view and interests, as distinct from national points of view and interests.

Another decided spurt in membership came in 1960 when eighteen new nations were admitted to membership—seventeen African states and Cyprus—which boosted the member nations to ninety-nine. Five new states were admitted in 1961, and six new states in 1962—Ruanda, Burundi, Algeria, Jamaica, Trinidad-Tobago, and Uganda. By 1963, then, the United Nations membership stood at 110, of which 32 were African states. It was rather ironic that of all the continents the last to get nationalism was the one which furnished the largest number of nations to the world organization.

Still the United Nations had not attained universality. The nations partitioned by the Cold War were not members—West and East Germany, North and South Korea, North and South Vietnam. The world's most populous nation and one of its very oldest—mainland China—was still not a member.

The admission of so many new states from the former colonial areas of the world shifted the balance of power within the United

Nations away from the Western countries. In general, the views of the new nations differed from American policies in several ways. In the disarmament debates these nations tended to put much less emphasis on the importance of effective international inspection and control. They were forever pushing for the establishment of new international agreements to stabilize commodity prices. They pressed for the rapid liquidation of all that remained of colonialism, and in this they were frequently backed by the Latin American bloc and the Communist bloc. On questions of disarmament the Asia-African bloc was often supported by the Communist bloc, and on questions of international economic aid by the Latin American bloc. The new nations were also clamoring for an enlargement of the number of seats in the Security Council and in the Economic and Social Council, so that more of them would have the opportunity to serve on these bodies.

The United Nations was clearly within its legal rights in laying down general policies with respect to territories under United Nations trusteeship, and the Assembly prodded the administering powers to hasten the conversion of their trust territories into independent nations. By 1963 almost all of the trust territories had become independent states and members of the United Nations. The United Nations was also clearly within its rights in insisting that the Union of South Africa give an accounting of the administration of its old League of Nations mandate in South West Africa. But the Assembly often boldly pushed on into less clearly defined fields and demanded that the colonial powers rapidly liquidate their rule in their own remaining dependent territories. Animated Assembly debates had taken place over the British position in Cyprus, Indonesia's claims to Dutch West New Guinea, French policies in Tunisia, Morocco, and Algeria, Portugal's maladministration in Angola, and so forth.

However, when the shoe was on the other foot and India seized Portuguese Goa, the new nations regarded this illegal action as a mere continuation of the Indian national revolution which was justified in taking over an Indian national "irredenta." In this case the United Nations was unable to take action. The United States time and again had been confronted with the difficult role of mediating between its allies, the old colonial powers of Western Europe, and the anti-colonial nations of Asia and

Africa, which it hoped to win to its side or at least keep out of the Soviet camp. The Soviet bloc, with no allies among the old colonial powers, had been free to throw its influence to the Asian-African bloc.

However, the Western powers and the United States had not suffered the setbacks in the United Nations which had generally been feared as more and more new and neutral states were admitted to that body. It will be recalled that most of the new nations had not entirely cut their ties with their former imperial rulers; most of the former British colonies were members of the British Commonwealth and most of the former French colonies in Africa were either members of the French Community or continued in close treaty relations with France. Most of the Latin American countries could usually still be counted on to support United States policies when America's vital interests were at stake. The Brazzaville group of former French colonies in Africa, along with Nigeria, Sierra Leone, Tanganyika, and Liberia, could usually be depended to take moderate views. And in any clear-cut East-West confrontation, the West's military allies, such as Formosa, the Philippines, Thailand, Pakistan, Iran, and Turkey, were of course in the Western camp. Doubtlessly the underdeveloped countries were often motivated, too, by their desires for American economic aid.

As a result, among other evidence of America's continued power and prestige in the United Nations, the United States escaped condemnation for its U-2 flight. The Western-supported candidates for the six non-permanent seats on the Security Council continued to fare surprisingly well, and the customary staggering of the six seats among geographical regions or political associations—Western Europe, Eastern Europe, Latin America, the Commonwealth, Asia, the Middle East, and Africa—and among the nations within them was left essentially unimpaired. Most unexpectedly of all, Red China was still refused admission to the United Nations, although in 1961 the United States had to play some shrewd politics to that end and, in deference to the wishes of the new nations, pressure Nationalist China into withholding its usual veto in the Security Council to the admission of Communist Outer Mongolia to the United Nations.

In its main function, the keeping of the peace among the nations, the United Nations' record was a mixed one. It had done better than its critics surmised. In every year since its existence it had contributed valuable work in restraining, moderating, or settling international conflicts. Among the instances of its serving the peace were its pressuring Britain and France to evacuate Syria and Lebanon in 1946; its exerting influence on the Soviet Union to withdraw from northern Iran that same year; its arranging of cease-fires between the Netherlands and Indonesia in 1947 and again in 1949 and its hastening of Indonesian independence; its conclusion of a cease-fire in Kashmir between India and Pakistan in 1949; its work in helping to stop the fighting between Israel and the Arab states in 1948 and 1949 and the part it played in securing an Israeli-Arab truce in 1949; the policing by its emergency military force along the Israel-Arab borders since 1956 and its checking of violence and commando raids there; the moderating influence of its observers in Lebanon and Jordan in 1958; U Thant's "persuading" Khrushchev in October 1962 to divert his ships away from Cuba, thus allowing him to save face while in effect capitulating by avoiding a showdown at sea.

By far the most notable accomplishments of the United Nations were its checking of aggression in Korea in 1950 and 1951; its stopping of the British-French-Israeli attack on Egypt in 1956 (although, of course, the fact that both the United States and Soviet Union exerted their top influence to this end was the prime factor); and its intervention in the Congo in 1960 to prevent a direct confrontation and clash of the Soviet Union and the United States.

Even when the United Nations was unable to insinuate itself effectively into major conflicts and developments involving the big powers, the services provided by that organization in furnishing headquarters and liaison facilities for conferences and negotiations in New York and Geneva and the continuing impact of personal contact among United Nations representatives and personnel were of incalculable value. Even more to the point, during the October 1962 Cuban crisis, the United Nations provided a site where both the United States and the Soviet Union could enter into bilateral negotiations, with no need for either party to yield prestige.

The United Nations made little headway in directly restraining the super-powers—the Soviet Union and the United States. And although the nuclear-weapons test ban and the disarmament discussions were held under the sponsorship of the United Nations Disarmament Commission, the negotiations were really in the hands of the United States and the U.S.S.R., and these failed to make headway. However, opinion in the Disarmament Commission and in the Assembly helped keep the American-Soviet negotiations alive. The continued failure of the United Nations Security Council to implement Articles 43 and 45 of the Charter, under which the member nations, particularly the big powers, were to set aside a portion of their armed forces for the United Nations, was a disappointment. However, this had not prevented the creation of an emergency United Nations military force in the Middle East and in the Congo, drawn from the small and neutral countries.

Some felt that it was unjust to restrain the little powers and not the big ones, to vote sanctions against the lesser powers and allow the United States and the U.S.S.R. to go unscathed. For a time in 1956 it appeared that sanctions might be voted against Israel, when it was well known that even if sanctions were voted against Russia for the brutal suppression of the Hungarian rising that same year they would be of little avail. The cry arose: "The same morality for the big power as for the little one." Again: "Why punish the little country and let the big one go scot free?" But this was an attitude which might well wreck all collective security, for in the present stage of international development it was wise to state frankly that effective sanctions were well-nigh impossible against a big power like the Soviet Union or the United States, that collective security had to be developed where it could be made to work. It could be made to work against the smaller powers (at least in some cases), and it was worth enforcing against the smaller powers because the conflicts of the smaller powers often reflected the rivalry of the big powers, and if the conflicts of the smaller countries could be settled, such settlements would prevent the smaller conflicts from ripening into bigger ones directly involving the super-powers. The localizing, checking, and settling of the lesser conflicts prevented their developing into major ones.

The United Nations was slowly evolving methods for making

peaceful changes in international situations. It was important to remove the causes of international conflicts, and conflicts often came out of situations which demanded change rather than mere adjudication of existing legal rights. The legal machinery emphasized the *status quo;* the political machinery would have to provide the means of peaceful change. One of the methods used by the United Nations was to send a team of observers or mediators to a trouble spot to gather information, or operate as a moderating influence, or suggest a basis for settlement. The team of United Nations observers sent to Lebanon in 1958 may have helped the Lebanese political leaders make the internal compromise in which President Chamoun gave up his plan to remain in office and agreed to a government take-over by the opposition. The internal civil war in Lebanon, which had grave international repercussion, was a political one and yielded to political compromise. The United Nations' growing use of plebiscites appeared on the way to becoming institutionalized as a method for making peaceful change. In 1956 the United Nations conducted a plebiscite in British Togoland to determine whether that territory would remain under British administration or join Ghana. The people voted 93,000 to 67,000 to join Ghana. In United Nations plebiscites held in the British Cameroons in 1961, the northern part of the territory voted for union with Nigeria, while the southern part voted to join the new nation of Cameroun. In 1962 the United Nations worked out a compromise between the Netherlands and Indonesia in which Dutch West New Guinea (West Irian) was peacefully transferred to the United Nations to be administered by the international organization for a time and then transferred to Indonesia. War was averted, "face" was saved, and change was made peacefully.

A most important step toward making the internal machinery of the United Nations effective to maintain peace was taken on November 3, 1950, when the General Assembly passed the "Uniting for Peace" resolution sponsored by the United States. This attempted to make sure that the United Nations would be able to take hold in an emergency even though action was blocked by a veto in the Security Council. Under the "Uniting for Peace" rule, if a crisis arose and action was blocked in the Security Council, the Assembly could be called into emergency session by

any seven members of the Security Council. Once the Assembly
was in session it could pass resolutions, demand a cease-fire, dispatch special observers or mediators to the scene, call on member
nations to apply economic sanctions or military sanctions or both,
create its own emergency police or military force, or do anything
else appropriate to the situation. In passing this "Uniting for
Peace" rule, the Assembly in effect asserted that the veto blocked
action only in the Council, that non-action by the Council left
the Assembly free to handle the crisis.

The Assembly also created an Interim Committee, composed
of the representatives of all the member states, to carry on when
the Assembly was not sitting. One of its most important duties was
to watch for dangers to the peace and to provide for calling the
Assembly into emergency session. The Assembly also established
the Peace Observation Commission, comprised of fourteen states,
including the five permanent members of the Security Council.
The Commission, at the service of the Interim Committee, the
Assembly, and the Security Council, developed the practice of
sending observers to trouble spots, with the consent of a nation
whose territory was under observation, so that the United Nations might have trustworthy information.

The "Uniting for Peace" rule not only enhanced the effectiveness of the United Nations but it also illustrated how institutions
evolve organically to meet changing conditions and new chal-
lenges. The United Nations Charter seemed destined to undergo
the same kind of enlarging process experienced by the United
States Constitution. "Uniting for Peace" also increased the prestige and power of the General Assembly. However, very frequently the Assembly tended to think it had done its duty when
it debated a question and indicated the proper policy to be pursued, whether that policy was actually implemented or not. In
1956, Secretary-General Hammarskjold recommended "greater
emphasis on the United Nations as an instrument for negotiations
of settlements, as distinct from the mere debate of issues." Others
warned of the excesses of "microphone diplomacy," of the danger
that debates in the Assembly might exacerbate rather than allevi-
ate tensions, and in some cases (for instance, the Assembly debates and resolutions condemning the Soviet suppression of the
Hungarian uprising) arouse expectations that could not be ful-

filled. However, there was no doubt that the debates, resolutions, and actions of the Assembly had come to have great moral weight, and that sometimes they contributed to effective settlements. And most important, unlike the experience of the League of Nations, the increasing activities of the Assembly had not seriously impaired the influence of the Security Council. For instance, during 1960 the Security Council held more than seventy sessions, gave much consideration to the U-2 and RB-47 incidents, and initiated some of the United Nations' important work in the Congo.

As the United Nations' functions expanded so also did its administrative responsibilities. Among the more important of its administrative activities of a political nature were the clearing of the Suez Canal, the upkeep of around 1 million Arab refugees along the Israel-Arab borders, the maintenance of an emergency military police force of over 5000 men along the Israeli-Egyptian demarcation line and the Gulf of Aqaba, the deployment of a military force of around 20,000 men in the Congo, and the sustaining of administrative and technical services in that country. At the same time, the United Nations' permanent administrative and specialized agencies had multiplied and extended their work.

The Evolution of International Administrative Agencies

A large number of commissions and specialized agencies—some of them pre-League of Nations, some of them coming out of the League, and some of them founded at the time the United Nations was established or thereafter—were connected with the United Nations, either directly or indirectly. Some of these agencies were composed of all the members of the United Nations, but some of them were made up of only a part of the United Nations membership. Not infrequently the Communist member nations of the United Nations refused to join certain of the agencies, and sometimes non-Communist nations declined to join this or that agency. Some of the agencies were financially sustained from the United Nations budget; some of them by assessments on the individual member states; and some of them by voluntary contributions.

A number of international agencies were almost entirely technical and removed from political coloration. The International Telecommunication Union dealt with international telephone, telegraph, radio, and television services. It worked to get nations to agree to a practical allocation of radio frequency bands. The radio spectrum had to be allocated to maritime and aeronautical communications, weather reports, radio and television broadcasting, amateur radio, and various kinds of scientific work. The Universal Postal Union administered the international agreements whereby every member nation for a reasonable charge had the right to send its mail over every other member's transport services and use its postal facilities, so that mail coming in from abroad was delivered at no extra charge. The Intergovernmental Marine Consultative Organization promoted the highest standards of navigation and safety at sea. The World Meteorological Organization promoted a quick exchange of weather information, standardization of weather observations, uniform methods of reporting, and improved ways of applying meteorology to shipping, aviation, and agriculture. The International Civil Aviation Organization helped member states coordinate air rights, safety, weather reports, traffic control, radio beacons, and communications. The United Nations Commission on Narcotic Drugs, the Permanent Central Opium Board, and the Drug Supervisory Body dealt with the estimates and trade statistics that determined the quantities of various drugs that could be legally shipped to the various countries and developed methods for detecting violations. All of these organizations promoted scientific and technical research in their respective fields and encouraged international standardization of practices.

Some of the agencies were social in character and dealt with ordinary people and problems at the grass roots. The Food and Agriculture Organization sent information and experts to advise member nations on how to increase the productivity of their land, forests, and fisheries. It was concerned with conservation, erosion, the use of fertilizer, the experimenting with and introducing of new kinds of crops, how to control pests and plant and animal diseases. In 1960 the FAO was asked to broaden President Eisenhower's "food-for-peace" program and become a clearinghouse to facilitate the transfer of surplus foods from surplus to deficit countries. The World Health Organization made war on the widespread diseases and plagues, particularly in the underdeveloped countries. It sent information and technicians to help fight malaria, tuberculosis, syphilis, yaws, leprosy, typhus, polio, and other maladies. The International Labor Organization promoted laws for the protection of wage-workers by holding annual conferences and proposing international agreements which the delegates submitted to their respective governments for ratification. A government which signed one of these agreements promised to work to enact its substance into domestic law. For instance, in 1958 the conference of the ILO adopted a formal convention designed to eliminate discrimination in occupations and employment in signatory countries through pursuit of national policies aimed at promoting equality of opportunity and treatment of the labor force. The United Nations International Children's Emergency Fund supplied medicines, food, and equipment for maternal and child welfare services, for child nutrition, for the control of diseases especially affecting children, and for the relief of children of refugees and children caught in famine and other disaster situations. Its activities sometimes overlapped those of FAO and WHO, and the three organizations frequently worked together.

One of the most far-reaching of the agencies was the United Nations Educational, Scientific, and Cultural Organization. UNESCO required that each of its member nations bring its educational, scientific, and cultural organizations into touch with UNESCO headquarters, thus facilitating international cultural cross-fertilization. UNESCO sponsored the International Copyright Convention of 1952 to protect the rights of authors and artists in all the ratifying countries. It facilitated international exchanges in research findings, books and other publications, educational equipment, phonograph records, and motion pictures. It encouraged teacher training, educational surveys, traveling scientific exhibitions, and national and international associations and meetings of teachers and scientists. Its representatives encouraged the governments of underdeveloped countries to send out itinerant teachers to instruct adults and children of the agricultural villages in health, sanitation, cleanliness, vocational matters, and the rudiments of reading and writing, thus laying the groundwork for systems of more formal education later on. Since more than half of the world's children still did not go to school, these UNESCO activities were of inestimable value. UNESCO's revenues came from direct assessments on its member nations.

The International Law Commission of the United Nations was

carrying on a monumental work of codifying international law. A notable gain for international cooperation was achieved in 1960 when the Antarctic Treaty, initiated in the United Nations, was ratified by the United States, the Soviet Union, and other countries. This treaty provided for a moratorium on the assertion of all national territorial claims in the Antarctic and the outright prohibition of any form of military activity in the Antarctic area, a prohibition enforced by international inspection. This illustrated how much could be accomplished in an area where there was an absence of big-power rivalry.

However, there was an increasing disagreement among the nations about extending the breadth of the territorial sea and the related issue of national fishing rights. The United States and the other Western maritime powers wanted to maintain the existing three-mile limit to territorial waters but the Soviet Union and most of the underdeveloped countries wanted to extend territorial waters to at least twelve miles. Some of the smaller countries even attempted unilaterally to broaden their territorial waters beyond the twelve-mile distance. At a United Nations Conference on the Law of the Sea held in 1958 and another in 1960, the United States and other Western maritime powers were able by narrow votes to prevent changes in the traditional territorial sea, but the consensus was that the three-mile limit was now outmoded and would eventually be extended.

Additional United Nations agencies were created as new needs arose. The International Atomic Energy Agency, which came out of President Eisenhower's suggestion of 1953 that the nations develop an "atoms for peace" program, began operating in 1957 with eighty nations as members. To get the project started, the United States supplied 5000 kilograms of uranium 253, the Soviet Union 50 kilograms, and other nations smaller amounts. International inspection was provided to make sure that stocks of nuclear materials supplied to the Agency were not diverted to weapons purposes. Among other things, the Agency was designed to help those nations which did not have sufficient economic and scientific resources to develop atomic-energy programs on their own. A research laboratory was constructed at Vienna, seat of the Agency. The Agency provided facilities for the advanced training of researchers and technicians. Experts supplied by the

Agency helped the various countries plan their use of atomic power. Under Agency sponsorship, studies were made of the application of radioactive materials in agriculture, industry, and medicine, of the protection of workers and the public from harmful radiation, of the safe disposal of waste materials, and of the safeguards against illicit use. The program for supplying uranium to member states had not progressed far. It seemed that the actual building and use of atomic power plants was being delayed by their high cost compared with coal and oil burning plants. Atomic power might soon be economically useful in countries where coal and oil were scarce or expensive, but it appeared that it was something for the future in the countries where the older fuels were still plentiful.

In 1959 the United Nations General Assembly established a special United Nations Committee on the Peaceful Uses of Outer Space, with strong representation for Communist and neutral countries as an inducement to Soviet participation, for the purpose of probing into the legal and scientific aspects of international cooperation in outer space. The dimensions of the problem were being constantly extended by the development of new types of rockets and satellites. Many questions had already been raised: the legitimacy of satellite overflights, the possible use of reconnaissance satellites and of photographic and radar observation of another country's territory, traffic controls, damage liability, and so forth. The Committee got off to a bad start and little was yet accomplished. As a guide to the Committee's labors, the United Nations Assembly in 1961 passed a resolution endorsing the principle that international law, including the United Nations Charter, applied to outer space and celestial bodies. These were declared free for exploration and use by all states and not subject to national appropriation. The resolution also called for notification to the United Nations of all space launchings.

Some of the most important international agencies were concerned with trade and economic development. The International Monetary Fund, whose reserve was supplied by the member nations on a quota basis, advised each member state how it might stay out of balance-of-payment difficulties which arose when for several years running the people of a given nation sold less abroad than they bought. The nations were counseled to make long-time adjustments by lowering their trade barriers with a view of increasing the total flow of world trade, to prevent inflation (so that they did not price themselves out of the world market), and to keep their currencies freely convertible into the currencies of other countries. A nation in difficulties, however, was usually advised to undergo an austerity program by cutting its imports temporarily, and in extreme cases to devalue its currency by reducing its value in ounces of gold, so that a foreign buyer could buy more of the devalued money than before, thus enjoying a kind of special discount. But most nations did not join the Monetary Fund to get advice but to get emergency help when they continued to suffer a deficit in foreign trade. A member nation with balance-of-payment difficulties went to the Fund to get the foreign currency or currencies it needed, paying in its own currency. When it had passed its difficulties and had re-established its own reserve, the nation restored its position in the Fund by buying back its own currency in dollars, or other convertible currencies, or in gold.

Following the failure of the United States to ratify the International Trade Organization, the preparatory committee of the United Nations' Economic and Social Council went ahead with a less formal arrangement known as the General Agreement on Tariffs and Trade, which set up periodic conferences where the United States and other leading trading countries met to bargain on reciprocal tariff reductions. These conferences were animated by the liberal and non-discriminatory trade principles of the aborted ITO. An important rule was that if two countries agreed to reduce certain tariffs for each other's benefit, then all the GATT members were given the opportunity for the same reciprocal reductions. It was when the European Common Market entered these bargainings and proposed across-the-board reductions in whole series of items that the United States had to amend its own Trade Agreements Act to permit such practice by the United States.

Under the eighteen-member Organization for European Economic Cooperation, demanded by the Marshall Plan, European countries had additional facilities for encouraging intra-European trade, convertibility of currencies, and the easing of balance-of-payment difficulties. In 1961 the OEEC was replaced by the Organization for Economic Cooperation and Development in which the United States and Canada joined eighteen European nations in a North Atlantic organization which provided machinery for the discussion of the mutual economic and trading problems of the twenty signatory nations. Within this organization there was the eleven-member Development Assistance Group composed of the leading nations of the North Atlantic and Japan. The United States encouraged each member of the Development Assistance Group to set aside at least 1 per cent of its annual gross national product for economic aid to underdeveloped countries.

The International Bank for Reconstruction and Development (World Bank) was designed originally to help in the economic recovery of war-torn Europe, but after the Marshall Plan took over, the Bank turned to basic projects in the underdeveloped countries such as roads, railroads, electric power plants, flood control, irrigation, and so forth. Each member nation, in proportion to its wealth, subscribed to the Bank's stock, but up to 80 per cent of this was merely in the form of guarantees to cover the Bank's liabilities. Actually, most of the money loaned by the Bank was obtained by selling its bonds on the money markets of the world. The Bank made loans to member governments, or their agencies, or to private enterprises in member states when the governments guaranteed the loans. The Bank made only "hard" loans, those that gave every indication of repayment in business-like fashion. By 1960 the Bank's members had doubled their subscriptions, and its subscribed capital had risen from about 10 billion to about 19 billion dollars.

In 1956 the International Finance Corporation was organized, a separate agency closely affiliated with the Bank. Its purpose was to encourage the development of private enterprise in the underdeveloped countries. It made loans to private ventures, and there were no government guarantees of the loans. Most loans went to processing industries and to enterprises which turned out such things as rubber and lumber products, cement and concrete, cotton textiles and rayon, and electrical equipment.

The International Development Association, although closely affiliated with the Bank, was a separate United Nations specialized agency established in 1960. The underdeveloped countries had reached their capacity to absorb "hard" loans, and the IDA was set up to make "soft"' loans to the governments of the member states for large projects which could not qualify for regular World Bank financing. The IDA had an authorized capitalization of 1 billion dollars.

In 1950 the United Nations Expanded Program of Technical Assistance was inaugurated. Its funds were raised each year by the voluntary contributions of the member nations. The United Nations and eight related agencies shared the funds available each year. The Technical Assistance Board, established within the Secretariat to administer part of the program, took care that priority was given to projects which did not fall to FAO, WHO, or other related agencies. From 1950 to 1960 the Expanded Program sent 8000 experts to 140 countries and territories and gave 14,000 fellowships for students from underdeveloped countries to study abroad.

In 1959 the United Nations Special Fund was established to cover gaps in the other technical assistance programs. Administered by a Governing Council, the Fund concentrated on research surveys of underdeveloped countries to determine economic potentialities, and helped organize urgent training courses for administrators, teachers, engineers, and other technicians. The budgets of both the Expanded Program and the Special Fund were raised by voluntary contributions of member nations, and each ran around 30 million dollars a year, not counting the amounts added to specific projects by the countries assisted.

However, the underdeveloped peoples were not satisfied with the existing international agencies for giving them economic aid. In most cases they could not qualify for the "hard" loans of the Bank, the resources of the International Development Association were regarded as inadequate, and technical assistance was thought to be far less important than capital for economic development. In 1960 the underdeveloped countries in the United Nations unanimously asked for a Special United Nations Fund for Economic Development (SUNFED) on the grounds that existing agencies for supplying capital were inadequate, that receipt of economic aid was more palatable when given by an international body than by an individual nation, and that a United Nations agency was the only authority in which the underdeveloped countries would have an effective voice in the uses of the fund. But the opposition of the United States, which felt it was unprepared to carry the major portion of another burden, defeated the project.

It should be recalled that the most important economic assistance by the United States came from its own economic-aid program administered by its Agency for International Development, that the parts of that program most concerned with supplying capital for development projects centered largely upon the Development Loan Fund and the Inter-American Fund for Social Progress. The Export-Import Bank, a United States institution, also frequently supplied loans for the economic development of the emerging societies.

Sometimes an individual underdeveloped country would be getting economic aid in one form or another from various United States sources—agricultural surpluses and "food for peace," the United States Agency for International Development and the Development Loan Fund, and the Export-Import Bank; and it would also be getting aid from various international agencies—the International Monetary Fund, the World Bank, the International Development Association, and the International Finance Corporation. If it were a Latin American country it might in addition be getting aid from the Inter-American Development Bank. If it were a south Asian country it might in addition be getting aid from the Colombo Plan. If it were a former colony of Britain or France it might in addition be getting aid from the country which until recently had governed it. And it also might be getting aid from the Soviet Union. Sometimes support for a single project was given in the form of a package plan in which some American government economic aid and some funds from several of the international agencies were pooled.

The Emergence of a United Nations Executive

As the technical and political administrative functions of the United Nations multiplied, the work of the Secretariat and of the Secretary-General greatly increased. The Secretary-General was no longer a mere co-ordinator; he was becoming a creative executive. The tenure of Dag Hammarskjold illustrated the large possibilities of that office for constructive endeavor. But as the office gained in power, the Soviet Union became disturbed. Although the Soviet bloc was in a more favorable position than in the earlier years of the United Nations, it was still usually in the minority on the various issues before that body, and the Soviet Union looked with misgivings on the widening activities of the Secretary-General, which were felt to be too often contrary to its own views. Differences of opinion came to a head over Congo policy. Therefore Khrushchev proposed that the functions of the Secretary-General be taken over by a three-man commission, one man representing the Western bloc, one the Communist bloc, and one the neutrals. Thus the single coordinator and executive would become a plural one. This was known as the *troika* plan.

This weakening of the Secretariat drew little support from even the neutrals. They viewed this Soviet proposal as one which would lead not only to an impairment of the Secretariat but also to that of the United Nations itself. The new states had come to regard the United Nations with increasing enthusiasm, for that organization furnished them many practical services, constantly brought their representatives into intimate contact with world leaders, gave their countries a world arena in which to express their opinions, and offered protection from both the old colonialism and the new satellitism. When the *troika* plan failed to win support, the Soviet Union suggested three under-secretaries, one from each of the three groups, whose agreement would be necessary before any action could be taken by the Secretary-General. But this, too, was unpopular with United Nations representatives.

However, as a propitiatory gesture, when U Thant of Burma was elected to fill the unexpired term of Dag Hammarskjold, it was decided that the Secretary-General should choose a limited number of advisers from various sections of the world to serve as his principal coadjutors, a step which might actually increase the powers of the Secretary-General, for it might be the beginning of an executive cabinet chosen by the executive himself. U Thant announced the choice of eight under-secretaries, representative of various geographical areas and ideological shades of opinion.

The behavior of the Soviet Union, in casting repeated vetoes in the Security Council and in making demands not only for a tripartite Secretariat but also for representation in the Security Council and the Economic and Social Council on a *troika* basis, was characteristic of the minority in a political body. In any political organization the majority usually pressed for integration and centralization and the minority for non-integration and decentralization. The situation was reminiscent of the history of American federalism. John C. Calhoun, it will be recalled, developed elaborate theories of "the concurrent majority" and of nullification to protect the Southern minority from the "tyranny" of the Northern majority.

Many heads of state and premiers of Communist and neutral countries, at the suggestion of Khrushchev, attended in person the meetings of the United Nations Assembly in 1960. Led by Khrushchev himself, the debates were frequently acrimonious, like those in national legislatures. Many feared that these heated wrangles presaged the disintegration of the United Nations, but on the contrary they seemed evidence of the vigorous vitality of that body. The United Nations had become an arena in which the leading statesmen from the various countries debated in person the prime realities of world politics. Despite often expressed fears that the Soviet Union would secede from the United Nations, there appeared little likelihood that this would happen.

An immediate threat was the failure of some of the member nations to pay the assessments levied against them to maintain the United Nations military forces in the Middle East and the Congo. The practice was growing of members refusing to pay for United Nations activities of which they as individual nations disapproved, even though those activities were duly authorized. This was the same old problem that the leagues and confederations of the past had faced, and it was the rock on which many of them had foundered. The Soviet Union, France, Belgium, Portugal, and some other countries refused to pay their Congo assessments, and the United Nations ran heavily in arrears.

The International Court handed down a decision saying that member nations were responsible for assessments for authorized activities which were not placed on a voluntary financial basis, as some of the United Nations activities were; but ways of enforcing the Court's decision had not been found. The United Nations was temporarily saved from bankruptcy when in 1962 the American Congress voted to allow the United States government to buy a substantial part of a U.N. bond issue of 200 million dollars. This afforded only temporary relief. Congress was in no mood to modify its edict that the U.S. pay no more than one-third of the upkeep of any international organization. But by mid-1963 the threat to enforce the Charter provision that members financially delinquent for two years be deprived of their votes in the Assembly seemed to be getting results.

The Future of the United Nations

At first Americans expected too much of the United Nations, but in 1947, when the United States took over responsibility for the defense of Greece and Turkey, Americans realized that "power politics" would continue along with collective security and that the effectiveness of the United Nations was still severely limited. This rude awakening produced some adverse reaction to the United Nations among Americans.

On the other hand, in the late 1940's and early 1950's many people abroad and many of the representatives of other countries in the United Nations were disappointed that the United States still maintained high tariff policies, attached "buy American" and "transport in American ships" to their foreign economic-aid programs, administered the McCarran-Walter immigration law in an hysterical anti-Communist fashion (even such distinguished non-Communist leftists as Gunnar Myrdal and Alberto Moravia were denied admission to the United States), rejected the compulsory jurisdiction of the World Court, refused even to consider ratification of the United Nations covenants on human rights and on genocide, and seemed sometimes on the verge of adopting the Bricker Amendment to the United States Constitution, which would have required specific Congressional legislation or specific legislation by all of the state legislatures to implement treaty provisions affecting internal law. To foreigners the Bricker Amendment meant that the treaty process of the United States, already more difficult than that of most countries, would be made even more difficult at the very time the United States was involved as a leader in all parts of the world.

But as the years rolled by there was a more realistic understanding on all sides. Americans came to realize that power politics and collective security were not incompatible and that the development of effective collective security would take years of evolution. They also became convinced by events that the

Communists or the neutralists would not take over control of the world organization.

On the other hand, foreigners came to see that although United States officials had to throw sops now and then to America's ultra-nationalists and that although the United States could not be expected to ratify any United Nations covenants on universal human rights, genocide, or freedom of information, for fear of strengthening the nationalist contention that the United Nations wanted to invade the realm of internal law and "socialize" the United States, there was no real danger that the extreme nationalists would control the American government, despite the ebb and flow of McCarthyism and right-wing extremism in American opinion. Foreigners were also pleased that with the passing of the years the American trade and tariff policies were liberalized, American foreign-aid programs expanded, and American policy better adjusted to the problems of the commodity-producing nations. Then too, American financial support was decisive in keeping afloat many of the international agencies and organizations and sometimes the United Nations itself. Indeed, the Communists often charged that for this and other reasons the United Nations was a mere appendage of American foreign policy.

Sometimes even internationally-minded Americans gave expression to the belief that American interests would be better served in a North Atlantic regional organization than in the United Nations, but on second thought it was usually seen that the world was now too interdependent for regional organizations alone, that a North Atlantic community without world organization would only widen the gap between the rich nations and the poor nations, and that if a North Atlantic community ever materialized it would have to be in addition to the United Nations and not a substitute for it.

In the absence of a world war, which could destroy the United Nations, many saw in that organization an embryonic world government. On the other hand, it was possible that a cataclysmic war would bring actual world government much more quickly than was expected. But it was far more likely that world government would evolve gradually from a league of states to a confederation and from a confederation to an international federal state, as the result of the United Nations' widening functional activities at the grass roots, its assumption of the enforcement of future international arms-control agreements, and the slow equalizing of the standards of living of all peoples. (Fear that the high standards of living in the advanced industrial countries would be submerged in the low standards of the rest of the world was one of the chief inhibitors of international government.) If arms-control agreements were made and their enforcement put in the United Nations, that organization would then emerge from a peripheral to a central element in world politics.

The most conclusive evidence that an international *community* was being transformed into an international *society* would be the practice of national delegations at international meetings and organizations splitting within themselves, groups within the national delegations making alliances with like groups in other national delegations against unlike groups in their own delegations —the supranational, multilateral criss-crossing of groups within the national delegations—just as political parties cut across the state delegations in the American Congress. As yet, there was little of this in international organizations. National delegations still presented solid fronts *vis-à-vis* one another.

Meantime, the United Nations was operating an already considerable international community, sometimes at a functional grass roots level.

[11]

WHITHER MANKIND?

_____

"Victory" for Neither Side

How well had the United States acquitted itself as a world leader? About that there were differences of opinion.

The outstanding fact of the postwar world was the containment of Communism. The Russians had not made any territorial gains or acquired European satellites—since 1948; indeed in the meantime they had lost two satellites—Yugoslavia and Albania, for different reasons. After the Chinese Revolution of 1949 no further countries were won by the Communists in Asia except little Vietminh, on the border of China, which would probably have been saved but for the intransigence of French colonialism, which allowed the Communists to identify themselves with Vietnamese nationalism. Except for Vietminh, none of the former European colonies had gone Communist. And by the 1960's the breach between Russia and China had become so wide as to split the Communist world wide open.

What had caused this containment of Communism? There were those who contended that American foreign policy had not been the chief factor, that there were other factors of more importance. Marxism, it was argued, unlike Nazism, had no ideological compulsion to military aggression but held rather that Communism was not exportable, that it must be generated from within by "objective conditions"; that nowhere in the whole body of Soviet Marxist doctrine was there the implication that the Soviet Union for ideological reasons should initiate a war. It was pointed out that the Soviet Union was both a national state and leader of a world revolutionary movement, that Russia's expansion over the satellites in 1945 was not Communist but national, in response to national interests, in fulfillment of the traditional Russian urge for a defense zone in Eastern Europe, and that after that was achieved, Russian expansion had ceased.

But even had Marxism been aggressive in the military sense, it was contended that at the end of the war Russia was too weak to have undertaken military conquests in behalf of Communist world revolution. Professor Fred Warner Neal, representing the point of view that while Marxism was aggressive in the social and economic revolutionary sense it was not aggressive in the military sense, and that therefore Western rearming and the building of a network of additional military alliances encircling the Communist powers was superfluous, put the case this way: "To the Soviet Union, Western fears of Soviet military aggression right after the end of the war must have appeared ridiculous as well as insincere. Although the U.S.S.R. came out of the war with its armies extended into Eastern and Central Europe as well as Far Eastern Asia, it was weak. The destruction wrought by conflict in both human and material terms was indescribable. The Soviet people, without adequate food, shelter, or clothing, were exhausted physically and psychologically. While it is true that the Soviet army was large numerically, much of it was still unmechanized and intently preoccupied in Germany and Eastern Europe. Its air force was inadequate. Except for a few submarines it had virtually no navy. As against this situation the United States ended the war with its war-making potential not only undamaged but greater than ever before. It is often implied that American demobilization right after the war lessened our comparative military strength. Nothing could be further from the truth. The American navy controlled the seas. The American air force controlled the skies. American bases, together with those of our British ally, were firmly ensconced around much of the periphery of the Soviet Union. And the United States, and it alone, possessed the atom bomb."

Others pointed out that Communist China, too, was hardly in a condition to wage a war for world Communism. China in 1949 had been through several decades of foreign and civil war and faced the tremendous internal problems of reconstruction, industrialization, and building a new system. China's wars, too—the one in Korea when that war came too close to her own borders for comfort and the one in the Himalayas against India in support of China's frontier claims—were not ideological but national, it was argued.

Historical forces, particularly the strength of nationalism, and not the specifics of foreign policy, seemed largely responsible for the splitting of the Communist world, and the determination of most of the new nations not only to cast off colonialism but escape satellitism as well.

As we receded from the immediate postwar years, critics of American foreign policy were no less insistent on the "misplaced emphasis" in American foreign policy. They contended that the policy of military alliances and bases became increasingly irrelevant after both the leading powers had nuclear weapons; that the continued emphasis on foreign alliances and bases into the age of intercontinental missiles became even more of a distortion and represented an expensive diversion from the more important economic and social factors, especially in the underdeveloped countries; that the United States had contributed its share to the arms race and the balance of terror; and that after Stalin's death, during "the Spirit of Geneva," and again in 1959 and 1960, during "the Spirit of Camp David," the United States had openings for a *détente*, for some relaxation of tensions and arms-limitations agreements, and had failed to take advantage of them.

However, the majority view in the United States and even in Western Europe was that the American emphasis on the military was not misplaced. Defenders of American policy insisted that in actual practice Marxism was conspiratorial, aggressive, and violent, and that "testing internal objective conditions" to determine whether a country was "ripe" for revolution involved all sorts of subversive methods, including fomenting strikes and other disturbances, infiltrating guerrilla and other civil wars, sending military "volunteers," and waging outright frontal war as in Korea. These contended that if the Communist powers had not been more militarily aggressive it was because the United States was militarily strong and had built a powerful system of military alliances. The way to keep the big Communist powers contained, they insisted, was to maintain the military defenses, build NATO to its full fighting strength, which had never yet been done, and convince the Communists that Americans and their allies had the will to fight and actually use the strategic nuclear weapons if need be.

The climate of world opinion in the 1960's was so different from what it had been in 1945 that it was easy to take the shift more or less for granted, to underrate the importance of American activities and pressures in bringing it about. It was the Americans who had alerted the world to the drastic differences between Communist and non-Communist systems and who had done much to modify the "objective conditions" to make European and Asian societies less amenable to internal Communist revolution and more resistant to Marxism. It will be recalled that in the minds of many Asian leaders in the 1940's and early 1950's the differences between Communism, socialism, social democracy, welfarism, and agrarian reform were blurred. Many at that time still regarded Mao Tse-tung as a mere agrarian reformer. Others, who saw him as a real Communist, believed that in their own countries they could be "creative Marxists" and mix and dilute Communism with other systems. But by the 1960's the line between Communism and other systems was more clearly perceived, and American policy had contributed much to this clarification. However, as late as the 1960's the specifics of American policy in Asia still suffered because almost all of America's alliances there were with authoritarian right-wing governments.

In Europe, the Depression of the 1930's and two world wars had weakened the middle classes, caused the spread of collectivist ideas, and put capitalism on the defensive. In the hour of victory over Hitlerism, there was general indignation that the ultra-conservatives, the appeasers, and "the grave-diggers" had "sold out" their countries to the Nazis, and a widespread belief that Nazism-Fascism and its collaborators represented the decadent stage of capitalism and that the alternative was Communism. The Communists had taken the lead in the underground wars of liberation. At the end of the war even Europe's conservatives were reconciled to drastic changes and some in France and Italy were saying that their cultures could "assimilate" Communism, that Communism in Western Europe would be different from

Communism in Russia. It was American policy, military as well as economic, which changed this thinking, stiffened the European determination not to succumb to Communism but to resist it.

In the light of the many differences among the European countries, the climate of opinion, the European softness toward collectivism, the strength of Communist, Socialist, and labor parties, the ardent hope that the war alliance of the Soviet Union and the West would continue on in peacetime, and the marked disinclination to divide Germany and Europe into two separate camps, America's success in building its Western European military alliances and in guiding Western Europe to greater economic and political cooperation was indeed impressive. And after NATO had been built, it required a skilled and continuous diplomacy to convince Western Europeans that on the one hand Americans were not aggressive warmongers and on the other that they had no intention of eventually abandoning the heart of Europe by retreating to a defense periphery of that continent or to the Western Hemisphere.

There was almost universal agreement that the Marshall Plan had been an outstandingly creative policy and undeniably successful. Marshall Plan aid had spurred a rapid economic recovery in Europe. It had resulted in the adoption of mass production and mass consumption methods which had given Europe a new economic birth. It had achieved this within the framework of a mixed economy that was more capitalist than collectivist, more free market than administered market. The appeal of Communism had declined and Communist parties in Western Europe had been weakened. The cooperation among the European nations demanded by the Marshall Plan sparked those movements toward Western European economic and political integration which held out such bright prospects for the future.

However, the possibility of Communist revolution in some countries of Western Europe had not entirely disappeared. All countries and all classes did not share appreciably in Western Europe's new economic prosperity. There was pervasive mass poverty in Spain, in Portugal, and in some areas of Italy. In France, the Communists had survived the smashing of the other old parties in the Gaullist elections; in Italy, the Communists, bereft of their old alliance with the Nenni Socialists, had won one fourth of the

Italian voters in the 1963 election; and in Spain, the middle way between rightist and leftist extremism was perilously weak.

In the rivalry for the friendship of the underdeveloped peoples, which largely revolved around the contests between West and East in extending them aid for modernization and industrialization, the United States, judged by what the other advanced industrial countries of the West had done, had indeed been generous. But judged by the needs, the added difficulties produced by the population explosion, the wealth of America, and the growing economic competition with the Communist powers, it had been inadequate.

As we have seen, giving economic aid effectively involved a host of difficulties. In what countries would the aid be most advantageously spent? How honest, reliable, energetic, dedicated, and popularly representative were the recipient governments? How might American technicians with political and social sense be recruited for service in the underdeveloped areas?

Up to now, America's economic-aid program had been a crazy quilt. Aid was given to democratic and to non-democratic countries, to social-democratic governments and to right-wing dictatorships, to countries ready for industrial projects and to countries with such primitive social and economic structures and such low per capita gross national product that any aid beyond the Peace Corps, the "food for peace" program, and technical and advisory services of the United Nations agencies was waste. Aid given to non-popular governments bent on preserving the economic and social *status quo*—and the United States had given much aid to such governments—was bad ideological propaganda; it was bad economically because such governments were unable to carry out programs of industrialization; and it was bad politically because such governments were untenable, sooner or later they would collapse.

Even under the best of circumstances, could the Herculean breakthrough from pre-industrialism to industrialism be achieved within a reasonably short time without resort to the regimentation and ruthless discipline of economic and political totalitarianism? Not a single non-Communist, pre-industrial society had yet achieved a breakthrough comparable to the Russian and perhaps the Chinese achievement. If just one underdeveloped non-Communist country with a popular government and relatively sufficient economic underpinning to justify prospects for successful results—say India or Egypt or Brazil—would demonstrate that it was well on the way to a stabilized and balanced modernization and industrialization, then the West might breathe easier.

Even so, the long-run trend was not unfavorable to the West. The contention that the people in all the underdeveloped countries were panting for industrialization and threatening to turn to Communism if this were not accomplished forthwith was an exaggerated one. The changes would usually not have to be extreme and immediate to satisfy popular demands for betterment. A moderate but visible rise in the standard of living would generally suffice to give people a sense of satisfaction. There was probably more time than was often supposed.

In Red China there was not only grueling sacrifice demanded but also many difficulties in reaching agricultural and industrial goals. The Russian experience in rapid industrialization did not guarantee that the Communists had a foolproof way of achieving industrialization in a hurry, although it seemed that China in its industrialization program was well ahead of India.

Despite the appeal to underdeveloped peoples of totalitarian economics as a way of getting rapid industrialization, the startling fact was that after two decades of anti-imperialist revolutions few of the new nations had gone Communist. This must have been most galling to Communist leaders in Moscow and Peiping, who spoke the language of anti-imperialist revolution and had believed with Lenin that the anti-colonial revolutions were certain to merge with Communist revolution. It now seemed clear that, provided reasonable progress was made toward modernization and industrialization, most of the underdeveloped peoples were willing to accept a slower-than-Communist pace if by so doing they could escape an all-inclusive and drastic collectivism, a police state, and satellitism. The former colonial areas of the world were evidencing the cultural impact on them of Western civilization, produced by long years of European rule; their trade and intercourse were still much more with the West than with the Communist countries; if the West retained its economic and cultural vitality it was likely to exert a continuing strong influence. It seemed clear that the West was being given a second chance. But the West did not have endless time. Western indifference, delays, and blunders might well tip the scales the other way. Then national anti-imperialist revolutions might in time be followed by second revolutions, Communist revolutions.

In 1945 many had feared that Communist revolutions would sweep Europe and that outside Europe most of the anti-imperialist revolutions would merge with Communist revolutions, as they actually did in China and Vietminh. But the threat that a large part of the world would be a Communist monolith had failed to materialize. Others had feared "an American century," "an American imperium," but this had not developed either. We had escaped a one-world monolithism.

But we had also escaped a two-world monolithism. The world had moved away from the immediate postwar bipolarization, from duality, from a tight Soviet sphere and a tight American sphere. Depolarization had taken place; the influence of both Moscow and Washington in their respective "worlds" had declined. The Western orbit had been fissured; the Communist orbit had suffered rifts which might even become chasms. And as more and more new nations had emerged into statehood most of them had refused to join either bloc, had asserted their neutrality, and thus the world became even more depolarized.

However, a multiple balance of power had not revived, although some day an integrated Western Europe might represent a "third force," and a strong China might represent a "fourth force." Although a multiple balance of power in the traditional sense appeared to be an anachronism, it was not inconceivable, nightmarish though it would be, that three or four new centers of power, all armed with nuclear weapons, would eventually develop.

Soviet Communism and American capitalism were exerting a mighty influence on the emerging peoples, but there was likely to be "victory" for neither system. Instead, an historical synthesis, a variety of systems showing the influence of both, was emerging. Most of the underdeveloped countries, new and old, were groping toward a mixed economy, a varying blend of indigenous collectivism, state enterprise, private enterprise, and welfarism. Even the Marxist countries were national as well as collectivist and differed in their methods, their stages of revolutionary development, their "roads to socialism," and their degrees of collectivism. However, in one sense the twentieth century *was* the

American century, for all the revolutions, even the Communist ones, were profoundly influenced by American methods of mass production, distribution, and consumption, and all considered the American standard of living as an ultimate goal to be approximated if not always achieved.

Not monolithism but pluralism was the cardinal political fact of the middle and later twentieth century: depolarization, fissures in the Western world, rifts in the Communist world, national self-determination of nations, political fragmentation and the existence of more independent political states than at any time in modern history, the emergence of scores and scores of new societies with fluid and mixed economies. But this in turn was forcing the nations to regional cooperation, federation, and even integration and to international organization.

Since the Americans never wanted a monolithic world or even two coexisting monolithic worlds but continued to adhere to national self-determination, the prevailing trend to a new pluralism, a world of proliferating new societies with varying mixed economies, was much closer to American views than to Marxist ones. But it would be difficult to make out a case for the proposition that the prevailing trend to pluralism was *chiefly* the result of the American foreign policy in action. Rather it would have to be put down as produced *mainly* by deeper historical and cultural forces. In the absence of egregious American blunders and a third world war, this trend was likely to continue.

Three times monolithism had threatened the twentieth-century world: the Communist threat to Europe in 1918, 1919, and 1920, following World War I; the Nazi-Fascist threat, which reached its climax in World War II; and the second threat of Marxism following World War II, when it appeared that Communism might win in Europe, spread to the colonial areas, and merge with anti-imperialist revolutions. Each time these monolithic threats miscarried.

The Balance of Terror

The haunting threat of nuclear war, the balance of terror, was the world's overriding problem. If somehow a *détente* between the United States and the Soviet Union could be reached, a settlement made with respect to Berlin and the German problem, and tensions relaxed sufficiently for beginning agreements in the limitation and control of armaments, the present trend to a plural world would likely continue. Such agreements, if implemented and progressively enlarged, would relieve the world's terror and release wealth for accelerated economic growth in the advanced industrial countries and more rapid progress in the underdeveloped areas. They would also arrest the trend to "the warfare state," the distorted dependence of the economy on armaments production together with the growth of a potentially dangerous industrial-military power complex, against which President Eisenhower warned in his farewell message to the nation.

But what was just as likely was a continuation of the Cold War, the trend to a plural world despite the Cold War, no arms agreements, and an intensification of the arms race and the balance of terror. Still, in practice, this might be a *pax atomica* of a sort. Both the super-nuclear powers increasingly shied away not only from major war but from limited war, in the fear that a little war might become the Big One. Even in the most daring brinkmanship, there was always a last minute recoil from war—witness Berlin, Cuba, Quemoy, and the Sino-Indian Himalayan border— and not only by the Soviet Union and the United States but also by Red China. There were still internal revolutions and civil wars, but outside intervention on behalf of revolution or counter-revolution was becoming increasingly hazardous. The world seemed moving toward a frozen *status quo*. The first part of the century was characterized by great world wars and excessive revolutionary and counter-revolutionary mobility; the end of the century might well be characterized by a nuclear-imposed immobility. This would be stability of a sort, but it would be a frustrating stability. How could change, even desirable change, take place? Would the world find substitutes for the great change-makers of the past— international wars and the revolutions and civil wars which often spilled over into world politics to produce such wars?

War might be sublimated; it might be waged vicariously. With the development of a new streamlined weapon, one side would say to the other: "See what I could do to you if I were to use this." And the other side would produce a still more stupendous and *de luxe* weapon and say to the other: "Now the victory is mine." Arms tournaments in the form of sensational weapons testings would supersede war; unlike the medieval tournaments with their warriors weighted down with armor, the new tournaments would be without warriors and without actual combat. Instead there would be contests between two sets of scientists, technicians, and operational forces engaged in competitive spectacular testings. But the cost in nerves, terror, wasted wealth, and economic and social slow-down would be incalculable. Irrational? Of course. It would be a manifestation of man's perennial irrationality "adjusted" to the technological "realities" of today. And the great wealth of highly developed technological societies could "afford" such "luxurious" spectacles.

However, the arms race and the emotion-packed displays of spectacular mutual might could result ultimately in cataclysmic war, and the proliferation of nuclear powers would multiply the chances of war by accident or miscalculation. Nuclear war might come, too, out of a "limited" war, or a crisis which got out of hand, or a momentary weakening of the will or simulation of the will of one side or the other to actually fight, or a notable lag in the technology of one side, an upsetting of the balance of terror, which encouraged an attack by the other. Never before had warfare and foreign policy been so tightly in the grip of technological developments, and any predictions about tomorrow's events and trends would have to be hedged by a prudent regard for future technological breakthroughs—anti-missiles, interceptors of anti-missiles, and so forth.

The American Right Wing and American Foreign Policy

There even remained a possibility, but it was no more than a possibility, that right-wing nationalist attitudes might spread in America and a right-wing government come to power which would pursue a "get tough" foreign policy, which would be followed by a "get tougher policy" on the other side—and this might lead to nuclear war. A segment of American opinion, lately strong, particularly outside the eastern United States, seemed increasingly to feel that the United States was losing the Cold War. It viewed neutral countries as enemies and mixed economies as "Communist." It believed that the United Nations had fallen into the hands of the "colored" and "backward" peoples. It called for an end of the "no-win" foreign policy, for the adoption of a "win" foreign policy. Should this segment of American opinion come to power it might pursue an unilateralist policy which had scant regard for neutral, allied, or world

opinion. It might adopt a "Fortress America" policy, an abandonment of America's allies, and a concentration of American defense in North America, made seemingly plausible by the development of intercontinental missiles. Or, more likely, it might take the
form of an aggressive American unilateralism in world affairs,
which however would appeal to right-wing elements the world
over. Such an aggressive American unilateralism might lead to
"the Fascist-Communist apocalypse" still predicted by the Stalinists and other "orthodox" Marxists.

An aggressive American unilateralism would confirm the Stalinists in their belief in the inevitability of war with the "capitalist
imperialists," would undermine the anti-Stalinists, would restore
the Stalinists to power, would force Russia and Red China back
into firm alliance, would aggravate Communist intransigence,
exacerbate international tensions, enormously increase the chances
of all-out nuclear war, and move America to the garrison state. It
would be a tragic paradox if Americans swallowed the Marxist
myth that world trends were against them, when in reality such
trends, on balance, were favorable to them—and thus lost the
world contest.

After 1945 America's right-wing nationalists had been strong
enough to influence some events and to affect the American image
abroad: their Congressional investigations, using totalitarian
methods, during the McCarthy era; their advocacy of preventive
war, of the Bricker amendment, and of a widening of the Battle
Act in such a way as to cut off foreign aid even to countries which
traded with Communist countries only in non-strategic materials;
their capacity to pass "captive nations" resolutions in Congress
which only irritated America's opponents while raising false hopes
among satellite peoples, to stop all attempts to modify the Con-
nally Amendment whereby the United States still refused to submit to the compulsory jurisdiction of the International Court, and
to prevent America's ratifying the United Nations covenants on
human rights and genocide and amending its immigration laws
to allow the United States to take foreign refugees in numbers
comparable to those taken by the other free nations; their part
in producing racial incidents such as those at Little Rock and
Oxford, which raised doubts abroad about American democracy.
However, America's nationalists, neo-mercantilists, and rightists
were a declining influence in trade and tariff policies, and, except

for China policy, in which they had the support of many other elements, they had not decisively affected major postwar policies; and it was not probable that they would do so in the future, let alone capture control of the presidency and Congress.

America's nationalists believed in "the policy of the free hand," in unilateralism, in little cooperation with allies abroad. In some individuals unilateralism took the form of isolationism, in others of crypto-imperialism, and very often within a single individual there was oscillation between isolationist impulses and crypto-imperialist impulses. Both isolationists and crypto-imperialists were not really reconciled to American participation in World War I or World War II (both Wilson and F.D.R. were still villains), and they were suspicious of the course of American foreign policy since 1945. As individuals, some of them represented the oldest traditions of the Republic, but they had not adjusted to the modern world and to America's place in it, and they were irritable, nostalgic, frustrated, and schizophrenic.

However, most Americans were cooperationists, putting their faith in alliances both inside and outside the United Nations. But the cooperationists were still roughly divided into two groups, and this division revealed itself inside the Kennedy administration. One group, represented by Adlai Stevenson, Averell Harriman, Chester Bowles, and Mennen Williams (the ex-governors), emphasized social politics and economic aid in the underdeveloped countries, and was inclined to take a somewhat optimistic view about *rapprochement* with the Soviet Union. The other, represented by Dean Acheson and McGeorge Bundy (and the Alsops), put more emphasis on the power struggle between the United States and the Soviet Union, stressed the importance of effective military alliances, and took a harder view with respect to negotiating *rapprochement* with the Russians. By 1963, there was an increasing tendency for informed Americans of all shades of opinion to reappraise American foreign policy in its totality, to question whether it was over-extended, whether it was attempting too much in too many areas of the world.

The Twentieth Century in Historical Perspective

The twentieth century was one of the watersheds of history, like the late fifteenth and early sixteenth centuries, when a new civilization emerged. That earlier epoch witnessed the rise of capitalism and the early national state on the decay of feudalism; the release of the individual from the corporative group life of the Middle Ages; the humanism of the Renaissance; the religious turmoil of the Reformation; notable gains in scientific thinking; and the revolutionary widening of man's horizon by the discovery and exploration of the remote parts of the earth.

In the twentieth century, in all countries, in varying degrees and under whatever label, the public sector of the economy was growing at the expense of the private sector; government and economy were becoming more or less indistinguishable; men were being subjected to bigger and bigger political, economic, and social organizations; life was becoming more bureaucratic, impersonal, and non-autonomous; society was more massive and other-directed; political and economic decisions were increasingly being made by specialists and technicians; individual and social life was becoming less intuitive and insightful and more technological, quantitative, and objectively measurable.

There was still a sharp and fateful distinction between totalitarian Communist societies with their omnivorous police states and non-totalitarian societies, but as the Communist societies industrialized they pluralized and were under pressures to liberalize. Among the non-totalitarian societies, the differences between democratic and non-democratic ones were becoming more difficult to distinguish. Some were authoritarian without being totalitarian. Some with all the formal apparatus of democracy were in fact undemocratic, and others without that apparatus were responding to popular aspirations. But in all states, parliamentary and non-parliamentary, the administrative functions were expanding and governmental decisions were increasingly administrative ones. As the demarcation between the private and the public sectors became less distinct, it was increasingly difficult to label an economy "capitalist" or "socialist." A basic question of the future would be the source and nature of the controls over managers, administrators, and technicians.

But labels aside, the old racial and class lines were falling, leveling egalitarianism was on the march, there was a widening of basic human rights, and despite the population explosion a determination to enjoy the higher living standards promised by the technological revolution. It was the century of Ortega's "mass man," of Henry Wallace's "common man." Whether one viewed this with the misgivings of an Ortega or the optimism of a Wallace depended upon one's values.

The new pluralism was shot through with a new uniformity. There were many new societies, and as these industrialized the kinds of economic activities multiplied, new groups and classes proliferated, and the internal economic and social order became more heterogeneous. Economies were becoming internally more diverse, and more like other economies in their diversity; societies more complex, and more like other societies in their complexity. And at the very time the kinds of economic activities, specialties, and careers multiplied, the new interdependence, the growth of organization, and the elimination of old class, racial, and sectional differences produced a novel oneness, an unprecedented sameness.

Despite the emergence of many new nations and societies and the asperity of the ideological and power conflict, there was more regional and even international cooperation. Despite the international anarchy, an international community and even society was haltingly emerging. The disastrous consequences of a general nuclear war might even bring world government with dramatic suddenness.

The second age of discovery and exploration, the conquest of outer space, would doubtlessly prove more revolutionary in all phases of life than even the earlier one. If outer space and its planets were somehow reserved for all the nations, for mankind, and not for individual nations, such community of interest would probably become a bond of unity similar to that which resulted when the thirteen American states became joint owners of the domain beyond the Appalachians. On the other hand, if a contest for outer space developed among the great powers, the result might well be a colossal new rivalry and imperialism.

To most, man's release from the earthbound was a climactic vindication of both rationalism and the unquenchable spirit of human adventure. But to others, among them traditional humanists, man's explorations of the heavens and his touching of the stars were robbing the universe of its last shred of mystery and represented the ultimate disillusionment, the crowning indignity.

EPILOGUE

DURING LATE 1963 and early 1964 the trend to pluralism continued, the Sino-Soviet rift widened, the implications of the nuclear revolution in war became increasingly impressive, and the United States and the Soviet Union moved cautiously toward a détente.

In the summer of 1963, after years of negotiation, the United States, Russia, and Britain signed a treaty banning all nuclear explosions in any place under their control in the atmosphere, in outer space, or under water, and each party pledged not to encourage non-underground nuclear explosions anywhere. There was to be no inspection. The treaty was ratified by the United States Senate with nineteen senators voting against it. All the nations were invited to become parties and most of them accepted. France and Communist China refused to sign, for the treaty would make their plans for becoming nuclear powers more difficult, which was one of the purposes of the treaty. Why did Russia and the United States finally come to this limited agreement? The Sino-Soviet rift freed Khrushchev from having to consider Chinese interests, put pressures on him to move closer to the West, and made the United States less fearful that Chinese territory might be used by the Russians to cheat on any test-ban agreement. The American government felt that because of the improvements in United States detection capability the chances of the Soviet Union's conducting tests which would remain undetected were "vanishingly small," even underground, and well-nigh nil for the kinds of tests banned by the treaty. The treaty was hailed as the first real break in the big-power deadlock, and some saw in it the first, small step to future comprehensive arms agreements, perhaps a general détente. However, underground testing was not affected and would continue, as would the arms and missiles race generally, and the opposition in the United States to the treaty, stirred by nationalists and rightists, indicated that future agreements might be difficult to achieve.

Nevertheless, the American and Soviet governments were publicizing the fact that their missiles and nuclear war-head stockpiles now had an enormous capacity for over-kill. Both governments announced defense cutbacks and reductions in military expenditures, and the impression grew that perhaps the way was being prepared for a Soviet-American agreement putting a ceiling on the number of nuclear weapons and carriers each might accumulate. Why continue adding to over-kill capacity after both countries had long since attained the power to blow up the other? However, even if such an agreement were made, it seemed certain that the search for technological improvements and new breakthroughs in nuclear weapons and carriers would continue.

The nuclear revolution in war continued to operate as an inhibition on the actual use of force in international affairs, and this tended increasingly to freeze the international *status quo*. Guerrilla warfare seemed to be the only "safe" form of force available, and it was being used here and there in an attempt to effect or to stop internal change. But even in these situations, intervention by outside powers on behalf of revolution or counter-revolution was more and more hazardous, for such intervention might escalate into full-scale "limited wars," like those which had been fought in Korea and Indochina in the early 1950's; and such limited wars in turn might escalate into the Big Nuclear War. (President de Gaulle's suggestion that the guerrilla war in South Vietnam should be ended by new international agreements neutralizing North and South Vietnam, Laos, and Cambodia found much support in the West, even in the United States.) This growing inhibition in the use of force in international affairs constituted a stupendous revolution in world politics, and it reemphasized the need to develop peaceful machinery for making even the ultimate decisions among the nations.

The existing political arrangements in Europe with respect to East Germany, the Oder-Neisse boundary, and the Soviet satellites seemed to be ripening into a more overt East-West *modus vivendi*, but one which remained merely tacit, one not actually formalized by over-all political agreements. Trade and intercourse between the countries of Western Europe and Eastern Europe were increasing at an accelerated pace, the satellite countries were operating more independently of Moscow, and an all-European economic and cultural cooperation was slowly replacing "the two Europes" of the postwar period. At the same time, the European Common Market had survived repeated crises, and in late 1963 and early 1964 agreements were reached among the Six to reduce a large number of internal agricultural tariffs. After this there was renewed talk of merging the three supranational communities—the EEC, the ECSC, and Euratom—and of electing the European Assembly by popular vote and giving it wider powers. But De Gaulle's insistence on the confederative approach, as opposed to the federal or supranational approach, was making political integration difficult. It now appeared that integration of the Six by way of supranational organizations would not include as many political and military matters, or even economic ones, as had been originally envisaged. (In the Arab world, too, political federation had been arrested; the second United Arab Republic announced in April 1963 had not materialized.)

The further decline of "the two worlds" and of tense ideological conflict was brought home with President de Gaulle's recognition of Communist China in early 1964, which, if the Chinese were not as intransigent as they sometimes seemed to be, would probably be followed by recognition from additional countries and an increase in trade and intercourse between Communist China and the West. This would tend to break down China's isolation and perhaps convince the Chinese Communists that the Westerners were not the aggressive "imperialists and war mongers" they had thought them to be, that the Capitalist-Communist Apocalypse was not inevitable. It might also allow the West to fill the void left in China by Russian withdrawal of aid and technicians, to wean the Chinese still further from the Russians. However, Sino-Soviet ideological affinities might still play a large part in world politics, and there were conceivable contingencies which might force Russia and China back into close alliance—for instance a right-wing victory in the United

States or a last desperate attack by Chiang Kai-shek on the mainland.

The West and Russia, then, seemed moving toward a détente, and in time Chinese-Western relations might take a similar direction. On the other hand, should China's revolutionary enthusiasm or, more likely, her drive to round out her national domain make a Sino-Western détente impossible, then Russia would probably move much more closely to the West, and both might unite against Chinese activism.

If the world was not yet safe for diversity, it was much safer than it had been. The nuclear deterrent was making Communist expansion increasingly difficult, and at the same time the availability of Polaris submarines and intercontinental missiles was making the United States less dependent on foreign allies, military alliances, and bases on foreign soil. It seemed clear, too, that any additional Communist revolutions would not be sweeping in their gains; that if they came they would be sporadic; that they would not be linked with any monolithic Communist center, that each would more or less go its own national way; and that even Communist economies would not be able to transform countries in Africa and Southeast Asia into industrial societies with technological might. The fact that Communist China and the Soviet Union were now rivals and working at cross purposes in their bid for Communist support in the new nations of the underdeveloped areas was certainly not helping the Communist cause in those areas.

Hence the United States, which had conducted a holding operation since the end of World War II, was modifying its containment strategy, contracting some of its commitments abroad, and rethinking foreign-policy priorities in more rigorous fashion. In many aspects of American foreign policy this made obvious good sense. However, if this should result in a general impairment of America's foreign economic aid (and not merely a more intelligent American selectivity), such impairment might revive the original threat of sweeping Communist gains by way of domestic revolutions, and it would certainly delay the stability and the increased economic productivity of the underdeveloped areas on which, in rather vital part, economic growth in even the old industrial societies depends.

BIBLIOGRAPHY

Comprehensive and Selective

I. ON THE NATURE OF POLITICS
   A. *The Contemporary Behavioral Approach*
      S. M. Lipset, *Political Man*, Doubleday, Garden City, N. Y., 1959
   B. *The Traditional, Personal, Humanistic Approach*
      F. S. Oliver, *The Endless Adventure*, Houghton Mifflin, Boston and New York, 1931

II. ON THE NATURE OF WORLD POLITICS
   A. *In General*
      W. G. Carleton, "Ideology or Balance of Power?" *The Yale Review*, Summer 1947
      E. H. Carr, *The Twenty Years' Crisis 1919-1939: An Introduction to the Study of International Relations*, Macmillan, London, 1946
      T. I. Cook and Malcolm Moos, *Power Through Purpose*, Johns Hopkins, Baltimore, 1954
      G. A. Craig, *From Bismarck to Adenauer: Aspects of German Statecraft*, Johns Hopkins, Baltimore, 1958
      A. B. Fox, *The Power of Small States: Diplomacy in World War II*, University of Chicago Press, Chicago, 1959
      C. J. Friedrich, *Foreign Policy in the Making*, Norton, New York, 1938
      Maurice Hankey, *Diplomacy by Conference*, Putnam, New York, 1946

J. H. Herz, *Political Realism and Political Idealism*, University of Chicago Press, Chicago, 1951

S. B. Jones, "The Power Inventory and National Strategy," *World Politics*, July 1954

George Liska, *International Equilibrium*, Harvard University Press, Cambridge, Mass., 1957

Niccolò Machiavelli, *The Prince and the Discourses*, Modern Library, New York, 1950

H. J. Morgenthau, *Dilemmas of Politics*, University of Chicago Press, Chicago, 1958

H. J. Morgenthau, *Politics Among Nations: The Struggle for Power and Peace*, 3rd edition, Knopf, New York, 1960

H. J. Morgenthau, *Scientific Man vs. Power Politics*, University of Chicago Press, Chicago, 1946

H. J. Morgenthau and W. T. R. Fox, "National Interest and Moral Principles in Foreign Policy," *American Scholar*, Spring 1949

R. B. Mowat, *The European State System*, Milford, London, 1923

H. G. Nicolson, *Diplomacy*, Oxford University Press, New York, 1950

H. G. Nicolson, *The Evolution of Diplomatic Method*, Macmillan, New York, 1955

Reinhold Niebuhr, *The Structure of Nations and Empires*, Scribner's, New York, 1959

Georg Schwarzenberger, *Power Politics, A Study of International Society*, Praeger, New York, 1960

Harold and Margaret Sprout, eds., *Foundations of National Power*, Van Nostrand, Princeton, N. J., 1951

A. J. P. Taylor, *The Struggle for Mastery in Europe, 1848-1918*, Clarendon Press, Oxford, 1957

C. W. Thayer, *Diplomat*, Harper, New York, 1959

Alfred Vagts, *Defense and Diplomacy*, King's Crown, New York, 1956

Sir Charles Webster, *The Art and Practice of Diplomacy*, London, 1952

Arnold Wolfers and L. W. Martin, eds., *The*

Anglo-American Tradition in Foreign Affairs, Yale University Press, New Haven, 1956

B. *The Tangled Complexity of World Politics as Seen by Those at the Center of It. (This did not become fully relevant to American experience until the presidencies of Woodrow Wilson and FDR, and not to sustained American experience until after World War II.) Here the bibliography is arranged not in alphabetical but in chronological historical order and represents a mere sampling.*

Thucydides, *The History of the Peloponnesian War* (There are several English-language editions; perhaps the most satisfactory is that prepared by Sir R. W. Livingston, published by the Oxford University Press in its series of The World's Classics. Also Plutarch on Pericles, in any of the numerous editions of Plutarch.)

Edward Gibbon, *The History of the Decline and Fall of the Roman Empire,* Vol. I, Chapters I, X, and XI, in any of the numerous editions of Gibbon

James Bryce, *The Holy Roman Empire,* Chapter XXII, Macmillan, New York, 1919

Dmitri Merejkowski, *The Romance of Leonardo Da Vinci* (fictional), Random House, New York, 1928 (Penetrating insights into power politics among the Italian principalities, the interplay of the nascent European state system with the Italian balance of power, and Machiavellian and anti-Machiavellian attitudes in politics.)

Hillaire Belloc, *Richelieu,* Lippincott, Philadelphia and London, 1929

Sir Richard Lodge, *Richelieu,* Macmillan, New York and London, 1914

Aldous Huxley, *Grey Eminence,* Chatto and Windus, London, 1942 (This is the life of Father Joseph, Richelieu's close collaborator, "the second head under the same cowl"; they were among the earliest of the masters of European power politics.)

Winston Churchill, *Marlborough* (6 vols.), Scribner's, New York, 1933

T. B. Macaulay, essay on Chatham and essay on the Younger Pitt in any of the editions of Macaulay's writings

J. H. Rose, *William Pitt and the Great War*, G. Bell, London, 1911

Crane Brinton, *Lives of Talleyrand*, Norton, New York, 1936

Sir Alfred Duff Cooper, *Talleyrand*, Harper, New York, 1932

A. Cecil, *Metternich*, Macmillan, New York, 1933

Harold Nicolson, *The Congress of Vienna*, Harcourt, Brace, New York, 1946

H. A. Kissinger, *A World Restored: Metternich, Castlereagh and the Problem of Peace*, Houghton Mifflin, Boston, 1957

A. J. P. Taylor, *Bismarck*, Knopf, New York, 1955

Maurice Paléologue, *The Tragic Empress*, Harper, New York, 1928 (In a series of intimate talks [1901-1919] with the Empress Eugénie, a distinguished French diplomat draws from the aged Empress her reflections on the foreign policies of the Second Empire and in his own asides makes penetrating and devastating comments about those policies.)

Bülow, Bernard von, *The Memoirs of Prince von Bülow*, (4 vols.), Little, Brown, Boston, 1931 and 1932 (The development of German foreign policy under Wilhelm II and the failure at home to bring into equilibrium the new commercial and industrial groups and the old feudal and military groups.)

III. THE HISTORY OF AMERICAN FOREIGN POLICY TO AROUND 1945

A. General

T. A. Bailey, *Diplomatic History of the American People*, 6th edition, Appleton, New York, 1958

C. A. Beard, *The Idea of National Interest*, Macmillan, New York, 1934

S. F. Bemis, *Diplomatic History of the United States*, 4th edition, Holt, New York, 1955

Jules Davids, *America and the World of Our Time: United States Diplomacy in the Twentieth Century*, Random House, New York, 1960

George F. Kennan, *American Diplomacy, 1900-1950* Mentor, New York, 1952

R. W. Leopold, *The Growth of American Foreign Policy*, Knopf, New York, 1962

Dexter Perkins, *Hands Off: A History of the Monroe Doctrine*, Little, Brown, Boston, 1946

J. W. Pratt, *History of United States Foreign Policy*, Prentice-Hall, New York, 1955

A. K. Weinberg, *Manifest Destiny: A Study of National Expansion in American History*, Johns Hopkins, Baltimore, 1935

B. *To Around 1900*

Bernard De Voto, *The Year of Decision: 1846*, Little, Brown, Boston, 1943

Walter Millis, *The Martial Spirit: A Study of Our War with Spain*, Houghton Mifflin, Boston and New York, 1931

Dexter Perkins, *The Monroe Doctrine, 1823-1826*, Harvard University Press, Cambridge, Mass., 1927

Dexter Perkins, *The Monroe Doctrine, 1826-1867*, Johns Hopkins, Baltimore, 1933

Dexter Perkins, *The Monroe Doctrine, 1867-1907*, Johns Hopkins, Baltimore, 1937

J. W. Pratt, *Expansionists of 1812*, Macmillan, New York, 1925

J. W. Pratt, *Expansionists of 1898*, Johns Hopkins, Baltimore, 1936

C. *Relations with the Far East from Around 1900 to Around 1945*

T. A. Bisson, *America's Far Eastern Policy*, Institute of Pacific Relations, New York, 1945

Tyler Dennett, *Americans in Eastern Asia*, Macmillan, New York, 1922

A. W. Griswold, *The Far Eastern Policy of the United States*, Harcourt, Brace, New York, 1938

S. K. Hornbeck, *The United States and the Far East*, World Peace Foundation, Boston, 1942

D. *Relations with Latin America from Around 1900 to Around 1945*

S. F. Bemis, *The Latin American Policy of the United States*, Harcourt, Brace, New York, 1943

C. W. Hackett, *The Mexican Revolution and the United States*, World Peace Foundation, Boston, 1926

H. C. Herring, *Good Neighbors*, Yale University Press, New Haven, 1941

L. H. Jenks, *Our Cuban Colony: A Study in Sugar*, Vanguard, New York, 1928

C. L. Jones, *The Caribbean Since 1900*, Prentice-Hall, New York, 1936

C. L. Jones *et al.*, *The United States and the Caribbean*, University of Chicago Press, Chicago, 1929

Scott Nearing and Joseph Freeman, *Dollar Diplomacy*, Huebsch and Viking, New York, 1925

Dexter Perkins, *The Monroe Doctrine: 1867-1907*, Johns Hopkins, Baltimore, 1937

Dexter Perkins, *The United States and the Caribbean*, Harvard University Press, Cambridge, Mass., 1947

G. H. Stuart, *Latin America and the United States*, 4th edition, Appleton, New York, 1943

E. *World War I and the Peace Settlement*

T. A. Bailey, *Woodrow Wilson and the Lost Peace*, Macmillan, New York, 1944

R. S. Baker, *Woodrow Wilson and World Settlement* (3 vols.), Doubleday, Garden City, N.Y., 1922

J. M. Blum, *Woodrow Wilson and the Politics of Morality*, Little, Brown, Boston, 1956

W. G. Carleton, "A New Look at Woodrow Wilson," *Virginia Quarterly Review*, Autumn 1962

Alan Cranston, *The Killing of the Peace*, Viking, New York, 1945

D. F. Fleming, *The United States and the League of Nations*, Putnam, New York, 1932

C. H. Grattan, *Why We Fought*, Vanguard, New York, 1929

Arthur Link, *Wilson: The Struggle for Neutrality*,

1914-1915, Princeton University Press, Princeton, N. J., 1960

Walter Millis, *Road to War,* Houghton Mifflin, Boston and New York, 1935

F. L. Paxson, *American Democracy and the World War,* Houghton Mifflin, Boston, 1936

Charles Seymour, *American Diplomacy During the World War,* Johns Hopkins, Baltimore, 1934

Charles Seymour, *American Neutrality, 1914-1917,* Yale University Press, New Haven, 1935

C. C. Tansill, *America Goes to War,* Little, Brown, Boston, 1938

F. *The Years Between World War I and World War II, and World War II*

C. A. Beard, *A Foreign Policy for America,* Knopf, New York, 1940

J. M. Burns, *Roosevelt: The Lion and the Fox,* Harcourt, Brace, New York, 1956

W. G. Carleton, "Isolationism and the Middle West," *The Mississippi Valley Historical Review,* December 1946

Herbert Feis, *The Road to Pearl Harbor,* Atheneum, New York, 1962

C. G. Fenwick, *American Neutrality: Trial and Failure,* New York University Press, New York, 1940

D. F. Fleming, *The United States and World Organizations, 1920-1933,* Columbia University Press, New York, 1938

Cordell Hull, *Memoirs of Cordell Hull* (2 vols.), Macmillan, New York, 1948

Kenneth Ingram, *Years of Crisis, 1919-1945,* Macmillan, New York, 1947

D. E. Lee, *Ten Years: The World on the Way to War, 1930-1940,* Houghton Mifflin, Boston, 1942

Walter Lippmann, *United States Foreign Policy: Shield of the Republic,* Little, Brown, Boston, 1943

Dexter Perkins, *America and Two Wars,* Little, Brown, Boston, 1944

W. E. Rappard, *The Quest for Peace Since the*

World War, Harvard University Press, Cambridge, Mass., 1940

Basil Rauch, *Roosevelt: From Munich to Pearl Harbor*, Creative Age Press, New York, 1950

R. E. Sherwood, *Roosevelt and Hopkins*, Harper, New York, 1948

IV. BASIC TWENTIETH CENTURY CONDITIONS AND TRENDS IN THE WORLD VITAL TO WORLD POLITICS

A. *Nationalism*

Ernest Barker, *National Character and the Factors in Its Formation*, Harper, New York, 1927

Salo W. Baron, *Modern Nationalism and Religion*, Harper, New York, 1947

Ruth Benedict, *Race: Science and Politics*, Viking, New York, 1940

I. L. Claude, *National Minorities, An International Problem*, Harvard University Press, Cambridge, Mass., 1955

Alfred Cobban, *National Self-Determination*, University of Chicago Press, Chicago, 1955

K. W. Deutsch, *Nationalism and Social Communication*, Wiley, New York, 1953

Rupert Emerson, *From Empire to Nation*, Harvard University Press, Cambridge, Mass., 1960

Hans Kohn, *The Idea of Nationalism*, Macmillan, New York, 1944

Hans Kohn, *Nationalism, Its Meaning and History*, Van Nostrand, Princeton, N. J., 1955

F. S. C. Northrop, *The Taming of the Nations*, Macmillan, New York, 1952

B. C. Shafer, *Nationalism, Myth and Reality*, Harcourt, Brace, New York, 1955

B. *Colonialism in General*

J. A. Hobson, *Imperialism*, Allen and Unwin, London, 1938

V. I. Lenin, *Imperialism, the Highest Stage of Capitalism*, International Publishers, New York, 1939

P. T. Moon, *Imperialism and World Politics*, Macmillan, New York, 1926

E. M. Winslow, *The Pattern of Imperialism*, Columbia University Press, New York, 1950

C. *Anti-Colonialism in General*

    H. C. Armstrong, *Grey Wolf* (Mustafa Kemal and the Turkish Revolution), Penguin, London, 1937

    M. K. Gandhi, *An Autobiography*, Beacon, Boston, 1957

    Jawaharlal Nehru, *Toward Freedom* (Nehru's autobiography), John Day, New York, 1941

    R. B. Restarick, *Sun Yat-sen, Liberator of China*, Yale University Press, New Haven, 1931

    Barbara Ward, *The West at Bay*, Norton, New York, 1948

D. *The Confrontation of Cultures*

    F. S. C. Northrop, *The Meeting of East and West*, Macmillan, New York, 1950

E. *The Ideological Conflict of the Economic and Political "Isms"—In General*

    G. A. Almond, *The Appeals of Communism*, Princeton University Press, Princeton, N. J., 1954

    Franz Berkenau, *Socialism, National or International*, Routledge, London, 1942

    William Ebenstein, *Today's Isms: Communism, Fascism, Capitalism, and Socialism*, Prentice-Hall, Englewood Cliffs, N. J., 1958

    Charles Frankel, *The Case for Modern Man*, Harper, New York, 1956

    R. L. Heilbroner, *The Future as History*, Evergreen edition, Grove, New York, 1961

    R. L. Heilbroner, *The Making of Economic Society*, Prentice-Hall, Englewood Cliffs, N. J., 1962

    Arthur Koestler, *Darkness at Noon* (fictional) Signet, New York, 1948

    Arthur Koestler, *Dialogue with Death*, Macmillan, New York, 1942

    Arthur Koestler, *The Invisible Writing*, Beacon, Boston, 1955

André Malraux, *Man's Fate* (fictional), Modern Library, New York, 1934

A. G. Meyer, *Communism*, Random House, New York, 1960

S. Neuman, "The International Civil War," *World Politics*, April 1949

George Orwell, *Homage to Catalonia*, Beacon, Boston, 1952

Karl Polanyi, *The Great Transformation*, Rinehart, New York, 1944

Karl Popper, *The Open Society and Its Enemies*, Routledge, London, 1945

J. S. Schapiro, *Movements of Social Dissent in Modern Europe*, Van Nostrand, Princeton, N. J., 1962

J. A. Schumpeter, *Capitalism, Socialism, and Democracy*, Harper, New York, 1950

A. M. Sievers, *Revolution, Evolution, and the Economic Order*, Prentice-Hall, Englewood Cliffs, N. J., 1962

A. B. Ulam, *The Unfinished Revolution*, Random House, New York, 1960

F. Communists and the Right-Wing in the United States

W. F. Buckley, Jr., and L. B. Bozell, *McCarthy and His Enemies*, Regnery, Chicago, 1954

Whittaker Chambers, *Witness*, Random House, New York, 1952

Richard Dudman, *Men of the Far Right*, Pyramid, New York, 1962

Barry Goldwater, *The Conscience of a Conservative*, Hillman, New York, 1960

J. E. Hoover, *Masters of Deceit*, Holt, New York, 1958

R. H. Rovere, *Senator Joe McCarthy*, Harcourt, Brace, New York, 1959

G. Egalitarianism and Mass Man

Erich Fromm, *Escape from Freedom*, Rinehart, New York, 1941

Walter Lippmann, *The Public Philosophy*, Little, Brown, Boston, 1955

José Ortega y Gasset, *The Revolt of the Masses*, Norton, New York, 1932

H. A. Wallace, *The Century of the Common Man*, Reynal and Hitchcock, New York, 1943

H. **World Resources, Population, and the Population Explosion**

Eugene Ayres and C. A. Scarlott, *Energy Resources —The Wealth of the World*, McGraw-Hill, New York, 1952

Harrison Brown, *The Challenge of Man's Future*, Viking, New York, 1954

Kingsley Davis, *The Population of India and Pakistan*, Princeton University Press, Princeton, N. J., 1951

P. M. Hauser, *The Study of Population: An Inventory and Appraisal*, University of Chicago Press, Chicago, 1959

Political and Economic Planning (PEP), *World Population and Resources*, Allen and Unwin, London, 1955

I. **The Central Problem of Economic Growth**

A. O. Hirschman, *The Strategy of Economic Growth*, Yale University Press, New Haven, 1958

Klaus Knorr and W. J. Baumol, eds., *What Price Economic Growth?* Prentice-Hall, Englewood Cliffs, N. J., 1961

W. W. Rostow, *The Process of Economic Growth*, Norton, New York, 1962

V. **CULTURAL AND INSTITUTIONAL CHARACTERISTICS WHICH AFFECT AMERICAN ATTITUDES IN INTERNATIONAL RELATIONS**

A. **The Traditional Characteristics**

G. A. Almond, *The American People and Foreign Policy*, Harcourt, Brace, New York, 1950

Max Beloff, *Foreign Policy and the Democratic Process*, Johns Hopkins, Baltimore, 1955

D. J. Boorstin, *The Genius of American Politics*, Phoenix edition, University of Chicago Press, Chicago, 1953

D. W. Brogan, *The American Character*, Vintage, New York, 1944

W. G. Carleton, "American Intellectuals and American Democracy," *The Antioch Review*, Summer 1959

W. J. Cash, *The Mind of the South*, Vintage, New York, 1960

D. S. Cheever and H. F. Haviland, Jr., *American Foreign Policy and the Separation of Powers*, Harvard University Press, Cambridge, Mass., 1952

H. S. Commager, *The American Mind*, Yale University Press, New Haven, 1950

Louis Hartz, *The Liberal Tradition in America*, Harcourt, Brace, New York, 1955

Will Herberg, *Protestant, Catholic, and Jew*, Anchor edition, Doubleday, Garden City, N.Y., 1960

Pendleton Herring, *The Politics of Democracy*, Norton, New York, 1940

F. M. Joseph, ed., *As Others See Us: The United States Through Foreign Eyes*, Princeton University Press, Princeton, N. J., 1959

Gunnar Myrdal, *An American Dilemma*, Harper, New York, 1944

Clinton Rossiter, *Conservatism in America*, Vintage, New York, 1962

Alexis De Tocqueville, *Democracy in America* (2 vols.) Knopf, New York, 1946

B. *Those Characteristics Developing in the Twentieth Century*

James Burnham, *The Managerial Revolution*, John Day, New York, 1941

J. K. Galbraith, *The Affluent Society*, Houghton Mifflin, Boston, 1958

C. W. Mills, *The Power Elite*, Oxford University Press, New York, 1956

C. W. Mills, *White Collar*, Oxford University Press, New York, 1953

Vance Packard, *The Hidden Persuaders*, Cardinal edition, Pocket Books, New York, 1958

D. M. Potter, *People of Plenty*, Phoenix edition, University of Chicago Press, Chicago, 1954

David Riesman, *The Lonely Crowd*, Anchor edition, Doubleday, Garden City, N. Y., 1956

W. H. Whyte, Jr., *The Organization Man*, Simon and Schuster, New York, 1956

VI. INTERNATIONAL RELATIONS SINCE WORLD WAR II—IN GENERAL

G. I. Arnold, *The Pattern of World Conflict*, Dial, New York, 1955

A. A. Berle, Jr., *Tides of Crisis: A Primer of Foreign Relations*, Reynal, New York, 1957

Hadley Cantril, *Tensions That Cause War*, University of Illinois Press, Urbana, 1950

J. B. Condliffe, *The Commerce of Nations*, Norton, New York, 1950

Isaac Deutscher, *The Great Conflict: Russia and the West*, Oxford University Press, New York, 1960

W. T. R. Fox, *The Super Powers*, Harcourt, Brace, New York, 1944

F. H. Hartmann, *The Relations of Nations*, 2nd edition, Macmillan, New York, 1962

J. H. Herz, *International Politics in the Atomic Age*, Columbia University Press, New York, 1959

Stephen Kertesz and M. A. Fitzsimmons, *Diplomacy in a Changing World*, Notre Dame Press, South Bend, 1959

Otto Klineberg, *Tensions Affecting International Understanding*, Social Science Research Council, New York, 1950

R. C. Macridis, ed., *Foreign Policy in World Politics*, Prentice-Hall, Englewood Cliffs, N. J., 1958

H. J. Morgenthau, *Politics Among Nations: The Struggle for Power and Peace*, 3rd edition, Knopf, New York, 1960

Gunnar Myrdal, *An International Economy: Problems and Prospects*, Harper, New York, 1956

Reinhold Niebuhr, *The Structure of Nations and Empires*, Scribner's New York, 1959

A. F. K. Organski, *World Politics*, Knopf, New York, 1958

J. N. Rosenau, *Public Opinion and Foreign Policy*, Random House, New York, 1961

Georg Schwarzenberger, *Power Politics, A Study of International Society*, Praeger, New York, 1951

Hugh Seton-Watson, *Neither War Nor Peace: The Struggle for Power in the Postwar World*, Praeger, New York, 1960

J. G. Stoessinger, *The Might of Nations, World Politics in Our Time*, Random House, New York, 1961

Robert Strausz-Hupé *et al.*, *Protracted Conflict*, Harper, New York, 1959

K. W. Thompson, *Political Realism and the Crisis of World Politics*, Princeton University Press, Princeton, N. J., 1960

UNESCO, *The Nature of Conflict*, Columbia University Press, New York, 1957

U. G. Whitaker, Jr., *Propaganda and International Relations*, Chandler Publishing Co., San Francisco, 1962

Arnold Wolfers, *Discord and Collaboration: Essays in International Politics*, Johns Hopkins, Baltimore, 1962

VII. AMERICAN FOREIGN POLICY SINCE WORLD WAR II—IN GENERAL

Dean Acheson, *Power and Diplomacy*, Atheneum, New York, 1962

Selig Adler, *The Isolationist Impulse, Its Twentieth Century Reaction*, Collier, New York, 1961

J. R. Beal, *John Foster Dulles*, Harper, New York, 1956

J. F. Byrnes, *Speaking Frankly*, Harper, New York, 1947

J. G. Campaigne, *American Might and Soviet Myth*, Regnery, Chicago, 1960

W. G. Carleton, "The American and the World," *The Round Table*, March 1955

W. G. Carleton, "American Foreign Policy: Myths and Realities," *Virginia Quarterly Review*, Spring 1961

W. G. Carleton, "An Atlantic Curtain?", *American Scholar*, Summer 1953

W. G. Carleton, "Braintrusters of American Foreign Policy," *World Politics*, July 1955

W. G. Carleton, "Europeans View Our Foreign Policy," *Antioch Review*, Winter 1950-1951

W. G. Carleton, "National Interest and the Balance of Power," *American Perspective*, Fall 1950

W. G. Carleton, "A New Era in World Politics?", *Virginia Quarterly Review*, Summer 1955

W. G. Carleton, "Price of American Failure," *American Scholar*, Spring 1950

W. G. Carleton, "Program for Survival," *Virginia Quarterly Review*, Winter 1959

W. G. Carleton, "There Is Still a Middle Way," *Virginia Quarterly Review*, Summer 1951

W. G. Carleton, "Wanted: Wiser Power Politics," *Yale Review*, Winter 1952

J. H. Cerf and Walter Pozen, *Strategy for the '60s*, Praeger, New York, 1961

V. M. Dean, *The United States and Russia*, Harvard University Press, Cambridge, Mass., 1947

Raymond Dennett and J. E. Johnson, *Negotiating with the Russians*, World Peace Federation, Boston, 1951

T. K. Finletter, *Foreign Policy: The Next Phase*, Harper, New York, 1958

T. K. Finletter, *Power and Policy: The United States Foreign Policy and Military Power in the Hydrogen Age*, Harcourt, Brace, New York, 1954

D. F. Fleming, *The Cold War and Its Origins, 1917-1960*, (2 vols.), Doubleday, Garden City, N. Y., 1961

N. A. Graebner, *Cold War Diplomacy*, Van Nostrand, Princeton, N. J., 1962

N. A. Graebner, *The New Isolationism*, Ronald, New York, 1956

L. J. Halle, *Civilization and Foreign Policy*, Harper, New York, 1955

G. F. Kennan, *Realities of American Foreign Policy*, Princeton University Press, Princeton, N. J., 1954

G. F. Kennan, "The Sources of Soviet Conduct," *Foreign Affairs*, July 1947

E. W. Lefever, *Ethics and United States Foreign Policy*, Meridian, New York, 1957

L. L. Leonard, *Elements of American Foreign Policy*, McGraw-Hill, New York, 1953

Walter Lippmann, *The Cold War*, Harper, New York, 1947

Walter Lippmann, *United States Foreign Policy: Shield of the Republic*, Little, Brown, Boston, 1943

John Lukacs, *A History of the Cold War*, Doubleday, Garden City, N. Y., 1961

C. B. Marshall, *The Limits of Foreign Policy*, Holt, New York, 1954

J. L. McCamy, *The Administration of American Foreign Affairs*, Knopf, New York, 1950

Max Millikan and W. W. Rostow, *A Proposal, Key to an Effective Foreign Policy*, Harper, New York, 1957

H. J. Morgenthau, *In Defense of the National Interest: A Critical Examination of American Foreign Policy*, Knopf, New York, 1951

F. W. Neal, *United States Foreign Policy and the Soviet Union*, Fund for the Republic, Center for the Study of Democratic Institutions, Santa Barbara, Calif., 1961

R. E. Osgood, *Ideals and Self-Interest in America's Foreign Relations*, University of Chicago Press, Chicago, 1953

Nathaniel Peffer, *America's Place in the World*, Viking, New York, 1945

Dexter Perkins, *The Evolution of Foreign Policy*, Oxford University Press, New York, 1948

D. K. Price, ed., *The Secretary of State*, Prentice-Hall, Englewood Cliffs, N. J., 1960

H. L. Roberts, *Russia and America*, Harper, New York, 1956

W. W. Rostow, *The United States in the World Arena*, Harper, New York, 1960

F. L. Schuman, *The Cold War: Retrospect and Prospect*, Louisiana State University Press, Baton Rouge, 1962

Laurence Sears, "American Foreign Policy and Its Consequences," *The American Scholar*, Autumn 1949

J. C. Slessor, *Strategy for the West*, Morrow, New York, 1954

N. J. Spykman, *America's Strategy in World Affairs*, Harcourt, Brace, New York, 1942

Adlai Stevenson, *Call to Greatness*, Atheneum, New York, 1962

Edmund Stillman and William Pfaff, *The New Politics: America and the End of the Post War World*, Harper and Row, New York, 1962

Robert Strausze-Hupé *et al.*, *A Forward Strategy for America*, Harper, New York, 1961

K. W. Thompson, *American Diplomacy and Emergent Patterns*, New York University Press, New York, 1962

H. S. Truman, *Memoirs* (2 vols.), Doubleday, Garden City, N. Y., 1955

J. B. Whitton, *The Second Chance: America and the Peace*, Princeton University Press, Princeton, N. J., 1944

W. A. Williams, *The Tragedy of American Diplomacy*, Delta, New York, 1962

Arnold Wolfers, ed., *Alliance Policy in the Cold War*, Johns Hopkins, Baltimore, 1959

VIII. WESTERN EUROPE

Dean Acheson, "The Illusion of Disengagement," *Foreign Affairs*, April 1958

Raymond Aron and Daniel Lerner, eds., *France Defeats the EDC*, Praeger, New York, 1956

Blair Bolles, *The Big Change in Europe*, Norton, New York, 1958

Alastair Buchan, *NATO in the 1960's*, Praeger, New York, 1960

W. G. Carleton, "Italy: Which Way?", *Virginia Quarterly Review*, Autumn 1952

W. G. Carleton, "What of the Council of Europe?", *Virginia Quarterly Review*, Spring 1951

Marquis Childs, *Sweden, The Middle Way*, Yale University Press, New Haven, 1938

Lucius Clay, *Decision in Germany*, Doubleday, Garden City, N. Y., 1950

Eugene Davison, *The Death and Life of Germany*, Knopf, New York, 1959

W. P. Davison, *The Berlin Blockade*, Princeton University Press, Princeton, N. J., 1958

Charles de Gaulle, *The War Memoirs of Charles de Gaulle* (2 vols.), Simon and Schuster, New York, 1959 and 1960

J. F. Deniau, *The Common Market*, Praeger, New York, 1959

K. W. Deutsch and L. J. Edinger, *Germany Rejoins the Powers*, Stanford University Press, Stanford, Calif., 1959

W. J. Diebold, *Trade and Payments in Western Europe*, Harper, New York, 1952

E. M. Earle, *Modern France*, Princeton University Press, Princeton, N. J., 1951

Anthony Eden, *Full Circle*, Houghton Mifflin, Boston, 1960

Mario Einaudi et al., *Nationalization in France and Italy*, Cornell University Press, Ithaca, N. Y., 1955

L. D. Epstein, *Britain—Uneasy Ally*, University of Chicago Press, Chicago, 1954

M. T. Florinsky, *Integrated Europe?*, Macmillan, New York, 1955

Gerald Freund, *Germany Between Two Worlds*, Harcourt, Brace, New York, 1961

E. S. Furniss, *France, Troubled Ally*, Harper, New York, 1960

John Gormaghtigh, "European Coal and Steel Community," *International Conciliation*, May 1955

E. B. Haas, *The Uniting of Europe, Political, Social, and Economic Forces, 1950-1957*, Stanford University Press, Stanford, Calif., 1959

R. L. Heilbroner, *Forging a United Europe, The Story of the European Community*, Public Affairs Committee, New York, 1961

Hajo Holborn, *The Political Collapse of Europe*, Knopf, New York, 1951

Alistair Horne, *Return to Power* (Germany), Praeger, New York, 1956

Michael Howard, *Disengagement in Europe*, Penguin, Baltimore, 1958

Serge Hurtig, "The European Common Market," *International Conciliation*, March 1958

J. M. Jones, *The Fifteen Weeks* (Truman Doctrine and Marshall Plan), Viking, New York, 1955

G. F. Kennan, *Russia, the Atom, and the West* (Kennan's proposal for disengagement), Harper, New York, 1957

Klaus Knorr, ed., *NATO and American Security*, Princeton University Press, Princeton, N. J., 1959

Joseph Kraft, "Europe Against de Gaulle," *Harper's Magazine*, August 1962

Kenneth Lindsay, *Toward a European Parliament*, International Secretariat, Paris, 1958

Karl Lowenstein, "Unity for Germany?", *Current History*, January 1960

Herbert Luethy, *France Against Herself*, Praeger, New York, 1955

H. L. Mason, *The European Coal and Steel Community: Experiment in Supranationalism*, Martinus Nijhoff, The Hague, 1955

Drew Middleton, *These Are the British*, Knopf, New York, 1957

B. T. Moore, *NATO and the Future of Europe*, Harper, New York, 1958

J. W. Nystrom and Peter Malof, *The Common Market*, Van Nostrand, Princeton, N. J., 1962

G. Patterson and E. S. Furniss, Jr., *NATO, a Critical Appraisal*, Princeton University Press, Princeton, N. J., 1957

Political and Economic Planning (PEP), *European Organizations*, Allen and Unwin, London, 1959

N. J. G. Pounds, *Divided Germany and Berlin*, Van Nostrand, Princeton, N. J., 1962

David Riesman, "Dealing with the Russians Over Berlin," *American Scholar*, Winter 1961-62

A. H. Robertson, *The Council of Europe—Its Structure, Functions, and Achievements*, Praeger, New York, 1956

C. B. Robson, ed., *Berlin—Pivot of German Destiny*, University of North Carolina Press, Chapel Hill, 1960

Royal Institute of International Affairs, *Atlantic Alliance*, London, 1952

Royal Institute of International Affairs, *Britain in Western Europe, WEU and the Atlantic Alliance*, London, 1956

J. E. Snell, *Wartime Origins of East-West Dilemma Over Germany*, Hauser, New York, 1959

Hans Speier, *The Soviet Threat to Berlin*, Rand Corporation, New York, 1960

Hans Speier and W. P. Davison, eds., *West German Leadership and Foreign Policy*, Row, Peterson, Evanston, Ill., 1957

A. P. Whitaker, *Spain and the Defense of the West, Ally and Liability*, Praeger, New York, 1962

Theodore White, *Fire in the Ashes*, Sloane, New York, 1953

David Wightman, *Economic Cooperation in Europe—A Study of the United Nations Economic Commission for Europe*, Stevens and Heinemann, London, 1956

René Williamson and Lee Greene, eds., *Five Years of British Labour, 1945-1950*, published by the *Journal of Politics*, Gainesville, Florida

IX. THE SOVIET UNION, COMMUNIST CHINA, AND THE COMMUNIST WORLD

H. F. Armstrong, *Tito and Goliath*, Macmillan, New York, 1951

F. C. Barghoorn, *The Soviet Cultural Offensive*, Princeton University Press, Princeton, N. J., 1960

R. H. Bass, *The Soviet-Yugoslav Controversy*, Prospect, London, 1959

Abraham Bergson, ed., *Soviet Economic Growth: Conditions and Perspectives*, Row, Peterson, Evanston, Ill., 1953

H. L. Boorman *et al.*, *Moscow-Peking Axis, Strengths and Strains*, Harper, New York, 1957

R. G. Boyd, *Communist China's Foreign Policy*, Praeger, New York, 1962

Conrad Brandt, *Stalin's Failure in China*, Harvard University Press, Cambridge, Mass., 1958

Z. K. Brzezinski, "The Sino-Soviet Dispute," *Problems of Communism*, September 1960

Z. K. Brzezinski, *The Soviet Bloc: Unity and Conflict*, Harvard University Press, Cambridge, Mass., 1960

Z. K. Brzezinski, "United States Foreign Policy in East Central Europe—A Study in Contradictions," *Journal of International Affairs*, Columbia University, Vol. 9, No. 1

C. A. Buss, *The People's Republic of China*, Van Nostrand, Princeton, N. J., 1962

W. G. Carleton, "Is Communism Going National?", *Virginia Quarterly Review*, Summer 1949

Edward Crankshaw, *Khrushchev's Russia*, Penguin, Harmondsworth, Middlesex, 1959

Alexander Dallin, *Soviet Conduct in World Affairs*, Columbia University Press, New York, 1960

David J. Dallin, *Soviet Foreign Policy After Stalin*, Lippincott, Philadelphia, 1961

Alexander Eckstein, "Conditions and Prospects for Economic Growth in China," *World Politics*, October 1954, and January and April 1955

Merle Fainsod, *How Russia Is Ruled*, Harvard University Press, Cambridge, Mass., 1953

R. L. Garthoff, *Soviet Strategy in the Nuclear Age*, Praeger, New York, 1962

R. L. Heilbroner, *The Future as History*, Evergreen edition, Grove Press, New York, 1961

A. L. Hsieh, *Communist China's Strategy in the Nuclear Age*, Prentice-Hall, Englewood Cliffs, N. J., 1962

G. F. Hudson *et al.*, eds., *The Sino-Soviet Dispute*, Praeger, New York, 1961

W. A. D. Jackson, *Russo-Chinese Borderlands*, Van Nostrand, Princeton, N. J., 1962

G. F. Kennan, *Russia and the West Under Lenin and Stalin*, Little, Brown, Boston, 1960

G. F. Kennan, *Soviet Foreign Policy, 1917-1941*, Van Nostrand, Princeton, N. J., 1960

S. D. Kertesz and M. A. Fitzsimmons, *The Fate of East Central Europe: Hopes and Failures of American Foreign Policy*, University of Notre Dame Press, South Bend, Ind., 1956

Flora Lewis, *A Case History of Hope, The Story of Poland's Peaceful Revolutions*, Doubleday, New York, 1958

Barrington Moore, Jr., *Soviet Politics, The Dilemma of Power*, Harvard University Press, Cambridge, Mass., 1950

R. Moorsteen, "Economic Prospects for Communist China," *World Politics*, January 1959

P. E. Mosely, *The Kremlin and World Politics*, Vintage, New York, 1960

R. P. Newman, *Recognition of Communist China?*, Macmillan, New York, 1961

N. D. Palmer and S. C. Leng, *Sun Yat-sen and Communism*, Praeger, New York, 1960

Royal Institute of International Affairs, *The Soviet-Yugoslav Dispute*, London, 1949

Russian Institute of Columbia University, ed., *The Anti-Stalin Campaign and International Communism*, Columbia University Press, New York, 1956

B. I. Schwartz, *Chinese Communism and the Rise of Mao*, Harvard University Press, Cambridge, Mass., 1951

Harry Schwartz, *Russia's Soviet Economy*, Prentice-Hall, Englewood Cliffs, N. J., 1954

Hugh Seton-Watson, *The East European Revolution*, Praeger, New York, 1956

Hugh Seton-Watson, *From Lenin to Khrushchev: The History of World Communism*, Praeger, New York, 1960

Edgar Snow, *Red Star Over China*, Random House, New York, 1938

A. B. Ulam, "Soviet Ideology and Soviet Foreign Policy," *World Politics*, January 1959

A. B. Ulam, *Titoism and the Cominform*, Harvard University Press, Cambridge, Mass., 1952

A. B. Ulam, *The Unfinished Revolution*, Random House, New York, 1960

Theodore White and Annalee Jacoby, *Thunder Out of China*, Sloane, New York, 1946

A. S. Whiting, *China Crosses the Yalu: The Decision to Enter the Korean War*, Macmillan, New York, 1960

B. D. Wolfe, *Three Who Made a Revolution*, Beacon, Boston, 1955

D. S. Zagoria, *The Sino-Soviet Conflict, 1956-1961*, Princeton University Press, Princeton, New Jersey, 1962

Howard Zinn, "Another Look at the Chinese Communists," *Antioch Review*, Spring 1962

X. THE UNDERDEVELOPED SOCIETIES, ECONOMIC FOREIGN AID, AND NEUTRALISM

Gabriel Almond and J. S. Coleman, eds., *The Politics of the Developing Areas*, Princeton University Press, Princeton, N. J., 1960

Joseph Berliner, *Soviet Economic Aid*, Praeger, New York, 1958

Chester Bowles, *Ambassador's Report*, Harper, New York, 1954

Chester Bowles, *The New Dimension of Peace*, Harper, New York, 1955

Z. K. Brzezinski, "The Politics of Underdevelopment," *World Politics*, October 1956

Eugene Burdick and W. J. Lederer, *The Ugly American* (fictional), Norton, New York, 1958

W. G. Carleton, "Leninism and the Legacy of Western Imperialism," *Yale Review*, Summer 1962

W. G. Carleton, "The New Nationalism," *Virginia Quarterly Review*, Summer 1950

W. G. Carleton, "The Primacy of Politics," *American Scholar*, Summer 1958

W. G. Carleton, "Social Politics—A Policy for America," *Antioch Review*, Summer 1947

V. M. Dean, *The Nature of the Non-Western World*, Mentor, New York, 1957

Graham Greene, *The Quiet American* (fictional), Viking, New York, 1956

R. L. Heilbroner, *The Future as History*, Evergreen edition, Grove Press, New York, 1961

Hans Heyman, Jr., "Soviet Economic Aid as a Problem for United States Policy," *World Politics*, July 1960

George Liska, *The New Statecraft: Foreign Aid in American Foreign Policy*, University of Chicago Press, Chicago, 1960

Laurence W. Martin, ed., *Neutralism and Nonalignment*, Praeger, New York, 1962

Massachusetts Institute of Technology, Center for International Studies, *Economic, Social, and Political Change in the Underdeveloped Countries*, U. S. Senate Committee on Foreign Relations, March 30, 1960

M. F. Millikan and D. L. M. Blackmer, eds., *The Emerging Nations, Their Growth and United States Policy*, Little, Brown, Boston, 1961

J. D. Montgomery, *The Politics of Foreign Aid*, Praeger, New York, 1962

W. W. Rostow, *The Process of Economic Growth*, Norton, New York, 1962

W. W. Rostow and M. F. Millikan, "Foreign Aid: Next Phase," *Foreign Affairs*, April 1958

L. A. Shonfield, *The Attack on World Poverty*, Vintage, New York, 1962

Eugene Staley, *The Future of Underdevloped Countries: Political Implications of Economic Development*, Harper, New York, 1954

Peggy and Pierre Streit, "Close-up of Foreign Aid," *New York Times Magazine*, April 13, 1958

A. B. Ulam, *The Unfinished Revolution*, Random House, New York, 1960

United States Department of State, *The Sino-Soviet Economic Offensive in the Less Developed Countries*, 1958

Barbara Ward, *The Interplay of East and West*, Norton, New York, 1957

Barbara Ward, *The Rich Nations and the Poor Nations*, Norton, New York, 1962

XI.   THE FAR EAST AND SOUTH ASIA

W. M. Ball, *Nationalism and Communism in East Asia*, Melbourne University Press, Melbourne, Australia, 1956

A. D. Barnett, *Communist China and Asia*, Harper, New York, 1960

Ruth Benedict, *The Chrysanthemum and the Sword*, Houghton Mifflin, Boston, 1946

Richard Butwell, *Southeast Asia Today and Tomorrow, A Political Analysis*, Praeger, New York, 1961

Sir Esler Dening, *Japan*, Praeger, New York, 1961

Michael Edwardes, *Asia in the Balance*, Penguin, Baltimore, 1962

J. K. Fairbank, *The United States and China*, revised, Harvard University Press, Cambridge, Mass., 1958

J. K. Fairbank and Ssu-yu Teng, *China's Response to the West*, Harvard University Press, Cambridge, Mass., 1954

Herbert Feis, *The China Tangle*, Princeton University Press, Princeton, N. J., 1953

Ellen Hammer, *The Struggle for Indochina*, Stanford University Press, Stanford, Calif., 1954

S. S. Harrison, *India: The Most Dangerous Decades*, Princeton University Press, Princeton, N. J., 1960

Ruth McVey, *The Soviet View of the Indonesian Revolution*, Cornell University Press, Ithaca, N. Y., 1957

G. D. Overstreet and Marshall Windmiller, *Communism in India*, University of California Press, Berkeley, Calif., 1959

R. L. Park and Irene Tinker, eds., *Leadership and Political Institutions in India*, Princeton University Press, Princeton, N. J., 1959

Guy Pauker, "Southeast Asia as a Problem Area in the Next Decade," *World Politics*, April 1959

H. S. Quigley, *China's Politics in Perspective, 1900-1949*, University of Minnesota Press, Minneapolis, 1962

E. O. Reischauer, *The United States and Japan*, Viking, New York, 1957

G. E. Taylor and F. H. Michael, *The Far East in the Modern World*, Holt, New York, 1956

W. L. Thorp, ed., *The United States and the Far East*, Prentice-Hall, Englewood Cliffs, N. J., 1962

H. M. Vinacke, *The United States and the Far East, 1945-1951*, Stanford University Press, Stanford, Calif., 1952

Barbara Ward, *India and the West*, Norton, New York, 1961

Myron Weiner, *Party Politics in India*, Princeton University Press, Princeton, N. J., 1957

H. J. Wiens, *Pacific Islands: Bastions of the United States*, Van Nostrand, Princeton, N. J., 1962

Theodore White, ed., *The Papers of General Joseph W. Stilwell*, Macfadden, New York, 1962

C. Wolf, Jr., "Soviet Economic Aid in Southeast

Asia: Threat or Windfall?", *World Politics*, October 1957

XII. THE MIDDLE EAST AND THE MOSLEM WORLD

H. C. Armstrong, *Grey Wolf* (Mustafa Kemal), Penguin, London, 1937

J. Baulin, *The Arab Role in Africa*, Penguin, Baltimore, 1962

J. C. Campbell, *Defense of the Middle East*, Harper, New York, 1960

Anthony Eden, *Full Circle*, Houghton Mifflin, Boston, 1960 (Eden's view of the Suez crisis)

John Gunther, *Inside Africa*, Harper, New York, 1953 (for the North African Moslem countries)

Maurice Harari, *Government and Politics in the Middle East*, Prentice-Hall, Englewood Cliffs, N. J., 1962

G. E. Kirk, *A Short History of the Middle East*, 6th edition, Praeger, New York, 1960

W. Z. Laqueur, *Communism and Nationalism in the Middle East*, Praeger, New York, 1957

W. Z. Laqueur, *The Soviet Union in the Middle East*, Praeger, New York, 1959

T. E. Lawrence, *Revolt in the Desert*, Doran, New York, 1927

T. E. Lawrence, *Seven Pillars of Wisdom*, Doubleday, Doran, New York, 1935

W. A. Leeman, *The Price of Middle East Oil: An Essay in Political Economy*, Cornell University Press, Ithaca, N. Y., 1962

George Lenczowski, *The Middle East in World Affairs*, 2nd edition, Cornell University Press, Ithaca, N. Y., 1956

Don Peretz, *The Middle East Today*, Holt, Rinehart, Winston, New York, 1963

H. B. Sharabi, *Governments and Politics in the Middle East in the Twentieth Century*, Van Nostrand, Princeton, N. J., 1962

Guy Wint and Peter Calvocoressi, *Middle East Crisis*, Penguin, Harmondsworth, Middlesex, 1957

XIII. AFRICA

Dennis Austin, *West Africa and the Commonwealth*, Penguin, London, 1957

Andrew Boyd and Patrick van Rensberg, *An Atlas of African Affairs*, Praeger, New York, 1962

J. S. Coleman, *Nigeria, Background of Nationalism*, University of California Press, Berkeley, Calif., 1958

Mamadou Dia, *The African Nations and World Solidarity*, Praeger, New York, 1961

Kwame Nkrumah, *I Speak of Freedom*, Praeger, New York, 1961

L. H. Gann and P. Duignan, *White Settlers in Tropical Africa*, Penguin, Harmondsworth, Middlesex, 1962

John Gunther, *Inside Africa*, Harper, New York, 1953

M. J. Herskovits, *Dahomey, an Ancient West African Kingdom*, (2 vols.), Augustin, New York, 1938

M. J. Herskovits, *The Myth of the Negro Past*, Harper, New York, 1941

Colin Legum, *Congo Disaster*, Penguin, Baltimore, 1961

Leo Marquard, *People and Policies of South Africa*, 3rd edition, Oxford University Press, London, 1962

Vernon McKay, *Africa in World Politics*, Harper and Row, New York, 1962

Roland Oliver and J. D. Fage, *A Short History of Africa*, Penguin, Baltimore, 1962

Arnold Rivkin, *Africa and the West*, Praeger, New York, 1962

Ronald Segal, *African Profiles*, Penguin, Baltimore, 1962

G. W. Shepherd, Jr., *The Politics of African Nationalism*, Praeger, New York, 1962

H. J. Spiro, *Politics in Africa*, Prentice-Hall,

Englewood Cliffs, N. J., 1962
Immanuel Wallerstein, *Africa: The Politics of Independence*, Vintage, New York, 1961

XIV. LATIN AMERICA

R. N. Adams *et al.*, *Social Change in Latin America Today*, Viking, New York, 1961
R. J. Alexander, *The Bolivian National Revolution*, Rutgers University Press, New Brunswick, N. J., 1958
R. J. Alexander, *Today's Latin America*, Anchor edition, Doubleday, Garden City, New York, 1962
Theodore Draper, *Castro's Revolution*, Praeger, New York, 1962
Laurence Duggan, *The Americas: the Search for Hemisphere Security, 1933-1945*, Holt, New York, 1949
C. G. Fenwick, *The Inter-American Regional System*, D. X. McMullen, New York, 1949
Gilberto Freyre, *Brazil, an Interpretation*, Knopf, New York, 1947
Lewis Hanke, *South America*, Van Nostrand, Princeton, N. J., 1959
E. P. Hanson, *Puerto Rico: Ally for Progress*, Van Nostrand, Princeton, N. J., 1962
C. H. Haring, *The Spanish Empire in America*, Oxford University Press, New York, 1947
Hubert Herring, *A History of Latin America*, 2nd edition, Knopf, New York, 1961
Ray Josephs, *Latin America: Continent in Crisis*, Random House, New York, 1948
T. V. Kalijarvi, *Central America*, Van Nostrand, Princeton, N. J., 1962
Edwin Lieuwen, *Arms and Politics in Latin America*, Praeger, New York, 1961
Salvador de Madariaga, *The Rise of the Spanish Empire*, Macmillan, New York, 1949
Salvador de Madariaga, *The Fall of the Spanish Empire*, Macmillan, New York, 1948
Karl E. Meyer and Tad Szulc, *The Cuban In-*

vasion, The Chronicle of Disaster, Praeger, New York, 1962

C. W. Mills, *Listen Yankee*, Ballantine, New York, 1961

Dexter Perkins, *The United States and Latin America*, Louisiana State University Press, Baton Rouge, 1961

Frank Tannenbaum, *The Mexican Agrarian Revolution*, Brookings, Washington, 1930

Frank Tannenbaum, *Mexico: The Struggle for Peace and Bread*, Knopf, New York, 1950

A. P. Whitaker, *The United States and South America*, The Northern Republics, Harvard University Press, Cambridge, Mass., 1948

A. P. Whitaker, *The Western Hemisphere Idea: Its Rise and Decline*, Cornell University Press, Ithaca, N.Y., 1954

M. W. Williams, *The People and Politics of Latin America*, Ginn, Boston and New York, 1945

XV. THE TECHNOLOGICAL REVOLUTION IN WAR

Raymond Aron, *The Century of Total War*, Beacon, Boston, 1955

Atoms for Power: the United States Policy in Atomic Energy Development, The American Assembly, New York, 1957

Hanson Baldwin, *The Great Arms Race*, Praeger, New York, 1958

Henri Barbusse, *Under Fire* (fictional), Dutton, New York, 1928

Bernard Brodie, *Strategy in the Missile Age*, Princeton University Press, Princeton, N. J., 1959

Karl von Clausewitz, *On War*, Modern Library, New York, 1943

F. J. Cook, *The Warfare State*, Macmillan, New York, 1962

Norman Cousins, *Modern Man Is Obsolete*, Viking, New York, 1945

H. S. Dinerstein, *War and the Soviet Union*, Praeger, New York, 1959

F. S. Dunn, *War and the Minds of Men*, Harper, New York, 1950

J. S. Dupré and S. A. Lakoff, *Science and the Nation, Policy and Politics*, Prentice-Hall, Englewood Cliffs, N. J., 1962

Cyril Falls, *A Hundred Years of War, 1850-1950*, Collier, New York, 1962

John Hersey, *Hiroshima*, Knopf, New York, 1946

C. J. Hitch and R. N. McKean, *The Economics of Defense in the Nuclear Age*, Harvard University Press, Cambridge, Mass., 1960

Herman Kahn, *On Thermonuclear War*, Princeton University Press, Princeton, N. J., 1960

Herman Kahn, *Thinking About the Unthinkable*, Horizon, New York, 1962

W. W. Kaufmann, ed., *Military Policy and National Security*, Princeton University Press, Princeton, N. J., 1956

H. A. Kissinger, *The Necessity for Choice: Prospects of American Foreign Policy*, Harper, New York, 1961

H. A. Kissinger, *Nuclear Weapons and Foreign Policy*, Harper, New York, 1957

Klaus Knorr, *The War Potential of Nations*, Princeton University Press, Princeton, N. J., 1956

Max Lerner, *The Age of Overkill: A Preface to World Politics*, Simon and Schuster, New York, 1962

Walter Millis, *Arms and Men, A Study in American Military History*, Putnam, New York, 1956

Oskar Morganstern, *The Question of National Defense*, Vintage, New York, 1961

J. U. Nef, *War and Human Progress*, Harvard University Press, Cambridge, Mass., 1950

W. F. Ogburn, ed., *Technology and International Relations*, University of Chicago Press, Chicago, 1949

R. E. Osgood, *Limited War*, University of Chicago Press, Chicago, 1957

Peter Paret and J. W. Shy, *Guerrillas in the 1960's*,

Praeger, New York, 1962

T. C. Schelling, *The Strategy of Conflict*, Harvard University Press, Cambridge, Mass., 1960

R. W. Tucker, *The Just War, A Study in Contemporary American Doctrine*, Johns Hopkins, Baltimore, 1960

G. B. Turner and R. D. Challenger, eds., *National Security in the Nuclear Age*, Praeger, New York, 1960

K. N. Waltz, *Man, the State, and War*, Columbia University Press, New York, 1959

Washington Center for Foreign Policy, *Developments in Military Technology and Their Impact on United States Strategy and Foreign Policy*, Government Printing Office, Washington, 1959

Quincy Wright, *A Study of War*, University of Chicago Press, Chicago, 1942

XVI. THE INTERNATIONAL CONTROL OF ARMAMENTS

D. G. Brennan, ed., *Arms Control, Disarmament, and National Security*, Braziller, New York, 1961

Louis Henkin, *Arms Control and Inspection in American Law*, Columbia University Press, New York, 1958

Louis Henkin, ed., *Arms Control, Issues for the Public*, Prentice-Hall, Englewood Cliffs, N. J., 1961

E. W. Lefever, ed., *Arms and Arms Control*, Praeger, New York, 1962

Seymour Melman, ed., *Inspection for Disarmament*, Columbia University Press, New York, 1958

Philip Noel-Baker, *The Arms Race, a Programme for World Disarmament*, Oceana, New York, 1958

T. C. Schelling and M. H. Halperin, *Strategy and Arms Control*, Twentieth Century Fund, New York, 1961

J. W. Spanier and J. L. Nogee, *The Politics of Disarmament*, Praeger, New York, 1962

Merze Tate, *The Disarmament Illusion*, Macmillan, New York, 1942

R. L. Worsnop, *Nuclear Testing Dilemmas*, Editorial Research Reports, Washington, 1962

XVII. THE UNITED NATIONS AND THE DRIVE TO PEACE THROUGH WORLD ORGANIZATION AND LAW

Crane Brinton, *From Many One: The Process of Political Integration and the Problem of World Government*, Harvard University Press, Cambridge, Mass., 1948

L. P. Bloomfield, *Evolution or Revolution? The United Nations and the Problem of Peaceful Territorial Change*, Harvard University Press, Cambridge, Mass., 1957

L. P. Bloomfield, *The United Nations and United States Foreign Policy*, Little, Brown, Boston, 1960

W. G. Carleton, "What Our World Federalists Neglect," *Antioch Review*, Spring 1948

D. S. Cheever and H. F. Haviland, Jr., *Organizing for Peace: International Organization in World Affairs*, Houghton Mifflin, Boston, 1954

Grenville Clark and L. B. Sohn, *World Peace Through World Law*, 2nd edition, Harvard University Press, Cambridge, Mass., 1960

I. L. Claude, Jr., *Swords into Plowshares*, Random House, New York, 1959

I. L. Claude, Jr., "The United Nations and the Use of Force," *International Conciliation*, March 1961

Commission to Study the Organization of Peace, *Strengthening the United Nations*, Harper, New York, 1957

Commission to Study the Organization of Peace, *Organizing Peace in the Nuclear Age*, New York University Press, New York, 1959

Commission to Study the Organization of Peace, *Peaceful Coexistence: A Challenge to the United Nations*, New York, 1960

D. C. Coyle, *The United Nations and How It Works*, Mentor, New York, 1955

Alexander Dallin, *The Soviet View of the United*

Nations, M.I.T. Center for International Studies, Cambridge, Mass., 1959

Alexander Dallin, *The Soviet Union at the United Nations*, Praeger, New York, 1962

Clyde Eagleton, *International Government*, Ronald, New York, 1948

C. M. Eichelberger, *The United Nations: The First Fifteen Years*, Harper, New York, 1960

A. H. Feller, *United Nations and the World Community*, Little, Brown, Boston, 1952

W. R. Frye, *A United Nations Police Force*, Oceana, New York, 1957

L. M. Goodrich, *Korea: A Study of United States Policy in the United Nations*, Harper, New York, 1956

L. M. Goodrich, *The United Nations*, Crowell, New York, 1959

E. A. Gross, *The United Nations: Structure for Peace*, Harper, New York, 1962

Thomas Hovet, Jr., *Bloc Politics in the United Nations*, Harvard University Press, Cambridge, Mass., 1960

P. C. Jessup and H. J. Taubenfeld, *Controls for Outer Space*, Columbia University Press, New York, 1959

Bertrand de Jouvenal, *Sovereignty: An Inquiry into the Good*, Cambridge University Press, Cambridge, 1957

Hans Kelsen, *The Law of the United Nations*, Praeger, New York, 1950

H. Lauterpacht, *International Law and Human Rights*, Praeger, New York, 1950

O. J. Lissitzn, *The International Court of Justice*, Carnegie Endowment, New York, 1951

A. Loveday, *Reflections on International Administration*, Clarendon Press, Oxford, 1956

John MacLaurin, *The United Nations and Power Politics*, Harper, New York, 1957

Walter Millis, Reinhold Niebuhr, Harrison Brown, James Real, and W. O. Douglas, *A World Without*

War, Washington Square Press, New York, 1961

David Mitrany, *A Working Peace System*, Royal Institute of International Affairs, London, 1946

Linus Pauling, *No More War*, Dodd, Mead, New York, 1958

J. G. Stoessinger, "Atoms for Peace: The International Atomic Energy Commission," in *Organizing Peace in the Nuclear Age*, New York University Press, New York, 1959

J. G. Stoessinger, "Financing the United Nations," *International Conciliation*, November 1961

Julius Stone, *Legal Controls of International Conflict*, Rinehart, New York, 1954

Amry Vandenbosch and W. N. Hogan, *The United Nations*, McGraw-Hill, New York, 1952

W. L. Willkie, *One World*, Simon and Schuster, New York, 1943

XVIII. THE ACTUAL NARRATIVE OF INTERNATIONAL EVENTS AND DEVELOPMENTS FROM YEAR TO YEAR AND FROM MONTH TO MONTH

The student will find valuable Andrew Boyd's *An Atlas of World Affairs*, Praeger, New York, 1962. The United Nations and the Council of Europe publish important year books. Penguin Reference Books, Harmondsworth, Middlesex, publish each year the *Annual Register*, which is most helpful. Invaluable for the student is the volume covering American foreign policy for each year published for the Council on Foreign Relations by Harper, New York. All of the volumes since 1945 are indispensable in a study of American foreign policy since World War II. All of them are written in a lively narrative style, cover American foreign policy in all parts of the world, and are objectively interpretive as well as factual. Many of the volumes in this series have been written by Richard P. Stebbins.

Among American newspapers the *Christian*

Science Monitor is excellent for foreign affairs, the *Washington Post* for official and Congressional developments in Washington which affect foreign policy, and the *New York Times* for both world and domestic politics. The reading of foreign newspapers is valuable not only for information but for seeing American policy in a different perspective. Among leading world newspapers are the *Times* of London, the *Manchester Guardian*, *Le Monde* of Paris, *Die Welt* of Hamburg, *Pravda* and *Izvestia* of Moscow, the *Asahi Evening News* of Tokyo (an English edition as well as a mass circulation vernacular edition), the *Times of India* (Bombay), *al-Ahram* of Cairo, *La Prensa* of Buenos Aires, and *El Tiempo* of Bogotá.

A number of American periodicals are devoted exclusively to international relations and foreign policy, such as *Foreign Affairs*, *World Politics*, and *Orbis*. The *American Political Science Review*, *Political Science Quarterly*, *Journal of Politics*, and *Western Political Quarterly* contain important articles on foreign policy and world politics; also *Harper's Magazine*, the *Atlantic*, *Current History*, and the general quarterlies—the *American Scholar*, the *Antioch Review*, *Commentary*, the *Virginia Quarterly Review*, and the *Yale Review*. Other periodicals are *Time*, *Newsweek*, and *U.S. News and World Report*, which are "right of center," the *Nation*, the *New Leader*, the *New Republic*, the *Reporter*, and the *Progressive*, which are liberal, and the *National Review*, which is conservative. The *New York Times Magazine* covers a variety of topics and opinions.

In Britain, the *New Statesman* interprets developments from the point of view of the European non-Communist left. The *Economist* is truly global in range, is highly perceptive and sensitively aware of all the cross-currents in the world, and the author of this book is much indebted to the file of that periodical.

INDEX

The Author

William G. Carleton taught for many years at the University of Florida, where he was Professor of Political Science and History and Head Professor of Social Science. He is now one of the youngest and busiest professors emeriti in the country, traveling, writing, and lecturing. He is also carrying on research in the history of American political parties under a Social Science Research Council grant. In the period after World War II, he traveled widely in Europe to gather material for articles. He has written extensively on both domestic and world politics and his work has appeared in numerous popular, scholarly and literary periodicals in the United States and abroad, among them the *Yale Review, The Nation,* the *American Scholar,* the *Virginia Quarterly Review* and *Harper's.*